W9-BXF-133

MARKETING THEORY: DISTINGUISHED CONTRIBUTIONS

THEORIES IN MARKETING SERIES
GERALD ZALTMAN, EDITOR

MARKETING THEORY:
DISTINGUISHED CONTRIBUTIONS

Stephen W. Brown
Arizona State University

Raymond P. Fisk
Oklahoma State University

John Wiley & Sons
New York   Chichester   Brisbane   Toronto   Singapore

**This book is dedicated to
Joanne, Tracey, and Erin (S. W. B.)
Jamie (R. P. F.)**

Copyright © 1984, by John Wiley & Sons, Inc.

All rights reserved. Published simultaneously in Canada.

Reproduction or translation of any part of
this work beyond that permitted by Sections
107 and 108 of the 1976 United States Copyright
Act without the permission of the copyright
owner is unlawful. Requests for permission
or further information should be addressed to
the Permissions Department, John Wiley & Sons.

Library of Congress Cataloging in Publication Data:

Main entry under title:

Marketing theory.

Includes indexes.
1. Marketing—Addresses, essays, lectures.
I. Brown, Stephen Walter, 1943–   II. Fisk,
Raymond P.
HF5415.M32323   1984   658.8′001   83-23452
ISBN 0-471-89085-5

Printed in the United States of America

10 9 8 7 6 5 4 3 2 1

PREFACE

On departing from our recent marketing theory seminars, some students remarked, "I'm more confused, but also more interested and challenged about our discipline than ever before." We find these observations an important and healthy sign of marketing's rekindled interest in theory. Marketing scholars are *thinking*, perhaps more than ever before, about the what, the how, and especially the why of thought development. Explicit and implicit assumptions of theory development and testing, research methodologies, and theory's relationship to research are being challenged and reexamined. Through these challenging and thought-provoking experiences, we are also beginning as a discipline to explore new and creative approaches to thought development and learning.

The rekindling of interest in marketing theory began in the second half of the 1970s, and this interest has expanded to the present. Books by Shelby D. Hunt (1976, 1983b), Richard P. Bagozzi (1980), and Gerald Zaltman, Karen LeMasters, and Michael P. Heffring (1983); four American Marketing Association theory conferences (1979, 1980, 1982, and 1984); and a special *Journal of Marketing* issue featuring marketing theory (Fall 1983) represent a few major examples of the renewed and broadened interest in theory among marketing scholars.

Within this setting of rekindled interest, *Marketing Theory: Distinguished Contributions* is the first compilation of outstanding marketing theory papers and articles in nearly fifteen years. As such, it represents the only collection of distinguished essays from the modern era of theory and marketing.

This book is not a comprehensive collection of all the many fine marketing theory essays. Instead, an attempt has been made to provide the reader with a representative sampling of some of the major contributions to the literature. The papers and articles selected for inclusion were chosen, in part, for their differing viewpoints. In assembling this collection, the editors planned that the reading of pairs and groups of the essays would spark considerable thinking and debate—such is the current state of development in marketing theory. Parenthetically, the existence of differing viewpoints also suggests that many of the positions taken in this volume are not necessarily those of the editors.

Marketing Theory: Distinguished Contributions has been developed for both the budding and the seasoned marketing scholar. The essays should serve as relevant source material for the graduate level marketing theory course as well as for other graduate, advanced undergraduate, and senior executive management offerings.

A special feature of this volume is the contributors' preface to their own articles. These prefatory observations were written for this book and most often represent the authors' rethinking about their contributions. Quite often these remarks provide special and revealing insight into the development of, and current thinking about, the essay. Another distinctive feature of the volume is the thought-provoking questions following each of the articles. For the most part these questions were author generated. This feature should help the reader to review the articles' contents and serve as an important catalyst to lively discussion. Following the articles and papers is a Taxonomical Bibliography of Marketing Theory. Stephen J. Grove, University of Mississippi, joined Professor Fisk in compiling this bibliography. This reference source should be especially valuable to the student of marketing theory.

Many individuals are responsible for this book. First and foremost are the authors whose articles and papers, prefaces, and discussion questions appear in this volume. Their publishers, by granting reprint permission, have also made this book pos-

v

sible. We also wish to recognize the imprint of our colleagues and current and former marketing theory students at Arizona State University and Oklahoma State University. Several people at Oklahoma State University whose diligent assistance was invaluable in bringing this book to completion deserve acknowledgment: Laura Davis, Patti Day, Dena Haimson, Kenna Metcalf, and Scot Williams. To Richard Esposito and John Wiley & Sons, we owe special appreciation. Finally, we wish to thank Gerald Zaltman, Editor of Wiley's Theories in Marketing Series, for challenging us with this opportunity and for supporting us throughout its development.

Stephen W. Brown
Raymond P. Fisk

SERIES EDITORS' FOREWORD

The field of marketing is moving toward a takeoff point with respect to the development of marketing theory. One indication of this is the increased attention being given to issues in marketing theory. For example, the past few years have witnessed the organization of conferences explicitly devoted to marketing theory, including issues in the modeling of marketing phenomena. The recent appearance of books by Bagozzi (1980); Zaltman, LeMasters, and Heffring (1982); and Hunt (1983b) has provided further stimulus, adding to that of the earlier volumes by Zaltman, Pinson, and Angelmar (1973) and Hunt (1976). Most doctoral programs in marketing now require students to have at least some exposure to scholarly work in the philosophy of science. There is also evidence that students in other marketing programs are increasingly being required to read seminal works in the history of marketing thought. In fact, it is partly because of the efforts of critical thinkers such as Alderson, Howard, Kotler, and several others that we can begin to approach a takeoff point. The notion that theory is important to practice in immediate and direct—as well as indirect—ways is an idea whose time is about to come.

Marketing Theory: Distinguished Contributions will undoubtedly play a major role in advancing marketing thought in general and marketing theory in particular. The editors, themselves true students of marketing thought, have collected some of the most seminal and provocative ideas in the field. Beyond providing an important kind of place utility, they have also asked contributors to revisit their original writings and add appropriate commentary. The result is valuable insight into thinking processes that we do not ordinarily see with collected readings and invited essays. Moreover, the editors have been most creative in selecting essays that have a synergy among them. Thus the collection is considerably more than the simple sum of its parts. This well-organized, comprehensive coverage of marketing theory provides a central source of scholarship that should be read carefully by any serious student of marketing. As the ideas in this volume are understood, argued, and extended, we will move one step closer to the point when theoretical issues are treated as central to both marketing practice and academic scholarship.

Gerald Zaltman

ABOUT THE EDITORS

Stephen W. Brown is Professor of Marketing at Arizona State University and National President-Elect of the American Marketing Association. Professor Brown is the coauthor of three books and over eighty articles and papers that have appeared in various publications, including the *Journal of Marketing Research, Journal of Advertising Research,* and *Journal of Advertising.* He also serves on the editorial boards of five professional journals, including the *Journal of Marketing* and the *Journal of Business Research.* He is a past president of the Southwestern Marketing Association and currently serves as consulting editor of Dryden Press's Marketing Series.

Professor Brown has been a student of, and contributor to, marketing theory for many years. In 1979 he helped originate and served as the cochair of the American Marketing Association's inaugural Marketing Theory Conference. He has also taught the doctoral theory seminar on a regular basis at Arizona State University since 1977. Many of his current and former students are contributors to the writings and teaching of marketing theory. Professor Brown is a graduate of Arizona State University.

Raymond P. Fisk is Assistant Professor of Mar-keting at Oklahoma State University. Professor Fisk received his doctorate from Arizona State University and has taught previously at Arizona State University and the American Graduate School of International Management. He was a 1979 American Marketing Association Doctoral Consortium Fellow and is a member of the American Marketing Association, the Association for Consumer Research, and the American Association for the Advancement of Science.

Professor Fisk's publishing and teaching activities have been oriented toward theoretical areas of marketing. His published works include conceptual articles in the *Journal of the Academy of Marketing Science* and the *Journal of Health Care Marketing,* theoretical papers in both of the American Marketing Association's Services Conferences, equity theory research for the Consumer Satisfaction/Dissatisfaction and Complaining Conference, and papers published in the first and third American Marketing Association's Theory Conferences Proceedings. His teaching activities include graduate courses in consumer behavior, promotion, and services marketing as well as the doctoral seminar in marketing theory at Oklahoma State University.

LIST OF CONTRIBUTORS

Alderson, Wroe, late of University of Pennsylvania

Anderson, Paul F., Virginia Polytechnic Institute and State University

Bagozzi, Richard P., Massachusetts Institute of Technology

Barksdale, Hiram C., University of Georgia

Baumol, William J., Princeton University and New York University

Bonoma, Thomas V., Harvard University

Brodbeck, May, University of Iowa

Brown, Stephen W., Arizona State University

Buzzell, Robert D., Harvard University

Calder, Bobby J., Northwestern University

Evans, Kenneth R., Arizona State University

Fisk, George, Emory University

Fisk, Raymond P., Oklahoma State University

Gardner, David M., University of Illinois, Urbana-Champaign

Gaulden, Corbett F., Jr., University of Texas-Permian Basin

Greyser, Stephen A., Harvard University

Grove, Stephen J., University of Mississippi

Hunt, Shelby D., Texas Tech University

Jacoby, Jacob, New York University

Kotler, Philip, Northwestern University

Leone, Robert P., University of Texas at Austin

Levy, Sidney J., Northwestern University

Lutz, Richard, University of Florida

Massy, William F., Stanford University

Meyers, Patricia, University of Massachusetts, Amherst

Mokwa, Michael P., Arizona State University

Morgan, Gareth, York University, Canada

Mowen, John C., Oklahoma State University

Myers, John G., University of California, Berkeley

Olson, Jerry C., Pennsylvania State University

Peter, J. Paul, University of Wisconsin, Madison

Phillips, Lynn W., Stanford University

Ryan, Michael J., University of Michigan

Schultz, Randall L., University of Texas at Dallas

Sheth, Jagdish N., University of Illinois, Urbana-Champaign

Shostack, G. Lynn, Bankers Trust Company

Smircich, Linda, University of Massachusetts, Amherst

Tybout, Alice M., Northwestern University

Walden, Kirk D., Ogilvy and Mather, Inc.

Zaltman, Gerald, University of Pittsburgh

CONTENTS

ONE

FOUNDATIONS OF SCIENCE AND THEORY

As indicated in the preface to this book, marketing scholars are *thinking*, perhaps more than ever before, about the what, the how, and the why of marketing thought and theory development. Explicit and implicit assumptions are being challenged and reexamined. An attempt to capture some of the tenor of these challenging and thought-provoking times for marketing theory is reflected in the three essays in Part 1.

The first essay is actually an editing of the transcript from a featured panel discussion at the 1982 American Marketing Association Theory Conference in San Antonio. The central focus of the essay is a debate over marketing's logical empiricism tradition and appropriate views of science in general and for marketing in particular. Chaired by J. Paul Peter, the panel represented a number of the leading thinkers in marketing as well as the noted philosopher of science May Brodbeck.

The Brodbeck paper summarizes the logical empiricist approach and reviews some of the criticism over the last twenty years of this approach to science. Brodbeck then points out some of the inherent shortcomings of some of the alternatives to logical empiricism and closes with some brief implications for a science of marketing. Paul F. Anderson's article is premised on the outdatedness of marketing's unilateral focus on logical empiricism. His objective is to expose the reader to the value of "post-positivistic models" and assess marketing's scientific status.

PREFACE TO

"Current Issues in the Philosophy of Science: Implications for Marketing Theory—A Panel Discussion"*

There has been a revolution in the philosophy of science literature in the past twenty years or so. While there are still those who cling to and attempt to shore up weaknesses in the traditional view of science, much of the philosophy of science literature involves approaches which bear little resemblance to logical empiricism. While perhaps not recognized as such, logical empiricism is the dominant philosophical approach employed in marketing and it has come to us in our borrowing of theory construction and research methods from psychology and economics.

With few exceptions, the revolution in philosophical thinking about science has gone unnoticed in marketing. Thus, the purpose of this panel was to open discussion about recent philosophical developments concerning the nature of science and to investigate the implications of these developments for marketing.

My personal concern with logical empiricism as the philosophical basis for seeking knowledge in marketing stems from three sources. First, philosophers of science have been unable to reconcile basic problems with the approach as Suppe explains in detail. Second, many leading philosophers of science have abandoned the approach and are instead investing their efforts in developing other approaches to explaining theory and the scientific enterprise. Third, logical empiricism does not give an adequate account of important scientific advances in the physical sciences and its norms seem far removed from the abilities of social science. Given these problems, it does not seem reasonable that we should embrace logical empiricism by default, i.e., because we are ignorant of any other approaches. Thus, if we are to be logical empiricists we should strive to be good ones, yet it is not clear that such an approach has led to much progress so far and it is unlikely to do so in the future.

The main thrust of this panel discussion involved a lively debate over appropriate views of science both in general and in marketing in particular. Unfortunately, due to technical difficulties in the recording of the panel, not all of the discussion was available for printing. Thus, the transcript . . . contains some usable portions of the tape as well as some summary position statements prepared after the conference. While the positioning of the materials may not be accurate chronologically, the reader will hopefully be able to discern the major positions and points presented.

Finally, I would like to personally thank the panel members for their hard work in preparing for this discussion and the insights each member provided.

Editors' Note: J. Paul Peter's original Editor's Note is the best preface for this panel discussion.

1

CURRENT ISSUES IN THE PHILOSOPHY OF SCIENCE: IMPLICATIONS FOR MARKETING THEORY—A PANEL DISCUSSION

J. PAUL PETER, Chairman and Editor
PAUL F. ANDERSON
MAY BRODBECK
SHELBY D. HUNT
RICHARD LUTZ
JERRY C. OLSON
MICHAEL J. RYAN
GERALD ZALTMAN

PAUL ANDERSON

While I was listening to Professor Brodbeck speak I wrote down a few notes and I apologize for perhaps not responding to all the points that she raised in her lengthy discussion. These are hastily scribbled notes but I thought that there were a couple of issues that really needed further duscussion as Jerry [Olson] suggested. I'm not at all sure that everyone in the audience fully appreciated the two viewpoints Professor Brodbeck was setting off against one another during her discussion, so let me briefly try to recount some of the issues that have emerged in the philosophy of science and sociology of science in the last twenty years. Logical empiricism, quite frankly, has been in decline for about twenty years within the philosophy/sociology of science and history of science area (the general area known as science studies). To a large extent it has been replaced by a kind of historicism. Basically, what this means is that philosophers and sociologists of science have decided to look at actual science and to test the norms that they derive for scientific processes against the actual history of science. It seems a reasonable thing to do. If I'm going to suggest to you that I have a scientific method, then I ought to be able to state that I have taken these norms, I have

Source: Reprinted with permission from *Marketing Theory: Philosophy of Science Perspectives,* Ronald F. Bush and Shelby D. Hunt, eds., Chicago, Ill.: American Marketing Association, 1982, 11–16.

put them up against what we could consider to be exemplary episodes in the actual history of science and I have demonstrated that these norms were followed. In fact, these are the norms which caused science to progress. Unfortunately, I think the record is clear both from the history of science and the sociology of science that logical empiricism simply will not do that. The historical record from the Copernican revolution, through the discovery of oxygen, through the development of Newtonian mechanics, through relativity, through plate tectonics—it simply will not wash. The processes which are supposed to operate according to the norms of logical empiricism simply don't describe the actual history of science. I think that is a crucial requirement for us to meet if we are going to suggest that there are, in fact, norms or that there is, in fact, a scientific method. Professor Brodbeck points out that critics of the logical empiricist view tend to make the progress of science a miracle. In other words, if you're a realist and if you believe that there is a reality out there that is discoverable by scientific method, then how do you explain that we can cure disease and put men on the moon? This is an argument that is frequently made against the historical perspective. But I think it misunderstands the historical perspective. I think that what relativists are saying is not that we are trying to debunk science. Indeed, most relativists are quite impressed by the progress of science. We are not trying to trivialize it. We're simply trying to understand how it actually works and how it actually works is through a web of sociological and psychological processes as well as a series of logical processes. I think it is fundamental for us to understand that science is a human activity. It is no different from any other human activity. It is carried out by humans who are subject to sociological factors and psychological factors. They also use reason and logical processes. It seems reasonable that we can draw on the sociology of science, the history of science and the traditional philosophy of science to come to some understanding of exactly how science progresses. Professor Brodbeck argues that the sociologists of science, in particular, are suspect because their science itself is subjective. Therefore, how can we believe them? The sociologists of science are not concerned with this kind of criticism because they recognize that all science is subjective. The fact that it works is the crucial aspect here, not the fact that it is in some sense subjective. The sociology of science and the more recent work in the philosophy and history of science have shown that we are not seekers after truth. We cannot define what truth is. We wouldn't know it if we found it. So, therefore, why do we constantly hold up this notion that science is objective knowledge, that it does seek truth and that any subjectivism in some sense debunks science or causes it to be less useful? Newtonian mechanics is now held to be false, but that does not mean it is not useful. It doesn't mean that it doesn't predict the behavior of macroparticles. It doesn't mean it doesn't predict the behavior of particles moving at some small percentage of the speed of light. But it is, nonetheless, considered false by contemporary physicists.

Basically, I think that the work in the past twenty years in the history, sociology and philosophy of science has shown us that the process of science is a consensus generation process. The real question is: "How can I convince my colleagues in the scientific community that my theory is correct?" I think, to some extent, we're about ten years behind the times in conducting this debate at this point in time. The fact that logical empiricism is, in Lakakos's terms, a degenerating research program doesn't mean that we should not consider it. But I think we have to look to the professionals in the field, the people who spend most of their time considering these issues and take a look at their literature and recognize that, in fact, they come to very different conclusions than the ones which were expressed today. I think that that probably offers enough criticism and enough issues to get us off the ground.

RICHARD LUTZ

I have four central points that I would like to make regarding the nature and role of philosophy of science, particularly as it relates to the marketing discipline.

First, I strongly agree with the school of thought which has been labeled *historicism*. I think that much of the confusion surrounding philosophy of science issues stems from the fact that the various approaches are comprised of rather stringent normative statements about how science *should* be done; each particular philosophical position aspires to achieve some sort of monolithic status whereby all scientific endeavor falls under its prescriptive umbrella. Unfortunately, these normative statements have apparently been derived in the absence of any consideration of how science is *actually* done. Books such as *The Double Helix* and Mittroff's *The Subjective Side of Science* have shown us that real scientists often deviate markedly from the tenets of philosophy of science. Yet, some of these same scientists have made enormous contributions.

Most of us ascribe to the notion that, in the behavioral sciences, description precedes explanation of behavior, which in turn permits prescriptions regarding appropriate behavior. Historicism is the only school of thought which seemingly follows the same logic in deriving its prescriptions for appropriate conduct of scientific inquiry; hence, I believe that some form of historicism (or any other approach which relies on description and explanation of scientists' behaviors as the basic input to prescriptions) is most likely to prove fruitful in the long run. One consequence of an historicist perspective on science may be somewhat troublesome, however. It is unlikely that, once we begin to carefully study the behavior of scientists, a *single* model of scientific behavior will emerge. Rather, it is likely that a sort of "contingency" model will be more appropriate, with a particular approach to science being useful in one context but not in others. Hence, an historicist position is not going to provide the sort of monolithic, all-encompassing approach to science which some would desire. Science is a highly complex human activity, and as such is probably not readily amenable to simple or inflexible approaches.

My second point concerns the so-called *holistic* school of thought, most closely associated with Duhem and Quine. The essential characteristic of this view is that science progresses only within the broader context of the total array of prior knowledge which has been generated. It is difficult to argue with this view, but it is more easily preached than practiced. I believe that acceptance of a holistic view of science implies that the scientist engage in a rigorous *program of research,* something which is all too rare in marketing today. However, it is my firm conviction that marketing will begin to make significant advances *as a science* only at such time as more of us dedicate ourselves to pursuing unified long-range research programs rather than grinding out one-shot studies on the latest hot topic.

Third, I would like to espouse the notion of *competitive support* first proposed, I believe, by Popper. Under the logic of competitive support, theories are tested *against* one another within a single experimental context in order to build a stronger body of research evidence. The most important aspect of competitive support is that it forces the scientist to consider at least two rival explanations for any phenomenon of interest. Thus, rather than taking our favorite pet theory and conducting an experiment designed to support it, we instead would pit our pet against a strong competing explanation and see which fared better. Platt, in his 1964 *Science* paper entitled "Strong Inference," takes the notion of competitive support a step further and argues that scientists should actually conduct research designed to *refute rather than support* their pet theories. An essential aspect of Platt's proposal is that competitive support for a theory is generated only by a *series* of studies and not by a single "crucial experiment." Therefore, the logic of competitive support seems to be highly compatible with the holistic school of thought I discussed earlier. An integrated research program testing a series of competing explanations would appear, at this point, to be the most likely scientific approach for generating new marketing knowledge.

My final point is that, in order to effectively utilize competitive support, we must first have competing theories. Thus, a large part of our task as scientists is to derive new theories for subsequent testing, a point emphasized by Feyerabend. In his study of moon scientists, Mitroff found that those scientists who were most highly respected by their colleagues were those who developed theories rather than those who conducted the highest quality and quantity of empirical research. I am not advocating that we all join what has been characterized as the "theory-of-the-month-club," but I am suggesting that we aspire to think, to reflect, to ponder (all those wonderful things professors are supposed to do), and to distill those thoughts into viable theories which may some day contribute to the science and practice of marketing.

MAY BRODBECK

Just let me say that, as I said in the paper, subjectivism or relativism is always with us. I think there are causal reasons for that going back to romanticism in the 19th century. It has partly the same roots here, generally in the climate of today which is anti-intellectual, anti-rational, within the social sciences—I don't refer to marketing. Within the social sciences in general there is strong support for some of these views. In fact, the relativists have had almost their only influence within a social science. There are reasons for that. When you have a field which doesn't have any well-developed theories that you have much reliance in, and Feyerabend might well say, "let a thousand theories grow," than it is psychologically very difficult not to say that all of these theories may have something good about them, in that each theory is good for something. Relativism is very seductive under those circumstances. None of this makes relativism true. Of course, science is a human activity, and of course scientists are human beings, and of course they fight among themselves; all of this is not to say that one can't learn something from this—that all of this is interesting, it's helpful, it's suggestive, it's useful to know.

By the way, I have to mention that not all sociologists of science are subjectivists or relativists. One who is not is Robert Merton, perhaps the most distinguished sociologist of science that this country has produced. What the logical empiricists are saying is that science is a human activity subject to all human frailties, in which we try to find out something about the world. If we're not trying to find out something about the world, then I don't know why we're in it. As far as this moon stuff goes, the interesting question there is not how did several scientists use the rather fragmentary pieces of evidence that the astronauts brought back, but how did we ever get them there? How we got them there was almost entirely through Newtonian mechanics, that's how we got them there, and by inferences from it. If there is any reason to believe that this isn't true, then we should never have taken a risk with those men's lives. It is interesting, as most of you probably know, space travel is almost entirely based upon classical mechanics, the only part that is not has to do with communications. The rest of it is all plain old 17th century science. I think that we want to go to science, science as an activity, to what people do to get suggestions, to learn why people change their concepts, and what are the things that are going on. All of this is peripheral to understand that once you had formulated an hypothesis, and this may be arrived at in all kinds of ways, once you have formulated a working hypothesis, then you have to say what kinds of things will, in fact, be evidence for or against it. If you find a negation of your hypothesis, then that hypothesis is false, and if you have a confirmation of it, then you have further reason to believe that it is true about things, not something that you ought to cling to simply because it is aesthetically desirable to do so, or because it is consistent.

Two people were mentioned, Duhem and Quine; Duhem is the 19th century philosopher of science and physics and Quine is the 20th century philosopher of science and physics. One of the things that Duhem, of course, is famous for is that he was presenting in a very interesting form a conventionalistic position. Duhem is very well worth reading; even though some of his conclusions were, I think, unacceptable. But what Duhem was struck by was that you cannot falsify in isolation. There is always another set of statements that could be taken as false. If I make a measurement and I say this disconfirms my hypothesis about how great the demand ought to be at this time, then there is always another possible source in your theory which could be wrong and not this one, as well as something wrong in your measuring instruments. What Duhem did was to point out the fact that in principle, certainly not in practice, but in principle and it's important to know this in practice, in principle it's always a whole theory that you're testing. In practice, of course, you're testing a single hypothesis,

but because there are always other components of that theory that could be wrong, your confirming evidence or your falsifying evidence is only tentative, although it is only tentative in a philosophical sense, in which we say it's only probable that the sun will rise tomorrow. There is always the fact that in a well-developed systematic theory, and even in a nonwell-developed theory in which you have a set of implicit assumptions running around, there's always something else that might be wrong and may account for the false prediction.

Quine is a distinguished philosopher and writes in the philosophical tradition of pragmatism. He's an instrumentalist with respect to theories. We've always had pragmatism; one has to ask "why does the theory work?" Not merely that it works, but why does it work? There must be something in the nature of things by virtue of which this theory works and that theory doesn't. I guess I have to come down on saying that, of course, science is an activity human beings are engaged in, and all goes on that we know goes on, that it's worthwhile knowing about these things. It's certainly worthwhile knowing the history of science, but when push comes to shove you have to have some firm principles which serve as guides, as ideals not as restrictions, not as something that binds you. I agree that if they bind you and keep you from getting other suggestions, this is bad. It's bad methods, but they have to be ideals against which you can say at some point I have confirmed this or I have disconfirmed it. For that you have to have the notions that we have been talking about, the notion of causal law, of hypothetical deductive theories, and of confirmation or disconfirmation in terms of whether the inferences drawn are, in fact, valid or invalid.

PAUL ANDERSON

I don't have time to respond to all the points you have raised, but I think I can at least identify the key points of disagreement between those of use who might be on the relativist side and those who are on the side of logical empiricism. I think it comes down to two key points; one is the presumption that because it works it must be true. Yes, we put men on the moon using Newtonian mechanics but Newtonian mechanics are considered to be false. The same goes for Ptolemaic astronomy. Ptolemaic astronomy is considered to have been falsified, but it worked quite well for a long time. It helped explain retrograde motion and so forth. I think that the key issue comes down to this: if we're going to provide norms of behavior for scientists we ought be able to take these norms and apply them to exemplary cases and demonstrate that these were, in fact, the norms that were used by scientists at the time. How else will you know that the norms are appropriate? Are you simply going to generate these norms logically and then say they are ideals that we will always strive toward but will never attain? How then do we know that these are worthwhile achieving if they have not been shown to work in cases which we consider to be exemplary science? I think this is the second key point of disagreement between the historical school and logical empiricists. The historicists do not want to take all the rationality out of science. The leading, I think, historicist philosopher of science today, Larry Laudan, is an extreme rationalist. He rejects almost all of the sociology of science. He is the chief antagonist of the relativists, but nonetheless he relies very heavily on the historical record to demonstrate that the norms that he identifies are, in fact, the actual norms employed by scientists.

There are a lot of different schools of thought which are in opposition to logical empiricism and they are not all relativistic. I think that most of them are informed either by the history of science or by the actual day-to-day practice of scientists (this being the realm of the sociologists of science). I think there's a sense in which logical expiricists, as Brown says, try to make automatons out of scientists. The assumption is that they blindly follow rules of good science and don't allow subjective factors to enter in. If that were the case, as Feyerabend and others have pointed out, some of the great advances in Western thought would not have come down to us today. This much is clear from historical record.

JERRY OLSON

I have been interested in philosophy of science for a long time, but in the last couple of years it seems to have grown into somewhat of a consuming interest. In my recent reading, I have found that there are several dramatically different points of view regarding scientific methods, theory, how to test theory, namely, how to do science. Over the last few months, I have been thinking about an overall "framework" into which all of these diverse perspectives can be fit in order to make sense of them—to see their relationships, their similarities and differences.

It seemed to me that most of the philosophers of science I have read are interested in describing how "science" works. That is, they want to explain the process by which science in general develops and progresses. (Most, of course, are concerned to develop a "rational" model for science.) But I wanted something more personal and immediately relevant from my study of sphilosophy of science. I wanted to find out how *I* could do my science work better. But not many philosophers of science (that I have read) were telling me very much about how an individual scientist could do better research and theory development work, on a day-to-day basis, in a particular domain. Instead, most philosophers proposed general models of science which implied rules of behavior for the ideal scientist. Some of these rules have become "codified" and are passed down to our students as prescriptive norms for how to do science. In marketing we can see this type of approach in the numerous attempts to come up with perscriptive rules for marketing research and theory development—"What is the philosophical way to do good marketing science?"

The problem with this tendency is that for every rule that has been proposed, some philosopher seems to have shown that, at least in some circumstances, it is not applicable, it doesn't work, or worse, that it is dysfunctional. So, I have come to agree with the essence of what Jerry [Zaltman] and Rich [Lutz] and others have said: It is unlikely that we will find a single perscriptive rule (or algorithm or method) that will guarantee success in marketing science. Rather, I think we ought to become familiar with many philosophical points of view and their corresponding methods. So, for example, I think we need to understand logical empiricism (even though it is largely mentioned). And, we need to understand all of the numerous alternatives to that perspective, including the so-called radical approaches.

There are two other things that I would like to briefly mention now and discuss in more detail later when we get down to specific issues. One is an idea that I have been exploring recently, not only in my thinking about philosophy of science, but also in my own empirical research. That is the issue of levels of analysis. Perhaps we may find that different philosophers of science are talking at slightly different levels of analysis and are not really meeting each other's ideas head on. So, maybe a levels-of-analysis distinction is a key component of an overall conceptual framework.

The second idea I want to raise is that in order to understand the different approaches to a philosophy of science—logical empiricism, historical realism, idealism or relativism, etc.—we ought to carefully examine the metatheoretical assumptions that these philosophers make about what they're doing. Often, of course, these basic assumptions are not explicitly stated—they are only implicit and one has to "read between the lines" in order to see them. To me, the most basic assumption has been alluded to several times today but has not yet been mentioned explicitly. I think this single presupposition can distinguish among many philosophers of science and the approaches they take, as well as differentiate the people in this room and the approaches you take in doing research. I'm referring to your basic assumptions about reality, and our ability to know it.

There are a wide variety of subtly different positions regarding reality, but for purposes of our discussion here, we might consider a dichotomous position. Some people—realists—believe in an objectively knowable world that exists independently of themselves. If you believe this, it will lead you to certain kinds of methods and research issues (such as logical empiricism). If you don't believe in an independent reality (or for purposes of doing science, you pretend that you don't believe in that), then your idealistic perspective will probably lead you in entirely different directions. Your philosophy and approach to research will be different from the "realists." Even the issues you select for study may be different. Since I believe in the latter perspective, I guess I am a relativist.

MAY BRODBECK

The fact that we have certain guides to which standards are acceptable and which are not, in terms of whether or not they will guide us to the truth, does not mean you can't use your feelings, your hopes, you dreams, you loves, your hates and all of this in your everyday scientific work in trying to construct

these competitive theories which we want. The second point refers to the view that Newtonian mechanics is "false." Newtonian mechanics is true of all ordinary magnitudes, velocities smaller than the velocity of light; magnitudes smaller than those in space. It is a limiting case, however, of a more general theory, namely, the Einsteinian theory of relativity which takes into account velocities that approach the velocity of light, which is constant, and magnitudes in space which are huger than anything we have here on earth. One can then make a derivation; while it is very complicated, you can show that Newtonian mechanics is a limiting case for ordinary dimensions, not real tiny and not real big, here on earth.

With respect to Duhem, that's a different story. Einstein pointed out in a very famous essay that besides the geometry you have to take into account the physics. Ptolemy worked fine, as long as you had Aristotelean physics. When you introduce Galilean physics, which says something different about the way in which particles fall, then you can no longer use the Ptolemaic description of the relations among the stars. What you need is both the physics and the geometry. This is part of the story I mentioned before, that you don't disconfirm one part in the case of physics or astronomy. You have two sets of beliefs or hypotheses; one about geometry which is physical but about space, and one about the other parts of physics-dynamics, velocities and so on. It depends on which of these you have as to whether or not Ptolemy is acceptable. It wasn't rejected just out of hand; it was rejected because with the introduction of the new physics it was no longer accurate. It is not merely that Ptolemy was just as good as Copernicus, given the new physics, it was not just as good as Copernican astronomy.

In one sense, method means the various techniques of laboratory research, experimental research, field observation, or just observing how people behave. There are as many different kinds of methods as there are sciences, and within sciences there are different kinds of methods. In that sense there is no unitary method. Another sense of method regards the principles (you might call it methodology or what I call the philosophy of science), in which we talk about what the criteria are that we use in order to introduce concepts, what are the criteria for a good, meaningful concept. What are the criteria we use for acceptance or rejection of a hypothesis? How do we go about theory construction and how do we validate or justify a theory? I tend to use that sense of method measuring broad general principles. I am an empiricist and I think all sciences, if they are to be sciences, are empirical; that is, they recognize that concepts have to have a relationship with reality. We have to be able to tell whether what we say is true or false. We try to test hypotheses by means of observations, directly or indirectly, and as our ambition grows we try to develop theories of wider and wider scope that will explain more and more phenomena. In that sense, I think all sciences are alike. In the sense of methodology of how you go about developing these concepts, how you go about talking to people or whether you derive hypotheses from already known theories or use your intuition, that is, your common sense about how you feel people will behave may be wrong. We use them as a source of hypotheses. All of this seems to me to be perfectly consistent with social science. For any social science which hopes to have broad scope, I think it is necessary to use hunches and insight in a perfectly meaningful sense of insight, not a mystical sense of insight, which draws upon experience. It is perfectly consistent with empiricist principles to use all of these different methods and I think they are absolutely essential. So that in one sense I say there is a unitary method; namely, we've got to be able to have empirically meaningful concepts and you've got to look for an hypothesis to test and then develop theories which, in turn, can be either tested or falsified. As to the other sense of method of using what you know from the past and what you learn from your colleagues or what you learn from common experience in order to formulate these concepts and hypotheses, it seems to me you would do everything that is helpful.

PAUL ANDERSON

As you might expect, I have some differences on these points, but I think there may be a middle ground, although I am sure that it would not be acceptable to Professor Brodbeck. My own position is, of course, that science is essentially a social activity and that scientific knowledge is every bit as affected by sociological and psychological criteria as it is by reality itself—whatever we take that to mean. As a result, I think that it is relatively uncontroversial in contemporary philosophy of science,

and certainly in sociology of science, that there is no single scientific method and certainly no demarcation criterion which exists to differentiate science from non-science. It seems to me that if we are looking for a middle ground, the best way to characterize science is as a consensus formation process. The important question we must ask is how can I convince my colleagues in the scientific community that my theory is correct. I think that the answer will differ from discipline to discipline and from time to time within the same discipline. I think that this is supported by the historical record. I think that in appraising theories our colleagues are going to use traditional criteria and psychological/sociological criteria. So I think there is a middle ground in the sense that I strongly believe that empirical testing has a role to play in science. Whether we call it confirmation following the logical empiricists, or corroboration following the falsificationists, or whether we're concerned with internal consistency or extensibility or simplicity, or all of the other traditional criteria—these all have a role to play. But I think we would be closing our eyes to the evidence that has been developed in the history and the sociology of science if we didn't also recognize that sociological criteria play an important role in the actual construction of knowledge. Things like the conjunction of a particular theory with professional interests—even class interests (if you can believe that some of the sociologists will go that far). The social acceptability of the results play an important role in determining the kinds of theories that scientists are willing to propose and the kinds of theories that scientists are willing to defend. The maintenance of prior agreements with colleagues concerning what is fact and what is not seems to play a role in this process. The nature of the presentational and rhetorical devices that are used by scientists to convince one another enters in as well. (Yes, there may actually be a role for marketing in science). And finally, there is this notion of the cost of challenging scientific theory. Latour and Woolgar, for example, conceptualize the scientific process as a kind of investment activity—we all invest in credibility. Our background knowledge, the theories that we are committed to, the facts that we take as given are the investments that we make. Our job as scientists is to enhance that credibility, to reinvest our credibility capital, and to advance our own status within the field. One of the things we do in developing that credibility is we make it very costly for others to challenge our credibility. The more costly the challenge the more difficult for other scientists to dislodge what we say is fact from its high epistemological status as fact.

It seems to me that it is reasonable for marketers to take an eclectic approach, as Jerry [Zaltman] suggests in the paper he's giving tomorrow. We need to recognize the role of traditional and sociological factors and we should not be tied to one particular philosophical approach. I think that there is no question that the sociological as well as the psychological factors enter in. There is also no question that traditional empirical factors enter in. I think that each one of us has to recognize that we have to play the game as we find it in the particular discipline we're in at the particular time in which we're trying to advance the discipline. The editors as well as the editorial boards have a particular idea of what is a good theory, what is a good notion, and how to go about presenting them. I think we've got to respond to that or we're simply not going to be able to communicate with our colleagues. At the same time, it is incumbent upon us to try to nudge those criteria a little bit. To try to raise issues such as: Is replication a good thing? That was an issue that was brought up last night, and very few people seem to be concerned at all about the fact that the issue of replication needs to be discussed. It seems to be clear to everyone that replication is a good thing. But there are alternative viewpoints on that issue. What I think we could do as metatheoriticians is to raise these issues and to try to change over time the evaluative criteria that we find in a particular discipline. But in the meantime, unfortunately, we're going to have to respond to the criteria as we find them.

JERRY OLSON

On numerous occasions I have suggested, asked, and sometimes demanded (usually in doctoral oral examinations) that people make explicit the basic, underlying, metatheoretical assumptions that provide the conceptual foundations for their research. Often they find it difficult to do so. It seems that we tend not to examine these general, very abstract assumptions very thoroughly. The examination I have in mind is, of course, at a conceptual and logical level, not empirical. In fact, empirical analyses are not of much help here, since these very basic assumptions are not testable, not even indirectly. This is why we call them metatheoretical. Perhaps this is what Lakatos meant by an inner hardcore of unassailable theoretical assumptions that "surround" and support a theoretical research program.

My point is that if it is good for empirical researchers to explicate the basic assumptions underlying their work, then it should be good for philosophers of science as well. At a metatheoretical level, we might then be able to see more clearly how alternative philosophies differ. We might have a basis for criticizing them and choosing among them. It might even be possible to begin with the metatheoretical assumptions that we like (believe in) and build a philosophy that is consistent with those abstract ideas.

Perhaps the most important metatheoretical assumption is how we think about the world (reality) and the relationship of our theories to that world. At one extreme we could see the world in an absolute sense—as an entity waiting there to be observed, whether or not we exist. Or, we could consider the world to be totally a construction of our own cognitive processes. If we believe in the former, then our theories are attempts to accurately represent that reality and we strive to develop theories that capture more and more of that reality. We might, for instance, try to develop theories that have increasing verisimilitude (greater truth content). However, if we believe that our theories "create" the reality we then "see," our perspective changes as does our criteria for theory evaluation. We then might strive to create theories that are increasingly functional in some important way—e.g., more elegant, predictive, integrative, or heuristic. We would not, however, think about whether our theories are "true"—that is, not even a meaningful question.

Some middle ground (but much closer to the latter position than the former) may be best for marketing. We might think that there is some "thing" out there, but that it can be "structured" or conceived of in a virtually infinite number of ways. There may be *a* reality (at any given time, from any given perspective), but it is one of many possible realities. Another way of saying this is that reality is relative—to a point of view, a perspective. A different perspective produces a somewhat different reality. Thus there are many different possible theories of any phenomenon, and many of these might be useful, valuable, or at least interesting.

This perspective is not as strange as it might first seem. Consider that as evolved human beings we are limited in the range of sensations that we can experience "directly." Our sense receptors (eyes, ears, touch, etc.) only respond to a limited range of the total range of variation. For example, we cannot see, in a direct visual manner, cosmic rays or radio waves. Yet, from the perspective that is provided by a measuring instrument (itself a manifestation of a theory, or several theories), we can "demonstrate" such "non-observable" phenomena. Thus most of us consider them real—a part of reality. In this rather obvious sense, our theories can be seen as "constructing" our reality.

It seems to me that positivism, in all its incarnations such as naive falsification, is based on the assumption of a stable reality that can be "directly" observed (although occasionally with difficulty). This leads to the notion that with better methods and theories we can come to know (or at least come closer to) the "truth." May Brodbeck and Shelby Hunt exemplify this perspective. Some people read Popper in this way. The so-called less "rational" approaches advocated by Lakatos and Kuhn are a bit looser. They allow, at least implicitly, that there may not be an absolute objective reality. Feyerabend comes out and says there isn't. So does Munevar and some other recent philosophers. A few theoretical physicists seem to say so more or less explicitly. That is to say, there is no one "truth." Instead there are numerous "truths" that are relative to different frames of reference.

Ok, so how does one do science in a world of multiple realities? Well, first we can realize there is a "working reality." It is defined by the frame of reference we adopt. Within that specific frame of reference we have a workable, researchable reality on which to do science—i.e., develop and test theory. The point is that we need to explicitly recognize the frame of reference we are working in and the metatheoretical assumptions embodied in it. Then we need to make sure it is the perspective we want to adopt!

This point of view leads us to recognize that there is no one "right way" to do science. I think Feyerabend is correct in suggesting that no rule, no perscriptive method, will insure success. However, this doesn't mean that there are no rules whatsoever. Instead we can consider that certain methods and rules may be appropriate and useful in certain circumstances, but as circumstances change (e.g., the theory develops or measurement techniques improve), different rules may be required. There are rules—many of them—but no single rule applies universally.

This is the relativistic perspective for the philosophy of science that I have been thinking about. To summarize, there are numerous rules for doing science. Most of these are useful for particular problems. That is, they are "good rules," *relative to certain applications*. No rule, however, can do it all. No single rule is absolutely appropriate for all situations in which scientists find themselves. Instead, we may need to match our philosophy, our prescriptive rules, our style of inquiry to the current "state of the art" of our theorizing and empirical research program. Here we would examine the current theories in use, in particular focusing on their levels of analysis, their precision and "fineness" of prediction, and on the clarity of the links between the theory's concepts and empirical data. Then we would match our philosophical perspective to that "state-of-the-art" situation.

Of course, a lot more work needs to be done to clarify these ideas before we can "count on them" in our own scientific work. Most philosophers seem to be interested in developing a more "absolutist" model of science than the relativistic ideas discussed above. Therefore, it isn't certain that much development of a relativist perspective will be undertaken. However, I think that some of us can begin to use that perspective in our own research just the same. It means that we must become familiar with several philosophical perspectives and be willing to use them selectively when the occasion warrants.

REFERENCES

Barnes, Barry (1979), *Natural Order: Historical Studies of Scientific Culture*, Beverly Hills, Calif.: Sage Publications.

Bloor, David (1976), *Knowledge and Social Imagery*, London: Routledge & Kegan Paul.

Feyerabend, Paul (1980), *Against Method*, London: Verso.

Lakatos, Imre (1974), "Falsification and the Methodology of Scientific Research Programs," in *Criticism and the Growth of Knowledge,* Imre Lakatos and Alan Musgrave, eds., Cambridge: At the University Press.

Laudan, Larry (1977), *Progress and Its Problems,* Berkeley: University of California Press.

Suppe, Frederick (1977), *The Structure of Scientific Theories,* 2nd edition, Urbana: University of Illinois Press.

Zukav, Gary (1979), *The Dancing Wuli Masters,* New York: William Morrow.

DISCUSSION QUESTIONS

Two major approaches to the philosophy of science are presented in this panel discussion:

1. Based on the information presented in the panel discussion, describe the essential characteristics of logical empiricism.

2. Based on the information presented in the panel discussion, describe the essential characteristics of subjectivism or relativism.

3. Compare and contrast, in tabular form, the beliefs of logical empiricism and subjectivism.

PREFACE TO

"Recent Developments in the Philosophy of Science"

During the past twenty years many philosophers sharply and exuberantly repudiated certain "received" views in the philosophy of science. These views were associated with logical positivist or empiricist doctrine whose proponents were the major force in developing the philosophy of science as a separate and powerful discipline after World War II. The "received" views were variously stated, not always in ways acceptable to the rather diverse philosophers who might reasonably be labeled as logical positivists and who differed among themselves on many significant matters.

In general, the main thrusts of the criticism were to reject the notion of a basic observation language, which was variously interpreted; the distinction between analytic and synthetic statements; the hypothetico-deductive analysis of the structure of scientific theories; the view of scientific explanation and prediction was deductive; and, not least, the emphasis on objective knowledge as supported by the role of observational and experimental evidence in the testing of hypotheses and theories.

The criticisms clearly cut a broad swath. Their prevalence and, for a time, broad acceptance paralleled other cultural currents of the 1960s and 1970s. Associated with the social critique of that period were vehemently antirationalistic and relativistic—even subjectivistic—views about the justification of knowledge, belief, and values. The replacement of objective truth by personal satisfaction as a criterion of acceptability had the singular merit of rendering the critique itself invulnerable to criticism. The inchoate popular expression of relativism was paralleled and, for those requiring sterner intellectual fare, undergirded by the resurgence of relativism in philosophy, as represented by the critique of logical empiricist views in the philosophy of science.

As generally happens, the critique has itself become "established" and, as also generally happens, about the time it is being questioned among philosophers, it has trickled down as new "received" doctrine to other disciplines, not least to the social sciences. This paper is a reaction against the new orthodoxy and, in particular, an attempt to demonstrate that the pronouncement of the demise of logical empiricist views is both premature and ill advised.

2

RECENT DEVELOPMENTS IN THE PHILOSOPHY OF SCIENCE*

MAY BRODBECK

Preparing for this talk, I became impressed by the sophistication of academic marketeers regarding issues in the philosophy of science and by your widespread concern that marketing take its place among the social sciences. I am far from clear that I have anything to contribute that you do not already know. In any case, I will summarize and comment on certain opposing views about the nature of scientific knowledge, concepts, and theories. It is my hope that my own particular emphasis, analysis, and evaluation will at least stimulate further discussion about the controversy and its implications for a science of marketing.

First, as a foil against which to examine recent views in the philosophy of science, I shall sketch the basic ideas of logical empiricism as I understand them. This position is not the same as the one that Suppe, in his helpful introductory essay (1974), calls the "Received View," for he includes certain doctrines which, though held by some individual philosophers identified with logical empiricism, do not constitute the core of logical empiricism. Indeed, some of these views are inconsistent with it. Logical postivism, which is also not a unitary view, is a special case of logical empiricism. In any case, logical empiricism, as I shall expound it, reflects certain fundamental ideas of modern empiricism as they derive from David Hume, but without the psychologism inherent in Hume's terminology of "impressions" and "ideas." Somebody once characterized logical empiricism as Hume plus symbolic logic. The apercu may not tell the whole story, but it reveals a lot.

Source: Reprinted with permission from *Marketing Theory: Philosophy of Science Perspectives,* Ronald F. Bush and Shelby D. Hunt, eds., Chicago, Ill.: American Marketing Association, 1982, 1–6.

*This paper was prepared while I was a Fellow at the Center for Advanced Study in the Behavioral Sciences at Stanford University. I am grateful for financial support provided by the National Endowment for the Humanities.

RECONSTRUCTION AND THE CONTEXT OF JUSTIFICATION

Logical empiricism is part of the twentieth-century movement in which philosophy took a linguistic turn. The turn to language arose from the conviction that many perennial philosophical problems or paradoxes can be traced to certain systematic ambiguities in the way we talk about the world. For example, in common speech "Tigers exist" and "Tigers growl" can be asserted with equal propriety and are both even true. "Tigers growl" is unproblematic, but reflect for a moment on "Tigers exist" and you are immediately led to philosophical perplexity. "Exists" is a grammatical predicate just like "growls." Yet to say "Tigers growl and exist" is surely redundant, for nonexistent tigers don't growl. Or consider "Tigers are real," which may be reformulated as "If something is a tiger, then it is real." Surely that is a tautology. Being real doesn't add anything to being a tiger. In consequence of a host of similar paradoxes and even absurdities, philosophers noticed that *some* philosophical problems are in some sense linguistic. Certain problems, not necessarily all, arise because of the way we talk about the world and about ourselves. Ordinary speech may be fine for routine communication, but under dialectical probing it can breed paradox and absurdity. To resolve such problems and in general to achieve philosophical clarity, philosophers distinguished between the grammatical and the logical form of statements. Although "Tigers exist" and "Tigers growl" have the same grammatical form, they differ in logical form. This distinction is a crucial step in the execution of the linguistic turn—that is, in the analysis of language as a tool for the clarification and at least partial resolution of philosophical problems.

The logical form of a sentence is the form of a sentence that replaces it after analysis for the purposes of philosophical clarification. The logical form must meet two conditions. First, it is true or false when the original statement is true or false, and, in that crucial sense, says the same thing. Second, it clarifies the original problem and does not give rise to philosophical perplexity. The contrast between logical and grammatical form is explicit in virtually all twentieth-century analytical philosophy. Indeed, it can be shown that classical philosophers as diverse as Aristotle, Hume, and Kant implicitly made a similar distinction. Logical empiricists also added the notion of logical reconstruction—that is, the replacement for philosophical purposes of one language by another, its ideal reconstruction. The reconstruction is not a true language that can be used for everyday communication or description. It is rather a schema, shorn of nuance, ambiguity, and rich idiomatic context, but a useful tool for clarifying certain philosophical issues.

Logical analysis thus replaces parts of ordinary language, which includes the technical language of science, by another "language" or schema, which is its reconstruction. The reconstruction need not be either formalized or complete. It is only metaphorically a language for we cannot speak it. The reconstruction is piecemeal, a way of talking about certain problematic notions that is free of the contextual variations in meaning to which common speech is subject.

The distinction between the context of discovery and the context of justification undergirds the adoption of logical reconstruction as a tool of clarification in the philosophy of science. The context of discovery includes the historical background and ambient social-psychological circumstances in which scientists select research problems, communicate with one another, formulate potentially significant concepts, and develop theories and hypotheses to explain phenomena. Historians and sociologists of science have enriched our understanding of these conditions. The context of justification, on the other hand, concerns those structural features of scientific theories, their constituent concepts and laws, by virtue of which theories describe and can be used to explain the observable world. Considerations of evidence for theories are relevant to these features. They are abstracted from the social context and the vagaries of tradition, circumstance, and personalities that may, at any given time, cause preoccupation with, but not be evidence for, one theory rather than another. Knowledge of the his-

torical, social, and psychological circumstances may of course be helpful in reconstructing the structure of scientific concepts, theories, and explanation. Yet, the resulting structure by virtue of which concepts are meaningful and theories productive is independent of the historical circumstances in which they are embedded. Or such is the logical empiricist reconstructionist view.

The philosophy of science is concerned to clarify certain key notions such as "cause," "explanation," and "theory." In the logical reconstruction or analysis, these notions are extracted from the everyday context, in which they have several different uses, and the diverse usages are distinguished from one another. Some recent philosophers stop there. For the logical empiricist or reconstructionist, however, probing the idiom for different usages is only preliminary to resolving or clarifying the philosophical issues. This clarification can be achieved only by identifying the usage that most closely corresponds to our preanalytic notions about, say, the distinguishing characteristics of scientific explanation. It then must be shown why this usage is basic to a scientifically sound explanation.

THREE CORE IDEAS OF LOGICAL EMPIRICISM

With this background, let me sketch some fundamental ideas of logical empiricism. These ideas are postanalytic reconstructions of the way we and scientists speak about the world. They are not descriptions of all the diverse and shifting ways language is used in the context of discovery. This presentation will serve us later, as we examine some recent criticisms.

Language has a vocabulary. This vocabulary has two kinds of words, descriptive and logical. The logical words, such as "or," "not," and "if . . . then . . . ." give the language its structure or form. The descriptive words give language its content. In particular, the subject matter or content of an area is indicated by its descriptive terms or concepts. Concepts are those terms which refer to the characters or attributes of individuals and the relations among them. They may refer to characters of inanimate physical things, of organisms, or of societies.

The meaning of descriptive words is stipulated by specifying the properties, including relational properties, to which they refer. Referential meaning is only one sense of the systematically ambiguous notion of meaning. But it is a crucial sense. The meaning of logical words is specified by stating the conditions for the truth or falsity of the compound sentences formed by means of them. The truth of the simple component sentence containing no logical words, like "Smith sells cars," is determined by specifiable observations. Such sentences are statements of individual fact. The truth of a compound sentence is then specified as a function of the truth of its constituents. The linguistic distinction between word and sentence parallels the nonlinguistic distinction between meaning and truth. To blur the former is to blur the latter; and if the distinction between meaning and truth is blurred, then intelligibility itself is forfeit. The meaning of some terms or concepts and the truth of some sentences does not depend upon the meaning or truth of other terms or sentences. Otherwise, we would be faced with a vicious regress in which language is a self-contained system having no contact with the world it is presumably about. I shall return to this point later.

A statement is meaningful if we know to what its descriptive terms refer and can therefore directly or indirectly determine by experience whether the sentence is true or false. Meaning precedes verification or confirmation. Logical empiricism rejects the verification theory of meaning associated with early positivism. A statement is verifiable because it is meaningful, not vice versa. Language is about the world and makes contact with it through our use of descriptive terms. Most scientific terms are either quantified or dispositional and refer to complex states of affairs. They must be defined before we can determine whether statements containing them are true or false.

The distinction between words and sentences implies another, that between synthetic and analytic statements. Some sentences are true by their form alone, that is, without knowledge of the meaning of their descriptive words. Such statements are also called tautologies. For example, "If P then P," or "P or not-P." All tautologies are compound statements. These statements are necessarily true, but they are without factual content. Synthetic statements, which may be simple or compound, are not true by form alone; their truth or falsity depends upon their content. Such statements may be statements of individual fact (simple or complex), or

they may be general statements. In either case, we cannot tell from examination of the sentence itself whether it is true or false; some observations have to be made. Definitions, strictly speaking, are not statements but rules about the use of words. However, it is frequently convenient to express them as statements. In that case, they are tautologies of the form "$P = P$." In common language, including the language of science in the context of discovery, we often cannot tell from an isolated sentence whether it is true by definition or a synthetic statement. Hence, the need for a reconstruction of how terms are being used at any given time in a given context. The relevance of this remark will become clearer later. All synthetic statements are only contingent or merely probable; that is, further experience may show them to be false. In brief, synthetic statements have content and say something about the world but are only contingently true. No knowledge about the world is certain, including our knowledge of the truth or falsity of the simplest statements. Analytic statements lack content, but are necessarily true by virtue of their form alone.

One further essential distinction is emphasized by logical empiricists, and not only by them. Among sentences, logical empiricists also distinguish the normative or prescriptive statements from descriptive statements. (In ordinary speech, of course, there are also questions, exclamations, and so on, but these do not concern an analysis of science.) Normative sentences contain words like "ought," "better," or "good" in their noninstrumental senses. They are statements about ends or goods-in-themselves, not about means. Descriptive statements do not contain any normative words. In ordinary speech and the context of discovery, the normative and descriptive are not always easy to separate. Analysis is required to determine that a statement is descriptive or, perhaps implicitly, normative. If it is descriptive, then its contingent truth or falsity can be determined by observation or inference from observation. If the sentence is normative, then other considerations about our ideals and ends enter, and the sentence is not, in the same sense, either true or false.

These then are the three basic tenets of logical empiricism. First, a distinction between terms or concepts and sentences and a distinction among terms between descriptive and logical words. All descriptive terms must ultimately be used to refer to some observable state of affairs, though the chain of definition may be long and complex. These terms have referential meaning. Second, among sentences, we distinguish the synthetic or factual, which are always only contingently true, from the analytic or tautological, which are necessarily true by their form alone. Finally, we distinguish the normative or evaluative use of language from the descriptive.

What is a sound scientific explanation and what are the grounds for it according soundness? What are the characteristics of a fruitful theory? Reconstruction starts with an insight, based on classical examples, into what counts as a sound explanation. The explication should reveal the general structure of sound explanation and clarify the intrinsic connections between the statements which explain and those that are explained so as to reveal the force of scientific explanation. For explanation, which may or may not provide "understanding," we need laws or generalizations.

An explanation of an individual fact always includes at least one law or generalization among its premises. This law may in turn be explained by deducing it from other laws. Although all the laws involved in an explanation are empirical generalizations or synthetic statements that may turn out to be false, the deductive connections among them are analytic, asserting that if the premises are true, then the statement to be explained must be true. A theory is such a deductively connected set of laws. In a theory, all the statements, both explained and explaining, are generalizations. Those that do the explaining are called the axioms of the theory. The laws that are explained are the theorems of the theory. The axioms are such only by virtue of their place in a theory. Neither self-evident nor otherwise privileged, they are empirical laws whose truth is, temporarily at least, taken for granted in order to see what other empirical assertions, the theorems, must be true if the axioms are true. An axiom in one theory may be a theorem in another of broader scope. Thus, what is an axiom in Galileo's theory about the free fall of bodies on earth is a theorem in the Newtonian theory of gravitation, which explains Galileo's laws. The Newtonian axiom is in turn explained, in conjunction with other statements, by Einstein's theory. (I shall presently turn to the critics' denial that this deduction is possible.) Explanation is always relative to a set of premises

that logically imply what is to be explained. We stop explaining when we don't know any more. There is no "ultimate" explanation (Brodbeck 1962; Hunt 1976).

Some auxiliary notions follow from the three core distinctions. Scientists seek and, within the limits of human fallibility, find objective knowledge of the external world. Indeed, if they did not, why should anyone pay attention to what they say? This knowledge is cumulative. A new theory replaces an old one, either because it has greater scope or because it explains and predicts with greater accuracy than the old one. Of course, it may have both greater scope and greater accuracy, as does Einstein's theory relative to Newton's. Theories can be compared by the difference in the observable events that are inferred from them. By our knowledge of scientific laws, we control and change nature in ways that can only be miraculous if in fact these laws do not describe the way things are. Despite the success, at least within the physical and biological sciences, apparent to every eye as reflected in technological accomplishment, the possibility of objective truth has persistently been denied. All three basic logical-empiricist distinctions and their associated views about concepts, laws, hypothetico-deductive explanation, and objective truth have been under attack. In some cases they are rejected only partially, in others totally; in some cases hesitantly, in others with gusto. I shall concentrate on the major criticisms, those that appear to have been most influential and are shared in some form by most critics, even though they disagree among themselves on various other particulars. I shall summarize the critics views against the foil of logical empiricism, and then discuss the grounds for the criticisms.

RECENT CRITICISMS OF LOGICAL EMPIRICIST PHILOSOPHY OF SCIENCE

First, the critics' major contention is that there is no "neutral" or theory-independent observation language that can be shared by all sorts of theories and can form the basis for choosing between them (Hanson 1958; Kuhn 1970). All terms are "theory-laden." The meaning of a term varies with its context, and it is "implicitly" defined by its connection with other terms in the theory. The same word may occur in different theories, but it will be used for a different concept because its "meaning" changes with its context. It follows that the distinction between words and sentences is rejected. This distinction requires that some terms have (referential) meaning independent of the context in which they occur. According to the empiricists, these terms are used in sentences that can be confirmed independently. For the critics, however, no statement can be independently true or false, because every statement is inseparable from the web of other statements in which it is enmeshed.

It follows from this view that the second tenet of logical empiricism, the distinction between analytic and synthetic statements, is greatly attenuated if not utterly abandoned. Recall that a synthetic statement is true by virtue of the truth or falsity of its constituent statements. If these constituent statements have no independent meaning, they cannot be determined to be true or false independently. In the regularity "If P then Q," if part of the meaning of P is Q (and other concepts of the theory), then P and Q are not independently true or false. Neither the regularity nor its constituents can be tested independently, which means they cannot be tested at all. The theory must be taken as a whole on other than observational grounds. Synthetic statements, therefore, though clearly not logical truths, nevertheless are not in any direct way true or false about the world. They are, the critics claim, true by "meaning."

Third, since concepts mean different things in different theories, alternative theories are incommensurable (Kuhn 1970). That is, there are no objective tests or rational grounds for choosing between theories, because comparison requires a common language in which conflicting assertions are made about the same phenomena. On the critics' view, if one theory implies that demand will rise and another that it will fall. These are not contradictory predictions because "demand" means something different in each theory. What "counts as a fact" is said to be determined by the theory in which it occurs. Accordingly, the choice between theories is based upon a variety of nonrational grounds, for no independent theory-free evidence can be stated. It follows that the third tenet of logical empiricism, the distinction between the normative or evaluative and the descriptive, also crumbles, since the rejection or acceptance of a theory follows from evaluative, normative considerations, which are held to be inseparable from whatever descriptive features the theory may have. The corollary belief of logical empiricists in realism and objective truth is of course replaced by subjectivism and relativism.

In the view of these critics, then, science is in effect a game, rather than an inquiry, disciplined by observation, into the way the world goes. Scientists adopt so-called "theories" or "paradigms," which incorporate, beyond the austere axioms and theorems of hypothetico-deductive theories, whole systems of thought, belief, myth, customs, and values, these broadly construed "theories" or "world views" cannot be said to be either true or false. Like games, they are first adopted or "played" and them abandoned by their adherents on essentially nonrational grounds. Such grounds may include aesthetic considerations, group loyalty, tradition, attitudes, values, or what-not, but not belief or doubt about their objective truth in the light of the best evidence.

The critics maintain that new theories spring up and old ones are abandoned for a variety of sociohistorico-psychological causes. The search for objective truth is an illusion. When an old theory is replaced by a new one, the latter is not a progressive extension of knowledge, but only a change in the accepted set of beliefs. Since new and old theories are incommensurable, the new cannot be said to be better, have broader scope, or be more accurate than the old. Even physics is but a game in which no two theories are comparable. All are equally viable until the community decides, for whatever reason, to quit and play another game.

This summary of the main tenor of the criticisms is ruthlessly brief, and perhaps does only rough justice to the views espoused. But it will serve. What are the grounds for these assertions, and what is to be said about their validity?

CRITIQUE OF THE CRITICS' VIEWS

Undergirding these criticisms is a conflation of the context of discovery with the context of justification. Two divergent sources are joined in a common set of criticisms. The first is the doctrine, now losing sway, that philosophical problems and particularly problems of meaning and understanding are to be resolved by analysis of the ways in which we ordinarily speak and communicate with one another (Winch 1958). The second source is the entry of erudite historians of science into the philosophy of science. The historians, quite naturally, stress the historical, social-psychological context of science. These two approaches intermingle in ways I shall not here explore. The contributions of both approaches can be illuminating, the historical rather more than the preoccupation with ordinary language. Each, in its own way, conflates science as an activity with its justifying logical structure. Both, not surprisingly, end in an unacceptable relativism.

The rallying cry of the analyst of ordinary language was "meaning is use." Differences of use signify differences of meaning. In science, it follows, the meaning of a term is defined by the role it plays within a particular law, theory, or even conversation. The term means something different in each different law, theory, or social context. How, then, do we state the negation of a hypothesis, if the term changes meaning with context? Indeed, we cannot state an exception. It follows that we cannot falsify a theory. We can only reject the whole system *in toto*. Hence, the doctrine "meaning is use" joins the historian's incorporation of social-psychological processes into the definition of meaning. Both groups (and they overlap as well as converge) confuse the two meanings of "meaning," reference, and significance.

A term is defined by declaring the observable state of affairs to which it refers. A term may have such reference but be useless; that is, we may know nothing about it, it may not be connected with anything else. When a concept occurs in a law or generalization, then that concept is also meaningful in a second sense. We know something about the reference of the term, and the concept is therefore significant. All "good" concepts are meaningful in both senses: they have a reference and they occur in laws. In marketing, we may define a term as referring to a group having certain features in common and be able to measure and count these features until the cows come home. But if those features, referred to by the concept, do not affect the group's marketing behavior, that is, its proclivity to enter into or desist from certain transactions, then the concept for all its empirical content is not worthwhile. It lacks significance. Without the independent referential meaning of a term we could not find out whether or not it was significant. In fact, we would not know what we were talking about. Referential meaning is a matter of convention. Terms do

not mean by themselves; we mean by using them. Of course we do. Significance or lawfulness is not a matter of convention, but a factual matter of the way things are. We can define any concept we wish to define. But we cannot endow a concept with significance. Either it has it or it hasn't.

To blur this distinction is to blur a contribution of the mind—the concepts we use—with what is not such a contribution, but, independent of the way we speak about it, a matter of the way the world goes. The formula "meaning is use" blurs this distinction. The doctrine that natural laws are true by virtue of the "meaning" of their constituent term obliterates it. For the two questions, what a thing is and what happens to it, are held by critics of empiricism to be not two questions, but one. The terms, we are told, cannot be identified apart from the laws in which they occur. In other words, given a law "If P then Q" we cannot know that we have P unless we simultaneously know that "it" has Q. This seems to make Q a definitional property of P. But definitions are tautologies and it is denied, even by the critics, that laws are tautologies. Yet the "meaning" of P is Q and denial of the law is "conceptually untenable."

Again, all terms are said to be "theory-laden." Their meaning is given by the entire theory, that is, the context in which they occur. Since the relevant context varies with each use and each user, no two people ever use a term in the same way. Lightning and thunder are said to mean something different to a youngster than to a meterologist. A clock means something different to Galileo's apprentice than to Galileo. The concept of mass means a different thing in Einstein's theory and in Newton's. *Accurately* stated, the meteorologist knows more about flashes and rumbles than does the boy, and Galileo knew more about clocks than did his apprentice. Otherwise, how would we even know that they were all talking about the same thing? Similarly, mass is a constant in Newton and varies with velocity in Einstein. These are conflicting laws or facts about mass, not part of its meaning. We can compare the two statements and show that Newton is wrong if taken universally, but right for the special initial conditions of ordinary earthly dimensions and velocities. The critics cannot have it both ways, namely, that Newton was wrong and that different theories are incommensurable. If, as mentioned above, an exception is held to be "conceptually impossible," then the statement itself is conceptually "necessary." Instead of the way we speak being determined by the way the world is, what is possible in the world is determined by the way we speak about it. If the "meaning" of a concept is always another concept, then the job of statements to describe the world, their connection with something nonconceptual, becomes inexplicable. Confusion of social-psychological description of language as communication with structural analyses of what this communication asserts about the world leads, not for the first time, to a philosophy that loses the world in a system of "meanings." If the system of laws is to be about the world—if it is to be a factual, descriptive system—its concepts must also have meaning in the sense of either designation or reference.

Nor can laws intelligibly be said to implicitly define their terms. The phrase "implicit definition" is most misleading. It can be used sensibly only when speaking of the axioms of an uninterpreted formal system, that is, a system of marks on paper. For such a system, the axioms implicitly define its terms only in the sense that, showing structure but not content, they delimit the range of possible meanings or interpretations that can be given to the primitive symbols of the system if true statements are to result. There may be many alternative sets of descriptive, referential concepts that result in either true or false statements (Brodbeck 1959, 1968).

The formulatized axioms of measurement, for instance, are true under some interpretations, false under others. Scientific theories share an important characteristic with formal systems, but are also significantly different from them. Like formal axiom systems, the axioms of scientific theories logically imply their theorems. Unlike formal systems, the axioms (and theorems) of a scientific theory have empirical content and are either true or false about the world. We may not know which; we may have pretty good evidence or none at all. But evidence is relevant to them. The assimilation of scientific theories to formal or mathematical systems combined with conventionalist-instrumentalist views about science to produce the confused notion that scientific theories "implicitly define" their terms. These instrumentalist-pragmatist currents were further reinforced by the ordinary-language or "conceptual analysis" school of philosophy. According to that school, all uses of language—for moral, religious,

or scientific purposes—fit the model of a game, reflecting different "forms of life," which may be played or unplayed but are neither true nor false.

The notion that all terms are "theory-laden" also gained specious plausibility from being confused with the quite different claim that no statements are "purely observational." This claim, properly understood, is correct even for simple or grammatically singular observation statements, though the early positivists may have thought otherwise. All knowledge, including knowledge of simple observable facts, is fallible because it contains an inferential component. The statement that something is a table, for instance, is not conclusively confirmed by a single observation or even by many observations. Even the simplest statement about material objects implies a regularity of behavior that is never fully present to the senses. The referential meaning of "table" includes reference to past and future behaviors. This means only that our knowledge of even singular statements involves generalizations. Such knowledge is therefore contingent and may be withdrawn on the basis of further evidence. To say this is not to say, as the critics do, that every way of describing the world makes a claim based on a particular theory.

The assertion that something is a table does not include the theory of particle mechanics from which it may be derived, nor does it include any other theory. To confirm the statement we have to test inferences, based on the meaning of the term table, about the object's past and probable future behavior. We do not have to study physics in order to know the meaning of "table" any more than we have to study economics in order to know that money is a medium of exchange. The referential meaning of these concepts is not dependent upon theories about them. All scientific knowledge requires evidence that, by its nature, is different from what it is evidence for—namely, the truth or falsity of an assertion about a certain state of affairs. One may confusingly express this fact by saying that every statement involves "interpretation" or is not "purely observational." In the sense I have indicated, this is true. However, it does nothing to support the notion that all descriptive statements rest on the theories from which they are derived, or even on theories at all. Different theories may, accordingly, talk about the same thing, whether it be tables, the planet Mercury, or money. These concepts are not "theory-laden" in the sense that their meaning is dependent upon the theories in which they occur. In short, the impossibility of a "pure observation" language does not support the notion that no two theories are commensurable or capable of test on the basis of theory-independent observations.

The ordinary-language philosopher focuses on language as communication as contrasted with the use of language for description. Communication is typically elliptical and context bound. The historian focuses on the social-psychological conditions of theory change and the dynamics of resistance to change. These preoccupations each confuse two senses of meaning and render inexplicable the confirmation or disconfirmation of hypotheses and the relation of theory to the world. Emphasis on resistance to change in the light of contrary evidence, whatever that can mean for our critics, results in denial of the line of continuity in science, as, say, from Galileo to Newton to Einstein. Instead, we are presented with the doctrine that every new theory constitutes a revolution so extreme that the victor cannot be compared with the vanquished. Each new theory is "incommensurable" with its predecessor, and the replacement of one by the other is explicable only on nonrational, relativistic grounds.

Scientists do, of course, frequently redefine their terms in the interests of greater precision and reliability. Tempered steel may be initially defined in terms of what was done to steel in the past. As we gain knowledge about the structure of steel, "tempered" is redefined to refer to a present molecular state of the steel. We draw upon theory in order to introduce a new concept, which replaces the old one. The new concept is now defined in terms of a different set of empirical conditions. That re-definition is not "theory-laden," but has been causally provoked by theoretical knowledge. The concept has not changed; it has been replaced by another one with determinable empirical content, independent of the laws in which it occurs.

Similarly, the historians of science rightly point out that scientists are often reluctant to abandon theories with great scope and explanatory power even in the face of disconfirming evidence, as we would normally say. There may be so much converging evidence for a law, or it may occupy so fundamental a place in a well-confirmed theory, that when something happens that seems to cast doubt upon its truth, rather than simply give it up, the scientists will look for interfering factors, or decide that perhaps his initial and boundary conditions were not those for which the law in question was affirmed to hold. In this sense, there are no "crucial experiments" for single, isolated hypotheses, as there may always be other sources of error in the theory. We can never conclusively falsify a theory, just as we can never conclusively confirm one. In principle, every experiment tests all the relevant hypotheses, but for the purposes of any particular research problem most of these are taken for granted. A new planet was discovered because the physicists were loath to abandon Newton's law of gravitation in the face of what appeared to be counterevidence. But next time around this expedient did not work. To explain later observations in conflict with predictions from the theory, a similar hypothesis of yet another planet was put forward. It had to be abandoned because no planet could be found. The theory was ultimately replaced by one that did explain the observed perturbations of the planet Mercury. We can tinker with and cling to old theories only up to a point, depending on the available evidence.

Certain "degrees of freedom" exist in theory-construction, but this does not ratify a conventionalist or instrumentalist view of theories. Not everything is a matter of choice. If certain conventions or definitions are adopted, then other parts of the theory are contingent. In a psychological sense, but only in a psychological sense, some laws of physics may, at some time, be called "necessary." To attribute this sort of necessity to a law, theory, or paradigm is to make a statement about the behavior of scientists in specified kinds of situations. The logical status of the law remains synthetic or contingent, whose truth or falsity must be, to the extent possible, independently determined.

As my final point, let me comment on the distinction between observational language and theoretical language. According to the critics, logical empiricists allow that some concepts, namely, those in basic theories about invisible particles, do not have referential meaning but are intelligible only in a given theoretical context. The critics reject the distinction, maintaining that all concepts are in the same boat, being all dependent for meaning on their "theoretical" contexts. Two senses of "theoretical" are conflated. One refers to concepts in any descriptive hypothetico-deductive system of laws. The other refers to the special case of theories in physical and closely bordering sciences whose concepts refer to invisible particles and quantities.

There is no canonical logical empiricist position on the dichotomy observational vs. theoretical. My own view is that no such distinction can be made *tout court* for science. Only by examining specific theories can we determine whether there is a difference to be discerned and, if so, the form it takes. For example, in classical Newtonian mechanics, which is a macroscopic (perceptual) experimental theory, no essential distinction exists between its theoretical terms and its experimental or observational ones. All its terms are defined ultimately in terms of observable properties of things. Its concepts, however, exhibit a difference in their degree of "abstractness," that is, in the length of the definitional chain that links the concept to measurable properties. In this respect, mass is more abstract than velocity, but it is no less observable concept.

On the other hand, in other physical theories, statements about invisible particles are introduced in order to explain the observable world. For example, the experimental law about the relation between the pressure, temperature, and volume of gases is explained by means of a theory about the behavior of invisible particles. It should be noted that the experimental law's meaning and truth is independent of the theory used to explain it. Even if the microscopic theory were abandoned, Boyle's law, in corrected form, would remain true. Various interpretations have been made of the logical connections between the microscopic theory of the invisible and the theory of macroscopic or perceptual phenomena, which it was introduced to explain. I have elsewhere proposed an analysis of the relation between theories about invisible particles and the visible world which they are introduced to explain (Brodbeck 1965). I will not elaborate on that relation here, but make one concluding comment.

The concepts of social science refer to observed behavior, either of individuals or of groups. Similarly, the terms of classical Newtonian theory and of the theory of gases all refer to what can be observed. The relatively simple structure of such powerful theories has not, to put it moderately, been deployed to its fullest advantage by social scientists. Why, then, should they hunger after the complexity of the invisible? In any case, it is yet to be claimed that the phenomena of social science are of atomic or subatomic dimensions. Marketing is or strives to be a social science. The critics' relativism trivializes all science. I would strongly urge that marketing stick to its last and strive for theories about observable patterns of behavior. For this important purpose, I suggest that the principles of logical empiricism are still the best guide to eventual success in the search for truth about how consumers behave.

The winds of doctrine in the philosophy of science flow as variably and fiercely as elsewhere. They come, they go, they return. The critics have stirred up the atmosphere. The logical empiricists have had to sharpen their tools, state more carefully their views. The hurricane has blown through. A calm remains. It is time to return to basics, to objectivity, reality, and fundamental empiricist doctrine.

REFERENCES

Brodbeck, May (1959), "Models, Meaning, and Theories," in *Symposium on Sociological Theory*, L. Gross, ed., New York: Harper & Row. (Reprinted in Brodbeck 1968.)

———(1962), "Explanation, Prediction, and 'Imperfect' Knowledge," in *Minnesota Studies in the Philosophy of Science III*, H. Feigl and G. Maxwell, eds., Minneapolis: University of Minnesota Press. (Reprinted in Brodbeck 1968.)

———(1965), "Mental and Physical: Identity vs. Sameness," in *Mind, Method, and Matter*, P. K. Feyerabend and G. Maxwell, eds., Minneapolis: University of Minnesota Press.

———(1968), *Readings in the Philosophy of the Social Sciences*, New York: Macmillan.

Hanson, N. R. (1958), *Patterns of Discovery*, Cambridge: At the University Press.

Hunt, Shelby D. (1976), *Marketing Theory: Conceptual Foundations of Research in Marketing*, Columbus, Ohio: Grid.

Kuhn, Thomas S. (1970), *The Structure of Scientific Revolutions*, 2nd ed., Chicago: University of Chicago Press.

Suppe, Frederick (1974), *The Structure of Scientific Theories*. Urbana: University of Illinois Press.

Winch, Peter (1958), *The Idea of a Social Science*, London: Routledge & Kegan Paul.

DISCUSSION QUESTIONS

1. Distinguish the context of justification from the context of discovery and explain why this distinction was defended by the logical empiricists and why it was rejected by their critics.

2. There are diverse meanings of "meaning." Explain why the *referential* meaning of a concept must be separated from other sorts of meaning.

3. How does a scientific theory permit the explanation or prediction of the behavior of individuals or groups? If a prediction about behavior does not materialize, why does this failure disconfirm or falsify the theory? Why can no theory be either falsified or confirmed *definitively?*

4. What are some of the observation concepts of marketing? Why are these independent of any theory in which they may occur? Can we have different theories containing the same concepts? What are the implications of your answer for the notion that all concepts are "theory-laden"?

5. How is observational evidence relevant to theories? In the light of this relevance, discuss the view that alternative theories are "incommensurable."

6. Critically discuss the view that alternative theories are accepted or rejected on socio-psychological grounds rather than on grounds of objective evidence for or against them.

PREFACE TO

"Marketing, Scientific Progress, and Scientific Method"

The genesis of this article may be traced to my early interest in the financial aspects of marketing management. In attempting to bring theories from financial economics to bear on marketing problems, I was struck by the disparate nature of the two disciplines. Although it was clear that the fields shared some common problem areas (e.g., investment analysis), it was also obvious that their approaches to these issues were radically different. I was particularly impressed by the contrasting nature of their respective research traditions. I found that within finance there was a considerable degree of consensus on the problems to be solved, the strengths and weaknesses of the theories proposed as solutions to these problems, and the methodologies, concepts, and procedures to be used in improving, modifying, or replacing existing theories. In short, the research program in finance displayed a coherence and structure that seemed to be lacking in marketing. At the same time, however, it was not clear that financial economists had been any more successful in generating useful, well-confirmed, or reliable knowledge than marketers. Indeed, financial theories were often criticized as unrealistic abstractions with little pragmatic value. Moreover, there appeared to be a significant level of incommensurability between theories in finance and marketing. That is, one could not simply apply finance theory to marketing problems without carting in a considerable amount of philosophical, ontological, and metaphysical baggage from financial economics. It was in an effort to determine the reasons for the marked differences between these two disciplines that led me to explore the philosophy, sociology, and history of science literature. In the course of this research, I discovered that existing notions of science and scientific method in marketing were out of step with contemporary thought in the field of science studies.

The major objective of the article was to acquaint marketers with this literature and to pursue its implications for scientific practice in marketing. The article concludes that there is no universal scientific method and that there is no clear cut demarcation between science and nonscience. This leads to an inescapable relativism that asserts scientific knowledge is generated within highly encapsulated research traditions. Finally, it is suggested that if marketing wishes to attain the status of a consensus science, it must change its cognitive aims and must commit itself to programmatic research aimed at solving important scientific problems. The article is essentially unaltered from the form in which it originally appeared.

24

3

MARKETING, SCIENTIFIC PROGRESS, AND SCIENTIFIC METHOD*

PAUL F. ANDERSON

INTRODUCTION

The debate concerning the scientific status of marketing is now in its fourth decade (Alderson and Cox 1948; Bartels 1951; Baumol 1957; Buzzell 1963; Converse 1945; Hunt 1976a, 1976b; Hutchison 1952; O'Shaughnessy and Ryan 1979; Taylor 1965; Vaile 1949). During this time much heat has been generated but relatively little light has been shed on the question of marketing's scientific credentials. The search for criteria that separate science from nonscience dates from the very beginnings of Western philosophy (Laudan 1980, 1982a). Popper labeled this question the "problem of demarcation," and asserted that its solution would be "the key to most of the fundamental problems of the philosophy of science" (1962, p. 42). Unfortunately, philosophers have been signally unsuccessful in their search for such criteria (Laudan 1982a). Indeed, there are many who consider the question to be a chimera.

Source: Reprinted with permission from the *Journal of Marketing,* 47, (4), 1983, 18–31, Chicago, Ill.: American Marketing Association.

*The author benefited greatly from the comments and suggestions of Jerry Olson, Paul Peter, Michael Ryan, two anonymous referees, and from conversations with numerous colleagues at Virginia Polytechnic Institute's Center for the Study of Science in Society. He wishes particularly to thank Larry Laudan for his comments on an earlier draft of this article.

The problem of demarcation is inextricably linked with the issue of scientific method. This can be seen, for example, in one of the more recent attempts to deal with the question in marketing. Hunt (1976a, 1976b) contends that the study of the positive dimensions (where the objective is explanation, prediction and understanding) of marketing qualifies as science. He reaches this conclusion by measuring the discipline against his own set of demarcation criteria. According to Hunt, a field of inquiry is a science if (1) it has a distinct subject matter, (2) it presupposes the existence of underlying uniformities in this subject matter, and (3) it employs the "scientific method." Brief reflection will reveal, however, that Hunt's demarcation standard depends entirely on this last criterion. The first two requirements are specious since astrologers, parapsychologists, and scientific creationists also study subject matters which they presuppose to exhibit regularities.

For Hunt, the key element in the scientific method is "intersubjective certification." On this view, science is epistemologically unique because different investigators with varying attitudes, opinions, and beliefs can ascertain the truth content of theories, laws, and explanations (Hunt 1976b). Elsewhere, Hunt (1983, p. 249) makes clear that his concept of scientific method is a version of positivism known as logical empiricism—an approach which has not held sway in the philosophy of science for more than a decade. During much of this century "positivism" dominated discussions of scientific method. The term was popularized by Comte, and generally refers to a strict empiricism which recognizes as valid only those knowledge claims based on experience (Abbagnano 1967; Brown 1977). In recent years, however, positivism has been challenged by insights drawn largely from the history and sociology of science. The historical and sociological perspective has revolutionized the field of science studies and has radically altered the traditional image of the scientific method.[1]

Since at least the early 1960s marketers have looked to the philosophy of science for guidance concerning scientific practice (Cox, Alderson, and Shapiro 1964; Halbert 1965; Howard and Sheth 1969; Hunt 1976a, 1983; Sheth 1967, 1972; Zaltman, Pinson, and Angelmar 1973). Indeed, it is clear that this literature has informed the actual construction of theory in marketing (Howard and Sheth 1969). More recently, some of the newer approaches from the science studies field have been making their way into the discipline (Olson 1981; Peter 1982, 1983; Zaltman, LeMasters, and Heffring 1982). This article will attempt to review both the traditional and contemporary literature bearing on the questions of scientific method and scientific progress. The objective will be to demonstrate the utility of post-positivistic models of the scientific process for an understanding of marketing's scientific status. The article begins with a discussion of the two pillars of positivism: logical empiricism and falsificationism.

LOGICAL EMPIRICISM

During the 1920s positivism emerged as a full-fledged philosophy of science in the form of logical positivism. Developed by the Vienna Circle, a group of scientists and philosophers led informally by Moritz Schlick, logical positivism accepted as its central doctrine Wittgenstein's verification theory of meaning (Brown 1977; Howard and Sheth 1969; Passmore 1967). The verification theory holds that statements or propositions are meaningful only if they can be empirically verified. This criterion was adopted in an attempt to differentiate scientific (meaningful) statements from purely metaphysical (meaningless) statements. However, logical positivism soon ran headlong into the age-old "problem of induction" (Black 1967; Hume

1911). According to the logical positivists, universal scientific propositions are true according to whether they have been verified by empirical tests—yet no finite number of empirical tests can ever guarantee the truth of universal statements (Black 1967, Brown 1977, Chalmers 1976). In short, inductive inference can never be justified on purely logical grounds (Hempel 1965).

As a result of these difficulties, Carnap (1936, 1937) developed a more moderate version of positivism which has come to be known as logical empiricism. Logical empiricism became the "received view" in the philosophy of science for approximately the next 20 years (Suppe 1974). Despite its decline during the 1960s, contemporary discussions of scientific method in marketing are still dominated by its influence (Hunt 1983).

Essentially, Carnap replaces the concept of verification with the idea of "gradually increasing confirmation" (1953, p. 48). He notes that if verification is taken to mean the "complete and definitive establishment of truth," then universal statements can never be verified (p. 48). However, they may be "confirmed" by the accumulation of successful empirical tests. This process can be illustrated with reference to Figure 1 (Savitt 1980; Zaltman, Pinson, and Angelmar 1973). According to the tenets of logical empiricism, the scientific process begins with the untainted observation of reality. This provides the researcher with his/her image of the real world structure from which he/she cognitively generates an a priori (i.e., untested) model of the process to be investigated. Hypotheses are derived from the model and are subjected to empirical tests. If the data are in accord with the hypotheses, a confirming instance has been identified. Thus, science progresses through the accumulation of multiple confirming instances obtained under a wide variety of circumstances and conditions.

Logical empiricism is characterized by the inductive statistical method. On this view, science begins with observation, and its theories are ultimately justified by the accumulation of further observations, which provide probabilisic support for its conclusions. Within marketing a classic example of this methodology is to be found in the PIMS studies. Based on observations of 57 corporations representing 620 individual "businesses,"[2] the PIMS researchers conclude that there is a positive linear relationship between market share and ROI

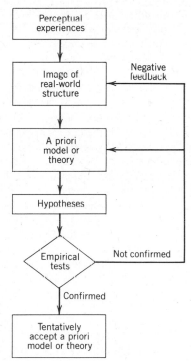

FIGURE 1

The logical empiricist model of scientific method.

(Buzzell, Gale, and Sultan 1975). This finding is generalized to a universal statement and is also converted into a normative prescription for business strategy.

Of course, the logical empiricist's use of a probabilistic linkage between the explanans and the explanandum does not avoid the problem of induction. It remains to be shown how a finite number of observations can lead to the logical conclusion that a universal statement is "probably true" (Black 1967). Moreover, attempts to justify induction on the basis of experience are necessarily circular. The argument that induction has worked successfully in the past is itself an inductive argument and cannot be used to support the principle of induction (Chalmers 1976).

In addition to the problem of induction, logical empiricism encounters further difficulties because of its insistence that science rests on a secure observational base. There are at least two problems here. The first is that observations are always subject to measurement error. The widespread concern in the

behavioral sciences with reliability and validity assessments attests to this. As observational procedures and measurement technologies improve, we can minimize but never eliminate these measurement errors.[3] The second, and perhaps more significant, problem concerns the theory dependence of observation (Howard and Sheth 1969). As Hanson (1958), Kuhn (1962), Popper (1972), and others have pointed out, observations are always interpreted in the context of a priori knowledge. The history of science provides numerous examples of the fact that "what a man sees depends both upon what he looks at and also upon what his previous visual-conceptual experience has taught him to see" (Kuhn 1970, p. 113). Thus, where Tycho Brahe saw a fixed earth and moving sun, Kepler saw a stationary sun and a moving earth (Hanson 1958). Similarly, where Priestley saw dephlogisticated air, Lavoisier saw oxygen (Kuhn 1970, Musgrave 1976); and where, today, geologists see evidence of continental drift, less than 20 years ago the very same observations yielded the conclusion that the continents are fixed in place (Frankel 1979).

The fact that observation is theory laden does not, by itself, refute the logical empiricist position. It does, however, call into question the claim that science is securely anchored by the objective observation of "reality." Indeed, the theory dependence and fallibility of observation constitute problems for any philosophy of science which admits a role for empirical testing. However, in his development of falsificationism, Popper has offered an alternative method of theory justification which is designed to overcome some of the difficulties inherent in logical empiricism.

FALSIFICATIONISM

Popper's alternative to the inductivist program can be illustrated with reference to Figure 2. Unlike the logical positivists, Popper accepts the fact that "observation always presupposes the existence of some system of expectations" (1972, p. 344). For Popper, the scientific process begins when observations clash with existing theories or preconceptions. When this occurs, we are confronted with a scientific problem. A theory is then proposed to solve the problem, and the logical consequences of the theory (hypotheses) are subjected to rigorous empirical tests. The objective of the testing is the refutation of

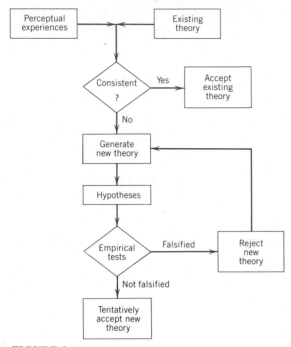

FIGURE 2

The falsificationist model of scientific method.

the hypotheses. When a theory's predictions are falsified, it is to be ruthlessly rejected. Those theories that survive falsification are said to be corroborated and are tentatively accepted.

In contrast to the gradually increasing confirmation of induction, falsificationism substitutes the logical necessity of deduction. Popper exploits the fact that a universal hypothesis can be falsified by a single negative instance (Chalmers 1976). In the Popperian program, if the deductively derived hypotheses are shown to be false, the theory itself is taken to be false. Thus, the problem of induction is seemingly avoided by denying that science rests on inductive inference.[4]

According to falsificationism, then, science progresses by a process of "conjectures and refutations" (Popper 1962, p. 46). On this view, the objective of science is to solve problems. Solutions to these problems are posed in the form of theories which are subjected to potentially refuting empirical tests. Theories that survive falsification are accepted as tentative solutions to the problems.

Popper's program has had a significant impact,

both on philosophers of science and on practicing scientists. The latter, in particular, have been attracted by falsification's image of science as a rational and objective means of attaining "truth" (Calder, Phillips, and Tybout 1981; Medawar 1979). However, despite the apparent conformity of much scientific practice with the falsificationist account, serious problems remain with Popper's version of the scientific method. For example, Duhem (1953) has pointed out that it is impossible to conclusively refute a theory because realistic test situations depend on much more than just the theory that is under investigation. Any empirical test will involve assumptions about initial conditions, measuring instruments, and auxiliary hypotheses (Chalmers 1976, Jacoby 1978, Pickering 1981). An alleged refutation of the theory can be easily deflected by suggesting that something else in the maze of assumptions and premises caused the result (Laudan 1977). Moreover, theories can be protected from falsification by ad hoc modifications.

A far more serious problem for the falsificationist view is the fact that the actual history of scientific advance is rarely in agreement with the Popperian account. For example, when D. C. Miller presented overwhelming evidence of a serious experimental anomaly for relativity theory in 1925, the reaction of the physics community was one of benign disinterest (Polanyi 1958). The historical record shows that most major scientific theories have advanced *in spite* of apparent refutations by empirical data. Copernican astronomy (Kuhn 1957), the theory of oxidation (Musgrave 1976), natural selection (Gould 1977, 1980), kinetic theory (Clark 1976), and continental drift (Frankel 1979) were all, at one time or another, in danger of drowning in an "ocean of anomalies" (Lakatos 1974, p. 135). The Popperian program of "conjectures and refutations" finds it difficult to account for the actual growth of scientific knowledge in the face of historical examples such as these.

The recognition that established theories often resist refutation by anomalies while new theories frequently progress despite their empirical failures, led a number of writers in the 1950s to challenge the positivistic views of Popper and the logical empiricists (Suppe 1974). Various philosophers and historians of science noted that scientific practice is often governed by a conceptual framework or world view that is highly resistant to change. In particular,

Thomas Kuhn pointed out that the established framework is rarely, if ever, overturned by a single anomaly (1962). Kuhn's model helped to initiate a new approach in the philosophy of science in which emphasis is placed on the conceptual frameworks that guide research activities. Moreover, Kuhn's work underlined the important role played by the history of science in the development and validation of philosophical analysis.

SCIENTIFIC REVOLUTIONS

Central to the Kuhnian position is the concept of a "paradigm."[5] Roughly, a paradigm constitutes the world view of a scientific community (Laudan 1977, Suppe 1974). The paradigm will include a number of specific theories which depend, in part, on the shared metaphysical beliefs of the community (Kuhn 1970). In addition, the paradigm will include a set of "symbolic generalizations" (like $E = mc^2$) and a set of shared "values" or criteria for theory appraisal (Kuhn 1970, 1977, p. 321). Finally, each paradigm will include "exemplars" or concrete problem solutions known to all members of the community (Kuhn 1970). Examples of paradigms in the natural sciences include Newtonian mechanics, Darwinian evolution, quantum theory, and plate tectonics. Within the social sciences, behaviorism, Freudian psychoanalysis, diffusion of innovation, and Marxian economics have often been referred to as paradigms.

Of particular importance are Kuhn's views on the paradigm shift that takes place during scientific revolutions. He likens the process to a conversion experience, which recalls a Kierkegaardian leap of faith. Some have objected that this approach implies that theory choice is essentially an irrational and subjective process (Lakatos 1974). However, this is an unfortunate misinterpretation of Kuhn's position. Kuhn argues that the actual criteria of theory appraisal are highly rational and fairly standardized within scientific communities. For example, he suggests that the requirements for accuracy, consistency, extensibility, simplicity, and fruitfulness are widely employed within most scientific disciplines (Kuhn 1977). Unfortunately, these attributes do not lead to unambiguous choices when applied to actual theories or paradigms. Thus, theory choice is said to be underdetermined by the data and the evaluative criteria.

The process of theory appraisal is further complicated by the incommensurability of paradigms (Kuhn 1970). Kuhn argues that scientists who pursue different paradigms are, in a sense, living in different worlds. They will be unable to agree on the problems to be solved, the theories to be employed, or the terminology to be used. More importantly, they will be unable to agree on any "crucial experiments" that would resolve their differences (Platt 1964). For example, Kuhn would argue that there is little prospect that a cognitive psychologist could be converted to a behaviorist by rational argument alone. The incommensurability of the paradigms requires too great a conceptual leap. Similar incommensurabilities exist between economics and marketing concerning the theory of consumer behavior (Becker 1971, Markin 1974) and between economics and management concerning the theory of the firm (Cyert and March 1963, Machlup 1967). Very often these paradigmatic conflicts are the result of the radically different philosophical methodologies and ontological frameworks employed by different disciplines or schools of thought (Anderson 1982). Another complication for the process of theory appraisal is the fact that new paradigms are rarely able to solve all the problems dealt with by the established paradigm. Indeed, new paradigms are typically pursued in spite of the many difficulties with which they are confronted. Thus, in Kuhn's view, the individual scientist's decision to pursue a new paradigm must be made on faith in its "future promise" (Kuhn 1970, p. 158).

For Kuhn, science progresses through revolutions, but there is no guarantee that it progresses toward anything—least of all toward "the truth" (Kuhn 1970, p. 170). Progression, in Kuhn's view, is synonymous with problem solving. From this perspective, "the scientific community is a supremely efficient instrument for maximizing the number and precision of the problems solved through paradigm change" (Kuhn 1970, p. 169). But this is all that it is—there is nothing in the process of scientific revolutions that guarantees that science moves ever closer toward absolute truth. Like Darwinian evolution, science is a process without an ultimate goal.

Philosophers of science have found much to criticize in the Kuhnian model (Feyerabend 1970, Lakatos 1974, Laudan 1977, Shapere 1964). However, only two specific points will be dealt with here. First, it has been alleged that Kuhn's account is historically inaccurate (Feyerabend 1970). Of particular concern is the fact that studies of the natural sciences rarely reveal periods in which a single paradigm has dominated a discipline. As Laudan points out, "virtually every major period in the history of [natural] science is characterized . . . by the co-existence of numerous competing paradigms" (1977, p. 74). Similarly, historical studies of the social sciences have found the Kuhnian approach lacking. For example, Leahy's (1980) study of the "cognitive revolution" in psychology concludes that the Kuhnian description of the process is deficient in almost all respects. Likewise, Bronfenbrenner (1971) and Kunin and Weaver (1971) raise serious questions concerning attempts to apply the model to economics.

The second major criticism of Kuhn has already been hinted at. Many philosophers of science object to his characterization of theory selection as an act of "faith." These writers are concerned that this seemingly removes the element of rational choice from the scientific process. As a result, alternative world view models have been developed which attempt to portray theory choice in rational decision-making terms. One such approach is the "methodology of scientific research programs" developed by Imre Lakatos (1974). Since this model is essentially a sophisticated version of falsificationism, it need not detain us here. However, more recently, Laudan (1977) has proposed the "research tradition" concept which attempts to restore rationality to theory selection by expanding the concept of rationality itself.

RESEARCH TRADITIONS

Following both Kuhn and Popper, Laudan argues that the objective of science is to solve problems— that is, to provide "acceptable answers to interesting questions" (Laudan 1977, p. 13). On this view, the "truth" or "falsity" of a theory is irrelevant as an appraisal criterion. The key question is whether the theory offers an explanation for important empirical problems. Empirical problems arise when we encounter something in the natural or social environment which clashes with our preconceived notions or which is otherwise in need of explanation.

Unfortunately, it is not possible to discriminate

among theories on the basis of solved empirical problems alone. As a result, Laudan suggests that there are two other types of problems that must enter into the appraisal process. The first of these is the "nonrefuting anomaly." This is a problem which has not been solved by the theory under consideration, but which has been solved by a rival theory. Laudan maintains that theory appraisal amounts to a process of comparing the merits of one theory with those of another. Thus, an anomaly that has been explained by a rival is a more damaging problem for an extant theory than an anomaly that has not been explained at all.

The other types of problems relevant to theory appraisal are known as conceptual problems. These include logical inconsistencies within the theory itself as well as inconsistencies between the theory under consideration and other scientific theories or doctrines. Examples of the latter include "normative" conceptual problems, in which a proposed theory clashes with the cognitive aims or philosophic methodologies of a rival theory or discipline (Anderson 1982).

Another type of conceptual problem arises when a theory clashes with an accepted world view of the discipline or the wider society. From this perspective, the decline of motivation research in marketing may be partly attributed to the fact that it assumes that "consumer behavior is triggered by subconscious motivations heavily laden with sexual overtones" (Markin 1969, p. 42). Similarly, the failure of behaviorism to gain a significant foothold in marketing may stem from the fact that it views consumer behavior as largely under the control of environmental stimuli (Nord and Peter 1980, Peter and Nord 1982, Rothschild and Gaidis 1981). Both the Freudian and Skinnerian perspectives are at variance with the established position that consumers are reasonably rational decision makers who "act on beliefs, express attitudes, and strive toward goals" (Markin 1974, p. 239). It can be seen that this "cognitive" world view constitutes a serious barrier to the acceptance of alternative theories of consumer behavior.

Thus, from Laudan's perspective, theory appraisal involves an assessment of the *overall* problem-solving adequacy of a theory. This may be determined by weighing the number and importance of the empirical problems solved by the theory against the number and significance of the anomalous and conceptual problems that the theory generates. On this view, motivation research and behavior modification are reasonably adequate theories at the empirical level. That is, they provide plausible answers to important empirical questions. However, both theories create such significant conceptual problems that it is unlikely that either will replace the cognitive orientation in the foreseeable future.

Like Kuhn and Lakatos, Laudan sees science operating within a conceptual framework that he calls a research tradition. The research tradition consists of a number of specific theories, along with a set of metaphysical and conceptual assumptions that are shared by those scientists who adhere to the tradition. A major function of the research tradition is to provide a set of methodological and philosophical guidelines for the further development of the tradition (Anderson 1982).

As in the case of its constituent theories, research traditions are to be appraised on the basis of their overall problem-solving adequacy. Thus, *acceptance* of a particular tradition should be based on a weighting of solved empirical problems versus anomalous and conceptual problems. However, it is very often the case that scientists choose to *pursue* (i.e., to consider, explore, and develop) research traditions whose overall problem-solving success does not equal that of their rivals. Moreover, there are many instances in which scientists have ostensibly accepted one research tradition while working within another.

To explain these phenomena, Laudan suggests that the context of pursuit must be separated from the context of acceptance. On this view, acceptance is a static notion. One compares the problem-solving adequacy of the tradition's existing theories with those of its competitors. Pursuit, on the other hand, is a dynamic concept. The pursuit of a research tradition should be based on its rate of problem-solving progress. Here one looks to the ability of the tradition's latest theories to solve more problems than its rivals. Very often the established tradition will have a more impressive record of overall problem solving. However, pursuit is not based on past success, but rather, on future promise. From Laudan's perspective, it is perfectly rational to pursue (without acceptance) a research tradition whose recent rate of problem solving offers the hope of future progress.

For example, the early work in marketing on

multiattribute attitude models seems to have been spurred by their promise as a diagnostic tool with managerial relevance (Lutz and Bettman 1977, Wilkie and Pessemier 1973). However, low coefficients of determination and questions concerning the prevalence of rational decision making by consumers (Kassarjian 1978, Sheth 1979) have raised doubts in some circles as to whether the promise has been fulfilled. Indeed, Nord and Peter (1980), Peter and Nord (1982), and Rothschild and Gaidis (1981) have recently suggested a reexamination of behaviorism by consumer researchers as an alternative to the cognitive orientation. Laudan's model implies that these writers will have to show a high rate of problem-solving progress if they wish to attract researchers to this program. In particular, they may need to demonstrate through empirical studies (e.g., Gorn 1982) the ability of behaviorism to solve some of the existing anomalies in the cognitivist program. At the same time, Laudan's approach suggests that conceptual problems associated with the notions of manipulation and control and the alleged primacy of environment over cognition may be the most serious barriers to the widespread adoption of the behaviorist model.

EPISTEMOLOGICAL ANARCHY

Unfortunately, Laudan's distinction between a context of pursuit and a context of acceptance fails to provide us with a rational basis for *initial* theory selection. As Feyerabend (1981) points out, there can be no decision to pursue a research tradition on the basis of its rate of progress unless it has already been pursued by someone who has demonstrated this progress. For his own part, Feyerabend argues for a kind of epistemological anarchy in which the only universal standard of scientific method is "anything goes." He claims that the historical record demonstrates, "there is not a single rule, however plausible, and however firmly grounded in epistemology, that is not violated at some time or another" (Feyerabend 1975, p. 23). Indeed, he believes that the violation of accepted scientific norms is essential for scientific progress.

On this view, every concrete piece of research is a potential application of a rule and a test case for the rule (Feyerabend 1978). In other words, scientists may allow standards to guide the research or they may allow the research to suspend the standards. Feyerabend argues that new appraisal criteria are introduced into research practice in piecemeal fashion. They are, in effect, partially invented in the process of carrying out research projects. For a time, new and old standards operate side by side until an alternative form of research practice (and a new rationality) is established. He believes that this process is necessary for scientific progress because conformity to rigid rules and procedures inhibits scientific imagination and creativity. He suggests that violations of conventional norms have led to some of the most significant advances in the history of thought (Feyerabend 1975).

This view suggests that there are no universal standards of scientific practice (Feyerabend 1978). Instead, knowledge claims are unique to specific "research areas" (the rough equivalent of paradigms or research traditions). Thus, what counts as scientific knowlege is relative to the group that produces the knowledge. Each research area is immune to criticism from the outside because of the incommensurability of appraisal criteria and because of the varying programmatic commitments of different research traditions.

THE COGNITIVE SOCIOLOGY OF SCIENCE

Similar conclusions have been reached by researchers working within the cognitive tradition in the sociology of science. Traditionally, sociologists of science have restricted their inquiry largely to the institutional framework of scientific activity (Ben-David 1971, Merton 1973). It has been taken for granted that the nature of the knowlege produced by scientific communities lies outside the purview of sociological analysis. Recently, however, this assumption has been challenged by a number of sociologists including adherents of the so-called "strong program" in the sociology of knowledge developed by David Bloor (1976) and Barry Barnes (1977).

While there are differences in the programs of Bloor and Barnes (Manier 1980), both agree that the production of scientific knowledge must be viewed as a sociological process. On this view, scientific beliefs are as much a function of cultural, political, social, and ideological factors as are any beliefs held by members of a society. Bloor argues that the role of the sociologist is to build theories which explain how these factors affect the generation of scientific knowledge, including knowledge in the sociology of science itself.

Bloor and Barnes criticize philosophers like Lakatos and Laudan for asserting that rational scientific beliefs need no further explanation (Barnes 1979, Bloor 1976). They point out that rationality implies reference to norms, standards, or conventions which they view as sociologically determined and maintained. As such, rationality is not simply a cognitive process common to all but, rather, a relative notion that is affected by external social factors. In particular, the strong program lays great stress upon the role of professional and class interests in affecting the nature of scientific knowledge (Barnes and McKenzie 1979; Barnes and Shapin 1979; MacKenzie and Barnes 1979; Shapin 1981).

Of course, many philosophers and sociologists of science are understandably sceptical of explanations of this sort (Laudan 1981, 1982b; Woolgar 1981). They point out that it will always be possible to construct a plausible explanation for the social interests which might sustain a particular scientific belief. At the same time, however, more sophisticated analyses emerging from other programs in the cognitive sociology of science have revealed interesting insights into the scientific process.[6] Thus, Pickering's (1981) study of experimental work in particle physics reveals the consensual nature of theory acceptance. He argues that science is inherently a social enterprise in which theories must be argued for "within a socially sustained matrix of commitments, beliefs and practices" (1981, p. 235). He demonstrates that these factors can actually impact the nature of the data produced by experimental studies because they determine, in advance, the acceptability of certain findings. This is not to suggest that the majority of scientists *consciously* adjust their apparatus and procedures to generate "marketable" results (Law and Williams 1982, Peter and Olson 1983). Rather, it implies that the design, implementation, and interpretation of experiments is always conducted with an eye to the acceptability of the findings.

The major implication of this sort of sociological analysis is to suggest that science is essentially a process of consensus formation. On this view, theories will be appraised not only on the basis of traditional criteria (e.g., confirmation, corroboration, novel predictions, etc.) but also on the basis of sociological criteria. These may include such factors as a conjunction of the theory with professional or class interests (Mackenzie and Barnes 1979, Shapin 1981), the social acceptability of the results (Pickering 1981), the nature of the rhetorical and presentational devices employed by scientists (Collins 1981b), the sociological "cost" of challenging established theory (Bourdieu 1975; Latour and Woolgar 1979), and the socially defined "workability" of results produced in the laboratory (Knorr-Cetina 1981, 1983).

Sociologists of science do not deny that traditional appraisal criteria appear to play a role in the process of theory acceptance. They simply argue that sociological factors may be every bit as important in determining which theories are accepted and which are rejected. The fact that science is ultimately a social activity cannot be denied. As such, it would appear fruitful to employ insights from both the philosophy and sociology of science in attempting to come to grips with the problem of scientific method within marketing.

IMPLICATIONS FOR THE DEVELOPMENT OF MARKETING SCIENCE

The foregoing review would appear to warrant a number of conclusions concerning science and scientific method. First, it is clear that positivism's reliance on empirical testing as the *sole* means of theory justification cannot be maintained as a viable description of the scientific process or as a normative prescription for the conduct of scientific activities. This point is essentially noncontroversial in contemporary philosophy and sociology of science. Despite its prevalence in marketing, positivism has been abandoned by these disciplines over the last two decades in the face of the overwhelming historical and logical arguments that have been raised against it.

Second, it should also be clear that no consensus exists as to the nature or the very existence of a unique scientific method. The decline of positivism has left us with a number of competing perspectives in the philosophy and sociology of science. Each has its following of loyal supporters, but it appears unlikely that any one perspective will assert its dominance in the near future. This suggests that it is

inappropriate to seek a single best method for the evaluation of marketing theory. As we have seen, appraisal standards will consist of both traditional and sociological criteria and will be subject to change over time. It is more important to ask what methodologies will convince the marketing community of the validity of a particular theory, than it is to ask what is the "correct" method.

Thus, a relativistic stance appears to be the only viable solution to the problem of scientific method. Relativism implies that there are few *truly universal* standards of scientific adequacy. Instead, different research programs (i.e., disciplines, subdisciplines, or collections of disciplines) will adhere to different methodological, ontological, and metaphysical commitments. These research programs are highly "encapsulated" and are immunized against attack from the outside. *Within* a program, knowledge is sanctioned largely by consensus. That is, theories are justified to the extent that they conform to programmatic commitments. However, appraisal standards as well as other programmatic entities will change over time. Indeed, it is not inconceivable that changes in cognitive aims, standards, and ontologies could lead to the eventual unification of competing programs (Laudan 1982c). Thus, research areas will tend to evolve as changes take place in methods, concepts, values, beliefs, and theories. Whether such changes can be viewed as progressive in any sense, will be judged differently by different research programs.

Finally, the lack of consensus on the issue of scientific method means that there is also no agreement on the question of demarcation between science and nonscience. Since the identification of a unique methodology for science is a necessary condition for demarcation, it appears that the search for such a criterion is otiose. As Laudan has put it, "The fact that 2,400 years of searching for a demarcation criterion has left us empty-handed raises a presumption that the object of the quest is nonexistent" (1980, p. 275). Thus, Hunt's (1976b) assertion that "intersubjective certifiability" can serve to distinguish science from nonscience is unsupportable.[7] As Gouldner points out, "Any limited empirical generalization can, by this standard, be held to be objective, however narrow, partial, or biased and prejudiced its net impact is, by reason of its selectivity" (1974, p. 57).

Gouldner uses the concept of sample bias to illustrate his point. He notes that a study using a consciously or unconsciously biased sample can easily be replicated by researchers wishing to justify a particular theory. Thus, replicability is nothing more than a "technical" definition of objectivity that does nothing to assure us that the knowledge it generates is "scientific." For example, disciplines which, by societal consensus, are taken to be non-scientific find it possible to meet the requirement of intersubjective certifiability. Scientific creationists regularly support one another's conclusions based on investigations of the same data. Similarly, para-psychologists maintain that they are able to replicate experiments with "some consistency" (Truzzi 1980, p. 43).

More importantly, however, intersubjective certifiability is by no means as unambiguous as it would appear. For example, what sense are we to make of this criterion in light of the history of the discovery of oxygen? Both Priestley and Lavoisier conducted the same experiment, and both produced the element that we now know as oxygen (Kuhn 1970, Musgrave 1976). Yet Priestley interpreted his discovery as "dephlogisticated air," while Lavoisier eventually saw his as oxygen. Each interpreted the same experiment and the same result in terms of competing research programs. Nor is this an isolated historical case. Numerous studies have demonstrated the inherent ambiguity of the intersubjective certifiability criterion (Collins 1975; Franklin 1979; Pickering 1981; Wynne 1976). Indeed, Collins has argued that experimenters in a field actually negotiate the set of tests that will be judged as competent and, in so doing, decide the character of the phenomenon under investigation.

Science$_1$ Versus Science$_2$

We have seen that the lack of a demarcation criterion makes it impossible to employ the term *science* unambiguously. It will be necessary, therefore, to dichotomize the term for analytical purposes. It is proposed that science$_1$ should refer to the idealized notion of science as an inquiry system which produces "objectively proven knowledge" (Chalmers 1976, p. 1). On this view, science seeks to discover "the truth" via the objective methods of observation, test, and experiment. Of course, it should be clear that no such inquiry system has ever existed—nor is it very likely that such a system will ever exist.

As a result, it will be necessary to define an alternative notion known as science$_2$. The defining element here is that of societal consensus. On this view, science is whatever society chooses to call a science. In Western cultures, this would include all of the recognized natural and social sciences. Thus physics, chemistry, biology, psychology, sociology, economics, political science, etc., all count as science$_2$. This definition bears a resemblance to Madsen's conceptualization of science as a socially organized information-producing activity whose procedures and norms are "socially established" (1974, p. 27). However, science$_2$ goes somewhat farther by emphasizing the importance of societal sanction. It suggests that society bestows a high epistemological status on science because it values its knowledge products, and because it believes that science *generally* functions in the best interests of society as a whole. In the remainder of this article, the terms *science* and *scientific* shall be understood in this sense unless otherwise noted.

The Quest for Science$_2$

The definition of science by societal consensus is not just a convenient method of avoiding a problem of demarcation. It provides us with a criterion that we can use to assess the scientific status of marketing. This is, we can compare marketing with the recognized social and natural sciences, to determine what marketing can do to become more scientific.[8] Of course, this begs the question of whether the objective is worth the effort. During the long debate over the scientific status of marketing, the desirability of becoming more scientific has never really been questioned. This is because the implicit definition of science has always been that of science$_1$. Given that the philosophy and sociology of science can no longer support the veridical status of science, how might we justify the quest for science$_2$?

One possible answer to this question recognizes that it can be in the interests of the discipline to achieve scientific status. An important goal of any area of inquiry with scientific pretensions is to ensure that its knowledge base is widely dispersed through the greater society, so that this knowledge can be used to benefit society as a whole. This is essentially a utilitarian argument (Jones et al. 1977, Reagan 1969.) It is clear that societal resources tend to flow to those disciplines that produce knowledge considered valuable for the accomplishment of societal objectives. The National Science Foundation and the National Institutes for Health are but two examples of institutional arrangements designed to allocate resources for this purpose. (In this regard, it is worth noting that the NSF only recently withdrew its blanket exclusion of research in business areas from funding consideration.) Beyond the pragmatic resource issues, however, it is also obvious that many within the marketing discipline would prefer to employ their knowledge to further society's goals and to enhance its citizens' quality of life. This deontological argument assumes that knowledge producers have special obligations and responsibilities vis-à-vis society (Jones et al. 1977, Ravetz 1971, Reagan 1969).

Within the last decade, the discipline has made enormous strides in the application of its knowledge to nonprofit organizations and to the marketing of social causes (Fine 1981; Fox and Kotler 1980; Kelley 1971; Kotler 1975, 1979; Levy and Zaltman 1975; Rothschild 1981; Shapiro 1973; Sheth and Wright 1974). Much of this has come about as a result of the proselytizing activities of marketers. However, social and nonprofit marketing appear to be informed by the view that marketing is ultimately a technology for influencing the behavior of customer groups (Kotler 1972, Kotler and Zaltman 1971). Tucker has referred to this perspective as the "channel captain" orientation. That is, marketing theorists have tended to focus on the implications of their knowledge for the marketer, rather than the consumer or the larger society (Olson 1981; Sheth 1972, 1979). Thus, Tucker suggests that marketers have had a tendency to study the consumer "in the ways that fishermen study fish rather than as marine biologists study them" (1974, p. 31).

The perception that marketing is simply a technology of influence may well inhibit the flow of its knowledge to segments of society that have no interest in marketing either goods and services or social causes. Increasingly, researchers whose primary interest is in consumer behavior have been called upon by public policy officials for their expert knowledge in such areas as children's advertising, information overload, deceptive advertising, and price perception. In part, this reflects the fact that consumer behavior has been evolving into a separate discipline, with a strong orientation toward knowledge for its own sake (Sheth 1972, 1979).

This shift in emphasis within consumer behavior has enhanced its legitimacy within the academic community, and has led a number of other disciplines to borrow some of its concepts and to employ some of its research findings (Sheth 1972). Marketing has also begun to experience this process of "reverse borrowing," especially in the areas of multivariate analysis and survey research. However, the amount of borrowing from marketing is not as great as one might expect, given its level of technical and methodological sophistication. We must ask ourselves if this reflects a lack of familiarity with marketing, the dearth of marketing theory, or if it suggests a perception that a normative (i.e., marketer-oriented) discipline has little to offer in the way of useful knowledge? It would appear likely that all three factors are operative. However, this need not be the case. There is no a priori reason to believe that marketing cannot continue to reverse the knowledge flow and inform, as well as be informed by more traditional academic disciplines (Sheth 1972).

It could be argued, therefore, that as marketing improves its scientific status in society, the knowledge it generates will be more acceptable within the society, and that additional resources will be made available for the further development of its knowledge base. However, this may require a reorientation within certain segments of the discipline. A focus on knowledge for its own sake (or, more appropriately, for the sake of society as a whole) may be the price which society demands before it is willing to offer full scientific legitimacy. Given the historical prejudice against marketing (Steiner 1976), this may not be too great a price to pay. Indeed, greater legitimacy in the eyes of society can only be viewed as salutary by marketing practitioners and academics alike.

Toward Science in Marketing

If the discipline of marketing wishes to move toward scientific status, it must look to the recognized social and natural sciences for guidance. A comparison with these other fields suggests a number of action implications. First, it is clear that marketing must be more concerned with the pursuit of knowledge as knowledge. Rightly or wrongly, society tends to reserve full scientific legitimacy for those inquiry systems which are perceived to be operating in the higher interests of knowledge and general societal welfare. The perception that marketing is primarily concerned with the interests of only one segment of society will surely retard its transition to a consensus science.

Of course, marketing can point with pride to its accomplishments in improving the efficiency and effectiveness of managerial practice in the private as well as the nonprofit and public sectors. We should not gainsay the ultimate benefits this has brought to society. Nevertheless, if the discipline truly wishes to implement the broadened concept of marketing (Bagozzi 1975, Kotler and Levy 1969), it is clear that it must adopt a different set of goals and a different attitude towards its ultimate purpose. Traditionally, marketers have viewed their discipline as an applied area concerned largely with the improvement of managerial practice. However, the broadening concept makes it clear that marketing is a generic human activity, which may be studied simply because it is an intrinsically interesting social phenomenon. On this view, the exchange process itself becomes the focus of attention in much the same way that communication is the focus of communications theorists, and administration is the focus of administrative scientists. The interest must lie in understanding and explaining the phenomenon itself, rather than understanding it from the perspective of only one of the participants. Marketing's preoccupation with the concerns of Tucker's ''channel captain''introduces an asymmetry into the study of the phenomenon that can only limit the discipline's perspective and inhibit its attainment of scientific status.

It should be noted that this change in focus need not create tension between academics and practitioners. The knowledge produced by the discipline will still be readily available for the practical pursuits of private, nonprofit, and social marketers. The difference is that the product of marketing science will also be readily available (and perhaps more palatable) to consumers, consumer groups, other academic disciplines, and a broader range of public policy officials. As Angelmar and Pinson (1975) note, other social sciences have seen fit to institutionalize this distinction by developing subdisciplines, such as applied psychology, applied anthropology, and applied sociology. Moreover, such a distinction already exists on a de facto basis within the fields of finance and management. As a discipline that already has an applied emphasis,

marketing's task is to develop its scientific dimensions further into a full-fledged subarea whose primary focus is on basic research.

Beyond the philosophical and attitudinal changes necessary for a full transition to marketing science, a number of more pragmatic considerations must also be addressed. The recognized sciences have achieved their status, in large part, because they have something to show for their efforts. As Kuhn (1970) or Laudan (1977) would express it, the sciences have shown a remarkable ability to solve important problems. They have done so, it would seem, through a commitment to theory-driven programmatic research. History demonstrates that scientific progress has emerged out of the competition among macro-structures variously known as paradigms, research programs, and research traditions. The established sciences can point with pride to the scientific problems they have solved and the exemplary theories which are their solutions. Indeed, Popper has argued that a discipline should be defined not by its subject matter, but by the theories it develops to solve the problems of its domain (1962, p. 67).

In contrast, much research in marketing remains scattered and fragmented (Jacoby 1978, Sheth 1967, Wind and Thomas 1980). It is often difficult to determine what problem the research is attempting to solve, or if the solution has any real significance for the advancement of knowledge or for the design of intervention strategies. Too often the focus is on what may be termed ''relationship studies.'' Here an attempt is made to determine if an independent and dependent variable are related, but there is little effort to link the result to an established research program or body of theory. More significantly, perhaps, it is rare that researchers engage in follow-up studies to further explore and develop the area. This approach appears to be informed by an empiricist model of science which assumes that, if enough scattered facts (relationships) are gathered, they will somehow assemble themselves into a coherent body of theory (Olson 1981). However, it should be clear that facts ''do not speak for themselves'' (Baumol 1957), and that the collection and interpretation of facts is always done in the light of some theory.

What is required in marketing is a greater commitment to theory-driven programmatic research, aimed at solving cognitively and socially significant problems (Howard and Sheth 1969, Jacoby 1978, Olson 1981). Only in this way will marketing achieve what is taken for granted in the recognized sciences, namely, an exemplary body of theory and a collection of scientific problems which it can count as solved. These two features will go a long way toward gaining scientific recognition for marketing. It is clear that this process has already begun in such areas as consumer behavior, sales management, and channel behavior. It can only be hoped that this will continue and will soon spread to other areas of the discipline.

REFERENCES

Abbagnano, Nicola (1967), "Positivism," *Encyclopedia of Philosophy*, 6, Paul Edwards ed., New York: Macmillan.

Alderson, Wroe and Reavis Cox (1948). "Towards a Theory of Marketing," *Journal of Marketing*, 13 (October), 137–52.

Anderson, Paul F. (1982), "Marketing, Strategic Planning, and the Theory of the Firm," *Journal of Marketing*, 46 (Spring), 15–26.

Angelmar, Reinhard and Christian Pinson (1975), "The Meaning of Marketing," *Philosophy of Science*, 42 (June), 208–13.

Bagozzi, Richard P. (1975), "Marketing as Exchange," *Journal of Marketing*, 39 (October), 32–39.

Barnes, Barry (1977), *Interests and the Growth of Knowledge*, London: Routledge & Kegan Paul.

—— (1979), "Vicissitudes of Belief," *Social Studies of Science*, 9, 247–63.

—— and Donald MacKenzie (1979), "On the Role of Interests in Scientific Change," in *On the Margins of Science: The Social Construction of Rejected Knowledge*, R. Wallis ed., Keele, U.K.: University of Keele, 49–66.

—— and Steven Shapin eds. (1979), *Natural Order*, Beverly Hills, CA: Sage Publications.

Bartels, Robert (1951), "Can Marketing Be a Science?," *Journal of Marketing*, 15 (January), 319–28.

Baumol, W. J. (1957), "On the Role of Marketing Theory," *Journal of Marketing*, 21 (April), 413–18.

Becker, Gary (1971), *Economic Theory*, New York: Alfred A. Knopf.

Ben-David, J. (1971), *The Scientist's Role in Society*, Englewood Cliffs, NJ: Prentice-Hall.

Bhaskar, Roy (1979), *The Possibility of Naturalism*, Brighton, U.K.: The Harvester Press.

Black, Max (1967), "Induction," *Encyclopedia of Philosophy*, 4, Paul Edwards, ed., New York: Macmillan.

Bloor, David (1976), *Knowledge and Social Imagery*, London: Routledge & Kegan Paul.

Bourdieu, Pierre (1975), "The Specificity of the Scientific Field and the Social Conditions of the Progress of Reason," *Social Science Information*, 14, 19–47.

Branch, Ben (1978), "The Impact of Operating Decisions on ROI Dynamics," *Financial Management*, 7 (Winter), 54–60.

Bronfenbrenner, Martin (1971), "The 'Structure of Revolutions' in Economic Thought," *History of Political Economy*, 3 (Spring), 136–51.

Brown, Harold I. (1977), *Perception, Theory and Commitment*, Chicago: University of Chicago Press.

Buzzell, Robert D. (1963), "Is Marketing a Science?," *Harvard Business Review*, 41 (January–February), 32–40, 166–70.

——, Bradley T. Gale, and Ralph G. M. Sultan (1975), "Market Share: A Key to Profitability," *Harvard Business Review*, 53 (January–February), 97–106.

Calder, Bobby J., Lynn W. Phillips, and Alice M. Tybout (1981), "Designing Research for Application," *Journal of Consumer Research*, 8 (September) 197–207.

Carnap, Rudolph (1936), "Testability and Meaning," *Philosophy of Science*, 3, 419–71.

—— (1937), "Testability and Meaning," *Philosophy of Science*, 4, 1–40.

—— (1953), "Testability and Meaning," in *Readings in the Philosophy of Science*, Herbert Feigl and May Brodbeck, eds., New York: Appleton-Century-Crofts, 47–92.

Chalmers, A. F. (1976), *What Is This Thing Called Sci-*

ence?, St. Lucia, Australia: University of Queensland Press.

Clark, Peter (1976), "Atomism Versus Thermodynamics," in *Method and Appraisal in the Physical Sciences,* Colin Howson ed., Cambridge U.K.: Cambridge University Press, 41–105.

Collins, H. M. (1975), "The Seven Sexes: A Study in the Sociology of a Phenomenon, or the Replication of Experiments in Physics," *Sociology,* 9, 205–24.

——— (1981a), "Stages in the Empirical Program of Relativism," *Social Studies of Science,* 11, 3–10.

——— (1981b), "Son of Seven Sexes: The Social Destruction of a Physical Phenomenon, *Social Studies of Science,* 11, 33–62.

Converse, Paul D. (1945), "The Development of a Science of Marketing," *Journal of Marketing,* 10 (July), 14–23.

Cox, Reavis, Wroe Alderson, and Stanley J. Shapiro (1964), *Theory in Marketing,* Homewood, IL: Richard D. Irwin.

Cyert, Richard M. and James G. March (1963), *A Behavioral Theory of the Firm,* Englewood Cliffs, NJ: Prentice-Hall.

Duhem, Pierre (1953), "Physical Theory and Experiment," in *Readings in the Philosophy of Science,* Herbert Feigl and May Brodbeck, eds., New York: Appleton-Century-Crofts, 235–52.

Feyerabend, Paul (1970), "Consolations for the Specialist," in *Criticism and the Growth of Knowledge,* Imre Lakatos and Alan Musgrave, eds., Cambridge, U.K.: Cambridge University Press, 197–230.

——— (1975), *Against Method,* Thetford, England: Lowe and Brydone.

——— (1978), "From Incompetent Professionalism to Professionalized Incompetence—The Rise of a New Breed of Intellectuals," *Philosophy of the Social Sciences,* 8 (March), 37–53.

——— (1981), "More Clothes from the Emperor's Bargain Basement," *British Journal for the Philosophy of Science,* 32, 57–94.

Fine, Seymour H. (1981), *The Marketing of Ideas and Social Issues,* New York: Praeger.

Fox, Karen F. A. and Philip Kotler (1980), "The Marketing of Social Causes: The First Ten Years," *Journal of Marketing,* 44 (Fall), 24–33.

Frankel, Henry (1979), "The Career of Continental Drift Theory," *Studies in History and Philosophy of Science,* 10, 21–66.

Franklin, Allan (1979), "The Discovery and Nondiscovery of Parity Nonconservation," *Studies in History and Philosophy of Science,* 10, 201–57.

Gorn, Gerald J. (1982), "The Effects of Music in Advertising on Choice Behavior: A Classical Conditioning Approach," *Journal of Marketing,* 46 (Winter), 94–101.

Gould, Stephen (1977), *Ever Since Darwin,* New York: Norton.

——— (1980), *The Panda's Thumb,* New York: Norton.

Gouldner, Alvin W. (1974), "Objectivity: The Realm of the 'Sacred' in Social Science," in *Values, Objectivity and the Social Sciences,* Gresham Riley, ed., Reading, MA: Addison-Wesley, 53–64.

Halbert, Michael (1965), *The Meaning and Sources of Marketing Theory,* New York: McGraw-Hill.

Hanson, Norwood R. (1958), *Patterns of Discovery,* Cambridge, U.K.: University Press.

Hempel, Carl G. (1965), *Aspects of Scientific Explanation,* New York: Free Press.

Howard, John A. and Jagdish N. Sheth (1969), *The Theory of Buyer Behavior,* New York: John Wiley.

Hume, David (1911), *A Treatise of Human Nature,* New York: Dutton.

Hunt, Shelby D. (1976a), *Marketing Theory: Conceptual Foundations of Research in Marketing,* Columbus, OH: Grid.

——— (1976b), "The Nature and Scope of Marketing," *Journal of Marketing,* 40 (July), 17–28.

——— (1983), *Marketing Theory: The Philosophy of Marketing Science;* Homewood, IL: Richard D. Irwin.

Hutchinson, Kenneth D. (1952), "Marketing as a Science: An Appraisal," *Journal of Marketing,* 16 (January), 286–93.

Jacoby, Jacob (1978), "Consumer Research: A State of the Art Review," *Journal of Marketing,* 42 (April), 87–96.

Jones, W. T., Frederick Sontag, Morton O. Beckner, and Robert J. Fogelin (1977), *Approaches to Ethics,* 3rd ed., New York: McGraw-Hill.

Kassarjian, Harold H. (1978), "Anthropomorphism and Parsimony," in *Advances in Consumer Research,* 5, H. K. Hunt, ed., Chicago: Association for Consumer Research, xiii–xiv.

Keat, Russell and John Urry (1975), *Social Theory as Science,* London: Routledge & Kegan Paul.

Kelley, Eugene J. (1971), "Marketing's Changing Social/Environmental Role," *Journal of Marketing,* 35 (July), 1–2.

Knorr-Cetina, Karin D. (1981), *The Manufacture of Knowledge,* Oxford, England: Pergamon Press.

_____ (1983), "The Ethnographic Study of Scientific Work: Toward a Constructivist Interpretation of Science," in *Science Observed,* K. D. Knorr and M. Mulkay eds., London: Sage Publications.

Kotler, Philip (1972), "A Generic Concept of Marketing," *Journal of Marketing,* 36 (April), 46–54.

_____ (1975), *Marketing for Nonprofit Organizations,* Englewood Cliffs, NJ: Prentice-Hall.

_____ (1979), "Strategies for Introducing Marketing into Nonprofit Organizations," *Journal of Marketing,* 43 (January), 37–44.

_____ and Sidney J. Levy (1969), "Broadening the Concept of Marketing," *Journal of Marketing,* 33 (January), 10–15.

_____ and Gerald Zaltman (1971), "Social Marketing: An Approach to Planned Social Change," *Journal of Marketing,* 35 (July), 3–12.

Kuhn, Thomas S. (1957), *The Copernican Revolution: Planetary Astronomy in the Development of Western Thought,* Cambridge, MA: Harvard University Press.

_____ (1962), *The Structure of Scientific Revolutions,* Chicago: University of Chicago Press.

_____ (1970), *The Structure of Scientific Revolutions,* 2nd ed., Chicago: University of Chicago Press.

_____ (1977), *The Essential Tension,* Chicago: The University of Chicago Press.

Kunin, Leonard and F. Stirton Weaver (1971), "On the Structure of Scientific Revolutions in Economics," *History of Political Economy,* 3 (Fall), 391–97.

Lakatos, Imre (1974), "Falsification and the Methodology of Scientific Research Programs," in *Criticism and the Growth of Knowledge,* Imre Lakatos and Alan Musgrave, eds., Cambridge, U.K.: University Press, 91–195.

Latour, Bruno and Steve Oolgar (1979), *Laboratory Life,* Beverly Hills, CA: Sage Publications.

Laudan, Larry (1977), *Progress and Its Problems,* Berkeley, CA: University of California Press.

_____ (1980), "Views of Progress: Separating the Pilgrims from the Rakes," *Philosophy of the Social Sciences,* 10, 273–86.

_____ (1981), "The Pseudo-Science of Science?," *Philosophy of the Social Sciences,* 11, 173–98.

_____ (1982a), "The Demise of the Demarcation Problem," paper presented at the Workshop on the Demarcation between Science and Pseudo-Science, Virginia Polytechnic Institute and State University, April 30–May 2.

_____ (1982b), "More on Bloor," *Philosophy of the Social Sciences,* 12, 71–74.

_____ (1982c), "Science and Values," Center for the Study of Science in Society, Blacksburg, VA: Virginia Polytechnic Institution and State University, unpublished paper.

Law, John and R. J. Williams (1982), "Putting Facts Together: A Study of Scientific Persuasion," *Social Studies of Science,* 12, 535–58.

Leahy, Thomas H. (1980), *A History of Psychology,* Englewood Cliffs, NJ: Prentice-Hall.

Levy, Sidney and Gerald Zaltman (1975), *Marketing, Society and Conflict,* Englewood Cliffs, NJ: Prentice-Hall.

Lutz, Richard J. and James R. Bettman (1977), "Multiattribute Models in Marketing: A Bicentennial Review," in *Consumer and Industrial Buying Behavior,*

Arch G. Woodside, Jagdish N. Sheth, and Peter D. Bennett, eds., New York: North-Holland, 137–49.

Machlup, Fritz (1967), ''Theories of the Firm: Marginalist, Behavioral, Managerial,'' *American Economic Review,* 57 (March), 1–33.

MacKenzie, Donald A. and Barry Barnes (1979), ''Scientific Judgment: The Biometry-Mendelism Controversy,'' in *Natural Order,* Barry Barnes and Steven Shapin, eds., Beverly Hills, CA: Sage Publications, 191–210.

Madsen, K. B. (1974), *Modern Theories of Motivation,* New York:John Wiley.

Manier, Edward (1980), ''Levels of Reflexivity: Unnoted Differences Within the 'Strong Programme' in Sociology of Knowledge,'' in *Proceedings of the 1980 Biennial Meeting of the Philosophy of Science Association,* P. D. Asquith and R. N. Giere, eds., East Lansing, MI: Philosophy of Science Association, 197–207.

Markin, Rom J. (1969), *The Psychology of Consumer Behavior,* Englewood Cliffs, NJ: Prentice-Hall.

——— (1974), *Consumer Behavior,* New York: Macmillan.

Medawar, P. B. (1979), *Advice to a Young Scientist,* New York: Harper & Row.

Merton, Robert K. (1973), *The Sociology of Science,* Chicago: University of Chicago Press.

Mill, John Stuart (1959), *A System of Logic,* London: Longman, Green & Company. (Originally published in 1843.)

Mulkay, Michael and G. Nigel Gilbert (1982), ''What Is the Ultimate Question? Some Remarks in Defense of the Analysis of Scientific Discourse,'' *Social Studies of Science,* 12, 309–19.

Musgrave, Alan (1976), ''why Did Oxygen Supplant Phlogiston?'', in *Method and Appraisal in the Physical Sciences,* Colin Howson, ed., Cambridge, U.K.: Cambridge University Press, 181–209.

Nord, Walter R. and J. Paul Peter (1980), ''A Behavior Modification Perspective on Marketing,'' *Journal of Marketing,* 44 (Spring), 36–47.

Olson, Jerry C. (1981), ''Toward a Science of Consumer Behavior,'' in *Advances in Consumer Research,* 9,

Andrew Mitchell, ed., Association for Consumer Research, v–x.

O'Shaughnessy, John and Michael J. Ryan (1979), ''Marketing, Science, and Technology,'' in *Conceptual and Theoretical Developments in Marketing,* O.C. Ferrell, Stephen W. Brown, and Charles W. Lamb, Jr., Eds., Chicago: American Marketing Association, 577–89.

Papineau, David (1978), *For Science in the Social Sciences,* London: Macmillan Press.

Passmore, John (1967), ''Logical Positivism,'' *Encyclopedia of Philosophy,* 5, Paul Edwards, ed., New York: Macmillan.

——— (1982), ''Current Issues in the Philosophy of Science: Implications for Marketing Theory—A Panel Discussion,'' in *Marketing Theory: Philosophy of Science Perspectives,* Ronald F. Bush and Shelby D. Hunt, eds., Chicago: American Marketing Association, 11–16.

Peter, J. Paul (1983), ''Some Philosophical and Methodological Issues in Consumer Research,'' working paper, Graduate School of Business, University of Wisconsin, Madison. in *Marketing Theory,* Shelby D. Hunt, ed., Homewood, IL: Richard D. Irwin, 382–94.

——— and Walter R. Nord (1982), ''A Clarification and Extension of Operant Conditioning Principles in Marketing,'' *Journal of Marketing,* 46 (Summer), 102–7.

Peter, J. Paul and Jerry C. Olson (1983), ''Is Science Marketing?'', *Journal of Marketing,* 47 (Fall).

Pickering, Andrew (1981), ''The Hunting of the Quark,'' *Isis,* 72 (June), 216–36.

Platt, John R. (1964), ''Strong Inference,'' *Science,* 46 (October), 347–53.

Polanyi, Michael (1958), *Personal Knowledge,* Chicago: University of Chicago Press.

Popper, Karl (1962), *Conjectures and Refutations,* New York: Harper & Row.

——— (1972), *Objective Knowledge,* Oxford, U.K.: The Clarendon Press.

Ravetz, Jerome R. (1971), *Scientific Knowledge and Its Social Problems,* New York: Oxford University Press.

Reagan, Charles E. (1969), *Ethics for Scientific Researchers,* Springfield, IL: Charles C. Thomas.

Rosenberg, Alexander (1980), *Sociobiology and the Preemption of Social Science,* Baltimore: John Hopkins University Press.

Rothschild, Michael L. (1977), *An Incomplete Bibliography of Works Related to Marketing for Public Sector and Nonprofit Organizations,* 3rd ed., Madison, WI: Graduate School of Business, University of Wisconsin.

———— and William C. Gaidis (1981), "Behavioral Learning Theory:Its Relevance to Marketing and Promotions," *Journal of Marketing,* 45 (Spring), 70–78.

Savitt, Ronald (1980), "Historical Research in Marketing," *Journal of Marketing,* 44 (Fall), 52–58.

Schoeffler, Sidney (1979), "SPI Seeks Science, Not Single 'Over Simplistic' Strategy Variable: Another Look at Market Share," *Marketing News,* 13 (February), 4.

Shapere, Dudley (1964), "The Structure of Scientific Revolutions," *Philosophical Review,* 73, 383–94.

Shapin, Steven (1981), "The History of Science and Its Sociological Reconstructions," working paper, Science Studies Unit, Edinburgh University.

Shapiro, Benson (1973), "Marketing for Nonprofit Organizations," *Harvard Business Review,* 51 (September–October), 123–32.

Sheth, Jagdish N. (1967), "A Review of Buyer Behavior," *Management Science,* 13 (August), B719–B56.

———— (1972), "The Future of Buyer Behavior," in *Proceedings of the Third Annual Conference,* M. Venkatensan ed., Association for Consumer Research, 562–75.

———— (1979), "The Surpluses and Shortages in Consumer Behavior Theory and Research," *Journal of the Academy of Marketing Science,* 7 (Fall), 414–27.

———— and Peter L. Wright, eds. (1974), *Marketing Analysis for Societal Problems,* Urbana, IL: University of Illinois, Bureau of Economic and Business Research.

Steiner, Robert L. (1976), "The Prejudice Against Marketing," *Journal of Marketing,* 40 (July), 2–9.

Suppe, Frederick (1974), *The Structure of Scientific Theories,* Urbana, IL: University of Illinois Press.

Taylor, Weldon J. (1965), "Is Marketing a Science? Revisited," *Journal of Marketing,* 29 (July), 49–53.

Thomas, David (1979), *Naturalism and Social Science,* Cambridge, U.K.: Cambridge University Press.

Truzzi, Marcello (1980), "A Skeptical Look at Paul Krutz's Analysis of the Scientific Status of Parapsychology," *Journal of Parapsychology,* 44 (March), 35–55.

Tucker, W. T. (1974), "Future Directions in Marketing Theory," *Journal of Marketing,* 38 (April), 30–35.

Vaile, Roland S. (1949), "Towards a Theory of Marketing—Comment," *Journal of Marketing,* 13 (April), 520–22.

Wilkie, William L. and Edgar A. Pessemier (1973), "Issues in Marketing's Use of Multi-Attribute Attitude Models," *Journal of Marketing Research,* 10 (November), 428–41.

Winch, Peter (1958), *The Idea of a Social Science,* London: Routledge & Kegan Paul.

Wind, Yoram and Robert J. Thomas (1980), "Conceptual and Methodological Issues in Organizational Buying Behavior," *European Journal of Marketing,* 14, 239–63.

Woolgar, Steve (1981), "Interests and Explanation in the Social Study of Science," *Social Studies of Science,* 11, 365–94.

Wynne, Brian (1976), "C. G. Barkla and the J Phenomenon: A Case Study in the Treatment of Deviance in Physics," *Social Studies of Science,* 6, 307–47.

Zaltman, Gerald, Christian R. A. Pinson, and Reinhard Angelmar (1973), *Metatheory and Consumer Research,* New York: Holt, Rinehart & Winston.

————, Karen LeMasters, and Michael Heffring (1982), *Theory Construction in Marketing: Some Thoughts on Thinking,* New York: John Wiley.

NOTES

[1] Philosophy, sociology, and history of science are often referred to collectively under the rubric of "science studies."

[2]In the best traditions of logical empiricism, the PIMS sample size has since been increased (Branch 1978, Schoeffler 1979).

[3]Of course, the same problems of masurement exist in the natural sciences. See, for example, Chalmers (1976), pp. 28–30.

[4]Of course, it has been noted that Popper's notion of corroboration itself depends on an inductive inference.

[5]Kuhn now refers to a paradigm as a "disciplinary matrix" (Kuhn 1970, p. 182). However, it has become conventional in discussion of his work to retain the original term.

[6]In addition to the strong program, there are at least three other recognizable "schools" in the cognitive sociology of science. These include adherents of the relativist (Collins 1981a), constructivist (Knorr-Cetina 1981), and discourse (Mulkay and Gilbert 1982) programs.

[7]Indeed, Hunt's demarcation standard is not even adequate on his own criteria for classification (Hunt 1983, p. 355).

[8]It should be noted that the question of the extent and nature of the differences between the natural and social sciences remains a highly contentious issue (Mill 1959; Winch 1958; Keat and Urry 1975; Papineau 1978; Bhaskar 1979; Thomas 1979; Rosenberg 1980).

DISCUSSION QUESTIONS

1. If science is essentially a process of consensus formation, need we despair for the concepts of truth and objectively certified knowledge?

2. What does the idea of the encapsulated research program imply for interdisciplinary criticism (e.g., criticisms of economics by marketers and of marketing by economists)?

3. If marketing adopts a knowledge-qua-knowledge perspective, how will this affect the nature of the problems it attempts to solve and the types of theories that it generates?

4. What do the criticisms of logical empiricism and falsificationism imply for the concepts of replication, experimentation, and the possibility of crucial experiments?

5. Does relativism imply that marketers are free to believe whatever they wish to believe?

TWO

FOUNDATIONS OF MARKETING THOUGHT
AND THEORY

Marketing theory is of relatively recent origin. Many issues raised among marketing theoreticians reflect the general youth of marketing theory efforts. Indeed, the papers in this section are concerned primarily with describing and classifying the phenomena of marketing. Such efforts are especially important in the early stages of a discipline's theory development.

The first section of Part 2 examines early contributors to marketing theory and considers an historical perspective on marketing. These papers provide an invaluable perspective on the development of marketing theory. The second section examines definition and classification issues. These issues were major topics of the 1970s. Today, many of the ideas developed in these papers are part of the generally accepted view of marketing.

A. EARLY CONTRIBUTORS AND HISTORICAL PERSPECTIVES

Wroe Alderson is widely regarded as the first great marketing theorist. The classic article presented here is a sampling of his prodigious output. In this piece, he discusses his analytical framework for marketing. The Barksdale paper summarizes and explains Alderson's contributions to marketing theory. The Baumol article, a classic on the role of marketing theory, was inspired by Wroe Alderson's thinking.

Buzzell's piece, part of an early debate in the marketing discipline, is concerned about whether marketing is an art or a science. Many of his thoughts are still timely. Sheth and Gardner provide an update on the history of marketing thought by succinctly displaying the major trends in marketing thought during the 1960s and 1970s.

PREFACE TO

"The Analytical Framework for Marketing"*

Alderson's analytic framework is one of the earliest attempts by a marketing scholar to develop a general paradigm for marketing. His ideas are broadly founded in the social and behavioral sciences. Three concepts are essential to Alderson's framework: heterogenous supply and demand, sorting processes, and organized behavioral systems.

---

*Editors' Note: The late Wroe Alderson was widely regarded as the premier marketing theorist of his day. In addition to his contributions to the literature, he was instrumental in initiating and coordinating a series of marketing theory seminars held during a number of summers in the 1950s.

4

THE ANALYTICAL FRAMEWORK FOR MARKETING

WROE ALDERSON

My assignment is to discuss the analytical framework for marketing. Since our general purpose here is to consider the improvement of the marketing curriculum, I assume that the paper I have been asked to present might serve two functions. The first is to present a perspective of marketing which might be the basis for a marketing course at either elementary or advanced levels. The other is to provide some clue as to the foundations in the social sciences upon which an analytical framework for marketing may be built.

Economics has some legitimate claim to being the original science of markets. Received economic theory provides a framework for the analysis of marketing functions which certainly merits the attention of marketing teachers and practitioners. It is of little importance whether the point of view I am about to present is a version of economics, a hybrid of economics and sociology, or the application of a newly emergent general science of human behavior to marketing problems. The analytical framework which I find congenial at least reflects some general knowledge of the social sciences as well as long experience in marketing analysis. In the time available I can do no more than present this view in outline or skeleton form and leave you to determine how to classify it or whether you can use it.

An advantageous place to start for the analytical treatment of marketing is with the radical heterogeneity of markets. Heterogeneity is inherent on both the demand and the supply sides. The homogeneity which the economist assumes for certain purposes is not an antecedent condition for marketing. Insofar as it is ever realized it emerges out of the marketing process itself.

The materials which are useful to man occur in nature in heterogeneous mixtures which might be called conglomerations since these mixtures have only a random relationship to human needs and activities. The collection of goods in the possession of a household or an individual also consitutes a heterogeneous supply, but it might be called an assortment since it is related to anticipated patterns of future behavior. The whole economic process may be described as a series of transformations from meaningless to meaningful heterogeneity. Marketing produces as much homogeneity as may be needed to facilitate some of the intermediate economic processes but homogeneity has limited significance or utility for consumer behavior or expectations.

The marketing process matches materials found in nature or goods fabricated from these materials against the needs of households or individuals. Since the consuming unit has a complex pattern of needs, the matching of these needs creates an assortment of goods in the hands of the ultimate consumer. Actually the marketing process builds up assortments at many stages along the way, each appropriate to the activities taking place at that point. Materials or goods are associated in one way for manufacturing, in another way for wholesale distribution, and in still another for retail display and selling. In between the various types of heterogeneous collections relatively homogeneous supplies are accumulated through the processes of grading, refining, chemical reduction and fabrication.

Marketing brings about the necessary transformations in heterogeneous supplies through a multiphase process of sorting. Matching of every individual need would be impossible if the consumer had to search out each item required or the producer had to find the users of a product one by one. It is only the ingenious use of intermediate sorts which make it possible for a vast array of diversified products to enter into the ultimate consumer assortments as needed. Marketing makes mass production possible first by providing the assortment of supplies needed in manufacturing and then taking over the successive transformations which ultimately produce the assortments in the hands of consuming units.

Source: Reprinted from *Proceedings: Conference of Marketing Teachers from Far Western States,* Delbert J. Duncan, ed., Berkeley: School of Business Administration, University of California, 1958, pp. 15–28.

45

To some who have heard this doctrine expounded, the concept of sorting seems empty, lacking in specific behavioral content, and hence unsatisfactory as a root idea for marketing. One answer is that sorting is a more general and embracing concept than allocation which many economists regard as the root idea of their science. Allocation is only one of the four basic types of sorting all of which are involved in marketing. Among these four, allocation is certainly no more significant than assorting, one being the breaking down of a homogeneous supply and the other the building up of a heterogeneous supply. Assorting, in fact, gives more direct expression to the final aim of marketing but allocation performs a major function along the way.

There are several basic advantages in taking sorting as a central concept. It leads directly to a fundamental explanation of the contribution of marketing to the overall economy of human effort in producing and distributing goods. It provides a key to the unending search for efficiency in the marketing function itself. Finally, sorting as the root idea of marketing is consistent with the assumption that heterogeneity is radically and inherently present on both sides of the market and that the aim of marketing is to cope with the heterogeneity of both needs and resources.

At this stage of the discussion it is the relative emphasis on assorting as contrasted with allocation which distinguishes marketing theory from at least some versions of economic theory. This emphasis arises naturally from the preoccupation of the market analyst with consumer behavior. One of the most fruitful approaches to understanding what the consumer is doing is the idea that she is engaged in building an assortment, in replenishing or extending an inventory of goods for use by herself and her family. As evidence that this paper is not an attempt to set up a theory in opposition to economics it is acknowledged that the germ of this conception of consumer behavior was first presented some eighty years ago by the Austrian economist Boehm-Bawerk.

The present view is distinguished from that of Boehm-Bawerk in its greater emphasis on the probabilistic approach to the study of market behavior. In considering items for inclusion in her assortment the consumer must make judgments concerning the relative probabilities of future occasions for use. A product in the assortment is intended to provide for some aspect of future behavior. Each such occasion for use carries a rating which is a product of two factors, one a judgment as to the probability of its incidence and the other a measure of the urgency of the need in case it should arise. Consumer goods vary with respect to both measures. One extreme might be illustrated by cigarettes with a probability of use approaching certainty but with relatively small urgency or penalty for deprivation on the particular occasion for use. At the other end of the scale would be a home fire extinguisher with low probability but high urgency attaching to the expected occasion of use.

All of this means that the consumer buyer enters the market as a problem-solver. Solving a problem, either on behalf of a household or on behalf of a marketing organization means reaching a decision in the face of uncertainty. The consumer buyer and the marketing executive are opposite numbers in the double search which pervades marketing; one looking for the goods required to complete an assortment, the other looking for the buyers who are uniquely qualified to use his goods. This is not to say that the behavior of either consumers or executives can be completely characterized as rational problem-solvers. The intention rather is to assert that problem-solving on either side of the market involves a probabilistic approach to heterogeneity on the other side. In order to solve his own problems arising from heterogeneous demand, the marketing executive should understand the processes of consumer decisions in coping with heterogeneous supplies.

The viewpoint adopted here with respect to the competition among sellers is essentially that which is associated in economics with such names as Schumpeter, Chamberlin and J. M. Clark and with the emphasis on innovative competition, product differentiation and differential advantage. The basic assumption is that every firm occupies a position which is in some respects unique, being differentiated from all others by characteristics of its products, its services, its geographic location or its specific combination of these features. The survival of a firm requires that for some group of buyers it should enjoy a differential advantage over all other suppliers. The sales of any active marketing organization come from a core market made up of buyers with a preference for this source and a fringe market which finds the source acceptable, at least for occasional purchases.

In the case of the supplier of relatively undifferentiated products or services such as the wheat farmer differential advantage may pertain more to the producing region than to the individual producer. This more diffused type of differential advantage often becomes effective in the market through such agencies as the marketing cooperative. Even the individual producer of raw materials, however, occupies a position in the sense that one market or buyer provides the customary outlet for his product rather than another. The essential point for the present argument is that buyer and seller are not paired at random even in the marketing of relatively homogeneous products but are related to some scale of preference or priority.

Competition for differential advantage implies goals of survival and growth for the marketing organization. The firm is perennially seeking a favorable place to stand and not merely immediate profits from its operations. Differential advantage is subject to change and neutralization by competitors. In dynamic markets differential advantage can only be preserved through continuous innovation. Thus competition presents an analogy to a succession of military campaigns rather than to the pressures and attrition of a single battle. A competitor may gain ground through a successful campaign based on new product features or merchandising ideas. It may lose ground or be forced to fall back on its core position because of the successful campaigns of others. The existence of the core position helps to explain the paradox of survival in the face of the destructive onslaughts of innovative competition.

Buyers and sellers meet in market transactions each side having tentatively identified the other as an answer to its problem. The market transaction consumes much of the time and effort of all buyers and sellers. The market which operates through a network of costless transactions is only a convenient fiction which economists adopt for certain analytical purposes. Potentially the cost of transactions is so high that controlling or reducing this cost is a major objective in market analysis and executive action. Among economists John R. Commons has given the greatest attention to the transaction as

the unit of collective action. He drew a basic distinction between strategic and routine transactions which for present purposes may best be paraphrased as fully negotiated and routine transactions.

The fully negotiated transaction is the prototype of all exchange transactions. It represents a matching of supply and demand after canvassing all of the factors which might affect the decision on either side. The routine transaction proceeds under a set of rules and assumptions established by previous negotiation or as the result of techniques of pre-selling which take the place of negotiation. Transactions on commodity and stock exchanges are carried out at high speed and low cost but only because of carefully established rules governing all aspects of trading. The economical routines of self-service in a supermarket are possible because the individual items on display have been pre-sold. The routine transaction is the end-result of previous marketing effort and ingenious organization of institutions and processes. Negotiation is implicit in all routine transactions. Good routines induce both parties to save time and cost by foregoing explicit negotiation.

The negotiated transaction is the indicated point of departure for the study of exchange values in heterogeneous markets. Many considerations enter into the decision to trade or not to trade on either side of the market. Price is the final balancing or integrating factor which permits the deal to be made. The seller may accept a lower price if relieved from onerous requirements. The buyer may pay a higher price if provided with specified services. The integrating price is one that assures an orderly flow of goods so long as the balance of other considerations remains essentially unchanged. Some economists are uneasy about the role of the negotiated transaction in value determination since bargaining power may be controlling within wide bargaining limits. These limits as analyzed by Commons are set by reference to the best alternatives available to either partner rather than by the automatic control of atomistic competition. This analysis overlooks a major constraint on bargaining in modern markets. Each side has a major stake in a deal that the other side can live with. Only in this way can a stable supply relationship be established so as to achieve the economics of transactional routines. Negotiation is not a zero sum game since the effort to get the best of the other party transaction by transaction may result in a loss to both sides in terms of mounting transactional cost.

In heterogeneous markets price plays an important role in matching a segment of supply with the appropriate segment of demand. The seller frequently has the option of producing a streamlined product at a low price, a deluxe product at a high price or selecting a price-quality combination somewhere in between. There are considerations which exert a strong influence on the seller toward choosing the price line or lines which will yield the greatest dollar volume of sales. Assuming that various classes of consumers have conflicting claims on the productive capacity of the supplier, it might be argued that the price-quality combination which maximized gross revenue represented the most constructive compromise among these claims. There are parallel considerations with respect to the claims of various participants in the firm's activities on its operating revenue. These claimants include labor, management, suppliers of raw materials and stockholders. Assuming a perfectly fluid situation with respect to bargaining among these claimants, the best chance for a satisfactory solution is at the level of maximum gross revenue. The argument becomes more complicated when the claims of stockholders are given priority, but the goal would still be maximum gross revenue as suggested in a recent paper by William J. Baumol. My own intuition and experience lead me to believe that the maximization of gross revenue is a valid goal of marketing management in heterogeneous markets and adherence to this norm appears to be widely prevalent in actual practice.

What has been said so far is doubtless within the scope of economics or perhaps constitutes a sketch of how some aspects of economic theory might be reconstructed on the assumption of heterogeneity rather than homogeneity as the normal and prevailing condition of the market. But there are issues raised by such notions as enterprise survival, expectations, and consumer behavior, which in my opinion cannot be resolved within the present boundaries of economic science. Here marketing must not hestiate to draw upon the concepts and techniques of the social sciences for the enrichment of its perspective and for the advancement of marketing as an empirical science.

The general economist has his own justifications for regarding the exchange process as a smoothly functioning mechanism which operates in actual markets or which should be taken as the norm and standard to be enforced by government regulation. For the marketing man, whether teacher or practitioner, this Olympian view is untenable. Marketing is concerned with those who are obliged to enter the market to solve their problems imperfect as the market may be. The persistent and rational action of these participants is the main hope for eliminating or moderating some of these imperfections so that the operation of the market mechanism may approximate that of the theoretical model.

To understand market behavior the marketing man takes a closer look at the nature of the participants. Thus he is obliged, in my opinion, to come to grips with the organized behavior system. Market behavior is primarily group behavior. Individual action in the market is most characteristically action on behalf of some group in which the individual holds membership. The organized behavior system is related to the going concern of John R. Commons but with a deeper interest in what keeps it going. The organized behavior system is also a much broader concept including the more tightly organized groups acting in the market such as business firms and households and loosely connected systems such as the trade center and the marketing channel.

The marketing man needs some rationale for group behavior, some general explanation for the formation and persistence of organized behavior systems. He finds this explanation in the concept of expectations. Insofar as conscious choice is involved, individuals operate in groups because of their expectations of incremental satisfactions as compared to what they could obtain operating alone. The expected satisfactions are of many kinds, direct and indirect. In a group that is productive activity is held together because of an expected surplus over individual output. Other groups such as households and purely social organizations expect direct satisfactions from group association and activities. They also expect satisfactions from future activities facilitated by the assortment of goods held in common. Whatever the character of the system, its vitality arises from the expectations of the individual members and the vigor of their efforts to achieve them through group action. While the existence of the group is entirely derivative, it is capable of operating as if it had a life of its own and was pursuing goals of survival and growth.

Every organized behavior system exhibits a structure related to the functions it performs. Even in the simplest behavior system there must be some mechanism for decision and coordination of effort if the system is to provide incremental satisfaction. Leadership emerges at an early stage to perform such functions as directing the defense of the group. Also quite early is the recognition of the rationing function by which the leader allocates the available goods or satisfactions among the members of the group.

As groups grow in size and their functions become more complex functional specialization increases. The collection of individuals forming a group with their diversified skills and capabilities is a meaningful heterogeneous ensemble vaguely analogous to the assortment of goods which facilitates the activities of the group. The group, however, is held together directly by the generalized expectations of its members. The assortment is held together by a relatively weak or derivative bond. An item "belongs" to the assortment only so long as it has some probability of satisfying the expectations of those who possess it.

This outline began with an attempt to live within the framework of economics or at least within an economic framework amplified to give fuller recognition to heterogeneity on both sides of the market. We have now plunged into sociology in order to deal more effectively with the organized behavior system. Meanwhile we attempt to preserve the line of communication to our origins by basing the explanations of group behavior on the quasi-economic concept of expectations.

The initial plunge into sociology is only the beginning since the marketing man must go considerably further in examining the functions and structure of organized behavior systems. An operating group has a power structure, a communication structure and an operating structure. At each stage an effort should be made to employ the intellectual strategy which has already been suggested. That is, to relate sociological notions to the groundwork of marketing economics through the medium of such concepts as expectations and the processes of matching and sorting.

All members of an organized behavior system occupy some position or status within its power structure. There is a valid analogy between the status of an individual or operating unit within the system and the market position of the firm as an entity. The individual struggles for status within the system having first attained the goal of membership. For most individuals in an industrial society status in some operating system is a prerequisite for satisfying his expectations. Given the minimal share in the power of the organization inherent in membership, vigorous individuals may aspire to the more ample share of power enjoyed by leadership. Power in the generalized sense referred to here is an underlying objective on which the attainment of all other objectives depends. This aspect of organized behavior has been formulated as the power principle, namely, "The rational individual will act in such a way to promote the power to act." The word "promote" deliberately glosses over an ambivalent attitude toward power, some individuals striving for enhancement and others being content to preserve the power they have.

Any discussion which embraces power as a fundamental concept creates uneasiness for some students on both analytical and ethical grounds. My own answer to the analytical problem is to define it as control over expectations. In these terms it is theoretically possible to measure and evaluate power, perhaps even to set a price on it. Certainly it enters into the network of imputations in a business enterprise. Management allocates or rations status and recognition as well as or in lieu of material rewards. As for the ethical problem, it does not arise unless the power principle is substituted for ethics as with Machiavelli. Admitting that the power principle is the essence of expediency, the ethical choice of values and objectives is a different issue. Whatever his specific objectives, the rational individual will wish to serve them expediently.

If any of this discussion of power seems remote from marketing let it be remembered that major preoccupation of the marketing executive, as pointed out by Oswald Knauth, is with the creation or the activation of organized behavior systems such as marketing channels and sales organizations. No one can be effective in building or using such systems if he ignores the fundamental nature of the power structure.

The communication structure serves the group in various ways. It promotes the survival of the system by reinforcing the individual's sense of belonging.

It transmits instructions and operating commands or signals to facilitate coordinated effort. It is related to expectations through the communication of explicit or implied commitments. Negotiations between suppliers and customers and much that goes on in the internal management of a marketing organization can best be understood as a two-way exchange of commitments. A division sales manager, for example, may commit himself to produce a specified volume of sales. His superior in turn may commit certain company resources to support his efforts and make further commitments as to added rewards as an incentive to outstanding performances.

For some purposes it is useful to regard marketing processes as a flow of goods and a parallel flow of informative and persuasive messages. In these terms the design of communication facilities and channels becomes a major aspect of the creation of marketing systems. Marketing has yet to digest and apply the insights of tbe rapidly developing field of communication theory which in turn has drawn freely from both engineering and biological and social sciences. One stimulating idea expounded by Norbert Wiener and others is that of the feedback of information in a control system. Marketing and advertising research are only well started on the task of installing adequate feedback circuits for controlling the deployment of marketing effort.

Social psychology is concerned with some problems of communication which are often encountered in marketing systems. For example, there are the characteristic difficulties of veritical communication which might be compared to the transmission of telephone messages along a power line. Subordinates often hesitate to report bad news to their superiors fearing to take the brunt of emotional reactions. Superiors learn to be cautious in any discussion of the subordinate's status for fear that a casual comment will be interpreted as a commitment. There is often a question as to when a subordinate should act and report and when he should refer a matter for decision upstream. Progress in efficiency, which is a major goal in marketing, depends in substantial part on technological improvement in communication facilities and organizational skill in using them.

The third aspect of structure involved in the study of marketing systems is operating structure.

Effective specialization within an organization requires that activities which are functionally similar be placed together but properly coordinated with other activities. Billing by wholesaler grocers, for example, has long been routinized in a separate billing department. In more recent years the advances in mechanical equipment have made it possible to coordinate inventory control with billing, using the same set of punch cards for both functions. Designing an operating structure is a special application of sorting. As in the sorting of goods to facilitate handling, there are generally several alternative schemes for classifying activities presenting problems of choice to the market planner.

Functional specialization and the design of appropriate operating structures is a constant problem in the effective use of marketing channels. Some functions can be performed at either of two or more stages. One stage may be the best choice in terms of economy or effectiveness. Decision on the placement of a function may have to be reviewed periodically since channels do not remain static. Similar considerations arise in the choice of channels. Some types of distributors or dealers may be equipped to perform a desired service while others may not. Often two or more channels with somewhat specialized roles are required to move a product to the consumer. The product's sponsor can maintain perspective in balancing out these various facilities by thinking in terms of a total operating system including his own sales organization and the marketing channels employed.

The dynamics of market organization pose basic problems for the marketing student and the marketing executive in a free enterprise economy. Reference has already been made to the competitive pursuit of differential advantage. One way in which a firm can gain differential advantage is by organizing the market in a way that is favorable to its own operations. This is something else than the attainment of a monopolistic position in relation to current or potential competitors. It means creating a pattern for dealing with customers or suppliers which persists because there are advantages on both sides. Offering guarantees against price declines on floor stocks is one example of market organization by the seller. Attempts to systematize the flow of orders may range from various services offered to customers or suppliers all the way to complete vertical integration. Another dynamic factor affecting the structure of markets may be generalized under the term "closure." It frequently happens that some marketing system is incomplete or out of balance in some direction. The act of supplying the missing element constitutes closure, enabling the system to handle a greater output or to operate at a new level of efficiency. The incomplete system in effect cries out for closure. To observe this need is to recognize a form of market opportunity. This is one of the primary ways in which new enterprises develop, since there may be good reasons why the missing service cannot be performed by the existing organizations which need the service. A food broker, for example, can cover a market for several accounts of moderate size in a way that the individual manufacturer would not be able to cover it for himself.

There is a certain compensating effect between closure as performed by new or supplementary marketing enterprises and changes in market organization brought about by the initiative of existing firms in the pursuit of differential advantage. The pursuit of a given form of advantage, in fact, may carry the total marketing economy out of balance in a given direction creating the need and opportunity for closure. Such an economy could never be expected to reach a state of equilibrium, although the tendency toward structural balance is one of the factors in its dynamics. Trade regulation may be embraced within this dynamic pattern as an attempt of certain groups to organize the market to their own advantage through political means. Entering into this political struggle to determine the structure of markets are some political leaders and some administrative officials who regard themselves as representing the consumer's interests. It seems reasonable to believe that the increasing sophistication and buying skill of consumers is one of the primary forces offsetting the tendency of the free market economy to turn into something else through the working out of its inherent dynamic forces. This was the destiny foreseen for the capitalistic system by Schumpeter, even though he was one of its staunchest advocates.

The household as an organized behavior system must be given special attention in creating an analytical framework for marketing. The household is an operating entity with an assortment of goods and assets and with economic functions to perform.

Once a primary production unit, the household has lost a large part of these activities to manufacturing and service enterprises. Today its economic operations are chiefly expressed through earning and spending. In the typical household there is some specialization between the husband as primary earner and the wife as chief purchasing agent for the household. It may be assumed that she becomes increasingly competent in buying as she surrenders her production activities such as canning, baking and dressmaking, and devotes more of her time and attention to shopping. She is a rational problem solver as she samples what the market has to offer in her effort to maintain a balanced inventory or assortment of goods to meet expected occasions of use. This is not an attempt to substitute Economic Woman for the discredited fiction of Economic Man. It is only intended to assert that the decision structure of consumer buying is similar to that for industrial buying. Both business executive and housewife enter the market as rational problem solvers, even though there are other aspects of personality in either case.

An adequate perspective on the household for marketing purposes must recognize several facets of its activities. It is an organized behavior system with its aspects of power, communication, and operating structure. It is the locus of forms of behavior other than instrumental or goal-seeking activities. A convenient three-way division, derived from the social sciences, recognizes instrumental, congenial, and symptomatic behavior. Congenial behavior is that kind of activity engaged in for its own sake and presumably yielding direct satisfactions. It is exemplified by the act of consumption as compared to all of the instrumental activities which prepare the way for consumption. Symptomatic behavior reflects maladjustment and is neither pleasure giving in itself nor an efficient pursuit of goals. Symptomatic behavior is functional only to the extent that it serves as a signal to others that the individual needs help.

Some studies of consumer motivation have given increasing attention to symptomatic behavior or to the projection of symptoms of personality adjustment which might affect consumer buying. The present view is that the effort to classify individuals by personality types is less urgent for marketing than the classification of families. Four family types with characteristically different buying behavior have been suggested growing out of the distinction between the instrumental and congenial aspects of normal behavior. Even individuals who are fairly well adjusted in themselves will form a less than perfect family if not fully adapted to each other.

On the instrumental side of household behavior it would seem to be desirable that the members be well coordinated as in any other operating system. If not, they will not deliver the maximum impact in pursuit of family goals. On the congenial side it would appear desirable for the members of a household to be compatible. That means enjoying the same things, cherishing the same goals, preferring joint activities to solitary pursuits or the company of others. These two distinctions yield an obvious four-way classification. The ideal is the family that is coordinated in its instrumental activities and compatible in its congenial activities. A rather joyless household which might nevertheless be well managed and properous in material terms is the coordinated but incompatible household. The compatible but uncoordinated family would tend to be happy-go-lucky and irresponsible with obvious consequences for buying behavior. The household which was both uncoordinated and incompatible would usually be tottering on the brink of dissolution. It might be held together formally by scruples against divorce, by concern for children, or by the dominant power of one member over the others. This symptomology of families does not exclude an interest in the readjustment of individuals exhibiting symptomatic behavior. Such remedial action lies in the sphere of the psychiatrist and the social worker, whereas the marketer is chiefly engaged in supplying goods to families which are still functioning as operating units.

All of the discussion of consumers so far limits itself to the activities of the household purchasing agent. Actually the term consumption as it appears in marketing and economic literature nearly always means consumer buying. Some day marketing may need to look beyond the act of purchasing to a study of consumption proper. The occasion for such studies will arise out of the problems of inducing consumers to accept innovations or the further proliferation of products to be included in the household assortment. Marketing studies at this depth will not only borrow from the social sciences but move into the realm of esthetic and ethical values. What is the use of a plethora of goods unless the buyer derives genuine satisfaction from them? What is the justification of surfeit if the acquisition of goods serves as a distraction from activities which are essential to the preservation of our culture and of the integrity of our personalities?

It has been suggested that a study of consumption might begin with the problem of choice in the presence of abundance. The scarce element then is the time or capacity for enjoyment. The bookworm confronted with the thousands of volumes available in a great library must choose in the face of this type of limitation.

The name hedonomics would appear to be appropriate for this field of study suggesting the management of the capacity to enjoy. Among the problems for hedonomics is the pleasure derived from the repetition of a familiar experience as compared with the enjoyment of a novel experience or an old experience with some novel element. Another is the problem of direct experience versus symbolic experience, with the advantages of intensity on the one hand and on [the] other the possibility of embracing a greater range of possible ideas and sensations by relying on symbolic representations. Extensive basic research will probably be necessary before hedonomics can be put to work in marketing or for the enrichment of human life through other channels.

This paper barely suffices to sketch the analytical framework for marketing. It leaves out much of the area of executive decision-making in marketing on such matters as the weighing of uncertainties and the acceptance of risk in the commitment of resources. It leaves out market planning which is rapidly becoming a systematic discipline centering in the possibilities for economizing time and space as well as resources. It leaves out all but the most casual references to advertising and demand formation. Advertising is certainly one of the most difficult of marketing functions to embrace within a single analytical framework. It largely ignores the developing technology of physical distribution. Hopefully what it does accomplish is to show how the essentially economic problems of marketing may yield to a more comprehensive approach drawing on the basic social sciences for techniques and enriched perspective.

DISCUSSION QUESTIONS

1. Using Alderson's concepts of organized behavioral systems, heterogenous supply and demand, the sorting processes, explain the most essential characteristics of a marketplace exchange between a corporate marketer and a household consumer.

2. If you were a marketing manager for a large consumer goods firm, how would you go about operationalizing Alderson's ideas for your business?

3. In Alderson's last paragraph, he notes several dimensions of marketing that are not captured by his analytic framework. Try to incorporate these missing pieces into Alderson's framework while adhering to the principle of parsimony.

PREFACE TO

''Wroe Alderson's Contributions to Marketing Theory''

I first learned the name Wroe Alderson some thirty years ago. He was a coauthor of the textbook used in the first marketing course that I took as an undergraduate. Later, when working with the Advertising Research Foundation (ARF), I met Alderson and had the opportunity to work with him on a large media research project that Alderson and Sessions did for ARF. Over the years, I attended several meetings of professional groups where Alderson was a featured speaker, including a seminar series that he gave at New York University during the spring of 1963. From time to time, during these years, I had the good fortune to visit with Alderson personally and discuss with him many of his ideas about marketing and marketing theory. This paper, written almost twenty years after his death, gives one assessment of Alderson's contributions to marketing theory.

Alderson was widely respected as a theoretician and was generally acknowledged as the most creative thinker in marketing of his day. He was an influential personality and his theoretical insights provide marketing scholars much to think about. Considering the contributions that Alderson made to marketing theory and the preeminent position that he held in the discipline, it is mystifying to discover how quickly interest in Alderson's theoretical concepts has dissipated.

5

WROE ALDERSON'S CONTRIBUTIONS TO MARKETING THEORY

HIRAM C. BARKSDALE

One of the striking characteristics about the growth and evolution of marketing as a discipline is the general lack of interest in theory development and the lack of concern about the theoretical side of the subject. Examination of the rough and tumble field of marketing during the twentieth century reveals many capable practitioners but relatively few scholars. Wroe Alderson was both a successful practitioner and a widely recognized scholar. In this respect, he holds a special place in the growth and development of marketing.

As a practitioner, Alderson began his career in 1925 with the United States Department of Commerce. Very early in this period he was involved with the Louisville and St. Louis surveys of food and drug stores. These two surveys were essentially pre-tests for the first Census of Business completed in 1929. In the middle 1930s he joined the research group at Curtis Publishing Company. There he worked with Charles Coolidge Parlin, frequently referred to as the father of marketing research, as well as Donald Hobart and other leaders in the research field. In 1944 after completing a war-time assignment with the government in Washington, Alderson joined with Robert E. Sessions to form Alderson and Sessions—a marketing research and consulting firm. In the operation of this business, Alderson attracted brilliant and thoughtful people as associates and consultants.

As a scholar, Alderson was frequently invited to lecture at universities in North America, Europe, and the Far East. He also served as a full-time teacher on two occasions. First, in 1953, he took a leave of absence from Alderson and Sessions and served as visiting professor of marketing at MIT for the academic year. In 1959, Alderson became professor of marketing at the University of Pennsylva-

nia. In the spring of 1963, Alderson served as Ford Foundation visiting professor at New York University.

Both as a practitioner and a scholar, Alderson was very much interested in advancing the science of marketing. He thought that the primary means of achieving this goal was the development of marketing theory.

Wroe Alderson played two roles in the development of marketing theory. First, Alderson was a producer or creator of marketing theory and, second, he was a promoter or catalyst in the development of marketing theory. These two roles are interrelated but they are also separate and distinct. I think it is necessary to examine both roles in order to understand Alderson's contributions to marketing theory.

ALDERSON AS A PRODUCER OF MARKETING THEORY

Alderson was a prolific writer. He was author or editor of a number of books.[1] He also published a number of important articles.[2] In addition, Alderson and Sessions (and later Alderson & Associates) published *Cost and Profit Outlook,* a newsletter that was widely circulated among academic people as well as business executives. In these publications Alderson presents what many consider the most comprehensive theory of marketing that has been constructed up to the present time.

A detailed statement of Alderson's theory will not be attempted here; however, a summary of his basic ideas will be given.

In the development of his general theory, Alderson adopted an ecological frame of reference, rather than an economic point of view, and drew heavily from biology, sociology, cultural anthropology, and other social sciences for perspectives and techniques. Therefore, Alderson's theory falls largely outside the bounds of traditional economics; however, it is not inconsistent with economic thought.

Source: Reprinted with permission from *Theoretical Developments in Marketing,* Charles W. Lamb and Patrick M. Dunne, eds., Chicago, Ill.: American Marketing Association, 1980, 1–3.

The underlying approach is functionalism which begins by identifying a system of related parts, stresses the operation of the total system and the dynamic relations among the component parts, and attempts to explain the component parts in terms of the contribution they make to the system's operation. In a few words, Alderson viewed marketing as an organized behavior system and emphasized the successive sorting transformations needed to match the diverse variety of goods produced by different firms with the heterogeneous product requirements of individual consumers. These three basic concepts—organized behavior systems, heterogeneous supply and demand, and sorting functions—form the core of Alderson's theory.

Organized Behavior Systems

An organized behavior system is defined as an ecological system composed of a group taken in conjunction with the environment in which it functions and has meaning. The group may be the individuals in a household, an association of people in a business firm, or a number of business firms. The distinguishing characteristic of ecological systems is the relations among its members; the participants are not rigidly connected as the parts in a machine, neither are they randomly associated as molecules in a gas chamber. Instead each member of an ecological system occupies a certain status in relation to other participants and tends to react in accordance with the general process of the system; still there is opportunity for independent action. Status links each member to the system and forms the basis for expectations about participation in its activities.

System performance depends upon coordination of participants, and even simple behavior systems exhibit some structural organization to facilitate the direction of effort. The expectations of individual members about the outcome of their association is the rationale explaining the formation and persistence of behavior systems. Behavior systems are organized because of the expected benefits, and participants cooperate to increase the output of the association. The expectations of participants are interrelated but not identical, and members may compete with one another for control of the system or to increase their share of the output.

Alderson postulated that systems do not have goals separate from those of individual members. Instead, systems are considered the means of expressing and realizing the aims of members who make up the association. In short, systems reflect the aims of their participants and they come into being and persist as long as members satisfy their individual goals.

Heterogeneous Markets

The second premise of Alderson's theory is heterogeneous markets. In contrast to economic models of perfect competition, which assume homogeneous markets, Alderson postulated heterogeneity on both the supply and demand sides of markets. On the demand side, the household is considered the most elementary behavior system. Each household, or its purchasing agents, accumulates goods to sustain anticipated patterns in behavior. It is assumed that the product requirements of each household are different and, in an industrial society, practically all of the goods required to create and replenish the assortment of goods desired by all households are purchased in the marketplace. Therefore, each family enters into the market as a problem-solver, seeking a unique assortment of goods needed to support expected patterns of behavior. In making buying decisions, household purchasing agents are guided by two factors. One is the conditional value of the good if used, and the other is the estimated probability of use. Both factors may vary widely from one product to another. For example, a fire extinguisher might have high conditional value but low probability of use. By taking both factors into account, the expected value of products may be compared. A clear distinction is made between the consumer of a product and the purchasing agent who buys it. In addition, it is recognized that the extent of deliberation and the amount of consultation among family members on purchase decisions vary from one product to another and from one family to another.

On the supply side, the behavior of sellers is interpreted as an effort to adjust to differences in product requirements among consumers. Sellers constantly seek to establish a competitive advantage by differentiating their products, services, locations or some combintation of these. To the extent that they are successful, each business firm occupies a unique position and satisfies some particular segment of demand. The never ending search for differential advantage explains the dynamics of competition.

The function of the market is to match up the differentiated products of sellers with the diverse requirements of buyers. The market is cleared when each segment of demand has been satisfied, but this never happens in the real world. Some goods always remain because consumers do not want them and some wants are not satisfied because the proper goods are not available.

Information is the means of clearing heterogeneous markets. Prices are treated as one part of the information flow needed to clear markets. Buyers require information about the goods available and sellers need facts about the products consumers desire. Usually both sides take some initiative in the transmission of information, and through these joint efforts buyers specify their product needs and sellers identify their goods. However, the transmission of information is costly and consumers' needs are never fully specified nor sellers' products completely identified. Since the information requirements vary from one selling situation to another and communication channels have restricted capacity, there are always the subtle questions of deciding how much information is enough and determining the methods of transmitting this information efficiently. Finally, the flow of information determines the efficiency with which the unique segments of supply and demand are paired in the market.

Sorting Functions

Given heterogeneous markets, the unique segments of supply and demand are matched by successive sorting transformations. More specifically, resources useful to man occur in heterogeneous mixtures in nature that are only randomly related to human needs and desires and are termed conglomerations. On the other hand, the supply of goods acquired by households are also heterogeneous collections, but they are related to anticipated behavior patterns and are called assortments. The purpose of marketing is to match segments of supply and demand. This end is achieved by successive sorting transformations which align small, heterogeneous segments of supply with appropriate segments of demand. Therefore, the basic functions of marketing are the sorting transformations which create meaningful assortments of goods from random mixtures of raw materials.

Sorting includes both the decisions that sellers make in assembling products for the market and the choices that buyers make in selecting goods to satisfy their wants. Alderson refers to the process as "double sorting" since sellers are looking for customers and buyers are searching for products.

Searching is defined as a form of pre-sorting which does not necessitate the physical movement of goods. The purpose of searching is to locate products which fall into specified categories. It may require considerable effort, but it is concerned with information and is basically a mental activity. Sorting, on the other hand, is a physical process and once completed cannot be reversed without the risk of some loss. Alderson identified four levels or states in the multiphase process of sorting: sorting out, accumulation, allocation, and assortment. Marketing is concerned with all four phases of sorting, but it is most interested in the final stage of building up assortments of goods. The other stages are important because they contribute to the final state which creates meaningful assortments of goods in the hands of consumers and takes products off the market.

Marketing institutions serve as specialists, performing the sorting functions and contributing to the matching of heterogeneous segments of demand with appropriate segments of supply.

Transactions are agreements concerning the exchange of goods which result from the double sorting process in which buyers search for goods and sellers look for customers. They reflect joint decisions in which buyers agree to take the products offered and sellers agree to supply the goods at stated prices.

All of the transactions and the related sorting transformations required to move a product from the raw material state to a finished product in the hands of a consumer are linked together by the concept of transvections. The term transvection was invented to describe the movement of a product through the entire marketing system.

In summary, the basic concepts of Alderson's theory are organized behavior systems, heterogeneous markets, and sorting functions. All aspects of marketing are explained in terms of these basic concepts. Marketing is considered an organized behavior system, operating in heterogeneous markets, and adapting to diverse market conditions by successive sorting functions.

Alderson viewed the marketing process as a series of sorting transformations which match heterogeneous segments of supply and demand. Transactions specify the terms and conditions under which products change hands and are defined in terms of the sorting process. All of the transactions for a product, beginning with producers of raw materials and ending with final consumers, and the related sorting transformations, form a sequence called a transvection which explains the flow of the product through the entire marketing system.

ALDERSON AS A PROMOTER OF MARKETING THEORY

Since Alderson was the major contributor of marketing theory, it is not surprising that he was also the leading promoter of theory development. Alderson believed that theory should play a fundamental role in advancing the science of marketing. It seems that he understood better than any of his contemporaries the importance of developing the theoretical side of the subject.

In 1948, Wroe Alderson (with Reavis Cox) published an important paper ''Towards a Theory of Marketing.'' This paper sets forth the proposition that marketing could be a science and explained the need for theory in order to reach this goal. In this classic article Alderson stated that the discipline was preoccupied with refining definitions and classifications and he explained that piling-up more facts about the institutions and activities of marketing would not lead to further progress. He argued that the development of theories to explain the accumulated facts about marketing was the way to advance the discipline.

One of Alderson's major contributions to marketing theory was his leadership of the Marketing Theory Seminars. In 1951, Alderson joined with Edmund McGarry, Leo Aspinwald, and H. W. Huegy to organize the first theory seminar at the University of Colorado. These meetings were held each summer until the middle 1960s.

Attendance at these annual meetings was by invitation only. Participants were recognized leaders in the field of marketing.

These seminars were the hot bed for discussions of marketing theory during the post-war period. Alderson was the mainspring in these seminars and was recognized as the undisputed leader of the group.

ASSESSMENT OF ALDERSON'S CONTRIBUTIONS TO MARKETING THEORY

It is now almost twenty years since a heart attack ended Wroe Alderson's life. With the passage of time, the number of references to Alderson in marketing textbooks has declined sharply. Most of the new books include few references to Alderson's publications and many do not include any reference at all to his work.

His books are out-of-print. This suggests that very few graduate students have to struggle through his publications and try to understand the theoretical concepts that Alderson created. With the passage of the years, interest in Alderson's theory of marketing continues to decline.

In his book *Dynamic Marketing Behavior,* Alderson included 150 hypotheses that he suggested others might test. Alderson called this section of the book a ''Research Agenda for Functionalism.'' These hypotheses should be a gold mine for Ph.D. students searching for dissertation topics, but as far as I know, little if any effort has been made to test any of them.

Alderson was a creative scholar and an innovative thinker; however, he was not a literary craftsman. His publications were difficult to read and understand. The concepts that he advanced were not fully developed and his ideas were not closely reasoned. Few if any of Alderson's concepts were picked up and used by practitioners.

Alderson was the acknowledged leader in marketing theory for twenty years. He had many followers; however, Alderson did not establish a tradition or school of scholars to continue his work. Consequently, when he died efforts to develop his concepts stopped.

If editors of journals and publishers of books receive any manuscripts that discuss what Alderson really said, or intended to say, then they are not published.

There is no doubt that Alderson's work contains many ideas, insights and suggestions, but his theorietical system never became the organizing concept for the mainstream of marketing thought. Today there is next to nothing of Alderson's theory that can be found in current textbooks.

As a promoter of marketing theory, Alderson understood the role of theory and argued that theory development was the way to further progress in the discipline. Most would agree that Alderson did more than anyone else to point up the importance of marketing theory and to focus attention on the need for theory development.

CONCLUSION

Wroe Alderson will continue to occupy an important place in the history of marketing. It is possible that his theoretical contributions will be rediscovered at some point in the future and be incorporated into the mainstream of marketing thought. However, this is not a prediction.

According to this analysis, Alderson's place in history will rest primarily on his role as a catalyst in theory development. Alderson understood the need to develop the conceptual side of marketing. This idea is as valid today as it was thirty years ago. I am optimistic that the discipline is coming to understand the importance of the theoretical side of the subject and as we do we will continue to appreciate the pioneering role that Alderson played in stimulating interest in theory development.

It may be an idle exercise to attempt assessment of the theoretical contributions of any scholar. It is difficult, if not impossible, to identify all of the things that an individual does and to judge the impact that he has on his discipline. Assessing the contributions that one makes to his profession is somewhat like a game that anyone can play. There are no definite rules to guide play. Therefore, the criteria by which each participant makes a judgment are likely to differ from one player to another. Consequently, the assessments of each individual differ in content and emphasis. Every play is challenged and discussed. After each round of play there is no agreement. This sets the stage for the next round of play and the game continues.

Alderson left us a legacy, but up to this time it has not had much impact on the life style of our discipline. In my opinion, this is our fault and our loss—not Alderson's.

NOTES

[1]Reavis Cox and Wroe Alderson (Editors), *Theory in Marketing*. Chicago: Richard D. Irwin, Inc.,

1950; Wroe Alderson, *Marketing Behavior and Executive Action*. Homewood Ill.: Richard D. Irwin, Inc., 1957; Wroe Alderson and Stanley J. Shapiro (Editors), *Marketing and the Computer,* Englewood Cliffs, N.J.: Prentice-Hall, Inc., 1963; Wroe Alderson and Paul Green, *Planning and Problem Solving in Marketing*. Homewood, Ill.: Richard D. Irwin, Inc., 1964; Reavis Cox, Wroe Alderson, and Stanley J. Shapiro (Editors), *Theory in Marketing* (Second Series). Homewood, Ill.: Richard D. Irwin, Inc., 1964; Wroe Alderson, *Dynamic Marketing Behavior: A Functionalist Theory of Marketing*. Homewood: Ill.: Richard D. Irwin, Inc., 1965; Wroe Alderson, Vern Terpstra, and Stanley J. Shapiro (Editors), *Patents and Progress*. Homewood, Ill.: Richard D. Irwin, Inc., 1965; and Wroe Alderson and Michael H. Halbert, *Men, Motives and Markets*. Englewood Cliffs, N.J.: Prentice-Hall, Inc., 1968.

[2]Wroe Alderson and Reavis Cox, "Towards a Theory of Marketing," *Journal of Maketing*. Vol. 13, October 1948, pp. 137–152; Wroe Alderson, "Scope and Place of Wholesaling in the United States," *Journal of Marketing*. Vol. 14, September 1949, pp. 145–155; Wroe Alderson, "A Systematics for Problems of Action," Philosophy of Science. Vol. 18, January 1951, pp. 16–25; Wroe Alderson, "Psychology for Marketing and Economics," *Journal of Marketing*. Vol. 17, October 1952, pp. 119–135; Wroe Alderson and Miles W. Martin, "Toward a Formal Theory of Transactions and Transvections," *Journal of Marketing Research*. Vol. 2, May 1965, pp. 117–127.

DISCUSSION QUESTIONS

1. Explain the two roles that Alderson played in the development of marketing theory.

2. Explain the basic concepts that form the core of Alderson's theory of marketing.

3. How do you explain the declining interest in Alderson's theoretical work?

4. What criteria should be used in evaluating theoretical contributions to marketing?

PREFACE TO
"On the Role of Marketing Theory"

"On the Role of Marketing Theory" was written during my period of close association with Wroe Alderson. This pioneer in marketing theory was a model of knowledge and insight into business practice, which were combined with an extraordinary ability to recognize general implications of particular observations. Add to this his great personal charm and it is easy to see how a young economist would be drawn to Alderson's interest in marketing theory. This paper was written in an attempt to see how far experience in economic theory could serve as guidance in the closely related field of marketing.

6

ON THE ROLE OF MARKETING THEORY*

W. J. BAUMOL

NATURE OF THEORY

The completion of a comprehensive work on marketing theory by Wroe Alderson[1] seems an appropriate occasion to review the aspirations and promise of a theoretical approach to marketing. There seems to be much misunderstanding about the nature of theory in general and that of marketing theory in particular, and this paper seeks to shed some light on these matters.

"Theory" in Popular Language

Words mean different things to different people and there is little point in arguing definitions. But meaningful discussion is only possible if the connotation of a word is the same to all who employ it. This has not been the case in the use of the word "theory," which means one thing to the layman and something entirely different to the theorist. As a result, the public has a distorted view of the goals and methods of theoretical research.

In common parlance "theoretical" is taken to be a contradictory either of "factual" or of "practical." "A theory" is the term often used to denote an allegation of fact for which no evidence has been presented. Unverified statements about the chemical composition of some compound, or about the behavior of some group of Australian aborigines, or about the nature of the so-called "canals" on Mars are all likely to be labeled theories. However, in the literature of scientific method, the statement, "the canals on Mars contain water," has nothing to do with astronomical or biological or any other theory. Rather, such an assertion would be referred to as an "unverified hypothesis."

The distinction is no mere quibble. A hypothesis is a pure question of fact while theory, to the theo-

rist, is concerned with explanation. The Martian canal hypothesis is either true or false and its validity can be settled one way or another by the first space ship to return from Mars, should one ever succeed in making the trip. Final disposition of the question on the Australians may be even simpler and may be contingent only on the financing of an anthropological expedition by one of the foundations. With theory, as we shall indicate presently, the question of verification is not so simple.

There is also a second common use of the term "theory," characterized by the frequently encountered statement: "That may all be very well in theory, but when we get down to practical matters. . . ." Of course, most theorists prefer to believe that their work can be immensely helpful to the practical man. Whether this is likely frequently to be the case, the reader must judge for himself from the sequel. At this point we only recall the rather hackneyed illustrations which are usually employed to show that in some cases at least theory can have enormous practical implications. We have often been reminded that the well-publicized developments in electronics and atomic energy would not now be possible without the work of the theoretical physicists. Even Edison's work, which itself was totally devoid of theory, depended heavily on earlier theoretical results which by his time had become part of the standard equipment of the technician.

"Theory" as Used by the Theorist

Roughly, the theorist uses the word "theory" to mean "systematic explanation." A theory is a structure which describes the workings and interrelations of the various aspects of some phenomenon. Philosophers tell us that the word "explanation" has a great variety of meanings, but this need not concern us here. We can avoid this expository difficulty by describing in some detail what the theorist seeks to do.

Essentially, his procedure involves the examination of some aspect of reality and the construction of a simplified small-scale model which behaves in at

Source: Reprinted with permission from the *Journal of Marketing,* 21, (April), 1957, 413–418, Chicago: American Marketing Association.

*This paper had its origins in a talk delivered before the Marketing Theory Seminar at Burlington, Vermont, which was held during the week of August 27, 1956.

least some ways like the phenomena under observation. The analyst can understand and trace out the workings of his model while reality is far too complicated and chaotic for this to be possible. In practice a particular day's demand for refrigerators may be conditioned by a family quarrel in Abilene, a case of mumps in South Bend, and the statement of a tea-leaf-reading gypsy to one of her clients in Jersey City. It is hopeless to seek to take all of these considerations into account in an investigation of the appliance market. Instead, one deals with a simplified make-believe market in which consumer demand is conditioned by income, advertising expenditure, and a few other variables.

This method is well established in the natural sciences. The physicist cannot predict just what path will be followed by a real automobile left free to roll down a real hill or the time a real chestnut will take to pop in a real fire. He can only tell us what will happen in the artificial circumstances described by a controlled experiment, where the elements carefully held constant in the laboratory are the aspects of reality from which his simplified model abstracts. Once he steps out of the laboratory, his conclusions must be treated with extreme caution. That is why the salaries of test pilots are high!

Basically, the need for theory arises because facts unfortunately do not speak for themselves. An inflationary movement in prices or a fall in the sales volume of a shoe manufacturer is compatible with a variety of hypotheses. Facts supply us with correlations, not with structural relationships. At times all of us are prepared to reject conclusions which appear to be implied by the facts because these conclusions conflict with the rudimentary theoretical structures which we implicitly accept. For example, no one ever treated seriously, as an explanation of prosperity and depression, the statistics which showed that at least for a time there was a high correlation between the level of national income and the height of feminine skirt hems. None of the theories of the business cycle to which we more or less unconsciously adhere allows for dictation of the level of America's industrial activity by Christian Dior.

Perhaps a better example is the relationship between interest rates and industrial construction. Statistics show that they tend to go up and down together and apparently imply that a rise in interest rates encourages the appearance of new factories and equipment. But economic theory usually denies this violently and argues plausibly that a rise in the cost of borrowing increases the businessman's construction costs and serves to deter this type of investment. The economist then accounts for the observed fact by pointing out that a third variable enters in and confuses matters. When national income is high, construction is profitable and the demand for funds to finance it raises interest rates. Which version of the facts is correct, we may never be sure, but the recent reaction of businessmen to Federal Reserve tight-money policies lends credence to the view that high interest costs are no stimulus to the creation of industrial capital goods.

We see then that since the facts themselves are silent, theory must be invented to describe their workings. If we desire to understand the structure of reality, we desire theory in the sense the theorist employs the term. This does not mean that non-theoretical research is undesirable or even less desirable than the work of the theorist. Their purposes are different—one supplies the data; the other, the explanations.

Illustration: An Empirical and a Theoretical "Law"

As an example of an empirical result in marketing, let us consider "Reilley's law." As originally formulated, this states that "Two cities attract retail trade from any intermediate city or town in the vicinity of the breaking point, approximately in direct proportion to the populations of the two cities and in inverse proportion to the square of the distances from these two cities to the intermediate town." [2]

When Reilley presented this result, he marshaled an impressive array of market data in its support but made no attempt at systematic explanation. The assertion was nevertheless useful and illuminating to marketing men.

Let us compare this with a somewhat related theoretical result which we owe to Fetter. [3] Consider two manufacturing centers A and B which produce a similar product at different unit costs. If they both pay the same cost of transportation per mile, what is the borderline between the territories that will be served by A and B? The answer is that if goods are sold at cost plus the same percentage markup, and customers buy from the man who sells most cheaply, the borderline will be a hyperbola whose formula is easily written down by a freshman mathematics student. For at every point, X, of equal price (cost), the difference between the distance of X to A and that of X to B will just make up for the difference in manufacturing cost at the two centers. In other words, there will be a constant difference between the distance of a point on the borderline to A and the distance from the point to B. But in analytic geometry, a hyperbola is defined as the locus of all points the difference in whose distances to two fixed points is a constant, and Fetter's conclusion follows at once.

Let us now see what the theoretical result does and what it does not do. Because we understand its workings we can easily see how the conclusion is affected by changes in the circumstances. If transportation cost is not strictly proportioned to the distance a cargo is carried, or if the pattern of pricing is not simply cost plus, or if in some other way the situation is known to differ from that postulated in the derivation of the original theorem, it may not be difficult to modify the analysis to take this into account. Should there be a proposed change in railroad rate structure, we could in advance examine the nature of its effects on competitive market areas with the aid of this theoretical analysis. Here, an empirical generalization would be of very little help because this can only tell us how things stand. Since it offers no clue as to how things work, it cannot tell us what will happen under changed conditions until after the change occurs and its results are observed. This, then, is a major advantage of the theoretical construct. It can help us in this way because it permits us to understand the *structure* of the situation.

On the other hand, the empirical law is—as a result of the way in which it is derived—virtually certain to be in closer agreement with the facts. The empirical law *states* the facts. The theoretical law describes not the facts, but a simplified model which at best only approximates them fairly well. We have said that a distinguishing feature of a factual hypothesis is that it is either right or wrong. By contrast, we may assert that a theoretical construct is sure to be more or less wrong in that it oversimplifies and hence distorts or omits some aspects of the circumstances under investigation.

Characteristics of "Good" Theory

Though all theory is in this sense wrong, it is not all of one quality. One piece of theoretic work is considered more successful than another. To account for this difference, we may list some of the desiderata of a theoretical model:

1. The model should be sufficiently simple version of the facts to permit systematic manipulation and analysis. This means that a more realistic model may often be a poorer model. It is, of course, always desirable to make a model more realistic if this can be done without seriously complicating the investigation.

2. On the other hand, the model must be a sufficiently close approximation to the relevant facts to be usable. How close an approximation is necessary and which facts are relevant depend, of course, on the problem under investigation. It follows, and this cannot be overemphasized, that a model which is appropriate for the examination of one problem arising out of a given set of circumstances may be totally useless and even misleading for the investigation of another problem arising out of these same circumstances.

How difficult it is to find a theoretical model which acceptably meets these two criteria is partly a matter of luck. Some problems may just be so complicated that any model which is sufficiently simple to be analytically useful must be too gross a misrepresentation of the situation which it seeks to describe. This observation is sometimes advanced as a partial explanation of the less than spectacular progress that has characterized the social sciences.

It is worth mentioning one more feature to be desired of a theory:

3. Its conclusions should be relatively insensitive to changes in its assumptions. An example which comes to mind is a pricing recommendation which was made to a client on the basis of an operations research analysis. The relevant cost data were not unambiguously indicated by the accounting records, so a wide variety of cost assumptions was investigated. It was shown that these had little effect on the computed optimum price—and the recommended price structure could consequently be regarded with considerably greater confidence. The basic point is that the assumptions of a model are never more than approximately valid, and if the structure of a model is such as seriously to magnify errors, this inaccuracy in the premises is likely to be translated into thoroughly independable conclusions.

Is There a Place for Marketing Theory?

Even when it is granted that theoretical work can play a useful role, questions are sometimes raised about the possibility of a distinctive marketing theory. It is pointed out that the problems of marketing now fall under the purview of various fields, including psychology, sociology, and economics, each of which already has developed a considerable body of theory. This is true, but it is not entirely relevant. Pursued to its limits, this argument might have economics and sociology as branches of psychology; the latter, in turn, might be labeled a field in biology; and all the sciences might end up reclassified as physics. It seems to me that economics and psychology may more usefully be taken to provide some bricks for the construction of marketing theory rather than constituting its sum and substance. The difference between two disciplines often lies in the point of view with which they view the same subject. Clinical pathology which makes up so much of the psychologist's subject matter is of little interest to the marketing man whose attention is focused more on the behavior of groups than of the individuals which constitute them and on behavior which is in some sense normal. The appropriate choice of theory is, as I have emphasized, a matter of the problem in which the investigator is interested. It must surely be admitted that marketing has its special problems and may, therefore, well find it useful to develop further its own body of theory.

The Functionalist Approach to Marketing Theory

The application of some of these criteria for theory is exemplified in the recent book by Wroe Alderson, which bears the subtitle "The Functionalist Approach to Marketing Theory." While it is rich in insights drawn from experience, it cannot be characterized as a description of marketing processes and institutions. It does not pretend to create a comprehensive new model for the marketing mechanism. Attainment of such a goal would be too much to expect of a pathbreaking work in any young discipline. But the book succeeds entirely in its more modest purpose: the provision of perspectives for model building directed either toward general interpretation of marketing or the solution of individual problems.

The fundamental theme of the book is problem solving in marketing, regarded as a function of organized behavior systems. The behavior system is said to function as if it were pursuing inherent goals or survival and growth, although it is recognized that the vital urge apparent in the system rests on the expectations of the individuals who participate in its activities in the effort to realize their own objectives.

The author describes his viewpoint as "functionalism" because he begins with an examination of the way in which organized groups function in continuous adjustment to an operating environment. The focal point of interest, however, is in the problems of adjustment which arise to threaten the security of the system and which must be solved to maintain or enhance its efficiency. The problem which faces the executive responsible for making a decision on behalf of any system lies in the uncertainty of success of any course of action which he chooses to adopt. Problem solving is the attempt to reduce uncertainty to tolerable limits so that action can be taken.

The author points out that uncertainty in marketing springs in part from the radical heterogeneity on both the demand side and the supply side of the market and from the stream of innovations which produce heterogeneity over time. The market mechanism undertakes to match each segment of demand with the appropriate segment of supply. Matching is difficult since the parties to be brought together are separated by distance and by lack of knowledge and contact. From the viewpoint of the agencies engaged in marketing functions, this may be described as the matching of opportunity with effort. Each segment of demand is potential opportunity for some supplier and all supply can be regarded as production and marketing effort expended to satisfy demand.

The matching of supply and demand is carried on through the shaping, fitting, and sorting of goods and services. Sorting in its various forms is held to be the essential marketing process and is taken to include allocation or the breaking down of supplies and assorting or the building up of assortments. Efficiency in production requires the development of marketing intermediaries to deal with sorting and related functions. Efficiency in marketing requires routinization of transactions and the development of specialized marketing channels.

The book reminds us that the structure of marketing agencies is constantly changing in response to changes in the scale and character of the marketing job to be done. The dynamics of this process arise from the economics of differential advantage.

Every vigorous competitor is constantly engaged in trying to gain an edge over his rivals. One way to gain a differential advantage in the performance of a marketing function is to be better organized to perform it. Freedom to compete includes freedom to organize the market. The most crucial function of all is the creation of structure through which to function. A marketing executive is not only concerned with action but with capacity for action. He follows the power principle in making decisions, which means that he acts in such a way as to promote the power to act.

The book also illuminatingly pictures consumers as coming into the market to solve problems and to reduce uncertainty as to the realization of their anticipations. Household commodity inventory assortments are created to meet future occasions of use, taking account of both the relative importance of these occasions and the probality of their occurrence. The housewife, too, makes executive decisions in her capacity as purchasing agent for the household. In a sense, her task is more complicated than that of the business executive since the family, which is her operating environment, is the principal setting for the congenial (inherently pleasant) behavior which is presumed to be the end and aim of all instrumental behavior including shopping. The seller can solve his problems only by helping buyers to solve their problems. The recognition of the consumer buyer as a problem solver is perhaps the most novel and characteristic aspect of this view.

Marketing theory in this version accepts the basic assumption of rational behavior posited in classical economics. It attempts to place rational problem solving in a broader theory of behavior derived from psychology and sociology. In addition to distinguishing between instrumental and congenial behavior, this theory recognizes a third category of symptomatic behavior springing from maladjustment. Yet, rational problem solving remains the central concept insofar as the book is truly theoretical. To the extent that it permits deductions about market behavior, they must rest on this concept. Since conscious and deliberate problem solving does not presumably occupy a large part of the time of either executives or housewives, a book

with this emphasis can scarcely be regarded as realistic description. To justify its claim as a beginning step in marketing theory, it does not have to mirror reality in all its complexity. The test will be whether it can fulfill its promise as a means of interpreting "market behavior and executive action" and for giving direction to further research.

NOTES

[1] Wroe Alderson, *Marketing Behavior and Executive Action* (Homewood, Ill.: Richard D. Irwin, Inc., 1957).

[2] William J. Reilley, *The Law of Retail Gravitation* (New York: Pilsbury Publishers, 1931), p. 9.

[3] Frank A. Fetter, "The Economic Law of Market Areas," *Quarterly Journal of Economics,* vol. 38, May 1924.

DISCUSSION QUESTIONS

1. Give some examples of hypotheses in marketing that are not theories. Why is the distinction important?

2. David Ricardo once rejected some statistical arguments by a critic on the grounds that the alleged facts were inconsistent with well-established theory and that the statistics therefore—in Ricardo's opinion—had to be erroneous. Stigler's more recent research confirmed that Ricardo' judgment about the statistics was correct. Is Ricardo's procedure generally justifiable? Under what circumstances is it an acceptable way of reasoning? When is it dangerous?

3. "Skillful theorizing involves the use of good judgment in the tradeoff between oversimplification which makes a model inapplicable to reality and excessive complication which makes it intractable analytically." Can you think of models which are excessively oversimple? Excessively complex? May a model be sufficiently complex for the analysis of one problem and yet too simple for another?

PREFACE TO
"Is Marketing a Science?"

When I wrote "Is Marketing a Science?" more than twenty years ago, scientific marketing seemed to be just around the next corner.

Applications of mathematical modeling to marketing seemed to offer virtually unlimited opportunities for improvement. Computers were, for the first time, being used not only for statistical analysis, but also to permit the development of marketing information systems with unprecedented levels of detail. New insights into customer behavior were being found, almost daily it seemed, from the behavioral sciences. Epitomizing all of these developments, the Marketing Science Institute (MSI) was established to serve as a catalyst for the movement toward scientific methods and general theory.

Looking back on the actual achievements of the past two decades, it is tempting to adopt a cynical attitude. Certainly the brave new world of scienctific marketing has not evolved as quickly as some envisioned in the early 1960s. Indeed, in the 1980s it has become fashionable to blame marketing, or the ways in which it has been implemented in most firms, for many of the economic and social ills of the U.S. and European economies. The chairman of a major corporation asks, "Where Is Marketing Now That We Really Need It?"* while two academicians bemoan "The Misuse of Marketing: An American Tragedy."† These and other critiques suggest either that scientific marketing has failed to materialize or that it has been misdirected to the solution of the wrong problems.

There have been some major disappointments, and *much* of the hoopla regarding marketing science in the early 1960s was no doubt grossly exaggerated in the first place. But I am still basically optimistic about our progress and about the prospects for the future. Marketing decision support systems (the descendants of MIS) *have* been developed in many companies and *have* led to tangible improvements. Techniques for market segmentation *are* vastly superior today when compared with the practices of earlier decades. Continuing improvements in information technology and telecommunication offer still greater potential for the years ahead.

So, although marketing is still far from being a true science, I believe that the application of the scientific method has contributed greatly to the state of the art and that it will continue to do so indefinitely.

---

*John F. Welch, Jr., presentation to the Conference Board 1981 Marketing Conference, New York, October 1981.

†Roger C. Bennett and Robert G. Cooper, in *McKinsey Quarterly*, Autumn 1982, pp. 52–69.

7

IS MARKETING A SCIENCE?*

ROBERT D. BUZZELL

If you ask the average business executive what the most important agent of progress in the contemporary society, the odds are good that he will answer, "science." There is a general respect, even awe, for the accomplishments of science. The satellites in orbit, polio vaccine, and television are tangible pieces of evidence that science conquers all.

To be against science is as heretical as to be against motherhood. Yet when executives are asked to consider the social and economic process of marketing as a science or prospective science, most confess to extreme skepticism. Is marketing a science? If not, can it ever become one? If so, what does this imply for management?

These questions are hardly new ones, but they have a special interest in light of several recent developments:

Perhaps the most noteworthy of these is the formation, in mid-1962, of the Marketing Science Institute [MSI], an organization supported by some twenty-nine large corporations and devoted to "fundamental research" in the field of marketing.

At the same time, the American Marketing Association, a professional group dedicated to "the advancement of science in marketing," has re-examined its own goals and taken stock of its accomplishments to date.

Finally, the issue of science in marketing—and especially the use of science or of its results by executives responsible for marketing decisions—also has received considerable attention in several recently published books.

Thus, it seems appropriate at this point to pause and consider the status of science in marketing, to sift out the claims and counter-claims, and to ask whether any basic changes are needed in management's approach to marketing problems.

WHAT IS MARKETING SCIENCE?

The [MSI] is headed by Dr. Wendell R. Smith, formerly Staff Vice President for Marketing Development at the Radio Corporation of America, and before that a university teacher. Smith stated in an address delivered to the Kansas City Chapter of the American Marketing Association on July 10, 1962, that the goals of the MSI were:

1. To contribute to the emergence of a more definitive science of marketing.
2. To stimulate increased application of scientific techniques to the understanding and solving of marketing problems.

It is useful to keep these two points separate. First, we can consider whether or not there is such a thing as a science *of* marketing, comparable in some sense to the sciences of physics, biology, and so on. Secondly, there is still remaining the question of how and to what extent scientific techniques can be applied *to* marketing—whether or not it is, or may be, a science in itself.

Of the two goals set forth by the MSI, certainly the first is the more ambitious. In order to qualify as a distinct science in its own right, marketing will have to meet some rather stringent requirements. For example, it is generally agreed that a science is

- A classified and systematized body of knowledge.
- Organized around one or more central theories and a number of general principles.
- Usually expressed in quantitative terms.
- Knowledge which permits the prediction and, under some circumstances, the control of future events.

Few believe that marketing now meets these criteria. True, there is a substantial body of classified

Source: Reprinted with permission from the *Harvard Business Review*, 41, (January/February), 32–40, 166–70, Boston: Harvard University Pres. Copyright © 1963 by the President and Fellows of Harvard College. All rights reserved.

*I gratefully acknowledge the assistance of Michael Halbert, who read the original version of this article and made many useful suggestions on it.

knowledge about marketing, but there certainly is no central theory; furthermore, there are few accepted principles, and our ability to predict is limited indeed. One reason for this state of affairs is that, for most of the fifty years since the beginnings of concerted efforts to study marketing, our emphasis has been predominantly on fact-gathering.

The story of attempts to describe and understand marketing phenomena, beginning in the early 1900s, is chronicled by Robert Bartels of Ohio State University in his new book, *The Development of Marketing Thought.*[1] Bartels sees the early study of marketing as an offshoot of economics, brought about by changes in economic conditions in the late nineteenth century. These changes produced a "growing disparity between facts and assumptions underlying prevailing [economic] theory," and one of the primary missions of the pioneer marketing students was to reconcile this disparity.

In particular, Bartels notes that while traditional economic theory assumed that producers could (and would) adjust to the market, by 1900 they increasingly sought to adjust the market to their own needs instead. Similarly, orthodox theory had little place for middlemen, and provided no key to understanding the growing size and diversity of such organizations as department stores and mail-order houses. In short, prevailing economic theory did not explain the observed facts about marketing, much less provide any basis for intelligent management.

Believing that economic theory was inadequate as a basis for understanding the marketing system, early students of marketing set out to describe existing institutions and practices and to discover, if possible, the rationale underlying them. Consequently, a spirit of thoroughgoing empiricism pervaded their efforts. For example, Bartels describes a project undertaken in the 1920s by the New York University School of Retailing in cooperation with a group of New York City department stores. This project culminated in the publication of the so-called "Retailing Series," which described the best contemporary practices in merchandising, retail credit, and so on.[2]

This empiricism of academic investigators was strongly reinforced by the philosophy of most business executives. Recently there have been indications that some executives are becoming more re-

ceptive to the notion of "theory." The willingness of its sponsors to support MSI provides an outstanding example of this. But most managers who are responsible for day-to-day decisions are still typically inclined to distrust generalizations. Charles Ramond of the Advertising Research Foundation pointed out in a paper, "Theories of Choice in Business," delivered at the Annual Convention of the American Psychological Association in St. Louis on September 5, 1962:

> The businessman's practical wisdom is of a completely different character than scientific knowledge. While it does not ignore generalities, it recognizes the low probability that given combinations of phenomena can or will be repeated. . . . In place of scientific knowledge, then, the businessman collects lore.

Both academicians and practitioners have concentrated on the accumulation of facts about marketing. To some extent, these facts have been systematized through a process of definition, classification, and analysis. But it must be admitted that few real principles have emerged. Bartels lists a number of generalizations drawn from the literature of marketing; but some of these are actually derived from traditional economic theory, while others are merely tautologies. As an example of the first type, we are told that sellers, under pure competition, will expand output until marginal cost equals marginal revenue. An illustration of a tautology is the assertion that "when conditions demand modification in the existing marketing structure, the change will be made."

RELATED SCIENCES

While marketing does not yet appear to qualify as a science in its own right, high hopes have been placed on the applications of findings and methods from other fields which are, presumably, further along the evolutionary trail. This optimism is reflected in several articles among those reprinted in a new revision of *Managerial Marketing: Perspectives and Viewpoints—A Source Book,* edited by William Lazer and Eugene Kelley.[3] First among these articles is one by Joseph W. Newman, originally appearing in *HBR,*[4] which asserts:

As marketers have become increasingly aware of how much they have to learn about the nature of buying and consumption, they have turned for assistance to the behavioral sciences, which have made great progress in recent times. Much can be gained from this move.

Some of the potential benefits of adopting and applying the results of scientific inquiry in psychology, sociology, and other fields are outlined by Lazer and Kelley in another of the papers in their collection, under the formidable title of "Interdisciplinary Contributions to Marketing Management." These quthors distinguish between "discovery disciplines" (i.e., those concerned with discovering regularities in specified aspects of nature) and "application disciplines" (i.e., those oriented to specific types of problems).

In these terms, marketing would appear to be primarily an area for application of findings *from* the sciences (especially behavioral sciences), and not a science in itself. Should the attempt to make it a science, then, be abandoned as a wild-goose chase?

No, it should be continued, W. J. Baumol argues in "On the Role of Marketing Theory," another article included in the Lazer and Kelley book. Baumol points out that while the problems of marketing do, in fact, fall within the spheres of such fields as economics, sociology, and psychology, it is also possible to argue that economics is merely a branch of psychology, and so on. He concludes that "marketing has its special problems and may, therefore, well find it useful to develop further its own body of theory."

But what form should this theory take? Baumol warns that it is too much to expect that theory will permit *exact* predictions of the future. Theory, of necessity, involves abstraction from, and simplification of, reality. Thus, the theorist's task includes:

. . . examination of some aspect of reality and the construction of a simplified small-scale model which behaves in at least some ways like the phenomena under observation. The analyst can understand and trace out the workings of his model while reality is far too complicated and chaotic for this to be possible. . . . The method is well established in the natural sciences. The physicist cannot predict just what path will be followed by a real automobile left free to roll down a real hill. . . . He can only tell us what will happen in the artificial circumstances described by a controlled experiment, where the elements carefully held constant in the laboratory are the aspects of reality from which his simplified model abstracts.

Has any useful theory in this sense been developed in marketing? One interesting attempt is described by Leo Aspinwall in "The Characteristics of Goods Theory" in the same book. Aspinwall's theory is designed "to predict with a high degree of reliability how a product will be distributed," that is, to predict the marketing channels that will be used to reach ultimate consumers or other end users. Five characteristics or "distinguishing qualities" are defined:

1. Replacement rate—the rate at which a good is purchased and consumed.

2. Gross margin—the total cost of moving a product from point of origin to final consumer.

3. "Adjustment"—the extent of services which must be "applied to goods in order to meet the exact needs of the consumer."

4. Time of consumption—durability of the product.

5. Searching time required to procure the product.

Aspinwall argues that these five characteristics are interrelated—in particular, replacement rate is inversely related to the other four, which in turn are directly related to each other. Hence, it is possible to combine the characteristics and derive a threefold classification of goods, arbitrarily designated as "red," "orange," and "yellow." Red goods, with a high replacement rate, low gross margin, low degree of adjustment, short consumption time, and low searching time, will be characterized by "broadcast distribution" and relatively long marketing channels. Yellow goods, with the opposite characteristics, will be distributed direct, while orange goods occupy an intermediate position.

Now, it is possible to criticize the Aspinwall theory on several counts. First, if it is true that replacement rate is invariably related to the other four characteristics, then the whole theory could be built on this single factor; the others are redundant. In the physical sciences, the principle of ''parsimony'' is well established. William of Ockham, a fourteenth century English scholastic, laid down the rule that theories should be as simple as possible, and the reasons for this seem as compelling in marketing as anywhere else.

A second criticism of the characteristics-of-goods theory is that, to some extent, it seems circular. It can be argued that the total gross margin required to distribute a product and the searching time required to obtain it are *results* of the marketing channels used, not underlying causes. Finally, there is some ambiguity as to whether Aspinwall is trying to explain how goods *are* distributed or how they *should be* distributed. If the implication is that these are one and the same, then there is a hidden premise in the theory.

But the point is not whether or not Aspinwall's theory is correct. In either case it may well be *useful,* because it provides a way of *organizing* facts about marketing. Lazer believes that this is the ultimate value of theory. In ''Philosophic Aspects of the Marketing Discipline,'' another selection included in the book, he argues:

> Marketing thought should not proceed merely by the accumulation of observations which are unregulated by theory. It is generally accepted that fruitful observations cannot be made, nor their results arranged and correlated, without the use of hypotheses which go beyond the existing state of knowledge.

MARKETING SCIENCE AND MANAGERS

At this point, the executive may well ask: ''What has all this to do with me?'' Many feel that the whole debate about science in marketing is strictly an academic red herring, and that the quest for science is really a roundabout form of academic status-seeking. Indeed, there is a certain unintentional irony in the plaint by Lazer and Kelley that ''as a discipline, marketing is often assigned a relatively low status in the academic spectrum.''

But there is more at stake than the vanities of professors. Some very ''practical'' men feel that even the modest progress to date toward science in

marketing calls for a new approach by management. On this score, Donald R. Longman, President of the American Marketing Association, said in a message to members of the association in September 1962:

> The concept of science in marketing and the idea of objective and thorough study of issues, acquisition and evaluation of relevant facts, are no longer the exclusive province in business of the researcher. The scientific approach has spread, permeating all senior levels of decision making. . . . This is a new thing—the marketing staff manager and decision maker as a researcher concerned with the science of marketing.

This viewpoint is strongly advocated by Edward C. Bursk in his new book, *Text and Cases in Marketing: A Scientific Approach.*[5] Bursk states flatly that ''old-fashioned judgmental decision making must be supplanted by a more scientific approach.''

What does such an approach entail? Bursk sets forth three requirements:

1. The use of scientific theories, and techniques based on them, wherever available.

2. Increased use of experimentation.

3. The use of analysis to decide on action in a ''systematic, planned way.''

Perhaps even more important than these prescriptions is the concept of *integration* between decision making and research activities which pervades this entire book. While many executives have long recognized the need for information on which to base intelligent decisions, and have spent substantial sums on research to get such information, all too often research is not really used effectively.

Joseph W. Newman, in another HBR article,[6] has noted:

> Only in a relatively small number of companies has marketing research become a regular part of the making of important policy and operating decisions.

> In companies with marketing research units, a wide gap typically separates research personnel and management personnel.

What typically happens, Newman observes, is that the role of marketing "research" is seen purely as one of fact gathering. The manager recognizes the need for information on market shares, advertising recall, extent of distribution, and the like. But the relationships between these things and a firm's marketing policies are seldom analyzed. When they are, in some massive "one-shot" study, the results are usually disappointing, and the atmosphere becomes antagonistic to further investigation fo several years.

Executives who distrust research per se take these failings as justification of their attitude. (Ha! You see? Even with all their formulas, they couldn't predict what would happen in Moline! What we need here is experienced judgment, not a lot of harebrained theories!)

It is probably unfortunate that the term "research" ever came to be used to describe the activities of most marketing research staff units. A much better designation would be "marketing intelligence," since the purpose of these activities is directly analogous to those of a G-2 unit in the Army. Military intelligence personnel are not expected to develop a science of warfare. Their mission, instead, is to obtain complete, accurate, and current information.

Such concentration on detailed, particularized data is, in fact, inconsistent with real scientific inquiry. For the same reason, it is probably hopeless to expect much progress in the development of science in marketing as a result of simply stockpiling more and more current facts. This does not mean that facts are unimportant. But they should be looked on as the raw materials of research, not its end results.

All of this suggests that what is needed is a very different kind of research, together with a very different approach to it by management. This approach will require, among other things, that research specialists and management "generalists" know more about each others' jobs. Beyond this, Newman advocates the use of "research generalists" who would serve as middlemen between executives and research technicians. A similar proposal has also been made by Marion Harper, Jr.[7] Finally, progress in marketing science will require a view of research as a continuous, cumulative process, with constant interaction between investigators and the decision-makers who utilize their findings.

DEVELOPMENT PROBLEMS

Granted for the moment that the goal of science in marketing is a desirable one, why does the task appear to be so difficult? There are essentially three schools of thought on this point.

1. That science in marketing can be achieved by continued application of the same methods used in other fields, but that results are harder to achieve because the phenomena being studied are more complex.
2. That marketing phenomena (and human behavior in general) differ in *kind* from those of the physical sciences, so that *different methods* will have to be employed in studying them.
3. That marketing (and, again, human behavior in general) can never become a science because of its inherent elusiveness. Thus, the search for science is well intentioned but doomed to failure.

Bursk subscribes to the first of these beliefs, asserting that "the material is so intricate and intangible that hitherto it has not been tackled consciously and formally." His reasons for believing as he does are based on these facts:

Buying and selling involve a "subtle, fluid interaction," with actions on each side affecting actions on the other.

The number of possible combinations of actions by a seller is very large.

General economic conditions are continually changing, and this clouds the effects of a firm's marketing programs.

The actions of competitors also influence marketing results.[8]

In brief, these reasons boil down to the idea that since observed behavior in marketing is influenced by *many variables,* it is very difficult to isolate the effect of any one or any small combination of variables. But is this not also true in the physical sciences? The behavior of a missile, for example, is subject to the influences of numerous factors, including some which are only dimly perceived.

In the speech referred to earlier, Charles Ramond suggested that the events studied by physical scientists are easier to understand and predict because physical systems are basically simpler than human behavior systems. First, physical systems are "loosely coupled." While many variables affect an event, it is possible to study one or a few as if they were, in fact, isolated. A statistician would term this a "low degree of interaction"; for example, while both temperature and atmospheric pressure may affect some event, it is possible to hold one of these constant and measure the effects of the other, and get good predictive results. In contrast, variables affecting human behavior interact to such an extent that the familiar "other-things-being-equal" assumption can lead to mistaken conclusions.

Further, according to Ramond, physical scientists have generally been able to represent real systems by *linear equations,* i.e., by relatively simple models which can readily be manipulated. But such simple models have not been found adequate to describe human behavior. For example, forecasts of sales, population growth, and so forth based on linear regression models have usually been very inaccurate.

And finally, while relationships among physical phenomena are characteristically *stable* over extended time periods, marketing is thought to be highly *dynamic.* Thus relationships which seem to describe a system at one time may not hold at some future time.

Because marketing deals with events which are, in Ramond's phase, "tightly coupled, nonlinear, and dynamic," the progress of science is slow and painful at best. An excellent illustration of the difficulties encountered in the "scientific approach" is afforded by Alfred R. Oxenfeldt in "Diary of a Research Project in the Television Set Industry."[9] Oxenfeldt describes, blow by blow, his efforts over a five-year period to explain changes in the market shares of TV set manufacturers.

He postulated that these changes resulted from differences in product quality, prices, dealer margins, and advertising efforts. To test this hypothesis, it was first necessary to get reasonably complete information on the "independent variables" as well as on market-share results. But Oxenfeldt-found that only partial information on any of the variables could be obtained; for instance, quality ratings by product-testing agencies were based on only one or two of the 15 or 25 models offered by a manufacturer. Worse still, many of the terms used in the industry (such as "margin") ". . . cannot be defined rigorously or even in a manner that would insure substantial uniformity of usage." Finally, it was discovered that no records at all were kept of some of the most important actions taken by manufacturers.

Further investigation led Oxenfeldt to the conclusion that it would probably be impossible to discover any meaningful regularities in the TV set market as a whole. He felt that in the end, each local market was a separate case, that each manufacturer was different from all the others, and that conditions changed significantly from one time period to the next. This in effect, supports the notion that marketing systems are *unstable;* and this, in turn, implies that conclusions reached from the study of the past have only limited applicability to the future.

Note that the assumption of stability underlies much of what is known in the physical sciences. For example, it has been found that certain substances undergo radioactive disintegration at a constant rate relative to time. This provides the basis for the "dating" methods used in geology and archaeology. Suppose, however, that radioactive disintegration were *not* a stable process; indeed, there is no way to prove that it is. If the rate of disintegration does change, then all of the dates applied to various epochs in the earth's history are, in fact, wrong.

Thus, there is a serious question about the belief, expressed by Harlan D. Mills in "Brand A Versus Brand B—A Mathematical Approach," that "marketing 'laws' can be derived in the same manner as the laws of physics [so that] the way is open for marketing to become, more and more, a science."[10]

If the concepts and methods of the physical sciences cannot be lifted bodily over to the study of marketing, what then? As noted earlier, one of the missions of the [MSI] is to promote the use of scientific *techniques* in marketing. Presumably this includes the development of new, special-purpose techniques. It is not possible to foresee just what form these new techniques may take.

It seems likely, however, that some of them will be based on the technology of the computer. Already some operations researchers have found that complex models of market behavior are best "solved" by simulation—that is, by generating artificial experience and testing the effects of changes by simulated experimentation. Since field experiments in marketing are so costly—and sometimes downright impossible—simulation may play an increasing role in the future.

Even if a new scientific tool kit can be developed, there are some who think marketing can never be a science. E. B. Weiss argues, first, that attempts to discover scientific principles over the past forty years have been unsuccessful, and that many of them have really been hoaxes. More important, he notes that even honest efforts involve the use of such concepts as "average behavior," i.e., the use of probability theory and statistical analysis. Weiss claims that there is "no such thing as an 'average mind' or 'average behavior'."

If this argument is meant to imply that knowledge expressed in terms of probabilities is essentially unscientific, then much of modern physics is also unscientific. The phenomenon of radioactive disintegration mentioned earlier, in fact, rests squarely on probability theory. The rate of disintegration used in dating objects is an *average* rate, and the only justification for using it is that the number of objects (atoms) involved is so large that individual deviations become unimportant.

To the extent that marketing deals with the behavior of large groups of people, the same reasoning applies to it. Certainly the notion of "average behavior" has been used effectively by insurance companies. Conclusions based on the probabilities of certain kinds of behavior among large groups cannot, of course, legitimately be applied to individuals, but predictions of individual responses may not be necessary for scientific marketing.

ART OF USING SCIENCE

Let us suppose for a moment that the millenium does arrive, and marketing does, indeed, become a full-fledged science. What then? Will marketing decisions become routine, with computers grinding out solutions in response to the proper inputs? Not so, is the view of Theodore Levitt, as expressed in his book, *Innovation in Marketing*.[12] Levitt points out that "management has always sought formulas and prescriptions for easier decision making." As a result, management has become susceptible to the "seductions of science," and has fallen easy prey

to the exaggerated claims of some researchers. Further, he believes that the root of the problem is that "all too often neither the researchers nor the corporate bosses really know what it is they are trying to do." This is another way of saying that marketing science—even in its relatively crude present state—is concerned with means, not ends. This is equally true of the most advanced branches of knowledge. Scientists can (presumably) tell us how to get a man to the moon, but do we really *want* a man on the moon? The main theme of *Innovation in Marketing* is the need for management to define just where it is trying to go. This need will remain regardless of how much progress may be made in developing marketing as a science.

For a long time to come, it seems clear that marketing science will not advance to a stage in which the element of risk is eliminated from decisions. Bursk says that risk is an integral part of marketing management. Levitt goes even further: "That is what management is all about—taking risks." While increased knowledge can help in *identifying* the risks involved in decisions, and in some cases provide *measures* of their magnitudes, it can never eliminate them altogether.

Because science is concerned with means, it does not offer any answers to the basic questions of *values* underlying marketing management. It is a commonplace that the results of science can be used rightly or wrongly. Consequently, no matter how scientific marketing may become, managers must still govern their actions, in part, by considerations of their ultimate effects on customers, employees, and society at large.

Indeed, advancements in marketing science will put ethical issues into even bolder relief than at present. To some extent, science usually implies *control*. A vision of "the hidden persuaders," only this time equipped with true scientific knowledge rather than just the dubious baggage of depth interviewing, is disturbing to many observers. It can only be hoped that along with increased knowledge will come increased competence to use it wisely.

In any case, at least for a long time to come, it will remain the responsibility of the manager to evaluate the worth of alleged advances in marketing science, and to decide whether and how new knowledge is to be used in administration. As Levitt phrases it:

The highest form of achievement is always art, never science. . . . Business leadership *is* an art worthy of [the manager's] own respect and the public's plaudits.

NOTES

[1]Robert Bartels, *The Development of Marketing Thought* (Homewood, Ill., Richard D. Irwin, Inc., 1962).

[2]This series included more than a dozen titles by various authors, such as James L. Fri, *Retail Merchandising, Planning, and Control* (New York, Prentice-Hall, Inc., 1925) and Norris A. Brisco and John W. Wingate, *Retail Buying* (New York, Prentice-Hall, Inc., 1925).

[3]William Lazer and Eugene J. Kelley, editors, *Managerial Marketing: Perspectives and Viewpoints—A Source Book* (Homewood, Illinois, Richard D. Irwin, Inc., 1962).

[4]Joseph W. Newman, "New Insight, New Progress, for Marketing," HBR [Harvard Business Review], November–December 1957, p. 95.

[5]Edward C. Bursk, *Text and Cases in Marketing: A Scientific Approach* (Englewood Cliffs, New Jersey, Prentice-Hall, Inc., 1962).

[6]Joseph W. Newman, "Put Research into Marketing Decisions," HBR, March–April 1962, p. 105.

[7]"A New Profession to Aid Marketing Management," *Journal of Marketing,* January 1961, pp. 1–6.

[8]Bursk, op. cit., pp. 6–7.

[9]Presented as a case in Bursk, op. cit., pp. 31–44 (adapted from "Scientific Marketing: Ideal and Ordeal," HBR, March–April 1961, p. 51).

[10]Presented as a case in Bursk, op. cit., pp. 23–30 (adapted from "Marketing as a Science," HBR, September–October 1961, p. 137).

[11]E. B. Weiss, "Will Marketing Ever Become a Science?" *Advertising Age,* August 20, 1962, pp. 64–65.

[12]Theodore Levitt, *Innovation in Marketing* (New York, McGraw-Hill Book Company, Inc., 1962).

DISCUSSION QUESTIONS

1. Assuming that marketing is an art, how should it be taught? Also, what kinds of research should be done if marketing is an art?

2. Assuming that marketing is a science, how should it be taught? Also, what kinds of research should be done if marketing is a science?

3. Given that Buzzell's article was originally written in 1963, has the question "Is Marketing a Science?" been resolved in the literature/discipline over the ensuing twenty years?

PREFACE TO

"History of Marketing Thought: An Update"

Historical issues have had few champions in marketing. The best known marketing history has been Robert Bartels's *The Development of Marketing Thought* published in 1962. However, many changes occurred in the discipline of marketing during the 1960s and 1970s. In chronicling these changes, Sheth and Gardner argue that six new schools of marketing thought have emerged since the 1960s.

8

HISTORY OF MARKETING THOUGHT: AN UPDATE

JAGDISH N. SHETH

DAVID M. GARDNER

INTRODUCTION

Since Bartels' classic summary of history of marketing thought in the early sixties (Bartels 1962), it is somewhat surprising to find that there is no update of marketing thought even though several new schools of marketing thought have emerged in the past quarter of a century. Accordingly, the purpose of this paper is to identify various new schools of marketing thought, examine their associated causal factors, and assess their contributions toward enriching marketing theory.

Bartels (1965) provided an elegant account of the development of marketing theory in terms of the periods of discovery (1900–1910), conceptualization (1910–1920), integration (1920–1930), development (1930–1940), reappraisal (1940–1950), and finally reconceptualization (1950–1960). During these periods, early pioneers made numerous conscious efforts to evaluate marketing above selling and distribution, to link marketing as an idea rather than a group of activities so that it could be recognized as a planning function and to generate several principles of marketing so that it could be labeled as a science rather than an art. The outcome of these pioneering efforts was the development and eventual integration of the functional, the commodity and the institutional schools of marketing thought.

These conventional concepts of marketing functions, channels and goods were questioned by a number of scholars (Breyer 1934; Alexander, Surface, Elder and Alderson 1940; Grether 1949; Duddy and Revzan 1947; Lazo and Corbin 1961; Howard 1957; Alderson and Cox 1948; Bartels 1944). It resulted in reappraising market thought away from the functions, institutions and products

Source: Reprinted with permission from *Marketing Theory: Philosophy of Science Perspectives,* Ronald F. Bush and Shelby D. Hunt, eds., Chicago, Ill.: American Marketing Association, 1982, 52–58.

and toward a more managerial and environmental orientation.

A closer look at the history of marketing thought including its development, integration and reappraisal during the first half of the twentieth century, however, indicates that two fundamental axioms seemed to dominate most thinking despite divergence of viewpoint.

The first axiom of consensus stemmed from the belief that marketing was essentially an economic activity, and that it was a subset of the discipline of economics. Therefore, marketing concepts (institutions, functions, products, managerial and environmental perspectives) were restricted to economic behavior of people and associated institutions. Marketing was not considered appropriate for such non-economic domains of human behavior as fine arts, religion, politics, public services, and such intangibles as ideas.

The second axiom of consensus stemmed from the belief that the initiator of marketing activities and programs was the marketer and not the consumer in the market place. While it was recognized that understanding customer behavior through market research was desirable and even essential, it was primarily regarded as an input to the design of marketing programs and activities so that the marketer can influence, manipulate and control market behavior with greater effectiveness through his professional skills of organization and management.

It would appear to us that the genesis of more recent schools of thought since the sixties comes from questioning those two fundamental axioms of marketing thought and replacing them with more comprehensive axioms.

For example, replacement of the axiom of economic exchange with *the axiom of exchange of values* by several scholars (Drucker 1974; Kotler and Levy 1969; Kotler 1972; Levy and Zaltman 1975; Bagozzi 1975; Carman 1980) literally broadened the marketing horizons to the nontraditional areas of human behavior including religion, politics, public services, and fine art.

Similarly, other scholars and practitioners (Katz and Kahn 1955; Howard 1963a,b; Cyert and March 1963; Katona 1960; Rogers 1965; Simon 1957; McKitterick 1957; Mayer 1958; Starch 1958; Dichter 1964) explicitly questioned the futility of the marketer as the initiator of marketing programs by suggesting that the consumer was more powerful than the marketer, that many other factors such as personal influences were more responsible for his decisions, and that it was best for the marketer to understand the *psychology* of the consumer and work backwards from the market to the factory to achieve more productivity and effectiveness out of marketing resources. In short, these scholars and practitioners encouraged *behavioral perspectives* in *place of economic perspectives* to develop a more realistic marketing theory.

The broadening of the marketing concept by the axiom of exchange of value seems to have triggered three distinct although related schools of marketing thought, all of them dealing with the issues of pervasiveness or marketing in the society. The first school of thought commonly referred to as *macromarketing*, for example, has attempted to focus on the potential and problems of marketing activities and programs from a more macro or societal perspective rather than from a more micro firm's perspective. The second school of thought, more commonly referred to as *consumerism*, emerged to provide an advocacy position in terms of developing and protecting the rights of the consumers. The third school of thought, commonly referred to as *systems approach* provided a framework for integrating both the supply and the demand factors into a single holistic theory. It argued that in an exchange of values, the customer has a more fundamental choice of self-making as a production unit, bartering it with other customers or buying in the market place which must be incorporated in any marketing thinking.

Similarly, the axiom of balance of power seems responsible for triggering another set of theory in marketing. The first and probably the most influential school of thought is commonly referred to as *buyer behavior*, which has tried to generate a behavioral theory of buying. It literally dominated the field of marketing ranging from theory to market research and practice. The second school of thought more commonly referred to as *behavioral organizations*, has focused on the behavioral aspects such as power, conflict, and interdependence among organizations and particularly among channels of distribution. The third school of thought, more commonly referred to as *strategic planning*, has focused on the balance of power issues between external environmental factors such as market values, competition, technology, resources and regulation, and the internal resource factors such as products, services, distribution and promotion.

The rest of the paper will provide a brief historical perspective on each of the six new schools of thought and at the end assess their contribution to marketing theory.

THE MACROMARKETING SCHOOL

With the exception of the managerial school of thought put forth in the sixties, little if any consideration had been given to exogenous variables by marketing theorists. While the managerial school of thought recognized exogenous variables, the emphasis was focused on *managing* the marketing organization to plan for uncontrollable variables while manipulating those that were controllable.

The genesis of macromarketing thought is closely linked with the developing concern of the role of business in society. The negative connotations toward the "military-industrial" complex and the big brother philosophy generated considerable early attention and interest by marketing scholars to systematically examine the role of marketing from a societal perspective rather than from the perspective of the profit oriented firm. For the first time, it was appropriate to question that the end all and be all of marketing is company's profit maximization. It was the macromarketing school of thought which literally elevated the discussion of short term vs. long term profit maximization to a higher level of corporate vs. societal goals associated with marketing practice.

The topic was of such contemporary concern that it simultaneously attracted the attention of knowledge generators (scholars) and knowledge disseminators (popular press).

While a number of scholars helped pioneer this school of thought, two are of particular interest.

Robert Holloway, in association with Robert Hancock, visualized marketing as an activity of society and consequently saw marketing as both being influenced by and influencing the society. A "rough schema" was developed around the broad exogeneous environmental variables of sociological, anthropological, psychological, economic, legal, ethical, competitive, economic and technological (Holloway and Hancock 1964). Holloway was also instrumental in publishing a textbook intended to give a clear choice to those who desired a more macro view of marketing (Holloway and Hancock 1968). In his award winning article with Grether, Holloway made a clear call for studies of the impact of governmental regulation on managerial decision making and the effect of regulation on the functioning of the market system (Grether and Holloway 1967).

George Fisk, heavily influenced by Wroe Alderson, brought a general systems perspective to the study of marketing. His pioneering work made the distinction between microsystems and macrosystems (Fisk 1967, p. 77). This dichotomy was a springboard for his focus on social marketing. His numerous papers have shaped the present school of macromarketing thought.

Other significant contributions have been made by John Westing (1967), Richard Bagozzi (1977), James Carman (1980) and Robert Bartels (1982). Other earlier, but more popular works were contributed by Sethi with his *Up Against the Corporate Wall* (Sethi 1971).

Fortunately, the early emphasis on broad environmental issues has recently given way to a more enduring issue of how marketing can become a means to achieving national goals such as economic development, population control, and redistribution of national income and wealth. In the process, it is generating excellent conceptual thinking (Bagozzi 1977; Shawver and French 1978). Simultaneously, many societal problems such as energy conservation, education, health care, population control and economic development are presently making use of marketing theory and practice (Kotler 1975).

The focus of this new thrust was first centered in a series of macromarketing seminars. The first seminar was held in Boulder, Colorado, in 1976 with Charles Slater as its organizer. These seminars, held every year since 1976 have greatly shaped this school of thought. But as one follows these seminars, the one issue that still remains open is the boundaries of this school of thought.

Out of these seminars grew the realization, however, that the school of macromarketing thought was broad enough and unique enough to support a journal of macromarketing. This journal, under the editorship of George Fisk, has the opportunity to have a major impact on marketing theory in the next decade.

It is clear that the macromarketing school of thought has made significant contributions to marketing theory. While the exact directions of its future are not clear, it is clear that applications to marketing practice will be impacted.

THE CONSUMERISM SCHOOL

This school of thought emerged as marketing scholars observed some obvious problems in the market place. These problems were dramatically illustrated by Ralph Nader (1965) in his book, *Unsafe at Any Speed*. However, it must be recognized that the foundation of consumer protection really rests in the concepts of welfare economics propagated by such great economists as Schumpeter, Keynes, Houthaker and Modigliani. And, it should be remembered that *Consumer Reports* as an advocacy magazine predates Ralph Nader by at least two decades.

The early writings on consumerism summarized in readings books (Aaker and Day 1971; Gaedeke and Etcheson 1972) clearly reflect the activist thinking commonly associated with people concerned with a specific cause or social problem. Both research and theory in the area tended to be highly ad hoc and specific to problems associated with marketing practice from the advocacy perspective of the individual consumer. It included areas of research such as deceptive advertising, high pressure sales tactics, product safety, and disclosure of information. It presumed that the average consumer was both educationally ignorant and technically incompetent to make rational choices which are good for him. Hence, the need for government regulation and for voluntary organization dedicated to the protection of consumer welfare. Such elitist attitudes may be more responsible for the recent decline in the movement than any other factor.

Fortunately, consumerism as a cause has given

way to more systematic and fundamental research and thinking in the area. This is manifested by the recent drive to understand and develop a theory of consumer satisfaction (Andreasen 1977; Day and Bodur 1977; Hunt 1977). Similarly, more comprehensive empirical research is undertaken to understand consumer complaining behavior as well as behavior of specialized segments such as the Blacks, the Hispanics, the handicapped, and the immigrants. A conspicuous absence of this new research trend is the lack of emotionally charged and value laden research which merely endorses prior judgments rather than become the basis for making those judgments.

This school of thought tends to overlap with both the buyer behavior and macromarketing schools. It overlaps with the buyer behavior school in that the research will often involve buyers. In that sense, the boundary between buyer behavior and consumerism is very fuzzy. For instance, the work of Bill Wilkie, sponsored by the National Science Foundation on Consumer Information Processing (Wilkie 1975) was clearly an application of well known buyer behavior research to the marketplace problem of consumer information.

This school overlaps with the macromarketing school in that it tends to deal with broader, more macro issues. If often focuses on regulation, market structure, education, competition and ethics.

The future of consumerism, however, is far more uncertain than macromarketing. On the one hand, there is the emergence of conservative social and political values which believes in less regulation and more personal initiatives. On the other hand, the more fundamental problems such as consumer satisfaction are getting integrated with the buyer behavior theory and marketing feedback mechanisms. It is, therefore, very likely that consumerism may not be able to survive a separate identity in marketing.

THE SYSTEMS APPROACH

Marketing scholars with strong quantitative interest in the early 1960s were able to bring to marketing the beginnings of a formal quantitative structure for defining and analyzing marketing problems.

The emergence of the systems approach can be directly identified with more recent economic concepts of attribute utility (Lancaster 1971) and time as the scarce resource (Becker 1965). In marketing, early efforts were manifested in highly complex simulation models of marketing which were highly interdependent between the demand and the supply factors (Amstutz 1967; Kuehn and Hamburger 1963; Forrester 1959). These were replaced by more interactive modeling efforts based on the concept of adaptive control pioneered by Little (1966). The latter models exemplified by names such as Demon, Sprinter, Hendry model, Adbudg and Mediac emphasized the need to incorporate a set of demand characteristics manifested in the generic concepts of elasticity and marginal utility.

A more recent effort, however, is focused on the more fundamental options available to the consumers. These include taking upon themselves the role of producers rather than buyers in the market place, as well as entering into barter exchange among themselves (Sheth 1982). In the process, it has generated concepts such as household as a production unit (Etgar 1978) and economic theory of consumption behavior (Ratchford 1975).

It appears that the systems approach to marketing theory is likely to grow in the near future for several reasons. First of all, it represents a more realistic utilization of the axiom of exchange of value. Second, today more than ever, we have the computerized capabilities to model and simulate more complex interdependencies. Third, the systems approach is closer to marketing theory and practice than either the buyer behavior theory or the consumerism movement. As such, it is likely to sustain its growth and separate identity.

BUYER BEHAVIOR THEORY

No other area in marketing has had a greater dominance for such a long time period as buyer behavior. While it seems to have peaked in recent years, it is still the most dominant area of research and theory in marketing.

A number of marketing scholars and their contributions can be identified as having made a major impact on this school (Bauer 1967; Howard 1963a; Howard and Sheth 1969; Bliss 1963; Britt 1966; Engel, Kollat, and Blackwell 1968; Nicosia 1966). While each take a different approach, the common denominator underlying their thinking was the applications of behavioral (psychological) principles to consumer behavior. This is clearly in sharp contrast to the descriptive approach of previous eras which was largely demographics and market size statistics. It is also in sharp contrast to attempts to explain buyer behavior by merely applying research findings from sociology (Martineau 1958; Levy 1963; Rogers 1965). It is the dominance of psychology which is largely responsible for bringing about a high level of scientific research traditions. It is no exaggeration to state that no other area of marketing has done so much to elevate marketing discipline from the status of professional practice to the status of scientific inquiry.

While the early buyer behavior pioneers were more interested in generating a grand theory of buyer behavior, several recent efforts have concentrated on scientific research and development of specific constructs of buyer behavior. These include brand loyalty, attitudes, intentions and information processing. At the same time, there has been increasing interest in understanding family buying decisions (Sheth 1974; Davis 1971) and industrial buying behavior (Sheth 1973; Sheth 1977; Webster and Wind 1972). Similarly, considerable degree of quantification of the area is also prevalent especially in terms of application of several mathematical models of choice behavior (McAlister 1982).

At the same time, however, buyer behavior theory has come under some criticism (Sheth 1979; Zielinski and Robertson 1982; Kassarjian 1982). It is criticized for the overemphasis of individual cognitive psychology and especially the use of multiattribute models. In our estimation, the future research in buyer behavior is likely to emerge from noncognitive perspectives as well as from more macro sociological perspectives.

BEHAVIORAL ORGANIZATION

Concurrently with scholars in other business disciplines, marketing scholars began to see that behavioral principles that had previously been primarily identified with human group behavior, could be used to explain the behavior of organizations. In particular, drawing upon emerging thinking in management of organizations with a strong sociological perspective (Etzioni 1961; Katz and Kahn 1966; Thompson 1967; March and Simon 1958; Cyert and March 1963) several marketing scholars applied this perspective to marketing channels. They were also influenced by several emerging social psychology theories (French and Raven 1960; Thibaut and Kelley 1959). The channel of distribution came to be viewed as an organization with behavioral patterns involving all the organizations in any way dependent on a channel.

A large part of research in the area is clearly identified with Stern (1969) and Stern and El-Ansary (1977), while a few others have recently contributed to the area (Etgar 1976; Frazier 1980), relatively few marketing scholars have made significant contributions. Two reasons probably explain this lack of participation. First is the great difficulty in obtaining data. In addition to the difficulty of obtaining hard data on actual relationships, most of the relationships are heavily influenced by perceptions of power. In addition, these relationships are dynamic. Secondly, much of the existing work in organizational behavior tends to focus on the workings of a given organization which offers little in the way of a conceptual base for studying interorganizational behavior. A notable exception is the much acclaimed work of Pfeffer and Salancik which stresses and offers conceptual foundations for the study of relationships with other organizations (Pfeffer and Salancik 1978).

The importance of this school of marketing thought is almost certain to not only increase, but attract more researchers from organization behavior area who are fascinated by the dynamics of the complexities of channels of distribution.

STRATEGIC PLANNING

Planning as an activity of the firm is well established. However, in recent years, planning has moved from just another of a list of activities to one of the most important. Furthermore, strategic planning, with its twofold emphasis on analysis of the dynamic environment and dynamic adaptation, has generally had the net impact of strengthening marketing planning. This is particularly true for firms that have separated corporate planning from strategic business unit planning.

This, the newest school of marketing thought, seems to be currently suffering from the usual confusion associated with most new schools of thought. Furthermore, it is beset by two additional difficulties. The first is that the majority of contributions to this school have come from consulting firms and their clients. The names of the Boston Consulting Group, Stanford Research Institute, and General Electric, for example, are familiar to most marketing scholars as proponents and contributors to strategic planning. But the second difficulty may be more troublesome. The most well publicized approaches, for the most part, are based on either in an implicit cash flow maximization basis or some form of capital asset pricing model. By their very nature then, they are not very useful for marketplace decisions. Rather they are most useful for corporate decisions.

So while we seemingly know much about strategic planning, we are not sure how much we know about strategic market planning. In fact, we lack competing conceptual frameworks that can be used to guide research and theory development in this area.

Nonetheless, we do have the beginnings of a school of thought. These beginnings fall into several overlapping categories. The first are those contributions that explicitly deal with one aspect of marketing strategy, but with a strategic reference point (Wind 1978; Pessemeir 1982; Thorelli 1977). Several texts have also appeared with a strategic focus (Hughes 1978; Constantine, Evans and Morris 1976; Luck and Ferrell 1979; Jain 1981; Cravens 1982) plus a readings book (Kerin and Peterson 1980) in addition to two monographs with strong marketing strategy implications (Hofer and Schendel 1978; Porter 1980). While these and other contributions give clear evidence that a school of thought is emerging, the real issues of what strategic marketing is and is not and what are its central concepts have not been definitely dealt with. One author, however, suggests that five contributions will be an important part of any future list of central concepts of strategic marketing (Biggadike 1981). He lists them as the marketing concept, market segmentation, positioning, mapping and the product life cycle.

In our opinion, strategic planning is likely to continue generating additional knowledge for marketing theory for several reasons. First, marketing has become more competition oriented rather than either technology or market oriented (Kotler 1980). Second, environmental factors are changing at an ever increasing pace forcing companies to design early warning systems. Finally, foreign competi-

tion especially from Japan and Europe has generated greater emphasis on planned approach to organizing marketing resources.

CONTRIBUTIONS TO MARKETING THEORY

Each of the six new schools of thought has made unique contributions to the development of marketing theory. At the same time, it would appear that some of the newer schools of thought may have directed talent and effort away from it. We will briefly assess each school's contribution in this section.

The single biggest contribution to [the] macromarketing school has been to redefine marketing objectives. It has clearly indicated why the unidimensional objections of profit maximization may not be appropriate for the organization. Instead, it has attempted to provide a multiobjective function for marketing effort. In addition, the macromarketing school has consistently emphasized the reality of constrained optimization of marketing objectives. These constraints relate mainly to the side effects of marketing practice from a more macrosocietal perspective.

A second major contribution of the macromarketing school has to do with increasing the importance and legitimacy of marketing objectives in noneconomic behaviors of society. For the first time, marketing is considered relevant to national economic and social plans in many underdeveloped countries. Similarly, it has removed the taboo associated with marketing as a commercial profit making activity in many spheres of noneconomic behaviors such as population control, energy conservation, religion and politics.

At the same time, macromarketing has also created the crisis of identity. By broadening its horizions through the concepts of exchange of value and taking broader societal perspectives, marketing is beginning to blur its boundaries with other disciplines such as business policy and public policy. It is our strong hope that macromarketing will attempt to delimit its sphere and more precisely define its boundaries in the very near future before the crisis of identity threatens the existence of marketing itself.

The consumerism school of thought has had far more impact on the marketing practice rather than on the marketing theory. Perhaps the single most important contribution can be attributed to Peter Druker (1974) who has labeled the existence of consumerism as a shame of marketing. It has also brought out the importance of market satisfaction as a far more important barometer of marketing success than either market share or profits. We believe that the concept of market satisfaction will become a major construct in the development of marketing theory.

Unfortunately, consumerism has generated more distraction from development of marketing theory. By concentrating on ad hoc and advocacy oriented issues, it has diverted attention away from the more fundamental and typical principles of marketing and toward the more atypical and isolated aspects of marketing practice.

The contribution of the systems approach toward marketing theory is largely methological. It has enabled scholars to think of quantification of marketing processes for simulation or optimization purposes. In the process, marketing has become more rigorous and more of a science. How much of this is illusionary and how much is real is yet to be determined. A second major contribution of the systems approach has been to provide a balance between the supply and the demand functions. It has clearly brought out the need to incorporate the mutual interdependence inherent in any economic exchange. Finally, this school of thought has enabled scholars to retain the identity of marketing despite incorporating higher levels of complexity in marketing theory. Unlike the macromarketing school, it has neither tried to broaden the horizons of marketing to noneconomic areas of behavior nor has it questioned the legitimacy of more traditional corporate objectives of profitability and market share. Finally, the systems approach has successfully integrated buyer behavior principles which are inherently at a more micro and behavioral level with the marketing principles which are inherently more macro and aggregate in scope.

In contrast, the buyer behavior school of thought has generated more alienation and division. In fact, it has acquired a separate identity of its own as manifested by a separate organization (ACR [Association for Consumer Research]) and a separate interdisciplinary journal (JCR [*Journal of Consumer Research*]). There is no question that understanding the psychology of the buyer is highly relevant to the development of a good marketing theory. Unfortu-

nately, buyer behavior theory has been perceived as somehow more scientific and rigorous than marketing theory. Therefore, many scholars working in the buyer behavior area have consciously avoided any association with marketing practice. Indeed, it is a shame that so much knowledge generated in buyer behavior is so little used in marketing practice except perhaps in industrial selling. It is our belief that the disassociation between the two disciplines as well as existence of a separate organization and a journal are very likely to generate a divorce between marketing and buyer behavior.

At the same time, the marketing discipline owes much to buyer behavior theory. First of all, it has brought a more scientific bent to marketing theory and practice through the process of borrowing both theory and research methodology from psychology, and especially social psychology. Second, it has attracted bright young scholars to the marketing discipline because it has consciously avoided being practice driven. Finally, it has generated a number of significant constructs which are likely to become good building blocks in the development of marketing practice. These include (a) redefinition of the marketing mix from the Four P's to the dichotomy of significant and symbolic communication (Howard and Sheth 1969), (b) rules of information processing, (c) psychological market segmentation, (d) rational vs. emotional needs, and (e) reference group influences as inhibitors or enhancers of marketing influences.

The behavioral organization school of thought has the potential to contribute but it has not so far attained its potential. The primary explanation probably lies in its disassociation with the traditional marketing objectives of profitability and market share (Frazier and Sheth 1982). It has generated a significant amount of descriptive research on interdependence among organizations but at the same time it has failed to show how to utilize this knowledge in marketing practice. We are, however, confident that in due course, interorganizational aspects associated with this school of thought will have strong influence in reshaping marketing theory from the traditional institutional and functional perspectives.

Finally, the contribution of the strategic planning school of thought is highly visible. First of all, it has clearly shifted attention from marketing tactics and activities to more strategic issues. Second, it has generated a more adaptive posture for marketing programs. Third, it has emphasized the concept of relative as opposed to the absolute power of marketing resources. However, the biggest impact of [the] strategic planning school on marketing theory is likely to be the integration of market research as part of marketing practice. The interface of market research and marketing plans is likely to reshape marketing theory from an unilateral to a bilateral approach of marketing activities and programs.

CONCLUSION

Two fundamental changes have generated at least six new schools of thought since Bartel's classic review of history of marketing thought up to [the] early sixties. These are (a) replacement of [the] economic exchange concept with the concept of exchange value, and (b) emergence of balance of power between the marketer and the customer as the initiator of marketing programs and activities.

REFERENCES

Aaker, David A. and George S. Day (1971), *Consumerism: Search for the Consumer Interest*, New York: The Free Press.

Alderson, Wroe and Reavis Cox (1948), "Towards a Theory of Marketing," *Journal of Marketing*, 13 (October), 139–152.

Alexander, Ralph, F. M. Surface, R. F. Elder and Wroe Alderson (1940), *Marketing*, Boston: Ginn.

Amstutz, Arnold E. (1967), *Computer Simulation of Competitive Market Response*, Cambridge, Mass.: MIT Press.

Andreasen, Alan R. (1977), "A Taxonomy of Consumer Satisfaction/Dissatisfaction Measures," *Journal of Consumer Affairs*, 12 (Winter), 11–24.

Bagozzi, Richard P. (1975), "Marketing as Exchange," *Journal of Marketing*, 39 (October), 32–39.

Bagozzi, Richard P. (1977), "Marketing at the Societal Level: Theoretical Issues and Problems," in *Macro Marketing: Distributive Processes from a Societal Perspective*, Charles C. Slater, editor, Boulder: University of Colorado.

Bartels, Robert (1944), "Marketing Principles," *Journal of Marketing*, 9 (October), 151.

Bartels, Robert (1962), *The Development of Marketing Thought*, Homewood, Ill.: Richard D. Irwin.

Bartels, Robert (1965), "Development of Marketing Thought: A Brief History," in *Science in Marketing*, George Schwartz, editor, New York: John Wiley & Sons.

Bartels, Robert (1982), "The Physics and Metaphysics of Marketing," in *Proceedings of the Eleventh Paul D. Converse Marketing Symposium*, David M. Gardner and Frederick Winter, editors, Chicago: American Marketing Association.

Bauer, Raymond A. (1967), "Consumer Behavior as Risk Taking," in *Risk Taking and Information Handling in Consumer Behavior*, Donald F. Cox, editor, Boston: Division of Research, Harvard Business School.

Becker, George (1965), "A Theory of the Allocation of Time," *Economic Journal*, 75, 493–517.

Biggadike, E. Ralph (1981), "The Contributions of Marketing to Strategic Management," *Academy of Management Review*, 6 (October), 621–632.

Bliss, Perry (1963), *Marketing and the Behavioral Sciences*, Rockleigh, N.J.: Allyn & Bacon.

Breyer, Ralph F. (1934), *The Marketing Institution*, New York: McGraw-Hill.

Britt, Steuart Henderson (1966), *Consumer Behavior and the Behavioral Sciences*, New York: John Wiley & Sons.

Carman, James M. (1980), "Paradigms for Marketing Theory," in J. N. Sheth, editor, *Research in Marketing*, Vol. 3, Greenwich, Conn.: JAI Press.

Constantin, James A., Rodney E. Evans and Malcolm L. Morris (1976), *Marketing Strategy and Management*, Dallas, Tex.: Business Publications.

Cravens, David W. (1982), *Strategic Marketing*, Homewood, Ill.: Richard D. Irwin.

Cyert, Richard M. and James G. March (1963), *A Behavioral Theory of the Firm*, Englewood Cliffs, N.J.: Prentice-Hall.

Davis, Harry L. (1971), "Measurement of Husband-Wife Influence in Consumer Decision Making," *Journal of Marketing Research*, 8 (August), 305–312.

Day, R. L. and M. Bodur (1977), ''A Comprehensive Study of Consumer Satisfaction with Services,'' in *Consumer Satisfaction, Dissatisfaction and Complaining Behavior,* R. L. Day, editor, Bloomington: Department of Marketing, School of Business, Indiana University.

Dichter, Ernest (1964), *Handbook of Consumer Motivations,* New York: McGraw-Hill.

Drucker, Peter A. (1974), *Management: Tasks, Responsibilities, Practices,* New York: Harper & Row.

Duddy, E. A. and D. A. Revzan (1947), *Marketing, An Institutional Approach,* New York: McGraw-Hill.

Engel, James F., David T. Kollat, and Roger D. Blackwell (1968), *Consumer Behavior,* New York: Holt, Rinehart & Winston.

Etgar, Michael (1976), ''Three Models of Distributive Change,'' in C. C. Slater, editor, *Macromarketing: Distributive Processes from a Societal Perspective,* Boulder: Business Research Division, Graduate School of Business, University of Colorado.

Etgar, Michael (1978), ''The Household as a Production Unit,'' in J. N. Sheth, editor, *Research in Marketing,* Vol. 1, Greenwich, Conn.: JAI Press.

Etzioni, E. (1961), *A Comparative Analysis of Organizations,* Glencoe, Ill.: The Free Press.

Fisk, George (1967), *Marketing Systems: An Introductory Analysis,* New York: Harper & Row.

Forrester, Jay W. (1959), ''Advertising: A Problem in Industrial Dynamics,'' *Harvard Business Review,* 59 (March–April), 10O–110.

Frazier, Gary L. (1980), ''A Conceptual Model of the Interfirm Power-Influence Process Within a Marketing Channel,'' in J. N. Sheth, editor, *Research in Marketing,* Greenwich, Conn.: JAI Press.

Frazier, Gary L. and Jagdish N. Sheth (1982), ''Impact of Goal Conflicts on Interfirm Interactions, Sentiments and Compatibility,'' Faculty Working Paper, University of Illinois.

French, J. R. P. and B. Raven (1960), ''The Basis of Social Power,'' in D. Cartwright and A. Zander, editors, *Group Dynamics: Research and Theory,* New York: Harper & Row.

Gaedeke, Ralph and Warren Etcheson (eds.), (1972), *Consumerism: Viewpoints from Business, Government, and the Public Interest,* 2nd ed., San Francisco: Harper and Row.

Grether, E. T. (1949), ''A Theoretical Approach to the Analysis of Marketing,'' in *Theory in Marketing,* Reavis Cox and Wroe Alderson, editors, Chicago: Richard D. Irwin.

Grether, E. T. and Robert J. Holloway (1967), ''Impact of Government upon the Marketing System,'' *Journal of Marketing,* 31 (April, 2, 1–5.

Hofer, Charles W. and Don Schendel (1978), *Strategy Formulation: Analytical Concepts,* St. Paul, Minn.: West Publishing Co.

Holloway, Robert J. and Robert S. Hancock (1964), *The Environment of Marketing Behavior,* New York: John Wiley & Sons.

Holloway, Robert J. and Robert S. Hancock (1968), *Marketing in a Changing Environment,* New York: John Wiley & Sons.

Howard, John A. (1957), *Marketing Management: Analysis and Decision,* Homewood, Ill.: Richard D. Irwin.

Howard, John A. (1963a), *Marketing: Executive and Buyer Behavior,* New York: Columbia University Press.

Howard, John A. (1963b), *Marketing Management: Analysis and Planning,* Homewood, Ill.: Richard D. Irwin.

Howard, John A. and Jagdish N. Sheth (1969), *The Theory of Buyer Behavior,* New York: JOhn Wiley & Sons.

Hughes, C. David (1978), *Marketing Management: A Planning Approach,* Reading, Mass.: Addison-Wesley.

Hunt, H. Keith (1977), ''Consumer Satisfaction/Dissatisfaction—Overview and Future Research Directions,'' in *Conceptualization and Measurement of Consumer Satisfaction and Dissatisfaction,* H. Keith Hunt, editor, Cambridge, Mass.: Marketing Science Institute.

Jain, Subhash C. (1981), *Marketing Planning and Strategy,* Cincinnati, Ohio: South-Western Publishing Co.

Kassarjian, Harold (1982), ''The Development of Consumer Behavior Theory,'' in *Advances in Consumer Research,* Vol. 9, Andrew Mitchell, editor, Chicago: Association for Consumer Research.

Katona, George (1960), *The Powerful Consumer: Psychological Studies of the American Economy,* New York: McGraw Hill.

Katz, Daniel and Robert L. Kahn (1966), *The Social Psychology of Organizations,* New York: John Wiley & Sons.

Kerin, Roger A. and Robert A. Peterson (1980), *Perspectives on Strategic Marketing Management,* Boston: Allyn & Bacon.

Kotler, Philip (1972), ''A Generic Concept of Marketing,'' *Journal of Marketing,* 36 (April), 46–54.

Kotler, Philip (1975), *Marketing for Nonprofit Organizations,* Englewood Cliffs, N.J.: Prentice-Hall.

Kotler, Philip (1980), *Marketing Management: Analysis, Planning and Control,* 4th edition, Englewood Cliffs, N.J.: Prentice-Hall.

Kotler, Philip and Sidney J. Levy (1969), ''Broadening the Concept of Marketing,'' *Journal of Marketing,* 33 (January), 10–15.

Kuehn, Alfred A. and Morris J. Hamburger (1963), ''A Heuristic Program for Locating Warehouses,'' *Management Science,* 9 (July), 643–666.

Lancaster, Kelvin (1971), *Consumer Demand: A New Approach,* New York: Columbia University Press.

Lazo, Hector and Arnold Corbin (1961), *Management in Marketing,* New York: McGraw-Hill.

Levy, Sidney J. (1963), ''Symbolism and Life Style,'' in S. A. Greyser, editor, *Toward Scientific Marketing,* Chicago: American Marketing Association.

Levy, Sidney J. (1966), ''Social Class and Consumer Behavior,'' in *On Knowing the Consumer,* Joseph W. Newman, editor, New York: John Wiley & Sons.

Levy, Sidney and Gerald Zaltman (1975), *Marketing, Society and Conflict,* Englewood Cliffs, N.J.: Prentice-Hall.

Little, John D. C. (1966), ''A Model of Adaptive Control of Promotional Spending,'' *Operations Research,* 14 (November–December), 175–197.

Luck, David J. and O. C. Ferrell (1979), *Marketing Strategy and Plans,* Englewood Cliffs, N.J.: Prentice-Hall.

March, James G. and Herbert Simon (1958), *Organizations,* New York: John Wiley & Sons.

Martineau, Pierre (1958), ''Social Classes and Spending Behavior,'' *Journal of Marketing,* 23 (October), 121–130.

Mayer, Martin (1958), *Madison Avenue, U.S.A.,* New York: Harper & Row.

McAlister, Leigh (1982), *Consumer Choice Theory Models,* Greenwich, Conn.: JAI Press.

McKitterick, J. B. (1957), ''What Is the Marketing Management Concept,'' in *The Frontiers of Marketing Thought and Science,* Chicago: American Marketing Association.

Nader, Ralph (1965), *Unsafe at Any Speed,* New York: Grossman Publications.

Nicosia, Francesco M. (1966), *Consumer Decision Processes: Marketing and Advertising Implications,* Englewood Cliffs, N.J.: Prentice-Hall.

Pessemier, Edgar A. (1982), *Product Management: Strategy and Organization* 2nd edition, New York: John Wiley & Sons.

Pfeffer, J. and G. R. Salancik (1978), *The External Control of Organizations,* New York: Harper & Row.

Porter, Michael E. (1980), *Competitive Strategy,* New York: The Free Press.

Ratchford, Bryan T. (1975), ''The Economic Theory of Consumer Behavior: An Interpretive Essay,'' *Journal of Consumer Research,* 2 (September), 65–75.

Rogers, Everett (1965), *Diffusion of Innovations,* Glencoe, Ill.: The Free Press.

Sethi, S. Prakash (1971), *Up Against the Corporate Wall,* Englewood Cliffs, N.J.: Prentice-Hall.

Shawver, Donald L. and Norman D. French (1978), ''Towards A Positive Theory of Macromarketing,'' in *Macromarketing: Distributive Processer from a Societal Perspective,* Philip D. White and Charles C. Slater, editors, Boulder: University of Colorado, Business Research Division.

Sheth, Jagdish N. (1973), ''A Model of Industrial Buying Behavior,'' *Journal of Marketing,* 37 (October), 50–56.

Sheth, Jagdish N. (1974), ''A Theory of Family Buying Decisions,'' in J. N. Sheth, editor, *Models of Buyer Behavior,* New York: Harper & Row.

Sheth, J. N. (1977), ''Recent Developments in Organizational Buyer Behavior,'' in Woodside, Sheth and Bennett, editors, *Consumer and Industrial Buying Behavior,* New York: North-Holland.

Sheth, Jagdish N. (1979), ''The Surpluses and Shortages in Consumer Behavior Theory and Research,'' *Journal of the Academy of Marketing Science,* 7 (Fall), 414–427.

Sheth, J. N. (1982), ''Discussion of the Three Papers on the Consumption of Consumer Goods,'' in A. Mitchell, editor, *Advances in Consumer Behavior,* Vol. 9, Chicago: Association for Consumer Research, pp. 313–14.

Simon, Herbert A. (1957), *Models of Man,* New York: John Wiley & Sons.

Starch, Daniel and Staff (1958), *Male vs. Female: Influence on the Purchase of Selected Products,* Greenwich, Conn.: Fawcett Publishing.

Stern, Louis W. (ed.), (1969), *Distribution Channels: Behavioral Dimensions,* Boston: Houghton Mifflin.

Stern, Louis W. and Adel El-Ansary (1977), *Marketing Channels,* Englewood Cliffs, N.J.: Prentice-Hall.

Thibaut, J. W. and H. H. Kelley (1959), *The Social Psychology of Groups,* New York: John Wiley & Sons.

Thompson, James D. (1967), *Organizations in Action,* New York: McGraw-Hill.

Thorelli, Hans B. (1977), *Strategy + Structure = Performance,* Bloomington: Indiana University Press.

Webster, Frederick E. and Yoram Wind (1972), *Organizational Buying Behavior,* Englewood Cliffs, N.J.: Prentice-Hall.

Westing, John H. (1967), ''Some Thoughts on the Nature of Ethics in Marketing,'' in *Changing Marketing Systems,* Chicago: American Marketing Association.

Wilkie, William L. (1975), *How Consumers Use Product Information,* Washington D.C.: National Science Foundation.

Wind, Yoram J. (1978), ''Issues and Advances in Segmentation Research,'' *Journal of Marketing Research,* 15 (August), 317–337.

Zielinski, Joan and Thomas S. Robertson (1982), ''Consumer Behavior Theory: Excesses and Limitations,'' in *Advances in Consumer Research,* Vol. 9, Andrew Mitchell, editor, Chicago: Association for Consumer Research.

DISCUSSION QUESTIONS

1. Sheth and Gardner critically evaluated the contributions to marketing theory of the six schools of marketing thought they identified. Do you agree that the six schools represent major streams of marketing thought? Do you agree with the contributions they described? Explain.

2. Critically evaluate the contributions of each of the six schools of marketing thought to marketing practice.

3. Contemplate the future of the six schools of marketing thought by the year 2000. Which will have survived and which will have expired? What changes in these schools of thought do you think may occur between now and the year 2000?

B. DEFINITION AND CLASSIFICATION ISSUES

Each of the articles in this section of the book addresses definitional or classificational issues in marketing. Several of these papers are part of what may be called the broadening literature.

Kotler, in the first of these selections proposes a generic concept of marketing that he argues is relevant to all organizations. Bagozzi, taking these ideas a step further, argues that marketing is exchange and that the concepts of exchange and marketing are universally applicable. Levy proposes that a distinction between theory and practice in marketing is necessary and that a science of marcology is needed.

Hunt presents a conceptual model of the scope of marketing that is useful in resolving issues concerning the nature of marketing and whether marketing is a science. Bagozzi initiates an attempt at a formal theory of marketing exchanges that seeks to describe them in terms of four determinants of exchange. Fisk and Walden argue that marketing is a fundamentally interpersonal phenomena, yet interpersonal exchanges are neglected by marketing scholars. They develop a conceptual analysis of interpersonal exchanges.

PREFACE TO
"A Generic Concept of Marketing"

Kotler's presentation of the generic concept of marketing stands as a landmark treatise on the broadening of marketing thought. The basic proposal is that all organizations do marketing and that marketing concepts apply to transactions between the organization and all of its publics. In developing this proposal, Kotler describes three levels of marketing consciousness, presents four axioms of marketing, and argues that new typologies are needed to describe marketing activity in nontraditional settings.

9

A GENERIC CONCEPT OF MARKETING

PHILIP KOTLER

One of the signs of the health of a discipline is its willingness to reexamine its focus, techniques, and goals as the surrounding society changes and new problems require attention. Marketing has shown this aptitude in the past. It was originally founded as a branch of *applied economics* devoted to the study of distribution channels. Later marketing became a *management discipline* devoted to engineering increases in sales. More recently, it has taken on the character of an *applied behavioral science* that is concerned with understanding buyer and seller systems involved in the marketing of goods and services.

The focus of marketing has correspondingly shifted over the years. Marketing evolved through a *commodity focus* (farm products, minerals, manufactured goods, services); and *institutional focus* (producers, wholesalers, retailers, agents); a *functional focus* (buying, selling, promoting, transporting, sorting, pricing); a *managerial focus* (analysis, planning, organization, control); and a *social focus* (market efficiency, product quality, and social impact). Each new focus had its advocates and its critics. Marketing emerged each time with a refreshed and expanded self-concept.

Today marketing is facing a new challenge concerning whether its concepts apply in the nonbusiness as well as the business area. In 1969, this author and Professor Levy advanced the view that *marketing is a relevant discipline for all organizations insofar as all organizations can be said to have customers and products.*[1] This "broadening of the concept of marketing" proposal received much attention, and the 1970 Fall Conference of the American Marketing Association was devoted to this theme.

Critics soon appeared who warned that the broadening concept could divert marketing from its true purposes and dilute its content. One critic did not deny that marketing concepts and tools could be

Source: Reprinted with permission from the *Journal of Marketing,* 36, (April), 1972, 46–54, Chicago, Ill.: American Marketing Association.

useful in fund raising, museum membership drives, and presidential campaigns, but he felt that these were extracurricular applications of an intrinsical business technology.[2]

Several articles have been published which describe applications of marketing ideas to nonbusiness areas such as health services, population control, recycling of solid wastes, and fund raising.[3] Therefore, the underlying issues should be reexamined to see whether a more generic concept of marketing can be established. This author concludes that the traditional conception of marketing would relegate this discipline to an increasingly narrow and pedestrian role in a society that is growing increasingly post-industrial. In fact, this article will argue that the broadening proposal's main weakness was not that it went too far but that it did not go far enough.

This article is organized into five parts. The first distinguishes three stages of consciousness regarding the scope of marketing. The second presents an axiomatic treatment of the generic concept of marketing. The third suggests three useful marketing typologies that are implied by the generic concept of marketing. The fourth describes the basic analytical, planning, organization, and control tasks that make up the logic of marketing management. The fifth discusses some interesting questions raised about the generic concept of marketing.

THREE STAGES OF MARKETING CONSCIOUSNESS

Three different levels of consciousness can be distinguished regarding the boundaries of marketing. The present framework utilizes Reich's consciousness categories without his specific meanings.[4] The traditional consciousness, that marketing is essentially a business subject, will be called *consciousness one.* Consciousness one is the most widely held view in the mind of practitioners and the public. In the last few years, a marketing *consciousness two* has appeared among some marketers holding that marketing is appropriate for all organizations that have customers. This is the thrust of the original broadening proposal and seems to be gaining adherents. Now it can be argued that even consciousness two expresses a limited concept of marketing. One can propose *consciousness three* that holds that marketing is a relevant subject for all organizations in their relations with all their publics, not only customers. The future character of marketing will depend on the particular consciousness that most marketers adopt regarding the nature of their field.

Consciousness One

Consciousness one is the conception that marketing is essentially a business subject. It maintains that marketing is concerned with *sellers, buyers,* and *"economic" products and services.* The sellers offer goods and services, the buyers have purchasing power and other resources, and the objective is an exchange of goods for money or other resources.

The core concept defining marketing consciousness one is that of *market transactions.* A market transaction involves the transfer of ownership or use of an economic good or service from one party to another in return for a payment of some kind. For market transactions to occur in a society, six conditions are necessary: (1) Two or more parties; (2) a scarcity of goods; (3) concept of private property; (4) one party must want a good held by another; (5) the "wanting" party must be able to offer some kind of payment for it; and (6) the "owning" party must be willing to forego the good or the payment. These conditions underlie the notion of a market

transaction, or more loosely, economic exchange.

Market transactions can be contrasted with nonmarket transactions. Monmarket transactions also involve a transfer of resources from one part to another, *but without clear payment by the other.* Giving gifts, paying taxes, receiving free services are all examples of nonmarket transactions. If a housekeeper is paid for domestic services, this is a market transaction; if she is one's wife, this is a nonmarket transaction. Consciousness one marketers pay little or no attention to nonmarket transactions because they lack the element of explicit payment.

Consciousness Two

Consciousness two marketers do not see *payment* as a necessary condition to define the domain of marketing phenomena. Marketing analysis and planning are relevant in all organizations producing products and services for an intended consuming group, whether or not payment is required.

Table 1 lists several nonbusiness organizations and their "products" and "customer groups." All of these products, in principle, can be priced and sold. A price can be charged for museum attendance, safe driving lessons, birth control information, and education. The fact that many of these services are offered "free" should not detract from their character as products. A product is something that has value to someone. Whether a charge is made for its consumption is an incidental rather than essential feature defining value. In fact, most of these social goods are "priced," although often

TABLE 1
Some Organizations and Their Products and Customer Groups

Organization	Product	Customer Group
Museum	Cultural appreciation	General public
National Safety Council	Safer driving	Driving public
Political candidate	Honest government	Voting public
Family Planning Foundation	Birth control	Fertile public
Police department	Safety	General public
Church	Religious experience	Church members
University	Education	Students

not in the normal fashion. Police services are paid for by taxes, and religious services are paid for by donations.

Each of these organizations faces marketing problems with respect to its product and customer group. They must study the size and composition of their market and consumer wants, attitudes, and habits. They must design their products to appeal to their target markets. They must develop distribution and communication programs that facilitate "purchase" and satisfaction. They must develop customer feedback systems to ascertain market satisfaction and needs.

Thus consciousness two replaces the core concept of *market transactions* with the broader concept of *organization-client transactions*. Marketing is no longer restricted only to transactions involving parties in a two-way exchange of economic resources. Marketing is a useful perspective for any organization producing products for intended consumption by others. *Marketing consciousness two states that marketing is relevant in all situations where one can identify an organization, a client group, and products broadly defined.*

Consciousness Three

The emergence of a marketing consciousness three is barely visible. Consciousness three marketers do not see why marketing technology should be confined only to an organization's transactions with its client group. An organization—or more properly its management—may engage in marketing activity not only with its customers but also with all other publics in its environment. A management group has to market to the organization's supporters, suppliers, employees, government, the general public, agents, and other key publics. *Marketing consciousness three states that marketing applies to an organization's attempts to relate to all of its publics, not just its consuming public.* Marketing can be used in multiple institutional contexts to effect transactions with multiple targets.

Marketing consciousness three is often expressed in real situations. One often hears a marketer say that his real problem is not *outside marketing* but *inside marketing;* for example, getting others in his organization to accept his ideas. Companies seeking a preferred position with suppliers or dealers see this as a problem of marketing themselves. In addition, companies try to market their

viewpoint to congressmen in Washington. These and many other examples suggest that marketers see the making problem as extending far beyond customer groups.

The concept of defining marketing in terms of *function* rather than *structure* underlies consciousness three. To define a field in terms of function is to see it as a process or set of activities. To define a field in terms of structure is to identify it with some phenomena such as a set of institutions. Bliss pointed out that many sciences are facing this choice.[5] In the field of political science, for example, there are those who adopt a structural view and define political science in terms of political institutions such as legislatures, government agencies, judicial courts, and political parties. There are others who adopt a functional view and define political science as the study of *power* wherever it is found. The latter political scientists study power in the family, in labor-management relations, and in corporate organizations.

Similarly, marketing can be defined in terms of functional rather than structural considerations. Marketing takes places in a great number of situations, including executive recruiting, political campaigning, church membership drives, and lobbying. Examining the marketing aspects of these situations can yield new insights into the generic nature of marketing. The payoff may be higher than from continued concentration in one type of structural setting, that of business.

It is generally a mistake to equate a science with a certain phenomenon. For example, the subject of *matter* does not belong exclusively to physics, chemistry, or biology. Rather physics, chemistry, and biology are logical systems that pose different questions about matter. Nor does *human nature* belong exclusively to psychology, sociology, social psychology, or anthropology. These sciences simply raise different questions about the same phenomena. Similarly, traditional business subjects should not be defined by institutional characteristics. This would mean that finance deals with banks, production with factories, and marketing with distribution channels. Yet each of these subjects has a set of core ideas that are applicable in multiple institutional contexts. An important means of achieving progress in a science is to try to increase the generality of its concepts.

Consider the case of a hospital as an institution.

A production-minded person will want to know about the locations of the various facilities, the jobs of the various personnel, and in general the arrangement of the elements to produce the product known as health care. A financial-minded person will want to know the hospital's sources and applications of funds and its income and expenses. A marketing-minded person will want to know where the patients come from, why they appeared at this particular hospital, and how they feel about the hospital care and services. Thus the phenomena do not create the questions to be asked; rather the questions are suggested by the disciplined view brought to the phenomena.

What then is the disciplinary focus of marketing? The core concept of marketing is the *transaction. A transaction is the exchange of values between two parties.* The things-of-values need not be limited to goods, services, and money; they include other resources such as time, energy, and feelings. Transactions occur not only between buyers and sellers, and organizations and clients, but also between any two parties. A transaction takes place, for example, when a person decides to watch a television program; he is exchanging his time for entertainment. A transaction takes place when a person votes for a particular candidate; he is exchanging his time and support for expectations of better government. A transaction takes place when a person gives money to a charity; he is exchanging money for a good conscience. *Marketing is specifically concerned with how transactions are created, stimulated, facilitated, and valued.* This is the generic concept of marketing.

The Axioms of Marketing

The generic concept of marketing will now be more rigorously developed. Marketing can be viewed as a *category of human action* distinguishable from other categories of human action such as voting, loving, consuming, or fighting. As a category of human action, it has certain characteristics which can be stated in the form of axioms. A sufficient set of axioms about marketing would provide unambiguous criteria about what marketing is, and what it is not. Four axioms, along with corollaries, are proposed in the following section.

Axiom 1. Marketing involves two or more social units, each consisting of one or more human actors.

Corollary 1.1. The social units may be individuals, groups, organizations, communities, or nations.

Two important things follow from this axiom. First, marketing is not an activity found outside of the human species. Animals, for example, engage in production and consumption, but do not engage in marketing. They do not exchange goods, set up distribution systems, and engage in persuasive activity. Marketing is a peculiarly human activity.

Second, the referent of marketing activity is another social unit. Marketing does not apply when a person is engaged in an activity in reference to a *thing* or *himself.* Eating, driving, and manufacturing are not marketing activities, as they involve the person in an interactive relationship primarily with things. Jogging, sleeping, and daydreaming are not marketing activities, as they involve the person in an interactive relationship primarily with himself. An interesting question does arise as to whether a person can be conceived of marketing something to himself, as when he undertakes effort to change his own behavior. Normally, however, marketing involves actions by a person directed toward one or more other persons.

Axiom 2. At least one of the social units is seeking a specific response from one or more other units concerning some social object.

Corollary 2.1. The social unit seeking the response is called the *marketer,* and the social unit whose response is sought is called the *market.*

Corollary 2.2 The social object may be a product, service, organization, person, place, or idea.

Corollary 2.3. The response sought from the market is some behavior toward the social object, usually acceptance but conceivably avoidance. (More specific descriptions of responses sought are purchase, adoption, usage, consumption, or their negatives. Those who do or may respond are called buyers, adopters, users, consumers, clients, or supporters.)

Corollary 2.4. The marketer is normally aware that he is seeking the specific response.

Corollary 2.5. The response sought may be expected in the short or long run.

Corollary 2.6. The response has value to the marketer.

Corollary 2.7 *Mutual marketing* describes the case

where two social units simultaneously seek a response from each other. Mutual marketing is the core situation underlying bargaining relationships.

Marketing consists of actions undertaken by persons to bring about a response in other persons concerning some specific social object. A social object is any entity or artifact found in society, such as a product, service, organization, person, place, or idea. The marketer normally seeks to influence the market to accept this social object. The notion of marketing also covers attempts to influence persons to avoid the object as in a business effort to discourage excess demand or in a social campaign designed to influence people to stop smoking or overeating.[6] *The marketer is basically trying to shape the level and composition of demand for his product.* The marketer undertakes these influence actions because he values their consequences. The market may also value the consequences, but this is not a necessary condition for defining the occurrence of marketing activity. The marketer is normally conscious that he is attempting to influence a market, but it is also possible to interpret as marketing activity cases where the marketer is not fully conscious of his ends and means.

Axiom 2 implies that "selling" activity rather than "buying" activity is closer to the core meaning of marketing. The merchant who assembles goods for the purpose of selling them is engaging in marketing, insofar as he is seeking a purchase response from others. The buyer who comes into his store and pays the quoted price is engaging in buying, not marketing, in that he does not seek to produce a specific response in the seller, who has already put the goods up for sale. If the buyer decides to bargain with the seller over the terms, he too is involved in marketing, or if the seller had been reluctant to sell, the buyer has to market himself as an attractive buyer. The terms "buyer" and "seller" are not perfectly indicative of whether one, or both, of the parties are engaged in marketing activity.

Axiom 3. The market's response probability is not fixed.

Corollary 3.1. The probability that the market will produce the desired response is called the *market's response probability.*

Corollary 3.2. The market's response probability is greater than zero; that is, the market is capable of producing the desired response.

Corollary 3.3. The market's response probability is less than one; that is, the market is not internally compelled to produce the desired response.

Corollary 3.4. The market's response probability can be altered by marketer actions.

Marketing activity makes sense in the context of a market that is free and capable of yielding the desired response. If the target social unit *cannot respond* to the social object, as in the case of no interest or no resources, it is not a market. If the target social unit *must respond* to the social object, as in the case of addiction or perfect brand loyalty, that unit is a market but there is little need for marketing activity. In cases where the market's response probability is fixed in the short run but variable in the long run, the marketer may undertake marketing activity to prevent or reduce the erosion in the response probability. Normally, marketing activity is most relevant where the market's response probability is less than one and highly influenced by marketer actions.

Axiom 4. Marketing is the attempt to produce the desired response by creating and offering values to the market.

Corollary 4.1. The marketer assumes that the market's response will be voluntary.

Corollary 4.2. The essential activity of marketing is the creation and offering of value. Value is defined subjectively from the market's point of view.

Corollary 4.3. The marketer creates and offers value mainly through configuration, valuation, symbolization, and facilitation. (Configuration is the act of designing the social object. Valuation is concerned with placing terms of exchange on the object. Symbolization is the association of meanings with the object. Facilitation consists of altering the accessibility of the object.)

Corollary 4.4. *Effective marketing* means the choice of marketer actions that are calculated to produce the desired response in the market. *Efficient marketing* means the choice of *least cost* marketer actions that will produce the desired response.

Marketing is an approach to producing desired responses in another party that lies midway between *coercion* on the one hand and *brainwashing* on the other.

Coercion involves the attempt to produce a response in another by forcing or threatening him with agent-inflicted pain. Agent-inflicted pain should be distinguished from object-inflicted pain in that the latter may be used by a marketer as when he symbolizes something such as cigarettes as potentially harmful to the smoker. The use of agent-inflicted pain is normally not a marketing solution to a response problem. This is not to deny that marketers occasionally resort to arranging a "package of threats" to get or keep a customer. For example, a company may threaten to discontinue purchasing from another company if the latter failed to behave in a certain way. But normally, marketing consists of noncoercive actions to induce a response in another.

Brainwashing lies at the other extreme and involves the attempt to produce a response in another by profoundly altering his basic beliefs and values. Instead of trying to persuade a person to see the social object as serving his existing values and interests, the agent tries to shift the subject's values in the direction of the social object. Brainwashing, fortunately, is a very difficult feat to accomplish. It requires a monopoly of communication channels, operant conditioning, and much patience. Short of pure brainwashing efforts are attempts by various agents to change people's basic values in connection with such issues as racial prejudice, birth control, and private property. Marketing has some useful insights to offer to agents seeking to produce basic changes in people, although its main focus in on creating products and messages attuned to existing attitudes and values. It places more emphasis on preference engineering than attitude conditioning, although the latter is not excluded.

The core concern of marketing is that of producing desired responses in free individuals by the judicious creation and offering of values. The marketer is attempting to get value from the market through offering value to it. The marketer's problem is to create attractive values. Value is completely subjective and exists in the eyes of the beholding market. Marketers must understand the market in order to be effective in creating value. This is the essential meaning of the marketing concept.

The marketer seeks to create value in four ways. He can try to design the social object more attractively (configuration); he can put an attractive terms on the social object (valuation); he can add symbolic significance in the social object (symbolization); and he can make it easier for the market to obtain the social object (facilitation). He may use these activities in reverse if he wants the social object to be avoided. These four activities have a rough correspondence to more conventional statements of marketing purpose, such as the use of product, price, promotion, and place to stimulate exchange.

The layman who thinks about marketing often overidentifies it with one or two major component activities, such as facilitation or symbolization. In *scarcity economies,* marketing is often identified with the facilitation function. Marketing is the problem of getting scarce goods to a marketplace. There is little concern with configuration and symbolization. In *affluent economies,* marketing is often identified with the symbolization function. In the popular mind, marketing is seen as the task of encoding persuasive messages to get people to buy more goods. Since most people resent persuasion attempts, marketing has picked up a negative image in the minds of many people. They forget or overlook the marketing work involved in creating values through configuration, valuation, and facilitation. In the future post-industrial society concern over the quality of life becomes paramount, and the public understanding of marketing is likely to undergo further change, hopefully toward an appreciation of all of its functions to create and offer value.

TYPOLOGIES OF MARKETING

The new levels of marketing consciousness make it desirable to reexamine traditional classifications of marketing activity. Marketing practitioners normally describe their type of marketing according to the *target market* or *product*. A *target-market classification of* marketing activity consists of consumer marketing, industrial marketing, government marketing, and international marketing.

A *product* classification consists of durable goods marketing, nondurable goods marketing, and service marketing.

With the broadening of marketing, the preceding classifications no longer express the full range of marketing application. They pertain to business marketing, which is only one type of marketing. More comprehensive classifications of marketing activity can be formulated according to the *target market, product,* or *marketer.*

Target Market Typology

A *target-market classification* of marketing activity distinguishes the various *publics* toward which an organization can direct its marketing activity. A *public is any group with potential interest and impact on an organization.* Every organization has up to nine distinguishable publics (Figure 1). There are three *input publics* (supporters, employees, suppliers), two *output publics* (agents, consumers), and four *sanctioning publics* (government, competitors, special publics, and general public). The organization is viewed as a resource conversion machine which takes the resources of supporters (e.g., stockholders, directors), employees, and suppliers and converts these into products that go directly to consumers or through agents. The organization's basic input-output activities are subject to the watchful eye of sanctioning publics such as government, competitors, special publics, and the general public. All of these publics are targets for organizational marketing activity because of their potential impact on the resource converting efficiency of the organization.

Therefore, a *target-market classification* of marketing activity consists of supporter-directed marketing, employee-directed marketing, supplier-directed marketing, agent-directed marketing, consumer-directed marketing, general public-directed marketing, special public-directed marketing, government-directed marketing, and competitor-directed marketing.

Product Typology

A typology of marketing activity can also be constructed on the basis of the *product* marketed. Under the broadened concept of marketing, the product is no longer restricted to commercial goods and services. An organization can try to market to a public up to six types of products or social objects. A product classification of marketing consists of goods marketing, service marketing, organization marketing, person marketing, place marketing, and idea marketing.

Goods and service marketing, which made up the whole of traditional marketing, reappear in this classification. In addition, marketers can specialize in the marketing of organizations (e.g., governments, corporations, or universities), persons (e.g., political candidates, celebrities), places (e.g., real estate developments, resort areas, states, cities), and ideas (e.g., family planning, Medicare, anti-smoking, safe-driving).

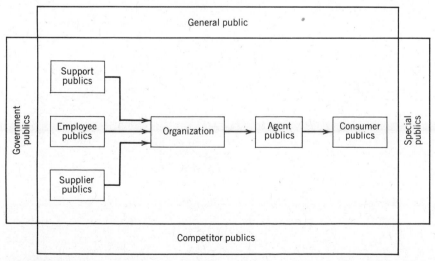

FIGURE 1
An organization's publics.

Marketer Typology

A typology can also be constructed on the basis of the *marketer,* that is, the organization that is carrying on the marketing. A first approximation would call for distinguishing between business and nonbusiness organization marketing. Since there are several types of nonbusiness organizations with quite different products and marketing tasks, it would be desirable to build a marketer classification that recognizes the different types of organizations. This leads to the following classifications: business organization marketing, political organization marketing, social organization marketing, religious organization marketing, cultural organization marketing, and knowledge organization marketing.

Organizations are classified according to their primary or formal character. Political organizations would include political parties, government agencies, trade unions, and cause groups. Social organizations would include service clubs, fraternal organizations, and private welfare agencies. Religious organizations would include churches and evangelical movements. Cultural organizations would include museums, symphonies, and art leagues. Knowledge organizations would include public schools, universities, and research organizations. Some organizations are not easy to classify. Is a nonprofit hospital a business or a social organization? Is an employee credit union a political or a social organization? The purpose of the classification is primarily to guide students of marketing to look for regularities that might characterize the activities of certain basic types of organizations.

In general, the purpose of the three classifications of marketing activity is to facilitate the accumulation of marketing knowledge and its transfer from one marketing domain to another. Thus political and social organizations often engage in marketing ideas, and it is desirable to build up generic knowledge about idea marketing. Similarly, many organizations try to communicate a program to government authorities, and they could benefit from the accumulation of knowledge concerning idea marketing and government-directed marketing.

BASIC TASKS OF MARKETING MANAGEMENT

Virtually all persons and organizations engage in marketing activity at various times. They do not all engage in marketing, however, with equal skill. A distinction can be drawn between *marketing* and *marketing management. Marketing* is a descriptive science involving the study of how transactions are created, stimulated, facilitated, and valued. *Marketing management* is a normative science involving the efficient creation and offering of values to stimulate desired transactions. Marketing management is essentially a disciplined view of the task of achieving specific responses in others through the creation and offering of values.

Marketing management is not a set of answers so much as an orderly set of questions by which the marketer determines what is best to do in each situation. Effective marketing consists of intelligently analyzing, planning, organizing, and controlling marketing effort.

The marketer must be skilled at two basic analytical tasks. The first is *market analysis.* He must be able to identify the market, its size and location, needs and wants, perceptions and values. The second analytical skill is *product analysis.* The marketer must determine what products are currently available to the target, and how the target feels about each of them.

Effective marketing also calls for four major planning skills. The first is *product development,* i.e., configuration. The marketer should know where to look for appropriate ideas, how to choose and refine the product concept, how to stylize and package the product, and how to test it. The second is *pricing,* i.e., valuation. He must develop an attractive set of terms for the product. The third is *distribution,* i.e., facilitation. The marketer should determine how to get the product into circulation and make it accessible to its target market. The fourth is *promotion,* i.e., symbolization. The marketer must be capable of stimulating market interest in the product.

Effective marketing also requires three organizational skills. The first is *organizational design.* The marketer should understand the advantages and disadvantages of organizing market activity along functional, product, and market lines. The second is *organizational staffing.* He should know how to find, train, and assign effective co-marketers. The third is *organizational motivation.* He must determine how to stimulate the best marketing effort by his staff.

Finally, effective marketing also calls for two

control skills. The first is *market results measurement,* whereby the marketer keeps informed of the attitudinal and behavioral responses he is achieving in the marketplace. The second is *marketing cost measurement,* whereby the marketer keeps informed of his costs and efficiency in carrying out his marketing plans.

SOME QUESTIONS ABOUT GENERIC MARKETING

The robustness of the particular conception of marketing advocated in this article will be known in time through testing the ideas in various situations. The question is whether the logic called marketing really helps individuals such as educational administrators, public officials, museum directors, or church leaders to better interpret their problems and construct their strategies. If these ideas are validated in the marketplace, they will be accepted and adopted.

However, academic debate does contribute substantially to the sharpening of the issues and conceptions. Several interesting questions have arisen in the course of efforts by this author to expound the generic concept of marketing. Three of these questions are raised and discussed below.

1. *Isn't generic marketing really using influence as the core concept rather than exchange?*

It is tempting to think that the three levels of consciousness of marketing move from *market transactions* to *exchange* to *influence as the succeeding core concepts. The concept of influence undeniably plays an important role in marketing thought. Personal selling and advertising are essentially influence efforts. Product design, pricing, packaging, and distribution planning make extensive use of influence considerations. It would be too general to say, however, that marketing is synonymous with interpersonal, intergroup, or interorganizational influence processes.*

Marketing is a particular way of looking at the problem of achieving a valued response from a target market. It essentially holds that exchange values must be identified, and the marketing program must be based on these exchange values. Thus the anticigarette marketer analyzes what the market is being asked to give up and what inducements might be offered. The marketer recognizes that every ac-

tion by a person has an opportunity cost. The marketer attempts to find ways to increase the person's perceived rate of exchange between what he would receive and what he would give up in freely adopting that behavior. The marketer is a specialist at understanding human wants and values and knows what it takes for someone to act.

2. *How would one distinguish between marketing and a host of related activities such as lobbying, propagandizing, publicizing, and negotiating?*

Marketing and other influence activities and tools share some common characteristics as well as exhibit some unique features. Each influence activity has to be examined separately in relation to marketing. *Lobbying,* for example, is one aspect of government-directed marketing. The lobbyist attempts to evoke support from a legislator through offering values to the legislator (e.g., information, votes, friendship, and favors). A lobbyist thinks through the problem of marketing his legislation as carefully as the business marketer thinks through the problem of marketing his product or service. *Propagandizing* is the marketing of a political or social idea to a mass audience. The propagandist attempts to package the ideas in such a way as to constitute values to the target audience in exchange for support. *Publicizing* is the effort to create attention and interest in a target audience. As such it is a tool of marketing. *Negotiation* is a face-to-face mutual marketing process. In general, the broadened concept of marketing underscores the kinship of marketing with a large number of other activities and suggests that marketing is a more endemic process in society than business marketing alone suggests.

3. *Doesn't generic marketing imply that a marketer would be more capable of managing political or charitable campaigns than professionals in these businesses?*

A distinction should be drawn between marketing as a logic and marketing as a *competence.* Anyone who is seeking a response in another would benefit from applying marketing logic to the problem. Thus a company treasurer seeking a loan, a company recruiter seeking a talented executive, a conservationist seeking an antipollution law, would all benefit in conceptualizing their problem in marketing terms. In these instances, they would be donning a marketer's hat although they would not be performing as professional marketers. A professional marketer is someone who (1) regularly works with marketing problems in a specific area and (2) has a specialized knowledge of this area. The political strategist, to the extent he is effective, is a professional marketer. He has learned how to effectively design, package, price, advertise, and distribute his type of product in his type of market. A professional marketer who suddenly decides to handle political candidates would need to develop competence and knowledge in this area just as he would if he suddenly decided to handle soap or steel. Being a marketer only means that a person has mastered the logic of marketing. To master the particular market requires additional learning and experience.

SUMMARY AND CONCLUSION

This article has examined the current debate in marketing concerning whether its substance belongs in the business area, or whether it is applicable to all areas in which organizations attempt to relate to customers and other publics. Specifically, *consciousness one marketing* holds that marketing's core idea is *market transactions,* and therefore marketing applies to buyers, sellers, and commercial products and services. *Consciousness two marketing* holds that marketing's core idea is *organization-client transactions,* and therefore marketing applies in any organization that can recognize a group called customers. *Consciousness three marketing* holds that marketing's core idea is *transactions,* and therefore marketing applies to any social unit seeking to exchange values with other social units.

This broadest conception of marketing can be called *generic marketing.* Generic marketing takes a functional rather than a structural view of marketing. Four axioms define generic marketing. *Axiom 1:* Marketing involves two or more social units. *Axiom 2:* At least one of the social units is seeking a specific response from one or more other units concerning some social object. *Axiom 3:* The market's response probability is not fixed. *Axiom 4:* Marketing is the attempt to produce the desired response by creating and offering values to the market. These four axioms and their corollaries are intended to

provide unambiguous criteria for determining what constitutes a marketing process.

Generic marketing further implies that marketing activity can be classified according to the *target market* (marketing directed to supporters, employees, suppliers, agents, consumers, general public, special publics, government, and competitors); the *product* (goods, services, organizations, persons, places, and ideas); and the *marketer* (business, political, social, religious, cultural, and knowledge organizations).

Marketers face the same tasks in all types of marketing. Their major analytical tasks are *market analysis* and *product analysis.* Their major planning tasks are *product development, pricing, distribution,* and *promotion.* Their major organizational tasks are *design, staffing,* and *motivation.* Their major control tasks are *market results measurement* and *marketing cost measurement.*

Generic marketing is a logic available to all organizations facing problems of market response. A distinction should be drawn between applying a marketing point of view to a specific problem and being a marketing professional. Marketing logic alone does not make a marketing professional. The professional also acquires competence, which along with the logic, allows him to interpret his problems and construct his marketing strategies in an effective way.

NOTES

[1] Philip Kotler and Sidney J. Levy, "Broadening the Concept of Marketing," *Journal of Marketing,* Vol. 33 (January, 1969), pp. 10–15.

[2] David J. Luck, "Broadening the Concept of Marketing—Too Far," *Journal of Marketing,* Vol. 33 (July, 1969), pp. 53–54.

[3] *Journal of Marketing,* Vol. 35 (July, 1971).

[4] Charles A. Reich, *The Greening of America* (New York: Random House, 1970).

[5] Perry Bliss, *Marketing Management and the Behavioral Environment* (Englewood Cliffs, N.J.: Prentice-Hall, Inc., 1970), pp. 106–108, 119–120.

[6] See Philip Kotler and Sidney J. Levy, "Demarketing, Yes, Demarketing," *Harvard Business Review,* Vol. 49 (November–December, 1971), pp. 71–80.

DISCUSSION QUESTIONS

1. The article describes three levels of marketing consciousness. Why do you think these levels occur? Can these levels be used to describe events during the twentieth century?

2. Kotler states that "A sufficient set of axioms about marketing would provide unambigious criteria about what marketing is, and what it is not." Do you believe that Kotler's axioms are sufficient for establishing parameters for the discipline? Develop a rationale for supporting or refuting the sufficiency of his axioms.

3. Develop a schematic representation of Kotler's discussion of three typologies of marketing. Represent or imply the four axioms within your schematic.

PREFACE TO

"Marketing as Exchange"

"Marketing as Exchange" was written while I was a doctoral student and actually was part of a longer essay. The other parts appeared as "Marketing as an Organized Behavioral System of Exchange"[*] and as "Science, Politics, and the Social Construction of Marketing.[†]" Three factors were instrumental in preparation of the essay. First I benefited greatly from the inspiration of Professor Richard M. Clewett who assigned the project as part of a doctoral seminar on marketing theory and who continually pushed for ever-deeper inquiry into the roots and meaning of marketing. Second, the role models and intellectual stimulation provided by my mentors, Professors Sydney J. Levy and Philip Kotler, were indispensable. Finally, dialectic exchanges with fellow students—especially Reinhard Angelmar, Nikhilesh Dholakia, Fuat Firat, and Christian Pinson—proved most useful. Any chord that this essay has struck in others is due largely to the influence of the aforementioned individuals and the central role that marketing exchanges play in our everyday lives.

[*]*Journal of Marketing*, Vol. 38 (October 1974), pp. 77–81.

[†]*Proceedings of the American Marketing Association*, 1976. Chicago: American Marketing Association, pp. 586–592.

10

MARKETING AS EXCHANGE*

RICHARD P. BAGOZZI

The exchange paradigm has emerged as a framework useful for conceptualizing marketing behavior. Indeed, most contemporary definitions of marketing explicitly include exchange in their formulations.[1] Moreover, the current debate on "broadening" centers on the very notion of exchange: on its nature, scope, and efficacy in marketing.

This article analyzes a number of dimensions of the exchange paradigm that have not been dealt with in the marketing literature. First, it attempts to show that what marketers have considered as exchange is a special case of exchange theory that focuses primarily on direct transfers of tangible entities between two parties. In reality, marketing exchanges often are indirect, they may involve intangible and symbolic aspects, and more than two parties may participate. Second, the media and meaning of exchange are discussed in order to provide a foundation for specifying underlying mechanisms in marketing exchanges. Finally, social marketing is analyzed in light of the broadened concept of exchange.

The following discussion proceeds from the assumptions embodied in the generic concept of marketing as formulated by Kotler, Levy, and others.[2] In particular, it is assumed that marketing theory is concerned with two questions: (1) Why do people and organizations engage in exchange relationships? and (2) How are exchanges created, resolved, or avoided? The domain for the subject matter of marketing is assumed to be quite broad, encompassing all activities involving "exchange" and the cause and effect phenomena associated with it. As in the social and natural sciences, marketing owes its definition to the outcome of debate and competition between divergent views in an evolutionary process that Kuhn terms a "scientific revolution."[3] Although the debate is far from settled, there appears to be a growing consensus that exchange forms the core phenomenon for study in marketing. Whether the specific instances of exchange are to be limited to economic institutions and consumers in the traditional sense or expanded to all organizations in the broadened sense deserves further attention by marketing scholars and practitioners. Significantly, the following principles apply to exchanges in both senses.

THE TYPES OF EXCHANGE

In general, there are three types of exchange: restricted, generalized, and complex.[4] Each of these is described below.

Restricted Exchange

Restricted exchange refers to two-party reciprocal relationships which may be represented diagrammatically as $A \leftrightarrow B$, where "$\leftrightarrow$" signifies "gives to and receives from" and A and B represent social actors such as consumers, retailers, salesmen, organizations, or collectivities.[5] Most treatments of, and references to, exchange in the marketing literature have implicitly dealt with restricted exchanges; that is, they have dealt with customer-salesman, wholesaler-retailer, or other such dyadic exchanges.

Restricted exchanges exhibit two characteristics:

First, there is a great deal of attempt to maintain equality. This is especially the case with repeatable social exchange acts. Attempts to gain advantage at the expense of the other is [sic] minimized. Negatively, the breach of the rule of equality quickly leads to emotional reactions. . . . Secondly, there is a *quid pro quo* mentality in restricted exchange activities. Time intervals in mutual reciprocities are cut short and there is an attempt to balance activities and exchange items as part of the mutual reciprocal relations.[6]

Source: Reprinted with permission from the *Journal of Marketing*, 39, (October), 1975, 32–39, Chicago, Ill.: American Marketing Association.

*The author wishes to acknowledge his gratitude to Professors Clewett, Kotler, and Levy and Associate Dean Westfall of Northwestern University, and to the reviewers, for the exchange of ideas that led to this article.

The "attempt to maintain equality" is quite evident in restricted marketing exchanges. Retailers, for example, know that they will not obtain repeat purchases if the consumer is taken advantage of and deceived. The "breach" in this rule of equality—which is a central tenet of the marketing concept—has led to picketing, boycotts, and even rioting. Finally, the fact that restricted marketing exchanges must involve a *quid pro quo* notion (something of value in exchange for something of value) has been at the heart of Luck's criticism of broadening the concept of marketing.[7] However, as will be developed below, there are important exceptions to the *quid pro quo* requirement in many marketing exchanges.

Generalized Exchange

Generalized exchange denotes univocal, reciprocal relationships among at least three actors in the exchange situation. Univocal reciprocity occurs "if the reciprocations involve at least three actors and if the actors do not benefit each other directly but only indirectly."[8] Given three social actors, for instance, generalized exchange may be represented as $A \rightarrow B \rightarrow C \rightarrow A$, where "$\rightarrow$" signifies "gives to." In generalized exchange, the social actors form a system in which each actor gives to another but receives from someone other than to whom he gave. For example, suppose a public bus company (*B*) asks a local department store chain (*A*) to donate or give a number of benches to the bus company. Suppose further that, after the department store chain (*A*) gives the benches to the bus company (*B*), the company (*B*) then places the benches at bus stops for the convenience of its riders (*C*). Finally, suppose that a number of the riders (*C*) see the advertisements placed on the benches by the department store chain (*A*) and later patronize the store as a result of this exposure. The sequence of exchange, $A \rightarrow B \rightarrow C \rightarrow A$, is known as generalized exchange; while it fails to conform to the usual notions of *quid pro quo,* it certainly constitutes a marketing exchange of interest.

Complex Exchange

Complex exchange refers to a system of mutual relationships between at least three parties. Each social actor is involved in at least one direct exchange, while the entire system is organized by an interconnecting web of relationships.

Perhaps the best example of complex exchange in marketing is the channel of distribution. Letting *A* represent a manufacturer, *B* a retailer, and *C* a consumer, it is possible to depict the channel as $A \leftrightarrow B \leftrightarrow C$. Such open-ended sequences of direct exchanges may be designated *complex chain exchanges.*

But many marketing exchanges involve relatively closed sequences of relationships. For example, consider the claim made by Kotler that a "transaction takes place . . . when a person decides to watch a television program."[9] Recently, Carman and Luck have criticized this assertion, maintaining that it may not exhibit an exchange.[10] The differences stem from: (1) a disagreement on whether exchange must consist of transfers of tangible (as opposed to intangible) things of value, and (2) a neglect of the possibility of systems of exchange. Figure 1 illustrates the exchange between a person and a television program and how it may be viewed as a link in a system termed *complex circular exchange.*[11] In this system of exchange, the person experiences a direct transfer of intangibles between himself and the program. That is, he gives his attention, support (for example, as measured by the Nielsen ratings), potential for purchase, and so on, and receives entertainment, enjoyment, product information, and other intangible entities. The person also experiences an indirect exchange with the television program via a sequence of direct, tangible exchanges. Thus, after being informed of the availability of a book through an exchange with the television program and its advertising, a person may purchase it for, say, $10.00. The book's publisher, in turn, may purchase the services of an advertiser, paying what amounts to a percentage of each sale, say, $1.00. Finally, the advertiser receives the opportunity to place a commercial on the air from the television network in exchange for what again amounts to a percentage of each sale, say $.80. In this particular example, the occurrence of the direct intangible exchange was a necessary prerequisite for the development of the series of indirect tangible exchanges. Thus, an exchange *can* occur between a person and a television program.

Complex chain and complex circular exchanges involve predominantly conscious systems of social and economic relationships. In this sense, there is an overt coordination of activities and expectations, which Alderson called an organized behavioral sys-

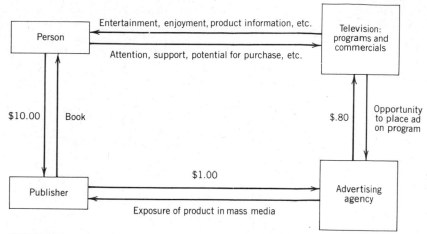

FIGURE 1

An example of complex circular exchange.

tem and which he reserved for the household, the firm, and the channel of distribution.[12] However, it should be evident that the designation "organized" is a relative one and that other exchange systems, such as the one shown in Figure 1, also evidence aspects of overt coordination in an economic, social, and symbolic sense.

Generalized and complex exchanges are also present in relatively unconscious systems of social and economic relationships. Thus, a modern economy may experience a covert coordination of activities through exchanges that occur when many individuals, groups, and firms pursue their own self-interest. This is what Adam Smith meant by his reference to an "invisible hand."[13] Similarly, in his analysis of primitive societies and marketing systems, Frazer has shown that exchange and the pursuit of self-interest can be the foundation for the web of kinship, economic, and social institutions.[14] The recent exchange theories of Homans and Blau are also based on the individualistic assumption of self-interest.[15] It should be stressed, however, that the exchange tradition developed by Levi-Strauss is not an individualistic one but rather is built on social, collectivistic assumptions associated with generalized exchange.[16] These differences will become more apparent when social marketing is analyzed below.

THE MEDIA AND MEANING OF EXCHANGE

In order to satisfy human needs, people and organizations are compelled to engage in social and economic exchanges with other people and organizations. This is true for primitive as well as highly developed societies. Social actors obtain satisfaction of their needs by complying with, or influencing, the behavior of other actors. They do this by communicating and controlling the media of exchange which, in turn, comprise the links between one individual and another, between one organization and another. Significantly, marketing exchanges harbor meanings for individuals that go beyond the mere use of media for obtaining results in interactions.

The Media of Exchange

The media of exchange are the vehicles with which people communicate to, and influence, others in the satisfaction of their needs. These vehicles include money, persuasion, punishment, power (authority), inducement, and activation of normative or ethical commitments.[17] Products and services are also media of exchange. In consumer behavior research, marketers have extensively studied the effects of these vehicles on behavior.

Moreover, it has been suggested that a number of these vehicles be used in conjunction with socio-psychological processes to explain the customer-salesman relationship.[18] It should be noted, however, that marketing is not solely concerned with influence processes, whether these involve manufacturers influencing consumers or consumers influencing manufacturers. Marketing is also concerned with meeting existing needs and anticipating future needs, and these activities do not necessarily entail attempts to influence or persuade.

To illustrate the multivariate nature of media in marketing exchanges, consider the example of the channel of distribution, a complex chain exchange. The firms in a channel of distribution are engaged in an intricate social system of behavioral relationships that go well beyond the visible exchange of products and money.[19] Typically, the traditional channel achieves its conscious coordination of effort through the mutual expectations of profit. In addition, each firm in the channel may influence the degree of cooperation and compliance of its partners by offering inducements in the form of services, deals, or other benefits or by persuading each link in the channel that it is in its own best interest to cooperate. A firm may also affect the behavior or decisions of another firm through the use of the power it may possess. Wilkinson has studied five bases of power in the channel of distribution—reward, coercive, legitimate, referent, and expert power—and has tested aspects of these relationships between firms.[20] Finally, a firm may remind a delinquent member in the channel of its contractual obligations or even threaten the member with legal action for a breach of agreement. This influence medium is known as the activation of commitments.

The Meaning of Exchange

Human behavior is more than the outward responses or reactions of people to stimuli. Man not only reacts to events or the actions of others but he self-generates his own acts.[21] His behavior is purposeful, intentional. It is motivated. Man is an information seeker and generator as well as an information processor. In short, human behavior is a conjunction of meaning with action and reaction.

Similarly, exchange is more than the mere transfer of a product or service for money. To be sure,

most marketing exchanges are characterized by such a transfer. But the reasons behind the exchange—the explanation of its occurrence—lie in the social and psychological significance of the experiences, feelings, and meanings of the parties in the exchange. In general, marketing exchanges may exhibit one of three classes of meanings: utilitarian, symbolic, or mixed.

Utilitarian Exchange   A utilitarian exchange is an interaction whereby goods are given in return for money or other goods and the motivation behind the actions lies in the anticipated use or tangible characteristics commonly associated with the objects in the exchange. The utilitarian exchange is often referred to as an economic exchange, and most treatments of exchange in marketing implicitly rely on this usage. As Bartels notes with regard to the identity crisis in marketing:

> Marketing has initially and generally been associated exclusively with the distributive part of the *economic* institution and function. . . .
>
> The question, then, is whether marketing is identified by the *field* of economics in which the marketing techniques have been developed and generally applied, or by the so-called marketing *techniques,* wherever they may be applied.
>
> If marketing relates to the distributive function of the economy, providing goods and services, that *physical* function differentiates it from all other social institutions.[22]

Most marketers have traditionally conceptualized the subject matter of the discipline in these terms, and they have proceeded from the assumptions embodied in utilitarian exchange.

In general, utilitarian exchange theory is built on the foundation of *economic man.*[23] Thus, it is assumed that:

1. Men are rational in their behavior.

2. They attempt to maximize their satisfaction in exchanges.

3. They have complete information on alternatives available to them in exchanges.

4. These exchanges are relatively free from external influence.

Coleman has developed an elaborate mathematical framework for representing exchange behavior that assumes many of the features of economic man.[24] His model is based on the theory of purposive action, which posits that each "actor will choose that action which according to his estimate will lead to an expectation of the most beneficial consequences."[25] Among other things, the theory may be used to predict the outcomes and degree of control social actors have for a set of collective actions in an exchange system.

Symbolic Exchange Symbolic exchange refers to the mutual transfer of psychological, social, or other intangible entities between two or more parties. Levy was one of the first marketers to recognize this aspect of behavior, which is common to many everyday marketing exchanges:

Symbol is a general term for all instances were experience is mediated rather than direct; where an object, action, word, picture, or complex behavior is understood to mean not only itself but also some *other* ideas or feelings.

The less concern there is with the concrete satisfactions of a survival level of existence, the more abstract human responses become. As behavior in the market place is increasingly elaborated, it also becomes increasingly symbolic. This idea needs some examination, because it means that sellers of goods are engaged, whether willfully or not, in selling *symbols,* as well as practical merchandise. It means that marketing managers must attend to more than the relatively superficial facts with which they usually concern themselves when they do not think of their goods as having symbolic significance. . . . *People buy things not only for what they can do but also for what they mean.*[26]

Mixed Exchange Marketing exchanges involve both utilitarian and symbolic aspects, and it is often very difficult to separate the two. Yet, the very creation and resolution of marketing exchanges depend on the nature of the symbolic and utilitarian mix. It has only been within the past decade or so that marketers have investigated this deeper side of marketing behavior in their studies of

psychographics, motivation research, attitude and multiattribute models, and other aspects of buyer and consumer behavior. Out of this research tradition has emerged a picture of man in his true complexity as striving for both economic and symbolic rewards. Thus, we see the emergence of *marketing man,* perhaps based on the following assumptions:

1. Man is sometimes rational, sometimes irrational.
2. He is motivated by tangible as well as intangible rewards, by internal as well as external forces.[27]
3. He engages in utilitarian as well as symbolic exchanges involving psychological and social aspects.
4. Although faced with incomplete information, he proceeds the best he can and makes at least rudimentary and sometimes unconscious calculations of the costs and benefits associated with social and economic exchanges.
5. Although occasionally striving to maximize his profits, marketing man often settles for less than optimum gains in his exchanges.
6. Finally, exchanges do not occur in isolation but are subject to a host of individual and social constraints: legal, ethical, normative, coercive, and the like.

The important research question to answer is: *What are the forces and conditions creating and resolving marketing exchange relationships?* The processes involved in the creation and resolution of exchange relationships constitute the subject matter of marketing, and these processes depend on, and cannot be separated from, the fundamental character of human and organizational needs.

SOCIAL MARKETING

The marketing literature is replete with conflicting definitions of *social marketing.* Some have defined the term to signify the *use* of marketing skills in social causes,[28] while others have meant it to refer also to "the *study* of markets and marketing activities within a total social system."[29] Bartels recently muddied the waters with still a new definition that is vastly different from those previously suggested. For him, social marketing designates "the *application* of marketing techniques to *non-marketing* fields."[30] Since these definitions cover virtually everything in marketing and even some things outside of marketing it is no wonder that one author felt compelled to express his "personal confusion" and "uncomfortable" state of mind regarding the concept.[31]

But what is social marketing? Before answering this question, we must reject the previous definitions for a number of reasons. First, we must reject the notion that social marketing is merely the "use" or "application" of marketing techniques or skills to other areas. A science or discipline is something more than its technologies. "Social marketing" connotes what is social and what is marketing, and to limit the definition to the tools of a discipline is to beg the question of the meaning of marketing. Second, social marketing is not solely the study of marketing within the frame of the total social system, and it is even more than the subject matter of the discipline. Rather, the meaning of social marketing—like that of marketing itself—is to be found in the unique *problems* that confront the discipline. Thus, as the philosopher of science, Popper, notes:

The belief that there is such a thing as physics, or biology, or archaeology, and that these "studies" or "disciplines" are distinguishable by the subject matter which they investigate, appears to me to be a residue from the time when one believed that a theory had to proceed from a definition of its own subject matter. But subject matter, or kinds of things, do not, I hold, constitute a basis for distinguishing disciplines. Disciplines are distinguished partly for historical reasons and reasons of administrative convenience (such as the organization of teaching and of appointments), and partly because the theories which we construct to solve our problems have a tendency to grow into unified systems. But all this classification and distinction is a comparatively unimportant and superficial affair. *We are not students of some subject matter but students of problems.* And problems may cut right across the borders of any subject matter or discipline.[32]

Social marketing, then, addresses a particular type of problem which, in turn, is a subset of the generic concept of marketing. That is, social marketing is the answer to a particular question: Why and how are *exchanges* created and resolved in *social* relationships? Social relationships (as opposed to economic relationships) are those such as family planning agent-client, welfare agent-indigent, social worker-poor person, and so on.[33] Social marketing attempts to determine the dynamics and nature of the exchange behavior in these relationships.

But is there an exchange in a social relationship? Luck, for example, feels that "a person who receives a free service is not a buyer and has conducted no exchange of values with the provider of the service."[34] It is the contention in this article that there is most definitely an exchange in social marketing relationships, but the exchange is not the simple *quid pro quo* notion characteristic of most economic exchanges. Rather social marketing relationships exhibit what may be called generalized or complex exchanges. They involve the symbolic transfer of both tangible and intangible entities, and they invoke various media to influence such exchanges.

Figure 2 illustrates a typical social marketing exchange. In this system, society authorizes government—through its votes and tax payments—to provide needed social services such as welfare. In return, the members of society receive social insurance against common human maladies. Government, in turn, pays the salaries of social workers, gives them authority to provide social services, and so on. It also distributes welfare payments directly to the needy. These relatively contemporaneous transfers make this marketing system one of generalized exchange. In addition, a number of symbolic and delayed transfers occur that make the system also one of complex exchange. For example, as shown by dotted lines in the figure, in many cases the needy and dependent have given to the government in the past, since they may have paid taxes and voted. Moreover, members of society anticipate that they, or a number of their members, will become dependent and that social services represent an investment as well as an obligation. Hence, in one sense there is a mutual exchange between society and the needy separated, in part, by the passage of time. Finally, it should be noted that there are other tangential exchanges and forces occurring in this social marketing system that, depending on their balance, give it stability or promote change. The system achieves stability due, first, to the pres-

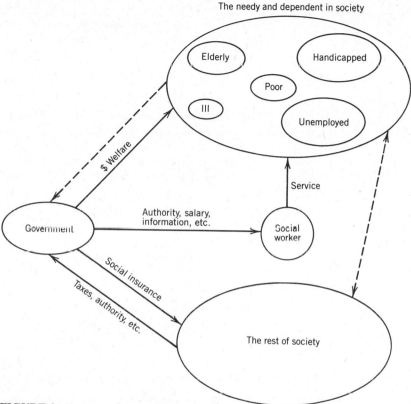

FIGURE 2

Social marketing and exchange.

ence of the exchanges described above, which create mutual dependencies and univocal reciprocities; and, second, to symbolic exchanges, which reinforce the overt transfers. For example, the social worker gives to the needy but also receives back gratitude and feelings of accomplishment. The system undergoes change due to the dynamics of competing interests, as is exemplified in the efforts of lobbies and pressure groups to bring their needs to bear on the legislative process.

Thus, social marketing is really a subset of the generic concept of marketing in that it deals with the creation and resolution of exchanges in social relationships. Marketers can make contributions to other areas that contain social exchanges by providing theories and techniques for the understanding and control of such transactions. They do not usurp the authority of specialists in areas such as social work, but rather they aid and complement the

efforts of these social scientists. It is not so much the fact that the subject matter of marketing overlaps with that of other disciplines as it is that the problems of marketing are universal. In answer to Bartels's query, "Is marketing a specific function with general applicability or a general function that is specifically applied?"[35]—one may state that it is neither. Rather, marketing is a general function of universal applicability. It is the discipline of exchange behavior, and it deals with problems related to this behavior.

CONCLUSIONS AND IMPLICATIONS

A number of broad research questions may be posed:

1. Why do marketing exchanges emerge? How do people and organizations satisfy their needs through exchange?

2. Why do some marketing exchanges persist in ongoing relationships while others fall apart?

3. What are the processes leading to changes in marketing exchange relationships? How do the social actors or third parties influence or control an exchange?

4. What are the consequences of imbalances in power, resources, knowledge, and so on, in a marketing exchange? What is an equitable exchange?

5. What are the relationships between conflict, co-operation, competition, and exchange?

6. At what level may marketing exchanges be analyzed? What are the consequences of viewing exchanges as single dyads or complex systems of relationships? What are the consequences of employing the individualistic reductionism of Homans versus the collectivistic orientation of Levi-Strauss for understanding exchange behavior?

7. Is the exchange paradigm universal? Does it apply to the free-enterprise countries of the western world, the planned economies of the communist countries, and the primitive economies of the third world?

8. How well does the exchange paradigm meet the requirements for theory as specified by philosophy of science criteria?

Although marketing seems to defy simple definition and circumscription, it is essential that marketers locate the distinctive focus (or foci) of the discipline. Failure to do so impedes both the growth of the discipline and the character of its performance. Exchange is a central concept in marketing, and it may well serve as the foundation for that elusive "general theory of marketing." This article has attempted to explore some of the key concepts in the exchange paradigm. Future research and discussion must search for specific social and psychological processes that create and resolve marketing exchanges.

NOTES

[1]See, for example, Marketing Staff of The Ohio State University, "A Statement of Marketing Philosophy," *Journal of Marketing,* Vol. 29 (January 1965), pp. 43–44; E. Jerome McCarthy, *Basic Marketing,* 5th ed. (Homewood, Ill.: Richard D. Irwin, 1975); Philip Kotler, *Marketing Management,* 2nd ed. (Englewood Cliffs, N.J.: Prentice-Hall, 1972), p. 12; and Ben M. Enis, *Marketing Principles* (Pacific Palisades, Calif.: Goodyear Publishing Co., 1974), p. 21.

[2]Philip Kotler, "A Generic Concept of Marketing," *Journal of Marketing,* Vol. 36 (April 1972), pp. 46–54; and Philp Kotler and Sidney J. Levy, "Broadening the Concept of Marketing," *Journal of Marketing,* Vol. 33 (January 1969), pp. 10–15.

[3]Thomas S. Kuhn, *The Structure of Scientific Revolutions,* 2nd ed. (Chicago: University of Chicago Press, 1970).

[4]The distinction between restricted and generalized exchange was first made by anthropologist Claude Levi-Strauss in *The Elementary Structures of Kinship* (Boston: Beacon Press, 1969). An extended critical analysis of restricted and generalized exchange may be found in Peter P. Ekeh, *Social Exchange Theory: The Two Traditions* (Cambridge, Mass.: Harvard University Press, 1974), Chap. 3.

[5]Ekeh, same reference as note 4, p. 50.

[6]Ekeh, same reference as note 4, pp. 51–52.

[7]David J. Luck, "Broadening the Concept of Marketing—Too Far" *Journal of Marketing,* Vol. 33 (July 1969), pp. 53–54; and Luck, "Social Marketing: Confusion Compounded," *Journal of Marketing,* Vol. 38 (October 1974), pp. 70–72.

[8]Ekeh, same reference as note 4, pp. 48, 50.

[9]Kotler, same reference as note 2, p. 48.

[10]James M. Carman, "On the Universality of Marketing," *Journal of Contemporary Business,* Vol. 2 (Autumn 1973), p. 5; and Luck, "Social Marketing," same reference as note 7, p. 72.

[11]A form of circular exchange in primitive societies was first suggested by Bronislaw Malinowski in *Argonauts of the Western Pacific* (London: Routledge & Kegan Paul, 1922), p. 93; but in his concept the same physical items were transmitted to all parties, while in complex circular exchange as defined here different tangible or symbolic entities may be transferred.

[12]Wroe Alderson, *Dynamic Marketing Behavior: A Functionalist Theory of Marketing* (Homewood, Ill.: Richard D. Irwin, 1965), Chap. 1.

[13]For a modern treatment of Adam Smith's contribution to exchange theory, see Walter Nord, "Adam Smith and Contemporary Social Exchange Theory," *The American Journal of Economics and Sociology,* Vol. 32 (October 1974), pp. 421–436.

[14]Sir James G. Frazer, *Folklore in the Old Testament,* Vol. 2 (London: Macmillan & Co., 1919).

[15]George C. Homans, *Social Behavior: Its Elementary Forms,* rev. ed. (New York: Harcourt Brace Jovanovich, 1974); and Peter M. Blau, *Exchange and Power in Social Life* (New York: John Wiley & Sons, 1964).

[16]Levi-Strauss, same reference as note 4. See also, Ekeh, same reference as note 4, Chaps. 3, 4.

[17]Talcott Parsons, "On the Concept of Influence," *Public Opinion Quarterly,* Vol. 27 (Spring 1963), pp. 37–62; and Parsons, "On the Concept of Political Power," *Proceedings of the American Philosophical Society,* Vol. 107 (June 1963), pp. 232–262. See also, Richard Emerson, "Power Dependence Relations," *American Sociological Review,* Vol. 27 (February 1962), pp. 31–40.

[18]Richard P. Bagozzi, "Marketing as an Organized Behavioral System of Exchange," *Journal of Marketing,* Vol. 38 (October 1974), pp. 77–81.

[19]See, for example, Louis W. Stern, *Distribution Channels: Behavioral Dimensions* (New York: Houghton Mifflin Co., 1969).

[20]Ian Wilkinson, "Power in Distribution Channels," *Cranfield Research Papers in Marketing and Logistics,* Session 1973–1974 (Cranfield School of Management, Cranfield, Bedfordshire, England); and Wilkinson, "Researching the Distribution Channels for Consumer and Industrial Goods: The Power Dimension," *Journal of the Market Research Society,* Vol. 16 (No. 1, 1974), pp. 12–32.

[21]This dynamic, as opposed to [a] mechanistic, image of human behavior is described nicely in R. Harré and P. F. Secord, *The Explanation of Social Behavior* (Totawa, N.J.: Littlefield, Adams & Co., 1973).

[22]Robert Bartels, "The Identity Crisis in Marketing," *Journal of Marketing,* Vol. 38 (October 1974), p. 75. Emphasis added.

[23]For a modern treatment of economic man, see Harold K. Schneider, *Economic Man* (New York: The Free Press, 1974).

[24]James S. Coleman, "Systems of Social Exchange," *Journal of Mathematical Sociology,* Vol. 2 (December 1972).

[25]James S. Coleman, *The Mathematics of Collective Action* (Chicago: Aldine-Atherton, 1973).

[26]Sidney J. Levy, "Symbols for Sale," *Harvard Business Review,* Vol. 37 (July–August 1959), pp. 117–119.

[27]It should be stressed that man is motivated by the hope or anticipation of *future* rewards, and these may consist of classes of benefits not necessarily experienced in the past. See Homans's individualistic exchange theory, a learning perspective, same reference as note 15; Levi-Strauss's collectivistic, symbolic perspective, same reference as note 4; and Ekeh, same reference as note 4, pp. 118–124, 163.

[28]Philip Kotler and Gerald Zaltman, "Social Marketing: An Approach to Planned Social Change," *Journal of Marketing,* Vol. 35 (July 1971), p. 5.

[29]William Lazer and Eugene J. Kelley, eds., *Social Marketing: Perspectives and Viewpoints* (Homewood, Ill.: Richard D. Irwin, 1973), p. 4. Emphasis added.

[30]Same reference as note 22. Emphasis added.

[31]Luck, "Social Marketing," same reference as note 7, p. 70.

[32]Karl R. Popper, *Conjectures and Refutations* (New York: Harper & Row, 1963), p. 67.

[33]For a conceptual framework comparing marketing and other social relationships, see Richard P. Bagozzi, "What Is a Marketing Relationship?" *Der Markt,* No. 51, 1974, pp. 64–69.

[34]Luck, "Social Marketing," same reference as note 7, p. 71.

[35]Same reference as note 22, p. 73.

DISCUSSION QUESTIONS

1. For each of the three types of exchange—restricted, generalized, and complex—select a real-world example. How are exchanges conducted in each situation? What lead to the formation of each exchange? What conditions external and internal to the relationships shape the

course and outcome of the exchanges? Why might the exchanges dissolve?

2. Provide a definition for the media of exchange. What are specific media in face-to-face encounters, for example, a customer-salesperson exchange? In mass communication situations?

3. Recall the last purchase you made. In what sense was it functional in a utilitarian way for you? In what sense was it symbolically meaningful for you personally? What do you think was your motivation for acquiring the product or service? In what ways were psychological or social needs met?

4. Discuss the similarities and differences in exchange relations in the United States versus the Soviet Union.

PREFACE TO

"Marcology 101 or the Domain of Marketing"

The paper, "Marcology 101 or the Domain of Marketing," came about in the following way. The immediate spur to writing it was an invitation from Keith Hunt to participate in the program of the 1976 AMA Educators' Conference in a session that he was to chair on "The Domain of Marketing." I took the opportunity to write down some thoughts that had been in my mind for some time. The marketing department at Northwestern University in the 1960s and early 1970s was (and still is) an enjoyable and stimulating environment. A group of faculty of diverse backgrounds and views had been brought together, and we had an exciting time exploring ideas. To the eager curiosity of Harper Boyd, the intellectual integrity of Ralph Westfall, and the careful, open minded attention of Richard Clewett, already established there, were joined the pioneering interdisciplinary experience of Steuart Henderson Britt, the encompassing mind of Philip Kotler, the broad understanding and vitality of Gerald Zaltman, the rich mind and urgency of Louis Stern, and the brilliance and discipline of Brian Sternthal and Bobby Calder.

Whether like adolescents or like mature philosophers, some of us spent endless hours ruminating on the nature of things, becoming intently absorbed in thinking about the question, What is marketing? As Spinoza was said to be a God intoxicated philosopher, we were marketing intoxicated. Some people find that foolish, immature, and futile—an early outside reviewer of "Marcology 101" dismissed it as just another impractical and useless essay on the nature of marketing. But out of such conversations, hoping to get at the heart of the matter, came such works as "Broadening the Concept of Marketing," "Social Marketing," and *Marketing, Society, and Conflict,*[*] which examined ideas about marketing as exchange, as a pervasive phenomenon, and as theoretically controversial. Not least of the results of these conversations was a stream of award-winning doctoral dissertations by Alice Tybout, Louis Chandon, Richard Bagozzi, and several others.

This experience indicates to me the value of raising what may seem simple-minded questions about phenomena that are otherwise taken for granted or pursued at superficial levels in our attempts to get at the deeper roots of meaning in our professional field. I have not changed the essay because it still seems very much to the point in justifying the distinction between the marcological level of inquiry and analysis and the level of marketing actions.

---

[*]Philip Kotler and Sidney J. Levy, "Broadening the Concept of Marketing," *Journal of Marketing*, 33, (January 1969), pp. 10–15; Philip Kotler and Sidney J. Levy, "Social Marketing: An Approach to Planned Social Change," *Journal of Marketing* (July 1971), pp. 3–12; Sidney Levy and Gerald Zaltman, *Marketing, Society, and Conflict*, Englewood Cliffs, N.J.: Prentice-Hall, 1975.

11

MARCOLOGY 101 OR THE DOMAIN OF MARKETING

SIDNEY J. LEVY

INTRODUCTION

There seems to be a great amount of conflict and brooding going on over the state of marketing, reflecting both old problems and new ones. Discerning a crisis in one's field is a common ploy, but some times do appear to be more critical than others, and the recent agitation is unusually lively. It may help in the search for clarity to discuss some main controversial ideas. There are three central issues that are here cast in the form of three major criticisms of marketing:

1. Marketing is a general evil.
2. Marketing trespasses on other fields.
3. Marketing theory is irrelevant.

These three negative ideas generate a noticeable degree of heat, and challenge all marketing educators to examine their field and its basic nature, and to clarify response to these criticisms. The endeavor may be foolish—perhaps unnecessary for thoughtful and reasonable people and futile for others. Still, these ideas have repercussions, they repel good students, affect the support of marketing scholars, and hamper the free expression of inquiry seeking to understand the human actions, structures, and pro-

cesses called marketing. These three problems radiate in many directions and involve numerous sub-issues and segments of society. They indicate that marketing is a controversial subject and source of conflict between marketers and non-marketers, among marketing thinkers, and between marketing thinkers and marketing doers.

The first proposition affects marketing in all its relations, stigmatizing it for existing in society; the second restricts its definition and application in a mean-minded and territorial fashion; and the third complaint denies the value of serious advanced study of marketing. The conflicts entailed are perhaps so deep and encompassing that they are ultimately irreconcilable, but they will probably gain from airing and dialogue, as Boris Becker [7] has pointed out, in our search for truth. Differences due to real opposed interests will undoubtedly continue, but those due to misunderstanding or confusion might be mitigated. It is not the purpose of this discussion to defend specific marketing actions against all comers, but to explore the issues and to suggest an ameliorative approach.

MARKETING STIGMATIZED

The general understanding of what constitutes marketing is both self-confident and negative. That is, most people do not doubt they know that marketing is the selling of goods and that the selling is con-

Source: Reprinted with permission from *Marketing: 1776–1976 and Beyond,* Kenneth L. Bernhardt, ed., Chicago, Ill.: American Marketing Association, 1976, 577–581.

ducted in a manner deserving of censure. This knowledge is ancient, going back to traditional attitudes toward those who sell. The root ideas of *mercari,* to trade, *mereri,* to serve for hire, *merere,* to earn, may seem neutral enough (or even positive, as in *merit*), but the use of these roots to form words such as *meretricious,* meaning like a prostitute, and *mercenary,* to indicate one who will do anything for money, shows the early attachment of negative value judgments to ideas of selling. Aristotle agreed with the opinion of the day when he wrote that "retail trade . . . is justly censured; for it is unnatural, and a mode by which men gain from one another."

Basic Motives

It is interesting to speculate on the sources of the degradation of marketing. They are presumably deep-rooted in being so pervasive and enduring. A common assumption in condemning marketing is that the buyer is taken advantage of by the seller. Even when the marketing exchange is supposed to be equal in value to both participants, dissatisfaction often remains. The many reasons for this go on at various levels. One problem is that the equation is comprised of units whose values are either not easily determined or compared. If the buyer receives the product and satisfaction of his need and the seller receives the payment for his cost and mark-up $(P + S = C + M)$, how can the two sides of the equation be judged truly equal? Even in a trade of goods where both parties are clearly buyer *and* seller, mutual suspicion may arise that one has yielded up a greater value than that received.

A second great source of difficulty relates to the perceived purposes of the seller, especially when a middleman exists and when money is involved. The distributor becomes divorced from basic production and is associated more narrowly with the goals of gaining and accumulating money, supposedly as much as possible. This motive is taken as unusually egocentric and damaging to other people, and therefore deserving of less admiration than other vocational aims. Those who grow or craft goods, whose work is healing, study, salvation, artistry, appear to have a commitment that is direct and socially valuable—although they, too, become suspect if money looms too large in their aims. Because the professions are supposedly self-denying in this respect, they have been ennobled. If the merchant, the paradigm of the marketer, sought only to provide, to be the selfless, dedicated quartermaster to the community, then his endeavor too might be exalted.

But even the most loving provider (e.g., the nursing mother) thwarts the fundamental desire to receive without return. Resist as one may, society insists on *quid pro quo* and socializes the young to believe it is more blessed to give than to receive, a precept that would not be needed if it were self-evident in one's feelings. But some giving becomes gratifying, a source of pride, sociability, greater receiving, and other benefits, so that not all exchange is condemned. Ideas of fair return become possible, as well as intellectual recognition of economic necessities relating to profit and accumulation of capital.

The Synechdochic Mechanism

Learning to adapt to the requirements of an elaborate system of giving and receiving, as society demands [9], leads to many complexities of outlook. In given economies, haggling may come to be admired, and bribery a way of life. In attempts to deny their own persistent desire to get, people do much blaming of others. Marketing is blamed for fostering materialism; and in case consumers seem overly fertile ground for its attractions and too eager to embrace it, the products are deemed shoddy, and the seduction credited to lies and aggressive selling. Implying that in some state of nature (sans marketing) one would have only virtuous spontaneous needs and wants, marketing is accused of brainwashing, forcing, and manipulating people to want things they do not need and to buy things they do not want.

Certainly, there are marketers who make inferior goods, sell aggressively, and tell lies in their advertising. And it is no defense of them to cite equally culpable quack physicians, destructive politicians, cheating customers, faithless ministers, and ignorant teachers. But it is worth noting the overgeneralizing that occurs when all marketing is stigmatized and the term becomes synonymous with doing bad things. All group prejudice is a form of this overgeneralizing, or fallacy of composition. To identify it here, the way a part of marketing is taken for the whole is called the synechdochic mechanism. A synechdoche is a rhetorical device wherein the singular is substituted for the plural: here the disapproved marketer is being used to define the category, substituted for those others who strive to make a fine product, offer an excellent service, price fairly, sell helpfully, and communicate honestly.

To refer to such positive marketing probably arouses cynical reactions even in an audience identified with marketing. It illustrates the deep-rooted nature of the problem to observe within the marketing professions signs of self-hatred, acceptance of the stigma, and casual use of the rhetoric that makes marketing a bad word. For example, W. T. Tucker cites critics of the marketing viewpoint who equate marketing activities with exploiting motives, and "more gimmickry and packaging than substantive change." He seems to accept their criticism and the verb *marketed* as a negative one when he says that the student is a special person who "must not be marketed into doing what the organizations want" [14].

Thus, it is that marketing is stigmatized because it is associated with the many frustrations of wanting and giving—with material things and guilt over the desire for them, with money and its deflection of direct interest in providing goods and services— leading to the projection of these frustrations onto marketing and marketers, and to the synechdochic equation of the whole field with its worst manifestations.

THE DOMAIN OF MARKETING

Another level of explanation of marketing's poor reputation may lie in confusion or misunderstanding as to what marketing actually is. Perhaps the conventional notion of marketing is not a good or accurate one, and redefinition could assist in making some useful distinctions. Partly, this is an academic exercise. As Robert Oliver says, in trying to offer a definition of the field of speech,

> Knowledge does not lend itself readily to segmentalization. Departmentalization is decreed on our campuses not for investigative, but administrative, convenience. The boundaries established around the various academic specialties are not strong enough to contain human curiosity [12].

In the field of speech, Oliver finds the heart of the matter in one purpose: to deal with influence as

exerted through oral discourse. He clings to this, despite his qualms.

> Like other professions, ours has been highly introspective, defensive, self-critical, and uncertain of its goals, its methods, and its boundaries. . . . When we replace the term "language" with the much more inclusive term "speech," the boundaries of our field tend to disappear. Yet within this complexity we must somehow establish our own identity of goals and methods. The task is appalling [13].

Territoriality

The marketing literature shows that marketing thinkers have trouble with finding their consistent locus, also, because their subject matter radiates so readily into and across other disciplines and ways of thinking about human behavior. In his discussion of "the identity crisis in marketing," Bartels raises this basic question:

> The crux of the issue is this: is the identity of marketing determined by the *subject matter* dealt with or by the technology with which the subject is handled? . . . Marketing has initially and generally been associated exclusively with the distributive part of the economic institution and function. In this capacity, marketing is identified by the *substance* and the *subject* of its area of concern [5].

Bartels seem open-minded about the issue, perhaps preferring the substantive definition rather than the methodological application one. He thinks the fresh interest in physical distribution, or *logistics,* may allow the word marketing to go on to refer to both economic and non-economic fields of application. Still, he sees marketing as but a species of generic behavioral activity, and one that is trying to trespass on someone else's territory: "From this standpoint, too, the idea that the fields of political campaigns, religious evangelism, or Red Cross solicitation are the province of marketers, rather than of social scientists, may also be questionable" [6].

David Luck also expresses his concern over the confusion of terminology and conceptualization created by the idea that "every sort of organization is engaged in marketing" [11], and hopes that an authoritative definition of marketing might come from a commission created for the purpose.

These territorial considerations are probably basically irrelevant. As Karl Popper says,

> All this classification and distinction is a comparatively unimportant and superficial affair. We are not students of some subject matter but students of problems. And problems may cut right across the borders of any subject matter or discipline [14].

That is, no one has any special right to a problem. Intellectual territoriality is not like the ownership of a piece of physical geography. Voting behavior may seem the province of political scientists, but that does not prevent sociologists from studying the behavior and need not inhibit marketers. That people like a particular food can be studied by biologists as a process of osmosis or hormonal secretions, by psychologists as a conditioned response or fixation due to trauma, by anthropologists as a cultural imperative, and by speech scholars as a reaction to the oral discourse, "Come and get it!" What makes sex political and politics sexual is the determined attention, analysis, and actions of feminists. To dismiss this as a "Feminist supremacy syndrome" (a la Luck's reference to those "with a sort of marketing supremacy syndrome") seems pointless and ostrich-like. To perceive or study the marketing content of a problem is not to say it is the marketer's province *rather than* the social scientist's, but that it is *also* the marketer's province.

Tucker implies that Kotler and Levy sought to broaden the boundaries of marketing in 1969 [10] in a desire to follow the action of important problems growing elsewhere [16]; but Levy studied such problems at Social Research, Inc. since starting his marketing research career in 1948. It may more properly be said that the action came to marketing for help rather than the other way around, as nonbusiness managers recognized that the marketing point of view might be useful with their problems. In some ways, to resist or resent this fact, is further agreement that marketing is an evil that socially virtuous causes ought not to turn to for help.

Exchange

It has been suggested above that the core issues in marketing arise from the coming together of *providing and needing or wanting*. That is, *exchange* comes about because one must always give something to get something one wants. The paradigm is the infant, reaching for anything available and trying to incorporate it. But experience soon teaches two conditions: one can't have everything, and one must give something in return. The first is the condition for making choices, and the second creates exchanges.

The issue of exchange has been much discussed—views have been presented by many, including Alderson, Kotler, Levy, and Zaltman [2], and two excellent recent articles by Bagozzi [3]. These will not be gone into here, except to reiterate and emphasize the latter's statement that marketing is "a general function of universal applicability. It is the discipline of exchange behavior, and it deals with problems related to this behavior" [4].

It seems important to insist on the issue of universal applicability, mainly because there seems no adequately consistent way to define marketing exchange that limits it short of universality. What is a marketing exchange as different from any other exchange? Some try to restrict marketing to the exchange of money for products, a distinction that fails immediately with consideration of markets in which money is exchanged for money, products for products, and money or product are exchanged for services. Then is there any way to limit which moneys, products, or services will be considered elements of marketing exchange, and which will not? Some use the word *economic* as the limiting adjective. But what is economic and what is non-economic? Economics texts wrestle with such definitions and mainly retreat to notions of scarce resources, utilities, production, consumption, usually trying to stay as close to money as possible. But again, universality of reference is hard to avoid, as what is not a scarce resource, what is not a utility? These concepts are all interwoven. Money is a measure and surrogate for value, for one's labor; labor is a form of energy, skill and service. Anything can be a commodity. All "utility" is a form of satisfaction. In a world in which there is no truly free air (although optimistically cited by Samuelson as a non-economic good in his classic text on economics), in which all exchanges are economic choices and all are exchanges of satisfactions, there can be no non-marketing exchanges. What is being exchanged may sometimes be hard to analyze, but marketing cannot be limited to being the science of *simple* exchanges.

It may be convenient, of course, to make distinctions between marketing exchanges that are culturally defined as commercial or economic, and other types. Some educators and most marketing practitioners in everyday business are more comfortable then. But that should not lead to the exclusion from marketing theory of the exchanges of goods and services in marriages, churches, politics, aesthetics, schools, government, and social causes.

MARKETING THEORY AND PRACTICE

Theorists and practitioners often develop tensions due to conflict of aims, procedures, concepts of scientific and professional standards, relevance, etc. Academic psychologists and clinical psychologists show this tension, and its recent flare-up in the marketing field is notable. For some time, marketing people have thought about the development of marketing as a science. Certainly, that ultimate state has not fully arrived; but various workers have been striving in that direction. The establishment of the Marketing Science Institute is one indication, as well as numerous conferences, symposia, and articles, fretting over marketing as a science, an art, a pseudoscience, as having theory, metatheory, etc. [17].

In the classical extreme, practitioners see theorists (viz., academicians) as ivory tower thinkers, impractical people who do not know the realities of the marketplace, who have ''never met a payroll,'' who teach because they can't do. The theorists return the compliment by regarding practitioners as concrete-minded people who are overly specialized and vocational, unable to generalize their experience, who want to know how-to-do-it rather than to understand why it works as it does. If a science is to work toward understanding, predicting, and controlling, the researcher and teacher tends to emphasize the first two aims, and the practitioner the last two.

The extremists write accusations about the uselessness of academic research or defend the validity and importance of the intellectual enterprise. Outstanding examples from the *Marketing News* are Newton Frank's rude and vituperative letter [3/14/75] on the uselessness of academic research,

the letter (12/1/74) from James F. Engel in which he says that marketing is not a pure science, that publications should face this fact and judge their contents only by their practical value in the applied marketer. He defines marketing as akin to an engineering discipline that draws upon several underlying disciplines; and regards the proposal of Randall Schultz (11/1/74) that there be separate journals of study and practice as a perpetuation of the travesty of educators talking to themselves.

Between the extremes are such moderating, judicious suggestions as a broader dialogue, by Professor Becker (3/31/75) who, however, also believes that if practitioners are determined to be so ignorant, then it is time to go our separate ways. Richard E. Homans (8/15/75) offers an accommodating discussion explaining the benefits of academic research. Thomas Lea Davidson's article shows alarm.

A schism exists today within the marketing community—with marketing academicians lined up on one side and marketing practitioners on the other. The continued growth of that schism—and it is growing—can only be detrimental to both sides.

His solution is indicated in the headline above his article:

One businessman's comments on marketing educators:
EDUCATORS MUST SEE MARKETING AS A 'DOING PROFESSION' AND ADD 'CLINICAL EXPERIENCE' TO 'CLASSROOOM VACUUM' [8].

The pressure is to get more practice into the classroom by inviting businessmen to talk to classes, by urging practitioners to write for the *Journal of Marketing*.

THE SCIENCE OF MARCOLOGY

It is evident that many of the problems discussed above are real ones that will not easily be solved. Marketing will always be regarded as an evil by those who refuse to recognize its universality or do not want to countenance its demands for a return and often a profit. There are manipulative marketers, deceptive ads, and high pressure salesmen. There are sincere disagreements about discipline boundaries and preferred definitions, and about the value of theory. All solutions are partial—the calls for dialogue, a commission to define marketing, an article giving business persons 10 guidelines to follow when invited to speak to students, and another by a young man exhorting marketers to be honest.

One source of these problems and the struggles with them lies in the idea of marketing as an *activity*. It is not surprising that educators are urged to see marketing as a "doing profession," when *marketing* is a *doing*. When one is a seller and markets, one is a marketer who *does* marketing; and a buyer *goes* marketing. Thus, if educators teach marketing, they should teach how to do it and how to go to it; then no wonder Engel says they are acting as engineers of the marketplace. Then it is reasonable that textbooks tend to be prescriptive writing, oriented to helping students to be profitable, successful marketers, good marketers who apply the marketing concept or virtuous marketers who consider their social responsibility in accordance with the latest ideas of how marketing ought to be done. Such prescriptions and applications are indeed not a "pure science," but the teaching of particular sets of marketing values, and they produce the faddishness and biases that Robert F. Agne deplores [1].

A marketing science should be demarcated that does not do *marketing research* but that does *research into marketing*. It should be a pursuit of knowledge, as distinguished from its application, candidly and proudly so. It should exist in relation to marketing as physics or chemistry are to their respective engineerings, as psychology is to counselling. Some have thought that marketing is applied economics, but economics shows little interest in marketing and marketing draws on economics mainly as it might on any other discipline—as sociology and economics draw on psychology and mathematics.

Marketing needs its own parent discipline and theoretical roots, its area of basic study. Despite being hampered by the confusions of being called marketers when they are trying to be teachers and researchers into marketing, such professionals have nevertheless been developing concepts, models, and a theoretical literature, and have doctoral students carrying out theoretical inquiries.

The name of such a science might draw on some appropriate linguistic roots and be called MARCOLOGY. Marcology could be the discipline of exchanges, operating at various levels of abstraction and in whatever contexts are of interest to the scholars. It could have its own focus and its interdisciplinary character, as all the behavioral sciences do. Marcology could study the history of exchanges, why marketing is evil, the various types of exchange, and such divisions of activity as commercial marketing, family or intimate marketing, social and political marketing—or their various marcologies. Abnormal or deviant marcology might study "unusual payments," as a study group recently called large-scale foreign bribery, without having to moralize about them. As *scientists,* marcologists should not teach their opinions about whether television or consumerism or emotional appeals or premiums or unit pricing are good or bad, but rather what these are, how and why they affect which participants in the exchange. They can study what is exchanged, by whom, where, when, and why, with what consequences personally, socially, nationally. They can do this like other scientists, *just to know,* and for those that wish, in order to share that knowledge without being condemned for having a journal that is not practical in character. And if they wish, like other scientists, marcologists can try to say what is likely to happen under given circumstances, so that practical people can learn from that and apply it as physics is applied to manufacturing and biology to medicine.

If there is to be a commission, let it convene marcologists to define their discipline and its curriculum. In this way, both marcology and the engineering activity that is marketing could be clarified, as well as the role identities that accompany the distinctions between research, teaching, and application.

REFERENCES

1. Agne, Robert F. "Businessman Proposes Conduct Code for Academicians," *Marketing News* (August 15, 1974), 4.
2. Alderson, Wroe. *Marketing Behavior and Executive Action.* Homewood, Ill.: Richard D. Irwin, 1957; Kotler, Philip. "A Generic Concept of Marketing," *Journal of Marketing,* 36 (April, 1972), 46–54; Levy, Sidney J. and

Gerald Zaltman, *Marketing, Society, and Conflict*. Englewood Cliffs, N.J.: Prentice-Hall, Inc., 1975.

3. Bagozzi, Richard P. "Marketing as an Organized Behavioral System of Exchange," *Journal of Marketing,* 38 (October, 1974), 77–81; Bagozzi, "Marketing as Exchange," *Journal of Marketing,* 39 (October, 1975), 32–39.

4. Bagozzi. (October, 1975), 39.

5. Bartels, Robert. "The Identity Crisis in Marketing," *Journal of Marketing,* 38 (October, 1974).

6. Ibid., 76.

7. Becker, Boris W. "Letters," *Marketing News* (April 25, 1975), 2.

8. Davidson, Thomas Lea. *Marketing News* (August 15, 1975), 1.

9. Firth, Raymond. *Symbols Public and Private.* London: George Allen & Unwin, Ltd., 1973, especially Chapter 11, "Symbolism in Giving and Getting," 368–402.

10. Kotler, Philip and Sidney J. Levy. "Broadening the Concept of Marketing," *Journal of Marketing,* 33 (January, 1969), 10–15.

11. Luck, David J. "Social Marketing: Confusion Compounded," *Journal of Marketing,* 38 (October, 1974), 71.

12. Oliver, Robert T. "Contributions of the Speech Profession to the Study of Human Communication," in Frank E. X. Dance, ed., *Human Communication Theory.* New York: Holt, Rinehart & Winston, 1967, 266.

13. Ibid., 265.

14. Popper, Karl R. *Conjectures and Refutations.* New York: Harper & Row, 1963, 67.

15. Tucker, W. T. "Future Directions in Marketing Theory," *Journal of Marketing,* 38 (April, 1974), 30–35.

16. Ibid., 31.

17. Tucker, Ibid.; Dawson, Leslie M. "Marketing Science in the Age of Aquarius," *Journal of Marketing,* 35 (July, 1971), 66–72; Bartels, Robert. *Marketing Theory and Metatheory.* Homewood, Ill.: Richard D. Irwin, 1970; Zaltman, Gerald, et al. *Metatheory and Consumer Research.* New York: Holt, Rinehart & Winston, Inc., 1973.

DISCUSSION QUESTIONS

1. What is the basic nature of marketing that is asserted and implied in "Marcology 101"? How does it differ from earlier ideas, such as the marketing concept?

2. How does the article explain the reasons for negative perceptions of marketing? What is the most fundamental reason? How else would you account for the problem?

3. Explain the distinction Levy is suggesting between marcology and marketing. How would you evaluate the validity or usefulness of that distinction?

4. Assuming there were a course entitled Marcology 101, what might be included in its subject matter?

PREFACE TO

"The Nature and Scope of Marketing"

Seven years have passed since the publication of "The Nature and Scope of Marketing" in the *Journal of Marketing*. During that time, the three dichotomies model of the marketing discipline has received a great deal of attention and has generated significant discussion on the fundamental characteristics of marketing. Much of the discussion has been spirited and all of it, in my opinion, has been undertaken by marketers who cared greatly for their discipline (even though they held widely divergent views as to its fundamental nature). The purpose of this introduction is not to rehash the controversy since it is thoroughly reviewed elsewhere (Arndt 1982; Etgar 1977; Gumucio 1977; Hunt 1978; Hunt 1983; Robin 1977; Ross 1977). Instead, the purpose is to provide some further observations on the marketing science controversy.

First of all, many of my colleagues in marketing misinterpreted my conclusion in the original article concerning the marketing science controversy. They seemed to believe that I concluded that the discipline of marketing is a science. However, a careful reading of the article clearly shows the following conclusion: "the study of the *positive* dimensions of marketing can be appropriately referred to as *marketing science*." Consistent with the viewpoint of the philosophy of science, I concluded that marketing management (the normative side of marketing) is not, and cannot be, a science since all sciences seek to explain and predict phenomena. It is true that the managerial side of marketing continues to develop increasingly sophisticated normative decision models for assisting marketing managers. It is also evident that these models are highly quantitative. Nevertheless, they differ from theories, in that normative decision models do not purport to explain and predict phenomena (Hunt 1979) and, therefore, are technically not science (at least not *empirical* science).

A second observation concerning the marketing science controversy concerns the nature of the question itself. Is the question positive or normative? That is, is the question, "*Is* marketing a science?" or is the question, "*Should* marketing be a science?" The article approached the controversy as if it were a *positive* issue. It delineated three characteristics of sciences: (1) a distinct subject matter drawn from the real world that is described and

classified, (2) underlying uniformities and regularities interrelating the subject matter, and (3) intersubjectively certifiable procedures for studying the subject matter. The article then discussed the extent to which the positive dimensions of marketing fit the criteria and drew the appropriate conclusions. As empirical evidence that there is a science side to the marketing discipline, one need only note the increasing attention being given to the development and testing of marketing theories in both the marketing journals and at professional conferences.

However, I believe there has always been a normative issue underlying the marketing science controversy. That is, the issue is: *Should* marketing be a science? What kind of discipline do marketers really want? What should we be teaching in our classes? What kinds of research should we be doing? What criteria should our journals use in the acceptance or rejection of manuscripts? The answers to these questions differ substantially, depending on whether the marketing discipline should be considered solely as marketing management or whether the discipline should include the scientific study of marketing phenomena.

There is no right or wrong answer to the underlying normative question concerning what should be the orientation of the marketing discipline. Reasonable people can disagree. Nevertheless, there does seem to be a growing consensus that we should *not* restrict our teaching exclusively to marketing management issues, that we should *not* confine our research just to exploring the current practices of marketing managers, and that we should *not* change the *Journal of Marketing* into a marketing clone of *Business Week*. That is, there *should* be a science side to marketing.

The marketing discipline has made significant progress in the last three decades. Much of that progress has come about because of the efforts to scholars willing to tackle the problems on the science side of marketing. In a 1965 address to doctoral students, Tom Staudt (then the Marketing Department Chairman at Michigan State University) declared, "Marketing *must* become more than just determining the brand loyalty differences between one-ply toilet paper users versus two-ply toilet paper users." And it has.

REFERENCES

Arndt, Johan (1982), ''The Conceptual Domain of Marketing: Evaluation of Shelby Hunt's Three Dichotomies Model,'' *European Journal of Marketing,* 16, 1, 27–35.

Etgar, Michael (1977), ''Comment on the Nature and Scope of Marketing,'' *Journal of Marketing,* 31 (October).

Gumucio, F. R. (1977), ''Comment on the Nature and Scope of Marketing,'' *Journal of Marketing,* 41 (January), 8.

Hunt, Shelby D. (1978), ''A General Paradigm of Marketing: In Support of the Three Dichotomies Model,'' *Journal of Marketing,* 42 (April).

Hunt, Shelby D. (1979), ''Positive vs. Normative Theory in Marketing,'' in *Conceptual and Theoretical Developments in Marketing,* O. C. Ferrell, Stephen W. Brown and Charles W. Lamb, Jr., eds., Chicago: American Marketing Association.

Hunt, Shelby D. (1983), *Marketing Theory: The Philosophy of Marketing Science,* Homewood, Ill.: Richard D. Irwin.

Robin, Donald P. (1977), ''Comment on the Nature and Scope of Marketing,'' *Journal of Marketing,* 41 (January), 136, 138.

Ross, Will H. (1977), ''Comment on the Nature and Scope of Marketing,'' *Journal of Marketing,* 41 (April), 10, 146.

12

THE NATURE AND SCOPE OF MARKETING*

SHELBY D. HUNT

During the past three decades, two controversies have overshadowed all others in the marketing literature. The first is the "Is marketing a science?" controversy sparked by an early *Journal of Marketing* article by Converse entitled, "The Development of a Science of Marketing."[1] Other prominent writers who fueled the debate included Bartels, Hutchinson, Baumol, Buzzell, Taylor, and Halbert.[2] After raging throughout most of the 1950s and 1960s, the controversy has since waned. The waning may be more apparent than real, however, because many of the substantive issues underlying the marketing science controversy overlap with the more recent "nature of marketing" (broadening the concept of marketing) debate. Fundamental to both controversies are some radically different perspectives on the essential characteristics of both *marketing* and *science*.

The purpose of this article is to develop a conceptual model of the scope of marketing and to use that model to analyze (1) the approaches to the study of marketing, (2) the "nature of marketing" controversy, and (3) the marketing science debate. Before developing the model, some preliminary observations on the controversy concerning the nature of marketing are appropriate.

THE NATURE OF MARKETING

What is marketing? What kinds of phenomena are appropriately termed *marketing phenomena?* How do marketing activities differ from nonmarketing activities? What is a marketing system? How can marketing processes be distinguished from other social processes? Which institutions should one refer to as marketing institutions? *In short, what is the proper conceptual domain of the construct "marketing"?*

The American Marketing Association [AMA] defines marketing as "the performance of business activities that direct the flow of goods and services from producer to consumer or user."[3] This position has come under attack from various quarters as being too restrictive and has prompted one textbook on marketing to note: "Marketing is not easy to define. No one has yet been able to formulate a clear, concise definition that finds universal acceptance."[4]

Although vigorous debate concerning the basic nature of marketing has alternately waxed and waned since the early 1900s, the most recent controversy probably traces back to a position paper by the marketing staff of the Ohio State University in 1965. They suggested that marketing be considered "the process in a society by which the demand structure for economic goods and services is anticipated or enlarged and satisfied through the conception, promotion, exchange, and physical distribution of goods and services."[5] Note the conspicuous absence of the notion that marketing consists of a set of *business activities* (as in the AMA definition). Rather, they considered marketing to be a *social process.*

Next to plunge into the semantical battle were Kotler and Levy. Although they did not specifically propose a new definition of marketing, Kotler and Levy in 1969 suggested that the concept of marketing be broadened to include nonbusiness organizations. They observed that churches, police departments, and public schools have products and customers, and that they use the normal tools of the marketing mix. Therefore, Kotler and Levy conclude that these organizations perform marketing, or at least marketing-like, activities. Thus,

the choice facing those who manage nonbusiness organizations is not whether to market or not to market, for no organization can avoid marketing. The choice is whether to do it well or poorly, and

Source: Reprinted with permission from the *Journal of Marketing*, 40, (July), 1976, 17–28, Chicago, Ill.: American Marketing Association.

*The author gratefully wishes to acknowledge the constructive criticisms of earlier drafts of this article by Professors George W. Brooker and John R. Nevin, both of the University of Wisconsin-Madison.

on this necessity the case for organizational marketing is basically founded.[6]

In the same issue of the *Journal of Marketing,* Lazer discussed the changing boundaries of marketing. He pleaded that: "What is required is a broader perception and definition of marketing than has hitherto been the case—one that recognizes marketing's societal dimensions and perceives of marketing as more than just a technology of the firm."[7] Thus, Kotler and Levy desired to broaden the notion of marketing by including not-for-profit organizations, and Lazer called for a definition of marketing that recognized the discipline's expanding societal dimensions.

Luck took sharp issue with Kotler and Levy by insisting that marketing be limited to those business processes and activities that ultimately result in a *market* transaction.[8] Luck noted that even thus bounded, marketing would still be a field of enormous scope and that marketing specialists could still render their services to nonmarketing causes. Kotler and Levy then accused Luck of a new form of myopia and suggested that, "The crux of marketing lies in a *general idea of exchange* rather than the narrower thesis of market transactions."[9] They further contended that defining marketing "too narrowly" would inhibit students of marketing from applying their expertise to the most rapidly growing sectors of the society.

Other marketing commentators began to espouse the dual theses that (1) marketing be broadened to include nonbusiness organizations, and (2) marketing's societal dimensions deserve scrutiny. Thus, Ferber prophesied that marketing would diversify into the social and public policy fields.[10] And Lavidge sounded a similar call to arms by admonishing marketers to cease evaluating new products solely on the basis of whether they *can* be sold. Rather, he suggested, they should evaluate new products from a societal perspective, that is, *should* the product be sold?

The areas in which marketing people can, and must, be of service to society have broadened. In addition, marketing's functions have been broadened. Marketing no longer can be defined adequately in terms of the activities involved in buying, selling, and transporting goods and services.[11]

The movement to expand the concept of marketing probably became irreversible when the *Journal of Marketing* devoted an entire issue to marketing's changing social/environmental role. At that time, Kotler and Zaltman coined the term *social marketing,* which they defined as "the design, implementation and control of programs calculated to influence the acceptability of social ideas and involving considerations of product planning, pricing, communication, distribution, and marketing research."[12] In the same issue, marketing technology was applied to fund raising for the March of Dimes, health services, population problems, and the recycling of solid waste.[13] Further, Dawson chastised marketers for ignoring many fundamental issues pertaining to the social relevance of marketing activities:

Surely, in these troubled times, an appraisal of marketing's actual and potential role in relation to such [societal] problems is at least of equal importance to the technical aspects of the field. Yet, the emphasis upon practical problem-solving within the discipline far outweighs the attention paid to social ramifications of marketing activity.[14]

Kotler has since reevaluated his earlier positions concerning broadening the concept of marketing and has articulated a "generic" concept of marketing. He proposes that the essence of marketing is the *transaction,* defined as the exchange of values between two parties. Kotler's generic concept of marketing states: "Marketing is specifically concerned with how transactions are created, stimulated, facilitated and valued."[15] Empirical evidence indicates that, at least among marketing educators, the broadened concept of marketing represents a *fait accompli.* A recent study by Nichols showed that 95% of marketing educators believed that the scope of marketing should be broadened to include nonbusiness organizations. Similarly, 93% agreed that marketing goes beyond just economic goods and services, and 83% favored including in the domain of marketing many activities whose ultimate result is not a market transaction.[16]

Although the advocates of extending the notion of marketing appear to have won the semantical battle, their efforts may not have been victimless. Carman notes that the definition of marketing plays a significant role in directing the research efforts of marketers. He believes that many processes (e.g., political processes) do not involve an exchange of values and that marketing should not take such processes under its "disciplinary wing."[17] Bartels has also explored the so-called identity crises in marketing and has pointed out numerous potential disadvantages to broadening the concept of marketing. These *potential* disadvantages include: (1) turning the attention of marketing researchers away from important problems in the area of physical distribution, (2) emphasizing methodology rather than substance as the content of marketing knowledge, and (3) an increasingly esoteric and abstract marketing literature. Bartels concluded: "If 'marketing' is to be regarded as so broad as to include both economic and noneconomic fields of application, perhaps marketing as originally conceived will ultimately reappear under another name."[18]

Similarly, Luck decries the "semantic jungle" that appears to be growing in marketing.[19] Citing conflicting definitions of *marketing* and *social marketing* in the current literature, Luck suggests that this semantic jungle has been impeding the efforts of marketers to think clearly about their discipline. He has challenged the [AMA] to create a special commission to clear up the definitional problems in marketing. Finally, a recent president of the [AMA] set the development of a consistent standard definition of marketing as a primary goal of the association.[20]

Three questions appear to be central to the "nature [broadening the concept] of marketing" controversy. First, what kinds of phenomena and issues *do* the various marketing writers perceive to be included in the scope of marketing? Second, what kinds of phenomena and issues *should* be included in the scope of marketing? Third, how can marketing be defined to both systematically encompass all the phenomena and issues that should be included and, at the same time, systematically exclude all other phenomena and issues? That is, a good definition of marketing must be both properly inclusive and exclusive. To rigorously evaluate these questions requires a conceptual model of the scope of marketing.

THE SCOPE OF MARKETING

No matter which definition of marketing one prefers, the scope of marketing is unquestionably broad. Often included are such diverse subject areas as consumer behavior, pricing, purchasing, sales management, product management, marketing communications, comparative marketing, social marketing, the efficiency/productivity of marketing systems, the role of marketing in economic development, packaging, channels of distribution, marketing research, societal issues in marketing, retailing, wholesaling, the social responsibility of marketing, international marketing, commodity marketing, and physical distribution. Though lengthy, this list of topics and issues does not exhaust the possibilities. Not all writers would include all the topics under the general rubric of marketing. The point deserving emphasis here, however, is that different commentators on marketing would *disagree* as to which topics should be excluded. The disagreement stems from fundamentally different perspectives and can best be analyzed by attempting to develop some common ground for classifying the diverse topics and issues in marketing.

The most widely used conceptual model of the scope of marketing is the familiar "4 P's" model popularized by McCarthy in the early 1960s.[21] The model is usually represented by three concentric circles. The inner circle contains the consumer, since this is the focal point of marketing effort. The second circle contains the marketing mix ("controllable factors") of price, place, promotion, and product. Finally, the third circle contains the uncontrollable factors of political and legal environment, economic environment, cultural and social environment, resources and objectives of the firm, and the existing business situation. As is readily apparent, many of the subject areas previously mentioned have no "home" in the 4 P's model. For example, where does social marketing or efficiency of marketing systems or comparative marketing belong?

During a presentation at the 1972 Fall Conference of the [AMA], Kotler made some observations concerning the desirability of classifying marketing phenomena using the concepts of *micro, macro, normative,* and *positive*.[22] These observations spurred the development of the conceptual model detailed in Table 1. The schema proposes that all marketing phenomena, issues, problems, models, theories, and research can be categorized using the three categorical dichotomies of (1) profit sector/nonprofit sector, (2) micro/macro, and (3) positive/normative. The three categorical dichotomies yield $2 \times 2 \times 2 = 8$ classes or cells in the

TABLE 1
The Scope of Marketing

		Positive	Normative
Profit Sector	Micro	(1) Problems, issues, theories, and research concerning: a. Individual consumer buyer behavior b. How firms determine prices c. How firms determine products d. How firms determine promotion e. How firms determine channels of distribution f. Case studies of marketing practices	(2) Problems, issues, normative models, and research concerning how firms *should:* a. Determine the marketing mix b. Make pricing decisions c. Make product decisions d. Make promotion decisions e. Make packaging decisions f. Make purchasing decisions g. Make international marketing decisions h. Organize their marketing departments i. Control their marketing efforts j. Plan their marketing strategy k. Apply systems theory to marketing problems l. Manage retail establishments m. Manage wholesale establishments n. Implement the marketing concept
	Macro	(3) Problems, issues, theories, and research concerning: a. Aggregate consumption patterns b. Institutional approach to marketing c. Commodity approach to marketing d. Legal aspects of marketing e. Comparative marketing f. The efficiency of marketing systems g. Whether the poor pay more h. Whether marketing spurs or retards economic development i. Power and conflict relationships in channels of distribution j. Whether marketing functions are universal	(4) Problems, issues, normative models, and research concerning: a. How marketing can be made more efficient b. Whether distribution costs too much c. Whether advertising is socially desirable d. Whether consumer sovereignty is desirable e. Whether stimulating demand is desirable f. Whether the poor should pay more g. What kinds of laws regulating marketing are optimal h. Whether vertical marketing systems are socially desirable

(continuea)

schema. Thus, the first class includes all marketing topics that are micro-positive and in the profit sector. Similarly, the second class includes all marketing activities that are micro-normative and in the profit sector, and so on throughout the table.

Some definitions are required to properly in-terpret the schema presented in Table 1. *Profit sector* encompasses the study and activities of organizations or other entities whose stated objectives include the realization of profit. Also applicable are studies that adopt the *perspective* of profit-oriented organizations. Conversely, *nonprofit* sector en-

TABLE 1—*Continued*

		Positive	Normative
		k. Whether the marketing concept is consistent with consumers' interests	i. Whether marketing should have special social responsibilities
Nonprofit Sector	Micro	(5) Problems, issues, theories, and research concerning: a. Consumers' purchasing of public goods b. How nonprofit organizations determine prices c. How nonprofit organizations determine products d. How nonprofit organizations determine promotion e. How nonprofit organizations determine channels of distribution f. Case studies of public goods marketing	(6) Problems, issues, normative models, and research concerning how nonprofit organizations *should:* a. Determine the marketing mix (social marketing) b. Make pricing decisions c. Make product decisions d. Make promotion decisions e. Make packaging decisions f. Make purchasing decisions g. Make international marketing decisions (e.g., CARE) h. Organize their marketing efforts i. Control their marketing efforts j. Plan their marketing strategy k. Apply systems theory to marketing problems
	Macro	(7) Problems, issues, theories, and research concerning: a. The institutional framework for public goods b. Whether television advertising influences elections c. Whether public service advertising influences behavior (e.g., "Smokey the Bear") d. Whether existing distribution systems for public goods are efficient e. How public goods are recycled	(8) Problems, issues, normative models, and research concerning: a. Whether society should allow politicians to be "sold" like toothpaste b. Whether the demand for public goods should be stimulated c. Whether "low informational content" political advertising is socially desirable (e.g., ten-second "spot" commercials) d. Whether the U.S. Army should be allowed to advertise for recruits

compasses the study and perspective of all organizations and entities whose stated objectives do not include the realization of profit.

The *micro/macro* dichotomy suggests a classification based on the level of aggregation. *Micro* refers to the marketing activities of individual units, normally individual organizations (firms) and consumers of households. *Macro* suggests a higher level of aggregation, usually marketing systems or groups of consumers.

The *positive/normative* dichotomy provides categories based on whether the focus of the analysis is primarily descriptive or prescriptive. *Positive* marketing adopts the perspective of attempting to describe, explain, predict, and understand the marketing activities, processes, and phenomena that actually exist. This perspective examines *what is*. In contrast, normative marketing adopts the perspective of attempting to prescribe what marketing organizations and individuals ought to do or what kinds of marketing systems a society ought to have. That is, this perspective examines what *ought to be* and what organizations and individuals *ought to do*.

ANALYZING APPROACHES TO MARKETING

An examination of Table 1 reveals that most of the early (circa 1920) approaches to the study of marketing reside in cell 3: profit sector/macro/positive. The institutional, commodity, and functional approaches analyzed existing (positive) business activities (profit sector) from a marketing systems (macro) perspective. However, not all the early marketing studies were profit/macro/positive. Weld's 1920 classic *The Marketing of Farm Products* not only examined existing distribution systems for farm commodities, but also attempted to evaluate such normative issues as: "Are there too many middlemen in food marketing?"[23] Thus, Weld's signally important work was both profit/macro/positive and profit/macro/normative. Similarly, the Twentieth Century Fund study *Does Distribution Cost Too Much?* took an essentially profit/macro/normative perspective.[24] Other important works that have combined the profit/macro/positive and the profit/macro/normative perspectives include those of Barger, Cox, and Borden.[25]

Although the profit/micro/normative (cell 2) orientation to marketing can be traced at least back to the 1920s and the works of such notables as Reed and White,[26] the movement reached full bloom in the early 1960s under proponents of the *managerial approach* to marketing, such as McCarthy.[27] The managerial approach adopts the perspective of the marketing manager, usually the marketing manager in a large manufacturing corporation. Therefore, the emphasis is micro and in the profit sector. The basic question underlying the managerial approach is: "What is the optimal marketing mix?" Consequently, the approach is unquestionably normative.

During the middle 1960s, writers such as Lazer, Kelley, Adler, and Fisk began advocating a *systems approach* to marketing.[28] Sometimes the systems approach used a profit/micro/normative perspective and simply attempted to apply to marketing certain sophisticated optimizing models (like linear and dynamic programming) developed by the operations researchers. Other writers used the systems approach in a profit/macro/positive fashion to analyze the complex interactions among marketing institutions. Finally, some used the systems approach in a profit/macro/normative fashion:

> The method used in this book is called the general systems approach. In this approach the goals, organization, inputs, and outputs of marketing are examined to determine how efficient and *how effective marketing is*. Constraints, including competition and government, are also studied because they affect both the level of efficiency and the kinds of effects obtained.[29]

During the late 1960s, the *environmental approach* to marketing was promulgated by writers such as Holloway, Hancock, Scott, and Marks.[30] This approach emphasized an essentially descriptive analysis of the environmental constraints on marketing activities. These environments included consumer behavior, culture, competition, the legal framework, technology, and the institutional framework. Consequently, this approach may be classified as profit/macro/positive.

Two trends are evident in contemporary marketing thought. The first is the trend toward *social marketing* as proposed by Kotler, Levy, and Zaltman[31] and as promulgated by others.[32] Social marketing, with its emphasis on the marketing problems of nonprofit organizations, is nonprofit/micro/normative. The second trend can be termed *societal issues*. It concerns such diverse topics as consumerism, marketing and ecology, the desirability of political advertising, social responsibility, and whether the demand for public goods should be stimulated.[33] All these works share the common element of *evaluation*. They attempt to evaluate the desirability or propriety of certain marketing activities or systems and, therefore, should be viewed as either profit/macro/normative or nonprofit/macro/normative.

In conclusion, it is possible to classify all the

approaches to the study of marketing and all the problems, issues, theories, models, and research usually considered within the scope of marketing using the three categorical dichotomies of profit sector/nonprofit sector, positive/normative, and micro/macro. This is not meant to imply that reasonable people cannot disagree as to which topics should fall within the scope of marketing. Nor does it even imply that reasonable people cannot disagree as to which cell in Table 1 is most appropriate for each issue or particular piece of research. For example, a study of the efficiency of marketing systems may have *both* positive and normative aspects; it may both *describe* existing marketing practices and *prescribe* more appropriate practices. Rather, the conceptual model of the scope of marketing presented in Table 1 provides a useful framework for analyzing fundamental differences among the various approaches to marketing and, as shall be demonstrated, the nature of marketing and marketing science controversies.

ANALYZING THE NATURE OF MARKETING AND MARKETING SCIENCE

The previous discussion on the scope of marketing now enables us to clarify some of the issues with respect to the "nature [broadening the concept] of marketing" controversy and the "Is marketing a science?" debate. Most marketing practitioners and some marketing academicians perceive the entire scope of marketing to be profit/micro/ normative (cell 2 of Table 1). That is, practitioners often perceive the entire domain of marketing to be the analysis of how to improve the decision-making processes of marketers. This perspective is exemplified by the definition of marketing Canton has suggested[34] and, somewhat surprisingly, by the definition proffered by Kotler in the first edition of *Marketing Management:* "Marketing is the analyzing, organizing, planning, and controlling of the firm's customer-impinging resources, policies, and activities with a view to satisfying the needs and wants of chosen customer groups at a profit."[35]

Most marketing academicians would chafe at delimiting the entire subject matter of marketing to simply the profit/micro/normative dimensions. Most would, at the very least, include all the phenomena, topics, and issues indicated in the top half of Table 1 (that is, cells 1 through 4). Kotler and others now wish to include in the definition of marketing *all* eight cells in Table 1.

Other fields have experienced similar discipline-definitional problems. Several decades ago, a debate raged in philosophy concerning the definition of philosophy and philosophy of science. Some philosophers chose a very narrow definition of their discipline. Popper's classic rejoinder should serve to alert marketers to the danger that narrowly circumscribing the marketing discipline may trammel marketing inquiry:

---

the theory of knowledge was inspired by the hope that it would enable us not only to know more about knowledge, but also to contribute to the advance of knowledge—of scientific knowledge, that is. . . . Most of the philosophers who believe that the characteristic method of philosophy is the analysis of ordinary language seem to have lost this admirable optimism which once inspired the rationalist tradition. Their attitude, it seems, has become one of resignation, if not despair. They not only leave the advancement of knowledge to the scientists: they even define philosophy in such a way that it becomes, by definition, incapable of making any contribution to our knowledge of the world. The self-mutilation which this so surprisingly persuasive definition requires does not appeal to me. There is no such thing as an essence of philosophy, to be distilled and condensed into a definition. *A definition of the word "philosophy" can only have the character of a convention, of an agreement; and I, at any rate, see no merit in the arbitrary proposal to define the word "philosophy" in a way that may well prevent a student of philosophy from trying to contribute,* qua *philosopher, to the advancement of our knowledge of the world.*[36]

Four conclusions seem warranted. First, definitions of the nature of marketing differ in large part because their authors perceive the total scope of marketing to be different portions of Table 1. Second, there is a growing consensus that the total scope of marketing should appropriately include all eight cells of Table 1. Third, it may be very difficult to devise a definition of marketing that would both systematically *include* all eight cells of Table 1 and, at the same time, systematically *exclude* all other phenomena. Especially difficult will be the task of including in a single definition both the normative dimensions of the *practice* of marketing and the positive dimensions of the *discipline* or *study* of marketing.

The fourth conclusion deserves special emphasis and elaboration. There is now a consensus among marketers that most nonprofit organizations, such as museums, zoos, and churches, engage in numerous activities (pricing, promoting, and so forth) that are very similar to the marketing activities of their profit-oriented cousins. There is also consensus that the marketing procedures that have been developed for profit-oriented organizations are equally applicable to nonprofit concerns. These are the two major, substantive issues involved in the debate over the nature (broadening the concept) of marketing. On these two issues there now exists substantial agreement.

The remaining two points of *disagreement* among marketers concerning the nature of marketing are minor when compared to the points of agreement. Issue one is essentially whether the activities of nonprofit organizations should be referred to as *marketing* activities or *marketing-like* activities. Given the agreement among marketers concerning the two previously cited substantive issues, the problem of distinguishing between marketing activities and marketing-like activities must be considered trivial to the extreme. The second issue on which disagreement exists concerns developing a definition of marketing. Although certainly nontrivial in nature, on this issue marketers would be well advised to take a cue from the discipline of philosophy, which has been around much longer and has yet to develop a consensus definition. That is, the discipline of marketing should not be overly alarmed about the difficulty of generating a consensus *definition* of marketing as long as there appears to be a developing consensus concerning its total *scope*.

The preceding analysis notwithstanding, there does remain a major, unresolved, substantive issue concerning the nature of marketing. Although *marketers* now recognize that nonprofit organizations (1) have marketing or marketing-like problems, (2) engage in marketing or marketing-like activities to solve these problems, and (3) can use the marketing policies, practices, and procedures that profit-oriented organizations have developed to solve marketing problems, we must candidly admit that most

nonmarketers have yet to perceive this reality. Sadly, most administrators of nonprofit organizations and many academicians in other areas still do not perceive that many problems of nonprofit organizations are basically marketing in nature, and that there is an extant body of knowledge in marketing academia and a group of trained marketing practitioners that can help resolve these problems. Until administrators of nonprofit organizations perceive that they have marketing problems, their marketing decision making will inevitably suffer. Thus, the major *substantive* problem concerning broadening the concept of marketing lies in the area of *marketing* marketing to nonmarketers.

IS MARKETING A SCIENCE?

Returning to the "Is marketing a science?" controversy, the preceding analysis suggests that a primary factor explaining the nature of the controversy is the widely disparate notions of marketing held by the participants. The common element shared by those who hold that marketing is not (and cannot) be a science is the belief that the entire conceptual domain of marketing is cell 2: profit/micro/ normative. Hutchinson clearly exemplifies this position:

> There is a real reason, however, why the field of marketing has been slow to develop an unique body of theory. It is a simple one: marketing is not a science. It is rather an art or a practice, and as such much more closely resembles engineering, medicine and architecture than it does physics, chemistry or biology. The medical profession sets us an excellent example, if we would but follow it; its members are called "practitioners" and not scientists. It is the work of physicians, as it is of any practitioner, to apply the findings of many sciences to the solution of problems. . . . It is the drollest travesty to relate the scientist's search for knowledge to the market research man's seeking after customers.[37]

If, as Hutchinson implies, the entire conceptual domain of marketing is profit/micro/normative, then marketing is not and (more importantly) probably *cannot* be a science. If, however, the conceptual domain of marketing includes both micro/positive and macro/positive phenomena, then marketing *could* be a science. That is, if phenomena such as consumer behavior, marketing institutions, marketing channels, and the efficiency of systems of distribution are included in the conceptual domain of marketing (and there appears to be a consensus to so include them), there is no reason why the study of these phenomena could not be deserving of the designation *science*.

Is marketing a science? Differing perceptions of the scope of marketing have been shown to be a primary factor underlying the debate on this question. The second factor contributing to the controversy is differing perceptions concerning the basic nature of science, a subject that will now occupy our attention.

The Nature of Science

The question of whether marketing is a science cannot be adequately answered without a clear understanding of the basic nature of science. So, what is a science? Most marketing writers cite the perspective proposed by Buzzell. A science is:

---

a classified and systematized body of knowledge, . . . organized around one or more central theories and a number of general principles, . . . usually expressed in quantitative terms, . . . knowledge which permits the prediction and, under some circumstances, the control of future events.[38]

Buzzell then proceeded to note that marketing lacks the requisite central theories to be termed a science.

Although the Buzzell perspective on science has much to recommend it, the requirement "organized around one or more central theories" seems overly restrictive. This requirement confuses the *successful culmination* of scientific efforts with *science itself*. Was the study of chemistry not a science before discoveries like the periodic table of elements? Analogously, would not a pole vaulter still be a pole vaulter even if he could not vault fifteen feet? As Homans notes, "What makes a science are its aims, not its results."[39] The major purpose of science is to discover (create? invent?) laws and theories to explain, predict, understand, and control phenomena. Withholding the label *science* until a discipline has "central theories" would not seem reasonable.

The previous comments notwithstanding, requiring a science to be organized around one or

more central theories is not completely without merit. There are strong *honorific* overtones in labeling a discipline a science.[40] These semantical overtones are so positive that, as Wartofsky has observed, even areas that are nothing more than systematized superstition attempt to usurp the term.[41] Thus, there are treatises on such subjects as the "Science of Numerology" and the "Science of Astrology." In part, the label *science* is conferred upon a discipline to signify that it has "arrived" in the eyes of other scientists, and this confirmation usually occurs only when a discipline has matured to the extent that it contains several "central theories."[42] Thus, chronologically, physics achieved the status of science before psychology, and psychology before sociology. However, the total conceptual content of the term *science* is decidedly not just honorific. Marketing does not, and should not, have to wait to be knighted by others to be a science. How, then, do sciences differ from other disciplines, if not by virtue of having central theories?

Consider the discipline of chemistry—unquestionably a science. Chemistry can be defined as "the science of substances—their structure, their properties, and the reactions that change them into other substances."[43] Using chemistry as an illustration, three observations will enable us to clarify the distinguishing characteristics of sciences. First, a science must have a distinct subject matter, a set of real-world phenomena that serve as a focal point for investigation. The subject matter of chemistry is *substances,* and chemistry attempts to understand, explain, predict, and control phenomena related to substances. Other disciplines, such as physics, are also interested in substances. However, chemistry can meaningfully lay claim to being a separate science because physics does not *focus on* substances and their reactions.

What is the basic subject matter of marketing? Most marketers now perceive the ultimate subject matter to be the *transaction*. Some subscribe to the *narrower thesis of marketing* and wish to delimit the basic subject matter to the *market* transaction. Others propose the *liberalized thesis of marketing* and wish to include within the subject matter of marketing all transactions that involve any form of *exchange of values* between parties.

Harking back to the chemistry analogue, marketing can be viewed as the *science of transactions*—their structure, their properties, and their relationships with other phenomena. Given this perspective, the subject matter of marketing would certainly overlap with other disciplines, notably economics, psychology, and sociology. The analysis of transactions is considered in each of these disciplines. Yet, only in marketing is the transaction the focal point. For example, transactions remain a tangential issue in economics, where the primary focus is on the allocation of scarce resources.[44] Therefore, the first distinguishing characteristic is that any science must have a distinct subject matter. Given that the *transaction* is the basic subject matter of marketing, marketing would seem to fulfill this requirement. Note that this conclusion is *independent* of whether one subscribes to the narrower or more liberal thesis of marketing.

A distinct subject matter alone is not sufficient to distinguish sciences from other disciplines, because all disciplines have a subject matter (some less distinct than others). The previously cited perspective of chemistry provides a second insight into the basic nature of science. Note the phrase, "their structure, their properties, and their reactions." Every science seeks to describe and classify the structure and properties of its basic subject matter. Likewise, the term *reactions* suggests that the phenomena comprising the basic subject matter of chemistry are presumed to be systematically interrelated. Thus, another distinguishing characteristic: *Every science presupposes the existence of underlying uniformities or regularities among the phenomena that comprise its subject matter. The discovery of these underlying uniformities yields empirical regularities, lawlike generalizations (propositions), and laws.*

Underlying uniformities and regularities are necessary for science because (1) a primary goal of science is to provide responsibly supported explanations of phenomena,[45] and (2) the scientific explanation of phenomena requires the existence of laws or lawlike generalizations.[46] Uniformities and regularities are also a requisite for theory development since theories are systematically related sets of statements, *including some lawlike generalizations,* that are empirically testable.[47]

The basic question for marketing is not whether there presently exist several "central theories" that serve to unify, explain, and predict marketing phenomena, as Buzzell suggests. Rather, the following should be asked: "Are there underlying unifor-

mities and regularities among the phenomena comprising the subject matter of marketing?" This question can be answered affirmatively on two grounds—one *a priori* and one empirical. Marketing is a discipline that investigates human behavior. Since numerous uniformities and regularities have been observed in other behavioral sciences,[48] there is no *a priori* reason for believing that the subject matter of marketing will be devoid of uniformities and regularities. The second ground for believing that the uniformities exist is empirical. The quantity of scholarly research conducted on marketing phenomena during the past three decades probably exceeds the total of *all* prior research in marketing. Substantial research has been conducted in the area of channels of distribution. Also, efforts in the consumer behavior dimension of marketing have been particularly prolific. Granted, some of the research has been less than profound, and the total achievements may not be commensurate with the efforts expended. Nevertheless, who can deny that *some* progress has been made or that *some* uniformities have been identified? In short, who can deny that there exist uniformities and regularities interrelating the subject matter of marketing? I, for one, cannot.

The task of delineating the basic nature of science is not yet complete. Up to this point we have used chemistry to illustrate that all sciences involve (1) a distinct subject matter and the description and classification of that subject matter, and (2) the presumption that underlying the subject matter are uniformities and regularities that science seeks to discover. The chemistry example provides a final observation. Note that "chemistry is the *science* of. . . ." This suggests that sciences can be differentiated from other disciplines by the method of analysis. At the risk of being somewhat tautologous: sciences employ a set of procedures commonly referred to as the scientific method. As Bunge suggests, "No scientific method, no science."[49] The historical significance of the development and acceptance of the method of science cannot be overstated. It has been called "the most significant intellectual contribution of Western civilization."[50] Is the method of science applicable to marketing?

Detailed explication of the scientific method is beyond the scope of this article and is discussed elsewhere.[51] Nevertheless, the cornerstone requirement of the method of science must be mentioned. The word *science* has its origins in the Latin verb *scire,* meaning "to know." Now, there are many ways *to know* things. The methods of tenacity, authority, faith, intuition, and science are often cited.[52] The characteristic that separates scientific knowledge from other ways to "know" things is the notion of *intersubjective certification.*

Scientific knowledge, in which theories, laws, and explanations are primal, must be *objective* in the sense that its truth content must be *intersubjectively certifiable.*[53] Requiring that theories, laws, and explanations be empirically testable ensures that they will be intersubjectively certifiable since different (but reasonably competent) investigators with differing attitudes, opinions, and beliefs will be able to make observations and conduct experiments to ascertain their truth content. "Science strives for objectivity in the sense that its statements are to be capable of public tests with results that do not vary essentially with the tester."[54] Scientific knowledge thus rests on the bedrock of empirical testability.

There is no reason whatsoever to presume that the scientific method of analysis is any less appropriate to marketing phenomena than to other disciplines. Similarly, scholarly researchers in marketing, although sometimes holding rather distorted notions concerning such topics as the role of laws and theories in research, seem to be at least as technically proficient as researchers in other areas. Finally, although some marketing researchers continue to cite "proprietary studies" as evidentiary support for their positions, the extent of this practice is now extremely small.

In summary, sciences (1) have a distinct subject matter drawn from the real world which is described and classified, (2) presume underlying uniformities and regularities interrelating the subject matter, and (3) adopt intersubjectively certifiable procedures for studying the subject matter. This perspective can be appropriately described as a consensus composite of philosophy of science views on science.[55] For example, Wartofsky suggests that a science is

an organized or systematic body of knowledge, using general laws or principles; that it is knowledge about the world; and that it is that kind of knowledge concerning which universal agreement can be reached by scientists sharing a common

language (or languages) and common criteria for the *justification of knowledge claims and beliefs.*[56]

Is Marketing a Science? A Conclusion

The scope of the area called marketing has been shown to be exceptionally broad. Marketing has micro/macro dimensions, profit sector/nonprofit sector dimensions, and positive/normative dimensions. Reasonable people may disagree as to which combination of these dimensions represents the *appropriate* total scope of marketing, although a consensus seems to be developing to include all eight cells in Table 1. If marketing is to be restricted to *only* the profit/micro/normative dimension (as many practitioners would view it), then marketing is not a science and could not become one. All sciences involve the explanation, prediction, and understanding of phenomena.[57] These explanations and predictions frequently serve as useful guides for developing normative decision rules and normative models. Such rules and models are then *grounded* in science.[58] Nevertheless, any discipline that is *purely* evaluative or prescriptive (normative) is not a science. At least for marketing academe, restricting the scope of marketing to its profit/micro/normative dimension is unrealistic, unnecessary, and, without question, undesirable.

Once the appropriate scope of marketing has been expanded to include at least some *positive* dimensions (cells 1, 3, 5, and 7 in Table 1), the explanation, prediction, and understanding of these phenomena could be a science. The question then becomes whether the study of the positive dimensions of marketing has the requisite characteristics of a science. Aside from the strictly honorific overtones of *nonmarketers* accepting marketing as a science, the substantive characteristics differentiating sciences from other disciplines have been shown to be (1) a distinct subject matter drawn from the real world and the description and classification of that subject matter, (2) the presumption of underlying uniformities and regularities interrelating the subject matter, and (3) the adoption of the method of science for studying the subject matter.

The *positive* dimensions of marketing have been shown to have a subject matter properly distinct from other sciences. The marketing literature is replete with description and classification. There have been discoveries (however tentative) of uniformities and regularities among marketing phenomena. Finally, although Longman deplores "the rather remarkable lack of scientific method employed by scientists of marketing,"[59] researchers in marketing are at least as committed to the method of science as are researchers in other disciplines. Therefore, the study of the *positive* dimensions of marketing can be appropriately referred to as *marketing science*.

NOTES

[1]Paul D. Converse, "The Development of a Science of Marketing," *Journal of Marketing*, Vol. 10 (July 1945), pp. 14–23.

[2]Robert Bartels, "Can Marketing Be a Science?" *Journal of Marketing*, Vol. 15 (January 1951), pp. 319–328; Kenneth D. Hutchinson, "Marketing as a Science: An Appraisal," *Journal of Marketing*, Vol. 16 (January 1952), pp. 286–293; W. J. Baumol, "On the Role of Marketing Theory," *Journal of Marketing*, Vol. 21 (April 1957), pp. 413–418; Robert D. Buzzell, "Is Marketing a Science?" *Harvard Business Review*, Vol. 41 (January–February 1963), pp. 32–40, 166–170; Weldon J. Taylor, "Is Marketing a Science? Revisited," *Journal of Marketing*, Vol. 29 (July 1965), pp. 49–53; and M. Halbert, *The Meaning and Sources of Marketing Theory* (New York: McGraw-Hill Book Co., 1965).

[3]Committee on Terms, *Marketing Definitions: A Glossary of Marketing Terms* (Chicago: American Marketing Assn., 1960).

[4]Stewart H. Rewoldt, James D. Scott, and Martin R. Warshaw, *Introduction to Marketing Management* (Homewood, Ill.: Richard D. Irwin, 1973), p. 3.

[5]Marketing Staff of The Ohio State University, "Statement of Marketing Philosophy," *Journal of Marketing*, Vol. 29 (January 1965), pp. 43–44.

[6]Philip Kotler and Sidney J. Levy, "Broadening the Concept of Marketing," *Journal of Marketing*, Vol. 33 (January 1969), p. 15.

[7]William Lazer, "Marketing's Changing Social Relationships," *Journal of Marketing*, Vol. 33 (January 1969), p. 9.

[8]David J. Luck, "Broadening the Concept of Marketing—Too Far," *Journal of Marketing*, Vol. 33 (July 1969), p. 54.

[9]Philip Kotler and Sidney J. Levy, "A New Form of Marketing Myopia: Rejoinder to Professor Luck," *Journal of Marketing*, Vol. 33 (July 1969), p. 57.

[10]Robert Ferber, "The Expanding Role of Marketing in the 1970's," *Journal of Marketing*, Vol. 34 (January 1970), pp. 29–30.

[11]Robert J. Lavidge, "The Growing Responsibilities of Marketing," *Journal of Marketing*, Vol. 34 (January 1970), p. 27.

[12]Philip Kotler and Gerald Zaltman, "Social Marketing: An Approach to Planned Social Change," *Journal of Marketing*, Vol. 35 (July 1971), p. 5.

[13]*Journal of Marketing*, Vol. 35 (July 1971): William A. Mindak and H. Malcolm Bybee, "Marketing's Application to Fund Raising," pp. 13–18; Gerald Zaltman and Ilan Vertinsky, "Health Services Marketing: A Suggested Model," pp. 19–27; John U. Farley and Harold J. Leavitt, "Marketing and Population Problems," pp. 28–33; and William G. Zikmund and William J. Stanton, "Recycling Solid Wastes: Channels-of-Distribution Problem," pp. 34–39.

[14]Leslie Dawson, "Marketing Science in the Age of Aquarius," *Journal of Marketing*, Vol. 35 (July 1971), p. 71.

[15]Philip Kotler, "A Generic Concept of Marketing," *Journal of Marketing*, Vol. 36 (April 1972), p. 49.

[16]William G. Nichols, "Conceptual Conflicts in Marketing," *Journal of Economics and Business*, Vol. 26 (Winter 1974), p. 142.

[17]James M. Carman, "On the Universality of Marketing," *Journal of Contemporary Business*, Vol. 2 (Autumn 1973), p. 14.

[18]Robert Bartels, "The Identity Crisis in Marketing," *Journal of Marketing*, Vol. 38 (October 1974), p. 76.

[19]David J. Luck, "Social Marketing: Confusion Compounded," *Journal of Marketing*, Vol. 38 (October 1974), pp. 70–72.

[20]Robert J. Eggert, "Eggert Discusses Additional Goals for His Administration, Seeks Help in Defining Marketing," *Marketing News*, September 15, 1974.

[21]E. J. McCarthy, *Basic Marketing* (Homewood, Ill.: Richard D. Irwin, 1960).

[22]These observations were apparently extemporaneous since they were not included in his published paper: Philip Kotler, "Defining the Limits of Marketing," in *Marketing Education and the Real World, 1972 Fall Conference Proceedings,* Boris W. Becker and Helmut Becker, eds. (Chicago: American Marketing Assn., 1972), pp. 48–56.

[23]L. D. H. Weld, *The Marketing of Farm Products* (New York: Macmillan, 1920).

[24]Paul W. Stewart, *Does Distribution Cost Too Much?* (New York: Twentieth Century Fund, 1939).

[25]Harold Barger, *Distribution's Place in the Economy Since 1869* (Princeton: Princeton University Press, 1955); Reavis Cox, *Distribution in a High Level Economy* (Englewood Cliffs, N.J.: Prentice-Hall, 1965); and Neil Borden, *The Economic Effects of Advertising* (Chicago: Richard D. Irwin, 1942).

[26]Virgil Reed, *Planned Marketing* (New York: Ronald Press, 1930); and P. White and W. S. Hayward, *Marketing Practice* (New York: Doubleday, Page & Co., 1924).

[27]Same reference as note 21.

[28]William Lazer and Eugene Kelley, "Systems Perspective of Marketing Activity," in *Managerial Marketing: Perspectives and Viewpoints,* rev. ed. (Homewood, Ill.: Richard D. Irwin, 1962); Lee Adler, "Systems Approach to Marketing," *Harvard Business Review,* Vol. 45 (May–June, 1967); and George Fisk, *Marketing Systems: An Introductory Analysis* (New York: Harper & Row, 1967).

[29]Fisk, same reference as note 28, p. 3.

[30]Robert J. Holloway and Robert S. Hancock, *The Environment of Marketing Behavior* (New York: John Wiley & Sons, 1964); Robert J. Holloway and Robert S. Hancock, *Marketing in a Changing Environment* (New York: John Wiley & Sons, 1968); and Richard A. Scott and Norton E. Marks, *Marketing and Its Environment* (Belmont, Calif.: Wadsworth, 1968).

[31]Kotler and Levy, Same reference as note 6; Kotler and Zaltman, same reference as note 12; and Kotler, same reference as note 15.

[32]Mindak and Bybee, same reference as note 13; Farley and Leavitt, same reference as note 13; Zikmund and Stanton, same reference as note 13; Carman, same reference as note 17; and Donald P. Robin, "Success in Social Marketing," *Journal of Business Research,* Vol. 3 (July 1974), pp. 303–310.

[33]Lazer, same reference as note 7; Dawson, same reference as note 14; David A. Aaker and George S. Day, *Consumerism* (New York: Free Press, 1971); Norman Kangun, *Society and Marketing* (New York: Harper & Row, 1972); Frederick E. Webster, Jr., *Social Aspects of Marketing* (Englewood Cliffs, N.J.: Prentice-Hall, 1974); Reed Moyer, *Macromarketing* (New York: John Wiley & Sons, 1972); John R. Wish and Stephen H. Gamble, *Marketing and Social Issues* (New York: John Wiley & Sons, 1971); Ross L. Goble and Roy Shaw, *Controversy and Dialogue in Marketing* (Englewood Cliffs, N.J.: Prentice-Hall, 1975); Ronald R. Gist, *Marketing and Society* (New York: Holt, Rinehart & Winston, 1971); and William Lazer and Eugene Kelley, *Social Marketing: Perspectives and Viewpoints* (Homewood, Ill.: Richard D. Irwin, 1973).

[34]Irving D. Canton, "A Functional Definition of Marketing," *Marketing News,* July 15, 1973.

[35]Philip Kotler, *Marketing Management* (Englewood Cliffs, N.J.: Prentice-Hall, 1967), p. 12.

[36]Karl R. Popper, *The Logic of Scientific Discovery* (New York: Harper & Row, 1959), p. 19. [Emphasis added.]

[37]Hutchinson, same reference as note 2.

[38]Buzzell, same reference as note 2, p. 37.

[39]George C. Homans, *The Nature of Social Science* (New York: Harcourt, Brace & World, 1967), p. 4.

[40]Ernest Nagel, *The Structure of Science* (New York: Harcourt, Brace & World, 1961), p. 2.

[41]Marx W. Wartofsky, *Conceptual Foundations of Scientific Thought* (New York: Macmillan Co., 1968), p. 44.

[42]Thomas S. Kuhn, *The Structure of Scientific Revelations* (Chicago: University of Chicago Press, 1970), p. 161.

[43]Linus Pauling, *College Chemistry* (San Francisco: W. H. Freeman & Co., 1956), p. 15.

[44]Richard H. Leftwich, *The Price System and Resource Allocation* (New York: Holt, Rinehart & Winston, 1966), p. 2.

[45]Same reference as note 40, p. 15.

[46]Carl G. Hempel, *Aspects of Scientific Explanation* (New York: Free Press, 1965), pp. 354–364.

[47]Richard S. Rudner, *The Philosophy of Social Science* (Englewood Cliffs, N.J.: Prentice-Hall, 1966), p. 10; and Shelby D. Hunt, "The Morphology of Theory and the General Theory of Marketing," *Journal of Marketing,* Vol. 35 (April 1971), pp. 65–68.

[48]Bernard Berelson and Gary Steiner, *Human Behavior: An Inventory of Scientific Findings* (New York: Harcourt, Brace & World, 1964).

[49]Mario Bunge, *Scientific Research I: The Search for System* (New York: Springer-Verlag, 1967), p. 12.

[50]Charles W. Morris, "Scientific Empiricism," in *Foundations of the Unity of Science,* Vol. 1, Otto Newrath, Rudolf Carnap and Charles Morris, eds. (Chicago: University of Chicago Press, 1955), p. 63.

[51]Shelby D. Hunt, *Marketing Theory: Conceptual Foundation of Research in Marketing* (Columbus, Ohio: Grid Publishing Co., 1976).

[52]Morris R. Cohen and Ernest Nagel, *Logic and the Scientific Method* (New York: Harcourt, Brace & World, 1934), p. 193.

[53]Same reference as note 36, p. 44.

[54]Carl G. Hempel, "Fundamentals of Concept Formation in Empirical Science," in *Foundations of the Unity of Science,* Vol. 2, Otto Newrath, ed. (Chicago: University of Chicago Press, 1970), p. 695.

[55]See, for example: Nagel, same reference as note 40, p. 4; May Brodbeck, *Readings in the Philosophy of the Social Sciences* (New York: Macmillan Co., 1968), pp. 1–11; Richard B. Braithwaite, *Scientific Explanation* (Cambridge: At the University Press, 1951), pp. 1–21; B. F. Skinner, *Science and Human Behavior* (New York: Macmillan Co., 1953), pp. 14–22; Rudner, same reference as note 47, pp. 7–9; Abraham Kaplan, *The Conduct of Inquiry* (Scranton, Pa.: Chandler Publishing Co., 1964), p. 32; Popper, same reference as note 36, pp. 44–48; and Hempel, same reference as note 54, p. 672.

[56]Same reference as note 41, p. 23.

[57]Nagel, same reference as note 40, p. 15; Henry E. Kyburg, Jr., *Philosophy of Science* (New York: Macmillan Co., 1968), p. 3; Carl G. Hempel, "The Theoretician's Dilemma," in *Aspects of Scientific Explanation* (New York: Free Press, 1965), p. 173; and Nicholas Rescher, *Scientific Explanation* (New York: Free Press, 1970), p. 4.

[58]Mario Bunge, *Scientific Research II: The Search for Truth* (New York: Springer-Verlag, 1967), p. 132.

[59]Kenneth A. Longman, "The Management Challenge to Marketing Theory," in *New Essays in Marketing Theory,* George Fisk, ed. (Boston: Allyn & Bacon, 1971), p. 10.

DISCUSSION QUESTIONS

1. Many of the articles in the *Journal of Marketing Research* (JMR) can be classified as having a high degree of quantitatively sophisticated profit/micro/normative content. At the same time, *JMR* is often criticized as being too scientific. Are the preceding two statements contradictory? Is the discipline called management science, a science? Could it possibly be a science? Is marketing management a science? Is accounting a science? Could accounting be a science?

2. Some marketers believe that marketing is an art, not a science. Others have observed that marketing people have been neither good artists nor good scientists. Finally, some have pointed out that truly great scientists have also been great artists since genius in both emanates from the taking of great care. Evaluate these positions. Be sure to define carefully what you mean by art, science, artist, and scientist.

3. The three dichotomies model purports to be a classificational schema that encompasses the entire scope of marketing. Examine several issues of the *Journal of Marketing* and the *JMR*. Determine which articles fall into which categories. Can some fall into several categories simultaneously? Conduct the same procedure for the chapters and major issues in a marketing textbook. Whenever an article, chapter or issue cannot be classified satisfactorily, propose a modification of the schema to accommodate the issue.

PREFACE TO

"Toward a Formal Theory of Marketing Exchanges"

"Toward a Formal Theory of Marketing Exchanges" reflects another step in my search for a theory of marketing based on *social* exchange and builds on an earlier article.* The primary goal is to forge a conceptualization of the central constructs of a theory of exchange and to suggest one possible direction for theory construction. Reflecting my strong commitment to the history of ideas, I have attempted to tie my ideas to prior work by social scientists as well as by marketers. At the same time, an effort was made to forge a unique perspective. The framework advocated here is conducive to either axiomatic or nonaxiomatic (e.g., causal, functional, structural, processual, systems) programs of theory construction.

---

*Richard P. Bagozzi, "Marketing as Exchange: A Theory of Transactions in the Marketplace," *American Behavioral Science* (March–April 1978), pp. 535–536.

13

TOWARD A FORMAL THEORY OF MARKETING EXCHANGES

RICHARD P. BAGOZZI

The idea of exchange is central to the meaning of marketing. Indeed, marketing scholars generally agree that the fundamental phenomenon to be explained, predicted, and controlled in the marketplace is the exchange relationship (Kotler, 1972; Hunt, 1976). Disagreements surrounding the role of the idea of exchange in marketing primarily center on the scope or breadth of the concept rather than on its content (cf., Bagozzi, 1977; Ferrell and Zey-Ferrell, 1977). Nevertheless the discipline lacks both a coherent conceptualization of exchange and a well-developed theory for explaining exchange.

This article has two objectives. The initial goal is to outline the substance of exchange and discuss a number of dimensions not treated before in the marketing literature. A second purpose is to present a formal theory of exchange in the marketplace. The theory is an elaboration and extension of a model proposed earlier by the author (Bagozzi, 1978).

THE CONCEPT OF EXCHANGE

The notion of exchange is universal and as ancient as man himself. Unfortunately, this aspect of the concept has lead marketers to take it for granted and regard it as a primitive concept, not requiring further definition. Reliance on the common-sense, every day idea of exchange has prevented the development of the concept itself and its role in marketing theory. In order to understand, explain, and influence exchanges, it will be necessary to begin with an abstraction of what it is and means.

Existing Conceptualizations

Nearly every behavioral science studies exchange as an accepted domain of its respective dis-

Source: Reprinted with permission from *Conceptual and Theoretical Developments in Marketing*, O. C. Ferrell, Stephen W. Brown, and Charles W. Lamb, Jr., eds., Chicago, Ill.: American Marketing Association, 1979, 431–447.

cipline. Well-developed ideas on exchange exist in economics, sociology, psychology, and anthropology. The pervasiveness of the concept in different academic circles suggests its fundamental character, placing it in the company of other key ways of representing human behavior such as functionalism, structuralism, or general systems theory. A by-product of this state of affairs is the apparent overlap in subject matter between marketing and the various behavioral sciences. To better understand the implications of this overlap for marketing theory, it will prove useful to examine its nature and extent.

Five points deserve mention as to the nature of the commonality in subject matter. First, no single, systematic exchange paradigm can be identified across the behavioral sciences. Rather, each discipline has conceived of exchange in a narrow, specialized way. Typically, the conceptualization found in a particular discipline is tied implicitly or explicitly to the *Weltanschauung* of that discipline. To economists, exchange entails a transfer of money for a product or service. The motivation for trade is one of self-gain; the process is rational; and the most well-developed theory applies to exchanges in perfectly competitive markets. Economic theories of exchange are asocial in the sense that the actual processes of interaction among actors are not modeled. Rather, the outcomes of exchanges are predicted, and the social process is presumed operative. Further, as exemplified in bilaterial monopoly and other forms of economic exchange, the exact outcome of any transaction is left indeterminate, given the theory. Finally, economic models of exchange focus on two actors who each possess only a single physical entity desired by the other, and the relationship between actors is regarded as an impersonal, one-shot affair.

To psychologists and some sociologists, exchange is regarded as the joint outcome in a relationship resulting when both parties choose from among two or more actions potentially affecting each other (e.g., Thibaut and Kelley, 1959). The exchange is defined to occur in relatively restricted and contrived settings such as the prisoner's dilemma game. The vast majority of research has examined exchanges wherein two actors interact, only two mutually exclusive actions by each are allowed, the actors cannot leave the relationship, the range and domain of choices are identical for both actors, choices are made simultaneously, communication with the other actor is not allowed, only four possible outcomes exist, and the motivation and/or rewards for transacting are limited to monetary gain. Unlike economic exchange, however, the possibility exists for the development of on-going transactions, and various interpersonal processes such as social influence, conflict, and bargaining can be modeled.

Finally, to anthropologists and many sociologists, the defining characteristic of exchange is its social nature. That is, rather than focusing on the objects of exchange, the decision calculus of the actors, or the actual transfer, per se, emphasis is placed on the function of exchanges for a specific group or society at large. The functions of exchange are typically symbolic and often reflect normative constraints on actors or positions in a social system. Exchange, then, is used metaphorically to refer to implicit transactions. Some anthropologists even stress that apparent one-way transfers constitute instances of exchange (e.g., gift-giving, theft) and that psychic or social entities are often more important than physical ones to the relationship (cf., Sahlins, 1965; Firth, 1973).

In sum, no uniform notion of exchange exists in the behavioral sciences, and many narrow, idiosyncratic viewpoints can be identified. This is, perhaps, to be expected, given the different histories and purposes of each discipline. However, the commonality of subject matter is a surface one—in name only—in that the substance of the overlap is minimal.

A second, related point to note about the overlap is that seldom is a formal definition of exchange provided. Many theorists use the term in a loose, descriptive sense to refer to any relationship in which tangible things change hands. Others use the term, as noted above, metaphorically. More often than not, the meaning of exchange is taken for granted. In addition, some researchers use the term in titles to their articles but then proceed to ignore it and investigate other phenomena such as power (cf., Cook and Emerson, 1978). On balance, it is difficult to say in what sense and to what degree the overlap in subject matter is genuine, given the vague and ambiguous use of the term.

Third, it should be noted that the study of exchange constitutes only part of the entire realm of the subject matter in each respective behavioral science. In some disciplines, the concept of exchange represents one of a number of ways for examining more basic or more general phenomena. In this sense, exchange constitutes a methodology or conceptual orientation. Sociologists, for example, investigate social behavior from the viewpoints of conflict theory, structural-functionalism, or role-theory, as well as exchange "theory." In other instances, exchange, itself, is the dependent variable for study, but only one of many others to be found in a discipline. Thus, in addition to social exchanges, psychologists study attitudes, small group processes, and decision-making, among other subjects.

A fourth point to stress is that many disciplines examine exchange behaviors but do so primarily to shed light on other issues. The study of exchange plays a subordinate role. For example, some anthropologists investigate the meaning that exchange has for kinship systems or other aspects of primitive societies. Similarly, sociologists studying macrosocial phenomena often use structural concepts as explanatory variables, but simultaneously employ exchange concepts as assumed *premises* with which to build their theories (e.g., Blau, 1964). Anthropologists and sociologists are typically interested more in the larger question of social order and not so much in the exchanges between individuals or institutions.

Finally, it should be noted that no discipline in the behavioral sciences claims exchange as its fundamental subject matter. Given this fact and the fact that exchange performs a limited, varied, subordinate, and vaguely defined role in the behavioral sciences, the opportunity exists for marketers to develop a relatively unique, general, and fundamental phenomenon for study. Already, the weight of historical precedence and an emerging consensus among marketing scholars recognizes exchange as the core of the discipline. The task remains for marketers to identify general characteristics and principles of exchange and to explain variation in exchange behavior with a general theory or theories.

The Elements of Exchange

We know very little about exchange behavior and lack a formal conceptualization of its parts. Alderson (1965) does provide a "law of exchange" and suggests the centrality of the concept in marketing. But he never defines what he means by exchange. Kotler (1972) presents certain axioms describing exchanges, Bagozzi (1975) discusses the types of exchange and their meaning, and Hunt (1976) helps us to view the discipline as "the science of transactions." But none of these authors has examined the content of exchange in great depth. Although such an examination is beyond the scope of this article, an attempt will be made to point out several key aspects of the concept that deserve further attention.

All exchanges involve a transfer of something tangible or intangible, actual or symbolic, between two or more social actors. For purposes of analysis, social actors might include actual persons, positions in a social network (e.g., roles), groups, institutions, or organizations, or any social unit capable of abstraction. The thing or things exchanged may be physical (e.g., goods, money), psychic (e.g., affect), or social (e.g., status). Rather than entailing a give-and-take of one thing for another, most exchanges are probably characterized by the transfer of bundles of physical, psychic, and social entities. The social actors may or may not be fully aware of all dimensions of what is exchanged or even their own motives or purposes for transacting. Usually, however, the things exchanged will be rewarding or punishing in some way to the parties involved. The values of the things exchanged may be sought as ends in themselves or as means to ends.

The determinants of exchange are varied. Often they arise out of the volition of individual social actors who function more or less as rational decision makers. Sometimes exchanges emerge out of compulsion, coercion, or habit. They may also result as a social response to norms or the expectations or pressures of others. One factor affecting the origin or course of an exchange is the availability of alternative sources for satisfaction. Whether one will enter or remain in an exchange and what and

how much one will give and get will depend on what the market will bear. Alternative sources of satisfaction act as constraints on the relationship as well as bargaining ploys. In different degrees, any social actor in an exchange will have alternative sources for the same object or for substitute sources of satisfaction. All of the above determinants of exchange will be discussed more fully later in the article.

If the concept of exchange is to be used in an explanatory—as opposed to a purely descriptive—sense, then it will have to be conceptualized as a phenomenon capable of variation in one or more ways. This author believes that exchanges might be fruitfully conceived as a threefold categorization of *outcomes, experiences,* and *actions,* each varying in degree and occurring to the actors as individuals, jointly or shared, or both. Outcomes in an exchange refer to physical, social, or symbolic objects or events accruing to the actors as a consequence of their relationship. Each person might receive separate outcomes such as a buyer and seller obtain in a consummated exchange. Or the parties might achieve mutual, shared rewards, as well as individual gains. The increase in sales connected to a new promotion campaign and resulting from give-and-take between the marketing and sales departments would be an example of joint outcomes. Individuals in both departments might share in the direct profit and social prestige of the successful campaign, as well as the salary regularly earmarked for them for performing their respective everyday roles. In any event, outcomes in an exchange refer to the things the actors get, either as individuals, a unit, or both.

Another important variable representing an exchange is the experiences the actors feel. Experiences are psychological states and consist of affective, cognitive, or moral dimensions. They typically are conveyed symbolically through the objects exchanged, the functions performed by the exchange, or the meanings attributed to the exchange. Again, experiences can be felt by each actor individually, as well as jointly. Joint experiences entail what sociologists term "social contructions," in that both actors in the exchange are thought to produce a mutual, shared understanding as a consequence of their interchanges. The common joy or feeling of accomplishment felt by a husband and wife as they interact in a consumer decision-making process would be an example of a joint experience in this sense.

The final variable with which to represent an exchange is the actions performed by the actors as a product of their interchange. Actions might represent individual choices and responses or joint commitments. Examples include the degree of cooperation, competition, or conflict in the dyad; and the intensity, duration, and timing of actions. For instance, one measure of the conflictual nature of exchange between wholesaler and retailer might be the number of threats transmitted between them in a period of time.

The goal of conceptualizing exchanges as specific outcomes, experiences, or actions is to provide a set of dependent or endogenous variables for study. With these as the subject matter of marketing, efforts can be made to specify explanatory variables and relate these to exchange in an overall theory.

THE ANTECEDENTS TO EXCHANGE

To explain exchange (i.e., variation in individual or joint outcomes, experiences, or actions), four classes of determinants are hypothesized: social influence, social actor characteristics, third party ef-

fects, and situational contingencies (see Figure 1). Each is briefly described below.

Social Influence Between the Actors

It is hypothesized that the parties to an exchange satisfy individual needs and reach mutual accommodations through a process of social negotiation. This process involves a give-and-take wherein the parties communicate their desires, intentions, and purposes; and adjustments in offers, counteroffers, and standards of acceptability are made throughout the process until an agreement to exchange or not is made. The process occurs both covertly and overtly, and the parties may or may not be fully aware of its dynamics or their role and outcomes during the negotiations.

The process of social negotiation entails a communication of rewarding or punishing stimuli through one or more of four modes of influence: threats, promises, warnings, or mendations (Tedeschi, Schlenker, and Bonoma, 1973). A threat is made when one social actor sends a message conveying a punishment to the other social actor and the message is conveyed under conditions wherein the sender can actually mediate the punishment and no attempt is made to conceal the influ-

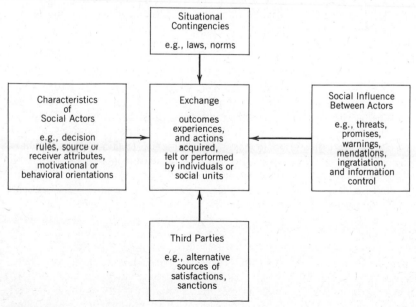

FIGURE 1
The determinants of exchange.

ence. For example, if a manufacturer were to state in a communication to a retail customer, "If you reduce the shelf space devoted to brand *X,* then we will discontinue our promotion credit to you," then he or she would be employing a threat mode of influence. In contrast, a promise is made when one social actor sends a rewarding message to another such that the sender actually mediates the reward and no attempt is made to conceal the influence. The statement by a manufacturer, "We will give you a promotion credit of 5 percent of sales," would be an example of a promise in the above sense.

Threats and promises (and all modes of social influence) can be contingent/noncontingent, request-specific/nonspecific, and consequences-specific/nonspecific. A contingent message uses the if-then implicative form to specify what will happen to the receiver of the message under certain conditions. The noncontingent message omits the conditions and relies solely on an assertion of intent or opinion on the part of the sender. The threat example in the previous paragraph is a contingent one, while the promise example is noncontingent. Further, the threat example is relatively specific as to its request and consequences.

A warning is said to occur when a sender communicates that a punishment will befall a target under certain conditions. The sender does not attempt to conceal his or her influence attempt under this mode; however, unlike the threatener, the sender of a warning does not directly mediate the punishing stimulus. Rather, either an external agent is involved and/or the punishment is contingent on the action or inaction of the target. The use of fear advertisements by the Heart Association is perhaps the best example of a warning in the sense defined here. A mendation is said to occur when a sender implies that a reward will accrue to a target should he or she act or fail to act. Again, the sender does not attempt to conceal his or her influence attempt; however, unlike the promiser, the sender of a mendation does not directly mediate the reward but a third party and/or the target does. An example of the mendation mode of influence might be the following statement made by a salesperson to a potential customer: "If you buy machine *Y* before July 1, when the law changes, then you will be able to realize the special income tax credit."

Threats and promises usually imply the potential for the exercise of power by one actor over another. Warnings and mendations, in contrast, are, perhaps, best exemplified by the general mode of influence termed "persuasion," where the element of force or coercion is presumed absent and the ideal of "free choice" is approached. Behavior in the marketplace is, of course, characterized by all four modes in varying degrees. These modes share the attribute that influence attempts are not concealed. Influence can also be employed when the source of communication desires to hide his or her attempts. Under these conditions, the clandestine influence takes on a distinct manipulatory flavor. Reinforcement control, information control, and ingratiation are three types of influence in this sense. A final point to note with respect to the use of social influence between actors in an exchange is that the impact of any mode depends on the characteristics of the social actors as well as the situation surrounding the exchange. It is to these that we now turn.

Characteristics of the Social Actors

The starting point for any exchange is the needs of the individual actors, the values of things that can be exchanged, and the give-and-take reflected in the social influence comprising the negotiations. The exact course of any exchange, including its final outcome, will depend, in part, on the unique interface of the characteristics of the actors.

Two kinds of characteristics seem salient. The first is termed source/receiver characteristics and has been studied extensively by communication researchers (cf., McGuire, 1969, 1972). Source characteristics include such variables as attraction, expertise, credibility, prestige, trustworthiness, or status. Receiver characteristics comprise such variables as self-confidence, background attributes, cognitive styles, and certain personality traits. In general, source and receiver characteristics influence exchanges through their ability to authenticate or deauthenticate the subjective expected utility associated with communicated threats, promises, warnings, or mendations (e.g., Tedeschi, et al., 1973: 65–83). For example, one study indicates that the greater the perceived similarity of a salesperson (a source characteristic akin to attraction), the greater the probability of purchase (Brock, 1965). The premise is that mendations from a similar salesperson were believed more, while those from the dissimilar salesperson were discounted. In a similar manner, other source/receiver characteristics interact with the modes of social influence to affect evaluative behavior and compliance.

A second kind of social actor characteristic influencing exchanges is the interpersonal orientation of the actors. Interpersonal orientations refer to the degree of motivational predispositions or behavioral tendencies the actors bring to an exchange. Research in bargaining and negotiation suggests that the conduct and outcomes of the exchange depend on the degree to which the parties (1) have a positive interest in the welfare of the other as well as one's own, (2) are oriented toward equitable or joint gain as opposed to doing better than the other or maximizing individual gain, regardless of what or how the other does, and/or (3) are sensitive to interpersonal aspects of relationships with the other (e.g., Rubin and Brown, 1975). Some individuals come to an exchange with cooperative, competitive, malevolent, rigid, responsive, etc., orientations, and these dispositions constrain the course of give-and-take by dictating the conditions for trade. One way in which interpersonal orientations are manifest is through the decision rules followed independently or jointly by the actors. Decision rules include, among others, maximize one's own gain; maximize the gain of the other; maximize the joint gain; from each according to one's ability, to each according to one's need; and balance outcomes over inputs (equity). A second way interpersonal orientations function is through affective processes such as is reflected in empathy, altruism, and charity motivated decisions.

Third Party Effects

Exchanges are also influenced by the constraints or opportunities afforded by third parties, i.e., social actors outside an exchange but with an actual or potential interest in activities or outcomes of the exchange. Following Thibaut and Kelley (1959), two standards held by the actors in an exchange seem salient. First, the parties to an exchange evaluate potential offers in light of their comparison level (CL) which represents the degree of satisfaction required or desired by the parties. The CL will be a function of the needs of the actors; their history of reinforcement, satiation, or deprivation; and their expectations tempered by the rewards that relevant others receive. Although the CL indicates the amount of benefits the parties would like to obtain

in an exchange relationship, the acceptable amount may be less than this, particularly if the rewards available from other sources of satisfaction are lower yet. Thus, each party to an exchange also has a comparison level for alternatives (CL_{alt}) which represents the amount of rewards potentially accessible from a third party. The hypothesis is that, if the level of outcomes actually received by an exchange partner is below one's CL_{alt}, then he or she will leave the relationship for the more satisfying alternative.

Third parties also serve as influences on exchanges in two other respects. First, through social comparison processes with third parties, the actors in an exchange arrive at standards of equity with which they evaluate their actual and anticipated outcomes. Second, third parties use social influence (e.g., persuasion, coercion) to affect the outcome of exchanges. Over the years, for example, the executive branch of the federal government has used moral persuasion to induce manufacturers to limit their price increases. Similarly, environmentalists use influence tactics to alter the exchange relationship between polluters and consumers.

Situational Contingencies

Situational contingencies represent another class of determinants facilitating or constraining exchanges. Four categories may be identified: the physical environment, the psychological climate, the social milieu, and the legal setting. The physical environment places limitations on the actions the parties to an exchange can make. Time pressures; the structure and content of issues, alternatives, and actions; and the quantity and quality of lighting, air, and noise are all instances to physical environment constraints affecting exchanges. Closely related to this factor is the psychological environment which encompasses the level of emotional (e.g., anxiety provoking) and cognitive (e.g., informational) stimuli surrounding an exchange and potentially disrupting it. The social milieu also influences exchanges and includes social class, peer group, and reference group pressures. This aspect of situational contingencies differs from third party influences in that the former deals with generalized expectancies that the parties feel and do not necessarily attribute to specific social actors, while the latter refers to relatively specific, felt pressures identified with particular social actors. Further, the social milieu typically entails internalized compulsions in the form of norms, morals, or ethics, while third party influences are more external and tied to the actions of others. Nevertheless, the force of the social milieu is backed often by incentives or sanctions, should one stray from social expectations. Finally, the legal setting constitutes a particularly potent type of influence on exchange. Laws govern, in part, how, when, where, what, and why parties exchange.

TOWARD A FORMAL THEORY

Overview of an Earlier Theory

In another article (Bagozzi, 1978), the author derived a theory which hypothesizes that marketing exchanges are a social process functioning under economic and psychological constraints. The unit of analysis was the dyadic relationship between two actors, and the dyad was also assumed to interact with other buyers and sellers. To explain exchanges, a utility function for the dyad was hypothesized, and a budget constraint and production functions were specified. In this sense, the theory is similar in form to that proposed by economists in "the new theory of consumer behavior," although the unit of analysis in this latter tradition is the individual decision maker rather than the exchange relationship itself (cf., Becker, 1965; Lancaster, 1971; Rosen, 1974). The nature of that part of the theory based on the new theory of consumer behavior may be summarized in words as follows:

In order to achieve desired levels of satisfaction from the consumption of goods and services, the [actors in an exchange relationship] are assumed to interact with each other and the providers of goods and services. Through decision-making processes and interpersonal influence within the dyad and similar exchanges between the dyad and outsiders, it is hypothesized that the [actors] combine time and market goods and services to produce [a] theoretical construct termed "subjective satisfaction" which represents the joint, negotiated outcome of decision-making and exchange for the [dyad]. The entire exchange process occurs subject to the constraints on the dyad's resources of time and wealth. (Bagozzi, 1978, 545–546)

Two important departures from the new theory of consumer behavior should be noted. First, unlike economists who have not conceptualized the arguments to the utility function very well and who have failed to operationalize these, the theory proposed by Bagozzi (1978) explicitly models the arguments as theoretical constructs consisting of affective, cognitive, and moral mental events shared by the actors. Further, correspondence rules and measurements are suggested and integrated with the theory in an overall model. Second, the theory developed by Bagozzi formally introduces psychic and social costs in the budget constraint equation, rather than allowing these to remain as strictly mathematically, assumed "shadow prices," as done in the economic theory. Operationalizations and correspondence rules are also proposed within the context of the overall model.

The modified theory was then extended to encompass social psychological processes such as those listed in Figure 1. This was accomplished through the use of a structural equation model. In this model, subjective satisfaction from goods, psychic and social costs, and the perceived resources of the dyad (e.g., permanent income) are endogenous variables, while social influence, situational contingencies, characteristics of the actors, and third party effects are exogenous determinants.

Extension of the Theory

In their interactions with each other and with other social actors, the parties to an exchange are presumed to maximize

$$U_d = U(Z_a, Z_c, Z_{mb}) \qquad (1)$$

where U_d is the utility for the dyad, and the Z_i's represent the joint, subjective "satisfactions" produced by the actors through their interdependencies and actions. The subjective satisfactions are hypothesized to occur as three basic, shared mental events[1]: affect (Z_a), cognitions (Z_c), and moral beliefs (Z_{mb}). Using an argument somewhat similar to that made in the new theory of consumer behavior (e.g., Becker, 1965), each dyad is posited to possess a set of production functions that determine in what way and in what amount the Z_i's are "produced" by certain inputs such as market goods and services (x_j), time (t_k), psychological characteristics of the actors (pc_l), and social-forces (s_m):

$$Z_i = Z(x_j, l_k, pc_l, s_m, \ldots) \qquad (2)$$

Notice that the Z_i's and the variables on the right-hand side of equation (2) constitute theoretical concepts which may be operationalized. The exact forms for the production functions are thus amenable to theoretical development and testing. Although this is a necessary prerequisite for the attainment of an explanatory theory, the conditions are not met by current conceptualizations in the new theory of consumer behavior.

To complete the development of the theory, the utility of the dyad, U_d, must be maximized subject to both the production functions and psychological and social constraints on the dyad.[2] Rather than assuming that social influence, situational contingencies, psychological characteristics, and third party efforts are exogenous as done in Bagozzi (1978), however, these variables may be treated as endogenous processes by introducing them into the production functions.

As a simple example, consider the case where a single satisfaction (Z_a) is produced with a single good (x) and a single social-force construct (s). Thus, maximizing U_d is equivalent to maximizing the output of Z_a:

$$U_d^* - Z_a(x, s) \qquad (3)$$

Following a logic paralleling Becker (1974), it is possible to represent the social-force influencing the exchange as the following additive function:

$$s = d + e \qquad (4)$$

where d represents the social-force due to the interaction within the dyad (e.g., through the modes of social influence), and e stands for the amount of social-force from other factors and not as a function of the dyad (e.g., situational contingencies, third party effects).

The income constraint for this situation can then be written as

$$p_x x + p_s d = I \qquad (5)$$

where p_x is the price of a unit of x; p_s is the expenditure on social influence between the parties to an exchange; and I is money income. Combining equations (4) and (5) yields:

$$p_x x + p_s s = I + p_s e = S \qquad (6)$$

where S represents "social" income.

Thus maximizing equation (3) subject to equation (6), produces the following marginal utilities for an equilibrium:

$$\left. \frac{\partial U_d^*}{\partial x} \right\} \frac{\partial U_d^*}{\partial s} = \frac{p_x}{p_s} \qquad (7)$$

That is, the parties in the dyad, as a producing and consuming unit, equate the ratio of the marginal utilities for x and s to their respective marginal costs. Similarly, following Becker (1974: 1070), it is possible to show that

$$w_x \eta_x + (1 - w_x)\eta_s = 1 - \alpha \qquad (8)$$

where $w_x = \frac{p_x x}{S}$, i.e., the total expenditure on x expressed as a fraction of S; η_x is the own-income elasticity of x; η_s is the own-income elasticity of s: and $\alpha = \frac{p_s e}{S}$, i.e. the share of e in S. Thus, an increase in income—holding prices constant—would increase the demand for x and s. However, given equation (8), a one percent change in income will produce a change of less than one percent in x and s. The exact change will be equal to $1 - \alpha$; i.e., the change due to an increase in income will be reduced by the percentage share of social-forces from outside the dyad (e.g., due to situational contingencies and third party effects). As a result, the relative impact of a change in income on utility will be mitigated the more potent are external social-forces.

Suggestions for Future Research

The theory outlined above provides a framework for modeling social exchange, including the impact of individual differences and social and environmental factors. A number of issues deserve further consideration, however. First, the topic of decision rules demands study. Rather than relying solely on a joint maximization rule, it would be useful to examine such alternatives as reciprocity, altruism, distributive justice, status consistency, or competitive advantage (cf. Meeker, 1971). Second, the nature of temporal constraints deserves scrutiny. Although the new theory of consumer behavior is innovative in this regard, it does not go far enough. By relying on a fixed, physical conceptualization of time, it fails to recognize the subjectivity and malleability of temporal concerns. Third, the theory is too shortsighted in that it models decision making in a static sense. Because situations change and people's tastes and demands ebb and flow, a dynamic theory would have more face validity. Finally, to make the theory testable, operationalizations and correspondence rules need to be specified. Some recommendations in this regard have been proposed by Bagozzi (1978).

CONCLUSIONS

Marketing thought is at a crossroads. For most of its history, marketing has existed as a technology for solving problems of the manager. The small amount of conceptual work found in the literature has either addressed narrow methodological concerns or else regarded the discipline in an applied sense as an appendage of business, management, or economics. Very little effort has been expended toward the goal of examining the philosophical and theoretical bases of the discipline. Yet such a step is necessary if a theory of marketing is to grow and flourish. Presently, an undercurrent of interest and enthusiasm exists for the subject matter of marketing. Rather than focusing exclusively on the boundaries of the discipline, however, it is perhaps time to redirect our intellectual energies toward the development of a general theory of marketing. The ideas proposed in this article are designed to provoke debate with the ultimate goal of stimulating a dialogue among theoretically concerned marketers.

REFERENCES

Alderson, Wroe (1965), *Dynamic Marketing Behavior: A Functionalist Theory of Marketing,* Homewood, Ill.: Richard D. Irwin, Inc.

Bagozzi, Richard P. (1975), "Marketing as Exchange," 39, *Journal of Marketing* (October), 32–39.

_____ (1978), "Marketing as Exchange: A Theory of Transactions in the Marketplace," *American Behavioral Scientist,* 21 (March/April), 535–556.

_____ (1977), "Is All Social Exchange Marketing? A Reply," *Journal of the Academy of Marketing Science,* 5 (Fall), 315–326.

_____ (1980), *Causal Models in Marketing.* New York: John Wiley & Sons.

Becker, Gary S. (1965), "A Theory of the Allocation of Time," *The Economic Journal,* 75 (September), 493–517.

_____ (1974), "A Theory of Social Interactions," *Journal of Political Economy,* 82 (November/December), 1063–1093.

Blau, Peter (1964), *Exchange and Power in Social Life,* New York: John Wiley & Sons.

Brock, Timothy C. (1965), "Communicator-Recipient Similarity and Decisions Change," *Journal of Personality and Social Psychology,* 1, 650–654.

Cook, Karen S. and Richard M. Emerson (1978), "Power, Equity, and Commitment in Exchange Networks," *American Sociological Review,* 43 (October), 721–739.

Ferrell, O. C. and Mary Zey-Ferrell (1977), "Is All Social Exchange Marketing?" *Journal of the Academy of Marketing Science,* 5 (Fall), 307–314.

Firth, Raymond (1973), *Symbols: Public and Private,* Ithaca, New York: Cornell University Press.

Hunt, Shelby D. (1976), "The Nature and Scope of Marketing, *Journal of Marketing,* 40 (July), 17–28.

Kotler, Philip (1972), "A Generic Concept of Marketing," *Journal of Marketing,* 36 (April), 46–54.

Lancaster, Kelvin (1971), *Consumer Demand: A New Approach,* New York: Columbia University Press.

McGuire, William J. (1969), "The Nature of Attitudes and Attitude Change," in G. L. Lindzey and E. Aronson (eds.), *Handbook of Social Psychology,* Vol. 3, Reading, Mass.: Addison-Wesley, 136–314.

_____ (1972), "Attitude Change: The Information-Processing Paradigm," in C. G. McClintock (ed.), *Experimental Social Psychology,* New York: Holt, Rinehart & Winston, 108–141.

Meeker, Barbara F. (1971), "Decision and Exchange," *American Sociological Review,* 36 (June) 485–495.

Rosen, Sherwin (1974), "Hedonic Prices and Implicit Markets: Product Differentiation in Pure Competition," *Journal of Political Economy,* 82 (January/February), 34–55.

Rubin, Jeffrey Z. and Bert R. Brown (1975), *The Social Psychology of Bargaining and Negotiation,* New York: Academic Press.

Sahlins, Marshall (1965), "On the Sociology of Primitive Exchange,'' in M. Banton (ed.), *The Relevance of Models for Social Anthropology*, A. S. A. Mon. I, London: Tavistock, 139–236.

Tedeschi, James T., Barry R. Schlenker, and Thomas V. Bonoma (1973), *Conflict, Power and Games*, Chicago: Aldine.

Thibaut, John W. and Harold H. Kelley (1959), *The Social Psychology of Groups*, New York: John Wiley & Sons.

NOTES

[1]Three generic kinds of subjective satisfactions are chosen here because these are the ones suggested by social psychologists as fundamental to most, if not all, human behavior. For a discussion of the meaning of affect, cognitions, and moral beliefs from a philosophical and social psychological perspective, see Bagozzi (1980). It should be recognized that other satisfactions might exist, and thus, the number of arguments in equation (1) should be left as an open question.

[2]Traditional budget and time constraints are assumed to influence the psychological and social constraints which are regarded as more fundamental.

DISCUSSION QUESTIONS

1. What does exchange mean to an anthropologist? A sociologist? A psychologist? An economist? And finally, a marketer?

2. Describe the three ways that exchange can be conceptualized as a phenomenon to be explained (i.e., as a dependent variable)? Contrast the idea of exchange as an action or outcome of one party with exchange as a relationship between parties.

3. Given the above notion of exchange as a dependent variable, what are the four classes of determinants that affect exchanges? Define each and list their subdimensions.

4. Take one real-world exchange in the marketplace and elaborate on its particular nature and the specific forces influencing it. Try to identify instances from each of the categories listed in Figure 1.

PREFACE TO

"Naive Marketing: A Neglected Dimension of Human Behavior"

A pedagogical desire to explain more clearly the universal nature of marketing exchanges inspired the ideas contained in this article. One semester, the first author decided to stir up his introductory marketing students by finishing off a lecture on the broadening of marketing by espousing the idea that dating was a marketing activity. This idea proved most controversial with the students.

The idea stimulated further contemplation of the interpersonal aspects of marketing. These thoughts percolated for two years until they became obsessive. The second author was drawn into this obsession at that time. After considerable discussion, we then decided to seek some sort of catharsis by writing a paper on the subject of naive marketing.

In developing the paper, we were particularly inspired by ideas from three sources. Our inspiration for the term naive marketing came from the concept of naive psychology developed by Fritz Heider (1958). Heider believed that all humans, by necessity, develop naive explanations about how people think and behave. Second, we found that McKenzie and Tullock's (1975) analyses of sex,

dating, marriage, death, and crime in economic terms were quite effective in demolishing our stereotypes concerning economics. Third, in the field of communication research, we stumbled on the concept of symbolic merchantry (developed by Phillips and Metzger, 1976) as our paper was nearing completion. Marketing by any other name is still marketing.

In revisiting our paper, we chose to expand and clarify several aspects of our thinking. First, we expanded our comments on the natural history of marketing. Second, we made some refinements in our diagrams and their explanation. Third, we expanded and updated our discussion of practical applications for our naive marketing analysis. Finally, we felt compelled to add a section to our paper after having had several graduate classes read the original paper. Many of those students foresaw dire consequences if people started thinking of their personal exchanges in marketing terms. We believe that such concerns necessitate addressing the ethical issues raised by our concept.

14

NAIVE MARKETING: A NEGLECTED DIMENSION OF HUMAN BEHAVIOR

RAYMOND P. FISK
KIRK D. WALDEN

During the past decade, marketing scholars sought to expand the concept of marketing (e.g. Kotler and Levy 1969; Kotler 1972b; Bagozzi 1975; and Levy 1976). At least two major ideas have emerged from these broadening attempts and the controversy surrounding them. First, marketing is seen as a discipline whose conceptual tools may be applied to the operations of any organization (profit or nonprofit). Second, the major focus of marketing activities is the exchange process. Bagozzi (1975, p. 39) has further proposed that "marketing is a general function of universal applicability." We agree! However, to date, the focus of analysis in marketing publications has been almost exclusively on organizational exchanges. Consequently, the universal applicability of marketing has not been explicated.

This paper expands our conceptualization of marketing from its present focus on organizational exchanges to the realm of interpersonal exchanges. First, the marketing activities in interpersonal exchange are defined and described as naive marketing. Naive marketing is a neglected dimension of human behavior. Second, two illustrations of naive marketing are expounded and analyzed with traditional marketing concepts. Third, practical applications of this new conceptualization of marketing are considered for marketing practitioners and academicians. Finally, the implications of naive marketing are examined for marketing as a discipline and for its relationship with other social sciences.

NAIVE MARKETING

Naive marketing[1] is intuitive, yet purposeful, marketing attempts or activities used by individuals in exchanges with other persons. Hence, we are refer-

Source: Revised for this volume from *Conceptual and Theoretical Developments in Marketing,* O. C. Ferrell, Stephen W. Brown, and Charles W. Lamb, Jr., eds., Chicago, Ill: American Marketing Association 1979, 459–473. Originally titled "Naive Marketing: Further Extension of the Concept of Marketing."

ring to the marketing activities that are performed in the everyday interpersonal lives of the public. Common examples would include making a friend, getting a job, or finding a marriage partner. In essence, we are referring to the marketing of oneself; however, naive marketing may include the marketing of personal possessions (such as selling a sofa or car). Marketers have generally noted that people can be products (Kotler and Levy 1969). Politicians and movie stars are common examples of people as products. The concept of naive marketing implies that all people are products and that most of us are not as sophisticated in marketing ourselves as are politicians or movie stars. Thus, naive marketing activities are not the result of the complex, highly formalized thought processes that have commonly characterized organizational marketing efforts.

Naive marketing is characteristic of most interpersonal marketing. Generically, interpersonal marketing refers to marketing activities among individuals acting on their own behalf, regardless of their level of marketing sophistication. Kotler and Levy (1969, p. 15) commenting on organizational marketing, noted:

> The choice . . . is not whether to market or not to market, for no organization can avoid marketing. The choice is whether to do it well or poorly, and on this necessity the case for organizational marketing is basically founded.

Regardless of the level of sophistication of one's knowledge about the occurrence of marketing, every individual markets himself or herself to others. Thus, like an organization, an individual cannot avoid marketing; and the analysis of naive marketing is based on the necessity of choosing to do it well or poorly. Indeed, we propose that marketing, whether interpersonal or organizational, is a necessary and fundamental characteristic of all human exchanges. Therefore, a key role in the marketing discipline is improving the marketing skills of all who use marketing.

Marketing evolved out of the basic human need to create exchange relationships. Consequently, naive marketing exchanges are the historical antecedent of all that is now called marketing. At an early stage in prehistory, primitive man discovered the advantages of exchange. These early exchanges may have had their origins in the biological unit of the family. Probably, an example of this was an exchange between man and woman wherein the man gathered food for the family and the woman raised the children. Primitive men and women conducted exchanges on the basis of barter. This was true whether they bartered for food, clothing, shelter, or a mate. As centuries passed and civilizations progressed, humankind developed organizations whose purposes were the production, transport, and sale of economic goods. However, the activities now known as marketing were not sufficiently complex nor sophisticated enough to develop into a distinctive subset of economic behavior until the twentieth century. The emergence of sophisticated corporate marketing has so dazzled its practitioners, academicians, and the public that we have overlooked the roots of marketing in interpersonal exchange. This oversight is particularly glaring when we consider that naive marketing is the most pervasive of all forms of marketing because of the vast numbers of the human population.

One possible explanation for the neglect of interpersonal marketing as a topic can be derived by analogy. In early times, the field of chemistry was concerned, by necessity, with the basic chemical processes. Chemists had no significant understanding of how chemical reactions occurred. Today chemists are able to identify and study the most minute physical elements that control chemical reactions. In the same fashion, perhaps it was necessary for marketers to come to an understanding of the nature of marketing through the more obvious large scale of organizations before they could fully comprehend the smaller scale of interpersonal marketing exchanges.

Explicating naive marketing requires three classification schemes to specify the level of analysis. First, Bagozzi (1975) proposed that there are three types of exchanges: restricted (two parties), generalized (three or more parties forming a circular exchange), and complex (three or more parties in a web of exchanges). For simplicity, only restricted exchanges will be discussed in this analysis. A second classification based on the role behavior of dyad members in restricted exchanges focuses the analysis. Four categories of role-behavior dyads are proposed: *A.* Organizational-Organizational; *B.* Organizational-Individual; *C.* Individual-Organizational; and *D.* Individual-Individual.

A. Organizational --------------→ Organizational
B. Organizational --------------→ Individual

C. Individual --------------------→ Organizational
D. Individual --------------------→ Individual

A third classification (Kotler 1972a) simplifies the directionality of the exchange. In unilateral marketing, one or the other party to the exchange initiates and attempts to create demand for the exchange. In bilateral marketing, both parties to the exchange actively enter into an exchange. Only unilateral marketing exchanges will be considered in this analysis.

Category *A* of the role-behavior dyads occurs when both parties to the exchange are fulfilling some sort of organizational role behavior. For example, one person might be a corporate salesperson and the other a purchasing manager. This category of role behaviors is characteristic of most industrial market exchanges. Categories *B* and *C* of the role-behavior dyads both occur when one party to the exchange is fulfilling an organizational role while the other party is fulfilling an individual role. However, two distinctly different types of unilateral exchanges occur. Category *B* occurs when a person performing an organizational role markets to a person performing an individual role. Category *B* might occur, for example, when a salesperson sells a physical good to a consumer. This type of exchange characterizes exchanges in consumer markets. Hence, to this point, our role-behavior categories have enabled us to identify exchanges characteristic of either industrial or consumer markets. Note that these exchanges are the regular and traditional province of marketing thought.

The remaining role behavior classifications forge new ground for marketing thought. The unilateral exchange in category *C* occurs when a person performing an individual role markets to a person performing an organizational role. An example of category *C* would be when an individual sells his or her job skills to a prospective employer. Category *D* of the role-behavior dyads occurs when both parties to the exchange are fulfilling individual roles rather than organizational roles. An example of such role behavior would be a man asking a woman for a date. These last two examples fall exclusively into the province of naive marketing and will be used as illustrations in the next section. However, please note that naive marketing behavior may occur in any of these role-behavior categories because in every case, the parties to the exchange are individuals whose levels of marketing sophistication will vary.

Further clarification of naive marketing as a broadening effort requires a brief examination of the economic foundations of marketing as a discipline. Marketing is commonly viewed as having developed from economics. Critics of the broadening efforts in marketing (Luck 1969; Arndt 1978) have charged that broadening attempts stray from the necessary economic foundations of marketing. In so arguing, these critics have relied on a somewhat traditional and simplistic distinction between economic and noneconomic exchanges. Economic exchanges occur when a good is exchanged for money. Noneconomic exchanges occur when things (usually intangibles) are exchanged without monetary payment. Hence, these critics argued that the proper focus of marketing is on economic exchanges. But the economics discipline did not remain static after marketing evolved from it. Economists have sought to enlarge the boundaries of their discipline. McKenzie and Tullock (1975) have demonstrated that so-called noneconomic exchanges (such as sex, dating, or marriage) may be analyzed with the traditional economic tools of utility and supply-and-demand analysis. For example, they analyzed the economic characteristics of sex as a service, the implicit costs of sex, sex as an exchange relationship, and sex as a marketed product. The following quotation from McKenzie and Tullock (1975, p. 261) regarding the expansion of the economics discipline would ring true for the marketing discipline as well:

> The vast expansion of economics as a discipline is one of the more interesting intellectual developments of this generation. The number of economists involved in this expansion and the variety of topics analyzed is on the increase; there is every reason to believe that this trend will continue, blurring the traditional boundaries which have separated economics from the other social sciences.

If the marketing discipline is to be viewed as founded on economics, marketing scholars must realize that the discipline of economics has expanded beyond its traditional boundaries and continues to expand. Consistent with the expansion of economics, two naive marketing illustrations are considered—one that falls within and one that falls outside the traditional boundaries of economics.

NAIVE MARKETING ILLUSTRATIONS

Marketing concepts and terminology developed in organizational marketing are extended to an analysis of naive interpersonal exchanges. The first exchange concerns the economic exchange of getting a job, one that is restrictive, unilateral, and that involves individual to organizational role behavior. This illustration was chosen as a starting point because it falls within the traditional boundaries of economic behavior, if not of marketing behavior. The second analysis illustrates the noneconomic exchanges involved in dating. This exchange is also restrictive and unilateral, but it involves individual-to-individual role behavior. Noneconomic exchanges are of interest because they are the most divergent from traditional marketing exchanges of goods and services. For this reason, an illustration of naive noneconomic exchange is perhaps the best test of the universal applicability of marketing. For each naive marketer illustration, a target market is identified and a marketing mix is described.

Job Hunting

The marketing activities of a man seeking a job provides the illustration for our discussion.[2]

Target Market Because marketing efforts by individuals are typically less conscious than those of organizations, the target market for our job seeker will be less formally defined. He will segment the market on criteria, such as industry, company, and the type of jobs available. He may choose to target on an entire industry that is attractive to him, with little concern for a specific job, thus using a relatively undifferentiated strategy. Or he may further segment the market by defining an industry, a company, and a job, for example, as sales representative for American Airlines in San Francisco.

In all cases, the potential of the target market is evaluated on the basis of its accessibility to the job market and its ability to purchase the job seeker's skills. The individual must also determine how well his own resources can be adapted to meet the needs of the target market.

Product   The job seeker's product is himself. In the short run, the product is relatively unalterable; therefore, decisions on the market target will be largely predetermined. Unlike most common consumer products, brand names cannot be easily changed or a new and improved model introduced.

In the long run, the job seeker may invest in education or job skills to improve himself as a product. As he obtains these, he implicitly classifies himself. A tax accountant who is an expert in oil well equipment could be considered a specialty good, whereas a manufacturer's purchasing agent might be considered a shopping good. Note that the job seekers' product classification can change depending on his education and work experience relative to the target market selected.

The individual also has a definite product life cycle determined by his age, income, and other relevant "product" characteristics. The individual's specific stage in the product life cycle will strongly affect the pricing, promotion, and distribution strategies he chooses.

Price   The job seeker intuitively sets his price consistent with economic price theory. Associated with a new job is the opportunity cost of quitting the current job. Unconsciously balancing free time, job satisfaction, and pay, the individual will seek to maximize his "profit" by setting his marginal cost equal to his marginal revenue. Even if the pay level is substantial, jobs will be rejected by the job hunter if perceived costs exceed perceived benefits.

Generally, the job seeker will employ a demand-backward pricing strategy. He will first determine the compensation level from a particular market segment and then work backward to adjust his price to the market.

Promotion   Normally, the persuasive communications of the job hunter will be aimed at stimulating selective demand by stressing his unique product characteristics. Initially, promotion will be impersonal, taking the form of a resume whose content is chosen to generate sufficient interest to warrant an interview. The target company may also receive other promotional messages, such as letters of references.

Personal communications occur at the interview stage. The interviewee will attempt to present the proper image to the company by carefully "packaging" himself in attire suitable to the company with which he interviews. In additional, the job seeker will have researched the company to adjust his promotional message to the specific target and thereby explain how he can best meet its needs. From resume through interview, he will attempt to attract attention, generate interest, stimulate desire, and obtain action.

Distribution   The individual's distribution strategy will be closely tied to the size of his target market. He may follow an exclusive strategy by limiting himself to a specific geographic region or a specific company. As he relaxes such restrictions, his strategy shifts toward selective distribution.

The job seeker may choose among several "retail" outlets by using an employment agency. Alternatively, he can assume the channel responsibility by contacting companies himself, thereby retaining greater control.

Dating

For the second illustration, the marketing activities of a man seeking a date with a woman will be used.

Target Market   The man seeking a date intuitively selects a target market, although that target market is not easily quantified. Characteristics of women (such as age, occupation, education, or appearance) serve as criteria that are both consciously and unconsciously weighed by the man, frequently on a situational basis, in choosing his target market. Because of the intuitive, individualized nature of dating, it is improbable that the man has established identifiable and consistent target market criteria. For this reason, he is likely to use a relatively undifferentiated strategy that is adjusted to the characteristics of the women in close proximity to him.

The size of the target market of potential dating partners probably declines after the early twenties, bringing fewer opportunities to interact in the marketplace. Therefore, within this constraint, the man will tend to seek the largest possible target market.

Product   As in the job-hunting illustration, the man's product is himself. He has a product life cycle based on his age (typically dating occurs in the growth stage—teens and early twenties). Intuitively, the man also classifies himself as a convenience, shopping, or specialty good. His classification will likely be based on such factors as income, occupation, education, and self-image. A highly educated, affluent man is likely to consider himself more important and, hence, a specialty good.

Price The price of dating includes time, emotional involvement, and money spent as well as the opportunity costs of dating or not dating or of choosing one date over another. Depending on an individual's overall goals, one of several pricing objectives can be set by him. If he chooses to date as many women as possible, regardless of the expected returns, he is following a volume pricing objective. To attain this volume, he would be willing to sacrifice disproportionately larger amounts of money and free time. Conversely, he may set a prestige pricing objective by severely limiting the time and money allotted to general dating, so that he might increase the profit per date. Finally, he could pursue a status quo objective by maintaining a balance between price factors equivalent to his "industry" of peers.

Promotion The persuasive communication of the man may stimulate primary demand in the early stages of his product life cycle. In the latter stages, the man may stimulate selective demand by emphasizing unique product characteristics. In addition, he will tend to work harder at promoting himself in the later stages of his product life cycle.

A major promotional tool is the man's use of "packaging" to merchandise and differentiate himself to the woman. His choice of clothing presents a particular image to the woman. Also, his use of deodorants, aftershaves, and colognes are part of the "package." Further, the length of his hair and the condition of his physique are relevant "package" aspects.

Distribution The distribution decision concerns how many women he chooses to date in a given time. If he chooses to date one woman to the exclusion of all others, he would be following an exclusive distribution strategy. If he chooses to date many women, he would then be using an intensive distribution strategy. The use of a selective distribution strategy could be based on evaluative criteria, such as hair color, age, physique, and intelligence of the target market of women.

The above analyses of naive marketers' behavior demonstrate some strong similarities between organizational marketing and interpersonal marketing. The tools and concepts developed in one help us better understand the other.

PRACTICAL APPLICATIONS

A major goal of this analysis of naive marketing is the improvement of interpersonal marketing skills. Indeed, it is hoped that an understanding of interpersonal marketing will help eliminate or at least reduce the naiveté that characterizes these exchanges. With this in mind, several areas of practical application of naive marketing analysis can be identified for both the marketing academician and the practitioner. For the practitioner, an understanding of naive marketing is important because even though sales personnel fulfill organizational sales roles, they must still market themselves during their exchanges. If they market themselves badly, this hampers and detracts from their organizational role. For the academician, an understanding of naive marketing can be used in his or her teaching in two ways: (1) It can be used to improve the instructor's interpersonal skills in the classroom, and (2) it can be used as a teaching device. For both the practitioner and the academician, an understanding of naive marketing becomes more critical as our economy shifts toward a service economy.

Selling

Despite the fact that the corporate salesperson is performing an organizational role, we must assert that all salespersons find it necessary to sell themselves to a prospective customer before they attempt to sell their company's product. Most salespersons intuitively recognize this and attempt to dress and act in such a manner that they will be trusted and favorably received by the prospective customer. The customer is not likely to buy from the salesperson he or she does not trust. Hence, an explicit understanding of naive marketing can be important in the improvement of the salesperson's performance and should be considered for inclusion in sales training programs.

Researchers in services marketing are increasingly sensitive to the interpersonal nature of services. Three presentations at the Second American

Marketing Association Services Marketing Conference dealt explicitly with interpersonal issues and the necessity of interpersonal marketing (Berry 1983; Gronroos 1983; Grove and Fisk 1983).

Teaching

The marketing academician, as Enis (1978, p. 422) has noted, is a "salesperson for the product marketing education." Like the corporate salesperson, the academician must sell himself or herself in addition to the product. Enis (1978) suggested that three characteristics are needed for an academic to be an effective teacher: empathy, the desire to teach, and the ability to communicate. We would suggest a fourth characteristic—enthusiasm for the subject matter. Nothing deadens a student's interest more quickly than a bored and boring instructor. These characteristics are important, and we contend that a major task of teachers is to convince the students that they have these characteristics. Indeed, for marketing academicians, it is imperative that they not be naive marketers. It is troubling to observe academicians who have a firm grasp of the fundamentals of corporate marketing, yet are ineffectual in their interpersonal marketing attempts. Maximum effectiveness as a teacher requires that academicians be adept at interpersonally marketing themselves as well as adept in marketing knowledge.

The marketing academician may also use naive marketing as a teaching device. One of the authors has devoted a day's lecture and discussion to naive marketing (specifically, dating behavior) in his introductory marketing classes. On each occasion, the topic was met with strong interest, astonishment, and humor by the students. Teaching the naive marketing approach enables the professor to demonstrate the fundamental applicability of marketing to the daily lives of each student. At the same time that the student grasps this relevance, he or she begins to understand the universality of marketing in human behavior.

Service Economy

Trends in gross national product (GNP) data show that service industries are the largest and fastest growing component of our economy. Examples of such industries include airlines, insurance, and health care. People are the tangible performers of these services. Therefore, their interpersonal marketing skills are critical to the marketing success of service industries. As a result, service industry mar-

keters will be placing greater emphasis on improving the interpersonal marketing skills of any personnel who work directly with the public. The growth of the service economy suggests to the marketing academician that more research effort must focus on analyzing service marketing. The marketing academician will, consequently, become more concerned with understanding the role interpersonal marketing skills have in the success of service industries.

IMPLICATIONS FOR MARKETING

The naive marketing concept proposed in this paper has significant implications for marketing as a discipline and for marketing's relationship with other social science disciplines. The first implication concerns ethical issues that arise when discussing interpersonal marketing. The second implication concerns potential applications of marketing ideas to the study of interpersonal relations. The third implication concerns traditional barriers between marketing and related social science disciplines.

Ethical Issues

The field of marketing suffers from some deep-seated prejudices against the exchange behaviors that characterize marketing phenomena (Steiner 1976). Fisk (1982, p. 255) has argued:

> Much of this prejudice results from persistent criticism of the ethics of marketing. The marketing discipline has not done a very good job of justifying its behaviors, nor has much yet been accomplished in creating a formal structure for marketing ethics. A great many vagaries still need to be resolved in marketing ethics.

Espousing the concept of naive marketing requires that the ethical issues inherent in all marketing be addressed. Ethical decisions are inherently individual decisions. Each individual must make such choices.

This paper's attempt at shifting interpersonal exchanges from their current naivety to sophistication is *not* intended to provide individuals with new ways of abusing each other's rights. Instead, we believe that part of being a sophisticated interpersonal marketer is the recognition that there is no long-term profit in exploiting other people. The marketing concept applies equally well to interpersonal marketing and organizational marketing.

Indeed, those who practice interpersonal marketing must learn how to practice the highest possible ethics. The current state of naive marketing is notoriously unethical. The exploitation of women by men is legendary. Misrepresentations by job seekers are also common. If interpersonal marketing is properly practiced, such abuses should decline rather than increase.

Applications to Interpersonal Relations

Based on the concept of naive marketing, marketing ideas may have potential applications to the study of interpersonal relations. Researchers in interpersonal relations (Bennis, et al., 1973; Swensen 1973) note that a broad range of disciplines have been drawn on in developing concepts, definitions, and theories of interpersonal relations. Bennis, et al. (1973, p. 2) point out:

> There is as yet no single, comprehensive theory of interpersonal relations. Sociology, social psychology, and psychiatry have offered important insights to the understanding of its phenomena, but the area has resisted successful theoretical comprehension.

It is a field ripe for further research and new insights.

Recently, Phillips and Metzger (1976) proposed a theory of communication in interpersonal relations that is of striking interest to a marketer. Their basic assumptions about man follow:

> Man is capable of making symbols about himself and the world, he is capable of using will to exert some control over the world and the things in it. . . . In addition to all this, he persuades. He actively seeks behavior from others. We allege that any and every relationship between two or more people is a persuasive engagement, in which one party is contending with others (who are contending with him) for some accommodating behavior change. (pp. 361–362)

Based on these assumptions about man, they identify their theory:

> Our basic metaphor emerges very clearly; Man Is A Symbolic Merchant! He buys and sells, trades and cons, advertises and delivers. (p. 360)

The parallels between Phillips and Metzger's theory of man as a symbolic merchant in interpersonal relations and the conception of naive marketing in interpersonal exchanges as proposed in this paper are readily apparent. In each instance, the researchers maintain that man actively engages in persuasion attempts and both contend that these persuasion attempts are fundamental to human behavior in exchange relationships. These parallels strongly suggest that the marketing discipline can contribute to the study of interpersonal relations. Moreover, these contributions may help the psychiatrist, the psychologist, and the sociologist better understand the interpersonal relationships they study. The insights gained from applying marketing concepts to the study of interpersonal relations would help the marketing discipline by improving the understanding of the interpersonal nature of all marketing exchanges.

Barriers to Knowledge

A third implication of naive marketing is that such a conceptualization of marketing tears down some of the traditional barriers between marketing and related social science disciplines. Before the inveterate fence menders rush in to restake these barriers, let us consider abandoning our attempts to stake out a unique territory for marketing thought. No discipline has unqualified claim to any aspect of human behavior. Consider this observation by Kenneth Boulding (cited in Kuhn 1974, p. ix):

> I became convinced at least twenty-five years ago that all the social sciences were studying the same thing, which is the social system, even though they were studying it from different points of view and with different vocabularies.

Many other disciplines study aspects of human exchange behaviors. Only the marketing perspective on these exchanges is unique; and perhaps it is only our perspective that has value. The marketer's perspective on exchanges is a focus on persuasion attempts to facilitate exchange by individuals or organizations. But, the marketing discipline should not yield to the temptation that ours is the only way to look at a specific human exchange or that we have exclusive right to look or even that there are some exchanges among human beings at which we cannot look. If marketing and other social science disciplines are to understand human behavior in all its multidimensional complexity, we must abandon our provincial territorial disputes and work toward better communication and cooperation among the social sciences.

CONCLUSIONS

Naive marketing represents a neglected dimension of human behavior. As such, naive marketing extends the concept of marketing from its present focus on organizational marketing to interpersonal marketing. Marketing is the use of activities that facilitate human exchanges. Interpersonal marketing is the subset of marketing by which individuals acting on their own behalf engage in activities that facilitate human exchanges. Naive marketing exchanges are interpersonal exchanges characterized by relatively intuitive, unconscious marketing activities. Historically, naive marketing activities are the predecessor of contemporary corporate marketing. The discipline of marketing evolved from economics. The coincident expansion of the economic discipline gives credence to the many broadening efforts in marketing.

The analysis of two illustrations of naive marketing demonstrated the applicability of marketing concepts developed in organizational marketing to interpersonal marketing. Naive marketing analysis is conceptually useful and offers practical benefits to the marketing practitioner for improving selling skills, to the marketing academician for enhancing the teaching of marketing, and to both in coping with and comprehending an emerging service economy. The concept of naive marketing has significant implications for the potential applicability of marketing concepts to the study of interpersonal relationships and for removing some of the traditional barriers that have previously separated marketing from other social science disciplines. However, the concept also requires careful attention to the ethical issues it raises.

Marketing activities are necessary and fundamental characteristics of human exchanges. This is true, whether they be organizational or interpersonal exchanges. Individual marketing behavior is no less legitimate or important than organizational marketing behavior. Indeed, interpersonal marketing exchanges are ubiquitous in human society. If marketing is truly "a general function of universal applicability," it should embrace the concept of naive marketing.

Several broad research questions are suggested by the concept of naive marketing:

1. What are the unique and coincident characteristics of interpersonal marketing and organizational marketing?

2. How applicable are marketing concepts and research techniques to the study of interpersonal relations? Are new concepts needed?

3. How can the skills of the naive marketer be improved?

Research is needed in each of these areas. A better understanding of naive marketing will reduce the naivety that characterizes interpersonal exchanges. Improving the quality of interpersonal marketing skills in society would offer positive benefits to both individuals and organizations.

Demonstrating the generalizability and practicality of marketing concepts to interpersonal exchanges by means of naive marketing verifies the "universal applicability" of marketing. Kotler (1972a, p. 48) notes: "An important means of achieving progress in a science is to try to increase the generality of its concepts." The analysis of naive marketing generalizes marketing concepts to interpersonal exchanges. Hunt (1976) argues that theory is and should be practical. The concepts on which a theory is based should also be practical. Marketing concepts are eminently practical because we can apply them to the interpersonal exchanges of our daily lives.

REFERENCES

Arndt, Johan (1978), "How Broad Should the Marketing Concept Be?" *Journal of Marketing,* 42 (January), 101–103.

Bagozzi, Richard P. (1975), "Marketing as Exchange." *Journal of Marketing,* 39 (October), 32–39.

Bennis, Warren G., David E. Berlew, Edgar H. Schein,

and Fred I. Steele (1973), *Interpersonal Dynamics,* 3rd ed., Homewood, Ill.: Dorsey Press.

Berry, Leonard L. (1983), "Relationship Marketing," in *Emerging Perspectives on Services Marketing,* Leonard L. Berry, G. Lynn Shostack, and Gregory D. Upah (eds.), Chicago: American Marketing Association, pp. 25–28.

Enis, Ben M. (1978), "Marketing Marketing by Teaching Teaching," in *Research Frontiers in Marketing: Dialogues and Directions,* Chicago: American Marketing Association, 422–425.

Fisk, Raymond P. (1982), "Toward a Theoretical Framework for Marketing Ethics," in *Marketing Theory: Philosophy of Science Perspectives,* Ronald F. Bush and Shelby D. Hunt (eds.), Chicago: American Marketing Association.

Gronroos, Christian (1983), "Innovative Organizational Strategies for Services," in *Emerging Perspectives on Services Marketing,* Leonard L. Berry, G. Lynn Shostack, and Gregory D. Upah (eds.), Chicago: American Marketing Association, pp. 9–21.

Grove, Stephen J., and Raymond P. Fisk (1983), "The Dramaturgy of Service Exchanges: An Analytical Framework for Services Marketing," in *Emerging Perspectives on Services Marketing,* Leonard L. Berry, G. Lynn Shostack, and Gregory D. Upah (eds.), Chicago: American Marketing Association, pp. 45–49.

Heider, Fritz (1958), *The Psychology of Interpersonal Relations,* New York: Wiley.

Hunt, Shelby D. (1976), *Marketing Theory: Conceptual Foundations of Research in Marketing,* Columbus, Ohio: Grid.

Kotler, Philip (1972a), "Defining the Limits of Marketing," in *Marketing Education and the Real World: 1972 Fall Conference Proceedings,* Boris W. Becker and Helmut Becker (eds.), Chicago: American Marketing Association, 48–56.

———— (1972b), "A Generic Concept of Marketing," *Journal of Marketing,* 36 (April), 46–54.

———— and Sidney J. Levy (1969), "Broadening the Concept of Marketing," *Journal of Marketing,* 33 (January), 10–15.

Kuhn, Alfred (1974), *The Logic of Social Systems,* San Francisco: Jossey-Bass.

Levy, Sidney (1976), "Marcology 101 or the Domain of Marketing," in *Marketing 1776–1976 and Beyond,* Kenneth L. Bernhardt (ed.), Chicago: American Marketing Association, 577–581.

Luck, David J. (1969), "Broadening the Concept of Marketing—Too Far," *Journal of Marketing,* 33 (July), 53–54.

McKenzie, Richard B., and Gordon Tullock (1975), *The New World of Economics,* Homewood, Ill.: Richard D. Irwin.

Phillips, Gerald M., and Nancy J. Metzger (1976), *Intimate Communication,* Boston: Allyn & Bacon.

Steiner, Robert L. (1976), "The Prejudice Against Marketing," *Journal of Marketing,* 40, (July), 2–9.

Swenson, Clifford H., Jr., (1973), *Introduction to Interpersonal Relations,* Glenview, Ill.: Scott, Foresman & Co.

NOTES

[1] Inspiration for the term naive marketing came from the fruitful and challenging ideas that developed in social psychology from Fritz Heider's (1958) conception of naive psychology. The word naive is used in exactly the same sense as used by Heider.

[2] No sex discrimination is intended by this illustration or the next. The authors chose to discuss the behavior of men only to avoid unintended misrepresentation of the behavior of women.

DISCUSSION QUESTIONS

1. Many scholars and laypeople have taken offense at the idea that human beings can be marketed. Many, also, take offense at the authors' assertion that human beings *should* market themselves. Why do you think these negative reactions occur?

2. Compare and contrast organizational versus individual marketing. What are the most essential differences between the two forms of marketing? What are their strongest similarities?

3. Examine the importance of individual role behavior to the success of organizational marketing and individual marketing. Would the importance change if you were a marketer of services rather than physical goods?

4. Examine the concept of symbolic merchantry. (If possible, obtain a copy of the Phillips and Metzger [1976] book.) What can marketing concepts offer to the study of interpersonal relations?

THREE

DEVELOPMENTS IN MARKETING THEORY

As indicated in a number of the previous essays, marketing is in its infancy stage in terms of theory development. Yet, our need for a stronger, more eclectic theory orientation is increasingly being recognized. The articles in Part 3 contribute to meeting this need.

The first section of Part 3 offers a variety of papers on the need for, and methods of, theory building in marketing. The articles in the second section explore the relationships between theory and practice, including an assessment of the research contributions of academia to marketing management. The final section of Part 3 scrutinizes the important links between theory and research.

A. THEORY BUILDING

The opening article in this section is by Leone and Schultz, and it challenges marketing scholars regarding what we actually *know* about marketing.

The authors find marketing in want of scientific foundations for our generalizations. The article also illustrates the process by which marketing knowledge can be formed. The Mokwa and Evans paper expands on their 1982 American Marketing Association Theory Conference work. The paper argues for a multimethod system of marketing inquiry by discussing basic dimensions of inquiry and knowledge systems, including the psychology of inquiry.

Hunt's article explores the nature of theory in marketing and then addresses the potential characteristics of a general theory of marketing. Fisk and Meyers's paper reviews the evolved and potential adoption of marketing paradigms under which macromarketing theories can be classified. In the last paper of this section, Mowen offers a process for theory discovery that integrates the logical processes of induction, deduction, and retroduction.

PREFACE TO

"A Study of Marketing Generalizations"

Anyone who in the mid-1970s looked dispassionately at the state of marketing knowledge would be forced to conclude that there was little *real* knowledge in the sense of generalizable findings. This insight motivated us to begin a search for the same kind of generalizations that characterize the physical sciences. We rejected the apology that marketing was so different from natural sciences, like chemistry or physics, that such thinking was impossible. What seemed to be nearer to the truth was that few marketing scholars ever thought to look for such generalizations. Certainly few studies were replicated and most research focused on methodology rather than substance.

Interestingly, after this paper was written, the simple point that it made was still often misunderstood. Many marketing researchers seemed to confuse scientific propositions with scientific generalizations and, so, concluded (correctly) that

there are many of these speculations on marketing behavior. What we do not know, of course, is *how* things are related. Such laws or generalizations have been the starting point for scientific advancement since Galileo. A tradition almost 400 years old seems worth preserving.

Progress in finding such generalizations in marketing will occur when (1) the concept is understood, (2) the approach of the physical sciences is learned, and (3) someone does it. This latter point today worries us most. There is virtually no long-term, ongoing, systematic research by individuals or groups of individuals that is being done in marketing as it is in the sciences. Such programmatic work is usually slow, painstaking, difficult—and important. The fact that we have made marketing research so "easy" is the reason why we have so little to show for our efforts.

15

A STUDY OF MARKETING GENERALIZATIONS

ROBERT P. LEONE

RANDALL L. SCHULTZ

SCIENTIFIC GENERALIZATIONS

Why is it that when marketing researchers think of philosophers of science they are more likely to recall the ideas of Kaplan, Blalock or perhaps Popper rather than, say, Hume, Whitehead, or even Einstein? How is it that scientific generalizations, the bedrock of knowledge in natural science, are so elusive in marketing literature? When will marketing scientists, so presently occupied with the development of methodology, turn to the fundamental question: What do we *know* about marketing behavior?

The answer to each of these questions is complex, but a simple insight comes from the fact that we have generally relied on what may be called "derivative" sources for our methodology and philosophy of method. In short, we have borrowed without examining deeply enough the nature of the debt. Let us be clear from the onset that we are not referring so much to the work of individual researchers or to such introspective works as Zaltman, Pinson, and Angelmar's (1973) treatise on methodology, or more recently Hunt (1976), as we are to the general residual, such that it is, of marketing "knowledge." This body of knowledge, mortgaged to other sciences by its reliance on *their* method and *their* theory is, unfortunately, meager, ill defined, and, interestingly enough, unappreciated.

In 1964, Bernard Berelson and Gary Steiner published *Human Behavior: An Inventory of Scientific Findings,* a commendable (and not uncontroversial) effort to pull together what was then known about human behavior. Their purpose was to report on scientific generalizations, i.e., *laws* of behavior. All modern science, particularly natural science, has been characterized since 1600 by a conception of Galileo: that the first goal of science

is to *describe* phenomena independently of any explanations. In this scheme, which accounts for the success of the "exact" sciences (cf. [sic] Kline 1953), speculation on why something happens necessarily follows documentation on how something happens. So Berelson and Steiner tried to duplicate the inventory of knowledge that seems to accumulate so (deceptively) easily in the natural sciences.

We initiated a similar search for marketing knowledge a few years ago; in fact, a book was planned for a series on marketing theory. It soon became apparent, however, that when the same standards used to define generalizations in other fields were applied to marketing, our scientific foundation appeared to be more marsh than bedrock. This paper is one outcome of that project. In it, we hope to illustrate the process by which marketing knowledge can be formed, if not gathered.

Some Qualifications

As we have noted, it is not presently possible to provide on paper an inventory of scientific generalizations in marketing. The fact that so few studies replicate and thus may corroborate earlier (tentative) findings is, it turns out, the least of all problems associated with this task. The greatest problem is the lack of conformity of methodology and hence definition of what can legitimately be considered "evidence" for generalization. A smaller problem is the apparent confusion that surrounds the idea of generalization in marketing vis à vis the development of marketing theory.

Two points about knowledge versus empirical research need to be clarified. First, a reviewer commented that "there seems to be no attempt to present a balanced analysis of support for and against each of the generalizations" in this paper. But when there is both support for and against an empirical statement, there is no generalization! Boyle's Law is a scientific generalization precisely because it summarizes, for certain well-defined conditions, the inverse relationship between pressure and vol-

Source: Reprinted with permission from the *Journal of Marketing,* 44, (Winter), 1980, 10–18, Chicago, Ill.: American Marketing Association.

ume for a fixed weight of gas. The evidence *supports* this statement: that is why we call it a law. Otherwise, it would still be Boyle's hypothesis or, worse, Boyle's folly.

Second, and this follows from our first point, a study of marketing generalizations is different *in kind* from a literature survey of empirical results. Reviews of empirical literature on a given subject should and do cover the gamut of research experience. But review articles (and this is mostly their purpose) tend to raise more questions than they answer. They are excellent guides to future research. Surveys of marketing generalizations, on the other hand, take stock of what we really know about marketing. The work of Ehrenberg (1966, 1972) provides an exemplary case of defining marketing knowledge. If a student or colleague asked you what is a generalization (not theory, not hypothesis, not proposition) in your own area, what would you say? What *could* you say? This is exactly the distinction between knowledge (generalization) and a series of research findings.

So for marketing we have the following situation: there is a great deal of empirical research, but very little is generalizable. Hence, we have very little knowledge of marketing phenomena. As we search for generalizations, we should not be unduly concerned with methodology per se, particularly since marketing research tools are in a state of evolution. It would be nice to evaluate the validity or reliability of every study (assuming that an observer could even do this), but whose methodological bias are we to choose as "correct"? Should we only admit as evidence of generalization the results of experiments? Or econometric studies? Or, more specifically, field experiments? Or "state-of-the-art" econometric/time series studies? Who, in other words, is to judge what is good or bad?[1]

Because we feel that it is far more useful to marketing science at this stage in its development to produce knowledge and not simply more hypotheses or methodology, we propose a scheme for weighing evidence that, if anything, tends to err on the side of admitting a finding as positive support of a proposition. By defining replication and corroboration broadly, we hope to illustrate that, even in such a widely researched area as sales response, our knowledge is thin. The attempt to lay out what we know about marketing should be at least as important, if not more so, as our continual attempts to expand the boundaries of marketing theory.

EVIDENCE AND GENERALIZATION

A final preliminary consideration is how a statement is to be regarded as an empirical generalization, i.e., how is it to be tested and how is the evidence to be weighed? Given any two concepts, A and B, we may be interested in the proposition (hypothesis), if A then B. This could be written as a methematical expression of the form $B = f(A)$. Through well-defined correspondence rules, we would find the operational form of the proposition, $B^1 = f(A^1)$, where B^1 and A^1 are the constructs which are purported to measure B and A. It is this class of operational propositions which can be tested (which are capable of being falsified) and should command our attention.

A scientific test of an operational proposition will be defined as a "method" of bringing evidence to bear on a "situation" of the proposition. These methods can range from simple observation of nonexperimental data to analysis of experiments or axiomatic systems. In a general way, we can speak of the viewpoint (bias) of an observer-researcher as instrumental to the "method," while the "situation" refers to a particular *empirical form* of the proposition. For example, if Sales = f(Advertising), then an empirical form of this proposition would specify both the mathematical and substantive conditions of the proposition. One such form could be Sales = α Advertising with α and all of the conditions under which this relationship is expected to hold specified.

Three different tests can be specified:

- Experimental Replication: same "method"— same "situation"
- Nonexperimental Replication: same "method"—different "situation"
- Corroboration: different "method"—same "situation," and different "method"—different "situation"

To illustrate, consider again the relationship between advertising and sales. In experimental replication the same experiment is conducted more than once, although there can be (especially with social systems) no perfect replication. In nonexperimental replication, the same method (econometrics) is applied to different situations (data). For example, the finding that advertising was related to sales holds for a number of situations, e.g., markets, products, etc., will be classified as nonexperimental replication. The "method" could be simple observation of nonexperimental data, but it would have to be extended beyond the original data. In corroboration, an experiment concerning sales and advertising may augment the finding of a regression study for the same situation. Alternatively, different methods may be used to generalize from a variety of situations. Notice it is the case of different situations which leads implicitly to broader generalizations.

If one or more of these tests is applied to an empirical proposition, then a positive result will be called a scientific generalization or a scientific finding. A negative result will produce something akin to a historical fact. This approach to testing generalizations is compatible with Simon's (1968) notion that a generalization is falsifiable or testable when "(a) it is extended beyond the data from which it was generated or (b) an explanatory theory is constructed from which the generalization can be derived, and the explanatory theory has testable consequences beyond the original data" (p. 449). This has been seen in the work of Bass and Parsons (1969) where they employed Basmann's (1965) concept of predictive testing in simultaneous-equation regression analysis.

FINDINGS ON SALES RESPONSE

The influence of marketing mix variables on sales is a matter of scientific and practical interest and there is a growing research tradition in this area. The only prior attempt to collect scientific data on sales response was by Clarke (1976). He presents a discussion of the literature concerning cumulative advertising effects and the important question of the duration of advertising effects. Using the criteria of evidence that we have set forth, we present research findings that represent scientific generalizations in this area. Since this is an illustration, we focus on aggregate sales or market share response to advertising expenditures, distribution, and shelf space. Although we make no claim of completeness, these three marketing decision variables have been rather thoroughly explored and our lack of comment on all other marketing mix variables except price is due to lack of evidence. The effect of price and product-related price elasticities is widely reported in the economics literature. In the marketing literature, Monroe (1973) provides a review of the studies concerning individuals' perceptions of price.

There are no *universal* generalizations in marketing. When we report, for example, that advertising has a positive influence on sales, we do not imply that this is true in every circumstance. It simply means that there is corroboration for this proposition from a number of sources for particular types of goods. The conditions under which the generalizations hold are, strictly speaking, limited to the evidence reported herein.

In conducting our search, a number of studies could not be used to substantiate the generalizations being studied. These ranged from one which reported no parameters at all (Rao 1972) to those that were internally inconsistent. For example, Sexton (1970) reports both positive and negative results and most of the coefficients as not significant.

We do not report any evidence for carryover effects of advertising or advertising goodwill, although they clearly exist and have been reviewed by Clarke (1976). We also do not report on the various types of models employed by the various researchers. It has been shown that the Koyck, partial adjustment, and customer holdover models are observationally equivalent; however, the implications of the models are quite different from a theoretical point of view. In addition, model estimates may be biased due to specification problems such as multicollinearity, which arises with polynomial lag models, aggregation bias, failure to consider the simultaneous nature of sales and advertising, or failure to account for serial correlation. These problems have been discussed in both the econometric literature (Theil 1971, p. 540) and in the marketing literature (Clarke 1976; Houston and Weiss 1975; Parsons and Schultz 1976). Many of the articles presented represent attempts to solve some of these problems. For example, the degree of statistical sophistication evident between the earliest work of Palda (1964) and the recent work by Leone (1978) is representative of attempts to find better estimates of advertising effectiveness. These problems exist and deserve to be brought to the reader's attention, but the statistical sophistication of the works will not be compared, only the results.

To simplify the findings, we regard sales and market share as equivalent measures of "sales" response. The qualitative impact of the marketing mix variables has not been considered, largely because it has not been studied since Buzzell (1964) found that the content and presentation of advertising messages, as reported by the Schwerin Research Corporation test for measuring the effectiveness of television commercials, is related to short-term changes in market share. Finally, the amount of advertising is measured by advertising expenditures and the elasticities we report are short run.[2]

A1. Primary advertising has a direct and positive influence on total industry (market) sales.

To test this proposition, data on *generic* advertising and total industry sales of a product are needed. The main support for this generalization consequently comes from studies of trade association advertising, as for beverages or fruits. Evidence comes from Nerlove and Waugh (1961) for oranges; Hochman, Regev, and Ward (1974) for orange juice; Ward (1975) for grapefruit juice; and Thompson and Eiler (1975) for milk. Somewhat weaker evidence is reported by Ball and Agarwala (1969) for tea. Although it cannot be generalized, Nerlove and Waugh report a short-run advertising elasticity of .17 for oranges.

Employing data at the brand level, Clarke (1972) and Leone (1978) studied the competitive environment for a frequently purchased good which can be placed in well-defined industry categories. Both of these studies found that the advertising of an individual brand, along with stimulating selective demand, tends to increase industry sales of other brands within a category, or a form of the primary demand effect.

It should be mentioned that Schultz and Wittink (1976) have developed a theory for testing the effects of industry advertising which can be used to investigate the influence of selective advertising on primary demand. While it was not applied, it provides an interesting analytical framework for investigating this question.

A2.1 Selective advertising has a direct and positive influence on individual company (brand) sales.

There is a good deal of evidence that, for particular markets and for particular brands, this proposition holds. This is not to say that insignificant relationships do not appear in studies of advertising effectiveness, for they do. Rather, broad and general support has been found in the following studies: Bass and Clarke (1972), Bass and Parsons (1969), Beckwith (1972), Black and Farley (1977), Clarke (1972, 1973, 1976), Cowling and Cubbin (1971), Erickson (1977), Helmer and Johansson (1977), Houston and Weiss

(1974, 1975), Johansson (1973), Lambin (1969, 1970, 1972a, 1972b, 1976), Lambin, Naert, and Bultez (1975), Leone (1978), McCann (1974), Montgomery and Silk (1972), Moriarty (1975), Palda (1964), Parsons (1975, 1976), Peles (1971), Sawyer and Ward (1977), Schultz (1971), Telser (1962), Weiss (1968), Wildt, (1974, 1976), Wittink (1975, 1977), and Yon and Mount (1975).

This research area represents the strongest generalization since it passes the strongest scientific test. That is, these articles represent studies which employed simple regression (Palda 1964), used simultaneous-equation regression analysis (Bass and Parsons 1969), attempted to adjust for serial correlation problems (Houston and Weiss 1975), and employed Box-Jenkins analysis (Helmer and Johansson 1977), not only on different data bases which provided supporting evidence, but also on the same data base (i.e., Lydia Pinkham). Therefore, we find both nonexperimental replication and the strongest form of corroborating evidence.

A2.2 The elasticity of selective advertising on company (brand) sales is low (inelastic).

For frequently purchased branded goods (FPBG), excluding cigarettes and gasoline, reported elasticities range from .003 to .23. For all products all elasticities are less than .5, as can be seen in Table 1. It should be noted that some of the elasticities in Table 1 come from direct measurements, such as double-log regression equations, and others are derived from the parameter estimates from other types of models.

B1. Increasing store shelf (display) space has a positive impact on sales of nonstaple grocery items.

The research investigating the relationship between shelf space and sales has concentrated on determining the *existence* of a relationship, rather than measuring its magnitude. In one of the earliest conceptual works in this area, Brown and Tucker (1961) proposed that for some products, sales were related to shelf space by an increasing concave function that reaches a maximum at some finite amount of shelf space. Cairns (1963, p. 43) concluded in another theoretical paper, "The more space allocated to an item, the more likely it is to be seen by a shopper, and, hence, the more likely to be purchased. This is particularly true in the case of items likely to be purchased on impulse." Howev-

TABLE 1
Reported Advertising Elasticities

Study	Product	Elasticity[a]
Bass and Parsons (1969)	FPBG[b]	.04 and .09
Clarke (1973)	FPBG	.02–.11
Cowling and Cubbin (1971)	Automobiles	.31
Erickson (1977)	Household Cleaner	.04
Houston and Weiss (1974)	FPBG	.09
Johansson (1973)	Women's Hair Spray	.07–.12
Lambin (1976)	Various[c]	.003–.482[d]
Lambin (1972a)	FPBG	.03–.05
Lambin (1972b)	Gasoline	.15–.43
Lambin (1970)	Small Electrical Appliance	.18–.21
Lambin (1969)	FPBG	.19–.23
Lambin, Naert, and Bultez (1975)	FPBG	.15–.18
Leone (1978)	FPBG	.034–.067
Montgomery and Silk (1972)	Prescription Drugs	.16–.19
Moriarty (1975)	FPBG	.003–.04
Parsons (1976)	FPBG	.11
Parsons (1975)	Household Cleaner	.107
Schultz (1971)	Air Travel	.12
Telser (1962)	Cigarettes	.47 and .46
Weiss (1968)	FPBG	.004–.022
Wildt (1976)	FPBG	.025–.15
Wildt (1974)	FPBG	.02–.03
Wittink (1977)	FPBG	.078[e]
Wittink (1975)	FPBG	.08
Yon and Mount (1975)	FPBG	.02

[a]"—" implies range of estimates for one or more brands or models; "and" implies estimates for separate brands.

[b]Frequently purchased branded good.

[c]This study is based on the analysis of 25 product-markets and 78 brand-countries. The average advertising elasticity for 40 significant coefficients was .10; more than 60% of the elasticities were less.

[d]The high end of the range are elasticities for electric shavers. With this infrequently purchased product excluded, the range is from .003–16.

[e]Pooled estimate. Range for unpooled data was .09–.66.

er, Cox (1964) found little difference in the sales of impulse goods and staples when shelf space was varied. Then, in a latter study (Cox 1970), a difference was found between various impulse goods contingent on whether an individual had a high or low acceptance for the brand. This divergence between the theoretical and empirical works led Anderson (1979) to state, "The literature concerned with the conceptual development of brand demand as a function of display area shows a higher degree of consistency than does the empirical research done to test various functional specifications."

Nonetheless, the empirical research in this area is in general agreement that there is a positive relationship between shelf space and unit sales. The evidence does point out, however, that this relationship is not uniform among products, nor across stores. Support for this comes from Cairns (1962), Chevalier (1975), Curhan (1972, 1974a, 1974b), Frank and Massy (1970), Kennedy (1970), Kotzan

TABLE 2
Reported Products Used in Articles Supporting the Shelf Space Generalization

Study	Product(s)
Chevalier (1975)	Bleach, mayonnaise, light-duty liquid detergent, cooking oil, storage bags, fabric softener, semi-moist dog food, and facial tissue.
Cox (1964)	Baking soda, hominy, "Tang," and powdered coffee creamer.
Cox (1970)	"Coffeemate," "Creamora," Morton's salt and Food Club salt.
Curhan (1972, 1974b)	500 grocery product.[a]
Curhan (1974a)	Sixteen selected fresh fruits and vegetables.
Frank and Massy (1970)	Frequently purchased and heavily promoted grocery item.
Kennedy (1970)	Cigarettes.
Kotzan and Evanson (1969)	Crest toothpaste, Preparation H suppositories 12's, Hook's Red Mouth Wash, and Johnson and Johnson Assorted "Band Aids."
Mueller, Kline, and Trout (1953)	Cigarettes, packaged soaps, candles, canned beans, paper products, aluminum foil, coffee, and frozen foods.
Pauli and Hoecker (1952)	Canned fruits and vegetables.
Progressive Grocer (1963–64)	Peanut butter, canned corn, catsup, scouring powder, facial tissues, toothpaste, and bleach.

[a]Curhan states in the article, "an average space elasticity of .212 for all items (was found), showing a positive relationship between shelf space and unit sales."

and Evanson (1969), Mueller, Kline, and Trout (1953), Pauli and Hoecker (1952) and *Progressive Grocer* (1963–64). Table 2 provides a list of these works and the products used in the studies.

It should be mentioned that this area has also not escaped methodological criticism. Peterson and Cagley (1973) pointed out some of the statistical problems with these studies, as well as the possibility of a nonlinear relationship existing between sales and shelf space. Lynch (1974) criticized studies in this area for failure to develop any theory of what was found and the possibility of the existence of a simultaneous system of equations.

C1. Distribution, defined by number of outlets, has a positive influence on company sales (market share).

This generalization is supported by the work of Parsons (1974) who investigated a frequently purchased branded good newly introduced on the market and Lambin (1972a) who investigated gasoline station locations. Although the magnitude of the elasticities is not generalizable, Lambin found elasticities of .15 and .59.

DISCUSSION

It is clear that empirical generalizations in marketing can be sorted out from historical facts and from theories and speculations. But what are the implications for the practice of marketing research? There seem to be two main points: the first relates to knowledge gaps and the second to replication studies.

By specifying what is known about marketing behavior, the vast gaps of what is *not known* are revealed and an agenda for future research is provided. For example, in the area of sales response, we have very little knowledge of the effects of marketing mix variables other than advertising. We know almost nothing about the interaction effects of these variables. And for marketing decision variables such as sales force effort, there are virtually no generalizable results.

A research editorial (Boyd 1976) recently noted that "too often manuscripts tend to replicate earlier studies with but a small difference in either the research design or in the product class involved." But we have seen that replication is the key to generalization for without it, in the broadest sense, we have no corroboration of research results. We are left with one-shot studies that represent historical facts. Only by extending findings to other data sets do we perceive the generality of marketing relationships.

A final point about theory is essential. Marketing theory provides the means for interpreting the laws and facts of marketing behavior. But theory development *depends* on current marketing knowledge. Basic answers to questions of *how* marketing variables are related lead logically to new questions of *why* they are related. Like our fellow scientists, we must first describe marketing behavior in order to bring us closer to explaining it.

REFERENCES

Anderson, Evan E. (1979), "An Analysis of Retail Display Space: Theory and Methods," *Journal of Business,* 52 (January), 103–118.

Ball, R. J. and R. Agarwala (1969), "An Econometric Analysis of the Effects of Generic Advertising on the Demand for Tea in the U.K.," *British Journal of Marketing,* 4 (Winter), 202–217.

Basmann, R. L. (1965), "On the Application of the Identifiability Test Statistic in Predictive Testing of Explanatory Economic Models," *The Econometric Annual of the Indian Economic Journal,* 13, 387–423.

Bass, Frank M. and Darral G. Clarke (1972), "Testing Distributed Lag Models of Advertising Effect," *Journal of Marketing Research,* 9 (August), 298–308.

———, and Leonard J. Parsons (1969), "Simultaneous-Equation Regression Analysis of Sales and Advertising," *Applied Economics,* 1 (May), 103–124.

Beckwith, Neil E. (1972), "Multivariate Analysis of Sales Responses of Competing Brands to Advertising," *Journal of Marketing Research,* 9 (May), 168–176.

Berelson, Bernard and Gary Steiner (1964), *Human Behavior: An Inventory of Scientific Findings,* New York: Harcourt, Brace and World.

Black, T. R. L. and John U. Farley (1977), "Responses to Advertising Contraceptives," *Journal of Advertising Research,* 17 (October), 49–56.

Boyd, Harper W. Jr. (1976), "The JMR's Editorial Objectives," *Journal of Marketing Research,* 13 (February), 1–2.

Brown, William M. and W. T. Tucker (1961), "Vanishing Shelf Space," *Atlantic Economic Review,* 9 (October), 9–13, 16, 23.

Buzzell, Robert D. (1964), "Predicting Short-Term Changes in Market Share as a Function of Advertising Strategy," *Journal of Marketing Research,* 1 (August), 27–31.

Cairns, J. P. (1962), "Suppliers, Retailers and Shelf Space," *Journal of Marketing,* 26 (July), 34–36.

——— (1963), "Allocating Space for Maximum Profits," *Journal of Retailing,* 39 (Summer), 41–45.

Chevalier, Michel (1975), "Increase in Sales Due to In-Store Display," *Journal of Marketing Research,* 12 (November), 426–431.

Clarke, Darral G. (1972), "An Empirical Investigation of Advertising Competition," unpublished doctoral dissertation, W. Lafayette, Ind.: Purdue University.

——— (1973), "Sales-Advertising Cross-Elasticities and Advertising Competition," *Journal of Marketing Research,* 10 (August), 250–261.

——— (1976), "Econometric Measurement of the Duration of Advertising Effect on Sales," *Journal of Marketing Research,* 13 (November), 345–357.

Cowling, K. and J. Cubbin (1971), "Price, Quality and Advertising Competition: An Econometric Investigation of the U.K. Car Market," *Economica,* 38 (November), 378–394.

Cox, Keith K. (1964), "The Responsiveness of Food Sales to Shelf Space Changes in Supermarkets," *Journal of Marketing Research,* 1 (May), 63–67.

——— (1970), "The Effect of Shelf Space upon Sales of Branded Products," *Journal of Marketing Research,* 7 (February), 55–58.

Curhan, Ronald C. (1972), "The Relationship Between Shelf Space and Unit Sales in Supermarkets," *Journal of Marketing Research,* 9 (November), 406–412.

——— (1974a), "The Effects of Merchandising and Temporary Promotional Activities on the Sales of

Fresh Fruits and Vegetables in Supermarkets," *Journal of Marketing Research,* 11 (August), 286–294.

———— (1974b), "Shelf Space Elasticity: Reply," *Journal of Marketing Research,* 11 (May), 221–222.

Ehrenberg, A. S. C. (1966), "Laws in Marketing—Tailpiece," *Applied Statistics,* 15 (November), 257–267.

———— (1972), *Repeat-Buying: Theory and Application,* Amsterdam: North-Holland Publishing Company.

Erickson, Gary (1977), "The Time-Varying Effectiveness of Advertising," in *1977 Educators' Proceedings,* Barnett A. Greenberg and Danny N. Bellenger, eds., Chicago: American Marketing Association, 125–128.

Frank, Ronald E. and William F. Massy (1970), "Shelf Position and Space Effects on Sales," *Journal of Marketing Research,* 7 (February), 59–66.

Helmer, Richard M. and Johny K. Johansson (1977), "An Exposition of the Box-Jenkins Transfer Function Analysis with an Application to the Sales-Advertising Relationship," *Journal of Marketing Research,* 14 (May), 227–239.

Hochman Eithan, Uri Regev, and Ronald W. Ward (1974), "Optimal Advertising Signals in the Florida Citrus Industry," *American Journal of Agricultural Economics,* 56 (November), 697–705.

Houston, Franklin S. and Doyle L. Weiss (1974), "An Analysis of Competitive Market Behavior," *Journal of Marketing Research,* 11 (May), 151–155.

———— and ———— (1975), "Cumulative Advertising Effects: The Role of Serial Correlation," *Decision Sciences,* 6 (July), 471–481.

Hunt, Shelby D. (1976), *Marketing Theory: Conceptual Foundations of Research in Marketing,* Columbus, Ohio: Grid Publishing, Inc.

Johansson, Johny K. (1973), "A Generalized Logistic Function with an Application to the Effect of Advertising," *Journal of the American Statistical Association,* 68 (December), 824–827.

Kennedy, John R. (1970), "The Effect of Display Location on the Sales and Pilferage of Cigarettes," *Journal of Marketing Research,* 7 (May), 210–215.

Kline, Morris (1953), *Mathematics in Western Culture,* New York: Oxford University Press.

Kotzan, Jeffrey A. and Robert V. Evanson (1969), "Responsiveness of Drug Store Sales to Shelf Space Allocation," *Journal of Marketing Research,* 6 (November), 465–469.

Lambin, Jean-Jacques (1969), "Measuring the Profitability of Advertising: An Empirical Study," *Journal of Industrial Economics,* 17 (April), 86–103.

———— (1970), "Optimal Allocation of Competitive Marketing Efforts: An Empirical Study," *Journal of Business,* 43 (October), 468–484.

———— (1972a), "A Computer On-Line Marketing Mix Model," *Journal of Marketing Research,* 9 (May), 119–126.

———— (1972b), "Is Gasoline Advertising Justified?" *Journal of Business,* 45 (October), 585–619.

———— (1976), *Advertising, Competition and Market Conduct in Oligopoly Over Time,* New York: North-Holland Publishing Company.

————, Philippe A. Naert, and Alain Bultez (1975), "Optimal Marketing Behavior in Oligopoly," *European Economic Review,* 6 (April), 105–128.

Leone, Robert P. (1978), "Time-Series Model Building and Forecasting: An Empirical Analysis of the Relationship Between Sales and Advertising," unpublished doctoral dissertation, W. Lafayette, Ind.: Purdue University.

Lynch, Michael (1974), "Comment on Curhan's 'The Relationship Between Shelf Sapce and Unit Sales in Supermarkets'," *Journal of Marketing Research,* 11 (May), 218–220.

McCann, John M. (1974), "Market Segment Response to the Marketing Decision Variables," *Journal of Marketing Research,* 11 (November), 399–412.

Monroe, Kent B. (1973), "Buyers' Subjective Perceptions of Price," *Journal of Marketing Research,* 10 (February), 7O–80.

Montgomery, David B. and Alvin J. Silk (1972), "Estimating Dynamic Effects of Market Communications Expenditures," *Management Science,* 18 (June), 485–501.

Moriarty, Mark (1975), "Cross-Sectional, Time Series Issues in the Analysis of Marketing Decision Variables," *Journal of Marketing Research,* 12 (May), 142–150.

Mueller, Robert W., George E. Kline, and Joseph J. Trout (1953), "Customers Buy 22% More When Shelves Are Well Stocked," *Progressive Grocer,* 32 (June), 40–48.

Nerlove, Marc and F. V. Waugh (1961), "Advertising Without Supply Control: Some Implications of a Study of the Advertising of Oranges," *Journal of Farm Sciences,* 43 (October), 813–837.

Palda, K. S. (1964), *The Measurement of Cumulative Advertising Effects,* Englewood Cliffs, N.J.: Prentice-Hall, Inc.

Parsons, Leonard J. (1974), "An Econometric Analysis of Advertising, Retail Availability, and Sales of a New Brand," *Management Science,* 20 (February), 938–947.

―――― (1975), "The Product Life Cycle and Time Varying Advertising Elasticities," *Journal of Marketing Research,* 12 (November), 476–480.

―――― (1976), "A Rachet Model of Advertising Carryover Effects," *Journal of Marketing Research,* 13 (February), 76–79.

――――, and Randall L. Schultz (1976), *Marketing Models and Econometric Research,* New York: North-Holland Publishing Company.

Pauli, Hans and R. W. Hoecker (1952), "Better Utilization of Selling Space in Food Stores: Part I: Relation of Size of Shelf Display to Sales of Canned Fruits and Vegetables," Marketing Research Report No. 30, Washington, D.C.: U.S. Government Printing Office.

Peles, Yoram (1971), "Economies of Scale in Advertising Beer and Cigarettes," *Journal of Business,* 44 (January), 32–37.

Peterson, Robert A. and James W. Cagley (1973), "The Effect of Shelf Space upon Sales of Branded Products: An Appraisal," *Journal of Marketing Research,* 10 (February), 103–104.

Progressive Grocer (1963–64), "The Colonial Study," 42 (September), 43 (March).

Rao, Vithala R. (1972), "Alternative Econometric Models of Sales-Advertising Relationships," *Journal of Marketing Research,* 9 (May), 177–181.

Sawyer, Alan and Scott Ward (1977), "Carry-Over Ef-

fects in Advertising Communication: Evidence and Hypotheses from Behavioral Science," in "Cumulative Advertising Effects: Sources and Implications," Darral G. Clarke, ed., Marketing Science Institute Report No. 77–211, September.

Schultz, Randall L. (1971), "Market Measurement and Planning with a Simultaneous-Equation Model," *Journal of Marketing Research,* 8 (May), 153–164.

――――, and Dick R. Wittink (1976), "The Measurement of Industry Advertising Effects," *Journal of Marketing Research,* 13 (February), 71–75.

Sexton, Donald E. (1970), "Estimating Marketing Policy Effects on Sales of a Frequently Purchased Product," *Journal of Marketing Research,* 7 (August), 338–347.

Simon, Herbert A. (1968), "On Judging the Plausibility of Theories," in *Logic, Methodology, and Philosophy of Science III,* B. Van Rootselaar and J. F. Staal, eds., Amsterdam: North-Holland Publishing Company.

Telser, Lester (1962), "Advertising and Cigarettes," *Journal of Political Economy,* 70 (October), 471–499.

Theil, Henri (1971), *Principles of Econometrics,* New York: John Wiley & Sons.

Thompson, Stanley R. and Doyle A. Eiler (1975), "Producer Returns from Increased Milk Advertising," *American Journal of Agricultural Economics,* 57 (August), 505–508.

Ward, Ronald W. (1975), "Revisiting the Dorfman-Steiner Static Advertising Theorem: An Application to the Processes Grapefruit Industry," *American Journal of Agricultural Economics,* 57 (August), 500–504.

Weiss, Doyle L. (1968), "Determinants of Market Share," *Journal of Marketing Research,* 5 (August), 290–295.

Wildt, Albert R. (1974), "Multifirm Analysis of Competitive Decision Variables," *Journal of Marketing Research,* 11 (February), 50–62.

―――― (1976), "The Empirical Investigation of Time Dependent Parameter Variation in Marketing Models," in *Marketing: 1776–1976 and Beyond,* Kenneth L. Bernhardt, ed., Chicago: American Marketing Association, 46–72.

Wittink, Dick R. (1975), "Systematic and Random Variation in the Relationship Between Marketing Variables," unpublished doctoral dissertation, W. Lafayette, Ind.: Purdue University.

―――― (1977), "Advertising Increases Sensitivity to Price," *Journal of Advertising Research,* 17 (April), 39–42.

Yon, Bernard and Timothy D. Mount (1975), *The Response of Sales to Advertising: Estimation of a Polynomial Lag Structure,* A. E. Res. 75–4, Department of Agricultural Economics, Cornell University, April.

Zaltman, Gerald, Christian R. A. Pinson, and Reinhard Angelmar (1973), *Metatheory and Consumer Research,* New York: Holt, Rinehart & Winston.

NOTES

[1]Some readers who might find fault with us for discounting the technical specifics of each reviewed study might be willing to serve on such a court, but this is a two-edged sword: the more deeply one looks into an econometric study, for example, the more doubts one may have about its particular validity. It is better to look at the forest now inasmuch as we have already seen so many trees.

[2]The articles reported in support for the following generalizations have been uncovered after a thorough search through academic journals, as well as professional meeting proceedings and working papers. It is, however, possible that some material was unintentionally overlooked, and to the author(s) we apologize.

DISCUSSION QUESTIONS

1. What is the relationship of marketing generalizations to marketing theory?

2. How is a search for marketing generalizations different from a search for marketing propositions?

3. Identify and evaluate the current approaches to theory development in the discipline of marketing.

4. A Nobel laureate in physics, Richard Feynman recently commented that the social sciences are not science because there are no laws or generalizations. Comment on this view.

PREFACE TO

"Knowledge and Marketing: Exploring the Foundations of Inquiry"

One night, shortly after we met, we had a serious conversation about current directions in, and influences on, marketing research and scholarship. Our mood was critical, but constructive and committed. Our criticism was not anchored in the phenomena of marketing. We shared a perspective that marketing phenomena and contexts were robust and exciting. Instead, our criticisms were anchored in frustrations with the discipline of marketing, particularly its overwhelming emphasis on conventional science as "*the*" method to direct and sanction disciplinary research and scholarship. Although we each possessed a respect for science and its conventions, we found science to be incomplete and often inadequate as "*a*" method to pursue and construct marketing reality.

Throughout our educations, we each had considerable exposure to systems thought. It had significant impact. Yet, we found that as we advanced in our formal educations, systems thought became increasingly neglected and frequently discussed as

inappropriate. *Why?* And, what does it *mean* to disregard, or at least neglect, this powerful perspective of inquiry?

The reflective work of C. West Churchman (especially 1968, 1979) provided necessary inspiration and insight to address such questions. We feel that systems thought, particularly its philosophical and methodological basis, are not developed well nor understood extensively in marketing.

In this paper, we decided to strengthen our personal understanding of the search for knowledge in marketing by exploring the foundations of inquiry. We view inquiry as the system of seeking, constructing, and validating knowledge. It is the pursuit of meaning and its human realization. We have chosen to anchor our search for knowledge in individuals, yet we consider its relevance and realization across social and general systems. We share this exploration in the mood of serious conversation.

16

KNOWLEDGE AND MARKETING: EXPLORING THE FOUNDATIONS OF INQUIRY

MICHAEL P. MOKWA

KENNETH R. EVANS

> The central task of the designer [of an inquiring system] is to come in touch with and work through the unconscious of the inquiring system.
>
> *(Churchman 1971: 265).*

INTRODUCTION

The marketing discipline has exhibited strong normative concern for developing valid and relevant knowledge. This has generated extensive acceptance of the ideals, norms, and procedures of conventional scientific methodology to direct and sanction formal inquiry within the discipline. Two dominating perspectives of the discipline have emerged. One portrays marketing as a discipline struggling toward becoming a science, whereas the other perspective suggests that marketing is a science struggling toward maturity (e.g., O'Shaughnessy and Ryan 1979; Myers, Massy, and Greyser 1980). Both perspectives appear to agree that marketing inquiry will comprehend reality most effectively when it is *disciplined* according to the norms and methods of conventional science. Strong arguments have been articulated to ground the formal inquiring system of the marketing discipline within the philosophy of science (e.g., Hunt 1976a, 1976b, 1979). Although we agree that there are significant benefits to be gained through a higher consciousness of the role and nature of traditional philosophy of science in marketing inquiry, we believe that a conventional philosophy of science perspective is neither a complete nor comprehensive framework for grounding and guiding marketing inquiry (e.g., Bagozzi 1976; Carman 1980; Sweeney 1972; Zaltman, Lawther, and Heffring 1982).

Source: Revised for this volume from *Marketing Theory: Philosophy of Science Perspectives*, Ronald F. Bush and Shelby D. Hunt, eds., Chicago, Ill: American Marketing Association, 1982, 34–38. Originally titled "In Pursuit of Marketing Knowledge: An Exploration Into Philosophies of Inquiry."

In the remainder of this paper, we consider the pursuit of marketing knowledge from a broad philosophy-of-inquiry perspective. We believe that the phenomena of marketing, the state of marketing knowledge, and the many, varied orientations and demands of marketing-knowledge producers and users indicate a need consciously to accept, encourage, and develop a multimethod system of marketing inquiry. To elaborate our perspective, we discuss some fundamental dimensions of inquiry and knowledge systems, emphasizing ontological issues and the psychological dimensions of inquiry. We explore distinct archetype philosophic systems that ground and guide inquiry, and we highlight implications of our perspective for the future development of marketing knowledge.

KNOWLEDGE AND INQUIRY

Knowledge has been an enduring topic for reflective thinking. Questions about the nature of knowledge—about knowing and about relating thought and action—are seldom novel. What does change are those who raise the questions and search for resolution and the contexts in which the questions and resolutions are considered.

Currently, there is a resurgence of interest in questions about knowledge and inquiry within most social and administrative disciplines (e.g., Mitroff and Kilmann 1978; Holzner and Marx 1979; Van Maanen 1979). Many factors appear to be driving this resurgence, for example, there is recognition of disciplinary information and data proliferation, yet there are critical gaps between the production of disciplinary knowledge and its utilization (e.g.,

Weiss 1977; Lindblom and Cohen 1979); there are increasing demands on both knowledge producers and users—many social and management problems appear to be getting more difficult (e.g., Mason and Mitroff 1981); there is more competition for resource investments in knowledge development and greater accountability for justifying efforts, outcomes, and consequences (e.g., Weiss 1977); there are open discussions of the psychological tensions encountered by some knowledge producers and users regarding the acceptance and enactment of their disciplinary socialization (e.g., Mitroff 1974; Pirsig 1974; Reinharz 1979).

The classic questions concerning knowledge, therefore, are being reconsidered in contemporary contexts: What do we know? How do we know? Can we verify or justify what we know and how we know? Moreover, the *unconscious* side of knowledge and inquiry is becoming increasingly important, and the classic questions can be stretched to consider: What *can* we know? How *can* we know? Can we *effect* (design) our knowledge and inquiry to hold up, or potentially lead, across time and social development?

Ontology

Knowledge and inquiry, which are basic elements of epistemology, are embedded within ontol-ogy—general, core assumptions about, or apperceptions of, the fundamental nature of phenomena and reality. In marketing, ontological issues have seldom been discussed explicitly, despite persistent exploration of epistemological concerns.

Morgan and Smircich (1980) characterize ontological perspectives along a continuum that is anchored at one extreme by the purely subjectivist orientation that reality is a projection of imagination and anchored at the other extreme by the purely objectivist orientation that reality is a concrete structure. The subjectivist views man as spirit, consciousness, or being, whereas the objectivist considers man as a responder. Subjectivists seek phenomenological insights; objectivists attempt to construct positivist science. Four other dominant ontological/epistemological patterns are identified along the continuum. An adaptation of the continuum is presented in Figure 1. Morgan and Smircich (1980) conclude:

> Our analysis affirms the need for a more reflexive approach to understanding the nature of social research . . . a need to approach discussions of methodology in a way that highlights the vital link between theory and method—between the world view to which the researcher subscribes, the type of research question posed, and the technique that

The Ontological Continuum				
	Perspective of reality	Perspective of human nature	Methodological orientation	Accepted metaphors
Subjectively oriented ↑	Projection of human imagination	Transcendental consciousness	Phenomenology	Spiritual being and consciousness
	A social construction	Symbol creator	Ethnomethodology and hermeneutics	Meaning and mythology
	Symbolic interaction	Symbol user and actor	Social action theory	Role playing and rituals
	Field of information and learning	Information processor	Cybernetics and contextual analysis	Patterns, feedback, and learning
	Concrete processes	Adaptor	Open systems theory	Boundaries and contingencies
Objectively oriented ↓	Concrete structures	Responder	Positivism and experimentation	Control and causality

(Left vertical label: Ontological Dimensions)

*Adapted from Morgan and Smircich (1980).

FIGURE 1

Basic ontological patterns.*

is to be adopted . . . much of the debate and criticism over methodology involves researchers who are failing to communicate . . . basic assumptions about their subject. (p. 499)

Thus, inquiry and knowledge are grounded within an ontological perspective held by inquirers and communities of inquirers. To understand inquiry and knowledge, the ontological perspective of the inquirer should be communicated.

Toward a Hybrid Ontology

We find that most conventional ontological perspectives are limited, constrained by simple conceptualizations and metaphors that portray or emphasize fragments of reality (e.g., Brown 1977; Morgan 1980). Moreover, human nature is often portrayed awkwardly or even discussed separately within ontological statements. We feel that an ontological perspective should express core assumptions concerning personal and social human nature as well as the nature of nonhuman phenomena. We suggest that all phenomena might not possess the same invariant nature or at least the same relevant invariant blend of nature. Thus, reality may involve both transcendental and concrete structural properties in various blends and states. Our ontological perspective follows.

We use man as the anchor for our ontological perspective. We view man as an active and purposive participant involved in a complex, dynamic, and often ambiguous context—reality. Reality includes both objective and subjective elements and dimensions in continuous interaction and change. These elements (phenomena) can be conceived, perceived, and acted upon or with. Some phenomena are relatively proximate and accessible, whereas others are more distant or ephemeral and are less accessible. Personal consciousness, capability, experience, and encounters with phenomena generate symbolic apperceptions that meld to create *an* individual's personal, distinctive reality. Social and nonpersonal (physical as well as metaphysical) dimensions of contexts interact with and influence personal reality construction, and they produce shared social constructions and emerging general systems of reality. The structure of reality reflects intermingling and the process reflects unfolding.

This ontological statement blends a perspective of active, purposeful, and personal human nature

with an interactive, multipurposive, and systemic complex of reality and realization. Accordingly, knowledge and inquiry involve personal desires, capabilities, and standards; interpersonal desires, capabilities and standards; and general system requisites, capabilities and their evolution. Thus, inquiry is a process of realization, and knowledge is realization.

The Inquiring Process

Inquiry is an active human pursuit to know (Churchman 1971). Inquiry is the process in which phenomena are apprehended by individuals or social communities with the purpose of consciously realizing (knowing) the phenomena or elements of it. The parameters of inquiry emanate from phenomena, individuals, methods, and contexts of encounter, social systems, general systems and the environment as well as from the intermingling of these.

The distinguishing characteristics of inquiry relative to other possible processes of realization or knowing are its *directed* consciousness. Inquiry is active rather than passive; directed rather than determined; selective rather than reflexive. Inquiry includes: orienting, generating, enabling, enacting, and evaluating processes (Susman and Evered 1978) as well as processes of interpersonal communication, collaboration, and sanction. What constitutes knowledge is to be found in the processes and parameters of inquiry. No one process nor parameter provides a complete nor adequate framework for explaining knowledge (Churchman 1979). Likewise, no one conventional explanation seems to capture the breadth or robustness of inquiry.

Knowledge

Knowledge has many definitions, partially because inquiry occurs at a personal level, at various social system levels, and throughout the general system. These levels become interwoven at any time and across time. Thus, knowledge is constructed, developed, communicated, stored, and varied within and across individuals, across and within levels, and across time. Knowledge variability is related both to differences in perspectives, capabilities, and processes and to emergent changes in phenomena or inquiring systems. Emergent changes can be evolutionary or can involve purposive intervention, design, and evaluation.

The fundamental unit or basis of knowledge is a personal realization of a shared social reality construction (Holzner and Marx 1979). This reflects the tight connection between an individual inquirer and relevant social system dynamics, such as genetic issues, socialization and acculturation processes, linguistic/semantic restraints, and the unique experience base of each individual.

Four important general features of knowledge help to specify the concept. These are: utility (value), veracity (truth), formality (methodology), and pervasiveness (scope). As such, knowledge can be used, tested, developed, and shared. Thus, knowledge is often classified in terms of common sense, of socially sanctioned stores of formal explanation, and of individual or societal capabilities to act purposively (Churchman 1971; Holzner and Marx 1979).

In general, common sense is knowledge that is relatively pervasive, informal, situationally useful, and questionably truthful. Sanctioned disciplinary methodology and social systems underlie formal stores of explanation. These project strong concern for formality to generate veracity without necessarily considering utility or extensive communication. Finally, knowledge as a capability involves low formality but high instrumentality and a concept of truth that involves an active attachment of inquirer, phenomena, and system.

Knowledge as capability stretches the role of the inquirer from unattached observer and interpretor of phenomena into a purposive, active, and involved participant in the field of the phenomena.

Whenever phenomena are encountered, it appears that common sense, interpretations of stores of formal explanation to which the inquirer has been exposed, and distinct personal preferences, capabilities, and experiences coalesce in the inquiring process. The question, thus, becomes: Can the system and methodology of inquiry be developed to guarantee, or at least enhance, utility, truth, and extensive sharing of these? Understanding the psychology of inquiry and accepting a broad methodology of inquiry lead in the right direction.

THE PSYCHOLOGY OF INQUIRY

One of the most powerful norms—and myths—of conventional philosophy of science is the ascribed role of detachment for the scientist. Normatively, the inquiring scientist is reduced to a mechanistic state—an agent of operationalization and an extension of instrumentation in the process of pure science. This ideal norm is simply not enacted in most scientific endeavors according to recent studies (e.g., Mitroff 1974; Reinharz 1979). Most scientists appear to be selective, interpretive, and *attached* to their inquiry, despite accepting and often professing the norm of detachment. However, the norm of detachment seems to have directed attention away from considering the truly personal capabilities, preferences and methods of inquirers and the potential positive impact of these upon inquiring systems.

Mitroff and Kilmann (1978) have carefully reviewed and synthesized significant studies from the various disciplines that have considered science as a substantive subject matter—fields such as history, philosophy, sociology, and psychology. An important and interesting contribution of their work is a classification framework that describes and differentiates four archetype inquiring personalities or orientations. They draw heavily on Jung's theories of personal preferences for, and development of, information-acquisition capabilities and decision-making style.

Jung (1959, 1968) contended that individuals possess two antithetical modes of information—acquisition and processing—and two antithetical styles of decision making. A preferred information mode is interrelated with a preferred decision style within each individual. These interact to form a preferred inquiring orientation or personality, and this orientation is developed more extensively than orientations combining the other mode and style. Orientations that are not preferred are accessible to an inquirer but these become underdeveloped and uncomfortable to use.

Jung's two information modes are sensation and intuition. His two decision strategies are thinking and feeling. Each will be described briefly (and simplistically).

Sensation focuses on detailed, sensory input—data and hard facts about a divisible, concrete reality. Intuition relies on imagination and conceptualization to construct a holistic reality beyond the capabilities of direct sensation. It accepts possibilities and ideals as reality. Thinking seeks formal explanations that are general and relatively independent of human qualities and values. It is accepting of givens and has been portrayed best in traditional expressions of logic and conventional science. Thinking is a search for invariant truth. In contrast, feeling is a process of individuation and questioning. It is the search for justification and human realization. It has been portrayed best in conventional expressions of aesthetics, ethics, politics, and religion. Feeling is a process of accepting ambiguity and dealing with it.

A final dimension of Jung's pattern typology is ignored by Mitroff and Kilmann (1978). This dimension characterizes personal inquiring orientations as introverted or extroverted. An introverted inquirer is usually comfortable in an orientation and is driven by intrinsic rewards, incentives, and evaluations. An introverted inquirer may have to be drawn out to contribute to the broader systems. An extroverted inquirer is driven by extrinsic rewards, incentives, and evaluations. The extroverted inquirer seeks substantial involvement and support within the broader systems. If the orientation of the extroverted inquirer is compatible with the proximate social system, the extroverted inquirer may be quite comfortable and productive. However, if there is incompatability, the inquirer may attempt to change orientations or operate from an underdeveloped orientation. In either case, there is a high potential for personal and interpersonal conflicts and ineffective performance. Thus, there is a challenge to draw introverted inquirers into the broader system and a complementary challenge to channel extroverted inquirers into the development and expression of their personal orientation within the broader systems.

Inquirers can be classified relative to four archetypes according to Mitroff and Kilmann (1978):

- The Analytical Scientist—a sensing thinker who perceives science and logic as superior modes of inquiry.

- The Conceptual Theorist—an intuitive thinker who conceives science and logic as superior modes of inquiry that unfold into broader systems of realization.

- The Conceptual Humanist—an intuitive feeler who is oriented through idealistic purposes toward developing designs for human realization.

- The Particular Humanist—a sensing feeler who requires intense personal experiences to generate and share knowledge to realize and improve human individuation.

Each archetype possesses a different view of reality, inquiry, and knowledge. Each prefers different inquiring methods and establishes different aims and guarantees for knowledge. Figure 2 outlines some of the important distinctions. The conclusion is intriguing:

> The entire field of science is in need of revolution and revision. . . . Anything less than a systemic or wholistic approach (to inquiry) will fail to capture and do justice to the phenomena of science. . . . If we are ever to achieve an integrative theory of humanity, then our methods can be no less complex than the very phenomena we are studying; that is our methods must be psychologically sophisticated and diverse as humanity itself. (pp. 107, 130)

Greater awareness, appreciation, and cooperation among diverse styles of inquiry is necessary, yet very difficult to implement, given the sociology of science and its institutions and processes. We believe, however, a broadened consciousness of basic methodological issues in inquiry is a necessary basis.

THE METHODOLOGY OF INQUIRY

Living is a continuous encounter with phenomena, a continuous stream of realizations. However, much of the realization process operates at a subdued level of consciousness. When consciousness is raised and directed, we enter the domain of inquiry—an active, directed, and selective process of information acquisition, structuring, testing, translating, enacting, and evaluating. While in the domain of inquiry, we consider consciously the process, character, and quality of knowledge construction and application.

Conventional core epistemological assumptions stress the management or control of the form (methodology) of the inquiry system (Kaplan 1964). Formalization of methodology is expected to produce the most truthful, useful and just knowledge. For example, the history and philosophy of science depict the struggle to construct, communicate, and enact a formal methodology capable of producing the most verifiable (truthful) approximations of reality without necessarily considering utility or justice.

FIGURE 2
A comparison of inquiring personality patterns.*

Elements of Inquiry	Archetype Inquiring Personality Patterns			
	Analytical Scientist	**Conceptual Theorist**	**Conceptual Humanist**	**Particular Humanist**
Nature of knowledge	Impersonal, value free, precise, empirical	Technical, value related, uncertain, imaginative	Interpersonal, value constituted, ambivalent, empathetic	Personal, value dominated, A-rational, behavioral
Role of the inquirer	Detached, an agent of operationalization	Interested, a technical designer	Involved, a social planner	Embedded, a political actor
Aim or inquiry	Precision, search for invariance and truth	Bounded integration; generation, patterning and expression of ideas	Unbounded synthesis, general patterns for social actualization	Intense personal experience and realization
Preferred logic	Classical deductive methods	Closed systems—bounded dialectics	Open human systems—Unbounded dialectics	Unique determinants
Preferred ideology	Conventional disciplinary science	Technological adaptation and evolution	Social ecology and development	Individual differentiation and personal goal seeking
Preferred methodology	Controlled experimental tests and convengence	Invention and conflict resolution	Innovation and conflict tolerance	Formative evaluation and competition
Guarantor of knowledge	Internal and external validity, peer consensus	Commitment and cooperation	Purpose and conflict	Action-learning and self-determination

*Developed from Mitroff and Kilmann (1978).

Constructive debate concerning the methodology of inquiry has been an important catalyst in the development and evolution of the general inquiring system. Briefly, we explore the archetype philosophies of inquiry that have emerged as frames of reference in this debate. Our exploration is directed by, and grounded extensively within, the reflective work of Churchman (1968, 1971, 1979). Each archetype possesses inherent strengths and limitations as well as strengths and limitations in its enactment. Moreover, the archetype methodologies unfold into each other.

The Inquiring Encounter

The role, purpose, and capabilities of the inquirer and the apperceived nature and characteristics of the encountered phenomenon and its proximate field/context provide the elementary parameters of an inquiring experience.

The role assumed by the inquirer can be characterized by the extent of perceived detachment or attachment to the encountered phenomena and its field. A detached role emphasizes controlled observation and interpretation in which the inquirer and phenomena simply interface, whereas the attached role emphasizes involved participation in which the inquirer and phenomena interact. These roles can converge and overlap consciously or unconsciously. Moreover, these roles may form an important dialectic in the inquiring system (Rowan 1976) that can be resolved only through reflective inquiry after a focal encounter or experience (Churchman 1968).

The apperceived nature of phenomena is grounded within an inquirer's ontological perspective, but the situationally relevant characteristics of a phenomenon and its field are selected just as an encounter is consciously planned, unfolds, and is reflected on by the inquirer. Phenomena are apperceived and characterized along multiple, interconnected dimensions, for example, simple/complex, concrete/abstract, accessible/elusive, ambiguous/clear, malleable/rigid, static/dynamic, recursive/nonrecursive, and so on (Van Gigch 1974). Thus, the apperception of the basic properties of a phenomenon and its proximate field as well as the role, capabilities, and preferences of the inquirer influence the adoption and enactment of a methodology.

Conceptual Inquiry

Leibniz described and advocated an inquiring system that was totally oriented and controlled through introverted conceptualization. The system possessed innate ideas and the capability to apperceive and interrelate these ideas into patterns or models. Grand patterns could be broken into components through deductions. Elementary apperceptions could be inductively interrelated into grand patterns—fact nets. This inquiring system would be capable of constructing formal symbolic systems, using and storing them. The enduring accomplishments of this approach to inquiry include conventional systems of logic and mathematics as well as the admonition to communicate and store knowledge.

The guarantor of conceptual inquiry is the pattern builder and the ability of the pattern builder clearly and precisely to specify and articulate the pattern and its elements. This philosophy of inquiry extols human insight, introverted analysis and model building, and the ability to create reality.

Strict Empirical Inquiry

Locke vigorously opposed the conceptual inquiring system, especially its basis, innate ideas. He proposed that all knowledge was experiential and anchored empirically. The Lockean inquirer possessed no innate ideas nor imminent logic. It possessed only the capabilities to receive and process direct sensory data and to recognize elementary properties. It developed the ability to verify through consensus—consensus across experiences by the inquirer (learning), and, more important, consensus across experiences by different inquirers who would share their experiences. Thus, learning and communication are vital for verification and also serve as agents of generalization. Generalizations are produced by extrapolating a consensus developed across experiences to other experiences judged to be similar. Generalization through learning and communicated consensus is an awkward dimension of the Lockean system. Moreover, the Lockean system is severely limited to phenomena that can be observed. Yet, the Lockean system accentuates the role of sensation, the processes of learning and communication, and the significance of interobserver consensus. These are all important contributions.

Toward a Synthesis

Kant struggled to resolve the inherent inadequacies of the purely conceptual and empirical inquiring systems. His proposed resolution was synthesis. In his methodology, the conceptual and empirical are interrelated and ultimately integrated. There is an a priori recognition of givens, the construction of multiple-patterned conceptualizations, and the gathering of multiple-relevant data sets. The conceptualization and data sets are aligned within the givens, and the best fit is selected as the best *approximation* for truth. As such, conceptual models constructed from ideas and stores of prior experiences are used as paths to guide empiricism, and empirical content is used to validate conceptual models.

Kant was deeply concerned with the adequacy of truth approximations built on the synthesis of conceptual models and empirical observations within given domains. He questioned the ability to guarantee the given and, thus, to orient inquiry appropriately. Furthermore, he pondered the adequacy of truth as the guiding criteria for inquiry. He explored human justice, ethics, and aesthetics as significant criteria. Thus, Kant provided the foundation for conventional scientific methodology and a strong sense of concern regarding its adequacy.

Dialectic Inquiry and Synthesis

A dialectic approach to inquiry has been proposed by Hegel. This method involves preparation of at least two explanations of reality that are each considered feasible, even truthful according to the criteria of other inquiring systems. Ideally, the explanations vary only across an interpretative dimension, include diametrically opposed interpretations, and represent firmly held convictions.

A structured confrontation is used to present the explanations and serves as a forum for investigation, justification, attack and counterattack. The debate attempts consciously to push to the surface the basic assumptions, parameters, and interpretations underlying the explanations. Once the total explanations—givens, models, data, and interpretations—are exposed and debated, there is an opportunity to create a new, higher order explanation through synthesis of the prior explanations and interpretations. If higher order synthesis is not achieved, then a consensus may develop at the heightened level of consciousness generated by the dialectic or the inquiry may be reoriented and redesigned to seek a new set of explanations and interpretations.

The Hegelian inquiring system accentuates the need consciously to consider and even attack basic apperceptions, parameters, and interpretations as well as the need to seek and offer counterexplanations. The system guarantor involves the open, persistent, creative, and committed conflictual search for knowledge through the conscious recognition of the unconscious elements of inquiry.

Purposive Inquiry and Progress

Singer critically investigated the orienting of inquiry, the role of inquirers, the capability of inquirers accurately to measure or portray realizations, and the contribution of inquiry to the evolution of human systems. He concluded that truth is always an *approximation*—there is not ultimate realization. Truth is specified pragmatically by human systems. Multiple-truth approximations emerge when human systems fail to communicate and cooperate. This constrains evolution and may even be dysfunctional. Thus, Singer proposed a complex, cooperative, and comprehensive philosophy for developing inquiry.

Above all, the Singerian inquiring system is purposive. It is oriented to finding purpose; then, to using purpose to seek, develop, and evaluate enabling realizations; and finally, to enact the purpose. The inquirer is an attached and inseparable element of the inquiring system with responsibilities to the system. Inquiry and action are indivisible. Ideals, such as aesthetics, ethics, and justice, must be considered just as carefully as veracity or other system referents. Methodology should be interdisciplinary (or better, beyond disciplines or other contrived boundaries), recognizing the unfolding of one discipline into another; furthermore, methodology is synthetic, indicating that all methodologies are interconnected.

Singer describes the system guarantor in terms of serious inquirers who are deeply committed and attached to their inquiry, continuously sweeping in new realizations to increase the system's capabilities to comprehend its purpose, develop its means, and actively move to higher order purposes and means. As such, the inquiring system is dynamic and continuous. It seeks higher order states for the system and guides the system through its realizations. The inquirer must possess and enact a heroic spirit.

The General System of Inquiry and Human Ecology

Churchman has exemplified the heroic mood of the serious inquirer—the guarantor within the Singerian system. He has contributed significantly to our realization of the inquiring system through the content of his work and by the example that he has set through his work. The indivisibility of inquiry, action, and person are manifested clearly in his methodology and its philosophy.

The logic of the Churchman methodology is quite complex. It is grounded in the general systems approach. However, it is a unique denotation of general systems thought that appears to have emerged from a strong ontological orientation that emphasizes a human ecology that is filled with purpose, perspective, prospective, realization, and mystery—all fascinatingly interconnected and unfolding into each other. This grasp and enactment of the systems approach is much different than the rudimentary connotative representations of the systems approach to which most of us have been exposed. Furthermore, Churchman's logic accentuates an imminent dialectic dimension and a reflective perspective of design and development in which orientation, construction, action, and evaluation meld into meaning and significance. A distinctive methodological synthesis emerges across Churchman's work. It extends, operationalizes and implements the philosophy of Singerian inquiry and integrates it with the contemporary unfolding of human ecology. As such, the substantive focus of the inquiry and the inquiring processes are synthesized. The inquiring system unfolds into all other human systems and beyond into general systems. Inquiry reflects and radiates all other systems, and all other systems reflect and radiate inquiry.

Churchman projects a view of inquiry as a (maybe, *the*) vital and critical potential that we can engage to make a difference in ourselves and our systems. Knowledge is personal realization (including enactment) of this potential. The guarantor . . . it is a serious conversation within time across time; it involves all who heroically strive to actualize their individuation as well as all who could; and the topic might be *"to make a difference, or not. . . ."*

INQUIRY, KNOWLEDGE, AND MARKETING

We began by noting a strong concern for knowledge development in the marketing discipline and by highlighting the focal role of conventional scientific methods and norms in the disciplinary institution of marketing. These are the general *conscious* dimensions of marketing inquiry. However, marketing knowledge and inquiry exceed institutional boundaries and norms. Moreover, within our boundaries, there are many *unconscious* dimensions, and there is substantial space to challenge, change, or simply raise our current consciousness.

We have explored some fundamental areas of low consciousness in marketing—ontology, the psychology of inquiry, and the philosophic archetypes underlying inquiring methods. We suggest that there are strong relationships among ontological orientations, inquiring personalities, and the acceptance and enactment of different methodologies in inquiring encounters. We need to deepen our realization of these fundamental elements of inquiry and how they unfold into an inquiring system.

Reality is multidimensional and richly faceted. Thus, the challenge of inquiry and knowledge is seriously to seek to enable, enact, evaluate, and express the broadest and deepest realizations of which individuals and our systems are capable. As such, all facets of knowledge—utility, veracity, form, and scope—and all methods of inquiry require more intensive consideration in contemporary contexts.

In marketing, we need to encourage articulation of the nature, scope, and characteristics of both our methods and our phenomena, from different ontological orientations. We need to accept and encourage the active development of diverse inquiring personalities, respecting personal capabilities, preferences, and contributions. We should continue to probe the role of conventional science in marketing, but we need to adopt a much broader and deep-

er philosophy of inquiry to realize all that *is* and *can be* marketing. A better understanding of the archetype inquiring methods, the conscious dimensions and enactments of each, and the unconscious unfolding of each into the others appears to be a serious direction for marketing inquiry.

REFERENCES

Bagozzi, Richard P. (1976), "Science, Politics and the Social Construction of Marketing," in *Marketing: 1776–1976 and Beyond,* Kenneth L. Bernhardt (ed.), Chicago: AMA, 586–592.

Brown, Richard H. (1977), *A Poetic for Sociology,* Cambridge: At the University Press.

Carman, James M. (1980), "Paradigms for Marketing Theory," in Jagdish N. Sheth (ed.), *Research in Marketing,* Vol. 3, Greenwich, Conn.: JAI Press, 1–36.

Churchman, C. West (1968), *Challenge to Reason,* New York: McGraw-Hill.

Churchman, C. West (1971), *The Design of Inquiring Systems,* New York: Basic Books.

Churchman, C. West (1979), *The Systems Approach and Its Enemies,* New York: Basic Books.

Holzner, Burkhart and John H. Marx (1979), *Knowledge Application: The Knowledge System in Marketing,* Boston: Allyn & Bacon.

Hunt, Shelby D. (1976a), *Marketing Theory: Conceptual Foundations of Research in Marketing,* Columbus, Ohio: Grid.

Hunt, Shelby D. (1976b), "The Nature and Scope of Marketing," *Journal of Marketing,* 40 (July), 17–28.

Hunt, Shelby D. (1979), "Positive vs. Normative Theory in Marketing: The Three Dichotomies Model as a General Paradigm for Marketing," *Conceptual and Theoretical Developments in Marketing,* Chicago: AMA, 567–576.

Jung, Carl G. (1959), *Psychological Types,* New York: Pantheon.

Jung, Carl G. (1968), *Analytical Psychology: Its Theory and Practice,* New York: Pantheon.

Kaplan, Abraham (1964), *The Conduct of Inquiry: Methodology for Behavioral Science,* San Francisco: Chandler.

Lindblom, Charles E. and David K. Cohen (1979), *Usable Knowledge,* New Have, Conn.: Yale University Press.

Mason, Richard O. and Ian I. Mitroff (1981), *Challenging Strategic Planning Assumptions,* New York: Wiley.

Mitroff, Ian I. (1974), *The Subjective Side of Science: A Philosophical Inquiry into the Psychology of the Apollo Moon Scientists,* Amsterdam, The Netherlands: Elsevier Scientific Publishing.

Mitroff, Ian I. and Ralph H. Kilmann (1978), *Methodological Approaches to Social Sciences,* San Francisco: Josscy-Bass.

Morgan, Gareth (1980), ''Paradigms, Metaphors and Puzzle Solving in Organization Theory,'' *Administrative Science Quarterly,* 25 (December), 605–622.

Morgan, Gareth and Linda Smircich (1980), ''The Case for Qualitative Research,'' *Academy of Management Review,* 5 (October), 491–500.

Myers, John G., William F. Massy, and Stephen A. Greyser (1980), *Marketing Research and Knowledge Development: An Assessment for Marketing Management,* Englewood Cliffs, N.J.: Prentice-Hall.

Pirsig, Robert M. (1974), *Zen and the Art of Motorcycle Maintenance: An Inquiry into Values,* New York: Morrow-Quill.

O'Shaughnessy, John and Michael J. Ryan (1979), ''Marketing, Science and Technology,'' *Conceptual and Theoretical Developments in Marketing,* Chicago: AMA, 577–589.

Reinharz, Shulamit (1979), *On Becoming a Social Scientist,* San Francisco: Jossey-Bass.

Rowan, John (1976), *Ordinary Ecstasy: Humanistic Psychology in Action,* London: Routledge & Kegan Paul.

Susman, Gerald I. and Roger D. Evered (1978), ''An Assessment of the Scientific Merits of Action Research,'' *Administrative Science Quarterly,* 23 (December), 582–603.

Sweeney, Daniel J. (1972), ''Marketing: Management, Technology or Social Process,'' *Journal of Marketing,* 36 (October), 3–10.

Van Gigch, John P. (1974), *Applied General Systems Theory,* New York: Harper & Row.

Van Maanen, John (ed.) (1979), ''Qualitative Methodology,'' *Administrative Science Quarterly,* 4 (December).

Van Maanen, John (ed.) (1983), *Qualitative Methodology,* Beverly Hills, Calif.: Sage, Inc.

Weiss, Carol H. (ed.) (1977), *Using Social Research in Public Policy Making.* Lexington, Mass.: D. C. Heath.

Zaltman, Gerald, Karen Le Masters, and Michael P. Heffring (1982), *Theory Construction in Marketing: Some Thoughts on Thinking,* New York: Wiley.

DISCUSSION QUESTIONS

1. Should personal perspective be encouraged within formal marketing inquiry? Discuss the strengths and limitations of the attached and detached orientations of inquirers.

2. What are the conventional ontological/ epistemological patterns found in marketing? Why do these dominate? If diverse ontological perspectives would be accepted within marketing, what might be the implications? Which ontological perspectives appear to offer the most promise for further development in marketing inquiry?

3. What is your ontological perspective and how has it been developed?

4. What inquiring personality pattern best captures your personal preferences and capabilities?

5. Within the domain of marketing, what problems and issues would be most appropriately suited for distinctive inquiring personalities?

6. what are the traditional methodologies of inquiry? How are these interrelated? What are the strengths and limitations of each?

7. What is ''the'' guarantor of knowledge?

8. How has or could each method of inquiry be used in marketing? What problems within marketing are/could be most appropriately studied from each methodology?

PREFACE TO

"General Theories and the Fundamental Explananda of Marketing"

The paper "General Theories and the Fundamental Explananda of Marketing," has its origins in three earlier works. First, in the "Morphology of Theory and the General Theory of Marketing" (1971), I proposed certain characteristics, such as lawlike generalizations, that all theories (general or otherwise) must have. Second, the publication "The Nature and Scope of Marketing" (1976) developed a model that attempted to provide more structure of the discipline of marketing and, hopefully, to solve several long-standing debates in our discipline. Finally, in *Marketing Theory: Conceptual Foundations of Research in Marketing* (1976), I attempted formally to integrate mainstream philosophy of science into analyses of marketing theory. The present article is a natural follow-up of the preceding works and attempts to delineate the nature of general theories in marketing. However, to do so requires a further specification of the fundamental nature of the marketing discipline. Hence, the development of the fundamental explananda of marketing science.

It has been my belief that one of the major ways an academic discipline progresses is through a dialectical process of thesis-antithesis. That is, disciplines progress by having participants take unequivocal positions on various issues and then having other participants attack these positions. These kinds of debates result in a new thesis, which often shares elements common to both of its prede-

cessors. Unfortunately, scholarly journals often foreclose thesis-anthesis debates. By the time many manuscripts run the entire gauntlet of the reviewing process, the resultant article is so hedged with qualifying phrases that one cannot tell exactly where the author stands. Both conceptual/theoretical papers and empirical papers share this affliction.

The present article presents my thesis on the nature of general theories and the fundamental explananda of marketing in unhedged fashion. Note my contention that *every* phenomenon (not many, or most, or quite a few, but *every* phenomenon) that marketing science seeks to explain can ultimately be reduced to a phenomenon residing in one of the four sets. As I write this short preamble, the article has not yet appeared in print. I look forward to the antithesis.

REFERENCES

Hunt, Shelby D. "The Morphology of Theory and the General Theory of Marketing." *Journal of Marketing*, 35 (April 1971), pp. 65–68.

Hunt, Shelby D. *Marketing Theory: Conceptual Foundations of Research in Marketing*. Columbus, Ohio: Grid, 1976.

Hunt, Shelby D. "The Nature and Scope of Marketing." *Journal of Marketing*, 40 (July 1976), pp. 17–28.

17

GENERAL THEORIES AND THE FUNDAMENTAL EXPLANANDA OF MARKETING*

SHELBY D. HUNT

After a flurry of articles and books on marketing theory in the 1950s and 1960s, there occurred a hiatus in the development of the theoretical foundations of marketing. Marketing turned toward other directions, as Lutz (1979, p. 3) has observed:

> For the most part, I believe that we have been experiencing a technological revolution of sorts, with most of our energies being devoted to the discovery and application of increasingly sophisticated mathematical and statistical procedures. This revolution has been a necessary step forward for the discipline, but it has perhaps diverted our attention away from similarly important inquiry into the conceptual foundations of marketing.

Evidence abounds that the hiatus is over and that interest in developing marketing theory is increasing. For example, there have now been three special conferences on marketing theory sponsored by the American Marketing Association (Bush and Hunt 1982; Ferrell, Brown, and Lamb 1979; and Lamb and Dunne 1980). These conferences have played a particularly significant role in encouraging marketing researchers to develop marketing theory. There have also been several books on marketing theory (Bagozzi 1980; Hunt 1976a, 1983; Zaltman, LeMasters, and Heffring 1982; Zaltman, Pinson, and Anglemar 1973). The works of Zaltman et al. and Hunt explore the philosophy of science foundations of marketing theory and Bagozzi's work attempts to

Source: Reprinted with permission from the *Journal of Marketing*, 47, (Fall), 1983, 9–17. Chicago, Ill.: American Marketing Association.

*The author wishes to acknowledge the assistance of Professors John J. Burnett, Larwrence Chonko, and Robert W. Wilkes, all of Texas Tech University, for reviewing an earlier draft of this article and to Professor A. C. Samli of Virginia Polytechnic Institute and State University for insightful observation on the fundamental explananda of marketing. Thanks also go the Professor Kenneth J. Roering, University of Minnesota, for providing the triggering cue for the development of this work.

integrate metatheoretical criteria with mathematical modeling techniques.

In addition to the special conferences and books on marketing theory, theorists have devoted significant attention to the conceptual domain of the marketing discipline (Ferber 1970; Hunt 1976b; Kotler 1972; Kotler and Levy 1969; Kotler and Zaltman 1971; Luck 1969, 1974). These debates on the nature of marketing concluded that (1) the primary focus of marketing is the exchange relationship, (2) marketing includes both profit sector and nonprofit sector organizations, and (3) all the problems, issues, theories, and research in marketing can be analyzed using the three categorical dichotomies of profit sector/nonprofit sector, micro/macro, and positive/normative (Arndt 1981a).

Consistent with the preceding writers, Bagozzi (1974) concurs that the basic subject matter that marketing science attempts to explain and predict is the exchange relationship. He proposes the foundations for a formal theory of marketing exchanges and suggests that "it is perhaps time to redirect our intellectual energy toward the development of a general theory of marketing" (Bagozzi 1979, p. 445). Is it time? The purpose of this article is to address the question "What would be the characteristics of a general theory of marketing if we had one?" In order to answer this question it will be necessary to (1) examine briefly the nature of theory in marketing, (2) explore the characteristics of general theories in the philosophy of science, (3) propose what a general theory of marketing would attempt to explain and predict, (4) delineate the structure of general theories in/of marketing, and (5) evaluate the status of general theories in/of marketing.

THE NATURE OF MARKETING THEORY

What is the nature of scientific theory? A consensus conceptualization of the characteristics of a theory is:

Theories are systematically related sets of state-

181

ments, including some law-like generalizations, that are empirically testable. The purpose of theory is to increase scientific understanding through a systematized structure capable of both explaining and predicting phenomena.

This conceptualization of theory (originally proposed by Rudner (1966) and first introduced into the marketing literature by Hunt (1971)) is characterized as consensus since it is consistent with the writings of (1) philosophers of science, (2) philosophers of social science, and (3) marketing theorists.

Philosophy of Science Perspectives on Theory

The stream of thought that dominated twentieth-century philosophy of science has been logical (or modern) empiricism, which owes its origins to the logical positivists of the 1920s. In fact the perspectives of the logical empiricists have been dubbed the "received view" of philosophy of science (Suppe 1977). Logical empiricism proposes that the "distinctive aim of the scientific enterprise is to provide systematic and responsibly supported explanations" (Nagel 1961, p. 15). Theories play a central role in explaining phenomena since a theory is "a system of hypotheses, among which law formulas are conspicuous" (Bunge 1967, p. 381). Similarly, Bergman (1957, p. 31) notes that "a theory is a group of laws deductively connected." Finally, Braithwaite (1968, p. 22) suggests that "a scientific theory is a deductive system in which observable consequences logically follow from the conjunction of observed facts with the set of the fundamental hypotheses of the system." Note that the views of all these "received view" philosophers of science are consistent with the previously suggested perspective. For a formal statement of the "received view" of theory, see Suppe (1977, p. 16–53).

In recent years, the proponents of logical empiricism have been vigorously attacked (for a discussion of the complete nature of these attacks, see Bush and Hunt 1982; Keat and Urry 1975; Suppe 1977). Although critics fail to speak with a single voice, most of these attacks have *not* centered on whether theories contain systematically related statements or law-like generalizations, or even whether theories should be empirically testable. Rather, the attacks have focused on issues like "what are the requirements for a generalization to

be considered law-like?" Proponents of the "received view" are content with the (essentially Humean) notion that "law-like" denotes nothing more than the observed regularity in the occurrence of two or more phenomena. Critics of logical empiricism, such as the scientific realists, insist that regularity is not enough; a kind of causal necessity must be shown (Harre and Madden 1975, p. 8). As Keat and Urry (1975, p. 44) have pointed out, both proponents and opponents of the "received view" hold that there are "general standards of scientificity, of what counts as an adequate explanation, of *what it is that we must try to achieve by scientific theories,* and of the manner in which *empirical evidence* should be used to assess their truth or falsity" (emphasis added). Thus, although they may differ as to technical details, both advocates and critics of the "received view" basically concur as to the *general* characteristics of theory.

Marketing and Philosophy of Social Science Perspectives

Both philosophers of social science and marketing theorists also agree as to the nature of theory. Thus, Kaplan (1964, p. 297) indicates that "a theory is a system of laws" and that "the laws are altered by being brought into systematic connection with one another, as marriage relates two people who are never the same again." Blalock (1969, p. 2) suggests that "theories do not consist entirely of conceptual schemes or typologies but must contain law-like propositions that interrelate the concepts or variables two or more at a time." The marketing theoretician Wroe Alderson (1957, p. 5) concludes that a "theory is a set of propositions which are consistent among themselves and which are relevant to some aspect of the factual world." Zaltman, Pinson, and Anglemar (1973, pp. 77–79) propose that a theory is a set of propositions, some of which are nonobservational, from which other propositions can be deduced which are at least testable in principle. Other contemporary writers in marketing theory use the same or similar conceptualization (Bagozzi 1980, pp. 63–65; El-Ansary 1979, p. 401; Ryan and O'Shaughnessy 1980, p. 47; Shoostari and Walker 1980, p. 100; and Solomon 1979, p. 377).

Starting from the perspective that theories are systematically related sets of statements, including some law-like generalizations, that are empirically testable, how do general theories differ from the ordinary kind? In short, what is it that makes a general theory "general"?

THE NATURE OF GENERAL THEORIES

There are several ways that one theory can be more general than another theory. Recalling that the purpose of theories is to explain and predict phenomena, general theories can be more general by explaining *more* phenomena. That is, general theories have a large extension or domain. Dubin (1969, p. 41) proposes that "the generality of a scientific model depends solely upon the size of the domain it represents." Zaltman et al. (1973, p. 52) concur: "a second formal syntactical dimension of a [theoretical] proposition is its *degree of generality*. All propositions purport to refer to a particular segment of the world, their universe of discourse."

As an example of how the extension of a theory affects its generality, consider the "hierarchy of effects" model. As originally proposed by Lavidge and Steiner (1961), and later developed by Palda (1966), the hierarchy of effects model attempts to explain how consumers respond to advertising through the hierarchy of cognition (thinking), affect (feeling), and conation (doing). Some empirical studies, such as those by Assael and Day (1968) and O'Brien (1971), have found support for the hierarchy of effects model.

Next consider the low involvement model originally proposed by Krugman (1965). The low involvement model suggests that for trivial products the consumers' interest is so low that they will respond to advertising through a hierarchy of cognition, conation, and affect (rather than cognition, affect, and conation). Empirical studies by Ray (1973), Rothschild (1974), and Swinyard and Coney (1978) have supported the low involvement hierarchy. The point here is that, according to the extension criterion, the low involvement model is more general than the traditional hierarchy of effects model, since there are many more "low involving" products than there are "high involving" products. That is, the domain of the low involvement model is larger than the domain of the original hierarchy of effects model.

A second way that theories can be more general is by systematically relating a larger number of law-like generalizations. Farber (1968, p. 173) suggests

that in psychology "comprehensive theories, i.e. those serving to organize a *considerable number* [emphasis added] of laws, depend on the state of knowledge in a given area." Similarly, Brodbeck (1968, p. 457) proposes that:

The more comprehensive a theory is, the more it unifies phenomena by revealing apparently different things to be special cases of the same kind of thing. The classic example of a comprehensive, unifying theory is Newton's. From the Newtonian theory of gravitation it was possible to derive Galileo's laws for the free fall of bodies on earth, Kepler's laws about the motions of the planets around the sun, the laws about the tides, and a host of other previously known but disparate phenomena. It explained all these and predicted new laws not previously known.

The preceding example suggested that the low involvement model was more general than the traditional hierarchy of effects model because it explained more phenomena. A recent model developed by Smith and Swinyard (1982), referred to as the "integrated information response model," attempts to unify both the traditional and low involvement models. Smith and Swinyard's model draws upon the expectancy-value model developed Fishbein and Ajzen (1975) and proposes that the key distinction between purchases for "trial" and purchases for "commitment" has been largely overlooked. Our purpose here is not to evaluate this new model, but rather, to point out that, to the extent that the model is validated by empirical testing, it represents a step forward in developing a more general theory of consumer behavior. This more general theory is brought about by incorporating into one theory all the law-like propositions of both the low-involvement and hierarchy of effects models.

A third way that theories can be general is that their constructs may be highly abstract. Blalock (1969, p. 141) states:

The general theory will be stated in highly abstract terms, with as few assumptions as possible as to the form of the equations, the values of the parameters, or (in the case of statistical theory) the specific distributions of the error terms. It will often be found that this very general theory can not yield useful theorems, and so additional assumptions will be made in order to study important special cases . . . the principal value of a highly general theoretical formulation is that it enables one to place the various special cases in perspective and to prove general theorems appropriate to them all.

Howard and Sheth were cognizant of the relationship between "level of abstraction" and "level of generalization." Thus, they (Howard and Sheth 1969, p. 391) indicate "first, the theory is said to be at a moderate level of abstraction, because it deals only with buying behavior, but nevertheless to be abstract enough to encompass consumer buying, institutional buying, distributive buying, and industrial buying."

Unfortunately, the phrase "high level of abstraction" does not have perfect antecedent clarity. At least three different meanings of "high level of abstraction" seem possible. First, high level of abstraction may indicate "more encompassing." This seems to be the usage suggested by Howard and Sheth when they propose that their theory of buyer behavior encompasses not only consumer buying, but also, other forms of buying as well. This meaning of level of abstraction would make it consistent with the notion that a general theory encompasses and explains a large number of phenomena.

A second possible meaning of high level of abstraction might be that the terms in the theory are "far removed" from directly observable phenomena. Thus, empirical referents or operational definitions for the "highly abstract" constructs may be difficult, if not impossible, to develop. Given the requirement that all theories must be empirically testable, there appears to be a significant danger in developing theories that are *too* abstract, or *too* far removed from observable reality. Even marketing theorists who have recently moved away from strict logical empiricism still hold empirical testing in high regard. Thus, Zaltman, LeMasters, and Heffring (1982, p. 107) propose:

Once a general theoretical statement has been made, the next step is to make a deduction and translate it into an *empirical* statement so that observations can be made and the "truth" of the statement tested. This testability of a statement

---

is of extreme importance to logical deductive analysis.

The original logical *positivist* position required all terms or constructs in a scientific theory to have direct empirical referents, i.e. be "observable." Recognizing that this position was untenable, the logical *empiricists* required all abstract or "theoretical" terms to be linked to directly observable terms via devices known as "correspondence rules." Current analysis in the philosophy of science suggests that even the logical empiricist position may be too stringent. Keat and Urry (1975) propose that attention be focused on the *testability* of statements rather than the *observability* of all terms *in* statements. Thus, they propose the following: "A statement is scientific only if it is possible to make observations that would count in some way for or against its truth or falsity" (Keat and Urry 1975, p. 38). This principle suggests that the constructs in a theory cannot be allowed to become so abstract (so far removed from reality) that they render the theory incapable of generating hypotheses capable of being empirically tested since such a theory would necessarily be explanatorily and predictively impotent.

There is a third possible meaning for "high level of abstraction." Sometimes it seems that the relationships among constructs in "highly abstract" general theories are very loosely specified. Consider the problem of a researcher attempting to "test" the general theory of consumer behavior proposed by Engel, Kollat, and Blackwell (1973). The researcher wishes to include in the experiment the construct "environmental influences." Unfortunately for the researcher, the model gives little guidance as to specifically which environmental influences should be included and how each should be related to other key constructs. When "high level of abstraction" means that the relationships between many of the key constructs in the "general" theory are very loosely specified, empirical testing is hindered and explanatory power is reduced. Therefore, it has been suggested elsewhere (Hunt 1976a) that many of these "highly abstract" general models may play their most significant role in what is referred to as the "context of discovery." That is, these kinds of general models or theories may be most useful in suggesting fruitful avenues for researchers to explore in generating or discovering theories that have direct explanatory power.

How then do general theories differ from ordinary theories? We may conclude that general theories explain a large number of phenomena and serve to unify the law-like generalizations of less-general theories. Theorists concerned with developing general theories should be alert to the problems involved in empirically testing their theoretical constructions. When key constructs in the theory become highly abstract in the sense of being too far removed from observable reality or in the sense that relationships among key constructs become too loosely specified, then empirical testability suffers, predictive power declines and explanatory impotence sets in. Despite these limitations, such theories or models might still serve the useful purpose of "road maps" for guiding the theoretical efforts of others.

THE FUNDAMENTAL EXPLANANDA OF MARKETING

If general theories in/of marketing have a broad domain and unify many law-like generalizations, what are the phenomena that these general theories would seek to explain and predict? In philosophy of science terminology, what are the *fundamental explananda* of marketing science? Alternatively, in experimental design terms, what are the fundamental *dependent variables?* Consistent with the perspective of most marketing theorists (Alderson 1965; Bagozzi 1974, 1978, 1979; Kotler 1972), this writer has proposed that the basic subject matter of marketing is the exchange relationship or transaction (Hunt 1976b). The discipline of marketing has its normative or "applied" side which is *technology,* rather than empirical science. The purpose of marketing technology is to assist marketing decision-makers by developing normative decision rules and models. Such rules and models are based on the findings of marketing science and various analytical tools (such as statistics and mathematics). The "basic" or positive side houses the empirical science of marketing (Hunt 1976b).

The preceding discussion implies that *marketing science is the behavioral science that seeks to explain exchange relationships.* Given this perspective of marketing science and adopting the customary (albeit

somewhat arbitrary) convention of designating one party to the exchange as the "buyer" and one party as the "seller," the fundamental explananda of marketing can be logically derived. The four interrelated sets of fundamental explananda (FE) of marketing science are:

FE1. The behaviors of buyers directed at consummating exchanges,

FE2. The behaviors of sellers directed at consummating exchanges,

FE3. The institutional framework directed at consummating and/or facilitating exchanges,

FE4. The consequences on society of the behaviors of buyers, the behaviors of sellers, and the institutional framework directed at consummating and/or facilitating exchanges.

As illustrated in Table 1, the first set of fundamental explananda indicates that marketing science seeks to answer *why do which buyers purchase what they do, where they do, when they do, and how they do?* The "which buyers" seeks to explain why certain buyers enter into particular exchange relationships and others do not. The "what" indicates that different buyers have different product/service mixes that they purchase. The "where" is the institutional/locational choice of buyers. That is, why do some buyers purchase at discount department stores and others at full service department stores and why do some buyers purchase in neighborhood stores and others in shopping centers? The "when" refers to the timing decisions of buyers. Why do buyers purchase differently in different stages in the family life cycle? Finally, the "how" refers to the processes that consumers use in making their purchasing decisions. That is, what are the identifiable stages in consumer decision making? The "how" also refers to any organizational systems that buyers develop to accomplish the purchasing task, for example, the sharing of buying responsibilities among various members of the household.

The second set of fundamental explananda of marketing concerns the behaviors of sellers. As Lutz (1979, p. 5) has pointed out, "It has been extremely unfortunate that the vast bulk of theory-based behavioral research in marketing has been on consumer behavior." He then concludes that "if we truly believe that exchange is the fundamental

TABLE 1
The Nature of Marketing Science

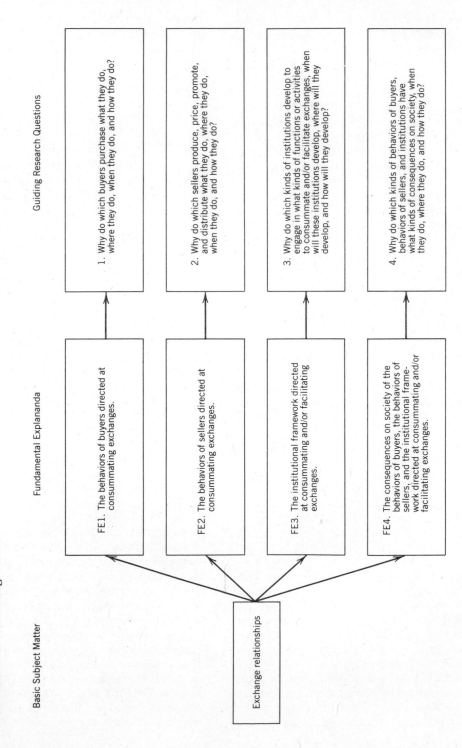

Basic Subject Matter

Fundamental Explananda

Guiding Research Questions

Exchange relationships

FE1. The behaviors of buyers directed at consummating exchanges.

FE2. The behaviors of sellers directed at consummating exchanges.

FE3. The institutional framework directed at consummating and/or facilitating exchanges.

FE4. The consequences on society of the behaviors of buyers, the behaviors of sellers, and the institutional framework directed at consummating and/or facilitating exchanges.

1. Why do which buyers purchase what they do, where they do, when they do, and how they do?

2. Why do which sellers produce, price, promote, and distribute what they do, where they do, when they do, and how they do?

3. Why do which kinds of institutions develop to engage in what kinds of functions or activities to consummate and/or facilitate exchanges, when will these institutions develop, where will they develop, and how will they develop?

4. Why do which kinds of behaviors of buyers, behaviors of sellers, and institutions have what kinds of consequences on society, when they do, where they do, and how they do?

building block of marketing, then, we have virtually ignored (in a scientific sense) the behavior of the party selling to the consumer.'' The guiding question is *why do which sellers produce, price, promote, and distribute what they do, where they do, when they do, and how they do?* The ''which'' points out that not all sellers participate in all exchanges. The ''what'' seeks explanations for the kinds of products produced, kinds of prices charged, kinds of promotions used, and kinds of distributors employed. The ''when'' seeks explanations for the timing of the behaviors of sellers. The ''where'' refers to the locations chosen by sellers to do business. The ''how'' refers to the processes involved and organizational frameworks developed by sellers when engaging in exchange relationships.

The third set of fundamental explananda suggests that marketing science seeks answers to *why do which kinds of institutions develop to engage in what kinds of functions or activities to consummate and/or facilitate exchanges, when will these institutions develop, where will they develop, and how will they develop?* The ''which'' points out that not all kinds of institutions participate in the consummation and/or facilitation of all kinds of exchanges and seeks to identify the kinds of institutions and ''what'' specific kinds of activities (functions) that will be performed by each. The ''when'' refers to the evolution or changing of the kinds of institutions through time and ''where'' these changes will take place. The ''how'' refers to the processes which bring about these institutional changes.

As used here, the term ''institution'' refers both to the intermediaries which either take title to the goods or negotiate purchases or sales, such as wholesalers and retailers, and also to purely facilitating agencies such as those solely engaged in transportation, warehousing, advertising, or marketing research. As suggested by Arndt (1981b, p. 37) marketing institutions can also be considered as ''sets of conditions and rules for transactions and other interactions.'' Note that the study of *marketing systems* can be considered the study of collections of interacting marketing institutions. In short, the third set of explananda seeks to explain the nature and development of all kinds of marketing systems.

The fourth set of fundamental explananda concerns the consequences of marketing on society.

The guiding question is *why do which kinds of behaviors of buyers, behaviors of sellers, and institutions have what kinds of consequences on society, when they do, where they do, and how they do?* The ''which'' directs the theorists to focus on specific kinds of behaviors and/or institutions and explain ''what'' kinds of consequences these behaviors or institutions will have on society. Again, the ''when'' refers to the timing of the consequences and the ''where'' focuses on *whom* the consequences will fall. For example, will the consequences fall disproportionately on the disadvantaged members of society? Finally, the ''how'' focuses on the processes and mechanisms by which various parts of society are impacted by marketing activities. The study of the kinds of consequences discussed here are generally subsumed under the term ''macromarketing.''

The preceding four sets of explananda are proposed to be *fundamental* in the sense that every phenomenon that marketing science seeks to explain can ultimately be reduced to a phenomenon residing in one of the four sets. A general theory *in* marketing would seek to explain all, or substantially all, the phenomena in a single set. For example, a theory which purports to explain all the behaviors of buyers directed at consummating exchanges would be characterized as a general theory *in* marketing. In contrast a general theory *of* marketing would purport to explain all the phenomena in all four sets.

GENERAL THEORIES: STRUCTURE AND STATUS

General theories can have two different structural forms, a hierarchical form or a collection of subtheories form. A hierarchical theory is one whose component laws are deductions from a very small subset of basic principles or axioms (Kaplan 1964, p. 298). The work of Bagozzi (1978) is an example of one attempt to develop a general theory from a very limited set of assumptions concerning exchange behaviors.

The second way to develop a general theory is to take several smaller theories and combine them in a systematic fashion. This is the approach taken by Bartels (1968) when he proposed that a general theory of marketing could be developed by combining the following seven sub-theories: (1) social initiative, (2) market separations, (3) expectations, (4) flows, (5) behavioral constraints, (6) marketing evolution, and (7) social control. This is also the approach taken by El-Ansary (1979), who suggested that the central organizing element for a general theory of marketing would be the channel of distribution. El-Ansary then identified 23 sub-theories which, if combined in a systematic fashion, would comprise a general theory of marketing.

The position adopted here is that the development of a general theory of marketing along strict hierarchical lines would be extraordinarily difficult and the possibility for the success of such an endeavor would be remote. Much more likely to be successful would be the procedure of developing a general theory for each of the four sets of fundamental explananda and then integrating each of the four theories into one comprehensive schema. Although we are not close to developing a general theory of marketing at this time, progress is being made. There have been several attempts to develop a general theory of buyer behavior. Although the works of Engel, Kollat, and Blackwell (1973); Howard and Sheth (1969); Nicosia (1966) have received the most attention, there have been other efforts at developing a comprehensive model of buyer behavior (Andreasen 1965; Bettman 1979; Hansen 1972; Markin 1974; Wind and Webster 1972). Some of these models have received empirical support; others remain to be tested. Note that most of these models were developed in the late 1960s and early 1970s. Perhaps the time is right for a new integrative model which would combine the best aspects of the various general models proposed to date.

As has been noted earlier, marketing has generally neglected theory concerning the behaviors of sellers directed at consummating exchanges. A notable exception was the work of Alderson (1965) on competition for differential advantage. This theoretical construction purports to explain the forces motivating firms in the marketplace by noting that in order to survive firms compete with other firms for the patronage of households. A firm can be assured of the patronage of a group of households only when the group has reasons to prefer the output of the particular firm over the output of competing firms. Therefore, each firm will seek some advantage over other firms to assure the patronage of a group of households, a process known as "competition for differential advantage." Competition consists of the constant struggle of firms to develop, maintain or increase their differential advantages over other firms. Unfortunately, very little has been done with the theory since the middle 1960s.

Several scholars have made major attempts to develop a general theory of marketing institutions. Using a microeconomic/functionalist approach, Bucklin (1966) has developed a "theory of distribution channel structure." Bucklin identifies the outputs of the channel distribution as delivery time, lot size and market decentralization. He then proposes that the channel functions necessary to produce these outputs are transit, inventory, search, persuasion and promotion. After determining the interrelationships among outputs and functions, Bucklin postulates the existence of a "normative channel" which the existing channel will tend toward in long-run equilibrium.

A second theoretical work by Baligh and Richartz (1967) builds a mathematical model of the channel of distribution drawing upon the original work by Balderston (1958). The Baligh and Richartz model is based on the key concepts of cooperation, competition, and their impact on "contactual" costs. The fundamental premise underlying their theory is that "exchange transactions are not costless and that in consequence there exists the possibility that these costs can be reduced" (Baligh and Richartz 1967, p. 6). Lastly, Robicheaux and El-Ansary (1975) have developed a general model for channel member behavior. The focal point of the model is the total performance of the channel of distribution which is postulated to be determined by both structural and individual characteristics. Shoostari and Walker (1980, p. 2) evaluate the model and conclude that "the model has the potential of becoming a highly valuable theory of channel performance." To the best of this writer's knowledge, none of the three general models concerning marketing institutions has been subjected to empirical tests. As with the general models of consumer behavior, most of the attempts to generate general theories concerning marketing institutions were developed in the 1960s. Again, as with consumer behavior, perhaps it is time to take a fresh look at the entire area and attempt to integrate the works of such authors as Baligh, Bucklin, El-Ansary, Richartz, and Robicheaux into a comprehensive model.

Unlike buyer behavior, seller behavior, and marketing institutions, there have been no attempts to develop a general theory of the consequences of marketing on society. The work of Beckman (1957) proposes that we can use "value added" as a measure of the total output of marketing activities. Similarly, the work of Bucklin (1978) postulates procedures for determining the efficiency with which marketing institutions perform their assigned tasks. A theory by Steiner (1973) explains the consequences on consumer prices of heavy advertising by national firms. Finally, Slater (1968) developed a model explaining the role of marketing in inducing economic development. Nevertheless, none of these theories in name or in fact constitute a general theory of the consequences of marketing activities and institutions on society. No one has even attempted a "general theory of macromarketing."

Two scholars have attempted to develop general theories *of* marketing. In 1968 Bartels suggested that a general theory of marketing should consist of seven sub-theories: (1) social initiative, (2) economic (market) separations, (3) market roles, expectations, and interactions, (4) flows and systems, (5) behavior constraints, (6) social change and marketing evolution, and (7) social control of marketing. An evaluation of these sub-theories (Hunt 1971) pointed out the lack of law-like generalizations in these sub-theories and concluded that the collection could not, therefore, be a general theory of marketing. This conclusion was also reached in the subsequent analysis by El-Ansary (1979).

Alderson (1965) also suggested that his work constituted a general theory of marketing. Although his efforts at developing a general theory have never been evaluated using the criteria contained herein, his work has been partially formalized and rendered amenable to systematic investigation (Hunt, Muncy, and Ray 1981). It is noteworthy that the partial formalization reveals that Alderson at least touched upon each of the four sets of fundamental explananda that a general theory of marketing would have to contain. In an attempt to explain the behavior of buyers, Alderson used the twin concepts of (1) the conditional value of a good if used and (2) the probability of use or the estimated frequency of use (Alderson 1965, p. 38). He used competition for differential advantage to explain seller behavior and the "discrepancy of assortments" to explain the

rise of intermediaries (Alderson 1965, p. 78). Finally Alderson's normative theory of marketing systems at least *explores* some of the effects of marketing systems on society (Alderson 1965, pp. 301–321). Although Alderson addressed each of the fundamental explananda of marketing, research in each separate area has gone well beyond the theoretical work of Alderson. For example, Alderson's theory of buyer behavior would be considered a somewhat naive approach today. Thus, although Alderson's efforts must be considered as extraordinary for his time, they cannot be considered a satisfactory general theory of marketing for today.

SUMMARY AND CONCLUSION

In summary, this article has attempted to explore the nature of general theories in/of marketing. Since theories are systematically related sets of statements, including some law-like generalizations, that are empirically testable, general theories should have these characteristics and "more." The extra dimension of general theories is that they should explain more phenomena and unify more laws. General theories *in* marketing would explain all the phenomena within one of the four sets of fundamental explananda of marketing: (1) the behaviors of buyers directed at consummating exchanges, (2) the behaviors of sellers directed at consummating exchanges, (3) the institutional framework directed at consummating and/or facilitating exchanges, and (4) the consequences on society of the behaviors of buyers, the behaviors of sellers, and the institutional framework directed at consummating and/or facilitating exchanges. A general theory *of* marketing would explain all the phenomena of all four sets. Such a general theory would probably be comprised of an integrated collection of sub-theories, rather a hierarchical theory.

Is a general theory of marketing possible? Given the progress that is being made on at least three of the four sets of fundamental explananda and given the increased emphasis being placed on theory development in marketing, there are grounds for optimism. There certainly is no logical reason for believing that it is *impossible* to develop such a general theory. Nevertheless, even if marketing should never generate a general theory of its total subject matter, the pursuit of such a general theory, like the pursuit of truth in general, would still be a worthy quest.

REFERENCES

Alderson, W. (1957), *Marketing Behavior and Executive Action,* Homewood, Ill.: Richard D. Irwin, Inc.

———— (1965), *Dynamic Marketing Behavior,* Homewood, Ill.: Richard D. Irwin, Inc.

Andreasen, A. R. (1965), "Attitudes and Customer Behavior: A Decision Model," in *New Research in Marketing,* L. Preston, ed., Berkeley, Calif.: Institute of Business and Economic Research, University of California, 1–16.

Arndt, Johan (1981a), "The Conceptual Domain of Marketing: An Evaluation of Shelby Hunt's Three Dichotomies Model," *European Journal of Marketing,* 16 (Fall), 27–35.

Arndt, J. (1981b), "The Political Economy of Marketing Systems: Reviving the Institutional Approach," *Journal of Macromarketing,* 1 (Fall), 36–47.

Assael, J. and G. S. Day, "Attitudes and Awareness as Predictors of Market Share," *Journal of Advertising Research,* 8 (December), 3–10.

Bagozzi, R. P. (1974), "Marketing as an Organized Behavioral System of Exchange," *Journal of Marketing,* 38 (October), 77–81.

———— (1978), "Marketing as Exchange: A Theory of Transactions in the Marketplace," *American Behavioral Scientist* 21 (March/April), 535–536.

———— (1979), "Toward a Formal Theory of Marketing Exchanges," in *Conceptual and Theoretical Developments in Marketing,* O. C. Ferrell, S. W. Brown, and C. W. Lamb, Jr., eds., Chicago: American Marketing Association, 431–447.

———— (1980), *Causal Models in Marketing,* New York: John Wiley & Sons, Inc.

Balderston, F. E. (1958), "Communication Networks in Intermediate Markets," *Management Science,* 4 (January), 154–171.

Baligh, H. H. and L. E. Richartz (1967), *Vertical Market Structures,* Boston: Allyn & Bacon, Inc.

Bartels, R. (1968), "The General Theory of Marketing," *Journal of Marketing,* 32 (January), 29–33.

Beckman, T. N. (1957), "The Value Added Concept as a Measurement of Output," *Advanced Management,* Vol. 22 (April), 6–9; reprinted in *Managerial Marketing: Perspectives and Viewpoints,* W. Lazer and E. J. Kelley, eds., Homewood, Ill.: Richard D. Irwin, Inc., 1962, pp. 659–67.

Bergman, G. (1957), *Philosophy of Science,* Madison: University of Wisconsin Press.

Bettman, James R. (1979), *An Information Processing Theory of Consumer Choice,* Reading, Mass.: Addison-Wesley Publishing Co.

Blalock, H. M. (1969), *Theory Construction,* Englewood Cliffs, N.J.: Prentice-Hall, Inc.

Braithwaite, R. B. (1968), *Scientific Explanation,* Cambridge: At the University Press.

Brodbeck, May (1968), *Readings in the Philosophy of the Social Sciences,* New York: The Macmillan Company.

Bucklin, L. P. (1966), *A Theory of Distribution Channel Structure,* Berkeley, Calif.: University of California, Institute of Business and Economic Research.

———— (1978), *Productivity in Marketing,* Chicago: American Marketing Association.

Bunge, M. (1967), *Scientific Research I: The Search for System,* New York: Springer-Verlag.

Bush, Ronald F. and Shelby D. Hunt eds. (1982), *Marketing Theory: Philosophy of Science Perspectives,* Chicago: American Marketing Association.

Dubin, R. (1969), *Theory Building,* New York: The Free Press.

El-Ansary, A. (1979), "The General Theory of Marketing: Revisited," in *Conceptual and Theoretical Developments in Marketing,* O. C. Ferrell, S. W. Brown, and C. W. Lamb, Jr., eds., Chicago: American Marketing Association, 399–407.

Engel, James, David B. Kollat, and Roger Blackwell (1973), *Consumer Behavior,* 2nd ed., New York: Holt, Rinehart & Winston, Inc.

Farber, I. E. (1968), "Personality and Behavioral Science," in *Readings in the Philosophy of the Social*

Sciences, M. Brodbeck, ed., New York: The Macmillan Company.

Ferber, Robert (1970), "The Expanding Role of Marketing in the 1970's," *Journal of Marketing,* 34 (January), pp. 29–30.

Ferrell, O. C., Stephen W. Brown, and Charles W. Lamb, Jr., eds. (1979), *Conceptual and Theoretical Developments in Marketing,* Chicago: American Marketing Association.

Fishbein, M. and I. Ajzen (1975), *Belief, Attitude, Intention and Behavior: An Introduction to Theory and Research,* Reading, Mass.: Addison-Wesley Publishing Co.

Hansen, Fleming (1972), *Consumer Choice Behavior,* New York: The Free Press.

Harre, R. and E. H. Madden (1975), *Causal Powers,* Totowa, N.J.: Rowman & Littlefield.

Howard, John A. and Jagdish N. Sheth (1969), *The Theory of Buyer Behavior,* New York: John Wiley & Sons, Inc.

Hunt, Shelby D. (1971), "The Morphology of Theory and the General Theory of Marketing," *Journal of Marketing,* 35 (April), 65–68.

—— (1976a), *Marketing Theory: Conceptual Foundations of Research in Marketing,* Columbus, Ohio: Grid.

—— (1976b), "The Nature and Scope of Marketing," *Journal of Marketing,* 40 (July), 17–28.

——, J. A. Muncy, and N. M. Ray (1981), "Alderson's General Theory of Marketing: A Formalization," in *Review of Marketing 1981,* B. M. Enis and K. J. Roering, eds., Chicago: American Marketing Association.

—— (1983), *Marketing Theory: The Philosophy of Marketing Science,* Homewood, Ill.: Richard D. Irwin, Inc.

Kaplan, A. (1964), *The Conduct of Inquiry,* Scranton, Penn.: The Chandler Publishing Company.

Keat, R. and J. Urry (1975), *Social Theory as Science,* London: Routledge & Kegan Paul.

Kotler, P. (1972), "A Generic Concept of Marketing," *Journal of Marketing,* 36 (April), 46–54.

Kotler, P. and S. J. Levy (1969), "Broadening the Concept of Marketing," *Journal of Marketing,* 33 (January), –15.

Kotler, P. and G. Zaltman (1971), "Social Marketing: An Approach to Planned Social Change," *Journal of Marketing,* 35 (July), 3–12.

Krugman, H. E. (1965), "The Impact of Television Advertising: Learning Without Involvement," *Public Opinion Quarterly,* 29 (Fall), 349–356.

Lamb, C. W., Jr., and P. M. Dunne, eds. (1980), *Theoretical Developments in Marketing,* Chicago: American Marketing Association.

Lavidge, R. C. and G. A. Steiner (1961), "A Model for Predictive Measurements of Advertising Effectiveness," *Journal of Marketing,* 25 (October), 59–62.

Luck, D. (1969), "Broadening the Concept of Marketing—Too Far," *Journal of Marketing,* 33 (July), 53–54.

—— (1974), "Social Marketing: Confusion Compounded," *Journal of Marketing,* 38 (October), 70–72.

Lutz, R. J. (1979), "Opening Statement," in *Conceptual and Theoretical Developments in Marketing,* O. C. Ferrell, Stephen W. Brown, and Charles W. Lamb, Jr., eds., Chicago: American Marketing Association, 3–6.

Markin, R. J. (1974), *Consumer Behavior: A Cognitive Orientation,* New York: The Macmillan Publishing Company.

Nagel, E. (1961), *The Structure of Science,* New York: Harcourt, Brace and World, Inc.

Nicosia, F. W. (1966), *Consumer Decision Processes: Marketing and Advertising Implications,* Englewood Cliffs, N.J.: Prentice-Hall, Inc.

O'Brien, T. (1971), "Stages of Consumer Decision Making," *Journal of Marketing Research,* 8 (August), 283–289.

Palda, K. S. (1966), "The Hypothesis of a Hierarchy of Effects: A Partial Evaluation," *Journal of Marketing Research,* 3 (February), 13–24.

Ray, M. (1973), "Marketing Communications and the Hierarchy of Effects," in *New Models for Mass Com-*

munications Research, Vol. 2, P. Clark, ed., Beverly Hills, Calif.: Sage Publications.

Robicheaux, R. and A. El-Ansary (1975), "A General Model for Understanding Channel Member Behavior," *Journal of Retailing,* 52 (Winter), 13–30, 90–94.

Rothschild, M. L. (1974), "The Effects of Political Advertising on the Voting Behavior of a Low-Involvement Electorate," Ph.D. dissertation, Stanford University, Calif.: Graduate School of Business.

Rudner, R. (1966), *Philosophy of Social Science,* Englewood Cliffs, N.J.: Prentice-Hall, Inc.

Ryan, Michael and John O'Shaugnessy (1980), "Theory Development: The Need to Distinguish Levels of Abstraction," in *Theoretical Developments in Marketing,* Charles W. Lamb, Jr., and Patrick M. Dunne, eds., Chicago: American Marketing Association, pp. 47–50.

Shoostari, Nader and Bruce Walker (1980), "In Search of a Theory of Channel Behavior," in *Theoretical Developments in Marketing,* Charles W. Lamb, Jr., and Patrick M. Dunne, eds., Chicago: American Marketing Association, pp. 100–103.

Slater, C. C. (1968), "Marketing Processes in Developing Latin American Societies," *Journal of Marketing,* 32 (July), 50–55.

Smith, R. E. and W. R. Swinyard (1982), "Information Response Models: An Integrated Approach," *Journal of Marketing,* 46 (Winter), pp. 81–93.

Solomon, Paul (1979), "Marketing Theory and Metatheory," in *Conceptual and Theoretical Developments in Marketing,* O. C. Ferrell, Stephen W. Brown, and Charles W. Lamb, Jr., eds., Chicago: American Marketing Association, pp. 374–382.

Steiner, R. L. (1973), "Does Advertising Lower Consumer Prices?" *Journal of Marketing,* 37 (October), 19–26.

Suppe, F. (1977), *The Structure of Scientific Theories,* 2nd ed., Chicago: University of Illinois Press.

Swinyard, William R. and Kenneth A. Coney (1978), "Promotional Effects on a High- versus Low-Involvement Electorate," *Journal of Consumer Research,* 5 (June), 41–48.

Wind, Y. and F. E. Webster (1972), "Industrial Buying as Organizational Behavior: A Guideline for Research Strategy," *Journal of Purchasing,* 8 (August), 5–16.

Zaltman, Gerald, Karen LeMasters, and Michael P. Heffring (1982), *Theory Construction in Marketing: Some Thoughts on Thinking,* New York: John Wiley & Sons, Inc.

Zaltman, Gearld, Christian R. A. Pinson, and Reinhard Anglemar (1973), *Metatheory and Consumer Research,* New York: Holt, Rinehart & Winston, Inc.

DISCUSSION QUESTIONS

1. In his preface, Hunt states, "It has been my belief that one of the major ways an academic discipline progresses is through a dialectical process of thesis-antithesis." Attempt to develop an alternative thesis to Hunt's thesis that there are four sets of fundamental explanada of marketing.

2. Hunt notes that no attempts have been made to develop a general theory of the consequences of marketing on society. Discuss the issues that such a theory would have to address.

3. Hunt argues that Alderson's theory of buyer behavior would be considered somewhat naive today. Attempt to modernize Alderson's theory by adding necessary theoretical constructs. Does the resulting theory differ markedly from existing buyer behavior models?

PREFACE TO
"Macromarketers' Guide to Paradigm Development"

The initial motivation for the "Macromarketers' Guide to Paradigm Development" arose from the need to encourage manuscript production for the *Journal of Macromarketing* (JMM), which began publication in the Spring of 1981. At that time, few marketing scholars knew where logical boundaries could be drawn to distinguish macromarketing from not-for-profit marketing, government marketing, consumer behavior, or even international business. Philosophers had debated the effects of trade and commerce on social institutions for centuries. From the knowledge thus accumulated, the fields of jurisprudence and political science had developed well-established disciplines in university curricula. However, the effects of the new technologies of marketing on society and of the responses of many impacted groups to marketing remain unclassified.

Today, scholars in many disciplines are attempting to develop theories that can be used to understand and manage the consequences of marketing technology. To bring order into the production of theories being developed in the physical and social sciences, the editors of the JMM needed some framework for evaluating the manuscripts submitted to this new journal. The problem had become so critical that a "Contributors' Guide" had to be developed quickly. The paper presented here provided the basis for preparing the "Contributors' Guide for Choice of Topics for Papers" (JMM 2:1, Spring 1982). This "Contributors' Guide" explains how the JMM solicits, selects, and positions manuscripts using the "Network Flow," "Evolutionary Change" and "Entropy" paradigms. These guidelines and categories are important, in that they demonstrate one contemporary synthesis of marketing thought viewed from a theory of knowledge and social impact perspective, not solely a managerial one.

18

MACROMARKETERS' GUIDE TO PARADIGM DEVELOPMENT

GEORGE FISK
PATRICIA MEYERS

The view we hold of the world governs the way we try to explain and predict outcomes of marketing interactions. Our theories of marketing are developed from these world views or ''paradigms'' as they are termed in the scientific community. We trace here the gradual adoption of marketing paradigms under which macromarketing theories can be catalogued. Because of their organizing power in conceptualizing theoretical gaps, paradigms promise to save much random effort in creating the theoretical basis for hypothesis development and testing. In this paper we examine paradigms that have proven productive or that promise to become so within the domain of macromarketing.

First, we describe four widely used paradigms: (1) the network flow paradigm, earliest of the organizing structures for macromarketing, (2) the market scarcity paradigm underlying the sales concept, (3) the competitive marketing management paradigm whose implicit behavioral limitation is described in its title and (4) the evolutionary systems change paradigm, the most recent to gain wide usage. Next, we identify (5) the general systems and (6) dissipative structures paradigms whose potential is yet to be determined but whose promise is alluring for macromarketing theorists. We then present in tabular form the time pattern of appearance of the first four paradigms in award winning papers. We conclude with our vision of paradigm developments possible in the future. Throughout this discussion it is necessary to recall that paradigms are not theories, but frameworks for developing them. Paradigms do not advance propositions or test hypotheses, but they do suggest the questions that can be posed to develop theories.

Source: Reprinted with permission from *Marketing Theory: Philosophy of Science Perspectives,* Ronald F. Bush and Shelby D. Hunt, eds., Chicago, Ill.: American Marketing Association, 1982, 281–285.

FOUR WIDELY USED PARADIGMS

Historically, the *network flow paradigm* appeared when early traders like Phoenicians sent cargoes of dyestuff, spices and wine to deficit production areas. Archeological digs are today uncovering sunken vessels and their cargoes along harborsides and in river channels. From such evidence we know that the first channels of distribution were literally ship channels and canals. These network channels of distribution were activated by the emergence of discrepancies in assortments desired and available from local supply areas. Assortment discrepancies arose as resource bases became inadequate to provision populations dependent on them (Alderson 1965). Marketers first traced the physical routes and channel organizations required to bridge the producer-consumer assortment discrepancies. The dominant idea in the network flow paradigm is that of equalizing supply-demand assortment discrepancies by moving goods and use rights from surplus supply areas to deficit demand areas, thus forming markets in the sense that buyers and sellers were placed into effective trading contracts (Alderson 1957).

The persistence of scarcity as populations grew exponentially in the post-feudal era aggravated the discrepancies in assortments experienced in many nations and triggered an age of exploration and commercial expansion. Here we find the roots of the *market scarcity paradigm*. Expansion led to reorganization of production first by specialization, then by mass production with its round-about capital investment requirements. Mass distribution was developed to sustain mass production during the period of European development characterized as the ''Commercial Revolution.'' By making possible larger market areas for sale of industrial goods, mass distribution permitted producers to reduce total unit costs of distribution plus manufacture by substituting low cost mass marketing for high cost small scale manufacture for the bundle of utilities delivered to buyers. However, under conditions of persistent scarcity, "Supply creates its own demand," as J. B. Say noted. Not until mechanization had advanced to the point of oversupplying the limited market areas of industrial nations was the market scarcity paradigm challenged by newer perspectives. The dominant idea in the market scarcity paradigm is that mass distribution expands markets to stimulate mass production. Markets can expand to the limits of quantities salable at prices in the vicinity of minimum long run average costs. Modern theories of production are still based on this paradigm.

When supply catches up to demand you can't sell what you have at a profit, so you have to find ways to have what you can sell. Thus the *competitive marketing management paradigm* emerged next. Developed as a strategy for managerial units within a firm, this perspective is basically perceived as "competition among the few." Competitive marketing theory in the U.S. assumes a behavior paradigm of competition in which a few large sellers face many small buyers, usually segregated into segments whose homogeneous demand characteristics match the differential advantage of a particular seller or industry group. Arndt (1979) called into question the marketing management conception, arguing that in Europe where industrial export marketing was as central as consumer goods marketing, governments often represent the only buyer facing oligopolistic cartelized industries in bilateral monopolistic exchanges. The fruitfulness of a broadened competitive marketing management paradigm as advocated by Arndt is evident in the number of theoretical variations displayed in Figure 1. Matched numbers of buyers and sellers may be read down the main diagonal. Kotler's version of the competitive marketing management paradigm is represented only by cell 34.

The spectrum of competitive behaviors range from price rivalry under perfect competition to a broad repertoire of product and enterprise differentiation. The core idea of the competitive marketing management paradigm is that entrepreneurial survival and growth is via efficiency of response in

Number of Sellers	Number of buyers			
	One	**Two**	**Few**	**Many**
ONE	11 Monopoly Monopsony	12 Monopoly Duopsony	13 Monopoly Oligopsony	14 Monopoly Perfect competition
TWO	21 Duopoly Monopsony	22 Duopoly Duopsony	23 Duopoly Oligopsony	24 Duopoly Perfect competition
FEW	31 Oligopoly Monopsony	32 Oligopoly Duopsony	33 Oligopoly Oligopsony	34 Oligopoly Perfect competition
MANY	41 Perfect competition Monopsony	42 Perfect competition Duopsony	43 Perfect competition Oligopsony	44 Perfect competition Perfect competition

FIGURE 1
The competitive market exchange paradigm.

matching competitors' offerings to fit buyers' want specifications most exactly at times, places and prices more advantageous to customers than terms of exchange offered by rivals. Only the swift and smart survive in this kind of competition. Theories developed from this perspective are basically explanations of adjustment mechanisms relative to the birth, growth and decline of rival enterprise.

In addition to competing with rivals, members of marketing channels also cooperate with their trading partners in mutually beneficial or "symbiotic" behavior. Sometimes one organization also lives on the cost-effort inputs of others—in a word, parasitism. Often new kinds of organizations emerge. Hence, to explain competition, cooperation, parasitism and mutation, a more sophisticated paradigm than the competitive marketing management framework is needed. Following Boulding (1981), paradigm 4 is the *evolutionary systems change paradigm*. The dominant idea in the evolutionary systems change paradigm is that competitive, cooperative and parasitic interactions between supply and demand behavior selects for survival and mutation those marketing organizations whose behavior is environmentally appropriate for existing market "niches." We will trace the appearance of these paradigms in award-winning articles and books after a brief description of the largely untried but promising general systems and dissipative structures paradigms.

TWO PROMISING PARADIGMS

A system is any set of interacting components. We are all familiar with the variety of adjectives identifying management information systems, social systems, political systems and so on. Von Bertalanffy (1968, pp. 32–33) says that

> we postulate a new discipline called General Systems Theory. Its subject matter is the formulation and derivation of those principles which are valid for systems in general . . . we can ask for principles applying to systems in general, irrespective of whether they are physical, biological or sociological. . . . A consequence of the existence of general system properties is the appearance of structural similarities or isomorphisms in different fields. . . . This correspondence is due to the fact that the entities can be considered in certain re-

spects, as "systems," i.e., complexes of elements standing in interaction.

Von Bertalanffy approached theory by emphasizing principles. He went on to found with others the Society for General Systems Research. The subsequent outpouring of papers included Kenneth Boulding's (1956) "General Systems Theory—The Skeleton of Science." As a "skeleton of science," General Systems Theory has furnished a framework or paradigm for integrating physical with biological and social science isomorphisms. The *general systems framework or paradigm* includes goals, organization structure, input/output transformations and performance monitoring and evaluation linked by feedback loops.

In marketing, simulation models of aggregate marketing processes for the full channel dimension for products, industries and even national and global economies employ the systems framework. These models are exercised to make comparisons between marketing systems in different economies. Efficiency comparisons of markets, channels, governmental regulations and consumption are made to aid public policy formulation and to improve understanding of different forms of marketing organization. These comparisons permit transfer of knowledge across disciplinary boundaries. Thus the promise of a general systems paradigm seems greatest in its capacity for organizing knowledge rather than in operational applications (Jain 1981), though governmental policies have been influenced by them.

The potential for crossing disciplinary boundaries with useful knowledge is not limited to general systems theory, but appears to characterize the "self-organization in nonequilibrium systems" of Illya Prigogine—what may be termed a *dissipative structures paradigm*. Although stated in physical science terms (Nicolis and Prigogine 1977), Prigogine advanced the idea that nonlinear fluctuations or discontinuities may be the source of self-organization as a system is forced further away from equilibrium towards disequilibrium until it reaches a critical point at which a sudden change in qualities emerges. The emergence of these new properties is a consequence of continuous interaction between a macroscopic level of behavior and statistical properties of a more microscopic level based on the laws of nonequilibrium thermodynamics. The promise of this nonequilibrium systems approach lies in the explanation of discontinuity and the sudden appearance of new kinds of organization.

In marketing, for example, the gradual accumulation of individuals willing to adopt a product and those willing to sell it becomes a critical mass large enough to form a new market for the commodity. Sellers form the critical mass large enough to offer a supply schedule of prices and quantities when the potential of expected buyers rises to the number needed to form a continuous demand and the number willing to sell. If these relations are stated in stochastic terms, fluctuations in the number of potential buyers and sellers become the mechanism for introducing the change in "market state." The system can reach price equilibrium as postulated in traditional economic theory only if environmental disturbances are absent. Most of the time, however, the system is moving away from equilibrium states because of many forms of energy exchange with the environment, ranging from the continuous market substitution effects of other products, to the disruptive effects of technological advances, and the export of bound energy as waste into the physical environment (entropy).[1]

While the direct applicability of self-organization in nonequilibrium states awaits wider awareness and understanding of Prigogine's work, increased market activity is measured by fluctuations in entropy exports to the external environment. The appearance of new structures is associated with emergence of a critical mass as fluctuations reach a macrosystemic amplitude. Fluctuation measurements are most operational at subcellular biochemical levels, but all or none phenomena are observable at the societal levels of organization. Characteristically, transaction flows, market sanction behavior, and marketing externalities all entail fluctuations in entropy exports. Potentially, the prediction, explanation and description of change in market organization and innovations could also profit from this perspective.

TIME PATTERN OF PARADIGM DEVELOPMENT

The selection of a paradigm within which to formulate theories is seldom a matter of conscious choice for marketing investigators. Usually personal training and experience dominate a researcher's research design as well as theory design. Paradigms however comprise a common body of perception and experience. Thus, all of the paradigms extant are potentially available to researchers. Unconsciously theorists and researchers draw on their image bank to develop their theories and models of behavior. Consequently few award-winning publications contain ideas from only one paradigm and most of those other than the competitive marketing paradigm appear in conjunction with at least one other framework. (See Appendix Table 1.) This fact is basic to our vision of paradigm developments possible for the future, which we discuss below in the concluding section.

The appearance of each paradigm among award-winning publications varies in duration and amplitude. The *network flow paradigm* appeared early and continues to appear intermittently, whereas the *market scarcity paradigm* appeared with greatest frequency in the years following initiation of the Converse award. The *evolutionary systems change paradigm* has appeared with increasing frequency in more recent years while the disappearance of the market scarcity paradigm after Tosdal's first edition of *Sales Management* in 1933 suggests explanations for this configuration of paradigms over time.

Total mentions also tell an important part of the story. The *competitive marketing management paradigm* stressing managerial application is the perspective most often found among award-winning papers in the sample represented by Converse and Maynard awards. With 36 of the 53 award winners using this paradigm, it appears in 68 percent of the contributions honored. The evolutionary systems change paradigm was used by 21 of the award winners or 40 percent. Sixteen authors used the channel network flow paradigm in formulating their ideas and 13 used the market scarcity paradigm.

The explanation for this distribution and frequency lies at least in part with the problem solving needs of marketing authors. Thus the network flow paradigm appeared very early and remains useful because marketing writers are trying to provide a framework showing the initiating circumstances leading to conduct of marketing activities under a wide variety of environmental conditions. Scarcity relative to demand was an almost universal environmental condition in the earlier years of marketing scholarship. Early concern centered on converting production skills and materials into consumable goods and services at prices affordable by "average" consumers. Hence, the market scarcity paradigm based on high marketing margins gained wide acceptance until mass marketing based on the profitable volume philosophy explained volume centered marketing activity in mass markets more adequately. Understandably the replacement of the market scarcity concept by the idea that sellers should have what they could sell was relatively rapid and far reaching as shown in Appendix Table 2. The market scarcity paradigm may, however, see a resurgence if resource scarcity phenomena become more common.

The competitive marketing management paradigm based on finding customers' wants and filling them at a profit remains today the most widely accepted view of competitive marketing outside the Socialist nations. Its continuing popularity is mirrored in the statistics on awards. Valuable as this approach has been for managerial applications, it is seriously deficient as a scientific representation of the processes of change with which most prediction models of marketing behavior are concerned. To predict or adapt to discontinuities and mutations calls for a more complete description of behavior. Among replacement candidates, the evolutionary change paradigm that incorporates cooperation, symbiosis and parasitism along with competition in explaining mutation and growth has gained the most in use. The task ahead is conveyed by the gap between paradigm availability and paradigm application discussed in the concluding section on possible developments.

POSSIBLE DEVELOPMENTS

The usefulness of paradigms for studying marketing problems together with the availability of new scientific knowledge go far in guiding the "market penetration" of each of the paradigms thus far considered. The nature of the environment and the emergence of new analytical methods will also prove important in the future. We do not presume to predict even the broad contours of future developments, but we can now state with a high degree of confidence a configuration of interacting possibilities which we examine below.

By the criterion of usefulness, someone will try to extend the social exchange paradigms of Bagozzi (1975, 1976, 1978) and Carman (1980). Both of these are grounded too exclusively in the behavioral sciences to make use of recent conceptual advances in the physical and biological sciences. Even within the behavioral sciences social exchange must be related to developing concepts of negotiation (Raiffa 1982; Strauss 1980) to provide a sufficient as well as necessary categorization of transaction flows.

For macromarketing, comparative studies such as Leontief's input/output models using transaction flows to trace marketing in the world economy represent an upper limit to the size of organization unit whose marketing behavior affects human well-being. Studies of the world economy as a unit are not only useful and feasible, but they are the only means for bringing together for study political systems of every kind. Interest in paradigms useful for study of world models is prompted not only by public policy concern of national planning agencies, but also by the desire of a growing variety of multinational and transnational marketing agencies to develop new knowledge for planning their activities and controlling the consequences of marketing for external publics that are impacted.

Environmental influences on future paradigm development stem from the worldwide concern for resource availability and the growing anxiety over pollution (Fisk 1974). These marketing and economic externalities represent an awareness that there are no longer "free" resources in the environment, but only depletable resource bank accounts. Nature requires these to be replenished if human population is to be indefinitely sustained. Hence, environmental as well as utilitarian considerations are driving theorists toward future development of evolutionary change paradigms.

In the future, evolutionary change paradigms will have to permit reconciliation of the increasing complexity of organization observed in living systems with the decreasing complexity arising from decreasing availability of energy and materials observed in physical systems. It is tempting to say that more accessible conceptualizations of Prigogine's nonequilibrium systems will provide the reference paradigms for such developments. This would require a greater increase in the knowledge of physical sciences by people in marketing and other behavioral sciences than now seems probable. Unless the knowledge advance represented by Prigogine's conceptualization becomes substantially more accessible, its adoption seems many years away. It is possible that with the help of artificial intelligence, humans will begin to think in four dimensional and hyper-space, but for the time being limited accessibility inhibits the utilization of combined applications of physical and biological science models. Here is an area of strong desire but weak demand in which intellectual entrepreneurs could make a significant contribution.

We have considered usefulness, environmental pressure and accessibility of knowledge as determinants of the future developments of paradigms for macromarketing, and we now consider their interaction.

Earlier paradigms such as the network flow and market scarcity paradigm derived from common sense observation or from relatively narrow single discipline perspectives. Even now, marketing students view the addition of Arndt's "politics" as a fifth "P" something of a radical departure in the conventional 4 P's paradigm, "Product, Price, Promotion and Physical Distribution," popularized by McCarthy. Extending this micromanagerial focus to social exchange and transaction flow and transvection perspectives by Bagozzi, Carman and Alderson has earned for them high regard in the marketing theory community. The brief popularity of social physics in the marketing theory literature of the 1950s has dwindled, but has not died. Like the biological analogies popular among economists unfamiliar with the real isomorphic qualities between their science and living systems theory, it remains an undeveloped possibility. The creeping commitment of the marketing theory community to interdisciplinary borrowing, mainly from the behavioral sciences, is now approaching disequilibrium. If this disequilibrium evokes a "critical mass" of discernible relationships embracing physical and biological with social sciences, marketing knowledge could be transformed into a multidiscipline. Marketers focusing on this possibility could contribute to a quantum leap in the explanatory and predictive power of the theories and hypotheses such a transformation would permit.

REFERENCES

Alderson, Wroe (1957), *Marketing Behavior and Executive Action*, Homewood, Ill.: Richard D. Irwin.

_____ (1965), *Dynamic Marketing Behavior*, Homewood, Ill.: Richard D. Irwin, pp. 78–80.

Arndt, Johan (1979), "Toward A Concept of Domesticated Markets," *Journal of Marketing*, Vol. 43, Fall, pp. 69–75.

Bagozzi, Richard P. (1975), "Marketing as Exchange," *Journal of Marketing*, Vol. 39, October, pp. 32–39.

_____ (1976), "Science, Politics and the Social Construction of Marketing," in *Marketing: 1776–1976 and Beyond*, Kenneth L. Bernhardt (ed.), Chicago: AMA, 586–592.

_____ (1978), "Marketing as Exchange: A Theory of Transactions in the Marketplace," *American Behavioral Scientist*, 21, March/April, 535–536.

Boulding, K. E. (1956), "General Systems Theory—The Skeleton of Science," *Management Science*, Vol. 2, April, pp. 197–208.

_____ (1981), *Evolutionary Economies*, Beverly Hills, Calif.: Sage Publications.

Carman, James M. (1980), "Paradigms for Marketing Theory," in *Research in Marketing*, Vol. 3, Greenwich, Conn.: JAI Press, pp. 1–36.

Fisk, George (1974), *Marketing and the Ecological Crisis*, New York: Harper & Row.

Jain, Virender (1981), "Structural Analysis of General Systems Theory," *Behavioral Science*, Vol. 26, April, pp. 51–62.

Nicolis, G. and I. Prigogine (1977), *Self Organization in Nonequilibrium Systems: From Dissipative Structures to Order Through Fluctuations*, New York: John Wiley.

Raiffa, Howard (1982), *The Art & Science of Negotiation*, Cambridge: Harvard University Press.

Strauss, Anselm (1978), *Negotiations: Varieties, Contextism Processes and Social Order*, San Francisco, Calif.: Jossey-Bass.

von Bertalanffy, L. (1968), *General Systems Science*, New York: George Braziller.

NOTES

[1]Physicists refer to the unavailability of energy that has been used as an increase in entropy.

DISCUSSION QUESTIONS

1. How are paradigms distinguished from theories and models?

2. What criteria are useful for selecting paradigms for application to particular marketing problems?

3. Are macromarketing paradigms applicable to marketing management problems?

4. Are managerial micromarketing paradigms suitable for use in macromarketing issues?

5. What structural differences characterize macromarketing paradigms drawn from physical and social sciences?

6. How are marketing paradigms related to the needs of the user? Marketing researchers? The public at large?

APPENDIX TABLE 1
Representative Awards for Contributions to Marketing

Year(s) of Publication	Year of Award	Title/Subject	Author(s)	Order of Appearance Among Award Winning Papers				
				Channel Network Flow	Market Scarcity	Competitive Marketing Management	Evolutionary Systems Change	Paradigm Not Relevant
Paul D. Converse Awards								
1904	1949	*The Theory and Practice of Advertising*						
1908		*The Psychology of Advertising*						
1911, 1919		*Influencing Men in Business*	Walter Dill Scott			1		
1911		*Selling and Buying*						
1917	1949	*Marketing Methods and Policies*	Ralph Starr Butler	1	2			
1912		First quantitative study of department store sales volumes; development of city marketing maps; general leadership in development of marketing research through his work as manager of the Commercial Research Division of the Curtis Publishing Co.; and establishment of the first commercial research department of any publication						
1912	1961	"Some Problems in Marketing Distribution," *Quarterly Journal of Economics*	Charles C. Parlin	2	3	2		
1916	1949	*An Approach to Business Problems*	Arch W. Shaw		4	3		
1913		*Advertising as a Business Force*						
1920	1949	*Elements of Marketing*	Paul Cherrington		5	4		
1915		*Economics of Retailing*						
1929		*Economics of Consumption*						
1929	1949	*Economics of Fashion*	Paul N. Nystrom		6	5	1	
1916		*Marketing Farm Products*						
1917		"Marketing Functions and Mercantile Organizations," *American Economics Review* (June)						
1917		"Marketing Agencies Between Manufacturer and Wholesaler," *Quarterly*						

(continued)

APPENDIX TABLE 1—Continued

Spanning header over the last five columns: **Order of Appearance Among Award Winning Papers**

Year(s) of Publication	Year of Award	Title/Subject	Author(s)	Channel Network Flow	Market Scarcity	Competitive Marketing Management	Evolutionary Systems Change	Paradigm Not Relevant
1917	1949	Journal of Economics (August) Unfair Competition	L. D. H. Weld	3	7	6		
		Federal Trade Commission reports:						
1920–26		Report on the Grain Trade Furniture (with Walter Durand)						
1923–27								
1927		Bakery Combines and Profits						
1931–34	1949	Chain Stores	W. H. W. Stevens	4			2	
1919		Commercial Research						
1920	1949	Marketing: Its Problems and Methods	C. S. Duncan		8	7		
1920		Marketing Problems						
1923		"Relation of Consumer Buying Habits to Marketing Methods," Harvard Business Review						
1924	1949	Principles of Merchandising	Melvin T. Copeland		9	8		
1922		Principles of Marketing						
1932	1949	Marketing Agriculture Products (with L. D. H. Weld)	Fred E. Clark	5	10			
1923	1951	Principles of Advertising	Daniel Starch			9		
1925		Magazine Audience Studies Retail Inventory Method						
1926	1953	Series of Operating Results of Department and Specialty Stores Wholesaling	Malcolm P. McNair		11	10		
1929–32	1959	Work done while in charge of the Census of Wholesale Distribution	Theodore N. Beckman	6			4	
1927	1957	Economics of Advertising	Roland S. Vaile			11	3	
1927		Sample Census of Distribution						
1929	1949	First National Census of Distribution	Herbert Hoover	7			5	
1927		The Legal Status of Agricultural Cooperation						
1934	1955	America's Capacity to Produce	Edwin G. Nourse	8			6	
1929		Market Data Handbook (U.S. Dept. of Commerce)						
1939		Does Distribution Cost Too Much? (Joint authorship for Twentieth Century Fund)	Paul W. Stewart		12	12		
1931	1951	The Law of Retail Gravitation	William J. Reilly	9				
1932	1959	Louisville Grocery Survey, Part IV,						

	1955	*Wholesale Grocery Operations.* General leadership in development of theory in marketing	Wroe Alderson			13	7	
1938, 1936, 1938	1953	*The Theory of Monopolistic Competition*	Edward H. Chamberlin			14	8	
1933, 1940, 1950	1959	*Introduction to Sales Management*	Harry R. Tosdal		13	15		
1935	1957	Pioneering work through his American Institute of Public Opinion	George Gallup			16		
1935		*Resale Price Maintenance in Great Britain with an Application to the Problem in the United States*						
1939	1955	*Price Control Under Fair Trade Legislation*	Ewald T. Grether				9	
1936		Surveys on Consumer Finances						
1946		Work in establishing the Survey Research Center						
1949	1955	Institute for Social Research	Rensis Likert				10	
1937	1957	*Marketing Research and Analysis*	Lyndon O. Brown			17		
1938	1955	*The Theory and Measurement of Demand*	Harry Schultz					1
1938		*The Marketing of Textiles*						
1948		The Economics of Installment Buying						
1950	1961	Theory in Marketing (co-editor, Wroe Alderson)	Reavis Cox	10		18		
1940	1951	Nielson Food and Drug Indices	Arthur C. Nielsen, Sr.			18		
1942	1951	Economic Effects of Advertising	Neil H. Borden			20	11	
1944, 1947, 1953	1967	*Theory of Games and Economic Behavior*	Oskar Morganstern and John Von Newmann					2
1933	1957	*America's Needs and Resources*	J. F. Dewhurst	11		12		
1949	1967	*Social Class in America* (co-authors, Marcia Meeker and Kenneth Eells)	W. Lloyd Warner					3
1951	1959	*Managerial Economics*	Joel Dean			21		
1951	1961	*Psychological Analysis of Economic Behavior* General leadership in work of the Survey Research Center	George Katona			22	13	
1954	1975	*The Practice of Management*	Peter F. Drucker			23		
1955	1967	*Personal Influence: The Part Played by People in the Flow of Mass Communication* (co-author, Elihu Katz)	Paul F. Lazersfeld	12			14	

(*continued*)

APPENDIX TABLE 1—Continued

Year(s) of Publication	Year of Award	Title/Subject	Author(s)	Order of Appearance Among Award Winning Papers				
				Channel Network Flow	Market Scarcity	Competitive Marketing Management	Evolutionary Systems Change	Paradigm Not Relevant
1957	1967	*Marketing Behavior and Executive Action*	Wroe Alderson	13		24	15	
1960	1978	*Consumer Behavior as Risk Taking*	Raymond Bauer			25		
1960	1978	*Marketing Myopia*	Theodore Levitt			26		
1962	1975	*The Diffusion of Innovations*	Everett M. Rogers			27	16	
1963		*Marketing Management: Analysis and Planning*						
1963		*Marketing: Executive and Buyer Behavior*						
1965		*Marketing Theory*						
1969	1975	The Theory of Buyer Behavior (with J. N. Sheth)	John A. Howard			28		
1964–73	1978	A series of publications on Bayesian and multivariate analysis	Paul Green			29		
1966	1975	*Marketing and Public Policy*	Ewald T. Grether			30	17	
1967		*Marketing Management: Analysis, Planning and Control*						
1969–73	1978	Articles extending the domain of marketing	Philip Kotler			31		
Harold H. Maynard Awards[a]								
1974	1975	"Future Directions in Marketing Theory"	W. T. Tucker				18	
1975	1976	"Deception in Advertising: A Conceptual Approach"	David M. Gardner			32		
1976	1977	"The Nature and Scope of Marketing"	Shelby D. Hunt	14		33	19	
1977	1978	"Macromarketing"	Robert Bartels and Roger L. Jenkins	15			20	
1978	1979	"Consumer Research: A State of the Art Review"	Jacob Jacoby			34		
1979	1980	"Memory Factors in Consumer Choice: A Review"	James R. Bettman			35		
1980	1981	"A Study of Marketing Generalizations"	Robert P. Leone and Randall L. Schultz			36		
1980	1981	"Distribution Channels as Political Economies: A Framework for Comparative Analysis"	Louis Stern and Torger Reve	16			21	

[a] All published in the *Journal of Marketing*.

APPENDIX TABLE 2
Paradigm Distribution Among Award-Winning Publications[a]

Paradigm and Dominant Idea	Frequency of Appearance by Decade and Total Frequency[b]								Paradigm Mention Frequency Σ	Pre 1980 Total	1980 Awards	Grand Total
	1900–09	1910–19	1920–29	1930–39	1940–49	1950–59	1960–69	1970–79				
Channel Network Flow Equalizing supply and demand assortment discrepancies is accomplished by moving goods and use rights from surplus supply areas to deficit demand areas.	0	2	6	3	0	2	0	2	15	15	1	16
Market Scarcity Mass distribution stimulates mass production by expanding markets to the limits of demand quantities salable at prices in the vicinity of minimum long-run average costs. "Supply creates its own demand."	1	7	4	1	0	0	0	0	13	13	0	13
Competitive Marketing Management "Find a need and fill it at a profit." Entrepreneurial survival and growth is achieved by efficiency of competitive response in matching competitors' offerings to fit buyers' want specifications most exactly at times, places and prices more advantageous to customers than terms of exchange offered by rivals.	1	6	5	6	2	4	7	4	35	35	1	36
Evolutionary Systems Change "The fittest survive and change." Competitive, cooperative, and parasitic interactions between supply and demand behavior selects for survival and mutation marketing organizations whose behavior is environmentally appropriate for existing market "niches."	0	2	4	5	1	3	2	3	20	20	1	2
Paradigms not relevant to award				(1)								
Multiple paradigm mentions					(2)				(3)	(3)		
Total No. of Paradigms in Award Winning Papers	2	17	19	15	3	9	9	9	83 + 3 = 86	83 + 3 = 86		1900–1980 Grand total mentions

[a] Number of awards: 53 awards = 100%

[b] For authors receiving awards for multiple year publications, the award is counted in the first year of award without respect to specific article or book.

PREFACE TO

"Retroduction and the Process of Discovery in Consumer Behavior"

Legend has it that the discoverer of the structure of the benzene ring attributed his insight to a daydream. As he sat gazing into the fireplace, he half fell asleep. In front of his eyes, he saw the flames jump up, form into a snake, and make a hexagonal ring by catching its tail by its teeth.

No such brilliant flash of insight occurred to this author in developing the present paper. The article evolved slowly and painfully with the final product bearing little resemblance to my original ideas.

Originally, the paper began as an article arguing for the desirability of borrowing theories and applying them to marketing phenomena. It was conceived as a reaction to the somewhat pompous statements then being made that marketers had been borrowing too much from the behavioral sciences—that we should create our own theories.

As I began to do some reading on the topic, I slowly realized that I was really talking about the process of discovery in science. Seeking assistance, I walked across the mall to the philosophy department and met John Bosworth, who introduced me to the writings of Charles Peirce. Here I found the term *retroduction*, which immediately had great appeal to me.

The major original aspect of the article is the diagram in which the model of the research process is pictorially represented. The remainder consists of applications to consumer behavior of ideas found in the philosophy of science literature.

The fact that the paper, although competent and interesting in my view, breaks no new ground in the philosophy of science was vividly pointed out by my philosopher colleague. Just before leaving for the 1979 Theory Conference where the paper was presented, I asked Professor Bosworth if he would read it. On returning from the Conference, I was flushed with pride. The paper had been well received, and my ego was inflated. Waiting for me were Bosworth's comments. They can be summarized as saying, "A nice, but elementary summary of some of the literature on discovery."

After piecing my ego back together, I realized that one should not necessarily expect to make new contributions to the field from which he or she borrows theory. An academician who has been able to competently translate an idea from one field to another so that it advances the state of knowledge in its new environment has made a laudable achievement.

19

RETRODUCTION AND THE PROCESS OF DISCOVERY IN CONSUMER BEHAVIOR*

JOHN C. MOWEN

INTRODUCTION

Marketing academicians are increasingly recognizing the importance of theory development (Halbert 1965; Hostiuck and Kurtz 1973; Hunt 1976). It has been argued that theory should be the starting point of the marketing research process and that theory is useful both to marketing managers and public policy makers (Howard 1965). Hunt (1976) stated that theories are important because of their practicality, their utility for decision making coming from their inherent ability to explain and predict. A key indicator of the importance of theory in marketing is the number of articles, chapters, and monographs written on metatheory (Bennett 1976; Hunt 1976; Zaltman, Pinson, and Angelmar 1973), defined as the investigation, analysis, and description of theory. Indeed, the existence of this conference exemplifies the importance of theory in marketing.

Despite the exhortations to develop theory, some marketers have appropriately voiced concerns about theory development. At one extreme authors have argued that marketing is an art rather than a science, and theories should only prescribe action (Tucker 1974). Similarly, comments are sometimes voiced that theories are too impractical and not relevant to an applied discipline, such as marketing (Hunt 1976). Another pessimistic view is derived from the writings of Kaplan (1964). Kaplan argued that formal theory development in the behavioral sciences is highly difficult and in applied fields, such as consumer behavior, doomed. Others, while taking a less pessimistic perspective, have noted

Source: Revised for this volume from *Conceptual and Theoretical Developments in Marketing,* O. C. Ferrell, Stephen W. Brown, and Charles W. Lamb, Jr., eds., Chicago, Ill.: American Marketing Association, 1979, 590–604. Originally titled ''Retroduction and the Research Process in Consumer Behavior.''

*The author would like to thank John Bosworth, Maryanne Mowen, and James Gentry for their helpful comments and suggestions on the paper.

that insufficient connections exist between theoretical structures and extant empirical research in marketing (Sheth 1967). Sheth (1967) likened the failure to base research on theory to seven blind men touching seven parts of an elephant and deriving substantially divergent views of the beast.

The promise and problems of borrowing theories from the behavioral sciences has also been discussed. Robertson and Ward (1973) observed several problems in the practice of borrowing. Other authors have developed criteria for borrowing theories, particularly focussing on the problems and consequences of divergent behavioral science theories making conflicting predictions (Mittelstaedt 1971). The difficulties of utilizing extant personality inventories in marketing has also been discussed (Wells and Gubar 1966). Kassarjian (1971), in fact, argued that marketers should develop their own instruments for delineating personality variables rather than borrowing tests from psychology.

In commenting on the difficulties of formal theory generation in consumer behavior, Robertson and Ward (1973) advocated a problem-solving approach to research. The approach consists of isolating a particular problem, defining it in terms of a relevant conceptual framework (theory), specifying hypotheses, and planning the research. By emphasizing the problem-solving aspects of research, the framework addresses the twin issues in consumer behavior of seeking to solve practical problems (i.e., maintaining relevancy) while maintaining the needed theoretical background for the research.

The problem-solving approach to research, advocated by Robertson and Ward (1973), bears strong similarity to a process labeled ''retroduction'' by philosophers of science (Peirce 1968). Retroduction involves the process of reasoning from conclusions to the reasons for conclusions. This construction of an explanation (reason or theory) for why an event (conclusion) occurred often takes the form of attempting to explain an unexpected finding. The philosophers of science,

Charles Peirce (1968) and Norwood Russell Hanson (1958), viewed retroduction as an inference process of the same genre as induction and deduction. They argued that such historically important scientific discoveries as Kepler's recognition of the elliptical orbit of Mars and Galileo's insight of the constancy of gravitational acceleration resulted from the retroduction of an explanation for anomalous information.

If marketers extensively utilize retroduction, what roles do induction and deduction play in explaining, predicting, and understanding marketing phenomena? In order to answer this question, a model of research process is developed. The next section presents the model, which differentiates the roles of deduction, induction, and retroduction, as well as, presents the discovery and justification phases of the research process. The final section of the paper applies the model of the research process to consumer behavior.[1] Opportunities for theory development are identified. In addition, some problems in taking advantage of these opportunities are discussed.

A MODEL OF THE RESEARCH PROCESS

The model of the research process (MRP) is composed of three types of logical processes and their component steps. Each process is linked to the goal of developing and testing theory, which stands at the apex of the MRP. Theory is defined in the manner of Hunt (1976). Thus, a theory is: (a) a structure capable of both explaining and predicting, (b) composed of a systematically related set of statements, some of which are lawlike generalizations, and (c) empirically testable. Figure 1 presents the processes of deduction, induction, and retroduction as well as their linkages.

The Deductive Process

Moving clockwise in the model, one begins the deductive process. Through the process the empirical testing and logical analysis of a theory occurs. Thus, one moves from extant theory to bridge laws, to hypothesis generation, and finally to empirical testing. Bridge laws refer to laws derived from the theory which span the gap between the theory and the hypotheses. Neither theories nor bridge laws are directly testable. They are only indirectly verifiable through the direct testing of research hypotheses.

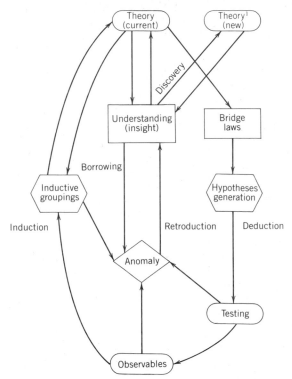

FIGURE 1
A model of the research process.

For further information readers are referred to Hunt's (1976) excellent treatment of the empirical testing process.

If the empirical test confirms the theory, one obtains support for its truth. This support is then joined with the other observable events or information to form the empirical framework of the theory. Thus, with the observation stage the model moves into the inductive process of research.

The Inductive Process

Induction in research involves moving from the specific to the general. Classically, philosophers have viewed theory development as the end result of induction. Thus as Hunt (1976) noted, one may move through the phases of observation, recording of data, classification, and induction of generalizations to obtain a theory.

A number of philosophers and scientists, however, have argued that theory does not result from a process of inductively observing, recording, and classifying. Einstein (1949) stated that while theories may be tested by experience, they may not be developed through experience. In contrast, Hanson (1958) believed that theories result from inferences from data. However, the law is not a summary of the data, as induction would suggest, but an explanation of the data. Whewell (1968) went farther to state that "inductive discoveries" or theories are a "conception of the mind." Thus the theory results from a "new thought" binding together previously detached cases and facts. Popper (1963) argued that theory development through pure induction is logically impossible because it leads to an infinite regress.

Each of the above writers pointed to a fundamental problem of the inductive process. How does one decide what to observe and which categories to develop? The answer lies in the fact that to observe, record, and classify requires a preliminary theory of the ordering of the phenomena. Thus, induction is impossible without theory. As shown by Figure 1, the inductive phase of the MRP consists of the stages of: (a) observing events, (b) inductively grouping the data, and (c) fitting groupings of data into an existing theoretical framework. Thus, the arguments of Einstein, Whewell, and Popper are accepted in the MRP. Theories are not viewed as "discovered" through induction but merely elaborated and extended. To more fully explicate such a view, a brief summary of Kuhn's (1970) discussion of theory development is presented.

Induction, Deduction, and Normal Science

Kuhn (1970) in his classic text *The Structure of Scientific Revolutions* discussed the nature of scientific advancement. In his view scientific progress moves through a series of stages: pre-paradigm science, normal science, anomaly, and revolution. A key concept in Kuhn's thought is the term "paradigm," defined as the "accepted examples of actual scientific practice—examples which include law, theory, application, and instrumentation." (p. 10) Paradigms develop from scientific achievements and consist of the theory and methods that a scientific community accepts as a satisfactory explanation of phenomena.

For Kuhn "pre-paradigm science" represents the stage at which no unifying theory or paradigm exists on which the scientific community agrees. In this phase numerous "schools of thought" coexist interpreting phenomena through divergent theories, and utilizing different methodologies of investigation. Kuhn gives an example of pre-paradigm science the state of knowledge in physical optics prior to Sir Isaac Newton's work. In this phase a number of schools of thought existed concerning the nature of light, such as the Epicurean, Aristotelian, and Platonic. The result was that no common body of belief existed, and each scientist had to build new foundations for his work.

According to Kuhn (1970), the move from pre-paradigm to "normal" science occurs when an individual or group develops a new conceptualization which accounts for the phenomena and synthesizes the previously scattered approaches. Individuals, then, slowly begin to accept the new viewpoint, its methods, and instruments. When the paradigm is eventually established, general agreement in the scientific community exists on what the world is like.

Kuhn (1970) describes normal science as the "mopping-up" operations. However, while only "mopping-up," important advances occur in the normal science phase. By working within an established paradigm researchers focus on esoteric problems in the depth and detail otherwise impossible. Scientists develop apparatus (e.g., synchotrons) to determine with great precision the facts shown important by the theory. Predictions derived from the theory are tested, and work is conducted to resolve the theory of its residual ambiguities.

Kuhn (1970) also emphasized the idea that in normal science researchers do not aim to produce major conceptual or phenomenal discoveries. In fact, the successful research project does not make new discoveries. The project which produces results inconsistent with the hypotheses developed from the theory reflects on the competency of the scientist, not on the nature of the phenomena. The purpose of normal science is to progress rapidly by accumulating, extending, clarifying, and limiting scientific knowledge within the scope of the paradigm.

The purpose of this digression into Kuhn's thoughts is to define more precisely the purpose of the deductive and inductive processes. Within the MRP the circular process of moving through successive deductive and inductive phases (i.e., deriving laws, developing hypotheses, testing, observing the factual phenomena, inductively grouping the data, and amending and extending the theory) is what Kuhn calls "normal science." Just as new theories and discoveries do not occur in normal science, they do not occur through the deductive or inductive processes. Thus, deduction is utilized to test and falsify theory, and induction is utilized to elaborate, articulate, and extend existing theory. Neither process generates discoveries.

Retroduction and Discovery

Popper (1963) in refuting what he called the myth of induction proposed that science operates by making conjectures and then attempting to refute them. In his view theory results, not by proceeding from observation to law, but from a problem-situation to law. The theory allows us to "explain" the observation which created the problem. The investigator, then, operates by trial and error to eliminate false theories by the empirical testing process. Writing prior to Popper, Peirce (1968) would have labeled the above process of theorizing by conjecture—"retroduction." Peirce viewed reasoning from consequent to antecedent as the first stage of inquiry with deduction and induction making up the second and third stages. Only by quoting this American philosopher can one obtain an understanding of his thinking by experiencing his remarkable prose.

> The inquiry begins with pondering these phenomena in all their respects, in the search of some point of view whence the wonder shall be resolved. At length a conjecture arises that furnishes a possible Explanation. . . . The whole series of phenomenon and the acceptance of the hypothesis, during which usually docile understanding seems to hold the bit between the teeth and to have us at its mercy, the search for pertinent circumstances and laying hold of them, sometimes without our cognizance, the scrutiny of them, the dark laboring, the bursting out of the startling conjecture, the remarking of its smooth fitting to the anomaly, as it turned back and forth like a key in a lock, and the final estimation of its Plausibility, I reckon as composing the First Stage of Inquiry. (pp. 143–144)

Also viewing discovery as resulting from problems, Hanson (1958) conceptualized a theory as constituting a "conceptual Gestalt" of an anomaly. The process is one of a struggle for intelligibility in which a new pattern is sought to fit the phenomena.

Such an approach is consistent with Peirce's thinking as well as with the work of Gestalt psychologists on insight and concept formation.

Kuhn (1970) also viewed discovery, or the formation of new theory, as a change in the way scientists viewed the world. In fact, he directly compared the process to the familiar classroom demonstrations of reversals of visual gestalt. Thus in Kuhn's view "normal science" proceeds to "extraordinary science" with the build-up of anomalies in the old paradigm. Discovery results from the impetus furnished by scientists perceiving that anomalies exist in the old paradigm. Such a view of scientific progress closely matches retroduction.

Figure 1 diagrams the retroductive process which begins with the presence of an anomaly acting as a stimulus to find the problem's solution. The arrow emerging from the "anomaly" and pointing to "understanding" and "current theory" depicts such a process. The application of "current theory" to explain new problems constitutes what marketers have previously called borrowing theory (Mittelstaedt 1971) and does not constitute discovery. Borrowing theory, however, is a retroductive process and, in fact, is the logical first step in attempting to explain problems. Much research productivity would be lost if new explanations were sought for every anomaly. The research climate conducive for discovery results from "current theory" not satisfactorily explaining the anomaly. After the unsuccessful application of current theories, researchers may develop insight into a new approach or theory to explain the problem. The arrow leading from Theory[1] through "understanding" to the anomaly represents "discovery." Thus, the explanation of an anomaly may result from the application of either a current theory, which had not been applied to the particular problem in question, or an entirely new explanatory mechanism. Importantly, with either the application of "current theory" or "new theory" the entire research process recycles with the initiation of the justification phase of normal science.

A Problem in MRP?

One problem exists with the integration of the Kuhnian analysis into the MRP. In the next section the MRP will be applied to consumer behavior. Yet, most individuals would place the study of consumer behavior (and for that matter most of the behavioral sciences) into the pre-paradigm phase of science. Thus, how can one apply to consumer behavior the MRP, which focuses mainly on normal science, when the discipline has not yet reached that stage?

The solution to the above problem comes from focussing on the middle-range theories, which Merton (1957) discusses. Middle-range theories are those intermediate to the working hypotheses evolving from the day-to-day research and the large, all-inclusive thinking comprising the master conceptualizations of such disciplines as physics and biology. Middle-range theories do meet Hunt's (1976) three criteria of theory; and they differ from the grand theories (e.g., Newtonian or Einsteinian physics) by focussing on a much narrower spectrum of phenomena. The pattern of behavioral sciences over the past 15 years has been to move from one middle-range theory to another in the various disciplines. Each of these changes may be viewed as mini-scientific revolutions. Thus, normal science in such a context consists of the justification of the current middle-range theory in vogue.

An example of such a mini-revolution occurred in social psychology. During most of the 1960s, experimental social psychologists viewed individuals from a cognitive consistency perspective. People were perceived as basically acting irrationally, balancing and dissonance reducing their way through life. Vast amounts of energy was expended in testing and extending the literature. However, anomalies began to appear in the cognitive consistency approach (Chapanis and Chapanis 1964). Then, in the late 1960s Bem (1967) and Kelley (1967) proposed that attribution processes can account for findings previously explained through cognitive consistency formulations as well as generate new predictions. Rapidly, the world perception of social psychologists changed such that individuals were viewed as cool information processors attributing causality to themselves and others. A mini-scientific revolution has occurred.

In summary, the MRP may be applied to two levels of the scientific enterprise. One is at the level of "grand" theory of the type found in the mature sciences of physics, chemistry, and biology. The second is at the middle-range theory level within which consumer behavior may be placed.

Summary of the MRP

The MRP depicts the processes through which justification and discovery occur in science. Justifi-

cation in this context is utilized in a broad sense, referring to the deductive and inductive processes involved in testing and extending extant theory. Thus, in the MRP justification is equated to the Kuhnian notion of the process of normal science.

The MRP depicts discovery as occurring through the process of retroduction, which begins with the identification of an anomaly. As depicted in Figure 1, the anomaly may result from the empirical testing of a theory, from the observation of an unexpected event, or from finding an observation which fails to fit past inductive groupings. The scientist then begins the process of attempting to explain the anomaly through various speculations. At some point an insight or understanding occurs in which the scientist is able to match the theoretical explanation to the anomaly, thereby, closing the "perceptual gestalt" by finding an explanation for the anomaly.

THE "MODEL" AND CONSUMER BEHAVIOR

As suggested by Robertson and Ward (1973), in their research programs consumer behaviorists first define a problem (e.g., what are the effects of working wives on family expenditures), and then attempt to shop for an extant theory capable of handling the problem. This retroductive approach to research differs from that often found in the more mature behavioral sciences, such as psychology and economics. In these disciplines researchers focus more extensively on taking established theory, deducing hypotheses, and testing these with the specific aim of elaborating and extending the theory. A question arises from such an analysis. Because consumer behaviorists tend to be problem oriented, does this relegate their research to the "minor leagues" of academia by being theory shoppers rather than theory developers, as some of my colleagues would suggest?

A Positive Prognosis for Discovery in Consumer Behavior

Based upon the model of the research process, the answer to the above question is clearly negative. Because consumer behaviorists focus on identifying problems or anomalies, they are in a unique position to: (a) compare the relative predictive validity of alternative theories, (b) apply existing theories in settings which test their generalizability, and (c) develop new theories to handle anomalies not accounted for by extant conceptualizations.

By attempting to explain an anomaly or problem through the application of existing theories, the researcher is in a position to compare and contrast the predictions made by alternative theories. Carefully designed studies can then be developed which allow for one of the competing theories to be falsified, if the other is supported. A related issue concerns the perspective taken by the researcher. An individual working from a single discipline sometimes becomes wedded to a small group of paradigms and theoretical approaches. Because of the interdisciplinary nature of consumer behavior, researchers have the opportunity to avoid such conceptual blinders by asking, "which approach best explains this anomaly."

Consumer behaviorists are also in an excellent position to test a theory's generalizability, because the anomaly investigated may occur in settings in which a theory has previously not been tested. For example, psychologists often test theory in the laboratory and fail to make further tests in more ecologically valid settings. In the area of attribution theory, social psychologists have tended to test the conceptualization using oversimplified stimuli (e.g., short sentences providing consistency, distinctiveness, and consensus information) in a laboratory setting. In contrast, marketers have used more complex stimuli (e.g., advertisements) in settings possessing greater ecological validity, such as shopping malls (Mowen and Brown 1979). By using more externally valid experimental settings and stimuli, the limitations and possible inconsistencies in a theory may emerge.

Consumer behaviorists are also in an excellent position to discover anomalies. They may discover anomalies through the "normal" science route of theory testing, just as do researchers in the theory-oriented disciplines. However, consumer behaviorists have a second route available often not used by scientists in the more "theory" oriented behavioral science disciplines. By tending to isolate problems from their experience with the "real world," consumer behaviorists observe the behavior of consumers or perhaps business and government and then attempt to categorize and explain the behavior. Thus, an anomaly may be perceived from either the observation process or the failure to develop a satisfactory grouping of events. In contrast, researchers solely involved in theory testing sometimes lose contact with "real world" phenomena. Indeed, this problem well represents the nexus of the debate still raging in experimental social psychology (Smith 1972). Thus, by taking a problem-solving, as well as a justification approach to research, a variety of avenues are available to discovery for consumer behavior researchers.

Some Difficulties with Discovery in Consumer Behavior

While the prognosis for theory building in consumer behavior is good, the process itself is difficult. One problem concerns developing researchers who can identify anomalies within the "noise" of the research environment. Jacoby (1976) and others have discussed the fact that consumer behavior has "progressed" relatively little in comparison to the amount of effort exerted. The lack of progress may be partially explained by the inability to select appropriate anomalies and apply relevant theoretical explanations.

A second issue concerns training researchers with interdisciplinary skills. Previously, I stated that with the identification of an anomaly, researchers merely had to find or develop appropriate theories to explain the aberration. Such a process, however, requires a sophisticated knowledge of relevant literature in multiple fields. Ferber (1977) specifically discussed the question of "Can Consumer Research Be Interdisciplinary?" Problems in the academic reward system, the lack of appropriate journals, and the sheer difficulty of keeping current in multiple fields severely retards an interdisciplinary focus. However, some positive portents brighten the outlook. Some academic departments are showing signs of encouraging interdisciplinary work, interdisciplinary journals are beginning to appear, and private foundations as well as the federal government are beginning to hire and fund such individuals. Thus, while difficult the interdisciplinary approach is not impossible.

A third issue concerns the dissemination of knowledge. As consumer behaviorists select and test theories for application to marketing problems anomalies certainly will appear. A question then occurs concerning how this information is fed back to the parent discipline. For example, in applying attribution theory to marketing phenomena, some aberrations have appeared in which significant findings failed to support derived hypotheses (Calder and Burnkrant 1977; Mowen and Brown 1979). With social psychologists not tending to read marketing journals, these researchers may remain unaware of the accumulation of anomalies. Some factors currently exist, however, which may alleviate the problem. Interdisciplinary journals, such as the *Journal of Consumer Research,* may provide such a function. Also, reference services, such as *Psychological Abstracts,* and organizations, such as the Division of Consumer Behavior in the American Psychological Association, probably restrict the potential problem. However, assuming that behavioral scientists have a supraordinate goal of advancing theory, the situation outlined is of concern. Only by empirical examination can the extent of the potential problem be determined.

SUMMARY

Previous discussions of metatheory by marketers have tended to omit an analysis of the discovery of theory. A model of the research process was developed to depict the manner in which discovery occurs in research. Borrowing heavily from the writings of the philosophers of science, Peirce (1968) and Hanson (1958), the concept of retroduction was introduced and defined as the process of identifying problems or anomalies and then developing theories or explanations for them.

Through the model of the research process, the relationship among deduction, induction, and retroduction was discussed. This relationship was shown to fit Kuhn's (1970) analysis of science into the phases of "normal" and "revolutionary" science. Thus, the justification of theories by successive stages of deductively testing and inductively elaborating them represents "normal" science. Revolutionary science results from retroductively accounting for anomalies by discovering an explanation not previously considered.

In applying the model, the paper noted that consumer behavior and other behavioral sciences move through a series of mini-revolutions rather than the "grand" scientific revolutions discussed by Kuhn (1970). Despite the smaller scale of operation, however, discovery can occur in consumer behavior. Indeed, the argument is made that consumer behaviorists, because of their problem-solving orientation to research, are in an advantageous position to engage in the discovery process. Reasons for

consumer behaviorists' ability to identify anomalies were discussed as well as some factors inhibiting the process.

REFERENCES

Bem, D. J. (1967), "Self-perception: An Alternative Interpretation of Cognitive Dissonance Phenomena," *Psychological Review,* 74, 182–200.

Bennett, Peter O. (1976), "Theoretical Developments in Consumer Buyer Behavior," *Work Series in Marketing Research,* College of Business Administration, Pennsylvania State University, 39 (April).

Calder, B. J. and R. E. Burnkrant (1977), "Interpersonal Influence on Consumer Behavior: An Attribution Theory Approach," *Journal of Consumer Research,* 4 (June), 29–38.

Chapanis, N. P. and A. Chapanis (1964), "Cognitive Dissonance: Five Years Later," *Psychological Bulletin,* 6 (January), 1–22.

Einstein, Albert (1949), "Autobiographical Notes," in P. A. Schillp, ed., *Albert Einstein, Philosopher-Scientist,* New York: Harper & Brothers.

Ferber, Robert (1977), "Can Consumer Research Be Interdisciplinary?" *Journal of Consumer Research,* 4 (December), 189–192.

Halbert, M. (1965), *The Meaning and Sources of Marketing Theory,* New York: McGraw-Hill Book Company.

Hanson, N. R. (1958), *Patterns of Discovery,* Cambridge: At the University Press.

Hostiuck, K. T. and D. L. Kurtz (1973), "Alderson's Functionalism and the Development of Marketing Theory," *Journal of Business Research,* (Fall), 141–156.

Howard, J. A. (1965), *Marketing Theory,* Boston: Allyn & Bacon, Inc.

Hunt, Shelby D. (1976), *Marketing Theory: Conceptual Foundations of Research in Marketing,* Columbus, Ohio: Grid, Inc.

Jacoby, Jacob (1976), "Consumer Research: Telling It Like It Is," *Advances in Consumer Research,* 3, 1–10.

Kaplan, A. (1964), *The Conduct of Inquiry: Methodology for Behavioral Science*, San Francisco: Chandler Publishing Co.

Kassarjian, H. H. (1971), "Personality and Consumer Behavior: A Review," *Journal of Marketing Research*, 8 (November), 409–419.

Kelley, H. H. (1967), *Attribution Theory in Social Psychology*, in D. Levine, ed., Nebraska Symposium on Motivation, Lincoln: University of Nebraska Press.

Kuhn, T. S. (1970), *The Structure of Scientific Revolutions*, Chicago: University of Chicago Press.

Merton, R. K. (1957), *Social Theory and Social Structure*, New York: The Free Press.

Mittelstaedt, R. A. (1971), "Criteria for a Theory of Consumer Behavior," in R. L. Holloway et al., eds., *Consumer Behavior: Contemporary Research in Action*, New York: Houghton Mifflin Co.

Mowen, John C., Stephen W. Brown, and Meg Schulman (1979), "Theoretical and Empirical Extensions of Endorser Effectiveness," in Neil Beckwith, Michael Houston, Robert Mittelstaedt, Kent B. Monroe, and Scott Ward, eds., *1979 Educator's Conference Proceedings*, Chicago, Ill: American Marketing Association, 258–262.

Peirce, Charles (1968), *Retroduction and Genius*, in B. Brody and C. Nicholas, eds., *Science: Men, Methods, Goals*, New York: W. A. Benjamin.

Popper, Karl (1963), *Conjectures and Refutations*, New York: Basic Books.

Robertson, T. S. and S. Ward (1973), "Consumer Behavior Research: Promise and Prospects," in S. Ward and T. S. Robertson, eds., *Consumer Behavior: Theoretical Sources*, Englewood Cliffs, N.J.: Prentice-Hall, Inc.

Sheth, J. N. (1967), "A Review of Buyer Behavior," *Management Science*, 13 (August), B718–B756.

Smith, M. B. (1972), "Is Experimental Social Psychology Advancing?" *Journal of Experimental Social Psychology*, 8, 86–96.

Tucker, W. T. (1974), "Future Directions in Marketing Theory," *Journal of Marketing*, 38 (April), 30–35.

Wells, W. D. and G. Gubar (1966), "Life Cycle Concept in Marketing Research," *Journal of Marketing Research*, 3 (November), 355–363.

Whewell, William (1968), "On Induction," reprinted in B. Brody and C. Nicholas, eds., *Science: Men, Methods, Goals*, New York: W. A. Benjamin.

Zaltman, G., C. Pinson, and R. Angelmar (1973), *Metatheory and Consumer Behavior*, New York: Holt, Rinehart, & Winston, Inc.

NOTES

[1] The model of the research process is applicable to any of the subareas of marketing. Consumer behavior was selected for specific application because among the various marketing subdisciplines, it has perhaps the greatest theoretical content.

DISCUSSION QUESTIONS

1. Compare and contrast the concepts of induction, deduction, and retroduction. What are their respective roles in the development and advancement of theory?

2. What are some current anomalies in marketing? Identify some possible approaches to solving these anomalies.

3. Consider the field of marketing or consumer behavior and its major theoretical constructs. (Loosely define theoretical constructs here!) How were these constructs "discovered" by marketers? Is it possible for marketers to discover new theory or will it have to be borrowed?

B. THEORY AND PRACTICE

The Myers, Greyser, and Massy article represents a critical assessment of the effectiveness of research and development for marketing management over a recent twenty-five-year period. Given this assessment, the authors offer a set of recommendations to strengthen the relationship between research and management.

Anderson proposes a new theory of the firm, specifying the role of marketing and other functional areas in the goal-setting and strategic-planning process. The Shostack article, premised on the increasing dominance of services in the American economy, argues for a creative and unique set of paradigms for service marketing.

PREFACE TO

''The Effectiveness of Marketing's 'R&D' for Marketing Management: An Assessment''

This article is one of the products of a ''blue ribbon'' American Marketing Association Commission on the Effectiveness of Research and Development for Marketing Management. Taking a retrospective look at marketing, Myers, Greyser, and Massy critique ''where we are and how we got there'' under the driving force of research accountability. Using a variety of methods and procedures, a series of objectives are addressed and suggestions are offered to help overcome the barriers that hamper new knowledge and research from being utilized in marketing practice.

20

THE EFFECTIVENESS OF MARKETING'S "R&D" FOR MARKETING MANAGEMENT: AN ASSESSMENT

JOHN G. MYERS
STEPHEN A. GREYSER
WILLIAM F. MASSY

INTRODUCTION

In 1976–1977, William F. Massy, then vice president of the American Marketing Association's Education Division, initiated a "blue ribbon" Commission to study the effectiveness of research and development for marketing management (Massy, Greyser, and Myers 1979). He enlisted Stephen A. Greyser to join the effort as co-chairman of the Commission. John G. Myers served as a Commission member along with many others[1] and became more deeply involved as the education Vice President following Massy. This article draws heavily on the work of the Commission and presents some of our own reflections on the state of research utilization in marketing and its "effectiveness" over the twenty-five-[year] period from the early 1950s to the present.[2] It represents a summary of and observations on those elements of the Commission's work that we believe to be of broadest interest.

BACKGROUND AND MISSION

The Commission considered a retrospective look at marketing—where we are and how we got there—to be of potential value in enhancing the process of creating new marketing knowledge and disseminating/utilizing it. By understanding the process of knowledge-creation and diffusion and the barriers and blocks to the process, marketers should be able to learn something about how to make it work more effectively. The Commission was charged with both an *evaluation* function—to assess the effectiveness of research and development in marketing[3]

Source: Reprinted with permission from the *Journal of Marketing,* 43, (January), 1979, 17–29, Chicago, Ill.: American Marketing Association.

for marketing management over the past quarter century—and a *prescriptive* function—to make recommendations of ways in which the generation and diffusion process could be improved.

The Commission accepted as a given the goal of the long-run relevance of knowledge created to practice in marketing. In this setting, knowledge implies all forms of academic and professional marketing research, and practice incorporates individuals and organizations such as line and staff marketing managers, senior corporation executives, and decision makers in government and nonprofit organizations. Its focus was thus on attempting to understand and evaluate the knowledge-creation and diffusion process in marketing. Where and how do changes originate? Where and with whom do ideas incubate and concepts become articulated? Where are the new methods tested and the techniques refined?

The concern for the study of these kinds of questions in marketing lies in the continuing serious debate as to the *relevance* of much of the knowledge-generating sector's activities to marketing management practice. It is obvious that a knowledge-creating sector does exist within marketing. Contrary to the views of many academics, the knowledge-creating sector is not solely, nor even largely, the province of academic researchers. Rather, it encompasses basic research mostly done in universities; applied and problem-oriented research in universities, research institutes, and government or nonprofit organizations; as well as problem-solving research in corporations, advertising agencies, marketing research firms, and consulting organizations. Attesting to a growth in quantity, albeit not necessarily in quality, of what is intended to be useful marketing knowledge over the past quarter-century was the creation of the AMA-sponsored *Journal of Marketing Research,* in addition to the *Journal of Marketing;* the advent of the multi-disciplinary *Journal of Consumer Research* with its large proportion of marketing-based content; and an expansion of marketing-related articles in journals such as *Management Science* and *Operations Research.* But a fundamental question is whether all or most of these segments do create *useful* knowledge. Although terms like "useful," "effective," and "relevant" are hard to define tightly, there is little question that a hard-headed demand for demonstrations of relevance to practical marketing problems has, to a considerable degree, replaced a post World War II faith that knowledge is useful "in its own right." This is not to deny that much research—particularly basic research—is difficult to manage and inherently "wasteful" by post hoc judgment. However, the Commission believed that it should be possible to trace *some* degree of impact of basic and other research on improvements in marketing management practice over a twenty-five-year period.

Another way of expressing the driving force behind the Commission's work is to say that it was fundamentally interested in research accountability. Is the investment in knowledge-generation in the field of marketing worthwhile? Is the process self-generating (like a breeder reactor), or does it require explicit and continuing investments of time, talent, and money? If the process is not now as effective as it should be, what are the barriers and blocks that prevent new knowledge and research from being utilized?

More specifically, the objectives of the Commission were:

• To identify changes in the marketing profession and practice over the past twenty-five years.

• To examine the nature and objectives of knowledge generation and R&D in marketing and provide examples of new knowledge developed during the period.

• To explain the process of knowledge-creation and the diffusion of knowledge in the field of marketing.

• To assess the contributions, or lack thereof, of marketing knowledge to marketing practice, and develop a list of recommendations directed to specific constituencies within the field.

The balance of this article is structured along these lines. Definitive conclusions in any of these areas are not easy, and not immediately amenable to the usual kinds of empirical research operations. The Commission employed a variety of methods and procedures to address each topic and illuminate the issues involved.

Methods

The work of the Commission involved five different operating methods and data generation procedures. First, commissioners and selected "friends" of the Commission[4] were polled for their opinions on four challenging questions: What were the major changes in the practice of marketing over the past twenty-five years? What major, new, useful approaches and techniques had been introduced over the period? What major problem areas remain? What major research approaches and techniques (in the commissioner's judgment) had failed to fulfill their promises?

Second, several face-to-face meetings of the commissioners were held during 1976 and 1977. Much attention, particularly in the later meetings, was given to the discussion and development of perspectives and viewpoints on the idea-generation and diffusion process in marketing.

Third, a study of changes in marketing journals and textbooks over the twenty-five-year period was undertaken by the Commission's staff. The journal study involved content analysis at five-year intervals of the *Journal of Marketing, Journal of Marketing Research, Harvard Business Review,* and *Journal of Consumer Research.* Examined were "hot topics" at the beginning and end of the period, topics that appeared to be an ongoing source of interest as well as topics that seemed to fade and others that were introduced, and the business/ academic affiliation of authors. Details of this study, as well as all other studies undertaken by the Commission, are given in its final report (Massy, Greyser, and Myers 1979). One self-evident watershed, however, was the 1964 founding of the *Journal of Marketing Research* with its emphasis on reports of empirical research and multivariate data analysis.

The textbook study involved content analysis of fifteen marketing textbooks (mostly those in multiple editions) ranging from Maynard and Beckman to Kotler, Enis, and Heskett. The period was characterized by a move from principles texts "about marketing" to managerial and decision-oriented texts "for marketing managers." Early texts covering institutional views and topics such as commodities and agricultural marketing were replaced by managerially oriented texts emphasizing components of the marketing mix. Kotler's first edition (1967) extended this focus by incorporating much more behavioral science and quantitative material and was, in some sense, a precursor to a decade of quantitatively rigorous management science and marketing books. Consumerism, environmental issues, multinational marketing, and marketing for nonprofit organizations are characteristic new topics introduced in textbooks towards the end of the period.

A fourth type of effort involved a survey of AMA members on various aspects of idea generation and diffusion. The focus was on determining the amount of awareness and usage of thirteen different types of analytical techniques, models, or research approaches. Here again, the details of this study are given in the main report (Massy, Greyser, and Myers, 1979).

Finally, attempts were made to elaborate on specific aspects of the overall project. Special interviews were conducted by the Commission staff to "track" the intellectual and applications evolution of new developments, in particular what many considered to be a highly successful example—that of conjoint analysis. Also, the Commission staff developed alternative skeletal views of the idea generation and diffusion process for use in Commission discussions of various conceptions of this process. Finally, the co-chairmen developed several "think pieces" on the types, nature, and functions of marketing research and the role of the marketing academic community.

HOW MARKETING PRACTICE HAS CHANGED

Readers who are old enough to remember marketing in the 1950s will appreciate the diversity of changes that have taken place both in the marketing manager's environment and in the nature of the marketing operations themselves. They also might appreciate the difficulty of attempting to capture the nature and type of these changes in a few paragraphs! From the viewpoint of managerial practice, much that has changed is traceable to a change in

managerial perspective contained in the familiar "marketing concept" with its emphasis on the identification and satisfaction of consumer wants and needs rather than on the "selling" of products. The implications of this externally focused attitude on how to run a business, and the basic idea that various components of marketing such as product, pricing, promotion, and distribution should be integrated into an overall comprehensive marketing plan, had far-reaching consequences for marketing practice and knowledge development over the period.

An external focus, for example, leads logically to a heightened awareness and stronger motivation for information-gathering and marketing research. This undoubtedly contributed to academic and professional concentration on understanding and predicting consumer behavior and was a major impetus in the creation of the consumer behavior field, the Association for Consumer Research, and numerous new consumer behavior textbooks and journals. The new focus gave increased stature and significance to marketing as a vital business function. Many of the aspects of a "profession" such as the scientific and explicit use of information in decision-making, the educational and university role in training managerial talent for marketing positions, and the numerous other trappings, are traceable to this change in overall managerial focus. The evolution of marketing research in some corporations from a purely data-gathering function to include complex decision models and multivariate analysis which characterize modern-day "marketing information systems" seems, in retrospect, a natural evolution of this fundamental idea. Another type of evolution is the application of marketing principles to nonprofit organization management, a trend particularly apparent in recent years.

An equally persuasive explanation for changes in marketing management practice and knowledge development can be found in technological innovations and in social, economic, and environmental changes that have occurred over the past twenty-five years. Perhaps the most significant innovations from the viewpoint of their effect on marketing management practice were the development of the computer and television. The twenty-five-year period spans the time in which each of these inventions came into being on a commercial scale and had far-reaching impact on marketing (as well as on other aspects of the nation as a whole). Computers made possible the management of very large amounts of data both in terms of accessibility and analysis. This, in turn, stimulated the need for models, theories, and perspectives to guide the data collection and analysis process. Highly complex multivariate methods became feasible analysis alternatives, and a whole generation of model-builders, statisticians, and computer specialists began to look at marketing as an applications area in which to pursue their interests. Progress in adapting the computer to basic discipline studies on which marketing researchers continued to draw their inspiration and insight—economics, psychology, sociology, and others—further emphasized and expanded the important role of the computer.

Parallel reasoning could be applied to assessing the impact of television (as well as many other types of period-specific innovations or product-line extensions such as jet air freight and travel, the space program, etc.). Television created entire industries of market-related specialists in advertising, research, production, and so on. Methodologies developed in basic social science ranging from econometrics to pupilometrics and psychometrics were quickly adopted, refined, and in some cases rejected by marketing academics and commercial research firms doing television and advertising research. The marketing manager, for the first time, could direct messages to a mass market of millions of households via a total communications package (both audio and visual channels) at a comparatively low cost-per-thousand viewers reached. The absolute costs of television usage involving hundreds of thousands of millions of advertiser dollars increased marketing budgets accordingly. Many commissioners identified an overall increase in the scale of marketing operations as a characteristic change over the period. Obviously, when a marketing manager's budget has increased significantly, the requirements and opportunities for the use of marketing research data differ greatly.

Many other environmental factors affected marketing management over the period. Commissioners noted the increased role of government in marketing decision-making. Consumerism was a movement of the 1960s which impacted greatly on marketing. Energy and other shortages characterized manager concern towards the end of the period. Along with an overall increase in the scale of marketing operations, decisions became much

more consequential or "risky" in terms of the stakes involved.

These are some of the major changes in marketing management practice and the forces that affected changes in practice over the period. The next question examined by the Commission concerned the nature and objectives of knowledge-generation and R&D in marketing and types of new knowledge that had been generated. The R&D on which the Commission focused does not refer to new technical inventions, chemical discoveries, and so on, flowing from the nation's laboratories or what might be called the research and development associated with production. Rather, it refers to marketing research developments and new knowledge pertaining to advancement of marketing management practices.

MARKETING'S R&D

Throughout the balance of the article, the terms marketing R&D and marketing knowledge are used interchangeably. The R&D term is introduced to emphasize the fact that much of what a marketing manager considers "state-of-the-art" knowledge is *not* limited to the literature. Professionals in an applied field, such as marketing, do not rely solely (or even primarily) on journal materials as their source of knowledge—a fact often overlooked by academics for whom journals represent the major storehouse of new and accumulated knowledge. For marketing professionals, the proprietary research information resident in their companies (from both the company's own research and outside commercial sources) as well as the folklore and accumulated experience of managerial colleagues are important components of the "state-of-the-art." As will be seen, it is possible to document changes in marketing knowledge by examining journal materials, but extremely difficult or impossible to document important aspects of the total storehouse of knowledge generated over the period.

An equally difficult question concerns the effectiveness measure. What are, or should be, the objectives of knowledge-generation in marketing? We examine this controversial question next.

Objectives of Knowledge-Generation in Marketing

Although a viable argument can be made that knowledge development should be pursued for "its own sake" and much basic research in marketing is generated in this way, the Commission took the position that the objectives of knowledge-generation in our field should be to improve marketing management practice. Thus, even basic research if it is to be considered "effective" should, over the long run, contribute something to improved decision-making or other aspects of management practice. But how should "good" practice and management be defined? What is an effective marketing manager? More generally, what is an effective marketing organization? In either case, the usual criteria of sales and profits are often suspect because of the dynamics of markets and marketing operations. Good sales and good profits can result from "good luck!" The Commission's position was that management should be evaluated also on the basis of "good judgment" and the specific ways in which budgets and people are managed, plans developed, actions implemented, and operations controlled. As one CEO is reported to have said: "Don't tell me about sales and profits, tell me whether or not I have a good marketing operation."

Entire books have been written on the qualities of a good manager or, more generally, the "functions of the executive" (Barnard 1968). A marketing manager needs to possess a whole bundle of qualities captured in the notion of "leader"—the capacity to motivate people working under him or her, the capacity to efficiently manage large amounts of funds and expenditures, and the capacity to make difficult and risky decisions in an environment of great uncertainty. Increasingly, however, marketing managers must be capable of managing large amounts of complex data which can be used to reduce the uncertainty in decision-making. To do so, they need to be able to recognize and conceptualize important problems, and to distinguish the important from the trivial. In the Commission's view, they need a capacity to develop good "theories" or "models" of their operations, to be able to distinguish cause and effect, and understand the implications of their decisions.

The modern manager, in other terms, must be a good planner. The development of a good marketing plan where realistic and worthwhile objectives are carefully specified, the resources marshalled to carry them out, and control mechanisms introduced to evaluate them, is an important characteristic of good management. To this, we believe, should be added the capacity to guide research efforts, to

marshall facts and data relevant to stated objectives, and the capacity to analyze and interpret complex information. The ideal manager must be able to bridge the gaps between an original theory/model specification, the research design actually used to generate data, and the interpretation of the final data results. The overriding point is that modern managers should display at least some of the characteristics of the scientist—a willingness to use theories, models, and concepts, a capacity to identify important problems, and a healthy respect for the value of objective information and research in seeking answers to problems. Managers need to know the "why" of their operations in the sense of a theory or model, the "what" in the sense of relevant facts and data that pertain to them, and the "how" in terms of the implications of implementation and control.

The difficulty of documenting that marketing managers were "better" at the end of the period than at the beginning should be obvious. The Commission did not attempt to test this proposition and we, frankly, don't know. We do know that more managers held the MBA degree, that there was much more marketing research information available, that the demands for in-company information systems and information to support decisions were higher, and that there was a marked rise in the size and scale of the marketing research industry generally. The criterion of "better practice" was thus left implicit rather than explicit in the Commission's deliberations, and the focus directed to better understanding the nature of marketing knowledge.

The Nature of Marketing Knowledge

Marketing "R&D" as referred to in this study encompasses a broad range of types of "knowledge" and ways in which it can be generated. Types of knowledge are in effect the "ends" to be achieved—the *objects* of research in marketing. The ways to generate knowledge represent the "means."

The Commission recognized two broad types of knowledge "objects" in this sense: (1) context-specific knowledge, and (2) context-free knowledge. Context-specific knowledge is specific to a particular firm or industry or specific to a particular managerial problem or situation: Does potato chip advertisement A generate more recall than advertisement B? Two subclasses of context-specific knowledge can be identified as (1a) product industry-specific, and (1b) situation-specific. Context-specific marketing knowledge is usually proprietary, particularly if it is current. It also is probably the most useful base of empirical evidence on which general facts and laws could eventually evolve. That is, by looking for regularities across product, industry, or situation-specific cases, we might come closer to more useful, relevant generalizations in the field of marketing. There are examples of this type of work (Clarke 1976; Haley 1970, but it is comparatively rare.

Context-free knowledge encompasses three subclasses referred to as: (2a) general facts and laws, (2b) theories or conceptual structures, and (2c) techniques. Examples are the advertising-to-sales ratios of Fortune 500 companies, theories of buyer behavior, and factor analysis, respectively. What we know about the duration effects of advertising, and patterns of brand loyalty and switching from stochastic brand choice research fit the 2a category, and contrasting theories of advertising effects (hierarchy, low-involvement, conflict, and so on) fit 2b. Conjoint analysis, to be discussed later, is an example of what is considered 2c, a technique, although there is certainly a model or theory which motivates this approach to data collection. These latter types of knowledge-generation are largely, but not exclusively, the domain of academics and university research and make up the content of much of our journal materials.

The means of knowledge-generation can be broadly classified as different kinds of marketing research. We note that many recent marketing research textbooks make a distinction between "Basic" research and "Decisional" research (Churchill 1976; Green and Tull 1978; Tull and Hawkins 1976). Basic research usually involves *hypothesis-testing* of some kind, a prediction based on the hypothesis, devising a test of the prediction, conducting the test, and developing an analysis plan to determine whether the results are statistically significant at some researcher-specified confidence level. Decisional research, on the other hand, begins with a specification of alternative *solutions* to a marketing problem, the possible outcomes of each alternative, the design of a method to predict actual outcomes, and data analysis which relies more on Bayesian-type reasoning than on that of classical statistics. The decision-maker is often mostly interested in how the information changes his/her pri-

or probabilities of likely outcomes than in statistical significance.

Although many "classic" data collection and analysis techniques are included in most marketing research textbooks, the decision-theory viewpoint, or "decisional" research, is becoming much more widely adopted, particularly where the emphasis is placed on the building of a model for which very specific demands are made on the data-collection process. Decisional research also differs in other fundamental ways. There is much more attention to considering trade-offs between the cost and value of the information which, in turn, implies less attention to replication and questions such as reliability and validity. The decision-maker is more interested in knowing the probability level of the results rather than whether they are statistically significant. Finally, the fact that the user of the research and researcher are in direct association with one another, distinguishes decisional from the basic or classical research. What seems evident is that marketing research textbooks are becoming more "decisional" than "basic" in these terms, and this appears to us to be a healthy trend.

A further delineation within the "decisional" category can provide a better understanding of a research taxonomy in marketing, namely distinguishing *problem-solving* research from *problem-oriented* research.

- Problem-*solving* research addresses a very specific applied issue or problem, and is usually proprietary in character; that is, it is usually done within a company or under contract by a commercial firm/consultant for a company. Advertising testing research is one example.

- Problem-*oriented* research addresses a *class* of issues or problems, and typically has at least limited generalizability across firms or situations. The topics examined are usually of a conceptual character, but oriented to applied problems—for example an effort to classify the kinds of products and consumer purchase situations in which the hierarchy of advertising effects might operate in different ways.

The major criterion for assessing problem-solving research in marketing is whether it helps improve a specific business decision. For problem-oriented research, the criteria are whether it improves our understanding of particular kinds of phenomena in marketing (as an applied social science) and whether it contributes to advancements of theory and method in a basic discipline. The narrowness of the problem, the time frame for utility, and the context of the application all are factors differentiating problem-solving from problem-oriented research.

Two important conclusions flow from these views on the means and ends of marketing's R&D. First, there has been a progressively stronger *leveraged role* for research in marketing practice. With larger markets, more dollars are riding on marketing decisions. With more complex, highly segmented and fragmented markets, there is a higher premium on developing and reaching one's distinctive part in the market. And those companies which know how to harness the array of research tools, help develop and apply them ahead of others, and employ them swiftly and effectively in marketing decisions have an advantage over competition. Second, the huge growth of marketing research information and techniques has resulted in a multi-faceted role for the marketing research manager. At least three separate missions can be discerned— facilitator, gatekeeper, and translator. *Facilitator* basically relates to planning and conducting studies and projects and bringing together managers and research specialists. *Gatekeeper* involves monitoring new research techniques and ideas, exploring, "filtering," and trying to apply some of them within the organization. The *translator* puts management issues and problems into researchable propositions and converts research findings into managerial terms.

Knowledge Development Over the Period

As noted earlier, it is impossible to document the full scope of new knowledge developed over the twenty-five-year period for much resides in the mind and mores of practicing managers. The overview in this section is largely confined to published materials. Suffice it to say, that marketing as a field is still characterized both by a management philosophy that emphasizes intuition, executive experience, and the "art" of marketing, and an emerging philosophy that emphasizes research, information-gathering, and what some call the "science" of marketing.

From this perspective, the Commission concluded that much had taken place during the twenty-

five years in the direction of increased use and dependency on scientific marketing research information. The increased size and sophistication of commercial marketing research services as well as a general expansion in the industry was noted. A marked shift from trade to consumer research and from secondary to primary research took place. Much more use was made of test marketing before new product introductions. By the end of the period, most of the large consumer packaged goods corporations had some form of marketing information system, and were making increasing use of models and methods to simulate consumer and competitive reactions.

The development of the computer and television noted earlier as impacting on management practice also impacted heavily on knowledge-generation. *Marketing and the Computer* (Alderson and Shapiro 1963) contained papers by a new generation of eager, young students such as Al Kuehn, Ralph Day, Paul Green, Hans Thorelli, Purnell Benson, Bill Massy, and Arnie Amstutz and was, in retrospect, a major precursor of things to come. The largest commercial marketing research service, A. C. Nielsen, Inc., is currently also one of the largest worldwide users of computers. Television required the development of new theories of consumer behavior and communication, new methods to study its effects (e.g., dozens of new commercial services such as Burke's DAR, AD-TEL, ASI In-Theater Testing, etc.), and significant new models of advertising decision-making such as MEDIAC (Little and Lodish 1969). ADBUG (Little 1970), POMSIS (Aaker 1968) and AD-ME-SIM (Gensch 1973) which utilized computer capacity to assist decision-making in television and mass media generally (for a recent review of related models, see Larreche and Montgomery 1977).

New knowledge in marketing, particularly that which has heavily impacted on changes in marketing practice, is very difficult to document. In medicine, the discovery of penicillen, X-rays, control of diseases like polio, tuberculosis, and syphilis are clearly definable events. In marketing, no "drug" has yet been invented that will "cure" the problem of new product failures. But it is, nevertheless, possible to trace some of the new ideas, theories, tools, and decision-aids introduced during the period.

Table 1 shows a listing of sixty-four examples of knowledge development in marketing from 1952 to

TABLE 1
Examples of Knowledge Development in Marketing, 1952–1977

Discipline-Based Theories	Managerial Frameworks and Approaches	Models and Measurement	Research Methods and Statistical Techniques
Demand and Utility Theory	Marketing Concept	Stochastic Models of Brand Choice	Motivation Research and Projective Techniques
Market Segmentation	Marketing Mix—4Ps	Market Share Models	Survey Research
General and Middle-Range Theories of Consumer Behavior	Development of Marketing Cases	Marginal Analysis and Linear Programming	Focus Groups and Depth Interviewing
Image and Attitude Theory	DAGMAR	Bayesian Analysis	Experimental and Panel Designs—ANOVA
Theories of Motivation, Personality, Social Class, Life Style, and Culture	Product Life Cycle	Advertising Models, e.g., MEDIAC, POMSIS, AD-ME-SIM, BRANDAID, ADBUG	Advances in Probability Sampling
Expectancy-Value Theory	Marketing Plan		Hypothesis Formulation, Inference, Significance Test
Theories of Advertising Processes and Effects	State Approaches to Strategy Development	Causal Models	Multivariate Dependence Methods—Multiple Regression and Multiple Discriminant Analysis, Canonical Correlation
Information Processing Theory	Product Portfolio Analysis	Sensitivity Analysis and Validity Tests	
Attitude Change Theories (consistency and complexity theories)	Physical Distribution	Response Functions	
	Marketing Information Systems	Weighted Belief Models, Determinant Attributes	Multivariate Interdependence Methods—Cluster and Factor Analysis, Latent Structure Analysis
	Product Positioning and Perceptual Mapping	Simulation and Marketing Games	
Attribution Theory	Segmentation Strategies		Advances in Forecasting Econometrics, and Time Series Analysis
Perceptual Processes	New Marketing Organization Concepts, e.g., Brand Management	Multidimensional Scaling and Attitude Measurement	
Advertising Repetition		Sales Management Models, e.g., DETAILER, CALLPLAN	
Distribution Theory	Territory Design and Salesman Compensation		
Refutation and Distraction Hypotheses	Marketing Audit	New Product Models, e.g., DEMON, SPRINTER, STEAM, HENDRY	Trade-Off Analysis and Conjoint Analysis
Theories of Diffusion, New Product Adoption and Personal Influence	Demand State Strategies		Psychographics and AIO Studies
	Creative Approaches and Styles	Bid Pricing Models	
Prospect Theory	New Search and Screening Approaches	Computer-Assisted Marketing Cases	Physiological Techniques—Eye Camera, GSR, CONPAAD
	Refinements in Test Marketing Approaches	Product Planning Models, PERCEPTOR, ACCESSOR	Unobtrusive Measures, Response Latency, Nonverbal Behavior

1977 organized into four categories: (1) Discipline-Based Theories, (2) Managerial Frameworks and Approaches, (3) Models and Measurement, and (4) Research Methods and Statistical Techniques. This listing is illustrative only and is intended to provide a sampling of the variety of identifiable new theories, concepts, methods, and techniques. It is interesting to note the degree to which much that is "new" in marketing is closely related to new developments in the basic disciplines, particularly economics and psychology. Much new marketing knowledge is by definition an application and refinement of basic theories and methods in these social sciences and, in some instances, has had major impacts on the development of their theory and method. An interesting characteristic is the comparative speed by which marketing academics and professional researchers have adopted or "tried out" those ideas. In general, marketing knowledge generated over the period 1952 to 1977 changed principally in the degree to which it increased in quantitative and behavioral science sophistication. The introduction of a management science/ engineering perspective to the field moved us closer to considerations of marketing as an applied science, and in general a "social engineering" view of the profession.

The next section deals with the third type of charge to the Commission: what is the nature of the knowledge-creation and diffusion process in marketing?

THE KNOWLEDGE-CREATION AND DIFFUSION PROCESS

The Commission recognized two major patterns by which new knowledge is created and diffused to line managers: knowledge that is essentially idea, concept, or methods-driven and problem-driven knowledge. The first can arise in the academic *or* professional sphere when someone has a good idea and the energy and persistence to pursue the research, testing, and publication required to disseminate it.[5] Examples of this in marketing are the idea of a "hierarchy of effects" and the subsequent expectancy-value models to explain consumer decision-making and information processing. Consumer information processing, in particular, is now a very popular marketing academic subject which, some might say, is being driven mostly by the inherent interest of researchers in attempting to understand this phenomenon.

The second type of new knowledge might arise when a manager needs to predict his brand share for a new product. This leads logically into sales forecasting techniques (and new developments in this area, Bass and Wittink 1975), which in turn leads to the concept and use of panel data and, for example, stochastic models of brand choice (Morrison 1965), basic concepts such as market segmentation (Frank, Massy, and Wind 1972; Myers and Nicosia 1968; Wind 1978a) and to a variety of other new models and methods developments (e.g., Silk and Urban 1978; Srinivasan and Shocker 1973). Much segmentation research during the early part of the period appeared to be basically "idea-driven" (researchers were more interested in testing new types of multivariate methods factor analysis, cluster analysis, latent structure analysis, Sheth 1977), whereas during the latter part, particularly with the publication of *Market Segmentation* (Frank, Massy, and Wind 1972), research appeared more problem-driven and efforts were concentrated on situation-specific-type variables.

To better understand the process, the Commission chose conjoint analysis as a means of studying one pattern of adoption and diffusion. It is an example of an idea or methods-driven pattern, even though the problem (deriving a preference function and/or determining the utilities, "part-worths," of attribute levels) has been a part of marketing since the days when marketers were told to "sell the sizzle and not the steak!" The example illustrates several important ideas such as the role of nonmarketing academics, the importance of consulting arrangements in the diffusion process, and the contributions of academic and professional researchers in getting a complex idea widely disseminated and used.

It is generally held that a breakthrough article on conjoint analysis was published in 1964 in the *Journal of Mathematical Psychology* (Luce and Tukey 1964). It was a breakthrough in the sense of a long tradition of psychological and attitude measurement perspectives going back to Thurstone and others (nonmarketing academics) who make up the field of psychometrics and mathematical psychology. The first major publication in marketing literature on the subject was a 1971 *Journal of Marketing Research* article (Green and Rao 1971).[6] Green and his colleagues focused on developing a "full-profile" approach to the fundamental task of generating part-worth utilities on sets of decision criteria or salient brand/product attributes. A professional researcher, Richard Johnson of Market Facts, Inc., Chicago, working independently from the Wharton group, developed a parallel procedure based on a "two-factor-at-a-time" approach which he called "trade-off analysis" and published the new procedure in *JMR* (Johnson 1974). What is important for our purposes is to note the location of each individual, one in a university environment and one in a commercial or "external" marketing research firm. Also of significance is the pattern, particularly of the marketing academic in this case, of essentially using real-world marketing applications as the laboratory for further testing and refining the methods reflected in numerous studies involving actual situation-specific decisions and data.[7] A similar pattern from the professional researcher viewpoint was going on through the normal process of a marketing research firm (Market Facts) dealing with numerous clients, many of whom were being introduced to the technique over the period via this channel. Both individuals also were appearing at conferences and presenting papers on the subject further enhancing the diffusion process. Robinson and Associates (Philadelphia), another "external" marketing research firm, was also an early adopter of conjoint analysis and introduced the technique to many of its clients. Wharton students, particularly graduating Ph.D.s who accepted positions at other universities across the country, were significant forces in the general refinement and diffusion of conjoint analysis. One estimate is that there have been, to date, over 300 commercial applications (separate and distinct studies) of conjoint analysis, and interest is still high and spreading to applications in the nonprofit and government sectors.

In sum, this is an example of one of the most successful types of new knowledge introduced over the period in terms of making a complex idea developed in a basic discipline of direct use and benefit to line marketing managers and marketing decision-making. The basic ingredients of the process are a methodological breakthrough in basic research, the adaptation and refinement of the ideas by a small "innovator group" of marketing academics and professionals, and subsequent diffusion to line managers involving external marketing research

companies, internal marketing research departments, students, journals, consultants, meetings, and conferences.

What can be said generally about the efficiency and effectiveness of this system over the twenty-five years? First, the Commission concluded that much innovation, particularly as perceived by academics, never reaches line managers, and in retrospect, has contributed little to improvements in marketing management practice. Second, and discussed in the next section, there is a great deal of "promising" development which is used little by managers. Third, important new developments have come from *both* academics *and* professionals. In marketing there is a relatively small "*innovator group*" made up of both professionals and academics from which a significant number of the major new, useful ideas flow. Finally, the Commission concluded that neither the idea nor the problem necessarily comes first at the initiation stage, and problems and ideas find themselves in different ways. There is no single, dominant pattern. In some cases, particularly among academics, a technique is developed and then applied to a real-world problem. In others, a problem is posed, and a search for new solution techniques is initiated. In either event, much effort is needed to test and hone the development before it becomes widely adopted or commercially useful. Unfortunately, problems often reside with management people who are not well trained to articulate them to research people unfamiliar with management life. The Commission was struck by the discrepancies between the volume of new knowledge generated over the period and the comparatively low rate of adoption at the line manager level. Is this type of "failure rate" endemic to the field? What causes it? What can be done about it?

Barriers to Innovation and Diffusion

The Commission recognized two types of barriers to the diffusion and adoption process broadly classified as Structural and Organizational (S/O) barriers and Substantive and Communication (S/C) barriers. On reflection, we have become impressed with the seeming rediscovery of C. P. Snow's "two cultures" within the field of marketing, not characterized so much as that of academic/business as that of researcher/manager. We are reminded of the "those who think and never act" and "those who act and never think" distinction. Into this mix must be poured the numerous types of research specialists that have arisen in marketing over the twenty-five years, many of whom communicate in a language inherently foreign to one another.

More specifically, the Commission recognized as S/O barriers the inherent differences in occupational roles and incentives among managers, researchers, and academics. In particular, the impact of the reward system and the drive to do research and publish for academics is a significant cause of the volume and type of research and new-knowledge generation in marketing. In some universities, only contributions to basic research carry any weight, and it is often nonmarketing academics (economists, psychologists, sociologists) who are doing the evaluating. Built in barriers between line and staff people within an organization, the proprietary and confidential nature of much marketing research information in corporations, the lack of exposure to and formal quantitative training of line managers,[8] and other characteristics of line managers and their positions (too busy, conservative, inherent inertia, etc.) were seen as S/O barriers to the process.

Numerous Substantive and Communication (S/C) barriers were identified. A common theme was the inappropriateness of many quantitative models and techniques to marketing problems as perceived by marketing managers. The length of time needed to test, adapt, and make a new idea useful was mentioned. Some commissioners recognized current marketing journals as a barrier—our journals represent mostly academics talking to one another, and reflect the *supply* of new knowledge rather than the *demand* for it. The credibility of much academic work comes into question when trivial problems are given treatment equal to that given important problems. The annual AMA conference structure was singled out as a barrier in the sense that two, separate conferences, one for educators and one for professionals, are held. The lack of line manager membership in the AMA, and/or the lack of time to participate actively in such organizations by line managers, was another type of S/C barrier. Particularly for managers, there are few incentives or rewards for contributing to new knowledge *per se,* and attention is often focused on short-run sales and profit generation.

Many of these barriers and blocks reduce to attitudinal factors residing in the make-up of each of the participants. Managers, often uncomfortable with complex quantitative and abstract materials, or with no time to learn about them, are prone to dismiss much that could be valuable as academic nonsense. Patterns such as the "not invented here" syndrome, anti-intellectualism, and other defenses develop to rationalize the basic position. Researchers, particularly those who are scholarly inclined, often write-off practical marketing problems as irrelevant to what they do, or as an interference with their scholarly progress. Patterns of "let them learn what I am doing" develop with little or no commitment to translating ideas into the practical world of the marketing decision-maker.

ASSESSMENT AND SOME RECOMMENDATIONS

Three broad observations appear germane to the overall charge to the Commission of assessing the effectiveness of marketing research and development for marketing management:

- Knowledge-generation in marketing, like in any other professional or academic field, is to some degree "inefficient." There will always be waste in the system in terms of false starts, blind alleys, and so forth. Throughout its work, the Commission held to an initial view that the most meaningful criterion—perhaps the only criterion—for assessing and making new investments in developing marketing knowledge was its ultimate contribution to marketing practice. At the same time, there was broad recognition that *basic* research both warranted and demanded support, even though many who engage in it do so with the principal (and sometimes sole) motivation of enriching knowledge rather than improving practice. The often indirect impacts on practice—despite the aforementioned inherent inefficiencies in and unpredictability of basic research to be "useful"—remain important enough to sustain and encourage it.

- All forms and types of marketing research increased in both quality and quantity over the twenty-five-year period. In quality terms, the direction has been toward greater quantitative and behavioral science sophistication. This has been manifested in the professional marketing and marketing research community and particularly in the ways marketing is taught in business schools. The latter, in turn, feeds the world of practice at the entry level.

- A significant amount of marketing research effort, new knowledge development, model-building, and theorizing has had relatively little impact on improving marketing management practice over the period. Although controversial, this observation represents our interpretation of a widely held belief among Commission members after many months of deliberation on events of the past twenty-five years. As one Commissioner noted, "There isn't a single problem area with regard to the practice of marketing management that marketing research or the world of technology and concepts has mastered." Another said, "The tendency (is) for many marketing decisions to be made either without any research or on the basis of extremely sloppy research. The fact that the vast majority of new products put on the market turn out to be failures may be a manifestation of the phenomenon."

In reflecting on these assessments, we recognize that marketing is still in a rather primitive state of development. Unlike our impression of some other business fields such as accounting and finance, there is still no unifying marketing theory or model which holds together the diversity of perspectives and viewpoints. Materials which are widely taught in the classroom such as Bayesian analysis do not appear to be widely used by practicing managers. Although there are numerous examples of what might be considered "successful" knowledge development, measured in terms of managerial adoption, we are struck by the degree to which much that has been developed and *could be* useful is *not* being used.

What the Commission in effect rediscovered in the management science/model-building area was a reaffirmation of what many model-builders themselves have long believed—comparatively few firms or practicing management people seem to be using their models. This is particularly true for early, complex model formulations that often went through a cycle of trial and rejection. The most recent model-building trend—to begin with relatively simple concepts and functions, to involve the manager in the model-building effort, and to establish long-run relationships with the client firm—appears to us to be a very healthy one. Many behav-

ioral researchers might well go through a similar type of introspective process with respect to how their work impacts on marketing practice, and the degree of its adoption or nonadoption by marketing decision-makers.

On a more optimistic note, we see marketing at somewhat of a turning-point with respect to the effectiveness of its R&D efforts. A major barrier to the diffusion process, particularly in terms of utilizing formal models, is largely one of scale of operations, the sizeable investments of funds required to develop and maintain on-going data bases, and the teams of specialists needed to achieve an effective utilization of research and knowledge-generation resources. The basic combination of scale and a willingness to invest now appears to us to exist in many corporations, and there are numerous examples of the fully integrated information system model which this implies.

In retrospect, then, the quarter-century contained a significant amount of "ineffectiveness" regarding marketing's R&D. *The contributions of research and knowledge-development at best can be characterized as mixed.* The impacts have been significant, but far less than "what might have been." The reasons lie primarily in the numerous types of barriers and blocks to the diffusion process. We think concerned people in the field should examine their own organizations with respect to both the S/O and S/C barriers. Many of the Commission's recommendations pertain to various ways to reduce these barriers.

Recommendations

There are numerous recommendations given in the Commission's full report. Many relate to the fundamental needs for open lines of communication between researchers and managers, the needs to find ways to break down the barriers and blocks to the idea-generation and diffusion process, and the needs for conscious effort, investment, and continuing funding to make the process work. In our view, the process is not like a breeder reactor, it is *not* self-generating; rather it requires conscious effort to sustain it. More sources need to be found for supporting research, particularly of the "problem-oriented" kind, and better ways need to be developed to bridge the gaps between knowledge-generation and knowledge-utilization.

Among the many recommendations, we view the following as particularly important and provide some of our own reflections on the implications and impact of each:

1. *More support should be provided for basic and "problem-oriented" research in marketing.* Both the professional and the academic marketing communities need to give "problem-oriented" research much more attention. The company role here goes beyond providing financial support, to contributing data and information on company experiences. In this way, more progress can be made to develop experience-based "conditional generalizations," i.e., knowledge and concepts that apply under specified kinds of product, market, or consumer conditions. On the academic side, more appreciation is needed of the "respectability" of such research for academic knowledge-building. (See item 5, below.)

On the whole, relatively few institutions—notably the Marketing Science Institute, the now phased-down National Science Foundation's Research Applied to National Needs program, the American Association of Advertising Agencies' Educational Foundation—exist with "problem-oriented" research as their major focus. Such marketing research typically is not "basic" enough to gain support from institutions principally geared to "harder" sciences; this appears to have been the experience at NSF. Yet problem-oriented research is usually not immediately practical enough to warrant support from company operating budgets. In short, "problem-oriented" research is a stepchild. So far, the limited success in gaining support for such research has been rooted in institutional systems, such as MSI's, that catalytically bring together conceptually oriented professionals with practically oriented academics (Greyser 1978).

This focus on "problem-oriented" research does not reduce the importance, in our view, of basic research. It *is* important over the long-run. We think, however, that business and academe alike have given too little recognition and value to problem-oriented research.

2. *Nontechnical reviews of new concepts, findings, and techniques in marketing should be published far more frequently. At the same time, publications that permit researchers to write to other researchers need to be preserved and encouraged.* This recommendation basically addresses both ends of the knowledge development/knowledge utiliza-

tion spectrum. For the former, we underscore the importance of having an "archival resource" that not only provides a medium where new research results can be published, but also permits such work to be accessed readily by other researchers over time. "Relevance" is not the appropriate criterion on which to assess such journals. The *Journal of Marketing Research* is obviously a specific example.

At the other end, nontechnical reviews represent one way of attempting to break the technical jargon block which many Commissioners thought was a major impediment to good communication. Complex ideas must often be expressed in formal, mathematical terms, but they should be capable of being communicated in terms that a broader audience can understand. The "annual reviews" in fields such as psychology were cited as illustrations, as were some of the "state-of-the-art" articles in current journals, and the concept of the *Review of Marketing*.

3. *Senior executives of major companies in the consumer, industrial, and services sector should be encouraged to develop a climate within their organizations which is amenable to exploration of and experimentation with new research ideas and techniques. Further, practicing managers must become more appreciative of the value of "good theory," and develop more capacity to conceptualize, supervise, and interpret information relevant to decision-making.* Unless the right climate of receptivity is developed within the organization, there is little chance of significant adoption of new knowledge. People simply won't want to take the necessary risks of introducing new ideas. Moreover, an attitude which assumes that new ideas and techniques are automatically of low or no relevance to one's operations needs to be guarded against. Anti-intellectualism, in whatever forms it may take and for whatever motivations it may arise, appears to us not to be in the best interests of either the firm or the manager. This recommendation may have a "motherhood" (maybe even a "Pollyanna") character, but we think it needs restatement here.

4. *A "clearinghouse mechanism" should be established in which company data files can be made available to academic and professional researchers.* This is not a new idea, but one which the Commission recommends receive attention and

effort. It would do much to meet the needs of academic researchers for empirical data, and consequently increase the usefulness (real and perceived) of their work.

The difficulties of implementing such an activity are widely recognized. Major difficulties include the concerns of companies regarding proprietary information, and the lack of congruence of categories and questions from study to study (even ones done by the same company). Although much time and careful effort is necessary, we think these problems can be mitigated.

One commissioner suggested that what is needed to facilitate a clearinghouse mechanism is some motivation for contributing companies. Conscious as we are that many company studies are underanalyzed (even in terms of their own objectives), we think one possible avenue would be for companies contributing data to suggest particular perspectives/approaches for consideration by researchers working with the data through the clearinghouse.

5. *Marketing educators and university administrators must be made aware of the crucial need to maintain open lines of communication with professional researchers and practicing managers. They should be persuaded to support teaching, consulting, and research activities which foster this communication and involve real-world marketing problems.* This recommendation relates in large part to our earlier comments on ''two cultures.'' In our view, too many academics think that ''being practical'' is not desirable (and may even be explicitly undesirable). For marketing academics, this tendency can become exacerbated when people from nonbusiness fields are involved, as in universitywide promotion reviews. Understanding practice, and contributing to it, can lead to major contributions to knowledge-development itself.

Conclusion

What do we hope will emerge from the Commission's work? First and foremost, our hope is for greater sensitivity to and concern for the state of research in marketing today—whether that research be basic, problem-oriented, or problem-solving. From such sensitivity and concern we think will emerge an improved climate for all research, both in universities and in the business community. In turn, professionalism in marketing decision-making will be enhanced—a goal that we believe should be shared by all in the field.

REFERENCES

Aaker, David A. (1968), ''A Probabilistic Approach to Industrial Media Selection,'' *Journal of Advertising Research,* 8 (September), 46–54.

Alderson, Wroe and Stanley J. Shapiro, eds. (1963), *Marketing and the Computer,* Englewood Cliffs, N.J.: Prentice-Hall, Inc.

Barnard, Chester I. (1968), *Functions of the Executive,* Cambridge: Harvard University Press.

Bass, Frank M. and Dick R. Wittink (1975), ''Pooling Issues and Methods in Regression Analysis with Examples in Marketing Research,'' *Journal of Marketing Research,* 12 (November), 414–425.

Churchill, Gilbert A. Jr. (1976), *Marketing Research: Methodological Foundations,* Hinsdale, Ill.: The Dryden Press.

Clarke, Darral G. (1976), ''Econometric Measurement of the Duration of Advertising Effect on Sales,'' *Journal of Marketing Research,* 13 (November), 345–357.

Frank, Ronald E., William F. Massy, and Yoram Wind (1972), *Market Segmentation,* Englewood Cliffs, N.J.: Prentice-Hall, Inc.

Gensch, Dennis H. (1973), *Advertising Planning: Mathematical Models in Advertising Media,* Amsterdam: Elsevier Publishing Co.

Gordon, Robert A. and James E. Howell (1959), *Higher Education for Business,* New York: Columbia University Press.

Green, Paul E. and Vithala R. Rao (1971), ''Conjoint Measurement for Quantifying Judgmental Data,'' *Journal of Marketing Research,* 8 (August), 355–363.

———and Donald S. Tull (1978), *Research for Marketing Decisions,* 4th ed., Englewood Cliffs, N.J.: Prentice-Hall, Inc.

Greyser, Stephen A. (1978), ''Academic Research Marketing Managers Can Use," *Journal of Advertising Research,* 18 (April), 9–14.

Haley, Russell I. (1970), "We Shot an Arrowhead (#9) Into the Air," *Proceedings,* 16th Annual Conference, Advertising Research Foundation, New York, 25–30.

Johnson, Richard M. (1974), "Trade-Off Analysis of Consumer Values," *Journal of Marketing Research,* 11 (May), 121–127.

Kotler, Philip (1967), *Marketing Management: Analysis, Planning & Control,* Englewood Cliffs, N.J.: Prentice-Hall, Inc.

Larreche, Jean-Claude and David B. Montgomery (1977), "A Framework for the Comparison of Marketing Models: A Delphi Study," *Journal of Marketing Research,* 14 (November), 487–498.

Little, John D. C. (1970), "Models and Managers: The Concept of a Decision Calculus," *Management Science,* 16 (April), B466–485.

———and Leonard M. Lodish (1969), "A Media Planning Calculus," *Operations Research,* 17 (January–February), 135.

Luce, Duncan R. and John W. Tukey (1964), "Simultaneous Conjoint Measurement: A New Type of Fundamental Measurement," *Journal of Mathematical Psychology,* 1 (February), 1–27.

Massy, William F., Stephen A. Greyser, and John G. Myers (1979), *Report of the Commission on the Effectiveness of Research and Development for Marketing Management,* Chicago, IL: American Marketing Association.

Morrison, Donald G. (1965), "Stochastic Models for Time Series with Applications in Marketing," *Program in Operations Research,* Stanford University, Technical Report No. 8.

Myers, John G. and Francesco M. Nicosia (1968), "On the Study of Consumer Typologies," *Journal of Marketing Research,* 5 (May), 182–193.

Pierson, Frank C. et al. (1959), *Education of American Businessmen: The Study of University-College Programs in Business Administration,* New York: McGraw-Hill (Carnegie Series in American Education).

Sheth, Jagdish N., ed. (1977), *Multivariate Methods for Market and Survey Research,* Chicago, Ill.: American Marketing Association.

Silk, Alvin J. and Glen L. Urban (1978), "Pre-Test Market Evaluation of New Packaged Goods: A Model and Measurement Methodology," *Journal of Marketing Research,* 15 (May), 171–191.

Srinivasan, V. and Allan D. Shocker (1973), "Linear Programming Techniques for Multidimensional Analysis of Preferences," *Psychometrika,* 38 (September), 337–369.

Tull, Donald S. and Del I. Hawkins (1976), "*Marketing Research: Meaning, Measurement, and Method,* New York: MacMillan Publishing Co.

Wind, Yoram (1978a), "Issues and Advances in Segmentation Research," *Journal of Marketing Research,* 15 (August), 317–337.

———(1978b), "Marketing Research and Management: A Retrospective View of the Contributions of Paul E. Green," in *Proceedings of the Tenth Paul D. Converse Awards Symposium,* Alan Andreasen, ed., Urbana: University of Illinois Press.

NOTES

[1]The Commission consisted of eighteen people, eight from universities, including the two co-chairmen, four from independent research, consulting, and advertising firms, and six from operating companies. The four from independent firms were professional researchers while the six from operating companies were evenly split between management and research functions. Other members were: Seymour Banks (Leo Burnett Co.), Frank Bass (Purdue University), Robert Burnett (Meredith Corporation), Robert D. Buzzell (Harvard University), Henry J. Claycamp (International Harvester), Robert Ferber (University of Illinois), Ronald E. Frank (University of Pennsylvania), John G. Keane (Managing Change, Inc., President, AMA, 1976–77), Philip Kotler (Northwestern University), Lawrence Light (BBD&O, Inc.), Elmer Lotshaw (Owens-Illinois), William T. Moran (Ad Mar Research), Bart R. Panettiere (General Foods), W. R. Reiss (American Telephone & Telegraph), and Dudley M. Ruch (The Quaker Oats Company). Christopher Lovelock (Harvard University) served as staff director, and John Bateson, an HBS doctoral candidate and Marketing Science Institute research assistant, served as project assistant.

[2]The twenty-five-year reference period was chosen as a useful time span for several reasons. It was considered long enough to provide evidence for a thoughtful review of changes in marketing practice and knowledge without being too long to be inaccessible to memory. It also encompassed several important events in the development of marketing. The computer was beginning to emerge onto the business scene at the beginning of the period. The Gordon and Howell (1959) and Pierson (1959) reports were completed during the early part of the period, significantly affecting curricula in business schools. An acceleration of change in the practice of marketing management and marketing research also took place during this period.

[3]By "research in marketing," we mean research addressed to any and all zones of the marketing field, rather than "marketing research" or "market research" alone, which typically imply research on consumers and/or on characteristics of markets.

[4]Particularly useful communications were obtained from Charles R. Adler of the Eastman Kodak Company, Paul N. Reis of the Procter and Gamble Company, C. R. Smith of Nabisco, Inc., and William D. Wells of Needham, Harper & Steers Inc.

[5]An academic administrator once correctly observed that even the most brilliant ideas contain no social value if they remain lodged in the heads of their proponents!

[6]This was preceded by several working papers and a paper published as early as 1968 by Green and his colleagues at Wharton.

[7]This process of refinement has continued to the present and involves different types of data-collection procedures, different types of scale assumptions (nominal, ordinal, interval, ratio), and basic extensions such as categorical conjoint measurement and second generation models such as componential segmentation. (See Wind 1978b).

[8]We note that the "average" brand or product manager in a major corporation may now be much more comfortable with quantitative techniques given the likely exposure to them in classroom situations over at least the past ten years. One estimate is that there are about 25,000 marketing majors produced annually in the United States. If only 1,000 per year are MBAs exposed to quantitative methods in our better business schools, there should be 10,000 managers out there for whom models and techniques are a familiar part of marketing knowledge.

DISCUSSION QUESTIONS

1. Table 1 presents examples of knowledge development in marketing. Based on your familiarity with the marketing literature, what major omissions from the 1952–1977 period do you see in the table? What major knowledge developments since 1977 would you add to the table?

2. Assume that the American Marketing Association wishes to update and expand the previous Commission's work. What modification, if any, would you propose for the new Commission? What operating methods and data-generation procedures would you propose?

3. Review the recommendations provided at the end of the article. Select two of the recommendations, and offer a searching critique of the appropriateness and possible operationalization of the suggestions you have chosen. What additional suggestions can you offer for encouraging more productive dialogue between marketing academic researchers and marketing management?

PREFACE TO

"Marketing, Strategic Planning, and the Theory of the Firm"

The research that led to this article grew out of my desire to understand a problem that has bothered me for a long time. Simply put, the problem concerns the incommensurability that seems to exist among the functional areas within the firm and among the various academic disciplines that seek to explain firm behavior. This incommensurability is most noticeable at the level of corporate goals. Here there appears to be little agreement on what the objectives of the firm are or what they ought to be. Moreover, the lack of consensus on goals seems to be closely linked to interfunctional rivalry within the organization and to the failure of academics to construct a unified theory of the firm.

The article traces the problem of interfunctional rivalry to the differing interests of the external constituencies that are both managed and served by the various functional areas. When these interests are embodied in the internal reward and measurement systems of the organization, conflict among these areas is a likely result. The incommensurability at the theoretical level is seen to be a function of the different research traditions that are brought to bear on the problem. It is suggested that marketers have uncritically adopted goals that have been reified by economic theories of the firm. However, it can be shown that these goals are simply putative assumptions that function heuristically in the construction of deductive-instrumentalist models. It is argued that marketing's commitment to a different research tradition (and consequently to different cognitive values) requires a theory of the firm at variance with received doctrine in economics and financial economics. To this end, the article develops the outlines of a constituency-based theory of the firm. The article appears here in its original form.

21

MARKETING, STRATEGIC PLANNING, AND THE THEORY OF THE FIRM

PAUL F. ANDERSON

> Would you tell me, please, which way I ought to go
> from here? asked Alice.
> That depends a good deal on where you want to go
> to, said the Cat.
> I don't much care where, said Alice.
> Then it doesn't matter which way you go, said the
> Cat.
>
> *Lewis Carroll, Alice's Adventures in Wonderland*

The obvious wisdom of the Cheshire's statement reveals an important fact concerning strategic planning: without a clear set of objectives, the planning process is meaningless. Two authorities on the subject refer to strategy as "the major link between the goals and objectives the organization wants to achieve and the various functional area policies and operating plans it uses to guide its day-to-day activities" (Hofer and Schendel 1978, p. 13). Other strategy experts generally agree that the process of goal formulation must operate prior to, but also be interactive with, the process of strategy formulation (Ackoff 1970; Ansoff 1965; Glueck 1976; Newman and Logan 1971). Given the growing interest of marketers in the concept of strategic planning, it would appear fruitful to assess the current state of knowledge concerning goals and the goal formulation process.

Over the years, the general area of inquiry has fallen under the rubric of the "theory of the firm." One objective of this paper is to review some of the major theories of the firm to be found in the litera-

Source: Reprinted with permission from the *Journal of Marketing,* 46, (2), 1982, 15–26, Chicago, Ill. American Marketing Association.

*The author wishes to thank George Day, Larry Laudan and two anonymous referees for their very helpful comments and suggestions. He also wishes to thank his colleagues at Virginia Tech's Center for the Study of Science in Society for their many helpful suggestions.

ture. The extant theories have emerged in the disciplines of economics, finance and management. To date, marketing has not developed its own comprehensive theory of the firm. Generally, marketers have been content to borrow their concepts of goals and goal formulation from these other disciplines. Indeed, marketing has shown a strange ambivalence toward the concept of corporate goals. The recent marketing literature pays scant attention to the actual content of corporate goal hierarchies. Even less attention is focused on the normative issue of what firm goals and objectives ought to be. Moreover, contemporary marketing texts devote little space to the subject. Typically, an author's perspective on corporate goals is revealed in his/her definition of the marketing concept, but one is hard pressed to find further development of the topic. There is rarely any discussion of how these goals come about or how marketing may participate in the goal formulation process.

This is not to say that received doctrine in marketing has been developed without regard for corporate objectives. The normative decision rules and procedures that have emerged always seek to attain one or more objectives. Thus it could be said that these marketing models implicitly assume a theory of the firm. However, the particular theory that serves as the underpinning of the model is rarely made explicit. More importantly, marketing theorists have devoted little attention to an exploration of the nature and implications of these theories.

For example, the product portfolio (Boston Consulting Group 1970; Cardozo and Wind 1980), and PIMS (Buzzell, Gale, and Sultan 1975) approaches that are so much in vogue today implicitly assume that the primary objective of the firm is the maximization of return on investment (ROI). This objective seems to have been accepted uncritically by many marketers despite its well-documented deficiencies (e.g., its inability to deal with timing, duration and risk differences among returns and its tendency to create behavioral problems when used as a control device [Hopwood 1976; Van Horne 1980]). However, the concern expressed in this paper is not so much that marketers have adopted the wrong objectives, but that the discipline has failed to appreciate fully the nature and implications of the objectives that it has adopted.

As a result, in the last sections of the paper the outline of a new theory of the firm will be presented. It will be argued that the theories of the firm developed within economics, finance and management are inadequate in varying degrees as conceptual underpinnings for marketing. It is asserted that the primary role of a theory of the firm is to act as a kind of conceptual backdrop that functions heuristically to guide further theory development within a particular discipline. As such, the proposed model is less of a theory and more a Kuhnian-style paradigm (Kuhn 1970). Moreover, for a theory of the firm to be fruitful in this respect it must be congruent with the established research tradition of the field (Laudan 1977). It will be demonstrated, for example, that the theories emerging from economics and finance are inconsistent with the philosophical methodology and ontological framework of marketing. However, the proposed model is not only fully consonant with marketing's research tradition, but, unlike existing theories, it explicitly considers marketing's role in corporate goal formulation and strategic planning. Thus it is hoped that the theory will be able to provide a structure to guide future research efforts in these areas.

ECONOMIC THEORIES OF THE FIRM

In this section three theories of the firm are reviewed. The first, the neoclassical model, provides the basic foundation of contemporary microeconomic theory. The second, the market value model, performs a similar function within financial eco-

nomics. Finally, the agency costs model represents a modification of the market value model to allow a divergence of interests between the owners and managers of the firm. In this sense, it operates as a transitional model between the economically oriented theories of this section and the behavioral theories of the section to follow. However, all three may be classified as economic models since they share the methodological orientation and conceptual framework of economic theory. Note that each postulates an economic objective for the firm and then derives the consequences for firm behavior under different assumption sets.

The Neoclassical Model

The neoclassical theory of the firm can be found in any standard textbook in economics. In its most basic form the theory posits a single product firm operating in a purely competitive environment. Decision making is vested in an owner-entrepreneur whose sole objective is to maximize the dollar amount of the firm's single period profits. Given the standard assumptions of diminishing returns in the short run and diseconomies of scale in the long run, the firm's average cost function will have its characteristic U-shape. The owner's unambiguous decision rule will be to set output at the point where marginal costs equal marginal revenues. The introduction of imperfections in the product market (such as those posited by the monopolistically competitive model) represent mere elaborations on the basic approach. The objective of the firm remains single period profit maximization.

The neoclassical model is well known to marketers. Indeed, it will be argued below that the profit maximization assumption of neoclassical economics underlies much of the normative literature in marketing management. It will be shown that this is true despite the fact that neoclassical theory is inconsistent with the basic research tradition of marketing. Moreover, the neoclassical model suffers from a number of limitations.

For example, the field of finance has challenged the profit maximization assumption because it fails to provide the business decision maker with an operationally feasible criterion for making investment decisions (Solomon 1963). In this regard, it suffers from an inability to consider risk differences among investment alternatives. When risk levels vary across projects, decision criteria that focus only on profitability will lead to suboptimal decisions (Copeland and Weston 1979; Fama and Miller 1972; Van Horne 1980). As a result of these and other problems, financial economists have generally abandoned the neoclassical model in favor of a more comprehensive theory of the firm known as the market value model.

The Market Value Model

Given the assumptions that human wants are insatiable and that capital markets are perfectly competitive, Fama and Miller (1972) show that the objective of the firm should be to maximize its present market value. For a corporation this is equivalent to maximizing the price of the firm's stock. In contrast to the profit maximization objective, the market value rule allows for the consideration of risk differences among alternative investment opportunities. Moreover, the model is applicable to owner-operated firms as well as corporations in which there is likely to be a separation of ownership and control.

The existence of a perfectly competitive capital market allows the firm's management to pursue a single unambiguous objective despite the fact that shareholders are likely to have heterogeneous preferences for current versus future income. If, for example, some stockholders wish more income than the firm is currently paying in dividends, they can sell some of their shares to make up the difference. However, if other shareholders prefer less current income in favor of more future income, they can lend their dividends in the capital markets at interest. In either case shareholder utility will be maximized by a policy that maximizes the value of the firm's stock.

The value maximization objective is implemented within the firm by assessing all multiperiod decision alternatives on the basis of their risk-adjusted net present values (Copeland and Weston 1979; Fama and Miller 1972; Van Horne 1980):

$$NPV_j = \sum_{i=1}^{n} \frac{A_i}{(1 - k_j)^i} \qquad (1)$$

where NPV_j equals the net present value of alternative j, A_i equals the net after-tax cash flows in year i, n is the expected life of the project in years, and k_j is the risk-adjusted, after-tax required rate of return on

j. In the absence of capital rationing, the firm should undertake all projects whose net present values are greater than or equal to zero. Assuming an accurate determination of k_j, this will ensure maximization of the firm's stock price. The discount rate k_j should represent the return required by the market to compensate for the risk of the project. This is usually estimated using a parameter preference model such as the capital asset pricing model or (potentially) the arbitrage model (Anderson 1981). However, it should be noted that there are serious theoretical and practical difficulties associated with the use of these approaches (Anderson 1981; Meyers and Turnbull 1977; Roll 1977; Ross 1976, 1978).

From a marketing perspective this approach requires that all major decisions be treated as investments. Thus the decision to introduce a new product, to expand into new territories, or to adopt a new channel of distribution should be evaluated on the basis of its risk-adjusted net present value. While similar approaches have been suggested in marketing (Cravens, Hills, and Woodruff 1980; Dean 1966; Howard 1965; Kotler 1971; Pessemier 1966), it has generally not been recognized that this implies the adoption of shareholder wealth maximization as the goal of the firm. Moreover, these approaches are often offered in piecemeal fashion for the evaluation of selected decisions (e.g., new products), and are not integrated into a consistent and coherent theory of the firm.

Despite the deductive logic of the market value model, there are those who question whether corporate managers are motivated to pursue value maximization. An essential assumption of the market value theory is that stockholders can employ control, motivation and monitoring devices to ensure that managers maximize firm value. However, in the development of their agency theory of the firm, Jensen and Meckling (1976) note that such activities by shareholders are not without cost. As a result, it may not be possible to compel managers to maximize shareholder wealth.

The Agency Costs Model

The separation of ownership and control in modern corporations gives rise to an agency relationship between the stockholders and managers of the firm. An agency relationship may be defined as ''a contract under which one or more persons (the principal[s]) engage another person (the agent) to perform some service on their behalf which involves delegating some decision making authority to the agent'' (Jenson and Meckling 1976, p. 308). In any relationship of this sort, there is a potential for the agent to expend some of the principal's resources on private pursuits. As such, it will pay the principal to provide the agent with incentives and to incur monitoring costs to encourage a convergence of interests between the objectives of the principal and those of the agent. Despite expenditures of this type, it will generally be impossible to ensure that all of the agent's decisions will be designed to maximize the principal's welfare. The dollar value of the reduction in welfare experienced by the principal along with the expenditures on monitoring activities are costs of the agency relationship. For corporate stockholders these agency costs include the reduction in firm value resulting from management's consumption of nonpecuniary benefits (perquisites) and the costs of hiring outside auditing agents.

The tendency of managers of widely held corporations to behave in this fashion will require the stockholders to incur monitoring costs in an effort to enforce the value maximization objective. Unfortunately, perfect monitoring systems are very expensive. Thus the stockholders face a cost-benefit trade-off in deciding how much to spend on monitoring activities. Since it is unlikely that it will pay the shareholders to implement a ''perfect'' monitoring system, we will observe corporations suboptimizing on value maximization even in the presence of auditing activities. This leads to implications for managerial behavior that are quite different from those predicted by the market value model. For example, the Fama-Miller model predicts that managers will invest in all projects that will maximize the present value of the firm. However, the agency costs model suggests that management may actually invest in suboptimal projects and may even forego new profitable investments (Barnea, Haugen, and Senbet 1981).

The recognition that a firm might not pursue maximization strategies is a relatively new concept to the literature of financial economics. However, in the middle 1950s and early 1960s, various economists and management specialists began to question the neoclassical assumption of single objective maximization on the basis of their observations of managerial behavior. This led directly to the development of the behavioral theory of the firm.

BEHAVIORAL THEORIES OF THE FIRM

In this section two behaviorally oriented theories of the firm will be reviewed. While other approaches could also be included (Bower 1968; Mintzberg 1979), these models will lay the foundation for the development of a constituency-based theory in the last sections of the paper. The first approach is the behavioral model of the firm that emerged at the Carnegie Institute of Technology. The behavioral model can best be understood as a reaction against the neoclassical model of economic theory. The second approach is the resource dependence model of Pfeffer and Salancik (1978). The resource dependence perspective builds on a number of ideas contained in the behavioral model. For example, both approaches stress the coalitional nature of organizations. Moreover, both models emphasize the role of behavioral rather than economic factors in explaining the activities of firms.

The Behavioral Model

The behavioral theory of the firm can be found in the writings of Simon (1955, 1959, 1964), March and Simon (1958), and especially in Cyert and March (1963). The behavioral theory views the business firm as a coalition of individuals who are, in turn, members of subcoalitions. The coalition members include ''managers, workers, stockholders, suppliers, customers, lawyers, tax collectors, regulatory agencies, etc.'' (Cyert and March 1963, p. 27).

The goals of the organization are determined by this coalition through a process of quasi-resolution of conflict. Different coalition members wish the organization to pursue different goals. The resultant goal conflict is not resolved by reducing all goals to a common dimension or by making them internally consistent. Rather, goals are viewed as ''a series of independent aspiration-level constraints imposed on the organization by the members of the organizational coalition'' (Cyert and March 1963, p. 117).

As Simon (1964) points out, in real world decision making situations acceptable alternatives must satisfy a whole range of requirements or constraints. In his view, singling out one constraint and referring to it as the goal of the activity is essentially arbitrary. This is because in many cases, the set of requirements selected as constraints will have much more to do with the decision outcome than the requirement selected as the goal. Thus he believes that it is more meaningful to refer to the entire set of constraints as the (complex) goal of the organization.

Moreover, these constraints are set at aspiration levels rather than maximization levels. Maximization is not possible in complex organizations because of the existence of imperfect information and because of the computational limitations faced by organizations in coordinating the various decisions made by decentralized departments and divisions. As a result, firm behavior concerning goals may be described as satisficing rather than maximizing (Simon 1959, 1964).

Cyert and March (1963) see decentralization of decision making leading to a kind of local rationality within subunits of the organization. Since these subunits deal only with a small set of problems and a limited number of goals, local optimization may be possible, but it is unlikely that this will lead to overall optimization. In this regard, the firm not only faces information processing and coordination problems but is also hampered by the fact that it must deal with problems in a sequential fashion. Thus organizational subunits typically attend to different problems at different times, and there is no guarantee that consistent objectives will be pursued in solving these problems. Indeed, Cyert and March argue that the time buffer between decision situations provides the firm with a convenient mechanism for avoiding the explicit resolution of goal conflict.

Thus in the behavioral theory of the firm, goals emerge as "independent constraints imposed on the organization through a process of bargaining among potential coalition members" (Cyert and March 1963, p. 43). These objectives are unlikely to be internally consistent and are subject to change over time as changes take place in the coalition structure. This coalitional perspective has had a significant impact on the development of management thought. Both Mintzberg (1979) and Pfeffer and Salancik (1978) have developed theories of the firm that take its coalitional nature as given. In the fol-

lowing section the resource dependence approach of Pfeffer and Salancik is outlined.

The Resource Dependence Model

Pfeffer and Salancik (1978) view organizations as coalitions of interests which alter their purposes and direction as changes take place in the coalitional structure. Like Mintzberg (1979) they draw a distinction between internal and external coalitions, although they do not use these terms. Internal coalitions may be viewed as groups functioning within the organization (e.g., departments and functional areas). External coalitions include such stakeholder groups as labor, stockholders, creditors, suppliers, government and various interested publics. Pfeffer and Salancik place their primary emphasis on the role of environmental (i.e., external) coalitions in affecting the behavior of organizations. They believe that "to describe adequately the behavior of organizations requires attending to the coalitional nature of organizations and the manner in which organizations respond to pressures from the environment" (Pfeffer and Salancik 1978, p. 24).

The reason for the environmental focus of the model is that the survival of the organization ultimately depends on its ability to obtain resources and support from its external coalitions. Pfeffer and Salancik implicitly assume that survival is the ultimate goal of the organization and that to achieve this objective, the organization must maintain a coalition of parties willing to "legitimize" its existence (Dowling and Pfeffer 1975; Parsons 1960). To do this, the organization offers various inducements in exchange for contributions of resources and support (Barnard 1938; March and Simon 1958; Simon 1964).

However, the contributions of the various interests are not equally valued by the organization. As such, coalitions that provide "behaviors, resources and capabilities that are most needed or desired by other organizational participants come to have more influence and control over the organization" (Pfeffer and Salancik 1978, p. 27). Similarly, organizational subunits (departments, functional areas, etc.) which are best able to deal with critical contingencies related to coalitional contributions are able to enhance their influence in the organization.

A common problem in this regard is that the various coalitions make conflicting demands on the organization. Since the satisfaction of some demands limits the satisfaction of others, this leads to the possibility that the necessary coalition of support cannot be maintained. Thus organizational activities can be seen as a response to the constraints imposed by the competing demands of various coalitions.

In attempting to maintain the support of its external coalitions, the organization must negotiate exchanges that ensure the continued supply of critical resources. At the same time, however, it must remain flexible enought to respond to environmental contingencies. Often these objectives are in conflict, since the desire to ensure the stability and certainty of resource flows frequently leads to activities limiting flexibility and autonomy. For example, backward integration via merger or acquisition is one way of coping with the uncertainty of resource dependence. At the same time, however, this method of stabilizing resource exchanges limits the ability of the firm to adapt as readily to environmental contingencies. Pfeffer and Salancik suggest that many other activities of organizations can be explained by the desire for stable resource exchanges, on the one hand, and the need for flexibility and autonomy on the other. They present data to support their position that joint ventures, interlocking directorates, organizational growth, political involvement and executive succession can all be interpreted in this light. Other activities such as secrecy, multiple sourcing and diversification can also be interpreted from a resource dependence perspective.

Thus the resource dependence model views organizations as "structures of coordinated behaviors" whose ultimate aim is to garner the necessary environmental support for survival (Pfeffer and Salancik 1978, p. 32). As in the behavioral model, it is recognized that goals and objectives will emerge as constraints imposed by the various coalitions of interests. However, the resource dependence model interprets these constraints as demands by the coalitions that must be met in order to maintain the existence of the organization.

RESEARCH TRADITIONS AND THE THEORY OF THE FIRM

In reflecting on the various theories of the firm presented herein, it is important to recognize that one of their primary roles is to function as a part of what Laudan calls a "research tradition" (Laudan 1977). A research tradition consists of a set of assumptions shared by researchers in a particular domain. Its main purpose it to provide a set of guidelines for theory development. In so doing it provides the researcher with both an ontological framework and a philosophical methodology.

The ontology of the research tradition defines the kinds of entities that exist within the domain of inquiry. For example, in the neoclassical model such concepts as middle management, coalitions, bureaucracy and reward systems do not exist. They fall outside the ontology of neoclassical economics. Similarly, the concepts of the entrepreneur, diminishing returns and average cost curves do not exist (or at least are not used) in the resource dependence model. The ontology of the research tradition defines the basic conceptual building blocks of its constituent theories.

The philosophical methodology, on the other hand, specifies the procedure by which concepts will be used to construct a theory. Moreover, it determines the way in which the concepts will be viewed by theorists working within the research tradition. For example, the neoclassical, market value and agency costs models have been developed in accordance with a methodology that could be characterized as deductive instrumentalism. The models are deductive in that each posits a set of assumptions or axioms (including assumptions about firm goals) from which implications for firm behavior are deduced as logical consequences (Hempel 1965, p. 336). The models are also instrumentalist in that their component concepts are not necessarily assumed to have real world referents. Instrumentalism views theories merely as calculating devices that generate useful predictions (Feyerabend 1964; Morgenbesser 1969; Popper 1963). The reality of a theory's assumptions or its concepts is irrelevant from an instrumentalist point of view.

It is essentially this aspect of economic instrumentalism that has drawn the most criticism from both economists and noneconomists. Over 30 years ago concerns for the validity of the theory among economists emerged as the famous "marginalism controversy" which raged in the pages of the *American Economic Review* (Lester 1946, 1947; Machlup 1946, 1947; Stigler 1946, 1947). More recently, much of the criticism has come from proponents of the behavioral theory of the firm (Cyert and March 1963; Cyert and Pottinger 1979). Perhaps the most commonly heard criticism of the neoclassical model is that the assumption of a rational, profit-maximizing decision maker who has access to perfect information is at considerable variance with the real world of business management (Cyert and March 1963; Simon 1955). Moreover, these critics fault the "marginalists" for concocting a firm with "no complex organization, no problems of control, no standard operating procedures, no budget, no controller, [and] no aspiring middle management" (Cyert and March 1963, p. 8). In short, the business firm assumed into existence by neoclassical theory bears little resemblance to the modern corporate structure.

Concerns with the realism of assumptions in neoclassical theory have been challenged by Friedman (1953) and Machlup (1967). In Friedman's classic statement of the "positivist" viewpoint, he takes the position that the ultimate test of a theory is the correspondence of its predictions with reality. From Friedman's perspective the lack of realism in a theory's assumptions is unrelated to the question of its validity.

Machlup, in a closely related argument, notes that much of the criticism of neoclassical theory arises because of a confusion concerning the purposes of the theory (1967). He points out that the "firm" in neoclassical analysis is nothing more than a theoretical construct that is useful in predicting the impact of changes in economic variables on the behavior of firms in the aggregate. For example, the neoclassical model performs well in predicting the *direction* of price changes in an industry that experiences an increase in wage rates or the imposition of a tax. It does less well, however, in explaining the complex process by which a particular firm decides to implement a price change. Of course, this is to be expected since the theory of the firm was never intended to predict the real world behavior of individual firms.

Thus the question of whether corporations really seek to maximize profits is of no concern to the economic instrumentalist. Following Friedman, the only consideration is whether such assumptions lead to "sufficiently accurate predictions" of real world phenomena (1953, p. 15). Similarly, the financial economist is unmoved by criticism related to the lack of reality in the market value and agency cost models. The ultimate justification of a theory from an instrumental viewpoint comes from the accuracy of its predictions.

In contrast to the instrumentalism of the first three theories of the firm, the behavioral and resource dependence models have been developed from the perspective of realism. The realist believes that theoretical constructs should have real world analogs and that theories should describe "what the world is really like" (Chalmers 1978, p. 114). Thus, it is not unexpected that these models are esentially inductive in nature. Indeed, in describing their methodological approach Cyert and March state that they "propose to make detailed observations of the procedures by which firms make decisions and to use these observations as a basis for a theory of decision making within business organizations" (1963, p. 1).

Thus it can be seen that the theories of the firm that have been developed in economics and financial economics emerged from a very different research tradition than the behaviorally oriented theories developed in management. This fact becomes particularly significant in considering their adequacy as a framework for marketing theory development. For example, the discipline of marketing appears to be committed to a research tradition dominated by the methodology of inductive realism, yet it frequently employs the profit maximization paradigm of neoclassical economic theory. Despite the recent trend toward the incorporation of social objectives in the firm's goal hierarchy, and the recognition by many authors that firms pursue multiple objectives, profit or profit maximization figures prominently as the major corporate objective in leading marketing texts (Boone and Kurtz 1980, p. 12; Markin 1979, p. 34; McCarthy 1978, p. 29; Stanton 1978, p. 13). More significantly perhaps, profit maximization is the implicit or explicit objective of much of the normative literature in marketing management. While the terms may vary from return on investment to contribution margin, cash flow or cumulative compounded profits, they are all essentially profit maximization criteria. Thus such widely known and accepted approaches as product portfolio analysis (Boston Consulting Group 1970), segmental analysis (Mossman,

Fischer, and Crissy 1974), competitive bidding models (Simon and Freimer 1970), Bayesian pricing procedures (Green 1963), and many others all adhere to the profit maximization paradigm. It may seem curious that a discipline that drifted away from the research tradition of economics largely because of a concern for greater "realism" (Hutchinson 1952; Vaile 1950) should continue to employ one of its most "unrealistic" assumptions. In effect, marketing has rejected much of the philosophical methodology of economics while retaining a significant portion of its ontology.

It would seem that what is required is the development of a theory of the firm that is consistent with the existing research tradition of marketing. Such a theory should deal explicitly with the role of marketing in the firm and should attempt to explicate its relationship with the other functional areas (Wind 1981) and specify its contribution to the formation of corporate "goal structures" (Richard 1978). In this way it would provide a framework within which marketing theory development can proceed. This is particularly important for the development of theory within the area of strategic planning. It is likely that greater progress could be made in this area if research is conducted within the context of a theory of the firm whose methodological and ontological framework is consistent with that of marketing.

TOWARD A CONSTITUENCY-BASED THEORY OF THE FIRM

The theory of the firm to be outlined in this section focuses explicitly on the roles performed by the various functional areas found in the modern corporation. There are basically two reasons for this. First, theory development in business administration typically proceeds within the various academic disciplines corresponding (roughly) to the functional areas of the firm. It is felt that a theory explicating the role of the functional areas will be of greater heuristic value in providing a framework for research within these disciplines (and within marketing in particular).

Second, a theory of the firm that does not give explicit recognition to the activities of these functional subunits fails to appreciate their obvious importance in explaining firm behavior. As highly formalized internal coalitions operating at both the corporate and divisional levels, they often share a common frame of reference and a relatively consistent set of goals and objectives. These facts make the functional areas an obvious unit of analysis in attempting to explain the emergence of goals in corporations.

The proposed theory adopts the coalitional perspectives of the various behaviorally oriented theories of the firm and relies especially on the resource dependence model. As a matter of analytical convenience, the theory divides an organization into both internal and external coalitions. From a resource dependence perspective, the task of the organization is to maintain itself by negotiating resource exchanges with external interests. Over time the internal coalitions within corporate organizations have adapted themselves to enhance the efficiency and effectiveness with which they perform these negotiating functions. One approach that has been taken to accomplish this is specialization. Thus certain coalitions within the firm may be viewed as specialists in negotiating exchanges with certain external coalitions. By and large these internal coalitions correspond to the major functional areas of the modern corporate structure.

For example, industrial relations and personnel specialize in negotiating resource exchanges with labor coalitions; finance, and to a lesser extent, accounting specialize in negotiating with stockholder and creditor groups; materials management and purchasing specialize in supplier group exchanges; and, of course, marketing specializes in negotiating customer exchanges. In addition, public relations, legal, tax and accounting specialize to a greater or lesser extent in negotiating the continued support and sanction of both government and public coalitions. In most large corporations the production area no longer interacts directly with the environment. With the waning of the production orientation earlier in this century, production gradually lost its negotiating functions to specialists such as purchasing and industrial relations on the input side and sales or marketing on the output side.

The major resources that the firm requires for survival include cash, labor and matériel. The major sources of cash are customers, stockholders and lenders. It is, therefore, the responsibility of marketing and finance to ensure the required level of cash flow in the firm. Similarly, it is the primary responsibility of industrial relations to supply the labor, and materials management and purchasing to supply the matériel necessary for the maintenance, growth and survival of the organization.

As Pfeffer and Salancik point out, external coalitions that control vital resources have greater control and influence over organizational activites (1978, p. 27). By extension, functional areas that negotiate vital resource exchanges will come to have greater power within the corporation as well. Thus the dominance of production and finance in the early decades of this century may be attributed to the fact that nearly all vital resource exchanges were negotiated by these areas. The ascendance, in turn, of such subunits as industrial relations and personnel (Meyer 1980), marketing (Keith 1960), purchasing and materials management (*Business Week* 1975) and public relations (Kotler and Mindak 1978) can be explained in part by environmental changes which increased the importance of effective and efficient resource exchanges with the relevant external coalitions. For example, the growth of unionism during the 1930s did much to enhance the role and influence of industrial relations departments in large corporations. Similarly, the improved status of sales and marketing departments during this same period may be linked to environmental changes including the depressed state of the economy, the rebirth of consumerism, and a shift in demand away from standardized ''Model-T type products'' (Ansoff 1979, p. 32). More recently, the OPEC oil embargo, the institutionalization of consumerism, and the expansion of government regulation into new areas (OSHA, Foreign Corrupt Practices Act, Affirmative Action, etc.) has had a similar impact on such areas as purchasing, public relations and legal.

Thus the constituency-based model views the major functional areas as specialists in providing particular resources for the firm. The primary objective of each area is to ensure an uninterrupted flow of resources from the appropriate external coalition. As functional areas tend to become specialized in dealing with particular coalitions, they tend to view these groups as constituencies both to be served and managed. From this perspective, the chief responsibility of the marketing area is to satisfy the long-term needs of its customer coalition. In short, it must strive to implement the marketing concept (Keith 1960; Levitt 1960; McKitterick 1957).

Of course, in seeking to achieve its own objectives, each functional area is constrained by the objectives of the other departments. In attempting to assure maximal consumer satisfaction as a means of maintaining the support of its customer coalition, marketing will be constrained by financial, technical and legal considerations imposed by the other functional areas. For example, expenditures on new product development, market research and advertising cut into the financial resources necessary to maintain the support of labor, supplier, creditor and investor coalitions. When these constraints are embodied in the formal performance measurement system, they exert a significant influence on the behavior of the functional areas.

In this model, firm objectives emerge as a series of Simonian constraints that are negotiated among the various functions. Those areas that specialize in the provision of crucial resources are likely to have greater power in the negotiation process. In this regard, the marketing area's desire to promote the marketing concept as a philosophy of the entire firm may be interpreted by the other functional areas as a means of gaining bargaining leverage by attempting to impress them with the survival value of customer support. The general failure of the other areas to embrace this philosophy may well reflect their belief in the importance of their own constituencies.

Recently, the marketing concept has also been called into question for contributing to the alleged malaise of American business. Hayes and Abernathy (1980) charge that excessive emphasis on marketing research and short-term financial control measures has led to the decline of U.S. firms in world markets. They argue that American business are losing more and more of their markets to European and Japanese firms because of a failure to remain technologically competitive. They believe that the reliance of American firms on consumer surveys and ROI control encourages a low-risk, short-run investment philosophy, and point out that market research typically identifies consumers' current desires but is often incapable of determining their future wants and needs. Moreover, the short-run focus of ROI measures and the analytical detachment inherent in product portfolio procedures tend to encourage investment in fast payback alternatives. Thus Hayes and Abernathy believe that

American firms are reluctant to make the higher-risk, longer-term investments in new technologies necessary for effective competition in world markets. They feel that the willingness of foreign firms to make such investments can be attributed to their need to look beyond their relatively small domestic markets for success. This has encouraged a reliance on technically superior products and a longer-term payoff perspective.

From a resource dependence viewpoint the Hayes and Abernathy argument seems to suggest that the external coalitions of U.S. firms are rather myopic. If the survival of the firm is truly dependent on the adoption of a longer-term perspective, one would expect this to be forced on the firm by its external coalitions. Indeed, there is ample evidence from stock market studies that investor coalitions react sharply to events affecting the longer-run fortunes of firms (Lev 1974; Lorie and Hamilton 1973). Moreover, recent concessions by government, labor and supplier coalitions to Chrysler Corporation suggest a similar perspective among these groups.

However, the real problem is not a failure by internal and external coalitions in recognizing the importance of a long-run investment perspective. The real difficulty lies in designing an internal performance measurement and reward system that balances the need for short-run profitability against long-term survival. A number of factors combine to bias these reward and measurement systems in favor of the short run. These include:

- Requirements for quarterly and annual reports of financial performance.

- The need to appraise and reward managers on an annual basis.

- The practical difficulties of measuring and rewarding the long-term performance of highly mobile management personnel.

- Uncertainty as to the relative survival value of emphasis on short-run versus long-run payoffs.

As a result of these difficulties, we find that in many U.S. firms the reward system focuses on short-run criteria (Ouchi 1981). This naturally leads to the use of short-term financial control measures and an emphasis on market surveys designed to measure consumer reaction to immediate (and often minor) product improvements. In some cases the market-

ing area has adopted this approach in the name of the marketing concept.

However, as Levitt (1960) noted more than two decades ago, the real lesson of the marketing concept is that successful firms are able to recognize the fundamental and enduring nature of the customer needs they are attempting to satisfy. As numerous case studies point out, it is the *technology* of want satisfaction that is transitory. The long-run investment perspective demanded by Hayes and Abernathy is essential for a firm that focuses its attention on transportation rather than trains, entertainment rather than motion pictures, or energy rather than oil. The real marketing concept divorces strategic thinking from an emphasis on contemporary technology and encourages investments in research and development with long-term payoffs. Thus, the "market-driven" firms that are criticized by Hayes and Abernathy have not really embraced the marketing concept. These firms have simply deluded themselves into believing that consumer survey techniques and product portfolio procedures automatically confer a marketing orientation on their adopters. However, the fundamental insight of the marketing concept has little to do with the use of particular analytical techniques. The marketing concept is essentially a state of mind or world view that recognizes that firms survive to the extent that they meet the real needs of their customer coalitions. As argued below, one of the marketing area's chief functions in the strategic planning process is to communicate this perspective to top management and the other functional areas.

IMPLICATIONS FOR STRATEGIC PLANNING

From a strategic planning perspective, the ultimate objective of the firm may be seen as an attempt to position itself for long-run survival (Wind 1979). This, in turn, is accomplished as each functional area attempts to determine the position that will ensure a continuing supply of vital resources. Thus the domestic auto industry's belated downsizing of its product may be viewed as an attempt to ensure the support of its customer coalition in the 1980s and 1990s (just as its grudging acceptance of the UAW in the late 1930s and early 1940s reflected a need to ensure a continuing supply of labor).

Of course, a firm's functional areas may not be

able to occupy all of the favored long-run positions simultaneously. Strategic conflicts will arise as functional areas (acting as units at the corporate level or as subunits at the divisional level) vie for the financial resources necessary to occupy their optimal long-term positions. Corporate management as the final arbiter of these disputes may occasionally favor one area over another, with deleterious results. Thus, John De Lorean, former group executive at General Motors, believes that the firm's desire for the short-run profits available from larger cars was a major factor in its reluctance to downsize in the 1970s (Wright 1979). He suggests that an overwhelming financial orientation among GM's top executives consistently led them to favor short-run financial gain over longer-term marketing considerations. Similarly, Hayes and Abernathy (1980) believe that the growing dominance of financial and legal specialists within the top managements of large U.S. corporations has contributed to the slighting of technological considerations in product development.

Against this backdrop marketing must realize that its role in strategic planning is not preordained. Indeed, it is possible that marketing considerations may not have a significant impact on strategic plans unless marketers adopt a strong advocacy position within the firm (Mason and Mitroff 1981). On this view, strategic plans are seen as the outcome of a bargaining process among functional areas. Each area attempts to move the corporation toward what it views as the preferred position for long-run survival, subject to the constraints imposed by the positioning strategies of the other functional units.

This is not to suggest, however, that formal-analytical procedures have no role to play in strategic planning. Indeed, as Quinn's (1981) research demonstrates, the actual process of strategy formulation in large firms is best described as a combination of the formal-analytical and power-behavioral approaches. He found that the formal planning system often provides a kind of infrastructure that assists in the strategy development and implementation process, although the formal system itself rarely generates new or innovative strategies. Moreover, the study shows that strategies tend to emerge incrementally over relatively long periods of time. One reason for this is the need for top management to obtain the support and commitment

of the firm's various coalitions through constant negotiation and implied bargaining (Quinn 1981, p. 61).

Thus, from a constituency-based perspective, marketing's role in strategic planning reduces to three major activities. First, at both the corporate and divisional levels it must identify the optimal long-term position or positions that will assure customer satisfaction and support. An optimal position would reflect marketing's perception of what its customers' wants and needs are likely to be over the firm's strategic time horizon. Since this will necessarily involve long-run considerations, positioning options must be couched in somewhat abstract terms. Thus the trend toward smaller cars by the domestic auto industry represents a very broad response to changing environmental, social and political forces and will likely affect the industry well into the 1990s. Other examples include the diversification into alternative energy sources by the petroleum industry, the movement toward "narrowcasting" by the major networks, and the downsizing of the single family home by the construction industry. The length of the time horizons involved suggests that optimal positions will be determined largely by fundamental changes in demographic, economic, social and political factors. Thus strategic positioning is more likely to be guided by long-term demographic and socioeconomic research (Lazer 1977) than by surveys of consumer attitudes.

Marketing's second major strategic planning activity involves the development of strategies designed to capture its preferred positions. This will necessarily involve attempts to gain a competitive advantage over firms pursuing similar positioning strategies. Moreover, the entire process is likely to operate incrementally. Specific strategies will focus on somewhat shorter time horizons and will be designed to move the firm toward a particular position without creating major dislocations within the firm or the marketplace (Quinn 1981). Research on consumers' current preferences must be combined with demographic and socioeconomic research to produce viable intermediate strategies. For example, Detroit's strategy of redesigning all of its subcompact lines has been combined with improved fuel efficiency in its larger cars (*Business Week* 1980).

Finally, marketing must negotiate with top management and the other functional areas to implement its strategies. The coalitional perspective suggests that marketing must take an active role in promoting its strategic options by demonstrating the survival value of a consumer orientation to the other internal coalitions.

Marketing's objective, therefore, remains long-run customer support through consumer satisfaction. Paradoxically, perhaps, this approach requires marketers to have an even greater grasp of the technologies, perspectives and limitations of the other functional areas. Only in this way can marketing effectively negotiate the implementation of its strategies. As noted previously, the other functional areas are likely to view appeals to the marketing concept merely as a bargaining ploy. It is the responsibility of the marketing area to communicate the true long-run focus and survival orientation of this concept to the other interests in the firm. However, this cannot be accomplished if the marketing function itself does not understand the unique orientations and decision methodologies employed by other departments.

For example, the long-run investment perspective implicit in the marketing concept can be made more comprehensible to the financial coalition if it is couched in the familiar terms of capital budgeting analysis. Moreover, the marketing area becomes a more credible advocate for this position if it eschews the use of short-term ROI measures as its sole criterion for internal decision analysis. At the same time, an appreciation for the inherent limitations of contemporary capital investment procedures will give the marketing area substantial leverage in the negotiation process (Anderson 1981).

In the final analysis, the constituency model of the firm suggests that marketing's role in strategic planning must be that of a strong advocate for the marketing concept. Moreover, its advocacy will be enhanced to the extent that it effectively communicates the true meaning of the marketing concept in terms that are comprehensible to other coalitions in the firm. This requires an intimate knowledge of the interests, viewpoints and decision processes of these groups. At the same time, a better understanding of the true nature of the constraints imposed by these interests will allow the marketing organization to make the informed strategic compromises necessary for firm survival.

REFERENCES

Ackoff, Russell (1970), *A Concept of Corporate Planning,* New York: John Wiley & Sons.

Anderson, Paul F. (1981), "Marketing Investment Analysis," in *Research in Marketing,* 4, Jagdish N. Sheth, ed., Greenwich, Conn.: JAI Press, 1–37.

Ansoff, Igor H. (1965), *Corporate Strategy,* New York: McGraw-Hill.

—————— (1979), "The Changing Shape of the Strategic Problem," in *Strategic Management: A View of Business Policy and Planning,* Dan E. Schendel and Charles W. Hofer, eds., Boston: Little Brown & Company, 30–44.

Barnard, Chester I. (1938), *The Functions of the Executive,* London: Oxford University Press.

Barnea, Amir, Robert A. Haugen, and Lemma W. Senbet (1981), "Market Imperfections, Agency Problems and Capital Structure: A Review," *Financial Management,* 10 (Summer), 7–22.

Boone, Louis E. and David L. Kurtz (1980), *Foundations of Marketing,* 3rd ed. Hinsdale, Ill.: Dryden Press.

Boston Consulting Group (1970), *The Product Portfolio,* Boston: Boston Consulting Group.

Bower, Joseph L. (1968), "Descriptive Decision Theory from the 'Administrative' Viewpoint," in *The Study of Policy Formation,* Raymond A. Bauer and Kenneth J. Gergen, eds., New York: Collier-Macmillan, 103–48.

Business Week (1975), "The Purchasing Agent Gains More Clout," (January 13), 62–63.

—————— (1980), "Detroit's New Sales Pitch," (September 22), 78–83.

Buzzell, Robert D., Bradley T. Gale, and Ralph G. M. Sultan (1975), "Market Share: A Key to Profitability," *Harvard Business Review,* 53 (January–February), 97–106.

Cardozo, Richard and Yoram Wind (1980), "Portfolio Analysis for Strategic Product—Market Planning," working paper, Wharton School, University of Pennsylvania.

Chalmers, A. F. (1978), *What is This Thing Called Science?* St. Lucia, Australia: University of Queensland Press.

Copeland, Thomas E. and J. Fred Weston (1979), *Financial Theory and Corporate Policy,* Reading, Mass.: Addison-Wesley Publishing Company.

Cravens, David W., Gerald E. Hills, and Robert B. Woodruff (1980), *Marketing Decision Making,* rev. ed., Homewood, Ill.: Richard D. Irwin.

Cyert, Richard M. and James G. March (1963), *A Behavioral Theory of the Firm,* Englewood Cliffs, N.J.: Prentice-Hall.

———— and Garrel Pottinger (1979), "Towards a Better Microeconomic Theory," *Philosophy of Science,* 46 (June), 204–222.

Dean, Joel (1966), "Does Advertising Belong in the Capital Budget?" *Journal of Marketing,* 30 (October), 15–21.

Dowling, John and Jeffrey Pfeffer (1975), "Organizational Legitimacy," *Pacific Sociological Review,* 18 (January), 122–36.

Fama, Eugene and Merton H. Miller (1972), *The Theory of Finance,* Hinsdale, Ill.: Dryden Press.

Feyerabend, Paul K. (1964), "Realism and Instrumentalism: Comments on the Logic of Facutal Support," in *The Critical Approach to Science and Philosophy,* Mario Bunge, ed., London; The Free Press of Glencoe, 280–308.

Friedman, Milton (1953), "The Methodology of Positive Economics," in *Essays in Positive Economics,* Chicago: University of Chicago Press.

Glueck, William (1976), *Policy, Strategy Formation and Management Action,* New York: McGraw-Hill.

Green, Paul E. (1963), "Bayesian Decision Theory in Pricing Strategy," *Journal of Marketing,* 27 (January), 5–14.

Hayes, Robert, H. and William J. Abernathy (1980), "Managing Our Way to Economic Decline," *Harvard Business Review,* 58 (July-August), 67–77.

Hempel, Carl G. (1965), *Aspects of Scientific Explanation,* New York: Macmillan Publishing Co.

Hofer, Charles W. and Dan Schendel (1978), *Strategy Formulation: Analytical Concepts,* St. Paul, Minn.: West Publishing Company.

Hopwood, Anthony (1976), *Accounting and Human Behavior,* Englewood Cliffs, NJ: Prentice-Hall.

Howard, John A. (1965). *Marketing Theory,* Boston: Allyn & Bacon.

Hutchinson, Kenneth D. (1952), "Marketing as a Science: An Appraisal," *Journal of Marketing,* 16 (January), 286–93.

Jensen, Michael C. and William H. Meckling (1976), "Theory of the Firm: Managerial Behavior, Agency Costs and Ownership Structure," *Journal of Financial Economics,* 3 (October), 305–60.

Keith, Robert J. (1960), "The Marketing Revolution," *Journal of Marketing,* 24 (January), 35–38.

Kotler, Philip (1971), *Marketing Decision Making,* New York: Holt, Rinehart & Winston.

———— and William Mindak (1978), "Marketing and Public Relations," *Journal of Marketing,* 42 (October), 13–20.

Kuhn, Thomas S. (1970), *The Structure of Scientific Revolutions,* 2nd ed., Chicago: University of Chicago Press.

Laudan, Larry (1977), *Progress and Its Problems,* Berkeley: University of California Press.

Lazer, William (1977), "The 1980's and Beyond: A Perspective," *MSU Business Topics,* 25 (Spring), 21–35.

Lester, R. A. (1946), "Shortcomings of Marginal Analysis for Wage-Employment Problems," *American Economic Review,* 36 (March) 63–82.

———— (1947), "Marginalism, Minimum Wages, and Labor Markets," *American Economic Review,* 37 (March), 135–48.

Lev, Baruch (1974), *Financial Statement Analysis: A New Approach,* Englewood Cliffs, NJ: Prentice-Hall.

Levitt, Theodore (1960), "Marketing Myopia," *Harvard Business Review,* 38 (July–August), 24–47.

Lorie, James H. and Mary T. Hamilton (1973), *The Stock Market: Theories and Evidence,* Homewood, Ill.: Richard D. Irwin.

Machlup, Fritz (1946), "Marginal Analysis and Empirical Research," *American Economic Review,* 36 (September), 519–54.

—— (1947), "Rejoinder to an Antimarginalist," *American Economic Review,* 37 (March), 148–54.

—— (1967), "Theories of the Firm: Marginalist, Behavioral, Managerial," *American Economic Review,* 57 (March), 1–33.

March, James G. and Herbert A. Simon (1958), *Organizations,* New York: John Wiley & Sons.

Markin, Rom (1979), *Marketing,* New York: John Wiley & Sons.

Mason, Richard O. and Ian I. Mitroff (1981), "Policy Analysis as Argument," working paper, University of Southern California.

McCarthy, E. Jerome (1978), *Basic Marketing,* 6th ed., Homewood, Ill.: Richard D. Irwin.

McKitterick, J. B. (1957), "What Is the Marketing Management Concept?" in *Readings in Marketing 75/76,* Guilford, Conn.: Dushkin Publishing Group, 23–26.

Meyer, Herbert E. (1980), "Personnel Directors Are the New Corporate Heros," in *Current Issues in Personnel Management,* Kendrith M. Rowland et al., eds., Boston: Allyn & Bacon, 2–8.

Meyers, Stewart C. and Stuart M. Turnbull (1977), "Capital Budgeting and the Capital Asset Pricing Model: Good News and Bad News," *Journal of Finance,* 32 (May), 321–36.

Mintzberg, Henry (1979), "Organizational Power and Goals: A Skeletal Theory," in *Strategic Management,* Dan E. Schendel and Charles W. Hofer, eds., Boston: Little, Brown & Company.

Morgenbesser, Sidney (1969), "The Realist-Instrumentalist Controversy," in *Philosophy, Science and Method,* New York: St. Martin's Press, 200–18.

Mossman, Frank H., Paul M. Fischer, and W. J. E. Crissy (1974), "New Approaches to Analyzing Marketing Profitability," *Journal of Marketing.* 38 (April), 43–48.

Newman, William H. and James P. Logan (1971), *Strategy, Policy and Central Management,* Cincinnati: South-Western Publishing Company.

Ouchi, William G. (1981), *Theory Z,* Reading, Mass.: Addison-Wesley.

Parsons, Talcott (1960), *Structure and Process in Modern Societies,* New York: Free Press.

Pessemier, Edgar A. (1966), *New-Product Decisions: An Analytical Approach,* New York: McGraw-Hill.

Pfeffer, Jeffrey and Gerald R. Salancik (1978), *The External Control of Organizations,* New York: Harper & Row.

Popper, Karl R. (1963), *Conjectures and Refutations,* New York: Harper & Row.

Quinn, James Brian (1981), "Formulating Strategy One Step at a Time," *Journal of Business Strategy,* 1 (Winter), 42–63.

Richards, Max D. (1978), *Organizational Goal Structures,* St. Paul, Minn.: West Publishing Company.

Roll, Richard (1977), "A Critique of the Asset Pricing Theory's Tests: Part I," *Journal of Financial Economics,* 4 (March), 129–76.

Ross, Stephen A. (1976), "The Arbitrage Theory of Capital Asset Pricing," *Journal of Economic Theory,* 13 (December), 341–60.

—— (1978), "The Current Status of the Capital Asset Pricing Model (CAPM)," *Journal of Finance,* 33 (June), 885–901.

Simon, Herbert A. (1955), "A Behavioral Model of Rational Choice," *Quarterly Journal of Economics,* 69 (February), 99–118.

—— (1959), "Theories of Decision Making in Economics and Behavioral Science," *American Economic Review,* 49 (June), 253–83.

—— (1964), "On the Concept of Organizational Goal," *Administrative Science Quarterly,* 9 (June), 1–22.

Simon, Leonard S. and Marshall Freimer (1970), *Analytical Marketing.* New York: Harcourt, Brace & World.

Solomon, Ezra (1963), *The Theory of Financial Management.* New York: Columbia University Press.

Stanton, William J. (1978), *Fundamentals of Marketing,* 5th ed., New York: McGraw-Hill.

Stigler, G. J. (1946), "The Economics of Minimum

Wage Legislation," *American Economic Review*, 36 (June), 358–65.

———— (1947), "Professor Lester and the Marginalists," *American Economic Review*, 37 (March), 154–57.

Vaile, Roland S. (1950), "Economic Theory and Marketing," in *Theory in Marketing*, Reavis Cox and Wroe Alderson, eds., Chicago: Richard D. Irwin.

Van Horne, James C. (1980), *Financial Management and Policy*, 5th ed., Englewood Cliffs, NJ: Prentice-Hall.

Wind, Yoram (1979), "Product Positioning and Market Segmentation: Marketing and Corporate Perspectives," working paper, Wharton School, University of Pennsylvania.

———— (1981), "Marketing and the Other Business Functions," in *Research in Marketing*, 5, Jagdish N. Sheth, ed., Greenwich, Conn.: JAI Press, 237–64.

Wright, Patrick J. (1979), *On a Clear Day You Can See General Motors*, Grosse Pointe, Mich.: Wright Enterprises.

DISCUSSION QUESTIONS

1. Are the economic theories of the firm trying to solve the same problems as the behavioral theories of the firm? Are they even talking about the same firm?

2. Is a unification of deductive-instrumentalist and inductive-realist theories of the firm possible?

3. What are the implications of the constituency-based theory of the firm for issues of corporate social responsibility?

4. Is it possible for a corporate reward and measurement system to encourage long-run goal setting and long-range strategic planning?

PREFACE TO

"A Framework for Service Marketing"

Over ten years of research, case analysis, and direct experience in management of service business provided the background for my initial observations regarding the nature of service marketing, which were set forth in 1977 in a paper entitled, "Breaking Free from Product Marketing" (Journal of Marketing, April 1977, pp. 73–80).

This revision incorporates several concepts from further investigations into the issues of modeling and service design, expands on the original framework, and has been edited to improve clarity.

Since 1977, a growing body of work on services has greatly expanded the relevant literature. Explorations of customer-service interactions (by Bateson, Berry, and Lovelock) and service selling (by George, Kelly, Booms, and Lewis) have been particularly noteworthy. I am happy to say that significant progress is being made in the evolution of a professional service-marketing discipline, and it is my expectation that the next five years will witness rapid expansion of the field.

22

A FRAMEWORK FOR SERVICE MARKETING

G. LYNN SHOSTACK

Despite the increasing dominance by services of the U.S. economy, service marketing remains an uncharted frontier.

The classic marketing "mix," the seminal literature, and the language of marketing all derive from the manufacture of physical goods. Practicing marketers tend to think in terms of products, particularly mass-market consumer goods. Some service companies even call their output products and have product-management functions modeled after those of experts, such as Proctor & Gamble.

Clearly, marketing is overwhelmingly product oriented. But many service-based companies are confused, uncertain as to the applicability of product marketing, and more than one attempt to adopt product marketing has failed.

Merely adopting product-marketing's labels does not resolve the question of whether product marketing can be overlaid on service businesses. Can corporate-banking services really be marketed according to the same basic blueprint that made Tide a success? Given marketing's current bias, there is simply no alternative.

Could marketing itself be myopic in having failed to create relevant paradigms for the service sector? Many marketing professionals who transfer to the services arena find their work fundamentally different, but have a difficult time articulating how and why their priorities and concepts have changed. Often, they find that marketing is treated as a peripheral function or is confused with one of its ingredients, such as research or advertising, and kept within a very narrow scope of influence and authority.[1]

This situation is frequently rationalized as being due to the ignorance of senior management in service businesses. Education is usually recommended as the solution. However, an equally feasible, although less comforting explanation is that service industries have been slow to integrate marketing

into the mainstream of decision making and control because marketing offers few principles, terminology, or practical rules that are clearly *relevant* to services.

MAKING ROOM FOR INTANGIBILITY

The American Marketing Association cites both goods and services as foci for marketing activities. Squeezing services into the Procrustean phrase "intangible products,"[2] is a distortion and a complete contradiction in terms.

It is wrong to imply that services are just like products, except for intangibility. By such logic, apples are just like grapes, except for their appleness. Although it is true that all fruits have certain similarities, it is not true that apples and grapes can be grown, harvested, or processed the same way. Each has unique properties that make generic definitions useless at the practical level.

Intangibility is not a modifier; it is a state. A service is rendered. A service is experienced. A service cannot be stored on a shelf, touched, tasted, or tried on for size because a service is not a *thing*. A service is a *process* or series of processes performed for the benefit of a consumer. This distinction has profound implications.

To truly expand marketing's conceptual boundaries requires a framework that accomodates intangibility instead of denying it. Such a framework must give equal descriptive weight to the realities of service as it does to the reality of product.

THE COMPLEXITY OF MARKETED ENTITIES

Examine, for instance, the automobile. Without question, it is a physical object, with a full range of tangible features and options. But another, equally important element is marketed in tandem with the steel and chrome, that is, the service of transportation. Transportation is an *independent* marketing element; in other words, it is not car-dependent but can be marketed in its own right. A car is only one

Source: Revised for this volume from the *Journal of Marketing*, 41, (April), 1977, 73–80, Chicago, Ill.: American Marketing Association. Originally titled "Breaking Free From Product Marketing."

alternative for satisfying the market's transportation needs.

This presents a semantic dilemma. How should the automobile be defined? Is General Motors marketing a service, a service that happens to include a by-product called a car? Levitt's classic "Marketing Myopia" exhorts businesspersons to think in exactly this generic way about what they market.[3] Are automobiles tangible services? It cannot be denied that both elements—tangible and intangible—exist and are vigorously marketed. Yet, they are by definition different qualities, and to attempt to compress them into a single word or phrase begs the issue.

Conversely, how will a service, such as airline transportation, be described? Although the service itself does not confer ownership of a tangible good, there are certain real things that belong in any description of airline services, including such important tangibles as interior decor, food and drink, seat design, and overall graphic continuity from tickets to attendants' uniforms. These items can dramatically affect the reality of the service in the consumer's mind. However, there is no accurate way to lump them into a one-word description.

If either/or terms (product vs. service) do not adequately describe the true nature of marketed entities, it makes sense to explore the usefulness of a new structural definition. This broader concept postulates that market entities are, in reality, combinations of discrete elements that are linked together in moleculelike wholes. Elements can be either products or services. The entity may have either a product or service nucleus. But the whole entity can only be described as having a certain dominance.

A molecular model offers opportunities for visualization and management of a total market entity. It reflects the fact that a market entity can be partly tangible and partly intangible without diminishing the importance of either characteristic. Not only can the potential be seen for picturing and dealing with multiple elements rather than a thing, but also the concept of dominance can lead to an enriched view of the priorities and approach that may be required of a marketer. Moreover, the model suggests the analogy that if market entities have multiple elements, a deliberate or inadvertent change in a *single* element may completely alter the entity, as the simple switching of FE_3O_2 to FE_2O_3 creates a new substance. For this reason, marketers must carefully manage *all* the elements, including some—especially for service-based entities—that they may not previously have considered within their domain.

DIAGRAMMING MARKET ENTITIES

A simplified comparison demonstrates the conceptual utility of a molecular modeling system. In Figure 1, automobiles and airline travel are broken down into their major elements. As shown, these

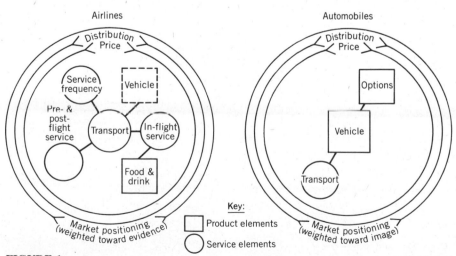

FIGURE 1
Molecular diagram of market entities.

two entities have different nucleii. They also differ in dominance.

Clearly, airline travel is service dominant, that is, it is a process performed for the benefit of the consumer rather than a physical good whose ownership is changing hands. Nearly all of the other important elements in the entity are services as well. Individual elements and their combinations represent unique satisfiers to different market segments. For some markets—students for example—pure transportation takes precedence over all other considerations. The charter flight business was based on this element. As might be expected during lean economic times, no-frills flying (priced accordingly) shows renewed emphasis on this nuclear core. On the other hand, for business travelers, schedule frequency may be paramount. Tourists, a third segment, may respond strongly to a combination of in-flight and post-flight services. There are even market segments that discriminate on the basis of the facilitating product. For these fliers, the issue of traveling in a DC10 versus a 727 is critical.

Airlines manage this mix of service and product elements according to changing market conditions. Reweighting can be observed, for example, in the marketing of airline food, which was once a battleground of quasi-gourmet offerings. Today, some airlines have stopped marketing food altogether, whereas others are repositioning it strictly for luxury markets.

In comparing airlines to automobiles, one sees obvious similarities. The element of transportation is common to both, as it is to boats, trains, buses, and bicycles. Tangible features of the vehicle also play a role in both entities. Yet, in spite of their similarities, the two entities are not the same either in configuration or in marketing implications.

The model can be completed by adding the remaining major marketing elements in a way that demonstrates their function vis-à-vis the organic core entity. First, the total entity is ringed and defined by a set value or price. Next, the valued entity is circumscribed by its distribution. Finally, the entire entity is encompassed according to its core configuration—by its public "face," that is, its positioning to the market.

The molecular concept makes it possible to describe and array market entities along a continuum according to the weight of the mix of elements that comprise them. Figure 2 shows several entities broken down into their key marketing elements. Figure 3 shows a series of entities placed along a scale of dominance. Entities at either end of the scale can, for convenience, be simply called products or services, because their dominance is so pronounced. Hybrid entities, toward the midpoint, must be treated especially carefully by the marketer, for here product and service elements are almost balanced and disrupting this balance can have a major impact on market perceptions. Such a scale accords ser-

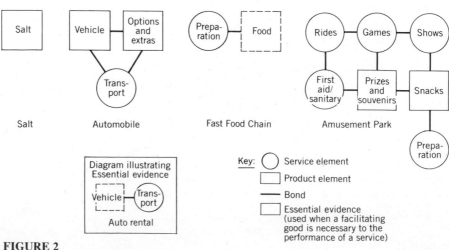

FIGURE 2

Basic molecular modeling.

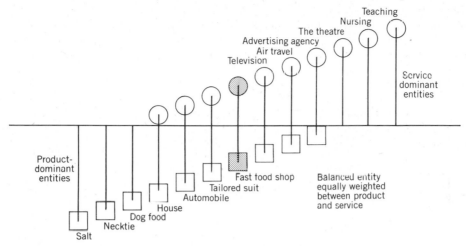

FIGURE 3

Scale of elemental dominance.

vice-dominant entities a place and weight commensurate with their true importance. The framework also provides a mechanism for comparison and positioning.

Molecular modeling and the scaling framework can be further extended to a refined analysis of alternative configurations. This is especially useful in the design of complex services. Figure 4, for example, shows how teaching, a basic service, can be analyzed and designed through use of a subscale that compares various mixes of elements—using various levels of facilitating product—to the pure Socratic form of the service. Through subscaling, a marketer can consider combinations of product and service elements to reach different markets effectively and profitably and can view these in the con-

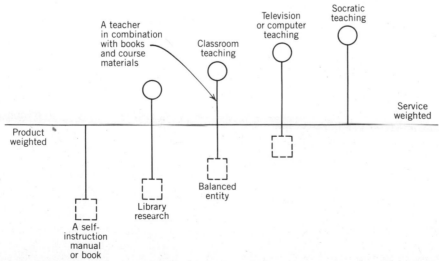

FIGURE 4

Subscale of a service-dominant entity (teaching) showing alternative configurations.

text of alternative or competitive structures. Needless to say, each entity will carry a complex and unique set of pricing, distribution, and promotional considerations.

SOME IMPLICATIONS OF THE MOLECULAR MODEL

Recognition that service-dominant entities differ from product-dominant entities allows consideration of other distinctions that have been intuitively understood but seldom articulated by service marketers. One important area of difference is immediately apparent, that is, that service knowledge cannot be gained in the same way as product knowledge. A product marketer's first task is to know his or her product. For tangible entities, this is relatively straightforward. A tangible object is subject to physical examination, photographic reproduction, and quantitative measure. Not only can it be exactly replicated, but also it can be modified in precise and scientific ways. It is not particularly difficult for the marketer of Coca-Cola, for example, to summon all the facts regarding the product itself. He or she can and does make reasonable assumptions about the product's behavior, for example, that it is consistent chemically to the taste, visually to the eye, and physically in its packaging. Any changes the marketer might make in these three areas can be deliberately controlled for uniformity because they will be tangibly evident. In other words, the marketer can take the product's reality for granted and move on to considerations of price, distribution, and advertising or promotion.

To gain service knowledge, however, or knowledge of a service element, where does one begin? Services cannot be touched, tried on for size, or displayed on a shelf. They are exceedingly difficult to describe with precision, particularly those services with high variability owing to high consumer-renderer interaction.

Product-biased marketers are in danger of assuming they understand a service-dominant entity when, in fact, they may only be projecting their own subjective version of reality. And because there is no good guidance on acquiring service knowledge, opportunities for error are multiplied.

Clearly, more than one version of service reality may be found in a service market. Therefore, the crux of service knowledge is the description of the major consensus realities that define the service entity to various market segments.

Because all services consist of processes, each process and subprocess of a service must be understood, and each process's relationship to, interaction with, and perception by the market must be documented. The way in which markets form mental pictures of services must be carefully investigated. How service realities vary from segment to segment must be outlined and mapped.

To understand what a service is to a market, the marketer must rely heavily on the tools and skills of psychology, sociology, and other behavioral sciences; tools that in product marketing usually come into play in determining image rather than fundamental reality.

In developing a definition of a service entity's main market realities, the marketer might find, for instance, that although tax-return preparation is analogous to accurate computation within an accounting firm, it means freedom from responsibility to one segment of the consuming public, opportunity for financial savings to another segment, and convenience to yet a third segment. For some markets, the subprocess involving client interaction with the tax preparer will be the main reality of the service. For other markets, this part of the process will be irrelevant, only the mathematics will matter.

Unless these realities are documented and ranked by market importance, no sensible plan can be devised to represent a service effectively or deliberately. When an entity is complex and involves multiple service/product elements, further research is required to define the interrelationships among elements and their priorities within markets. In Figure 2, all elements were shown at the same size. However, segmentation research can be applied to create prioritized models based on consumer preference. For example, in a complex entity, such as an amusement park, first aid and sanitary services will carry greater weight (and be drawn proportionally larger) for parents with children than for single adults. Similarly, research can help to prioritize the bonds connecting various elements. These bonds may be used to signify clusters of elements having a high correlation in purchase decisions or elements influencing usage or preference for other elements.

In new service development, the importance of service research is critical because the successful development of a new service—a molecular collection of intangibles—is so difficult that it makes new-product development look like child's play. Yet, most marketing research techniques either carry an underlying assumption of tangibility or are limited to dealing with services at the subjective level of opinion and emotion, with all the associated risks of imprecision and misinterpretation that word-oriented methodologies allow. Thus, existing research approaches are often superficial in dealing with the nuances and complexities of documenting services.

IMAGE VERSUS EVIDENCE—THE KEY TO SERVICE REPRESENTATION

The definition of service realities should not be confused with the creation of image. Image is a method of *differentiating* and *representing* an entity to its target market. Image is not product, nor is it service. Examination of cases suggests a common thread among effective representations of services that is a mirror-opposite contrast to product techniques.

Consumer product marketing most often approaches the market by enhancing a physical object through abstract associations. Coca-Cola, for example, is surrounded with visual, verbal, and aural associations with authenticity and youth. Whereas Dr. Pepper's image has been structured to suggest "originality" and "risk taking," 7-Up is "light" and "buoyant." A high priority is placed on linking these abstract images to physical items.

But a service is already abstract. To compound the abstraction dilutes the reality that the marketer is trying to build. Effective service representations appear to be turned 180° away from abstraction. The reason is that service images and even service realities appear to be shaped to a large extent by circumstantial evidence, that is, by the things consumers can understand with their five senses. Such evidence is what a service cannot be. It is tangible.

FOCUSING ON THE EVIDENCE

The management of tangible evidence is not articulated in marketing as a primary priority for service marketers. There has been little in-depth exploration of the range of authority that emphasis on tangible evidence would create for the service marketer. In product marketing, tangible evidence is pri-

marily the product itself. But for services, tangible evidence would encompass broader considerations, and in contrast to product marketing, different considerations than are considered marketing's domain today.

In product marketing, many kinds of evidence are beyond the marketer's control and are consequently omitted from priority consideration in the market-positioning process. Because of the biases of product marketing, service marketers often fail to recognize the unique forms of evidence they can normally control, and they fail to see that they should be part of marketing's responsibilities.

Environment is a good example. Because product distribution normally means shipping to outside agents, marketers have little voice in structuring the environment in which the product is sold. Their major controllable impact on the environment is usually product packaging. Services, on the other hand, are often fully integrated with environment, that is, the setting in which the service is distributed is controllable.

Environment can play an enormous role in influencing the reality of a service in the consumer's mind. Physicians' offices provide an interesting example of intuitive environmental management. Although the quality of medical service may be identical, an office furnished in teak and leather creates a totally different reality in the consumer's mind from one with plastic slipcovers and inexpensive prints.

Similarly, although the services may be identical, the consumer's differentiation between Bank A service and Bank B service can be materially affected by whether the environment is dominated by butcherblock and bright colors or marble and polished brass.

By understanding the importance of evidence management, service marketers can make it their business to review and take control of this critical part of their mix. Creation of environment can be deliberate rather than accidental or by leaving such decisions in the hands of interior decorators.

Going beyond environment, evidence can be integrated across a wide range of items. Airlines, for example, manage and coordinate tangible evidence better than almost any large service industry. Whether by intuition or design, airlines do not focus attention on trying to explain or characterize transportation itself. One never sees an ad that attempts to convey "the slant of takeoff," "the feel of acceleration,'' or ''the aerodynamics of lift.'' Airline transport is given shape and form through consistency of a firm's visible and tangible face: in its uniforms, the decor of its planes, its graphics, baggage tags, ticket envelopes, and color schemes. Differentiation among airlines, although they all provide the same service, is a direct result of differences in packages of evidence.

Using the scale developed in Figure 3, this concept can be postulated as a principle for service representation. As shown in Figure 5, once an entity has been analyzed and positioned on the scale, the degree to which the marketer will focus on either tangible evidence or intangible abstractions for market positioning will be found to be *inversely related to the entity's dominance.*

Some forms of evidence can seem trivial until one recognizes how great their impact can be on service perception. Correspondence is one example. Letters, statements, and the like are sometimes the main conveyers of the reality of a service to its market; yet, often these are treated as peripheral to any marketing plan. From the grade of paper to the choice of colors, correspondence is visible evidence that conveys a unique message. A mimeographed, unsigned letter contradicts any words about service quality that may appear in the text of the letter. Conversely, engraved parchment from the local dry cleaner might make one wonder about their prices.

HUMAN EVIDENCE

Services are often inextricably entwined with their human representatives. In many fields, a person is perceived to *be* the service. The consumer cannot distinguish between them. Product marketing is myopic in dealing with the issue of people as evidence in terms of market positioning. Consumer marketing often stops at the production of materials and programs for sales personnel to use. Some service industries, on the other hand, have long intuitively manged human evidence to marketing ends.

Examples of this principle have been the basis for jokes, plays, and literature. ''The Man in the Grey Flannel Suit,'' for example, was a synonym for the advertising business for many years. Physicians are uniformly packaged in smocks. Lawyers and bankers are still visualized in pinstripes and vests. IBM representatives were famous for adhering to a ''white shirt'' policy. Going beyond apparel, a firm, such as McDonald's, even achieves age uniformity—an extra element reinforcing its total market image.

These examples add up to a serious principle when thoughtfully reviewed. They are particularly instructive for service marketers. None of the above examples were the result of deliberate market planning. McDonald's, for instance, backed into age consistency as a result of trying to keep labor costs low. Airlines are the single outstanding example of

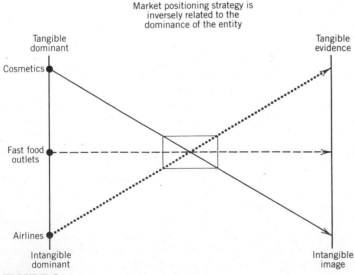

FIGURE 5
Principle of market positioning.

consciously planned standards for uniformity in human representation. The power of the human evidence principle is obvious, and the potential power of more deliberately controlling or structuring this element is clear.

SERVICES AND THE MEDIA

As previously discussed, services are abstract. Because they are abstract, the marketer must work hard at making them real, by building a case from tangible evidence. In this context, media advertising presents a particularly difficult problem.

The problem revolves around the fact that most media are already one step removed from reality. Media, as Marshall McLuhan would put it, abstracts the physical.

Thus, media work with the creation of product image and help in adding abstract qualities to tangible goods. A photograph is only a two-dimensional version of a physical object and may be visually misleading. Cosmetics, for example, are often positioned in association with an airbrushed or soft-focus filmed ideal of beauty. Were the media truly accurate, the wrinkles and flaws of the flesh to which even models are subject, might not create such an appealing product association. But product tangibility provides an anchor for all representations. The consumer has little difficulty recognizing the product by name or remembered appearance when he or she sees it or wants to buy it.

Because of their abstracting capabilities, the media often make service entities more hazy instead of more concrete, and the service marketer must work against this inherent effect. Unfortunately, many marketers are so familiar with product-oriented thinking that they go down precisely the wrong path and attempt to represent services by dealing with them in abstractions.

The worst examples attempt to describe the already-intangible service with more abstractions. Such compounded abstractions do not help the consumer form a reality, do not differentiate the service, and do not help to build credibility.

The best examples of service advertising are those that attempt to associate a service with some form of tangible evidence, working against the media's abstracting qualities. Merrill Lynch, for instance, has firmly associated itself with a clear visual symbol of bulls and concomitant bullishness. Where Merrill Lynch does not use the visual herd, it uses photographs of tangible physical booklets and invites the consumer to write for them. H&R Block uses the physical presence of its founders. TWA shows its comfortable seats. Numerous other examples illustrate the practice.

Therefore, the final principle offered for service marketers would hold that *effective media representation of intangibles is a function of establishing nonabstract manifestations of those intangibles.*

DESIGNING A SERVICE

The principles and methods suggested by the foregoing discussion all come together to form a workable and objective system for service design. Service design means rational and detailed design of complex processes. But process design is only part of total service design.

Service design must take into account evidence, the selection of methods of rendering (e.g., human rendering vs. machine), the time value of money, and the design of overall control mechanisms. Service design involves consideration of distribution as well as the fashioning of image. Unlike product marketing, in which a product concept might be suggested by marketing but the product's creation is left to the manufacturing arm, service design is part of service marketing.

Service design can be thought of as a form of architecture, but an architecture dealing with processes instead of bricks and timbers. Its objective is the creation of a complete blueprint for a service or service concept. It is not possible to discuss in full the details and nuances of total service blueprinting. However, the basic principles can be suggested here, along with some implications for creative and flexible use of both service blueprinting and molecular modeling.

DEVELOPING A SERVICE BLUEPRINT

To illustrate the basic concepts, consider the simple service of the corner shoeshine. In Figure 6, four process steps, proceeding left to right in time constitute the primary blueprint for the service. But clearly there is more to the service than simply the functional procedures. After diagramming the basic processes, the service designer must look for fail points, in other words, places where the service can go awry. In this example, there is one main error possibility, that is, application of the wrong color of

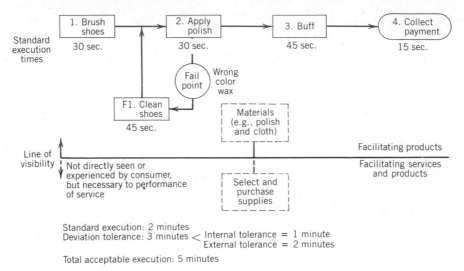

Standard execution: 2 minutes
Deviation tolerance: 3 minutes < Internal tolerance = 1 minute
External tolerance = 2 minutes
Total acceptable execution: 5 minutes

FIGURE 6

Blueprint for a simple service: The corner shoeshine.

wax. A corrective process (i.e., recleaning the shoes) is shown as being necessary to complete the service.

Other processes and evidence that are not visible to the consumer must also be considered. Purchase of supplies, for example, is shown below the line of visibility of the service as a subservice, necessary but not seen by the consumer. For many services, these back-office processes are important because a change in them may change the service identity. If, for example, a computer program is redesigned in such a way that a different account statement is produced for banking customers, this new piece of evidence may affect service image and may affect other perceptions of price/value as well. Thus, even invisible processes must be planned and monitored by the marketer.

A facilitating good, that is, wax, is necessary to the rendering of this service. This product (or piece of essential evidence) is visible to the consumer but is not part of the service process. Nevertheless, all products associated with a service must be selected and managed with care.

IDENTIFYING STANDARDS AND TOLERANCES

Because all services are time linked, understanding time costs is critical to a service designer. This particular design has a model execution time of 2 minutes. However, some deviation from the model can be expected and should be allowed for in-service design. The consumer's execution tolerance for this blueprint is shown at 180 seconds, or 3 additional minutes. Beyond 5 minutes, the consumer will show signs of dissatisfaction and begin materially to lower his or her judgment of quality.

Deviation tolerance, as a design and quality measure, is divided into two categories. Internal deviation occurs within the service process itself. For example, if buffing extends to 60 seconds, 15 seconds of internal deviation will have taken place. External tolerance occurs outside the service process. Waiting 2 minutes in line for the service would be an example of external deviation. Although both types of deviation can affect consumer perception, usually only internal deviation affects profitability. Therefore, the marketer, in designing a service, must set service tolerances to relate directly to profit.

As shown, an application of the wrong wax or spending too much time on any function can reduce pretax profit by half or more. At the 4-minute stage, the service loses money. This is true even though the customer will tolerate up to 5 minutes of total execution time. Thus, the temptation to relax productivity to the customer's level of tolerance has been deliberately offset by the profit dynamics of

TABLE 1
Profit Analysis

	Total Internal Execution		
	2 Min.	**3 Min.**	**4 Min.**
Price	50¢	50¢	50¢
Costs			
1. Time @ 10¢ per minute	20	30	40
2. Wax	3	3	3
3. Other (brush, cloth, etc.—amortized)	9	9	9
Total Costs	32	42	52
Pretax Profit	18	8	(−2)

doing so. When marketers set service standards and tolerances in this way, they establish not only a basis for measuring performance, but also a basis for managing uniformity and quality if the service is to be broadly distributed.

MODIFYING A SERVICE

Although Figure 6 may appear to be a simple service, it is subject to substantial change by the marketer. As Figure 7 shows, the marketer may add a repeat cycle of steps 2 and 3, thus creating a two-coat shine. This may be sufficient differentiation to allow a 20¢ price increase, thus increasing the margin by 1¢. Or, a marketer might decide to add service evidence in the form of a receipt or add product in the form of a sample of wax. Not only would the marketer create a reminder of the service (by perhaps printing his or her name and address on the sample), but the marketer might be able to raise prices even higher. Or he or she might be able to maintain the price, yet increase the margin, by buying a machine that lets the customer buff his or her own shoes. The time saved would allow greater profit, provided no perceived diminishment in quality occurred on the customer's part.

In addition to the controlled change suggested by Figure 7, both the service blueprint and the molecular model can be used even more flexibly to engineer market entities. Figure 8 shows how whole

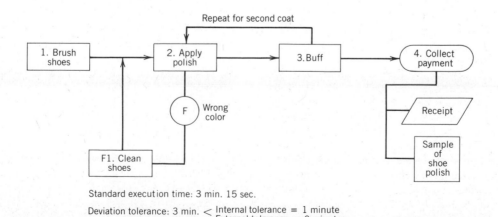

FIGURE 7
Modified design incorporating new service cycle, service evidence, and product element.

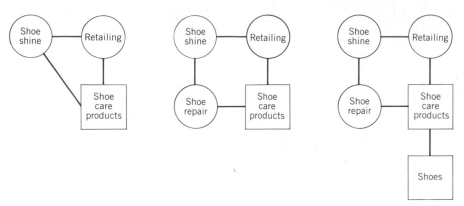

FIGURE 8
Alternative designs for more complex entities.

new market entities can be designed starting with a basic service and adding other service and product elements to it. Clearly, through blueprinting and modeling, a great deal of entity design can be done at the drawing board well before expensive formal market introduction. Moreover, it can be done objectively, quantifiably, and scientifically.

BENEFITS AND USES OF SERVICE BLUEPRINTING

The service blueprint accomplishes a number of objectives. First, it provides both a visual and a quantitative verbal definition that is less subject to interpretation or misinterpretation. Second, a service blueprint allows a service to be created on paper. Rather than resorting to subjective and imprecise concept testing as a means of service development, an actual blueprint can be tested in which the proposed service has been thoroughly and specifically worked out. A blueprint can even be mocked up into a prototype service, which can be trial tested by potential consumers in ways that give the marketer concrete and actionable feedback. This feedback can be used to make rational modifications before the service is retested. All this is possible because the blueprint allows the marketers to know exactly what they are testing, be it deviation tolerances, fail points, consumer values associated with specific functions, evidence, or any other feature.

Finally, the service blueprint provides a perma-

nent benchmark against which execution can be measured, modification proposals analyzed, competitors compared, prices established, and cogent promotional plans developed.

CONCLUSION

The service-marketing function is unique because services themselves are unique. This paper has suggested only a few of the many areas in which services offer exciting challenges and new marketing directions. But clearly, the service marketer must address not only the structure of services, but also their performance, pricing, distribution, and positioning in a different manner than consumer-product marketing allows. It is time traditional marketing took off its blinders and began the process of evolving to meet the needs of services and service marketers. Continued exploration of new concepts and new techniques is imperative if marketing is to achieve stature and influence in the post-industrial services economy. These hypotheses only scratch the surface of the issues presented by services. The frontier remains open for the adventurous.

NOTES

[1]See William R. George and Hiram C. Barksdale, ''Marketing Activities in the Service Industries,'' *Journal of Marketing*, 38 (October 1974), pp. 65–70.

[2]*The Meaning and Sources of Marketing Theory,* (Marketing Science Institute Series) New York: McGraw-Hill, 1965, p. 88.

[3]Theodore H. Levitt, "Marketing Myopia," *Harvard Business Review,* 38 (July–August 1960) pp. 45–56.

DISCUSSION QUESTIONS

1. According to the author, the basic distinction that causes services marketing to differ from product marketing is that services are processes, whereas products are things. Is this difference meaningful in terms of the application of existing marketing concepts and techniques?

2. Compare and contrast service development to product development. Discuss the use of tools, such as prototypes and trial-use test marketing, in terms of services. Are the requirements of service development adequately met by the marketing tools available?

3. Consider a service such as teaching. How can this service be designed to yield uniform quality at a competitively attractive price? What are the problems involved in distribution of this service to multiple locations while maintaining uniform quality and execution? What alternative service designs might a marketer consider to meet the market demand for learning?

4. What makes great service firms, such as H&R Block, American Express, Disney, McKinsey & Co., American Airlines, or Merrill Lynch, successful? Who controls policy, decision making, and management of these key success criteria? What role does marketing play in these organizations?

5. Does the nature of services suggest that the marketing function should be redefined for services? What new areas of control or responsibility should a service marketer have compared to a product marketer? Why? What new skills or knowledge does a service marketer need to deal adequately with service creation and management?

C. THEORY AND RESEARCH

Jerry Olson's 1981 Presidential Address to the Association for Consumer Research opens this subsection on theory and research. In this paper, Olson candidly shares his concerns about consumer behavior, research, and theory, and he offers some suggestions for strengthening the theory-research relationship. Although tailored to consumer behaviors, most of what Olson presents can be readily extended to marketing.

The Morgan and Smircich article is the only essay in this collection that was published outside the domain of marketing and consumer behavior. Yet, the article's case for qualitative research is especially timely, given marketing's current reexamining of the appropriateness of traditional methodologies and the exploration of new and creative approaches to thought development. The Calder, Phillips, and Tybout article clarifies the differences between two distinct types of generalizability in consumer and marketing research—effects application and theory application—and it shows how the failure to distinguish between the associated appropriate research designs can lead to incorrect research conclusions.

The Brown and Gaulden paper questions the validity of much of the body of thought that makes up the marketing discipline, based on the absence of a research-replication tradition. Replication is discussed in the context of theory building and theory testing, and suggestions are offered for building a replication tradition in the discipline. In an article that complements Olson's paper, Jacoby offers a searching and challenging critique of the research assumptions, methods, and findings of consumer behavior. Like Olson, much of what is observed could be extended to marketing research in general.

PREFACE TO

"Presidential Address: 1981, Toward a Science of Consumer Behavior"

I have been interested in the philosophy (and sociology) of science for many years, but during 1980 and 1981 I devoted more time to studying in this domain. Some of this work helped me clarify my ideas about how the field of consumer behavior was developing and how alternative styles of research might enhance our progress. I used this speech to the Association of Consumer Research (ACR) as an opportunity to think through and state my recommendations for conducting scientific research in consumer behavior. The paper accurately represents my ideas at that point in time (mid-1981); I have not changed any part of it for this volume.

My perspective on science places theory at center stage; theories should be our prime concern in consumer research. I put more emphasis on theory creation and development (sometimes called discovery) than do many philosophical perspectives that are more concerned with theory testing. I believe more consumer researchers (but not all of them) should be working at the earlier stages of research programs, creating theories and then developing them to a point where rigorous tests may be appropriate. In fact, even at the testing stage, we should be seeking to *develop* our theories further. My paper attempts to sketch out—in broad brush strokes only—some of the research behaviors and philosophical perspectives that might facilitate the creation and development of consumer behavior theory.

There are several important issues that I did not discuss explicitly, although they are implicit in the paper. One is a recommendation for a problem or phenomenon orientation in consumer research rather than the common, narrower focus on a particular methodology or analytical procedure or concern with a particular theory. This is partly what I meant when I argued for an increased emphasis on "bigger" issues. Also implicit throughout the paper is my relativistic perspective on science—the idea that the meanings of data, methods, and theories are relative to each other and to the sociohistorical context in which they are used. This view is in contrast to the absolutist, realist perspective taken by most approaches to science—basically, the idea that scientists are discovering the way the world actually is. The constructivist, relativistic perspective provides the basic metatheoretical foundation for my recommendations to develop multiple theoretical perspectives to any phenomenon and to compare theories with alternative theories (rather than just data) to determine their usefulness rather than their "truth." Finally, because meanings (and "truth") are relative, no one philosophy or scientific procedure (such as falsification) can insure our success. We need multiple philosophical approaches as well as multiple theories, methods, and measures.

23

PRESIDENTIAL ADDRESS: 1981, TOWARD A SCIENCE OF CONSUMER BEHAVIOR*

JERRY C. OLSON

INTRODUCTION

Developing a Presidential Address is an interesting process. For one thing, it forces the writer to consider what he or she feels strongly enough about to warrant inflicting on a few hundred people for thirty minutes or so. Although the process was a bit painful, I did find something I felt that strongly about. It is reflected in my subtitle, ''Toward a Science of Consumer Behavior.''

I will continue the recent trend in Presidential Addresses in which ACR Presidents proselytize for their own ideas and values. My talk is also an attempt to convert some of you to my way of thinking. I hope to convince most of you that the field of consumer research has problems with its theory. From what I've heard at this conference, I don't anticipate any great difficulty doing that. However, I have no illusions that most of you will agree with my particular assessment of our theory problems or with the partial solutions I will recommend. At minimum, I want to challenge some of our traditional ways of thinking about research and theory and consider a few alternative approaches to developing theories of consumer behavior. I will be satisfied if you think about these ideas—even if you ultimately reject them.

Source: Reprinted with permission from the *Advances in Consumer Research,* Andrew Mitchell, ed., Ann Arbor, Mich.: Association for Consumer Research, 1982, v–x.

*This paper was delivered as the Presidential Address at the 12th Annual Conference of the Association of Consumer Research held October 1981 in St. Louis.

There are many people who have helped me see the issues addressed here a bit more clearly, both by our spirited discussions (arguments) and by alerting me to books and articles I otherwise might have missed. Among these, I am particularly indebted to Jack Jacoby, Andy Mitchell, Paul Peter, William Ray, and Gerry Zaltman, and especially my students past and present. Thanks are also due to Alden Clayton, Jack Jacoby, Paul Peter, and Diane Schmalensee for their helpful comments on earlier drafts of this paper.

A SCIENCE OF CONSUMER BEHAVIOR?

I am not going to extensively defend the issue of whether we ought to aspire to have a science of consumer behavior. It seems to me that many (perhaps most?) of us either think consumer research is already a science or else we are trying to make it one. As my title implies, I am in the latter camp. I don't think we are quite there yet. But I do think that a science of consumer behavior is a worthwhile goal to pursue. I believe that many of us agree with Bill Wilkie in our aspirations to make consumer behavior more than an engineering-type discipline in which we apply concepts and theories developed elsewhere to solve specific problems.[1] Although most of us do lots of engineering-type work, many of us try to do science-type work, too.

What is science-type work? What would it mean to have a science of consumer behavior? Let me suggest that whatever else we think a science is, it has a lot to do with theory. *Theories* are a basic requirement for a science. To have a viable science of consumer behavior, we must have viable theories of consumer behavior. Thus, doing consumer behavior science involves working with theories—developing, testing, modifying, and improving theories of consumer behavior phenomena.

Current State of Consumer Behavior Theory

My basic contention is that we consumer researchers are not doing enough to *develop* theory. Moreover, what little theory development we do attempt is not being done well enough.[2] Several previous ACR Presidents, among others, have pointed out many of the reasons why we find ourselves in this impoverisehd theoretical state. Jack Jacoby cited a long list of problems in our field, many of which concerned our poor work with theory. Hal Kassarjian, Jerry Kernan, and Dave Gardner all tried to focus our efforts on specific topics in need of better theory. Bill Wilkie discussed the kind of scholarly commitment necessary to make contributions to knowledge, which I interpret as contributions to theory. For the most part, these problems and the proposed solutions are widely recognized, so I will not review them here.

Instead, I want to discuss a research approach to developing consumer behavior theory that is neither widely known nor commonly practiced. Although I believe this approach can help move us toward a science of consumer behavior, I recognize that it is at best only part of an overall solution to our problems. And I recognize that it is not for everyone. For one thing, this alternative research "style" requires adopting a somewhat different perspective on the procedures, methods, and philosophies of doing research than what most of us were taught in graduate school.

Why Is Theory So Important?

Before I elaborate on this research style though, let me deal with the counterarguments some of you already may be generating and try to convince you not to tune me out—yet. Perhaps some of you are saying things to yourself like, "Oh no, another talk about Theory, with a capital T." Or, "I've got all these problems to be solved before 2:00 P.M.; I just don't have time to mess around with theory." Or the best one of all, "Don't give me a theory, just show me the data."

Please note that I'm not just talking about practitioners here. Many academic researchers have an inappropriate, overly restricted view of theory, too. For instance, many of us tend to think that some of the things we do, do not involve theory. We may think that data, at least some data, stand alone. That is, we think some data are directly interpretable. We may think that some concepts are directly observable. These kinds of ideas reflect the basic underlying assumptions of empiricism and the positivist philosophy of science that still reigns in the social sciences (see Koch, 1981) and in consumer behavior. This approach to research is based on the assumption that only our sense impressions—in research terms, our empirical observations—provide useful knowledge of the world. It is as if characteristics of the world are sort of waiting around for researchers to come along and observe them.

But these ideas have been repudiated by many philosophers of science.[3] From their point of view, facts do not stand alone. Data do not have intrinsic meaning. No concept is directly observable. Even simple, apparently well-understood measures are based on complex, multichained, interconnected assumptions, which are really theories. Thus, in contrast to the empiricist perspective, this alternative view says that our abstractions—our ideas, our theories—provide the basic framework and rationale for everything we do as researchers, even for our supposedly "direct" empirical observations.[4]

Usually these theoretical assumptions are unstated. We seldom examine the "hidden" theories in our research; we seldom question them.[5] Often they are very difficult to recognize simply because we have taken them for granted for so long. But these theoretical assumptions need to be explicitly recognized. Perhaps we would find that some of these theories are not justified or cannot be supported. Then we could begin the work to improve the theories.

Make Implicit Assumptions Explicit

So, one of the simplest things we can do to develop a science of consumer behavior is to make explicit as many of our theoretical assumptions as we can, including those that have been long hidden from our consideration. Certainly, we will have to stop short of examining every theoretical assumption. But even so, the practice can be very healthy. Some of you, of course, are already expert practitioners of this style—often to the chagrin of your students and/or your colleagues. It is a wonderful habit for all of us to acquire. It can make our thinking more rigorous and precise, which should help us develop better theories of consumer behavior.

Our Current Use of Theory in Consumer Research

Perhaps some of you are a bit offended by this talk so far. Maybe you are generating counterarguments like: "Who's he talking about? I'm into theory! My studies always test some theoretically based hypothesis!"

I grant you that overt concern with theory in consumer behavior has probably never been higher. Just look back at the literature of ten years ago and see for yourself. Today nearly every article mentions some theory or another. Sometimes we even claim to be testing a theory! Hard-nosed business researchers and "softer nosed" public policymakers occasionally use theory to help make decisions. Why, we even have AMA Theory Conferences. And all of this has been going on for several years. But where is the progress in *developing* theories of consumer behavior?

In fact, we have become skilled at *borrowing* theories from other disciplines and *applying* them to our problems. This is fine, but I am concerned with what we do with those theories after we have applied them. Seldom do we do anything beyond either applying them again or dropping them. Our discipline applies borrowed theory, but does relatively little to *develop* theory. I echo the sentiments of Jag Sheth (1979), Jack Jacoby (1976), and others who have called for an end to mere borrowing and for beginning an extensive effort directed at theory development.

THEORY DEVELOPMENT

In the rest of my talk, I want to ge beyond a simple plea for more theory development in consumer behavior. I want to present several specific suggestions for how a research approach that is intended to develop theory might proceed.[6] I think these suggestions have the potential to improve our theories of consumer behavior. But the improvement will necessarily be gradual. It will take time. Developing good theory is a very complex process. There will be deadends. Some ideas won't pan out. Basically, we will be involved in a trial and error process. We will have to begin modestly, but we must begin. To paraphrase Bill Wilkie's (1981) message last year, more of us will have to commit ourselves to contribute to theoretical knowledge about consumer behavior in order to make an impact.

Basic Assumptions Regarding Theory

In keeping with my recommendation that we make our assumptions explicit, let me state the basic assumptions about theory that underlie the rest of my talk.

I consider (at least this year I do) theories to be *representations,* abstract conceptualizations that represent the phenomenon of interest. The phenomenon of interest can be virtually anything—a measure, a method, a data analysis procedure, a simple behavior, or a very complex behavior. There are, of course, many alternative ways to represent any event or phenomenon. Thus, there are many possible theories of anything. Any single theoretical representation will be flawed in that it will be incomplete; it will not capture all of the aspects of the phenomenon. In other words, we know from the beginning that our theories are problematic. This idea can cause a subtle (or perhaps not so subtle) change in our typical perspective on theory and scientific research. A researcher who adopts this perspective may become less interested in *TESTING* theory. Rather, a researcher who sees all theories as imperfect representations tends to be more concerned with *DEVELOPING* or improving theory, with trying to produce better representations of the domain or phenomenon of interest.

OK, but what is "better"? A better theory is not necessarily one that can be verified by data or that successfully survives some falsification attempt. Alternative theories could also be verified or avoid falsification. Rather a better theory is a more *useful* representation. But useful for what? Well, useful for whatever purpose it is you are theorizing about. For example, a theory may be useful for helping suggest solutions to a problem, or useful for explaining large bodies of complex data, or heuristically useful for generating new theories or stimulating new research directions (see Gergen 1978). Although we could argue about which aspect of usefulness is relevant for a particular case, these are all viable and appropriate criteria for evaluating theories. But they are not widely used as criteria in most of our research.

Instead, the dominant approach to theory research in our field seems to be concerned mainly with whether empirical data "fits" a theory (or vice versa). Generally, we test theories against data. More specifically, we usually "test" a theoretical prediction of "X" effect by comparing it against the null of no effect. Because the null is seldom given any theoretical meaning, all we have is a theory that predicts obtaining some effect, in contrast to a strawman null. Most of our studies, therefore, boil down to simple demonstrations that the anticipated effect was obtained. Much less frequently we try to "falsify" the theory (see Calder, Phillips, and Tybout 1981). Although both of these types of research may be useful and appropriate for certain purposes, I argue that neither approach has been very useful for developing new theory or for producing valuable modifications of "old" theory.

A null-hypothesis-testing style of research has many other dysfunctional consequences for developing a science of consumer behavior.[7] One is that it focuses the researcher's attention on obtaining statistical significance rather than on the magnitude of the effect itself—e.g., the strength of the relationship—which is more relevant to its usefulness.[8] A more serious problem is that sometimes we get lazy and let the results of our statistical inference analyses do our scientific inferencing or theorizing for us. Too often, we are content to let a statistically significant effect stand alone. We try to let the data "speak for themselves," something that data can not really do.

A Different Style of Inquiry

My major suggestion for breaking out of these patterns of behavior is that some of us adopt a different style of inquiry for at least that part of our research effort intended to develop theory. We need a research approach in which theory *development*, rather than merely collecting empirical support for a theory, is the primary goal. For such objectives, the traditional views of empirical research are not very useful.

Null Hypothesis Testing In particular, we should move away from a style of research based on simple null hypothesis testing. At best, such studies can provide only weak evidence about the usefulness of a theory. Moreover, they do not tend to generate the conceptual speculations that are necessary to modify and improve the theory.

Strong Inference As an alternative to a style of research based on simple verification or falsification doctrines and carried out by null hypothesis testing procedures, we might adopt (or adapt) a style of empirical research described almost twenty years ago by John Platt (1964) in an article entitled "Strong Inference." Basically Platt suggests that we should pit competing hypotheses against one another—where each is based on a different theory. Thus, in the ideal study, one theory will be supported and the other will not be. Such outcomes provide an empirical basis for making *strong inferences* about the usefulness of both theories.

In other words, in our empirical research we should test theory against theory, not theory against data. We should also be more concerned with comparing theories with each other at a conceptual level. As we become more familiar with this style of thinking and research, we will become more skilled at identifying the contradictory features of alterna-tive theories, some of which are likely to be implicit, metatheoretical assumptions. Then we can design better studies in which these discrepant features are compared against each other. If a test is well designed, we may have a critical experiment that clearly establishes the superiority of one idea over another.

An interesting wrinkle in this kind of study was recommended by Paul Feyerabend (1975), who suggested that we not drop the "losing" theory in such contests. Rather, our post-experimental efforts should go into modifying and improving the loser, as well as the "winning" theory. In other words, we should continually work to develop and improve alternative, competing theories, not just our favorite theory, not just the one enjoying general support at the moment.

Bootstrapping I also believe that we need to analyze our data more deeply, more carefully and more intensively. I mean this in both a theoretical, conceptual sense and in a statistical analysis sense, but I am not advocating more sheer number crunching. If our goal is to *develop* theory, then we will need better—i.e., more conceptually sophisticated—data about which to speculate in order to modify and improve our theories. Then, these improved theories can guide the collection of even more sophisticated data, which in turn can be used as a speculative basis for further developing the theory. And so on.

This approach to doing science and developing theory is called bootstrapping, and is described in a small book, *Theory and Evidence*, by Clark Glymore [1980]. Although this style is different from the traditional scientific method, there is fairly convincing evidence that successful theory developers follow a bootstrapping approach. Bootstrapping may seem uncomfortably like "cheating" to some of you. But not if you take the point of view that all theories are imperfect representations, and our objective is to develop better representations. From this perspective, the bootstrapping approach is quite appropriate for *developing* theory.

Proliferate Theories

Another, perhaps more controversial suggestion is related to these ideas. Rather than seek a single, overall theory—a single paradigm to tie the discipline together—we might intentionally proliferate theories. Especially given our present state of ignorance about consumer behavior, we should not rush to one point of view, to one paradigm. Real knowledge and understanding (not just apparent knowledge) is most likely to come from the application of many alternative points of view (see Feyerabend 1975).[9] This is another way of saying that we will learn more by comparing theoretical ideas with alternative theoretical ideas than by fitting data to single theoretical ideas.

Where are we supposed to get all of these alternative theoretical ideas? For one thing, we can start by doing more speculating. We should be speculating about the theoretical assumptions underlying our measures, our experimental procedures, and our analyses. In particular, we should do more speculating about the meaning, actually the alternative meanings, of our results.[10] Based on these speculations, new theories may develop and existing theories may be modified. Let's not be afraid to do it, and let's not dump on those who try.

Where else, besides our own speculation, can we find alternative ideas to contrast with our theories of interest? Feyerabend goes further than most of us are probably willing to go by suggesting that we look to the most bizarre sources for alternative theoretical perspectives. For instance, we could look to voodoo magic as an alternative to the germ theory of disease to explain why people get sick and sometimes die. Or, we could proceed counterinductively, as Feyerabend puts it, by intentionally postulating irrational theories and treating them as serious alternatives to our theory of interest. Consumer research may not be ready for such extreme steps, but there are less bizarre sources to which we can turn. We can generate alternate theoretical ideas from workable solutions to applied problems, from obtained data, from the theories that we borrow from other disciplines, and from everyday life.

As comforting (and seductive) as it is to have a widely accepted paradigm for conducting our research, we should tolerate and even encourage the gadflies among us to come up with alternative perspectives that may not square with our common sense. Moreover, we should *publish* these ideas *if* they are well reasoned and clearly presented (i.e., if they precisely describe how they differ from better known theories). By comparing these alternative theories with each other, both at a logical conceptual level and at an empirical level, we will have a strong inference basis from which to work to *devel-*

op both theories. In this sense, a plurality of theories and research paradigms, instead of a monolithic theoretical structure, can be seen as beneficial and as a positive indicator of progress toward a science of consumer behavior.

Address Bigger Issues

My next suggestion concerns the focus and content of our theorizing and our research. Although there are notable exceptions, to be sure, many of us need to tackle "bigger" issues. By bigger, I mean more important issues, issues that make a difference, issues that have broad ramifications at a theoretical level or broad implications at an applications level. Too much of our research and theory is concerned with "small" issues, issues that don't make a great deal of difference either for theory or for applications.[11]

We seem to prefer to study ". . . problems, theories, or research paradigms that appear simple and are easily studied rather than the more basic and important problems that are invariably complex and difficult to resolve" (Battig and Bellezza, 1979, p. 322). Does the following passage in which the late Bill Battig describes the typical "development" in cognitive psychology ring true as a descriptor of our own "progress" in developing a science of consumer behavior?

First somebody comes up with a new theory, research paradigm, or interesting and controversial empirical result, which appears quite simple, straightforward, and easy to investigate further. This catches on, creating a new "hot" research topic, which promises to be more productive than previous approaches, and therefore attracts the interest of a great many psychologists. But as more work gets done, the originally simple problem gets more complicated, because of failures to replicate the original findings, demonstrations that the original problem is inadequate or at best incomplete, and increasing evidence that the problem is more complicated and less general than originally thought. So as this relationship develops, it becomes apparent that any further progress will require a great deal of painstaking detailed research activity directed toward limited aspects of the overall problem or phenomenon as well as efforts to interrelate the topic appropriately with other previously distinct topics or phenomena. In other words, further research has reached a point of diminishing returns, because a threshold of too much complexity has been crossed, so the once hot topic now appears nonproductive or uninteresting, and soon dies out to be replaced by one or more different more simplistic types of research. So then the cycle starts all over again, often with almost total suppression of everything that was done or learned in the context of the previously "hot" research topic. (Battig and Bellezza 1979, p. 323)

In the brief twenty- twenty-five years of major research effort regarding consumer behavior, how many times has this happened? Think of all the theories, concepts, hypotheses, and ideas that have been dropped from favor when the going got tough, many of them probably prematurely. For starters, how about motivation research, stochastic modeling, perceived risk, brand loyalty, and attitude theory? Will attribution theory, information processing theory, causal modeling, or the next "hot" idea not yet even on the horizon go the same way? Probably, unless we begin to see our task as developing and improving these theories, rather than as testing them in the sense of finding one that seems to fit the data. Until more of us stop seeing consumer behavior as an engineering-type discipline and start seeing ourselves as scientists concerned with developing theory, I don't think we will make much progress.

Don't Drop Theories Prematurely

My next suggestion expands on this one. Perhaps we should not be so quick to drop a theory that runs into trouble. The trouble could be conceptual in that the theory has some vague aspects, or isn't elegant, or doesn't explain certain phenomena well. Or, the trouble could be empirical in that the theory is not consistent with certain aspects of the data. But all theories have problems.[12] In fact, such problems are expected, when we think of theories as imperfect representations. So, the idea is to give a theory lots of chances to show us its virtues, along with its faults.

As Thorton Roby suggested over twenty years ago in the *American Psychologist,* "Suggestive hypotheses should not be put directly to drudgery but should be entertained for awhile, as rare and welcome guests (1959, p. 131)." Perhaps we should

become a bit *less* concerned about whether we can produce data to support a theory, especially early in its life cycle. Early attempts to make data fit a theory are often disappointing. The resulting dissatisfaction can cause researchers to move on to other theories. But premature rejection of an idea with merit is a very serious error in terms of theoretical development. It is a kind of Type III error, which to the theory developer is much more important than the Type I and II errors of primary concern to the empirically oriented researcher. The Type III error is more critical because it tends to stop investigation altogether on ideas and concepts that may have merit.

I am not saying that a theory should not have to account for data. Useful theories should account for data, eventually. But there is an appropriate time and place to rigorously apply this criterion. A new theory may have to wait, perhaps for many years, until the necessary measuring procedures can be developed. Or, the theory may have to be modified, or more supportive data developed, perhaps using a bootstrapping approach.

More Tolerance

My next suggestion concerns the tolerance in our field that is necessary in order that a variety of theoretical perspectives can flourish. All of us—especially journal editors and reviewers—need to be more tolerant of new theoretical ideas.[13] The need for tolerance will increase as our discipline continues to mature. Specialized subareas of interest in consumer behavior are beginning to crop up now and will continue to develop. We should welcome these diverse views and encourage their proliferation. But we must guard against the champions of these specialities becoming so polarized and isolated from one another that there is no communication, no understanding, and no tolerance. Let's not get into the kinds of situations common in many of the disciplines from which we borrow— the "You're-either-with-us-or-against-us" syndrome. All types of researchers, with different perspectives and different preferred styles of inquiry, are necessary to develop a science of consumer behavior. We need the empiricist, the humanist, and the theorist. We need people interested in data analysis, methodology, modeling, marketing, psychology, sociology, and philosophy. But, to make it all work, each person needs to understand the perspectives of the others and appreciate their contributions.

A Non-Marketing Perspective

My final suggestion is somewhat more specific. I think that we should expand our beginning efforts to develop concepts and theories of consumer behavior from different perspectives than that of the marketing manager. For instance, what would a theory of brand loyalty look like from the perspective of the consumer as an effort minimizer? Or, what would individual difference theories of consumers be like if they were not consciously constructed to be useful for market segmentation? Until we start explicitly contrasting our marketing-oriented theories with theories based on different values and objectives, we probably won't realize how limiting the marketing perspective is.

CONCLUSION

In conclusion, the field of consumer behavior research has made progress and continues to mature. But how will our future progress be charted? Will we continue to borrow theories that have enjoyed success in other disciplines and adapt them to a consumer behavior context? Will we then be content to run demonstration studies in which we attempt to show that these theories are at least somewhat consistent with our data? Or, will we develop the conceptual skills, the necessary styles of inquiry, and the courage and self-confidence that will enable us to further develop these theories and to create our own theories? I hope we will not be afraid to modify, extend, and improve the theories we borrow. I hope we will encourage those who can to boldly speculate about consumer behavior phenomena. I hope we will nourish and develop these theoretical ideas, because they are necessary for us to move toward a science of consumer behavior.

REFERENCES

Baken, David (1966), "The Test of Significance in Psychological Research," *Psychological Bulletin*, 66(6), 423–437.

Battig, William F. and Francis S. Bellezza (1979), "Organization and Levels of Processing," in *Memory Organization and Structure*, C. Richard Puff (ed.), New York: Academic Press.

Calder, Bobby J., Lynn W. Phillips, and Arlice M. Tybout (1981), "Designing Research for Application," *Journal of Consumer Research*, 8, 197–207.

Capra, Fritof (1975), *The Tao of Physics*, Boulder, Colo.: Shambhala.

Ericsson, Anders K. and Herbert A. Simon (1980), "Verbal Reports as Data," *Psychological Review*, 87(3), 215–251.

Feyerabend, Paul (1975), *Against Method*, London: Verso.

Gergen, Kenneth J. (1978), "Toward Generative Theory," *Journal of Personality and Social Psychology*, 36(11), 1344–1360.

Glymore, Clark (1980), *Theory and Evidence*, Princeton, N.J.: Princeton University Press.

Greenwald, Anthony G. (1975), "Consequences of Prejudice Against the Null Hypothesis," *Psychological Bulletin*, 82(1), 1–19.

Jacoby, Jacob (1976), "ACR Presidential Address—Consumer Research: Telling It Like It Is," in *Advances in Consumer Research*, Vol. 4, W. D. Perreault, Jr., (ed.), Atlanta: Association for Consumer Research, 1–11.

Koch, Sigmund (1981), "The Nature and Limits of Psychological Knowledge: Lessons of a Century qua 'Science'," *American Psychologist*, 36(3), 257–269.

Lykken, David T. (1968), "Statistical Significance in Psychological Research," *Psychological Bulletin*, 70(3), 151–159.

Meehl, Paul E. (1967), "Theory-Testing in Psychology and Physics: A Methodological Paradox," *Philosophy of Science*, 34, 103–115.

Mitroff, Ian I. and Ralph H. Kilmann (1978), *Methodological Approaches to Social Science*, San Francisco: Jossey-Bass.

Platt, John R. (1964), "Strong Inference," *Science*, 146(3642), 347–353.

Roby, Thorton B. (1959), "An Opinion on the Construction of Behavior Theory," *American Psychologist,* 14(3), 129–134.

Sheth, Jagdish N. (1979), "The Surpluses and Shortages in Consumer Behavior Theory and Research," faculty working paper No. 573, College of Commerce and Business Administration, University of Illinois at Urbana-Champaign.

Suppe, Frederick (1977), *The Structure of Scientific Theories,* 2nd ed., Urbana: University of Illinois Press.

Wilkie, William (1981), "Presidential Address: 1980," in *Advances in Consumer Research,* Vol. 8, Kent B. Monroe (ed.), Ann Arbor, Mich.: Association for Consumer Research, 1–5.

Zukov, Gary (1979), *The Dancing Wu Li Masters,* New York: Bantam.

NOTES

[1]Usually we tackle marketing problems. Occasionally we address public policy problems. Seldom do we directly concern ourselves with consumer welfare problems.

[2]Although this talk may have a holier-than-thou tone, I don't really feel that way. I recognize that I have been part of the problem. In fact, I am directing this talk as much to myself and my research behavior as to you.

[3]In this brief talk I can not fully develop these ideas and present them in a completely compelling manner. However, a few basic references have been cited to which interested readers can refer and form their own conclusions and develop their own preferred style of inquiry. Suppe (1977) provides perhaps the best overall discussion of many of these issues. In fairness, there are philosophers who still adhere to many of the tenets of logical positivism, now reincarnated as critical rationalism (see Feyerabend 1975; Suppe 1977).

The metaphysics of this point of view can be extended even further. The idea that theories provide the logical rationale for everything we do as researchers leads to the metaphysical position that our theories actually *create* the reality we observe.

There are, at least in principle, an infinite number of ways in which we can theoretically represent some characteristic or phenomenon of the world. Therefore, there are an infinite number of alternative realities that we can create through our theories. (It may be easier to see this in other fields than in consumer behavior. Quantum theory and particle physics are good areas to contrast with our field. Two fascinating books that clearly illustrate these points are *The Dancing Wu Li Masters* [1979] by Gary Zukov and *The Tao of Physics* [1975] by Fritof Capra.) This point of view clearly implies that we ought to be working to improve our existing theories and develop new theories rather than just trying to fit data to existing theories.

[5]This is also true in psychology and sociology, fields from which we borrow most of our theories. A clear exception, however, is the work of Ericsson and Simon (1980) published in *Psychological Review.* Ericsson and Simon explicated the typically ignored assumptions underlying self-report behaviors, and developed an explicit theory to explain certain aspects of self-reports.

[6]Let me be clear about my goals. Although I can be as evangelistic as anyone when I get started on a topic that interests me, I am not trying to convert everyone to this point of view. For one thing, it would be impossible. In a very interesting book entitled *Methodological Approaches to Social Science,* Ian Mitroff and Ralph Kilmann, [1978] suggested that the style of inquiry adopted by a researcher is a function of many influences, including environmental, intellectual, and social variables. Also, a researcher's preferred style of inquiry is influenced by his or her personality or temperament. Many of you may not find the ideas presented here compatible with your own ideas about research or your intellectual temperament. This is fine. In fact, Mitroff and Kilmann argue, I think convincingly, that a viable science involves several types of scientists, with different values, working from multiple theoretical and methodological perspectives. A single approach is not sufficient to form a viable science. No one perspective has the inside track to "truth."

[7]There is a sizable literature that should convince you of this point, if you do not already agree with

me. If you are not familiar with it, why not take a look and form your own conclusions? For starters, see *Baken* (1966), Greenwald (1975), Lykken (1968), Meehl (1967), and Platt (1964).

[8]Occasionally, I have seen papers in which only the size of the obtained *p* values were reported. No mention was made of the absolute magnitudes of the effects themselves!

[9]This is similar to the *yin* and *yang* principle of oriental philosophies, which suggests that extreme contrasts are necessary for understanding (see Capra 1975).

[10]I'm not speaking to only my fellow academics here; applied researchers should do more speculating, too.

[11]This may be the most frequent criticism of academic consumer research by practitioners and of applied research by theoretically oriented researchers.

[12]Alternatively, most theories (even bizarre ones) probably have some value. At minimum, any theory can be useful as a counterpoint to a more reasonable theory.

[13]The field of consumer behavior has always been an eclectic discipline; thus, we are probably somewhat more tolerant of new ideas than other, more insulated fields of study. However, I don't think we can be characterized as *highly* tolerant of new ideas, or of their proponents. There is room for improvement.

DISCUSSION QUESTIONS

1. How does a focus on theory testing differ from a concern with theory development? When is each most useful? Do the two goals require different empirical methods or philosophical perspectives?

2. Select a research issue in your field and identify the basic, metatheoretical assumptions that provide the foundation for this work. Show how the typical thinking about theories, measures, interpretations of data, and so on, would change if different metatheoretical assumptions were adopted. (If you can't think of reasonable alternative assumptions, then just adopt assumptions opposite to those currently held.) Consider how this dialectical process makes you more aware of the critical concepts and procedures in that domain, concepts and procedures that are usually taken for granted.

3. Criticize the views expressed in this paper from a logical empiricist (realist) perspective. What is relativistic about the views advocated here? With which type of philosophical perspective are you most comfortable? Why?

4. What are big issues? How can we identify and pursue them instead of being sidetracked by small issues? Discuss how an emphasis on problems or phenomena rather than on methods or specific theories can help. Do you think a functional approach to science is useful?

PREFACE TO

"The Case for Qualitative Research"

The ideas presented in this paper originated in discussion between the authors about the possibility of communicating to the management researcher some of the major debates that have taken place in the philosophy of social science in as condensed and direct a way as possible. Specifically, the paper seeks to communicate ideas explored in much greater depth in *Sociological Paradigms and Organizational Analysis* (1979) by Gibson Burrell and Gareth Morgan. This book presents an in-depth analysis of the way in which various world views have evolved in the social sciences and also sets forth different analyses of the nature of social life along with their diverse implications for research practice. This reading builds on elements of this analysis to illustrate the complex assumptions that have shaped so-called quantitative and qualitative approaches to social research. It also seeks to demonstrate—in a way that allows the reader to understand the logic of the different approaches—the manner in which quantitative and qualitative approaches to research are based on different kinds of assumptions with regard to the nature of social life. The article is written to emphasize the importance of understanding the links between theory and method in social research and to permit us to get beyond the simple dichotomies that are often drawn between qualitative and quantitative approaches to research. The reader will quickly see that there are many styles of qualitative research underpinned by many different kinds of assumptions, many of which have an important contribution to make to the future of marketing research.

24

THE CASE FOR QUALITATIVE RESEARCH

GARETH MORGAN
LINDA SMIRCICH

INTRODUCTION

In recent years there has been growing concern regarding the longstanding debate on the adequacy of research methods in the social sciences. In particular, methods derived from the natural sciences have come to be seen as increasingly unsatisfactory as a basis for social research, and systematic attention has been devoted to a search for effective alternatives. This attention was recently highlighted in a special issue of *Administrative Science Quarterly* (December 1979), considering research based on so-called qualitative methods within the field of organization theory. In reaction against the way in which organizational research of the 1960s and 1970s has been dominated by the use of quantitative methods, it now seems that a call is being raised in favor of qualitative methods.

While there can be little doubt that a more balanced approach to research in organization theory is required, there are many problems involved in the choice of a method that current debates have failed to explore. In particular, there has been a failure to examine the important relationship between theory and method. There has been a tendency to argue the case for different methods almost as ends in themselves, abstracted from the wider issues that they are ostensibly designed to examine. Whereas the 1960s and 1970s have been dominated by an abstracted empiricism based on the use of quantitative methods, the threat now is that the 1980s may be dominated by a pendulum swing to an abstracted empiricism based on qualitative methods. There is a danger that one kind of abstracted empiricism will be replaced by another.

In this [reading], we seek to offset this possibility by exploring the core assumptions that underlie the arguments in favor of different methods. Our basic thesis is that the case for any research method, whether qualitative or quantitative (in any case, a somewhat crude and oversimplified dichotimization) cannot be considered or presented in the abstract, because the choice and adequacy of a method embodies a variety of assumptions regarding the nature of knowledge and the methods through which that knowledge can be obtained, as well as a set of root assumptions about the nature of the phenomena to be investigated. Our aim is to examine the issues relating to methodology within this wider and deeper context, and in so doing develop a framework within which debates about rival methods in social science might be fruitfully and constructively considered.

We take our lead in this endeavor from the scheme of analysis offered by Burrell and Morgan (1979), which suggests that all approaches to social science are based on interrelated sets of assumptions regarding ontology, human nature, and epistemology. Table 1 provides a general overview of the relationships between ontology, human nature, epistemology, and methodology in contemporary social science. In order to simplify presentation, . . . we shall restrict our attention to what Burrell and Morgan have described as the Interpretive and Functionalist paradigms. The social thought embraced by these two paradigms raises a number of important research issues, but they are wedded to ideological perspectives that overplay the tendency to spontaneous order and regulation in social affairs, while ignoring modes of domination, conflict, and radical change. This is a serious omission. A full discussion and critique of contemporary research practice should also consider perspectives characteristic of the Radical Humanist and Radical Structuralist paradigms, within which the qualitative/quantitative research issue would be regarded as an ideological debate or minor significance. With this qualification in mind, we shall now seek to show how assumptions about ontology and human nature, which provide the grounds of social theorizing, are captured metaphorically in ways

Source: Reprinted with permission from *Academy of Management Review*, 5(4), 1980, 491–500.

TABLE 1
Network of Basic Assumptions Characterizing the Subjective-Objective Debate Within Social Science

	Subjectivist Approaches to Social Science					Objectivist Approaches to Social Science
Core Ontological Assumptions	Reality as a projection of human imagination	Reality as a social construction	Reality as a realm of symbolic discourse	Reality as a contextual field of information	Reality as a concrete process	Reality as a concrete structure
Assumptions About Human Nature	Man as pure spirit, consciousness, being	Man as a social constructor, the symbol creator	Man as an actor, the symbol user	Man as an information processor	Man as an adaptor	Man as a responder
Basic Epistemological Stance	To obtain phenomenological insight, revelation	To understand how social reality is created	To understand patterns of symbolic discourse	To map contexts	To study systems, process, change	To construct a positivist science
Some Favored Metaphors	Transcendental	Language game, accomplishment, text	Theater, culture	Cybernetic	Organism	Machine
Research Methods	Exploration of pure subjectivity	Hermeneutics	Symbolic analysis	Contextual analysis of Gestalt	Historical analysis	Lab experiments, surveys

275

that define different epistemological and methodological positions. The quantitative/qualitative debate has arisen on the basis of these competing assumptions—which, for the most part, have gone unchallenged.

ASSUMPTIONS ABOUT ONTOLOGY AND HUMAN NATURE

The assumptions about ontology and human nature sketched out in Table 2 amplify the brief descriptions provided in Table 1. In essence, they are intended to provide a rough typology for thinking about the various views that different social scientists hold about human beings and their world. All the views have a distinguished history, are the products of long discussion and debate by their advocates, and their basic ideas are manifested in powerful kinds of social thought. Each has evolved in awareness of the existence of the other points of view, and indeed has to some extent developed in reaction to competing perspectives. As Table 2 seeks to show, most have left their mark on contemporary organization theory, although the influence

TABLE 2
Assumptions About Ontology and Human Nature

SUBJECTIVE APPROACHES ←

	Reality as a Projection of Human Imagination	**Reality as a Social Construction**	**Reality as Symbolic Discourse**
Core Ontological Assumptions	The social world and what passes as "reality" is a projection of individual consciousness; it is an act of creative imagination and of dubious intersubjective status. This extreme position, commonly known as solipsism, asserts that there may be nothing outside oneself: one's mind is one's world. Certain transcendental approaches to phenomenology assert a reality in consciousness, the manifestation of a phenomenal world, but not necessarily accessible to understanding in the course of everyday affairs. Reality in this sense is masked by those human processes which judge and interpret the phenomenon in consciousness prior to a full understanding of the structure of meaning it expresses. Thus the nature of the phenomenal world may be accessible to the human being only through consciously phenomenological modes of insight.	The social world is a continuous process, created afresh in each encounter of everyday life as individuals impose themselves on their world to establish a realm of meaningful definition. They do so through the medium of language, labels, actions, and routines, which constitute symbolic modes of being in the world. Social reality is embedded in the nature and use of these modes of symbolic action. The realm of social affairs thus has no concrete status of any kind; it is a symbolic construction. Symbolic modes of being in the world, such as through the use of language, may result in the development of shared, but multiple realities, the status of which is fleeting, confined only to those moments in which they are actively constructed and sustained.	The social world is a pattern of symbolic relationships and meanings sustained through a process of human action and interaction. Although a certain degree of continuity is preserved through the operation of rule-like activities that define a particular social milieu, the pattern is always open to reaffirmation or change through the interpretations and actions of individual members. The fundamental character of the social world is embedded in the network of subjective meanings that sustain the rule-like actions that lend it enduring form. Reality rests not in the rule or in rule following, but in the system of meaningful action that renders itself to an external observer as rule-like.

of approaches represented by positions on the right hand side of the continuum have been dominant. The transition from one perspective to another must be seen as a gradual one, and it is often the case that the advocates of any given position may attempt to incorporate insights from others. Consequently, the success of efforts to determine who advocates what may be limited to determining the relative emphasis an advocate gives to one or more adjacent positions. Much time could be spent engaged in this particular sport, but that is not the major objective here. The point is that the scheme provides a useful way for thinking about the kind of assumptions that underlie continuing research and debate within the social sciences, and the thorny problems regarding epistemological and methodological adequacy.

PROBLEMS OF EPISTEMOLOGY

The different assumptions regarding ontology and human nature pose interesting problems of epistemology. The different world views they reflect imply different grounds for knowledge about the social world. As we pass from assumption to as-

→ **OBJECTIVE APPROACHES**

Reality as a Contextual Field of Information
The social world is a field of ever-changing form and activity based on the transmission of information. The form of activity that prevails at any one given time reflects a pattern of "difference" sustained by a particular kind of information exchange. Some forms of activity are more stable than others, reflecting an evolved pattern of learning based on principles of negative feedback. The nature of relationships within the field is probabilistic; a change in the appropriate pattern and balance within any sphere will reverberate throughout the whole, initiating patterns of adjustment and readjustment capable of changing the whole in fundamental ways. Relationships are relative rather than fixed and real.

Reality as a Concrete Process
The social world is an evolving process, concrete in nature, but ever-changing in detailed form. Everything interacts with everything else and it is extremely difficult to find determinate causal relationships between constituent processes. At best, the world expresses itself in terms of general and contingent relationships between its more stable and clear-cut elements. The situation is fluid and creates opportunities for those with appropriate ability to mold and exploit relationships in accordance with their interests. The world is in part what one makes of it: a struggle between various influences, each attempting to move toward achievement of desired ends.

Reality as a Concrete Structure
The social world is a hard, concrete, real thing "out there," which affects everyone in one way or another. It can be thought of as a structure composed of a network of determinate relationships between constituent parts. Reality is to be found in the concrete behavior and relationships between these parts. It is an objective phenomenon that lends itself to accurate observation and measurement. Any aspect of the world that does not manifest itself in some form of observable activity or behavior must be regarded as being of questionable status. Reality by definition is that which is external and real. The social world is as concrete and real as the natural world.

(continued)

TABLE 2—*Continued*

SUBJECTIVE APPROACHES ←		
	Humans as Transcendental Beings	**Humans Create Their Realities**	**Humans as Social Actors**

Assumptions About Human Nature

Humans are viewed as intentional beings, directing their psychic energy and experience in ways that constitute the world in a meaningful, intentional form. There are realms of being, and realms of reality, constituted through different kinds of founding acts, stemming from a form of transcendental consciousness. Human beings shape the world within the realm of their own immediate experience.	Human beings create their realities in the most fundamental ways, in an attempt to make their world intelligible to themselves and to others. They are not simply actors interpreting their situations in meaningful ways, for there are no situations other than those which individuals bring into being through their own creative activity. Individuals may work together to create a shared reality, but that reality is still a subjective construction capable of disappearing the moment its members cease to sustain it as such. Reality appears as real to individuals because of human acts of conscious or unwitting collusion.	Human beings are social actors interpreting their milieu and orienting their actions in ways that are meaningful to them. In this process they utilize language, labels, routines for impression management, and other modes of culturally specific action. In so doing they contribute to the enactment of a reality; human beings live in a world of symbolic significance, interpreting and enacting a meaningful relationship with that world. Humans are actors with the capacity to interpret, modify, and sometimes create the scripts that they play upon life's stage.

Some Examples of Research

Phenomenology	Ethnomethodology	Social Action Theory

sumption along the subjective-objective continuum, the nature of what constitutes adequate knowledge changes. To take the extremes of the continuum by way of illustration, an objectivist view of the social world as a concrete structure encourages an epistemological stance that emphasizes the importance of studying the nature of relationships among the elements constituting that structure. Knowledge of the social world from this point of view implies a need to understand and map out the social structure, and gives rise to the epistemology of positivism, with an emphasis on the empirical analysis of concrete relationships in an external social world. It encourages a concern for an "objective" form of knowledge that specifies the precise nature of laws, regularities, and relationships among phenomena measured in terms of

social "facts" (Pugh & Hickson 1976a, 1976b; Skinner 1953, 1957).

At the other end of the continuum, the highly subjectivist view of reality as a projection of individual imagination would dispute the positivist grounds of knowledge in favor of an epistemology that emphasizes the importance of understanding the processes through which human beings concretize their relationship to their world. This phenomenologically oriented perspective challenges the idea that there can be any form of "objective" knowledge that can be specified and transmitted in a tangible form, because the knowledge thus created is often no more than an expression of the manner in which the scientist as a human being has arbitrarily imposed a personal frame of reference on the world, which is mistakenly perceived as lying in an exter-

Humans as Information Processors	**Humans as Adaptive Agents**	→ **OBJECTIVE APPROACHES** **Humans as Responding Mechanisms**
Human beings are engaged in a continual process of interaction and exchange with their context—receiving, interpreting, and acting on the information received, and in so doing creating a new pattern of information that effects changes in the field as a whole. Relationships between individual and context are constantly modified as a result of this exchange; the individual is but an element of a changing whole. The crucial relationship between individual and context is reflected in the pattern of learning and mutual adjustment that has evolved. Where this is well developed, the field of relationships is harmonious; where adjustment is low, the field is unstable and subject to unpredictable and discontinuous patterns of change.	Human beings exist in an interactive relationship with their world. They influence and are influenced by their context or environment. The process of exchange that operates here is essentially a competitive one, the individual seeking to interpret and exploit the environment to satisfy important needs, and hence survive. Relationships between individuals and environment express a pattern of activity necessary for survival and well-being of the individual.	Human beings are a product of the external forces in the environment to which they are exposed. Stimuli in their environment condition them to behave and respond to events in predictable and determinate ways. A network of causal relationships links all important aspects of behavior to context. Though human perception may influence this process to some degree, people always respond to situations in a lawful (i.e., rule-governed) manner.
Cybernetics	**Open Systems Theory**	**Behaviorism Social Learning Theory**

nal and separate realm (Husserl 1962). The grounds for knowledge in each of these perspectives are different because the fundamental conceptions of social reality to which the proponents of each position subscribe are poles apart.

Science as Metaphor

We thus encounter a fundamental issue that has attracted the attention of social philosophers for many centuries. It is the issue of whether or not human beings can ever achieve any form of knowledge that is independent of their own subjective construction, since they are the agents through which knowledge is perceived or experienced. A strong case can be made for the view that science of all kinds, whether nominalist or realist in its basic orientation, is primarily metaphorical (Brown 1977; Morgan 1980; Schon 1963). It is through the use of metaphor that scientists seek to create knowledge about the world. The metaphors that theorists choose as a basis for detailed theorizing usually derive from very fundamental, and often implicit, core assumptions about ontology and human nature. In selecting different metaphors for elaborating their theories, they implicitly commit themselves to an epistemological position emphasizing particular kinds and forms of knowledge. Debates about epistemology hinge largely on the advocacy of different kinds of metaphoric insight as a means of capturing the nature of the social world. It is worth examining this point in detail.

Reality as a Concrete Process   As we proceed from right to left along the subjective-objective continuum illustrated in the two tables, the epistemology of extreme positivism, derived from a mechanical conception of the universe as a closed structure, gives way to an epistemology emphasizing the need to understand process and change. It is a change in epistemology that reflects a move away from a conception of the world as a machine, or closed system, to a conception of the world as an organism, an open system. The metaphor of organism has exerted a dominant influence on the development of open systems theory within social science, providing a mode of conceptualization appropriate to theorizing about the social world as if it were a concrete process evolving through time. This epistemological position stresses the importance of monitoring process, the manner in which a phenomenon changes over time in relation to its context (e.g., Burns & Stalker 1961; Emery & Trist 1965). The metaphors of machine and organism call for different modes of research as a means of generating knowledge; they define different epistemologies, since the knowledge required to examine a view of the world as a closed mechanical structure is inadequate for examining the world as an organismic system.

Reality as a Contextual Field of Information
Similarly, the epistemological framework for examining the world as an organismic system proves inadequate for studying the world if it is regarded, in accordance with the next ontological position along the continuum, as a process of information. This ontological position calls for epistemologies based on cybernetic metaphors, which emphasize the importance of understanding contexts in a holistic fashion (Morgan 1979). The metaphor of organism encourages the theorist to draw boundaries around the subject of study, elevating it in importance against the wider background. Thus the organization theorist often is concerned with the somewhat arbitrary relationship between organization and environment, structuring the research process and knowledge thus generated around this conceptualization. A more context-oriented epistemology, such as that provided by the cybernetic metaphor, would consciously seek to avoid this abstraction of "figure" from "ground," and search for what Bateson had described as "systemic wisdom." As he points out, it is possible to attempt to explain the evolution of the horse (figure) in terms of a one-sided adaptation to the nature of grassy plains (ground); however, this is to miss the point that the grassy plains have evolved along with the horse and may equally well be seen as an adaptation to the horse, as the other way around (1972 p. 155). The same is true with "organization" and "environment."

The point is that it is *contexts* which evolve, and that an adequate understanding of the *process* entails grasping the ecological nature of the context as a whole. Epistemologies based on the organismic metaphor are inadequate for this end, and need to be replaced by epistemologies concerned with the mapping of contexts (Gadalla & Cooper 1978) and facilitating understanding of the patterns of systemic relationships inherent in the ecological nature of those contexts. Thus, as far as research in organization theory is concerned, the contextual approach would stress a need to understand how organizations and environment evolve together, rather than presuming that the adaptation of organization to environment is one way, as the organismic metaphor tends to presume. The contextual approach is not concerned with the notion of causality, which underlies positivist epistemology, because it becomes impossible to find a point at which causal forces begin. The nature of interaction and feedback between elements within a contextual field is such that there are always causes, which cause causes to cause causes (Wilden 1972, p. 39). The beginning of systemic wisdom lies in an awareness that relationships change in concert and cannot be reduced to a set of determinate laws and propositions, as positivist epistemology would have it. A view of social reality as a contextual field carries with it distinctive requirements as to what constitutes an adequate epistemology.

Reality as a Realm of Symbolic Discourse
The next position along our continuum, which characterizes the social world as a realm of symbolic discourse, implies yet another set of epistemological requirements. Emphasis is now placed on understanding the nature and patterning of the symbols through which individuals negotiate their social reality. It is an epistemological position that rejects the idea that the social world can be represented in terms of deterministic relationships, in favor of a view that knowledge, understanding, and explanations of social affairs must take account of

how social order is fashioned by human beings in ways that are meaningful to them. This epistemological position, which often draws on the metaphors of theatre (Goggman 1959; Silverman 1970) or culture (Pondy & Mitroff 1979; Turner 1971), emphasizes how social situations should be researched in a manner that reveals their inner nature. Thus, within the context of organizations there may be a concern for understanding the roles that language, symbols, and myths play in the shaping of any given reality, and a concern for generating ethnographic accounts of specific situations that yield insight with regard to the way reality works. The epistemology involved here does not hold that the findings thus obtained would be universally generalizable, but it does regard them as providing nonetheless insightful and significant knowledge about the nature of the social world. Such knowledge is inevitably seen as being relative and specific to the immediate context and situation from which it is generated, building what Glaser and Strauss call "substantive theory" (1967).

Reality as a Social Construction The epistemology that views reality as a social construction focuses on analyzing the specific processes through which reality is created. Here, reality resides in the process through which it is created, and possible knowledge is confined to an understanding of that process. Thus emphasis tends to be on the metaphors of text (Ricoeur 1971), accomplishment (e.g., Garfinkel 1967), and language game (e.g., Winch, 1958) as means of generating insight regarding the methods through which individuals make sense of their situation, thus creating and sustaining a semblance of reality. Garfinkel's term *ethnomethodology* aptly characterizes an important aspect of this approach to social inquiry, since the whole aim of inquiry is to understand the *methods* relevant to the production of common-sense knowledge in different (*ethno*) areas of everyday life. The task of epistemology here is to demonstrate the methods used in everyday life to create subjectively an agreed or negotiated social order. As Douglas (1970, p. 18) has indicated, the theoretical orientation that underlies ethnomethodology and other similar approaches to the study of society does not permit the generation of a form of knowledge that meets the demands of positivist epistemology; the ontological position implied here gives rise to an existential mode of social analysis the adequacy of which must be judged on quite different epistemological grounds.

Another Look at Extreme Subjectivism

The most subjectivist position on the continuum presented in our tables also carries with it its own particular grounds for knowledge. As has already been indicated in our general discussion of the nature of subjectivist epistemology, knowledge here rests within subjective experience. The appreciation of world phenomena is seen as being dependent on the ability to understand the way in which human beings shape the world from inside themselves. Epistemologies consistent with this position draw on a number of different sources. Some draw on the phenomenological tradition deriving from Husserl (1962, 1965) and emphasize the importance of obtaining understanding in terms of the nature of a transcendental form of consciousness. Others emphasize the importance of studying experiential learning phenomenologically (e.g., Torbert 1972, 1976). Yet others draw on non-Western modes of philosophy (e.g., Herriegel 1953). In each case, the grounds for knowledge demand that human beings transcend conventional scientific modes of understanding and begin to appreciate the world in revelatory, but as yet largely uncharted, ways.

It is convenient that we should end our discussion of possible epistemologies with a view rooted in such extreme subjectivism, because it stands in such stark contrast to positivism that many will regard it as antithetical to science. Far from pursuing the ideal of generating "objective" forms of knowledge, in terms of determinate relationships between facts, it denies that such knowledge is possible. Yet we have arrived at that position by merely following the epistemological implications of a gradual change in ontological assumptions. In so doing, we have sought to demonstrate how the whole of scientific activity is based on assumptions. Positivism follows from one particular set of ontological assumptions, as naturally as antipositivist epistemologies follow from others.

THE ISSUE OF METHODOLOGY

The case for qualitative research in social science begins as one departs from the objectivist extreme of our subjective-objective continuum. The quantitative methods used in the social sciences, which draw principally on the methods of the natural sciences, are appropriate for capturing a view of the social world as a concrete structure. In manipulating ''data'' through sophisticated quantitative approaches, such as multivariate statistical analysis, social scientists are in effect attempting to freeze the social world into structured immobility and to reduce the role of human beings to elements subject to the influence of a more or less deterministic set of forces. They are presuming that the social world lends itself to an objective form of measurement, and that the social scientist can reveal the nature of that world by examining lawful relations between elements that, for the sake of accurate definition and measurement, have to be abstracted from their context. The large-scale empirical surveys and detailed laboratory experiments that dominate much social research stand as examples of the principal types of method operating on assumptions characteristic of the objectivist extreme of our continuum.

Once one relaxes the ontological assumption that the world is a concrete structure, and admits that human beings, far from merely responding to the social world, may actively contribute to its creation, the dominant methods become increasingly unsatisfactory, and indeed, inappropriate. For if one recognizes that the social world constitutes some form of open-ended process, any method that closes the subject of study within the confines of a laboratory, or merely contents itself with the production of narrow empirical snapshots of isolated phenomena at fixed points in time, does not do complete justice to the nature of the subject. The very nature of the phenomena under investigation challenges the utility of such methodological closure. Historical change, contextual fields of information, and processes through which human beings engage in symbolic modes of discourse, create their reality, and project themselves from the transcendental to more prosaic realms of experience, can be captured and measured only through means of static techniques and only in the most partial and limited of ways. Different approaches and methods are required for studying these phenomena, and more often than not they focus on qualitative rather than quantitative features of the subject of study. Quantitative techniques may have an important but only partial role to play in the analysis and understanding of the process of social change, and in defining the informational properties of a cybernetic field; how-

ever, their utility is much more restricted in the more subjectivist positions identified on our continuum. The requirement for effective research in these situations is clear: scientists can no longer remain as external observers, measuring what they see; they must move to investigate from within the subject of study and employ research techniques appropriate to that task.

Many such techniques offer themselves as a basis for qualitative forms of investigation, each appropriate to different kinds of assumptions about ontology and human nature. These techniques have been forged by generations of social scientists who have long recognized the limitation of narrowly based quantitative methods and the positivist search for determinate laws and regularities as a basis for effective research. Historical methods of comparative analysis for capturing process and change, cybernetic methods for mapping fields of information, ethnography, language analysis, experiential learning, collaborative inquiry, phenomenological reduction and ''bracketing'' as a basis for appreciating phenomena in consciousness—all have their role to play within the context of the assumptions on which they have been developed. It would be tempting to demonstrate the precise way in which different techniques such as participant observation, content analysis, in-depth interviewing, biography, linguistic analysis, and psychotherapy fit the detailed scheme of analysis presented in Tables 1 and 2. But this would be to oversimplify the issues involved, and serve as a potential disservice, because any given technique often lends itself to a variety of uses according to the orientation of the researcher. For example, participant observation in the hands of a positivist may be used to document the number and length of interactions within a setting, but in the hands of an action theorist the technique may be used to explore the realms of subjective meaning of those interactions. This technique can be made to serve research requirements consistent with many different positions along the subjective-objective continuum. The same can be said of the other techniques referred to above; their precise nature ultimately depends on the stance of the researcher, and on how the researcher chooses to use them. As Geertz has noted in relation to ethnography:

From one point of view, that of the textbook, doing ethnography is establishing rapport, selecting informants, transcribing texts, taking genealogies, mapping fields, keeping a diary, and so on. But it is not these things, techniques, and received procedures that define the enterprise. What defines it is the kind of intellectual effort it is (1973, p. 6).

The virtues of techniques and methods cannot be determined and categorized in the abstract, because their precise nature and significance is shaped within the context of the assumptions on which the social scientist acts. It is for this reason that our presentation of methodological perspectives in Table 1, and in the above discussion, seeks to highlight broad differences in methodological approach rather than the place of specific techniques.

The range of possible approaches to qualitative research indicates clearly that the dichotomization between quantitative and qualitative methods is a rough and oversimplified one. Qualitative research stands for an approach rather than a particular set of techniques, and its appropriateness—like that of quantitative research—is contingent on the nature of the phenomena to be studied. Our analysis affirms the need for a more reflexive approach to understanding the nature of social research, with a focus on the way in which favored techniques are often linked to underlying assumptions. It emphasizes a need to approach discussions of methodology in a way that highlights the vital link between theory and method—between the world view to which the researcher subscribes, the type of research question posed, and the technique that is to be adopted as a basis for research. All these issues are related in the most fundamental of ways.

A preoccupation with methods on their own account obscures the link between the assumptions that the researcher holds and the overall research effort, giving the illusion that it is the methods themselves, rather than the orientations of the human researcher, that generate particular forms of knowledge. The development of organization theory, like other social science disciplines, would be better served if researchers were more explicit about the nature of the beliefs they bring to their subject of study. Much of the debate and criticism over methodology involves researchers who are failing to communicate with one another because they hold varying basic assumptions about their subject. When the varying assumptions become explicit, less effort can be devoted to arguing about

the relative superiority of this method over that, and greater effort devoted to more basic issues.

Everything that has been said here points to a neglected feature of *all* social research—that it is based on implicit and largely untested ground assumptions. All the ontological positions and views of human nature considered in this [reading] offer plausible, or at least useful, insights with regard to the nature of the social world. Indeed, it is the fact that they do that accounts for their presence and robustness within contemporary social science. The really important methodological issues revolve around the problems of testing the grounds of these rival views. For the most part, social scientists have been so concerned with generating research that articulates a view of the world consistent with their underlying assumptions that the more fundamental need to test these assumptions has passed almost unobserved. Here rests the main challenge of our analysis. We are calling for a focus of attention on the ground assumptions of social theory and research in order to transcend the abstract debate about methodology on its own account and the abstracted forms of empiricism, both qualitative and quantitative, that dominate the contemporary scene.

REFERENCES

Bateson, G. *Steps to an ecology of mind.* New York: Ballantine, 1972.

Brown, R. H. *A poetic for sociology.* Cambridge: At the University Press, 1977.

Burns, T., & Stalker, G. M. *The management of innovation.* London: Tavistock, 1961.

Burrell, G., & Morgan, G. *Sociological paradigms and organizational analysis.* London: Heinemann Educational Books, 1979.

Douglas, J. D. *Understanding everyday life.* Chicago: Aldine, 1970.

Emery, F. E., & Trist, E. J. The causal texture of organizational environments, *Human Relations,* 1965, *18*(1), 21–32.

Gadalla, I. E., & Cooper, R. Towards an epistemology of management. *Social Science Information,* 1978, *17*(3), 349–383.

Garfinkel, H. *Studies in ethnomethodology*. Englewood Cliffs, N.J.: Prentice-Hall, 1967.

Geertz, C. *The interpretation of cultures*. New York: Basic Books, 1973.

Glaser, B. G., & Strauss, A. L. *The discovery of grounded theory*. Chicago: Aldine, 1967.

Goffman, E. *The presentation of self in everyday life*. New York: Doubleday, 1959.

Herriegel, E. *Zen in the art of archery*. New York: Pantheon, 1953.

Husserl, E. *Ideas*. New York: Collier, 1962.

Husserl, E. *Phenomenology and the crisis of philosophy*. New York: Harper Torchbooks, 1965.

Morgan, G. *Cybernetics and organization theory: Epistemology or technique?* Unpublished manuscript, 1979.

Morgan, G. Paradigms, metaphors, and puzzle solving in organization theory. *Administrative Science Quarterly,* 1980, *25*(4), 605–622.

Pondy, L. R., & Mitroff, I. I. Open system models of organization. *Research in organizational behavior*. Greenwich, Conn.: JAI Press, 1979.

Pugh, D. S., & Hickson, D. J. *Organizational structure in its context (Vol. 1)*. Farnborough, Eng.: Saxon House, 1976. (a)

Pugh, D. S., Hickson, D. J. *Organizational structure: Extensions and replications (Vol. 2)*. Farnborough, Eng.: Saxon House, 1976. (b)

Ricoeur, P. The model of the text: Meaningful action considered as a text. *Social Research,* 1971, *38,* 529–562.

Schon, D. *The displacement of concepts*. London: Tavistock, 1963.

Silverman, D. *The theory of organizations*. London: Heinemann, 1970.

Skinner, B. F. *Science and human behavior*. New York: Macmillan, 1953.

Skinner, B. F. *Verbal behavior*. New York: Macmillan, 1957.

Torbert, W. R. *Learning from experience*. New York: Columbia University Press, 1972.

Torbert, W. R. *Creating a community of inquiry*. Wiley Interscience, 1976.

Turner, B. A. *Exploring the industrial subculture*. London: Macmillan, 1971.

Wilden, A. *System and structure: Essays in communication and exchange*. London: Tavistock, 1972.

Winch, P. *The idea of a social science*. London: Routledge & Kegan Paul, 1958.

DISCUSSION QUESTIONS

This article emphasizes that most researchers tend to neglect the implicit, untested assumptions on which they conduct their research. We hope that professional colleagues reading this article are stimulated to *clarify* the basic assumptions about knowledge and human nature that drive their own inquiry and to *examine critically* how those assumptions influence the way they pursue research issues. We are asking researchers to reflect on the hidden foundations from which they come to define some research questions as interesting and worthwhile as well as how they are led to choose certain methodological orientations over others.

A general discussion may be stimulated by asking: What is the significance of the argument developed in this paper for marketing theory and research? What problems are amenable to more objectivist orientations? What problems are amenable to more subjectivist orientations? Because our paper stresses the link between the researcher (his or her ground assumptions) and the researched (the kinds of questions explored), a serious discussion of this article must ultimately include self-reflection on the part of readers regarding their own ways of seeing their subject of study and how these ways of seeing facilitate and limit their research.

PREFACE TO

"Designing Research for Application"

The immediate impetus for this reading was a position paper by Robert Ferber appearing in the *Journal of Consumer Research* in 1977. Ferber—at that time the editor of the journal—argued cogently and trenchantly that researchers too often conducted research by convenience rather than with respect for the validity of their procedures. In his remarks, he echoed and crystalized thoughts that have been expressed in a number of articles on research methodology over the years. One example, and a major one, of Ferber's criticisms has to do with the use of samples of students in research. His contention was that such samples are not representative of the population at large and that they are used only because of their easy availability to researchers.

On first glance, and from some points of view, it appears obvious that methods, such as using student samples rather than randomly selected samples, are not good research practice. Yet, many experienced researchers have had doubts that the issues involved are quite so simple. Consider the case against homogeneous student samples in somewhat more detail. If the researcher has a question such as "For any universe of people, what is the percentage ownership of dogs?," the question clearly calls for some statistical sampling from that universe. The sample asked about dog ownership ought to be representative of the larger population.

But what if the researcher has a larger, more enduring question? In fact, suppose the researcher

has a theory—say she believes people who have certain personality traits are likely to own products, such as dogs and the like. Notice that it makes little sense to frame the question here in terms drawing a random sample. The question is universal. It applies to everyone. The theory says that a person's personality traits cause certain buying behaviors. The question can be tested with any group of people. There is nothing in the theory to suggest that it applies only to some particular group. Therefore, a student sample constitutes perfectly good research methodology, and as it turns out, there is much to recommend it.

On reflection, we came to the conclusion that research methodology must be considered from the point of view of the question being asked. Different procedures may be appropriate for different kinds of questions. The issues involved are complex and in need of much more debate. This reading along with articles that followed its original publication in the *Journal of Consumer Research* are our attempt to point out this complexity and to encourage debate.*

---

*Related pieces include: Calder, B. J., L. W. Phillips, and A. M. Tybout (1982), "Concept of External Validity," *Journal of Consumer Research*, Vol. 9, No. 3, pp. 240–44; Calder, B. J., L. W. Phillips, and A. M. Tybout (1983), "Beyond External Validity," *Journal of Consumer Research*, Vol. 10, No. 1, pp. 112–114.

25

DESIGNING RESEARCH FOR APPLICATION*

BOBBY J. CALDER
LYNN W. PHILLIPS
ALICE M. TYBOUT

INTRODUCTION

There is always the expectation in conducting research that the findings ultimately will be useful in addressing situations beyond the one studied. Yet, there exists a concern that much of consumer research, and behavioral research in general, is not generalizable. It frequently is argued that research procedures, particularly the use of student subjects and laboratory settings, necessarily limit the application of findings. Underlying this contention is a failure to recognize that generalizability is not a single issue. Two distinct types of application may be identified in consumer research. The purpose of this paper is to examine the two types of application, and to specify their implications for research design.

The first type of generalizability, which we term *effects application,* maps observed data directly into events beyond the research setting. That is, the specific effects obtained are expected to mirror findings that would be observed if data were collected for other populations and settings in the real world.[1] The second type, which we term *theory application,* uses only scientific theory to explain events beyond the research setting. Effects observed in the research are employed to assess the status of theory. But, it is the theoretical explanation that is expected to be generalizable and not the particular effects obtained.

The paper begins by elaborating the distinction between the goals of effects application and theory application. Then, the ramifications of this distinction are discussed by addressing the following questions:

Source: Reprinted with permission from the *Journal of Consumer Research,* 8 (September), 1981, 197–207.

    *The authors thank Joel Cohen, Claes Fornell, Louis W. Stern, and Brian Sternthal for comments on earlier drafts of this paper.

- What specific research procedures are appropriate when each type of application is intended?
- What are the resulting implications of these differences in research procedures for methodological controversies in the literature regarding the use of student subjects and laboratory settings?
- What philosophical assumptions underlie each type of application, and what then should be done to improve our ability to make each type?

In examining these issues, it is shown that the two types of application lead to different priorities when designing studies. It is argued that the failure to distinguish between the research designs optimum for each type has led to inappropriate conclusions regarding the impact of student subjects and laboratory settings on generalizability. Finally, it is observed that, despite the need for both effects application and theory application in consumer research, each rests on assumptions and can be improved by consideration of the validity of these assumptions.

DISTINGUISHING RESEARCH GOALS

Effects application and theory application have common elements as well as distinguishing features. Research seeking either type of generalizability necessarily involves some framework or reasoning that might be loosely referred to as "theory." And in both instances, research entails observations of some "effects" related to the theoretical framework. The distinction lies in whether the researcher's primary goal is to apply the specific effects observed or to apply a more general theoretical understanding. In this section, we examine the goals and procedures for achieving each type of generalization.

Effects application is based on a desire for knowledge about the events and relationships in a particular real-world situation. The primary goal of this type of research (hereafter referred to as "effects research") is to obtain findings that can be applied directly to the situation of interest. A theoretical framework may be used to identify and measure effects.[2] But it is the effects themselves that are generalized rather than being linked by inference to theoretical constructs and the hypothesized theoretical network then used to deduce patterns of outcomes.

Application of effects calls for correspondence procedures. It is necessary to assess effects in a research setting that corresponds to a real-world situation. Complete correspondence is difficult to achieve, however. The mere fact of data collection usually distinguishes the research setting from its real-world counterpart. And, because interest rarely is limited to present situations, temporal differences often exist as well. These differences, and others, between the research setting and the real world are inevitable. Effects application, nonetheless, is characterized by the premise and there is *sufficient* correspondence to expect the effects observed to be repeated in the real world.

In contrast, theory application is based on a desire for scientific knowledge about events and relationships that occur in a variety of real-world situations. The primary goal of such research (hereafter referred to as "theory research") is to identify scientific theories that provide a general understanding of the real world. Theory applications call for falsification test procedures. These procedures are used to test a theory by creating a context and measuring effects within that context that have the potential to disprove or refute the theory. The research context and effects are not of interest in their own right. Their significance lies in the information that they provide about the theory's adequacy. Theories that repeatedly survive rigorous falsification attempts are accepted as scientific explanation (subject to further more stringent testing), and are candidates for application.[3] Scientific theories typically are universal and, therefore, can explain any real-world situation within their domain.

The actual application of theory entails using the scientific explanation to design a program or intervention predicted to have some effect in the real world. In a marketing context, the intervention may take the form of a product, price, communication strategy, etc. It is crucial to note that, whatever the strategy, the process of translating from theory to intervention is necessarily a creative one. Theories neither specify how their abstract constructs can be embodied in real-world interventions nor identify the level(s) that uncontrolled theoretical variables will assume in a particular application. Moreover, theories are always incomplete—they deal with a subset of variables that exist in the real world. Consequently, the design process must rely on some assumptions about the operation of both theoretical and nontheoretical variables.

Because intervention design is creative, basing an intervention on theory that has survived rigorous falsification attempts is not sufficient to ensure that the intervention will yield the theoretically predicted outcome. Separate falsification procedures are required to test a theory and a theory-based intervention. Perhaps an example can best illustrate this. Theories of aerodynamics explain the processes underlying flight. It is not possible, however, to design an airplane solely from aerodynamic theory. Any number of stress studies and the like are necessary to calibrate the theory to conditions in a particular real-world situation. These studies, which we term efforts at intervention falsification, systematically subject the intervention to conditions that might cause it to fail in a particular situation. If the intervention does not perform as predicted by the theory, then its weaknesses are exposed. As in theory testing, failures are more informative than successes. But, the failure of an intervention need not imply inadequacies in the theory. Indeed, failure of the theoretical explanation can be implied only when theory falsification procedures are employed.[4] Theory falsification procedures are, thus, the foundation of any effort to apply theory.

If it succeeds, confidence that the intervention is viable increases. As a result, the intervention may be used in the real world. As a result, the intervention may be used in the real world. In contrast to effects application, however, *no attempt is made to generalize any particular outcomes observed in testing the theory or the intervention*. It is only the theoretical relationship that the intervention is presumed to represent that is applied beyond the research setting.

The goals of research leading to effects application and to theory application are summarized in Table 1. As we have indicated, different research procedures are necessary to achieve each of these

TABLE 1
Summary of Two Approaches to Applicability

	Effects Application	**Theory Application**
Research goal	To obtain findings that can be generalized directly to a real-world situation of interest.	To obtain scientific theory that can be generalized through the design of theory-based interventions that are viable in the real world.
Research procedure	Generalizing effects requires procedures to ensure that the research setting accurately reflects the real world. These are termed *correspondence procedures*.	Generalizing theory requires two stages of *falsification procedures*. First, *theory falsification procedures* are used to ensure that the abstract theoretical explanation is rendered fully testable. Theories that survive rigorous attempts at falsification are accepted and accorded scientific status.
		Accepted theory is used as a framework for designing an intervention. Then, *intervention falsification procedures* are used to test the intervention under conditions that could cause it to fail in the real world. Only interventions surviving these tests are implemented.

goals. We now examine these research procedures in greater detail.

COMPARISON OF CORRESPONDENCE AND FALSIFICATION PROCEDURES

Effects application relies on research methods not only different from, but also largely incompatible with, the methods leading to theory application.

The former requires correspondence procedures to ensure that all features of the real world are represented in the research setting. The latter requires falsification procedures to ensure, first, that the abstract scientific explanation is rendered fully testable, and, second, that the concrete theory-based intervention is viable under conditions present in the real world.

In this section, research procedures leading to

effects application and those leading to theory application are compared with respect to selecting respondents, operationalizing variables, choosing research settings, and selecting research designs. This entails contrasting correspondence, theory falsification, and intervention falsification procedures. Primary consideration is given to the comparison of correspondence and *theory* falsification procedures because they are maximally different, and their differences are particularly relevant to methodological controversies in the literature. Theory falsification procedures also are emphasized because they lie at the heart of any theory application. Discussion of the distinguishing features of intervention falsification procedures is deferred until the end of the section. (See Table 2 for a comparison of all three procedures.)

Selecting Respondents

When effects application is the goal, correspondence procedures require that research participants match individuals in the real-world setting of interest. Ideally, this is accomplished by carefully defining the relevant population for the effects of interest, and then employing in the investigation a strictly representative sample of individuals from this target population.[5] This procedure is necessary if any generalization from the sample to the population is to be statistically valid. But, because strict statistical sampling often is not feasible, other procedures may be invoked to enhance the representativeness of individuals in the research. For example, it may be possible to replicate the study with different subgroups of the target population. Alternatively, one might purposively sample individuals

TABLE 2
Comparison of Research Procedures Optimal for Correspondence, Theory Falsification, and Intervention Falsification

Methodological Issues	Correspondence Procedures	Falsification Procedures	
		Theory	**Intervention**
Selection of respondents	Use a sample statistically representative of the real-world population.	Use a sample homogeneous on nontheoretical variables.	Use a sample that encompasses individual differences that might influence performance of the intervention.
Operationalization of key variables	Operationalize variables in the research to parallel those in the real world.	Ensure that empirical operationalization of theoretical constructs cannot be construed in terms of other constructs.	Operationalize variables to reflect the manner in which an intervention is to be implemented in the real world.
Selection of a research setting	Choose a research setting statistically representative of the environmental variation present in the real world.	Choose a setting that allows operationalization of theoretical constructs and is free of extraneous sources of variation.	Choose a setting encompassing environmental heterogeneity that might influence the performance of the intervention.
Selection of a research design	Use a design that preserves the correspondence between the research environment, and provides the type of information required for decision making (e.g., descriptive, correlational, causal).	Use a design that affords the strongest possible inferences about the relationships between theoretical constructs.	Use a design that affords the strongest possible test of the intervention subject to constraints imposed by the need to represent real-world variation.

who vary on important dimensions that characterize members of the target population. Some degree of representativeness could even be achieved by sampling only the most prevalent type of individual in the target population (Cook & Campbell 1975).

The underlying theoretical framework may be useful in determining important dimensions for any nonrepresentative sample. When alternatives to statistical sampling are employed, however, the application of the results must rest on belief that the sample accurately reflects the population and not on any statistical principle. Thus, confidence in generalizing is severely weakened when statistical sampling is not used.

The criteria are quite different when theory application is the goal. The theory falsification procedures, which underlie this type of generalization, require only that research participants be selected to provide a rigorous test of the theory at issue. Because most scientific theories are universal in scope, any respondent group can provide a test of the theory's predictions (Kruglanski 1973; Webster and Kervin 1971).[6] The ideal theory falsification procedure, however, is to employ maximally homogeneous respondents.[7] This entails sampling from groups of individuals that are similar on dimensions likely to influence the variables of theoretical interest. (E.g., for some theories, students or housewives with similar profiles on relevant dimensions may qualify as homogeneous respondents.)

Homogeneous respondents are desired for two reasons. First, they permit more exact theoretical predictions than may be possible with a heterogeneous group. For instance, by employing a homogeneous student sample it might be possible to predict that purchases of a particular product known to be used by students would decrease with advertising exposure. In contrast, if a more heterogeneous sample were selected it might be possible only to predict a decline in some broad category of products. The greater variability in behavior associated with a heterogeneous group makes precise predictions more difficult. This makes failure of the theory harder to detect. Thus, heterogeneous respondents may weaken the theory test.

Homogeneous respondents also are preferred because they decrease the chance of making a false conclusion about whether there is covariation between the variables under study. When respondents are heterogeneous with respect to characteristics that affect their responses, the error variance is increased and the sensitivity of statistical tests in identifying the significant relationships declines. Thus, heterogeneous respondents constitute a threat to statistical conclusion validity (Cook and Campbell 1975). They increase the chance of making a Type II error and concluding that a theory was disconfirmed when, in fact, the theoretical relationship existed but was obscured by variability in the data attributable to nontheoretical constructs. By selecting maximally homogeneous samples, or by conducting full or partial replications of the research for each level or "block" of a respondent characteristic believed to inflate error variance, these random sources of error can be controlled, and the likelihood of making a Type II error decreased (Cook and Campbell 1975; Winer 1971). As a result, the researcher can be more confident that any negative results reflect failure of the theoretical explanation.

It should be noted that nothing in the theory falsification procedure rules out statistical sampling from a relevant population. But a representative sample is not required because *statistical* generalization of the findings is *not* the goal. It is the theory that is applied beyond the research setting. The research sample need only allow a test of the theory. And, any sample within the theory's domain (e.g., any relevant sample), not just a representative one, can provide such a test.

In summary, effects application requires correspondence between the research sample and the population of interest. This is best achieved through statistical sampling. Only such sampling justifies statistical generalization of the research findings. In contrast, theory application requires a research sample that permits falsification of the theory. Although any sample in the theory's domain can potentially falsify the theory, homogeneous samples are preferred because they typically provide a stronger test of the theory. Only the theory is applied and its applicability is determined by its scientific status, not by statistical sampling principles.

Operationalizing Independent and Dependent Variables

Whether the goal is effects application or theory application, valid operationalizations of the independent and dependent variables are necessary. The two types of application differ, however, in the nature of the variables they strive to capture and, thus, in their criteria and procedures for achieving this objective. When the goal is theory application, theory falsification procedures require that the operationalization of constructs (i.e., the independent and dependent variables) render the theory testable. This involves making certain that there is a high degree of correspondence between the empirical operationalizations and the abstract concepts they intend to represent, and that the empirical indicators used to represent the theory's constructs cannot be construed in terms of other constructs. This is necessary to ensure that any failure to disconfirm the theory is not due to the use of empirical operationalizations not measuring the theoretical constructs and, thus, not testing the relationship of interest. This mislabeling of operationalizations in the theory-relevant terms is referred to as a threat to the construct validity of research results (Cook and Campbell 1975).[8]

Attaining construct validity in theory research requires rigorous definition of the theoretical constructs so that empirical measures can be tailored to them. Further, because single exemplars of any construct always contain measurement components that are irrelevant to the theoretical construct of interest, validity is enhanced by employing multiple operationalizations of each construct (Campbell and Fiske 1959; Cook and Campbell 1975). Multiple exemplars of each construct should demonstrably share common variance attributable to the target construct, and should differ from each other in unique ways (Campbell and Fiske 1959). Such "multiple operationalism" allows one to test whether a theoretical relationship holds even though measurement error is present in each operationalization (Bagozzi 1979).

When the goal is effects application, the operationalization of variables is determined by the need for correspondence. Indices of the independent and dependent variables in the research setting are chosen to parallel events in the real world. They are not tailored to abstract theoretical constructs that these variables may be presumed to represent.

Similarity between the operationalizations of variables and their real-world counterparts is maximized by using naturally occurring events in the target setting as independent variables, and naturally occurring behaviors in the target setting as dependent variables (Tunnell 1977; Webb, Camp-

bell, Schwartz, and Sechrest 1966). Events and behaviors are considered to be "natural" if they occur in the real world. This does not necessarily imply that such events will be uncontrolled by the researcher. Price, advertising strategy, etc., are determined by decision-makers; thus, their systematic variation for research purposes would not compromise naturalness, provided that their variations reflected any real-world constraints (e.g., any practical constraints preventing disentangling related components of a marketing program in the real world). On occasion, however, the researcher may be concerned with effects on variables for which no naturally occurring measures are available, for example, attitudes. Then, measures must be designed to assess these variables, while still preserving the correspondence between the research setting and the real world. Generally, this is achieved by making these measures as unobstrusive as possible. Regardless of the variables being examined, measurement error is a concern. Therefore, multiple measures of variables also are desirable in research leading to effects application.

The objectives when operationalizing variables for theory research are largely incompatible with the objectives when operationalizing variables for effects research. As just noted, the correspondence needed for effects application is achieved best by employing naturally occurring events and behaviors as variables, whenever possible. However, naturally occurring events and behaviors generally are inappropriate variables in research testing theory. They do not permit the researcher much latitude in tailoring operationalizations to theoretical constructs. Moreover, naturally occurring events often serve as indicators of a complex package of several theoretically distinct constructs. Rarely can they be taken as indicators of a single unidimensional construct. Theory falsification procedures aim to untangle these packages into several distinct variables that can be labeled in theoretical terms. Correspondence procedures aim to preserve these packages as single variables to reflect events in the real world more accurately. Thus, these two types of construct validity typically cannot be pursued simultaneously.

Choosing a Research Setting

The goals of effects application and theory application also imply different criteria in choosing a research setting. The correspondence procedures associated with effects application lead to maximizing the similarity between the research setting and the real-world situation of interest (Ellsworth 1977; Tunnel 1977). This real-world situation usually is heterogeneous on a number of background factors. For example, it may include variation in the time of day, the season, the complexity of the products involved, or the characteristics of salespersons who deliver influence attempts. To enhance transfer of the research findings to the real world, the research setting must reflect the heterogeneity of the background factors. Ideally, a random sampling of background factors present in the real world would be employed (Brunswik 1956). From a statistical perspective, only this method of treating the heterogeneity in such factors allows generalizing the results from the research to the real world.

Often it is infeasible, if not impossible, to represent systematically all the variation in the real-world setting within a single study. In such circumstances, the researcher may try to identify the background factors most likely to impact the effects of interest. The underlying theoretical framework may be used for this purpose. Then, these factors may be represented in several ways. The study may be replicated in settings representing different levels of these background factors. Alternatively, variation on significant factors may be built into a single study without randomly sampling such factors. Or, some degree of representativeness might be achieved by including only the most frequent or typical setting factors found in the real world (Cook and Campbell 1975). When these approaches are employed, however, generalization of the effects must rest on judgment that all important background factors have been properly represented, and not on a statistical principle.

Regardless of which procedure for treating setting heterogeneity is followed, representativeness is best achieved through field research. Field research refers to ''any setting which respondents do not perceive to have been set up for the primary purpose of conducting research'' (Cook and Campbell 1975, p. 224). The idea is to conduct the research in the real world with as little intrusion as possible. When effects research must be conducted in nonfield (i.e., laboratory) contexts, efforts should be made to incorporate the critical background factors from the real-world setting into the laboratory setting (Sawyer, Worthing, and Sendak 1979).

The theory falsification procedures associated with theory application lead to selection of an entirely different research setting. To test a theory, its constructs must be tied to a particular set of observables in a specific circumstance. It is not important, however, that these events be representative of some set of events that occur in another setting. Rather, the particular events at issue in the research setting are only important as operationalizations of the theory. What is required is that a theory's operationalization in the test setting allow it to be falsified. Typically, this involves choosing a research setting relatively free of extraneous sources of variation, for example, free of variation on variables not of theoretical interest, and free of variation in treatment implementation. Extraneous variation can produce spurious effects on the dependent variable, and, at a minimum, inflates error variance (Cook and Campbell 1975). To the extent that theoretically irrelevant factors are at work, significant relationships between the phenomena under study may be obscured and the risk of Type II error may be increased. Insulated test settings miminize such irrelevancies.

Most often, the best procedure for reducing the number of random irrelevancies is to employ a controlled laboratory setting. In contrast to field settings, laboratory settings facilitate the use of standardized procedures and treatment implementation, and allow the researcher to control rigorously the stimuli impinging upon respondents. Moreover, laboratory settings possess other inherent advantages, relative to field settings, in conducting the strongest possible test of a theory. Homogeneous respondents are obtained more easily in the laboratory, because the investigator typically has greater control over who participates in a study. Similarly, the laboratory provides greater latitude for tailoring empirical operationalizations to the constructs they are meant to represent, because operationalizations in the laboratory are only limited by the ingenuity of the investigator, and not by naturally occurring variation and real-world constraints. And, the laboratory possess greater potential for achieving multiple operationalizations of independent and dependent variables, because the expense associated with exposing individuals to a number of independent variables and administering a number of dependent variable responses typically is lower for the laboratory than for the field. Thus, laboratory settings generally are better geared to achieving high degrees of statistical conclusion validity and theoretical construct validity.

The advantages of the laboratory in terms of increasing statistical power and enhancing construct validity are not without limit. Tests of certain theoretical hypotheses may lead to the field if they involve variables not easily examined in laboratory settings. Thus, the advantages of insulated settings may sometimes have to be given up in order to achieve adequate empirical realizations of a theory's constructs. Nevertheless, such limits to the utility of employing laboratory settings in theory tests do not contradict our thesis. They simply reaffirm the general rule that settings yielding the strongest test of the theory should be employed when the goal is theory application. In many cases, this will be the laboratory.

Selecting a Research Design

The choice of a research setting either determines or is determined by the research design to be used. For example, laboratory research is usually associated with "true" experimental designs wherein respondents are randomly assigned to treatments (Campbell and Stanley 1966; Cook and Campbell 1975). When the goal is theory application, and theory testing is being conducted, true experimental designs are preferred because they allow the strongest test. Unlike other designs, such as the survey method or the case study, true experiments permit the investigator to minimize the possibility that third variables cause any observed relation between the independent and dependent variables. This is necessary to ensure that any failure to disconfirm the theory linking the variables is not due to the spurious impact of irrelevant third variables. Moreover, true experiments allow the investigator to establish that the independent variable precedes the dependent variable in time, thus ruling out the possibility that the dependent variable initiates changes in the independent variable, rather than vice versa. The capacity for establishing temporal antecedence and for ruling out third variable rival explanations enables true experiments to elim-

inate most plausible threats to internal validity, that is, threats to the conclusion that a demonstrated statistical relationship between the independent and dependent variables implies causality (Cook and Campbell 1975). This is a critical aspect of theory falsification procedures because most theories are stated in a causal framework. True experiments, by ranking higher than other research designs on internal validity, allow the strongest test of causality.[9]

The general preference for true experimental procedures does not mean that all research testing theory will employ such designs. On occasion, the independent variables of interest [are] not subject to manipulation by the researcher, and conditions prevent random assignment of respondents to different treatments. When this occurs, correlational or quasi-experimental designs must be employed. In certain cases, these designs permit causal inferences (Bagozzi 1979; Cook and Campbell 1975), and even when they do not, they are often of sufficient probing value to be worth employing. However, research designs of less efficiency than true experiments should be used only when true experiments are not feasible (Campbell and Stanley 1966). This is in keeping with the criterion and the research design chosen be the one that offers the strongest test of the theory.

When the goal is effects application, the need for correspondence necessitates different research design priorities. The design depends on the nature of the event structure of interest and the particular information needed regarding that structure. If it is important to establish the causal sequence of the events in the real world, then true experiments are preferred whenever possible. Yet, true experiments may not be feasible to examine certain variables. And, true experiments may seriously compromise the naturalness of the research setting. In these circumstances, or when causal statements regarding the event structure are not required as a basis for decision making, research seeking effects application should opt for correlational or quasi-experimental designs. Such designs are far less intrusive and, hence, enhance correspondence between the research setting and the real-world situation.

Summary

Effects application and theory application differ sharply in the research procedures upon which they depend. When effects application is the goal, correspondence procedures are required to ensure that the findings are generalizable to some real-world situation of interest. These procedures allow *nothing* to be done that might cause an important mismatch between the research and the real-world situation. Ideally, this goal is achieved by employing a representative sample of respondents, using natural events and behaviors as variables in a field context, and selecting a research design that preserves the natural setting (see Table 2). To the extent that similarity between the research and the real world is achieved, the empirical outcomes observed may be applied in the real world.

When theory application is the goal, falsification procedures are required to assess the scientific status of the theory. These procedures allow *anything* to be done that will ensure a rigorous test of the theory. Such a test is provided when internal, construct, and statistical-conclusion validity are maximized. As summarized in Table 2, this entails selecting homogeneous respondent samples, tailoring multiple empirical operationalizations to the abstract theoretical concepts that they are meant to represent, and conducting true experiments in laboratory or other settings that are relatively free of extraneous sources of variation. If research provides a strong test of the theory, and if the theory escapes refutation, then the theory is accepted as a scientific explanation of real-world events.

Theory application is done through the design of a theory-based intervention. But, before such an intervention is implemented in the real world, intervention falsification procedures are required to test its performance. Like theory falsification procedures, intervention falsification procedures seek the most rigorous test possible. But, in contrast to a theory test, a rigorous intervention test is not provided by minimizing variation on nontheoretical factors. Instead, such a test is obtained by exposing the intervention to real-world variability that might cause it to fail. Thus, internal, construct, and statistical-conclusion validity are pursued within limits created by the need to reflect important dimensions of the real world. As summarized in Table 2, this entails selecting research respondents and choosing a research setting that are heterogeneous on variables likely to affect intervention outcomes, operationalizing variables to reflect the manner in which the intervention would be implemented in the real world, and employing the most rigorous research design possible given the need to capture aspects of real-world variability. Only interventions that yield outcomes predicted by the theory in such a test situation are applied in the real world.

Although superficially similar, intervention falsification procedures and correspondence procedures are distinct. Correspondence procedures demand that the research provide an *accurate representation* of the real-world situation of interest. This is necessary because the goal is to apply the particular effects observed in the research to the real world. Intervention falsification procedures only require that the research subject the intervention to *levels of variability* that it might encounter in the real world. The research need not mirror the real world because it is the theoretical relationship represented by the intervention, and not the particular effects observed in the research, that is applied.

THE METHODOLOGICAL LITERATURE

Much confusion in the methodological literature has resulted from a lack of realization that different procedures are optimal for achieving the two types of generalizability. This confusion is particularly evident in criticism of laboratory studies with student respondents. It is instructive to review this criticism with the research procedures underlying effects application and theory application in mind.

Objections to laboratory studies have traditionally centered on the "artificiality" of the findings obtained (Aronson and Carlsmith 1968; Opp 1970; Webster and Kervin 1971). But in recent years these objections have manifested themselves in two specific lines of criticism (Kruglanski 1975). One has been the concern that because much research employs student, volunteer, and other convenience samples, it cannot be generalized to broader population groups. In consumer research, this concern has prompted a number of investigations attempting to determine whether students' responses to marketing stimuli are representative of the responses made by individuals comprising some larger target population, such as housewives, businessmen, etc. (Albert 1967; Cunningham, Anderson, and Murphy 1974; Enis, Cox, and Stafford 1972; Khera and Benson 1970; Park and Lessig

1977; Sheth 1970; Shuptrine 1975). Moreover, it has led to the appeal for use of more relevant and more representative subject samples in laboratory research (Ferber 1977; McNemar 1946; Rosenthal and Rosnow 1969b; Schultz 1969; Shuptrine 1975) Relevance refers to the need for samples or target populations appropriate to the topic under investigation (Ferber 1977). Representativeness refers to how accurately the sample reflects characteristics of the target population.

A second major line of criticism has been the argument that, because the laboratory is characterized by unique features not found in the real world, laboratory studies necessarily yield nongeneralizable results. The unique features most commonly referred to include the unrealistic character of the interaction between the experimenter and the subject (Orne 1962; Reicken 1962; Sawyer 1975; Silverman 1968; Venkatesan 1967), and the unrealistic contextual features that make up the laboratory background (Banks 1965; Cox and Enis 1969; Green 1966; Uhl 1966). For example, it is often contended that studies of persuasion in laboratory settings differ from real-world persuasion situations in terms of such contextual factors as audience involvement, attention, noise, exposure time, motivation, and opportunity to make cognitive responses (Gardner 1970; Greenberg 1967; Ray 1977) and, thus, are limited in their relevance to the real world. This argument has been the impetus for suggestions that true experiments be conducted in field settings whenever possible (Banks 1965; Caffyn 1964; Cartwright and Zander 1968, p. 36; McGuire 1969; Ross and Smith 1968; Tunnell 1977; Uhl 1966), and that when laboratory settings are employed, research procedures be altered to take into account the real-world dimensions of the phenomenon under investigation (Fromkin and Streufert 1975; Ray 1977).

When effects application is the goal, the above concerns are well founded. Correspondence between the subjects and the setting used in the research and those in the real world is a necessary condition for effects application. To the extent that the use of student or other convenience samples and laboratory settings undermine this correspondence, applicability of the effects observed is limited. Thus, procedures that enhance the match between the research environment and the real world, such

as the use of relevant representative samples and field settings, are appropriate when effects application is desired.

Yet, when the goal is theory application, the call for research subjects and settings representative of the real world is inappropriate. The foundation of theory application is rigorous theory testing. It is a mistake to assume that the people and events in a theory test must reflect people and events in some real-world situation. Rather, the test circumstance simply must provide the strongest test of the theory possible. Features of the test are only constrained by the requirement that they not undermine the degree to which any demonstrated construct relationship can be generalized to other settings not ruled out by the theory. Any sample is relevant if it permits operationalization within the domain of the theory. Homogeneous convenience samples may thus be employed in theory research. In fact, homogeneous samples are preferred because their use enables more precise predictions and enhances statistical-conclusion validity, thereby increasing the rigor of the theory test.

Similarly, laboratory settings generally are desirable in theory testing research. The controlled environment of the laboratory typically allows the researcher to employ true experimental designs, to tailor variables to abstract theoretical constructs, and to minimize extraneous sources of variation. These features lead to high internal, construct, and statistical-conclusion validity, thereby providing a strong theory test.

The only damaging criticisms of the laboratory setting are those that specify why its unrealistic features might operate as plausible threats to internal, construct, or statistical-conclusion validity. For example, if the artificiality of the laboratory facilitates participants in guessing the experimental hypothesis, then internal validity may be threatened and the theory test weakened. If valid arguments can be made to this effect, generalizability of the observed construct relationship is impaired. Otherwise, the use of insulated environments, standardized procedures, and other "unrealistic" features may constitute perfectly acceptable theory-testing procedures.

Recommendations for alternatives to the controlled laboratory setting, such as the suggestions that true experiments be conducted in field settings or that real-world features be introduced into the laboratory, are detrimental to achieving a rigorous theory test. Conducting true experiments in field settings is likely to reduce internal validity because there are numerous obstacles to forming and maintaining randomly constituted groups in the field (Cook and Campbell 1975). Construct validity also may be lower because tailoring operationalizations to abstract constructs may be difficult in the field. In addition, statistical-conclusion validity is likely to suffer because the field affords less opportunity for using standardized procedures and controlling stimuli.

Likewise, attempts to incorporate real-world features into the laboratory may undermine construct and statistical-conclusion validity. These features can represent plausible sources of distortion regarding the theoretical labeling of the independent variables, as well as uncontrolled sources of error variance in dependent variable responses (Aronson and Carlsmith 1968; Cook and Campbell 1975; Webster and Kervin 1971). Thus, because these strategies could potentially decrease the internal, construct, and statistical-conclusion validity of research results, they should be avoided in theory-testing research whenever possible. Their implementation could compromise the severity of the theory test.

The conclusion is not that variation in people and events found in the real world is irrelevant to theory application, however. On the contrary, it simply assumes a different role than in effects application. In theory application, accepted theory is used to design an intervention. This intervention, then, must be shown to perform successfully in the face of variability that it is likely to encounter in the real world. To test the performance of an intervention, it may be implemented in an uncontrolled environment such as a field setting, or it may be exposed to extreme levels of important variables in a controlled (laboratory) environment. But, as we observed earlier, the test environment need not be *representative* of any particular real-world situation (as is the case when effects application is sought); it only must expose the intervention to stress that could cause it to fail. Repeated failure of interventions based on a particular theory may suggest the need for a better explanation. However, testing procedures for any new theory remain controlled. The applicability of an explanation is never improved by weakening its test.

PHILOSOPHIES UNDERLYING THE TWO TYPES OF APPLICABILITY

Clarification of the procedural implications of the two types of applicability does much to resolve the confusion in the methodological literature. The distinction between effects application and theory application is more than a procedural one however. Also at stake are two basic philosophies of how to go about application. Discussion rarely gets beyond the vague perception of research pursuing effects application as "intuitively practical" and research pursuing theory application as "academically respectable." Not surprisingly, many studies end up trying to embrace both, with little appreciation that they represent different philosophies. Accordingly, it is appropriate to end the present discussion with an explicit statement of the philosophical rationale underlying each approach to application.

Traditionally, the application of effects has rested philosophically on the principle of induction. The notion that observed effects will be repeated in the real world, given the use of correspondence procedures, is an inductive argument. The observation that something has happened is said to imply that it (or something similar) will happen again.

It must be pointed out, however, that, although intuitively plausible, induction turns out, on close examination, to be an extremely hollow form of argument. Induction actually has no basis in logic. With any logical argument, true premises should yield true conclusions. Yet even though the sun has come up every day so far, whether or not it comes up tomorrow is not a matter of logical necessity. True premises may yield a false conclusion. Induction is not a logical argument.

The intuitive appeal of an inductive argument is such that many researchers are willing to subscribe to it as a matter of experience, if not logic. After all, the sun appears to come up every day. Even the appeal from experience, however, is suspect. It amounts to using induction to justify itself. Because induction has seemed to work before, it will work in the future. The circularity of such reasoning is devastating in the case of effects of application. The researcher has only a few observations on which to base conclusions. Conclusions about the real world must really be based on an uncritical faith in induction rather than any experience with observations.

It might seem that the problem of induction could be escaped by resorting to probabilistic conclusions. Given observed effects, the occurrence of a real-world event is not proven, but it is made more highly probable. Under any standard concept of probability, however, this turns out to be not very helpful. In principle, the researcher could observe an effect an infinite number of times. The number of observations actually available is obviously finite. Thus, the probability of any effect must be zero if the number of possible observations of the effect is infinite. Probabilities are not meaningful in the context of infinite possiblity.

Our conclusion must be that effects application rests on very soft grounds. While this approach appears to be the epitome of rigorous application, it is mostly a matter of blind faith. Induction itself cannot support going from observed effects to conclusions about the real world.

Effects application might better be viewed as reasoning by analogy. There is no logical principle involved. Rather, outcomes observed in the research are related to outcomes of the real world. If the research conditions seem to be analogous to events in the real world, then the analogy is completed by concluding that observed effects will hold in the real world. Reasoning by analogy depends, not on logic, but on the researcher's insight. Although correspondence procedures may provide some basis for analogy, this process is ultimately qualitative in nature.[10] This argument cannot be pursued here; however, it is our opinion that effects application could be improved by the increased use of qualitative methods (Calder 1977).

In contrast to effects application, theory application rests on the logical principle that it is possible for observed effects to contradict a theory, thereby falsifying it. Theories are tested in situations where they can possibly fail. Only those that survive these tests, then, are accepted and are candidates for application.

The logical principle of falsification requires that theory testing be bound to formal methodological procedures. These procedures are designed to expose the theory to refutation, and should follow directly from the theoretical explanation itself. It is

only where theory fully dictates observation that observation can contradict theory. Thus, qualitative methods are not essential in testing theory.

The falsification procedures employed to test theory are not sufficient to ensure successful theory application however. Accepted theories can provide only a framework for designing interventions. These interventions also must be tested before they are applied in the real world. Again the logic of falsification is invoked. Research procedures are designed to expose the intervention to refutation. These procedures should follow directly from the underlying theory *and* the real-world circumstances that the intervention will face. If the intervention performs as predicted by the theory, it may be implemented. If, however, the intervention does not lead to expected outcomes, it must be modified. Careful assessment of theoretical and nontheoretical variables as part of the testing process may provide insight for this redesign.

Application of theory often stops short of efforts to falsify interventions. It is mistakenly assumed that accepted theories will yield usable interventions without further work. But, whereas such theories do provide efficient frameworks for design, testing the intervention designed is still necessary. Theory application in consumer research would be greatly improved by recognition of the need for, and role of, intervention falsification procedures.[11]

CONCLUSION

Consumer researchers pursue two distinct types of generalizability. One involves the application of specific effects observed in a research setting. The other involves the application of a general scientific theory. Although both types of generalization are tenable, it is important to determine which will be the primary goal prior to designing a study. Effects application and theory application are based on different philosophical assumptions and, therefore, require different research procedures.

Effects application rests on the presumption of correspondence between the research and some real-world situation of interest. If these two situations are analogous, then the outcomes observed in one can be expected to occur in the other. When effects application is the goal, the research subjects, setting, and variables examined must be representative of their real-world counterparts. Any procedures likely to impair the match between the research and the real world, such as convenience samples and laboratory settings, should be avoided. Because objective correspondence is impossible to achieve fully, and can never ensure equivalent *experience,* qualitative insight may assist the researcher in judging whether or not the research experience matches that of the real world.

Theory application rests on the acceptance of the scientific explanation itself. This acceptance is determined by the logical principle of falsification. Theories that survive rigorous efforts at disproof are accepted. The only requirement for research testing theory is that it provide the strongest test possible. Because homogeneous samples and laboratory settings often lead to a stronger test of the theory than heterogeneous samples and field settings, they may be preferred in this type of research. But, theory tests alone are not sufficient for theory application. Accepted theories must be calibrated to the real world through the design and testing of interventions.

In sum, the research procedures optimal for effects application and theory application are incompatible. This does not mean that there cannot be synergy between research pursuing each type of applicability. It does mean that research procedures can only be evaluated with reference to the type of generalizability being pursued. To do otherwise only leads to needless criticism and poor communication within the discipline.

REFERENCES

Albert, Bernard (1967), "Non-businessmen as Surrogates for Businessmen in Behavioral Experiments," *Journal of Business,* 40, 203–7.

Aronson, Elliot, and Carlsmith, J. Merrill (1968), "Experimentation in Social Psychology," in *Handbook of Social Psychology, Vol. 2,* eds. Gardner Lindzey and Elliot Aronson, Reading, Mass.: Addison-Wesley Publishing Co.

Bagozzi, Richard (1980), *Causal Models in Marketing,* New York: John Wiley & Sons.

Banks, Seymout (1965), *Experimentation in Marketing,* New York: McGraw-Hill Book Co.

Brunswik, Egon (1956), *Perception and the Representative Design of Psychological Experiments,* 2nd ed., Berkeley: University of California Press.

Caffyn, J. M. (1964), "Psychological Laboratory Techniques in Copy Research," *Journal of Advertising Research,* 4, 45–50.

Calder, Bobby J. (1977), "Focus Groups and the Nature of Qualitative Marketing Research," *Journal of Marketing Research,* 14, 353–64.

Campbell, Donald, and Fiske, Donald (1959), "Convergent and Discriminant Validation by the Multitrait-Multimethod Matrix," *Psychological Bulletin,* 56, 81–105.

———, and Stanley, John (1966), *Experimental and Quasi-experimental Designs for Research,* Chicago: Rand McNally & Co.

Cartwright, Dorwin, and Zander, Alvin (1968), *Group Dynamics,* New York: Harper and Row.

Cook, Thomas, and Campbell, Donald (1975), "The Design and Conduct of Experiments and Quasi-experiments in Field Settings," in *Handbook of Industrial and Organizational Research,* ed. Martin Dunnette, Chicago: Rand McNally & Co.

Cox, Keith, and Enis, Ben (1969), *Experimentation for Marketing Decisions,* Scranton, Penn.: International Textbook Co.

Cunningham, William, Anderson, W. Thomas, Jr., and Murphy, John (1974), "Are Students Real People?" *Journal of Business,* 48, 399–409.

Ellsworth, Phoebe (1977), "From Abstract Ideas to Concrete Instances: Some Guidelines for Choosing Natural Research Settings," *American Psychologist,* 32, 604–15.

Enis, Ben, Cox, Keith, and Stafford, James (1972), "Students as Subjects in Consumer Behavior Experiments," *Journal of Marketing Research,* 9, 72–4.

Ferber, Robert (1977), "Research by Convenience," *Journal of Consumer Research,* 4, 57–8.

Fromkin, Howard, and Streufert, Siegfried (1975), "Laboratory Experimentation," in *Handbook of Industrial and Organizational Psychology,* ed. Marvin Dunnette, Chicago: Rand McNally & Co.

Gardner, David (1970), "The Distraction Hypothesis in

Marketing,'' *Journal of Advertising Research,* 10, 25–30.

Green, Paul (1966), ''The Role of Experimental Research in Marketing: Its Potentials and Limitations,'' in *Science, Technology, and Marketing,* ed. Raymond Haas, Chicago: American Marketing Association.

Greenberg, Allan (1967), ''Is Communications Research Really Worthwhile?'' *Journal of Marketing,* 31, 48–50.

Khera, Inder, and Benson, James (1970), ''Are Students Really Poor Substitutes for Businessmen in Behavioral Research?'' *Journal of Marketing Research,* 7, 529–32.

Kruglanski, Arie (1973), ''Much Ado About the 'Volunteer Artifacts','' *Journal of Personality and Social Psychology,* 28, 348–54.

――― (1975), ''The Two Meanings of External Invalidity,'' *Human Relations,* 28, 653–9.

Kuhn, Thomas (1970), *The Structure of Scientific Revolutions,* Chicago: University of Chicago Press.

Lakatos, Imre (1970), ''Falsification and the Methodology of Science Research Programs,'' in *Criticism and the Growth of Knowledge,* eds. Imre Lakatos and Alan Musgrave, London: Cambridge University Press.

McGuire, William (1969), ''Theory-Oriented Research in Natural Settings: The Best of Both Worlds for Social Psychology,'' in *Interdisciplinary Relationships in the Social Sciences,* eds. M. Sherif and C. Sherif, Chicago: Aldine Publishing.

McNemar, Quinn (1946), ''Opinion-Attitude Methodology,'' *Psychological Bulletin,* 43, 289–374.

Opp, Karl-Dieter (1970), ''The Experimental Method in the Social Sciences: Some Problems and Proposals for Its More Effective Use,'' *Quality and Quantity,* 34, 39–54.

Orne, Martin (1962), ''On the Social Psychology of the Psychological Experiment with Particular Reference to Demand Characteristics and Other Implications,'' *American Psychologist,* 17, 776–83.

O'Shaughnessy, John, and Ryan, Michael J. (1979), ''Marketing, Science and Technology,'' in *Conceptual and Theoretical Developments in Marketing,* eds. O. C. Ferrell, Stephen Brown, and Charles Lamb, Chicago: American Marketing Association.

Park, C. Whan, and Lessig, V. Parker (1977), ''Students and Housewives: Differences in Susceptibility to Reference Group Influence,'' *Journal of Consumer Research,* 4, 102–10.

Popper, Karl R. (1959), *The Logic of Scientific Discovery,* New York: Harper Torchbooks.

――― (1963), *Conjectures and Refutations,* New York: Harper Torchbooks.

Ray, Michael (1977), ''When Does Consumer Information Processing Actually Have Anything to Do with Consumer Information Processing?'' in *Advances in Consumer Research, Vol. 4,* ed. William Perreault, Jr., Atlanta: Association for Consumer Research.

Riecken, Henry (1962), ''A Program for Research on Experiments in Social Psychology,'' in *Decisions, Values, and Groups, Vol. 2,* ed. Norman Washburn, New York: Pergamon Press, pp. 25–41.

Rosenthal, Robert, and Rosnow, Ralph (1969a), *Artifact in Behavioral Research,* New York: Academic Press.

―――, and Rosnow, Ralph (1969b), ''The Volunteer Subject,'' in *Artifact in Behavioral Research,* eds. Robert Rosenthal and Ralph Rosnow, New York: Academic Press.

Ross, J., and Smith, P. (1968), ''Orthodox Experimental Designs,'' in Methodology in Social Research, ed. Hubert Blalock and Ann Blalock, San Francisco: McGraw-Hill Book Co.

Sawyer, Alan (1975), ''Demand Artifacts in Laboratory Experiments in Consumer Research,'' *Journal of Consumer Research,* 1, 20–30.

―――, Worthing, Parker, and Sendak, Paul (1979), ''The Role of Laboratory Experiments to Test Marketing Strategies,'' *Journal of Marketing,* 43, 60–7.

Schultz, Duane (1969), ''The Human Subject in Psychological Research,'' *Psychological Bulletin,* 72, 214–28.

Sheth, Jagdish (1970), ''Are There Differences in Dissonance Reduction Behavior Between Students and Housewives?'' *Journal of Marketing Research,* 7, 243–5.

Shuptrine, F. Kelly (1975), ''On the Validity of Using Students as Subjects in Consumer Behavior Investigations,'' *Journal of Business,* 48, 383–90.

Silverman, Irwin (1968), "Role-Related Behavior of Subjects in Laboratory Studies of Attitude Change," *Journal of Personality and Social Psychology,* 8, 343–8.

Tunnell, Gilbert (1977), "Three Dimensions of Naturalness: An Expanded Definition of Field Research," *Psychological Bulletin,* 84, 426–77.

Uhl, Kenneth (1966), "Field Experimentation: Some Problems, Pitfalls, and Perspectives," in *Science, Technology, and Marketing,* ed. Raymond Haas, Chicago: American Marketing Association.

Venkatesen, M. (1967), "Laboratory Experiments in Marketing: The Experimenter Effect," *Journal of Marketing Research,* 4, 142–7.

Webb, Eugene, Campbell, Donald, Schwartz, Richard, and Sechrest, Lee (1966), *Unobtrusive Measures: Nonreactive Research in the Social Sciences,* Chicago: Rand McNally & Co.

Webster, Murray, and Kervin, John (9171), "Artificiality in Experimental Sociology," *Canadian Review of Sociology and Anthropology,* 8, 263–72.

Winer, B. J. (1971), *Statistical Principles in Experimental Design,* New York: McGraw-Hill Book Co.

Wright, Peter, and Kriewall, Mary Ann (1980), "State-of-Mind Effects on the Accuracy with Which Utility Functions Predict Marketplace Choice," *Journal of Marketing Research,* 17, 277–94.

NOTES

[1]The term "real world" is employed in reference to all situations not constructed for, or altered by, the conduct of research. It is not meant to imply that research settings do not have their own reality.

[2]The theoretical framework underlying effects research can be either scientific (i.e., a general theory that has survived rigorous testing) or intuitive (i.e., a theory generated to address a particular situation, which may be consistent with informal observations, but which has not undergone any rigorous testing). This is in contrast to theory research, which is restricted to the examination of general scientific theories. Although we subscribe to the view that scientific theory has advantages over intuitive theory even in effects research, this is obviously a debatable issue. Moreover, because this issue is only tangentially related to ones surrounding the conduct and application of effects research, we leave its discussion to some other forum.

[3]It should be noted that the view of theory testing outlined here is a falsificationist one (Popper 1959, 1963). Theories are not proven. They are accepted pending further research. Although many issues surround the falsificationist perspective (Kuhn 1970; Lakatos 1970), they are largely peripheral to the concerns of this paper. The important point is that theory tests must attempt to expose theories to refutation by observed data, and must be conservative in accepting theories that escape refutation.

[4]This is not to say that intervention-falsification procedures might not sometimes suggest theory-falsification procedures. Nor does it mean that in some cases the two procedures might not be identical.

[5]Although for ease in exposition we use the term "individuals" to refer to respondents, the issues discussed apply equally when the units of analysis are groups.

[6]Although any respondent group can be used to test a universal theory, characteristics of the particular group chosen affect, or are affected by, the operationalizations of theory variables. Operationalizations that are relevant for the subject population (Ferber 1977) should be employed to avoid the possibility that Type II errors will weaken the theory test.

[7]An exception to this preference for homogeneity occurs when an individual difference variable that cannot be manipulated by the researcher (e.g., extroversion) is of theoretical interest. Here, testing the theory requires that variability be achieved by sampling individuals who differ on the dimension of interest. This exception is consistent with providing the strongest possible test of the theory.

[8]For a more comprehensive discussion of construct validity, see Bagozzi (1979, Chap. 5).

[9]The major threats to internal validity that remain in laboratory experiments are participants uncovering the hypothesis and responding to it rather than to the independent variables alone, or participants responding to demand characteristics, that is, to inadvertent cues given by the experimenter regarding the appropriate behavior. Procedures such as care-

fully constructed cover stories, between subjects' designs, and "blind" experimenters can be used to reduce the plausibility of these threats; see Rosenthal & Rosnow (1969a) for a discussion of these procedures.

[10]See Wright and Kriewall (1980) for an empirical demonstration of the need for effects research to capture individuals' "state-of-mind" in the real-world setting of interest.

[11]O'Shaughnessy and Ryan's (1979) discussion of the distinction between science and technology in some ways parallels and compelments our discussion of the difference between theory testing and intervention design and testing.

DISCUSSION QUESTIONS

1. In contrast to the position advanced by Calder, Phillips, and Tybout, other researchers have argued that external validity must be a priority even when the researcher's goal is theory testing. To achieve external validity, it is suggested that theory-testing researchers strive to incorporate background factors into their research design and then block on their variables to avoid the problems of increasing extraneous variation and, thus, reduce statistical-conclusion validity. How would Calder, Phillips, and Tybout react to this recommendation?

2. Select a study from either the *Journal of Marketing,* the *Journal of Marketing Research,* or the *Journal of Consumer Research.* Discuss how this study should be classified according to the framework presented by Calder, Phillips, and Tybout (i.e., Is the goal to test theory, to apply theory, or to estimate specific effects?). Then, consider whether the research methods employed are consistent with the goal. Finally, in light of the goal and the research methods employed, assess the contribution of the research.

3. What do the arguments advanced by Calder, Phillips, and Tybout say about the distinction between academic and applied research? Specifically consider research techniques commonly employed in practical circumstances (e.g., day-after recall for advertisements). Are such measures also useful in academic settings when examining theoretical issues?

PREFACE TO

"Replication and Theory Development"

This paper was written for the 1980 American Marketing Association Theory Conference. The paper builds on and extends an earlier paper by the first author and the late Professor Kenneth Coney of Arizona State University (1976). Professor Coney brought to our attention the dangers inherent in marketing discipline's absence of a research replication tradition.

In this reading, we have taken our understanding of replication into the arena of theory development. After reviewing the nature of replication, the relationship of replication to theory, theory testing and instrumentation are discussed. The discussion closes with a call for a replication tradition and offers five recommendations on how such a tradition can be initiated.

In the last three to four years, we have seen some of the recommendations acted on, at least in a door-opening fashion. Our journals, in general, are more appreciative of, and receptive toward, replication manuscripts. Some of the academic conferences have openly called for and accepted replication efforts as part of their conference programs. Finally, casual observation indicates that more doctoral programs are using replications as a research-learning experience. These opportunities promote student learning while helping verify or refute previously performed research.

In conclusion, as we noted in 1980, the absence of a replication tradition raises questions about the validity of much of the marketing discipline's body of thought. We hope that the reprinting of our paper will make more marketing scholars aware of this shortcoming in our discipline and encourage additional consideration of our recommendations.

26

REPLICATION AND THEORY DEVELOPMENT

STEPHEN W. BROWN
CORBETT F. GAULDEN, JR.

INTRODUCTION

A renewed interest in marketing theory has developed among marketing academicians in the last several years. In fact, in some areas, marketing texts have begun to deal directly with the issue of self-identity in marketing. In particular, the area of buyer behavior has been heavily laced with appeals to theory construction. So specific have such requests become, that several volumes have been devoted exclusively to metatheory in marketing. Most recently, the editor of the *Journal of Marketing* has called for the preparation and submission of theoretical papers to the journal. According to Wind (1979), "the achievement of JM's primary objective—the advancement of the science and practice of marketing—calls for further development of marketing theory."

This attention to marketing self-identity has occurred elsewhere as well. Conferences of professional marketers have included topics which deal directly with issues surrounding the borrowing, use and development of theory in marketing. In fact, this had become such a common occurrence that a special American Marketing Association Theory Conference was held in 1979. So successful was this conference that we are attending the first of a probable series of sequels to that conference. The very existence of theory conferences highlights the need for serious consideration of the state of marketing thought and its continued development. Conferences are called to deal with existing problems, not solved ones. Self-assessment by members of the academic community seems to be required. It is the purpose of this paper to explore one area of such an assessment and to provide some suggestions. The issue to be considered is that of replication in marketing research.

Source: Reprinted with permission from *Theoretical Developments in Marketing*, Charles W. Lamb and Patrick M. Dunne eds., Chicago, Ill.: American Marketing Association, 1982, 240–243.

In a recent noteworthy publication, Jacoby (1978) has cited five broad but critical areas of shortcomings common to most marketing research: (1) theories and models, (2) methodology, (3) measurement, (4) statistical techniques, and (5) subject matter. It is not the purpose of this paper to proffer general solutions to these problem areas. Rather, the purpose is to suggest that a tradition of replication in marketing research efforts could contribute to suggestions toward improvement in all five problem areas. For instance, theories or models could become well grounded in the literature if they were found to be widely generalizable. This can appropriately be done only when a theory or model is applied in a number of different settings. On the other hand, such a program would also be useful in fixing the boundaries of applicability of the theory (or model) and thus suggesting new and "better" explanations.

It is important to note that a replication tradition does not exist among marketing academics today. We have definitely (even consciously) avoided just such a tradition. Academic researchers/writers seem much more intent on borrowing or intuiting novel approaches to the study of marketing phenomena than to establishing the usefulness and boundaries of the explanations. The literature in marketing today displays a conspicuous absence of attempts at replication, even though there have been repeated pleas for replication.

Madden, Franz, and Mittelstaedt (1979) addressed replication at the 1979 AMA Marketing Theory Conference but only in the context of communication among researchers. There was no argument by Madden or others participating in the 1979 conference with respect to the contributions to theory development which are inherent in replication. This, in spite of the implications for self-assessment and self-identity with which the issue of replication is so pregnant. Perhaps the idea of replication is dull and unglamorous. There is an air of "non-creativity" which surrounds this whole idea. It might be characteristic of academicians to shun that which appears to be routine. However, the other social sciences have indulged very heavily in replication in recent years. Those concerned with the development of the marketing discipline should follow suit. An orderly progression to self-discovery requires this at some point.

It is precisely the relationship between marketing theory and research replication that this paper explores. Replication will be considered in the context of theory building and theory testing. Past calls for a replication tradition will be considered and the sources noted. The paper will then turn to a consideration of the current effects of the failure of the marketing discipline to engage in the mechanics necessary to bring about even a token tradition of replication and implications of this failure. Finally, a selection of remedies will be discussed.

WHAT IS REPLICATION?

Before proceeding with a discussion of the promise and problems of replication as a tradition, it is appropriate to establish a definition for the term. There is divergence of opinion as to what a replication is. Various usages of the term will be considered and an attempt will be made to arrive at some sort of consensus of meaning.

Although not often used for the purpose, a dictionary is not a bad starting point in the hunt for a definition. Webster (1961) provides three meanings for the verb "replicate", two of which are useful for this discussion. These two meanings distill down to "repeat" and "reply." Further investigation reveals, however, that the noun "replication" restricts the repeat or copy to additional tests made at the same time under the same circumstances on additional test units. This latter is the sense in which the term replication is used in controlled experimental design studies such as those conducted in agricultural experimentation. In social science research this simultaneity requirement seems to have been relaxed. With adequate controls, repetitions which are temporally separated can be accepted as replications. This is true for both survey and experimental types of research. The "reply" meaning of replicate will be examined in conjunction with definitions proffered by Brown and Coney (1976).

Social psychologists have used the term replication in the two ways discussed above: applied to additional test-units in a single study and to entire repetitions of a study. In some cases, these repetitions may even involve some modifications in attempts to test various assumptions or conditions present in the initial experiment. Such a usage is in keeping with the "spirit" of replication as this paper uses the term. In fact, this is the sole meaning attached to the term by some researchers.

Bush et al. (1975) adopted precisely this meaning of replication in their definition. In fact, their primary emphasis is on study modifications rather than on the duplication of previous research. In this sense, the replication operates basically as a base line for a modified (or even new) research idea. However, the underlying idea of a repetition of a previous study is preserved.

Brown and Coney (1976) discuss two basic contexts for the term replication, both of which are embedded in their definition of rejoinder. The rejoinder is defined as a reply, either theoretical or empirical in nature, to ideas or results previously put into print. The definitions of replication which are put forth are essentially empirical rejoinders. They distinguish between two types: replication and replication with extension; the distinction being a function of the orientation of the study. The simple replication is concerned with internal validity and the replication with extension is concerned with external validity. Usually one of these two orientations determine the actual task undertaken by the "follow-up" researcher.

Bush et al. (1975, p. 30) define replication as an essential duplication of a previous effort with the intent of considering additional variables in the design. This is the sense of the replication with extension discussed in the previous paragraph. The definitions are not in disagreement, but are distinguished by degree of refinement. This is not a minor point. The Brown and Coney (1976) definitions provide for a broader category of phenomena and a potential for distinctions among replication types.

Madden, Franz, and Mittelstaedt (1979) discussed three aspects of simple replication as discussed by Brown and Coney [1976]. The descriptions they use do not consider the case of replication with extension since they are concerned with questions of internal validity. Thus, while further clarification is provided, the domain of replication is still unchanged by their definitions.

In order to avoid a normal tendency toward definitional landsliding, no new definitions will be put forward at this time. The Brown and Coney descriptions seem adequate, and in keeping with general usage of the terms involved. However, in the interest of accuracy and refinement, the authors wish to encourage dialogue on the point of definition.

REPLICATION AND THEORY

A central contention of this paper is that the construction and testing of theories, as well as their integration, are dependent on replication in a number of critical ways. In fact, certain of the basic assumptions in a metatheory contain explicit references to replication. A sampling of these implications should serve to illustrate the point. One might even say that the implication is so basic that it has been overlooked as a topic of concern. However, in the following section, some specific requests for replication will be brought into focus.

The question of replication is a methodological question, and hence, according to Hunt (1976), belongs to the context of justification (or validation) rather than to the context of discovery. This is reasonable, since the only logical route to discovery through replication would be serendipitous. In fact, Rudner (1966), takes the position that there is no demonstrable logic of discovery. Hunt concludes that there is no single logic and states that the debate over the context of discovery is actually misplaced and belongs in the context of justification to begin with, as the questions are methodological in nature.

This, then, narrows the focus of this discussion to the context of justification or validation. This context is concerned with testing and refinement of theories however they are "discovered." Hence, the following discussion will assume that the researcher has a theory in hand. The researcher's interest is in either using that theory to aid in constructing new theory, integrating the theory with other existing theories, or testing the theory for soundness or applicability to a particular set of conditions. In order for exercises of the first two types to have any scientific meaning, the results of those exercises must presuppose attempts to subject resultant theories to some sort of empirical testing.

Hunt (1976, p. 3) states that any theoretical structure must have empirically testable content. He goes on (Hunt 1976, pp. 26–27) to add the requisite characteristic of intersubjective certifiability to theoretical explanations. Regardless of the source of the theory, then, its construction requires that morphologically its builder must provide a statement set which possesses these two characteristics, as well as others. A stated theory must be testable by its builder, which implies a minimum of one research effort. The theory should also be stated in such a form that other scientists can understand it as it was intended, and then be able to produce support for the theory is an empirical setting. Hence, they should be able to "replicate" any findings produced by the theory's builder in any tests of the theory which he undertakes. In this sense, then, the potential for replicable results is implied in the very definition of theoretical explanation.

The concept of intersubjective certification does not strictly require that other scientists subject a theory to empirical testing. However, Reynolds (1971) argues that its purpose is to require that different scientists make similar predictions. Tests of the accuracy of the predictions are empirical in nature. Thus, the contention that theory building or integration (and building) imply empirical testing and replicability holds. A simple procedure for testing the implications is to test the theory and attempt empirical replications, preferably by different scientists.

Theory Testing

All research is directed toward testing some hypothesis or hypotheses about states of nature. The hypothetical statements are based on some "theory" or idea about the effect of the presence or absence of some set (one or more) of variables on the state of another set (one or more) of variables. That the theories which give rise to hypotheses are often ill formed and only implicitly available for scrutiny is unfortunate. But the fact remains that there is a testable idea. A good hypothesis, by definition, is grounded in theory and is, in fact, a statement of some portion of the "empirically testable" nature of the theory. The hypothesis should also be intersubjectively certifiable, that is, reasonable and testable in the evaluation of the researcher's peers.

No serious researcher should expect that hypotheses and their implications would be accepted at face value. In order to present hypotheses and have them accepted as reasonably factual, the researcher must present concurrently an empirical test of the content of the hypotheses. Implicit in presentation of such evidence is a reasonable degree of confidence in the results. Additionally, the researcher is implying that if another researcher conducted the same or similar research, similar results would be forthcoming. A fairly simple test of such assumptions (one very much used in psychology and social psychology and the physical sciences) is for other scientists to conduct the same or similar research, and either confirm or allay the original researcher's prediction of duplicate results.

Given the existence of a large body of precedent, it is reasonable to conclude that a very important aspect of theory construction and testing is the ability of the construction to withstand scrutiny by more than one researcher on more than one occasion. In other words, serious theory development seems to require rather straightforward tests of the characteristics of theory. Replication would seem to provide the most direct way of accomplishing a major part of such testing.

Along with the concern over the theoretical base in marketing research, there is currently considerable interest in methodological issues related to the theoretical constructs. Of particular interest to this paper is the concern over data collection. This concern centers around two important issues: validity and reliability.

Instrumentation

Validity and reliability are properties of a measurement instrument which relate the instrument to the constructs it is designed to measure. These constructs should be well grounded in theory and the relationships specified in some hypotheses should also be theoretically sound. Instrumentation is designed to test the soundness of the relationships. In order to increase confidence in theoretical constructs and their relationships as predictors of observable phenomena, it would seem desirable to test them empirically. This involves instrumentation.

Once suitable instrumentation is found, the researcher may be concerned with the accuracy and precision with which the instrument performs. If it can be ascertained that the instrument is both accurate and precise (valid and reliable), then the researcher can become concerned with results as indicators of quality in the theoretical statements. If not, then the researcher's results are suspect and no true evaluation can be made with respect to the hypotheses. Thus, measures of validity and reliability are necessary for evaluation of instrumentation.

While various statistical tests have been constructed, "proof" of those measures would certainly be enhanced if uses of an instrument in the same theoretical setting (as its construction) were forthcoming.

A discussion of the various aspects of validity is beyond the scope of this paper. However, it is interesting to note that the typology presented by Zaltman, Pinson, and Angelmar (1973, p. 44) implies reproducibility of results under varying conditions (replications). In fact, several of the types of validity require substantial duplication or near duplication of effort for their proof.

Similar reasoning holds true for reliability testing. In this case, however, the relationship is much closer. In fact, reliability is essentially a measure of the extent to which results are replicated when measurement is replicated, usually by the same researcher. How comforting it would be if a small number of other researchers could also reproduce the same results under similar conditions. The more recent concept of generalizability introduced by Cronbach et al. (1963) and popularized in the marketing literature by Peter (1979) can be thought of in precisely the same way.

In summary, while the originator of a measurement instrument is responsible for considering its validity and reliability, researchers in general would benefit from replications. Such efforts would contribute new points of view to consideration of the instrument and its use. They would also lend additional credibility to research using the instrument.

Conceptually, one can propose "increments" of credibility. The creator of an instrument can increase credibility for his instrument by demonstrating its validity and reliability. Another major increment of credibility can be assigned when an independent user confirms the instruments usefulness. Succeeding users and situations would add progressively smaller increments until all reasonable doubt was removed from use of the instrument. A fairly small number of consistent replications would yield a relatively high level of confidence. The greater the variance in method or results, the more lengthy the process would be.

The same line of reasoning holds for the theoretical bases of the empirical effort. A small number of replications, particularly by different researchers, should indicate the efficacy of the theoretical constructions *and* should simultaneously refine the constructions, if necessary. This, then, allows further theoretization.

CALLS FOR REPLICATION

The need for replication has not gone unnoticed. In particular, consumer behaviorists have asked for replication on the grounds that research is difficult enough without building on spurious results. Engel et al. (1978) have urgently requested a tradition of replication. Other requests have come from Jacoby (1978), Brown and Coney (1976), and Madden, Franz and Mittelstaedt (1979) among others. Marketing research texts (e.g., Wentz, 1979) also include indirect appeals to replication through consideration of reliability and validity. In short, the challenge has been issued. The discipline, unfortunately, has been very slow to pick up the challenge.

DEVELOPING A REPLICATION TRADITION

To this point we have taken an advocacy position for replication. It must be mentioned, however, that replication is not a panacea. No literal or true replication is possible. Something is always different resulting in the potential of error and possibly making the replication and original results differ when the phenomena being measured do not. In addition, some research does not lend itself to feasible replication. Furthermore, in decisional research both cost and time considerations may limit the feasibility of replications.

Despite these cautions, replications can and should be conducted with greater frequency and regularity. This is especially true in basic research. In succeeding paragraphs, ways in which the marketing discipline can encourage replication are explored.

A major step in easing the appearance of unverified research results is to perform the research in such a way as to reduce "evaluation apprehension" or uneasiness about the research results (Rosenberg 1969). This may be achieved by incorporating Campbell's heteromethod replication approach (1969) within the research process. This involved the routine programming of different methods into the initial research phase.

The plea for building a replication tradition

could also be eased if the discipline did less indiscriminant borrowing of concepts and techniques from other disciplines, particularly social psychology. Although such borrowing is often viewed as contributing new insight to the marketing discipline, the encouragement of these "novel" applications may very well be impeding progress toward self-discovery within the discipline itself. The aura of "non-creativity" sometimes associated with replication needs to be eliminated and replaced by a recognition of the contribution of replication to the maturing of the discipline.

Despite the case that can and has been made for replication, the pragmatic problem is how to encourage it with the marketing discipline. Specific recommendations for overcoming the problem are explored as follows.

First, the major marketing journals should editorially welcome and promote replication efforts. Meaningful efforts should then be published on a regular basis in these journals. The notes and communications sections of the journals would be a possible place to position this kind of research. Another alternative would be a separate section for replications. To conserve space, the replications could be limited to a maximum number of words.

The procedure outlined is quite common in many of the behavioral journals. The Editorial Board of the *Journal of Marketing Research* discussed establishing a replications section in August 1978. Although the idea was rejected, it was decided that quality replication with extension articles could be included in the "Notes and Communications" section. Unfortunately, the journal has not fully promoted this policy to potential contributors.

The recent call for theoretical papers in the *Journal of Marketing* could also implicitly encourage replication. According to Wind, "greater attention is needed . . . in the development of a sound conceptual rational for the use of certain methodologies and the design of specific studies" (1979). Earlier discussion in this paper has clearly established the contribution of replication to the theoretical development of any discipline. The *Journal of Marketing* should therefore be more explicit on its policy on replication manuscripts, thereby hopefully encouraging this kind of research.

Second, the marketing journals should foster the exchange of research designs. It is difficult to replicate most published studies because limited space is allocated to the discussion of methodological procedures. The journals should consider following a practice of the *Journal of Personality and Social Psychology*. The editor of the journal notes that information on methods and results is often insufficient for the interest of other scholars. Readers are therefore encouraged to request additional information or comment on criticism to the author(s) with copies of this correspondence being sent to the journal editor ("Editor's Note," 1975).

Third, the professional conferences of the various national and regional associations should provide for a special track or sessions devoted to replications. Results of replication efforts could be presented, thus giving those results, as well as the researcher, public exposure. In 1977 and 1979 the buyer behavior track for the AMA Educators' Conference specifically called for replications and a session devoted to this research was featured at the Conference. More such encouragement is needed by the American Marketing Association and other bodies.

Fourth, working paper series would be an excellent outlet for replication efforts. The American Marketing Association and/or Association for Consumer Research could sponsor and promote such a series through the journals, the *Marketing News* and *ACR Newsletter*. The Education Division of the AMA and the ACR could also simply act as an accumulator and disseminator of individual replication efforts. The *ACR Newsletter* has taken steps in this direction by publishing working paper titles and author addresses.

Fifth, replication offers an opportunity for doctoral students to do some "pre-dissertation" research. Departments offering doctoral degrees should consider incorporating replication research into their programs. Such research would prepare the student for many of the problems that might occur unexpectedly in the dissertation. The external value of such an effort would of course be the verification or refutation of previously performed research. Replication requirements are a part of the doctoral programs at Arizona State University and the University of Oregon.

CONCLUSION

The maturing of the marketing discipline and the extension of its theoretical base is contingent upon increased replication studies. The absence of a replication tradition raises serious questions regarding the validity of much of the discipline's body of thought. This paper has built a strong case for the contribution of replication to theory and also offered pragmatic suggestions for building a replication tradition in the discipline.

REFERENCES

Brown, Stephen W., and Kenneth A. Coney, "Building a Replication Tradition in Marketing," in Kenneth L. Bernhardt, ed., *Marketing: 1776–1976 and Beyond*, Chicago: American Marketing Association, 1976, 622–625.

Bush, Ronald F., Joseph F. Hair, Jr., Paul Busch, and Eric R. Pratt, "A Content Analysis and Critical Review of Methodological Issues in Consumer Behavior Research, 1964–1975," Working Paper 75–2, University, Mississippi: Bureau of Business and Economic Research, University of Mississippi, November 1975.

Campbell, Donald T., "Prospective: Artifact and Control," in Robert Rosenthal and Ralph L. Rosnow, eds., *Artifact in Behavioral Research*, New York: Academic Press, Inc., 1969, 365–367.

Cronbach, Lee J., Nagaswari Rajaratnam, and Goldine C. Gleser, "Theory of Generalizability: A Liberalization of Reliability Theory," *British Journal of Statistical Psychology*, 16 (November 1963), 137–163.

"Editor's Note," *Journal of Personality and Social Psychology*, 32 (October 1975), 761.

Engel, James F., Roger D. Blackwell, and David T. Kollatt, *Consumer Behavior*, 3rd ed., Hinsdale, Ill.: Dryden Press, 1978, 579.

Hunt, Shelby D., *Marketing Theory: Conceptual Foundations of Research in Marketing*, Columbus, Ohio: Grid, Inc., 1976.

Jacoby, Jacob, "Consumer Research: a State of the Art Review," *Journal of Marketing*, 42 (April 1978), 87–96.

Madden, Charles Stanley, Lori Sharp Franz, and Robert Mittelstaedt, "The Replicability of Research in Marketing: Reported Content and Author Cooperation," in O. C. Ferrell, Stephen W. Brown, and Charles W

Lamb, Jr., eds., *Conceptual and Theoretical Developments in Marketing*, Chicago: American Marketing Association, 1979, 76–85.

Peter, J. Paul, "Reliability: A Review of Psychometric Basics and Recent Marketing Practices," *Journal of Marketing Research*, 16 (February 1979), 6–17.

Reynolds, Paul Davidson, *A Primer in Theory Construction*, Indianapolis: The Bobbs-Merrill Company, Inc., 1971.

Rosenberg, Milton J., "The Conditions and Consequences of Evaluation Apprehension," in Robert Rosenthal and Ralph L. Rosnow, eds., *Artifact in Behavioral Research*, New York: Academic Press, Inc., 1969, 365–367.

Rudner, Richard S., *Philosophy of Social Science*, Englewood Cliffs, N.J.: Prentice-Hall, Inc., 1966.

Webster's Third New International Dictionary, Springfield, Mass.: G. & C. Merriam, Publishers, 1961.

Wentz, Walter B., *Marketing Research: Management, Methods and Cases, 2nd ed., New York: Harper and Row, Publishers, 1979.*

Wind, Yoram, "From the Editor: On the Status of Marketing Theory," *Journal of Marketing,* 43, (Fall 1979), 6–7.

Zaltman, Gerald, Christian R. A. Pinson, and Reinhard Angelmar, *Metatheory and Consumer Research,* New York: Holt, Rinehart and Winston, Inc., 1973.

DISCUSSION QUESTIONS

1. Brown and Gaulden build a case for the benefits of a replication tradition in the marketing discipline. What does the absence of such a tradition indicate about the discipline's existing body of thought?

2. The paper offers a number of recommendations for building a replication tradition in marketing. What additional suggestions can you offer for building such a tradition?

3. What is the relationship between replication and validity? Between replication and reliability?

PREFACE TO

"Consumer Research: A State-of-the-Art Review"

In this article, Jacoby presents a compelling state-of-the-art evaluation of consumer research. He proposes that considerable work is necessary to improve five aspects of consumer research: (1) theories, models, and concepts; (2) procedures and methods; (3) measures and indices; (4) statistics; and (5) subject matter.

27

CONSUMER RESEARCH: A STATE-OF-THE-ART REVIEW*

JACOB JACOBY

Whether one does, sells, and/or buys consumer research, it stands to reason one should be able to critically evaluate and distinguish that which is acceptable from that which is junk. However, judging from papers which continue to be published in our most prestigious journals and from research reports which often form the basis for important marketing management and public policy decisions, it is all too apparent that *too large a proportion of the consumer (including marketing) research literature is not worth the paper it is printed on or the time it takes to read.*

Nearly a decade ago, Kollat et al. wrote:

The consumer behavior literature has doubled during the last five years. This constitutes a remarkable achievement by almost any standard. Unfortunately, however, it would not be surprising if 90% of the findings and lack of findings prove to be wrong.[1]

Unfortunately, the same frank evaluation can be made today. Unless we begin to take corrective measures soon, we stand to all drown in a mass of meaningless and potentially misleading junk! This assertion can be documented by considering five broad categories of problems: the contemporary *theories* (and comprehensive models), *methods, measures, statistical techniques,* and *subject matter* in consumer research. Before doing so, a brief digression is needed to make three points:

1. The evaluation of consumer research should logically be predicated upon a definition of con-

Source: Reprinted with permission from the *Journal of Marketing,* 42 (April), 1978, 87–96, Chicago, Ill.: American Marketing Association.

*This article is based on the following presidential address delivered in 1975 to the Association for Consumer Research: Jacob Jacoby, ''Consumer Research: Telling It Like It Is,'' in *Advances in Consumer Research, Vol. 3,* B. B. Anderson, ed. (Atlanta: Georgia State University, 1976), pp. 1–11.

sumer behavior. Such a definition has been presented and described at length elsewhere.[2] In essence, it holds that *consumer behavior* encompasses the acquisition, consumption, and disposition of goods, services, time, and ideas by decision-making units (e.g., individuals, families, organizations, etc.). *Consumer research,* then, is simply research addressed to studying some aspect of consumer behavior.

2. I shout at the outset: MEA CULPA! I have committed many of the sins about to be described. No doubt, I will continue to commit at least some of them long after this is published and forgotten. No one of us who is a researcher is without guilt. This does not mean, however, that we should passively accept the status quo and thereby stifle the impetus toward improvement.

3. Except in one instance, naming names and citing specific articles as illustrations of the problems being iterated would probably serve few, if any, positive ends. The interested reader has only to examine the articles in our leading journals to find numerous suitable examples. On the other hand, because they may serve a guidance function for some, names are named and specific articles cited in order to illustrate *positive* examples addressed to the issue under consideration. However, citing an article as being positive in one respect does not mean that it is void of other deficiencies.

THEORIES, MODELS AND CONCEPTS

Over the past decade, an increasing amount of attention has been devoted to the development, presentation, and discussion of relatively comprehensive theories and models of consumer behavior.[3] Five years ago, Kollat et al.[4] noted: ''These models have had little influence on consumer behavior research during the last five years. Indeed, it is rare to find a published study that has utilized, been based on, or even influenced by, any of the models identified above.'' Unfortunately, not much has changed since then.

"Look Ma—No Theory"

Despite the availability of consumer behavior theories and models, the impetus and rationale underlying most consumer behavior research seems to rest on little more than the availability of easy-to-use measuring instruments, the existence of more or less willing subject populations, the convenience of the computer, and/or the almost toy-like nature of sophisticated quantitative techniques. Little reliance is place on theory, either to suggest which variables and aspects of consumer behavior are of greatest importance and in need of research or as a foundation around which to organize and integrate findings. It is still true that nothing is so practical as a good theory. However, while researchers (particularly in academia) talk a good game about the value and need for theory, their actions loudly speak otherwise.

The Post Hoc, Atheoretic, Shotgun Approach

By neglecting theory, the researcher increases the likelihood of failure to understand his own data and/or be able to meaningfully interpret and integrate his findings with findings obtained by others. This problem has elsewhere been referred to as "the atheoretical shotgun approach" to conducting research.[5] These papers tried to illustrate the nature of this problem by considering empirical attempts to relate personality variables to consumer behavior. The most frequently quoted passage is as follows:[6]

> Investigators usually take a general, broad coverage personality inventory and a list of brands, products, or product categories, and attempt to correlate subjects' responses on the inventory with statements of product use or preference. Careful examination reveals that, in most cases, the investigators have operated without the benefit of theory and with no *a priori* thought directed to *how,* or especially *why,* personality should or should not be related to that aspect of consumer behavior being studied. Statistical techniques, usually simple correlation of variants thereof, are applied and anything that turns up looking halfway interesting furnishes the basis for the Discussion section. Skill at

post-diction and post hoc interpretation has been demonstrated, but little real understanding has resulted.

These papers went on to illustrate why it was necessary to use theoretically derived hypotheses for specifying variables and relationships in advance. That is, they called on consumer researchers to (1) make specific predictions of both expected differences and *no* differences, (2) explain the reasoning underlying these predictions, and (3) do both *prior* to conducting their research. To illustrate:

> You're sitting with a friend watching Pete Rose at bat. Rose hits a home run and your friend says: "I knew he was going to hit that home run. He always hits a home run off right-hand pitchers when he holds his feet at approximately a 70° angle to each other and his left foot pointing directly at the pitcher."
>
> Think of how much greater confidence you would have had in your friend's forecast if he had made this as a *pre*diction just as Pete Rose was stepping into the batter's box. (Anticipating another issue raised below, replication, think of how much greater confidence you would have if your friend had predicted Rose would hit home runs on two subsequent occasions just before Rose actually hit home runs, and also predicted Rose would *not* hit a home run on eight other instances, and he did not.

Although considered in the context of relating personality variables to consumer behavior, it is clear that almost every aspect of consumer research reflects the atheoretic shotgun approach, particularly when it comes to utilizing concepts borrowed from the behavioral sciences. Most consumer researchers are still pulling shotgun triggers in the dark.

"Whoops! Did You Happen to See Where My Concept Went?"

Even in those instances where consumer researchers seem to be sincerely interested in conducting research based upon a firm conceptual foundation, they sometimes manage to misplace their concepts when it gets down to the nitty gritty. For example, Gardner states:[7]

> It is imperative that any definition of deception in advertising recognizes the interaction of the advertisement with the accumulated beliefs and experience of the consumer.

Two paragraphs later he provides a definition which *ignores* this imperative, and subsequently goes on to propose procedures which completely disregard the fact that deception may occur as a function of the prior beliefs of the consumer and not as function of the ad (or ad campaign) in question. The reason why we cite this paper here (and below) is because it has already been cited by others—receiving the 1975 Harold H. Maynard Award "for its contribution to marketing theory and marketing thought."[8]

Another equally frustrating example is provided by those who define brand loyalty as a hypothetical construct predicted upon the cognitive dynamics of the consumer—and then proceed to base their measure of brand loyalty *solely* on the buyer's overt behavior. The consumer behavior literature contains numerous such examples of our inability to have our measures of concepts correspond to these concepts.

The "Theory of the Month" Club

Interestingly, the failure to use existing models and theories has not discouraged some from proposing new models and theories, thereby generating a different kind of problem. Several of our most respected scholars seem to belong to a "theory of the month" club which somehow requires that they periodically burst forth with new theories and rarely, if ever, provide any data collected specifically to support their theories. Perhaps those with a new theory or model should treat it like a new product: either stand behind it and give it the support it needs (i.e., test and refine it as necessary)—or take it off the market!

Single-Shot vs. Programmatic Research

Another theory-related problem is the widespread avoidance of programmatic research. Judging from the published literature, there are fewer than a dozen individuals who have conducted five or more separate investigations in systematic and sequentially integrated fashion designed to provide incremental knowledge regarding a single issue. Instead, we have a tradition of single-shot studies conducted by what one scholar has termed "Zeitgeisters-Shysters."[9]

Rarely do single-shot investigations answer all questions that need to be answered or make definitive contributions on any subject of importance. Yet many consumer researchers seem to operate under the mistaken belief that such studies are capable of yielding payout of substance and duration. I am not advocating that we do *only* programmatic research. I appreciate the allure, excitement, and challenge often inherent in such studies and the potential that they *sometimes* have for providing resolution to a problem of immediate concern. However, to make contributions of substance, it is necessary that a greater proportion of our research efforts be programmatic.

PROCEDURES AND METHODS

The Ubiquitous Verbal Report

By far, the most prevalent approach to collecting consumer data involves eliciting verbal reports via interviews or through self-administered questionnaires.

Typically, verbal reports assess either (a) recall of past events, (b) current psychological states (including attitudes, preferences, beliefs, statements of intentions to behavior, likely reactions to hypothetical events), and/or (c) sociodemographic data. Of the 44 empirical studies in Schlinger,[10] 39 (87%) were based primarily or entirely on verbal report data. Of the 36 empirical studies in the first six issues of the *Journal of Consumer Research,* 31 (more than 85%) were also based primarily or solely on verbal reports. Given the numerous biases in verbal reports and the all-too-often demonstrated discrepancy between what people say and what they actually do, it is nothing short of amazing that we persist in our slavish reliance on verbal reports as the mainstay of our research.

The problems inherent in the ubiquitous verbal report approach can be organized into three categories: (1) interviewer error, (2) respondent error, and (3) instrument error.

Interviewer Error   We will disregard consideration of interviewer errors, since more than 75% of the published verbal report studies are based upon the self-administered questionnaires.

Respondent Error   Verbal report data are predicated upon many untested and, in some cases, invalid assumptions. Many of these concern the respondent. As examples, consider the following assumptions underlying attempts to elicit recall of factual information:

• Prior learning (and rehearsal) of the information has actually taken place; that is, something actually exists in memory to be recalled.

• Once information is stored in memory, it remains there in accurate and unmodified form.

• Said information remains equally accessible through time.

• There are no respondent differences in ability to recall which would be controlled or accounted for.

• Soliciting a verbal report is a non-reactive act; that is, asking questions of respondents is unlikely to have any impact on them and on their responses.

Analogous assumptions exist with respect to assessing psychological states (e.g., attitudes, preferences, intentions, etc.) via verbal reports. For example, Bogart noted that asking the respondent a question often ''forces the crystallization and expression of opinions where (previously) there were no more than chaotic swirls of thought.''[11] Actually, the assumptions underlying recall of factual material are few and simple relative to assumptions underlying verbal reports used as indicants of psychological states. Perhaps the most effective way to summarize the state of affairs is to say that many of the fundamental assumptions which underlie the use of verbal reports are completely invalid. The reader is asked to cogitate regarding the ramifications of this fact.

Instrument Error   Consider further the fact that instruments for collecting verbal reports often contribute as much error variance as do interviewers or respondents, or even *more*. In general, a large proportion of our questionnaires and interview schedules impair rather than enhance efforts to collect valid data. More often than not, we employ instruments which, from the respondent's perspective, are ambiguous, intimidating, confusing, and incomprehensible. Developing a self-administered questionnaire is one of the most difficult steps in the entire research process. Unfortunately, it is commonly the most neglected.

Formulating questions and questionnaires seems like such an easy thing to do that everyone is assumed to be an expert at it, or at least adequately capable. Yet many never become aware of the literally hundreds of details that should be attended to.[12] We assume that because *we* know what we mean by our questions and *we* are not confused by the lay-out and organization of our instrument, data collected using this instrument will naturally be valid; that is, any errors which result are obviously a function of the respondent and not a function of our instrument. As a consequence, we are often left with what computer technicians refer to as GIGO—Garbage In, Garbage Out. In most instances, the investigator is hardly even cognizant of the fact that this has occurred.

Please note that I am NOT proposing that we do away with verbal reports (i.e., interview and self-administered questionnaires). They are a valid and vital part of our methodological armamentarium. However, if we are to continue placing such great reliance on verbal reports, the least we ought to do is devote greater attention to the basics; that is, learn how to formulate questions and structure questionnaires. What does it mean if a finding is significant, or that the ultimate in statistical analytical techniques have been applied, if the data collection instrument generated invald data at the outset?

But do we actually have to place slavish reliance on the verbal report? Certainly not! One alternative is to devote less time to studying what people *say they do* and spend more time examining what it is that they *do do*. In other words, we can place greater emphasis on studying actual behavior relative to the amount of effort we place on studying verbal reports regarding behavior.

There have been several recent developments in this regard.[13] We would be well advised to begin using these as alternatives and/or supplements to the ubiquitous verbal report. As Platt notes: ''Beware the man of one method or one instrument . . . he tends to become method oriented rather than problem oriented.''[14]

Static Methods for Dynamic Process
We also need to begin studying consumer behavior in terms of the dynamic process that it is. Virtually all consumer researchers tend to consider

consumer behavior as a dynamic, information processing, decision-making, behavioral process. Yet probably 99+% of all consumer research conducted to date examines consumer behavior via static methods administered either before or after the fact. Instead of being captured and studied, the dynamic nature of consumer decision making and behavior is squelched and the richness of the process ignored. Our static methods are inappropriate for studying our dynamic concepts. This issue is treated in greater detail elsewhere.[15]

Roosters Cause the Sun to Rise

Consider, also, the necessity for greater reliance on the experimental method, particularly in those instances where cause-effect assertions are made or alluded to. Examination reveals a surprising number of instances in which causation is implied or actually claimed on the basis of simple correlation. It bears repeating that no matter how highly correlated the rooster's crow is to the sun rising, the rooster does not cause the sun to rise.

More and Richer Variables

A final set of methodological issues concerns the need for research which (1) incorporates measures of a variety of dependent variables, (2) explores the combined and perhaps interacting impact of a variety of independent variables, and (3) uses multiple measures of the same dependent variable.

With respect to the former, it is often possible to measure a variety of different dependent variables at little additional cost (e.g., decision accuracy, decision time, and subjective states).[16] Unfortunately, opportunities for substantially enhancing understanding through the inclusion of a variety of dependent variables are generally ignored. Equally important, we live in a complex, multivariate world. Studying the impact of one or two variables in isolation would seem to be relatively artifical and inconsequential. In other words, we need more research which examines and is able to parcel out the impact of a variety of factors impinging in concert.

It is also too often true that conclusions are accepted on the basis of a single measure of our dependent or criterion variable. The costs involved in incorporating a second or third measure of that *same* variable are usually negligible, particularly when considered in terms of the increased confidence we could have in both our findings and our

concepts if we routinely used a variety of indices and found that all (or substantially all) provided the same pattern of results.[17] This second issue (namely, using multiple measures of the same variable) relates more to the validity of our measure than to our methods, and is elaborated upon below.

MEASURES AND INDICES

Our Bewildering Array of Definitions

Kollat, Blackwell, and Engel[18] have referred to the "bewildering array of definitions" that we have for many of our core concepts.

As one example, at least 55 different and distinct measures of brand loyalty have been employed in the more than 300 studies comprising the brand loyalty literature.[19] Virtually no attempt has been made to identify the good measures and weed out the poor ones. Almost everyone has his own preferred measure and seems to blithely and naively assume that findings from one investigation can easily be compared and integrated with findings from investigations which use other definitions.

The same horrendous state of affairs exists with respect to many of our other core concepts. There are at least four different types of "innovator" definitions[20] and three different categories of "opinion leadership" definitions (i.e., self-designating, sociometric, and key informant). Each one of these categories is usually broken out into several specific forms. As examples, Rogers and Catarno,[21] King and Summers,[22] and Jacoby[23] all provide different operationalizations of self-designating opinion leadership.

More stupefying than the sheer number of our measures is the ease with which they are proposed and the uncritical manner in which they are accepted. In point of fact, most of our measures are only measures because someone *says* that they are, not because they have been shown to satisfy standard measurement criteria (validity, reliability, and sensitivity). Stated somewhat differently, most of our measures are not more sophisticated than first asserting that the number of pebbles a person can count in a ten-minute period is a measure of that person's intelligence; next, conducting a study and finding that people who can count many pebbles in ten minutes also tend to eat more; and, finally, concluding from this: people with high intelligence tend to eat more.

Wanted Desperately: Validity

A core problem is the issue of validity: Just how valid are our measures? Little attention seems to be directed toward finding out. Like our theories and models, once proposed, our measures take on an almost sacred and inviolate existence all their own. They are rarely, if ever, examined or questioned.

Several basic types of validity exist, although often described with somewhat varying terminology.[24] In a highly readable and almost layman-like presentation of the subject, Nunnally writes of three basic types:[25] (1) content validity which is generally irrelevant in consumer research, (2) predictive validity, (3) construct validity. Face validity, a non-psychometric variety, refers to whether a *measure looks like it is measuring what it is supposed to be measuring*. Examination of the core consumer behavior journals and conference proceedings since 1970—a body of literature consisting of approximately 1000 published articles—reveals the following:

Face Validity First, there are numerous examples of face validity. The measures used almost always look like they are measuring that which they are supposed to be measuring. However, the overwhelming majority of studies go no further, that is, provide no empirical support. Thus, face validity is often used as a substitute for construct validity.

Predictive Validity There are also a sizable number of studies which suggest the existence of predictive validity, that is, the measure in question seems to correlate, as predicted, with measures or other variables. Unfortunately, many investigators do not seem to recognize that predictive validity provides little, if any, *understanding* of the relationship. One can have a predictive validity coefficient of .99 and still not know why or what it means—other than the fact that the scores on one variable are highly predictive of scores on a second variable. The relationship may even be meaningless. As one example, Heeler and Ray note that Kuehn in 1963 comments that he:[26]

. . . improved the ability of the Edwards Personal Preference Schedule (EPPS) to predict car ownership. He did it with EPPS scores computed by subtracting "affiliation" scores from "domi-

nance" scores. Such a difference really has no psychological or marketing significance; it is just a mathematical manipulation that happened to work in one situation.

Obviously, high predictive validity doesn't necessarily have to be meaningful.

Cross-Validity One type of predictive validity, however, receives too little attention, namely, cross-validity. "Whereas predictive validity is concerned with a single sample, cross-validity requires that the effectiveness of the predictor composite be tested on a *separate* independent sample from the *same* population."[27] It should be obvious that unless we can cross-validate our findings, we may really have no findings at all. Again, examination of the literature reveals few cross-validation studies.[28]

Construct Validity The most necessary type of validity in scientific research is construct validity.

Examination of the recent literature indicates that a negligible proportion of our productivity has been directed toward determining construct validity. A large part of the problem lies in the fact that many researchers appear to naively believe that scientific research is a game played by creating measures and then applying them directly to reality. Although guided by some implicit conceptualization of what it is he is trying to measure, the consumer researcher rarely makes his implicit concepts sufficiently explicit or uses them as a basis for developing operational measures. Yet virtually all contemporary scholars of science generally agree that the concept must precede the measure.[29]

It is not our intention to provide a lengthy dissertation of the nature of scientific research. We simply wish to point out here that many of our measures are developed at the whim of a researcher with nary a thought given to whether or not it is meaningfully related to an explicit conceptual statement of the phenomena or variable in question. In most instances, our concepts have no identity apart from the instrument or procedures used to measure them.

As a result, it is actually impossible to evaluate our measures. "To be able to judge the relative value of measurements or of operations requires criteria beyond the operations themselves. If a concept is nothing but an operation, how can we talk about being mistaken or about making errors?''[30] In other words, scientific research demands that clearly articulated concepts (i.e., abstractions regarding reality) intervene between reality and the measurement of reality.

Probably the most efficient means for establishing construct validity is the Campbell and Fiske *multi-method × multi-trait* approach.[31] Despite the fact that numerous papers refer to this approach as something that ''could'' or ''should'' be applied, considerably less than 1% of our published literature has actually systematically explored construct validity using this approach.[32] ''Before one can test the relationship between a specific trait and other traits, one must have confidence in one's measure of that trait.''[33] If we cannot demonstrate that our concepts are valid, how can we act as if the findings based upon measures of these concepts are valid?

Convergent Validity   A basic and relatively easy-to-establish component of construct validity is convergent validity. This refers to the degree to which attempts to measure the same concept using two or more different measures yield the same results. Even if few construct validity investigations are available, it seems reasonable to expect that, since many of our core concepts are characterized by numerous and varied operationalizations, we should find many studies to demonstrate convergent validity.

Surely there must be many investigations which have concurrently used two or more measures of these concepts, thereby permitting us to assess convergent validity. Examination of the literature reveals that such is not the case. Somewhat incredibly, only two (out of more than 300) published studies have administered three or more brand loyalty measures concurrently to the same group of subjects, thereby permitting an examination of how these measures interrelate.[34]

Our other core concepts fare equally poorly. Data that are available often indicate that different ways of measuring innovators are negligibly related to each other.[35] Given that we cannot demonstrate adequate convergent validity, it should be alarmingly obvious that we have no basis for comparing findings from different studies or making generalizations using such measures. More widespread use

of multiple measures is urgently needed so that we can begin the relatively simple job of assessing convergent validity. We are being strangled by our bad measures. Let's identify and get rid of them.

Reliability and Replication

Another fundamental problem with our measures is that data regarding their reliability, particularly test-retest reliability, are rarely provided. As an illustration, only a single study appears in the entire brand loyalty literature which measures the test-retest reliability of a set of brand loyalty measures.[36] A similar state of affairs exists with respect to indices of other core constructs.

Consider also the case of the test-retest reliability of recall data. In the entire advertising literature, only two *published* articles can be found which provide data on the test-retest reliability of recall data.[37] Young notes that results obtained in ten retests were the same as those in the initial test *in only 50% of the cases.*[38] Assuming we were ill and actually had a body temperature of 103° Farenheit, how many of us would feel comfortable using a thermometer if, with no actual change in our body temperature, this thermometer gave us readings of 97.0°, 100.6°, 98.6°, and 104.4°, all within the space of one 15-minute period. Yet we persistently employ indices of unknown reliability to study consumer purchase decisions and behavior. More sobering, we often develop expensive nationwide promotional strategies and wide-ranging public policies based on findings derived from using such indices.

There is a strong necessity for replicating our findings using different subject populations, test products, etc. The name of the game is confidence in our findings.

Measurement Based on House-of-Cards Assumption

Another frequently appearing problem is the tendency to have one's measures (or proposed measures) rest on an intertwined series of untested and sometimes unverifiable assumptions so that the measures used are sometimes five or more steps removed from the phenomenon of interest. In such cases, if a single one of the many assumptions is rendered invalid, the entire measurement system must necessarily come cascading downward. Such is the case with the logic developed in the article on deceptive advertising noted above.[39]

The Folly of Single Indicants

A final measurement problem is easily illustrated by posing the following question: "How comfortable would we feel having our intelligence assessed on the basis of our response to a *single* question?" Yet that's exactly what we do in consumer research. Brand loyalty is often "definitively assessed" by the response to a single question; the same is true with respect to virtually all of our core concepts. The literature reveals hundreds of instances in which responses to a single question suffice to establish the person's level on the variable of interest and then serves as the basis for extensive analysis and entire articles.

Just as is true of such concepts as personality and intelligence, most of our core concepts (e.g., opinion leadership, brand loyalty, innovation proneness, perceived quality, perceived risk, etc.) are multi-faceted and complex. Intelligence and personality are generally measured through a battery of different test items and methods. Even single personality traits are typically assessed via 30 or 40 item inventories. Given the complexity of our subject matter, what makes us think that we can use responses to single items (or even to two or three items) as measures of these concepts, then relate these scores to a host of other variables, arrive at conclusions based on such an investigation, and get away calling what we have done "quality research?"

STATISTICS, STATISTICS

In general, our statistical techniques for analyzing data reflect the fewest number of problems and, in recent years, probably the greatest number of advances. However, at least four major problems remain.

Number Crunching

I have finally reached the point where I am no longer automatically impressed by the use of high-powered and sophisticated statistics. Why? Because too often the use of these statistics appears *not* to be accompanied by the use of another high-powered and sophisticated tool, namely, the brain. For example, what does it really mean when the fourteenth canonical root is highly significant and shows that a set of predictors including size of house, purchase frequency of cake mix, and number of times you brush your teeth per day is related to age of oldest child living at home, laundry detergent preference, and frequency of extra-marital relations? Examination of the recent consumer research literature reveals many more instances of such mindless applications.

Multi-Layered Madness

In its most sophisticated form, number crunching involves the multi-layering of statistical techniques so that the output from one analysis provides the input for the next analysis. Sometimes, this statistical version of musical chairs involves five to ten different techniques used in series. Again, given the nature of the data collected in the first place, what does the final output actually mean?

Measuring Giant Icebergs in Millimeters and Using Calipers to Measure Melting Marshmallows Perhaps what is most surprising about this number crunching is the fact that the data being crunched are usually exceedingly crude and coarse to begin with. As already noted, the large majority of our data are collected using the self-administered questionnaire. Yet many researchers haven't the foggiest idea about the basic DOs and DON'Ts of questionnaire construction. Consider also the fact that the reliability and validity of the data we collect are often assumed, not demonstrated.

Finally, consider the fact that trying to measure diffuse, complex, and *dynamic* phenomena such as attitudes, information processing, decision making, etc., may be like trying to measure melting marshmallows with Vernier calipers. In other words, what are we doing working three and four digits to the right of the decimal point? What kind of phenomena, measures, and data do we really have that we are being so precise in our statistical analyses?

Substantial developments in both our methodology (particularly in regard to questionnaire construction) and the psychometric quality of our measures (particular in regard to validity and reliability) are needed before use of high-powered statistics can be justified in many of the instances where they are now being routinely applied.

Static State Statistics

There is one area, however, in which our statistics can use improvement. By and large, most of our statistics are appropriate only for data collection using traditional, cross-sectional, static methodologies. Just as we have a need for the further development of dynamic methodologies, we need further development of statistics for analyzing the data collected using such methods. That is, we need statistics which do not force dynamic process data to be reduced to static-state representations. Trend analysis and cross-lagged correlations can and have been used in this manner. However, our repertoire of statistical techniques for handling dynamic data needs to be expanded, either by borrowing from disciplines accustomed to dealing with dynamic data, or through the creative efforts of statisticians working within the consumer research domain.

SUBJECT MATTER

Many (including Cohen[40]) have called much consumer research "trivial." In all too many ways, they are right.

Systematically Exploring the Varieties of Acquisition

Most definitions of consumer behavior shackle us by confining attention to purchase. Aside from the fact that purchase can itself take a variety of forms (e.g., buying at list price, bargaining, bidding at auction), purchase is only one form of acquisition. There are others (e..g, receiving something as a gift, in trade, on loan, etc.), each of which can have important economic, sociological and psychological consequences and dynamics different from purchase. For example, if one million more Americans this year than last suddenly decided to borrow their neighbor's rake to handle their fall leaf problems, the impact on the rake industry could be enormous.

What are the dynamics underlying being a borrower or being a lender? What are the dynamics underlying giving or receiving a gift?[41] Hardly any published data exist regarding these other forms of acquisition—or how they interact with and affect purchase behavior. Both for scholarly and practical reasons, we must begin to systematically explore the entire realm of consumer acquisition decisions and behavior.

Putting Consumption Back into Consumer Behavior

Although considerable research has focused on actual consumption, particularly by the home economists, this fact is not adequately reflected in the predominant theories and textbooks of consumer behavior. This is surprising inasmuch as what happens during consumption has a strong influence on subsequent acquisition (especially purchase) decisions. Consumption must be given greater salience and be more tightly integrated with the existing consumer behavior literature.

What About Disposition?

The third major facet of consumer behavior, disposition, appears to have been completely neglected. This neglect should be rectified for at least four reasons:[42]

1. Many disposition decisions have significant economic consequences for both the individual and society. Some (e.g., when and how to properly dispose of unused or outdated prescription drugs) even have important health and safety ramifications.

2. Since much purchase behavior is cyclical, a variety of marketing implications would most likely emanate from an understanding of the disposition subprocess.

3. We are entering an age of relative scarcity in which we can no longer afford the luxury of squandering resources. Understanding disposition decisions and behavior is a necessary (perhaps even logically prerequisite) element in any conservationist orientation.

4. There is some evidence that the study of consumer disposition could conceivably provide us with new "unobtrusive" macro-indicators[43]—both leading and trailing—of economic trends and the state of consumer attitudes and expectations.

Consumption and Production

Not only does our conception of what constitutes consumer behavior have to be expanded and its various facets studied, but the relationship between consumption and production should be explored. Consumption and production are integrally related. Studies are needed which examine this interrelationship by considering both domains simultaneously.

CONCLUSION

This compendium is by no means an exhaustive iteration of the problems in and confronting consumer research. It does, however, cover many of the most frequently occurring and severe problems.

Quite clearly, we think it is important to know that we don't know—important so that we don't delude ourselves and others about the *quality* of our research and validity of our findings as providing sound bases upon which to make decisions of consequence. One thing we most need to learn is that we must stop letting our existing methods and tools dictate and shackle our thinking and research. They are no substitute for using our heads. The brain is still the most important tool we have and its use should precede more than succeed the collection of data.

It is important to recognize that we are in the midst of a consumer research explosion; and unless we take corrective action soon, we stand to become immersed in a quagmire from which it is already becoming increasingly difficult to extricate ourselves. Fortunately, it is not yet too late.

NOTES

[1]David T. Kollat, Roger D. Blackwell, and James F. Engel, "The Current Status of Consumer Behavior Research: Development During the 1968–1972 Period," in *Proceedings of the Third Annual Conference of the Association for Consumer Research*, M. Venkatesan, ed. (1972), pp. 576–85, at p. 577.

[2]Jacob Jacoby, "Consumer Psychology as a Social Psychological Sphere of Action," *American Psychologist*, Vol. 30 (October 1975), pp. 977–87; Jacob Jacoby, "Consumer Research: Telling It Like It Is," in Advances in Consumer Research, Vol. 3, B. B. Anderson, ed., (Atlanta: Georgia State University, 1976), pp. 1–11.

[3]Alan R. Andreasen, "Attitudes and Consumer Behavior: A Decision Model," in *New Research in Marketing*, L. Preston, ed. (Berkeley, Calif.: Institute of Business and Economic Research, University of California, 1965), pp. 1–16; Francesco Nicosia, *Consumer Decision Processes: Marketing and Advertising Implications* (Englewood Cliffs, N.J.: Prentice-Hall, 1966); James F. Engel, David T. Kollat, and Roger D. Blackwell, *Consumer Behavior* (New York: Holt, Rinehart & Winston, 1968; 2nd ed., 1973); John A. Howard and Jagdish N. Sheth, *The Theory of Buyer Behavior* (New York: John Wiley & Sons, 1969); Flemming Hansen, *Consumer Choice Behavior: A Cognitive Theory* (New York: Free Press, 1972); Rom J. Markin, *Consumer Behavior: A Cognitive Orientation* (New York: Macmillan Publishing Co., 1974).

[4]Kollat et al., same as reference 1 above, p. 577.

[5]Jacob Jacoby, "Toward Defining Consumer Psychology: One Psychologist's Views," *Purdue Papers in Consumer Psychology*, No. 101, 1969. Paper presented at the 77th Annual Convention of the American Psychological Association, Washington, D.C. (1969); Jacob Jacoby, "Personality and Consumer Behavior: How NOT to Find Relationships," *Purdue Papers in Consumer Psychology*, No. 102 (1969).

[6]Engel et al., same as reference 3 above, pp. 652–53; Harold H. Kassarjian, "Personality and Consumer Behavior: A Review," *Journal of Marketing Research*, Vol. 8 (November 1971), pp. 409–19.

[7]David M. Gardner, "Deception in Advertising: A Conceptual Approach," *Journal of Marketing*, Vol. 39 (January 1975), pp. 40–46.

[8]Edward W. Cundiff, "Alpha Kappa Psi Foundation and Harold H. Maynard Awards for 1975," *Journal of Marketing*, Vol. 40 (April 1975), p. 2.

[9]Victor H. Denenberg, "Polixities A. Zeitgeister, B. S., M. S., PhONY," *Psychology Today*, Vol. 3 (June 1969), p. 50.

[10]Mary Jane Schlinger, ed., *Advances in Consumer Research, Vol. 2* Proceedings of the Association for Consumer Research, (Chicago: University of Illinois, 1975).

[11]Leo Bogart, "No Opinion, Don't Know, and Maybe No Answer," *Public Opinion Quarterly*, Vol. 31 (Fall 1967), p. 335.

[12]Paul Erdos, *Professional Mail Surveys* (New York: McGraw-Hill, 1970); Stanely L. Payne, *The Art of Asking Questions* (Princeton, N.J.: Princeton University Press, 1951); Arthur Kornhauser and Paul B. Sheatsley, "Questionnaire Construction and Interview Procedure," in *Research Methods in Social Relations*, C. Selltiz, M. Jahoda, M. Deutsch, and S. W. Cook, eds. (New York: Henry Holt & Co., 1959), pp. 546–87.

[13]Jacob Jacoby, Robert W. Chestnut, Karl Weigl, and William Fisher, "Pre-Purchase Information Acquisition: Description of a Process Methodology, Research Paradigm, and Pilot Investigation," in *Advances in Consumer Research, Vol. 3*, B. B. Anderson, ed. (Atlanta: Georgia State University, 1976), pp. 306–14; John Payne, "Heuristic Search Processes in Decision-Making," in *Advances in Consumer Research, Vol. 3*, B. B. Anderson, ed., (Atlanta: Georgia State University, 1976).

[14]John R. Platt, "Strong Inference," *Science*, Vol. 146 (1964), p. 351.

[15]Jacoby et al., same as reference 13 above; Peter L. Wright, "Research Orientations for Analyzing Consumer Judgment Processes," in *Advances in Consumer Research; Vol. 1*, S. Ward and P. L. Wright, eds. (Urbana, Ill.: Association for Consumer Research, 1974), pp. 268–79.

[16]Jacob Jacoby, Donald E. Speller and Carol A. Kohn Berning, "Brand Choice Behavior as a Function of Information Load: Replication and Extension," *Journal of Consumer Research*, Vol. 1 (June 1974), pp. 33–42.

[17]Jacob Jacoby and David B. Kyner, "Brand Loyalty vs. Repeat Purchasing Behavior," *Journal of Marketing Research*, Vol. 10 (February 1973), pp. 1–9.

[18]Kollat et al., same as reference 1 above.

[19]Jacob Jacoby and Robert W. Chestnut, *Brand Loyalty: Measurement and Management* (New York: John Wiley & Sons, 1978.

[20]Carol A. Kohn and Jacob Jacoby, "Operationally Defining the Consumer Innovator," *Proceedings, 81st Annual Convention of the American Psychological Association*, Vol. 8 (Issue 2, 1973), pp. 837–38; Thomas S. Robertson, *Innovative Behavior and Communication* (New York: Holt, Rinehart & Winston, 1971).

[21]Everett M. Rogers and David G. Cartano, "Methods of Measuring Opinion Leadership," *Public Opinion Quarterly*, Vol. 26 (Fall 1962), pp. 435–41.

[22]Charles W. King and John O. Summers, "Overlap of Opinion Leadership Across Consumer Product Categories," *Journal of Marketing Research*, Vol. 7 (February 1970), pp. 43–50.

[23]Jacob Jacoby, "Opinion Leadership and Innovativeness: Overlap and Validity," in *Proceedings of the Third Annual Conference of the Association for Consumer Research*, M. Venkatesan, ed. (1972), pp. 632–49.

[24]American Psychological Association, *Standards for Educational and Psychological Tests and Manuals* (Washington, D.C.: American Psychological Association, 1966); Reinhard Angelmar, Gerald Zaltman, and Christian Pinson, "An Examination of Concept Validity," in *Proceedings of the Third Annual Conference of the Association for Consumer Research*, M. Venkatesan, ed. (1972), pp. 586–93; Lee Cronbach, *Essentials of Psychological Testing*, 2nd ed. (New York: Harper & Bros., 1960); Roger M. Heeler and Michael L. Ray, "Measure Validation in Marketing," *Journal of Marketing Research*, Vol. 9 (November 1972), pp. 361–70; Jim C. Nunnally, *Psychometric Theory* (New York: McGraw-Hill, 1973).

[25]Nunnally, ibid., pp. 75–102.

[26]Alfred A. Kuehn, "Demonstration of a Relationship Between Psychologial Factors and Brand Choice," *Journal of Business*, Vol. 36 (April 1963), pp. 237–41; Heeler and Ray, same as reference 24 above.

[27]P. S. Raju, Rabi S. Bhagat, and Jagdish N. Sheth, "Predictive Validation and Cross-Validation of the Fishbein, Rosenberg, and Sheth Models of Attitudes," in *Advances in Consumer Research, Vol. 2*, M. J. Schlinger, ed. (Chicago: University of Illinois, 1975), pp. 405–25, at p. 407.

[28]Leon B. Kaplan, George J. Szybillo, and Jacob Jacoby, "Components of Perceived Risk in Product Purchase: A Cross-Validation," *Journal of Applied Psychology*, Vol. 59 (June 1974), pp. 287–91; Raju et al., same as reference 27 above; Donald E. Speller, "Attitudes and Intentions as Predictors of Purchase: A Cross-Validation," *Proceedings, 81st Annual Convention of the American Psychological Association*, Vol. 8 (Issue 2, 1973), pp. 825–26; David T. Wilson, H. Lee Mathews, and James W. Harvey, "An Empirical Test of the Fishbein Behavioral Intention Model," *Journal of Consumer Research*, Vol. 1 (March 1975), pp. 39–48.

[29]Dominic W. Massaro, *Experimental Psychology and Information Processing* (Chicago: Rand-McNally, 1975), p. 23; Robert Plutchik, *Foundations of Experimental Research* (New York: Harper & Row, 1968), p. 45; Selltiz et al., same as reference 12 above, pp. 146–47.

[30]Plutchik, ibid., p. 47.

[31]Donald T. Campbell and Donald W. Fiske, "Convergent and Discriminant Validation by the Multitrait-Multimethod Matrix," *Psychological Bulletin*, Vol. 56 (1959), pp. 81–105.

[32]Harry L. Davis, "Measurement of Husband-Wife Influence in Consumer Purchase Decisions," *Journal of Marketing Research*, Vol. 8 (August 1971), pp. 305–12; Jacob Jacoby, "The Construct Validity of Opinion Leadership," *Public Opinion Quarterly*, Vol. 38 (Spring 1974), pp. 81–89; Alvin J. Silk, "Response Set and the Measurement of Self-Designated Opinion Leadership." *Public Opinion Quarterly*, Vol. 35 (Fall 1971), pp. 383–97.

[33]Campbell et al., same as reference 31 above, p. 100.

[34]Jacoby et al., (1978), same as reference 19 above.

[35]Kohn et al., same as reference 20 above.

[36]Jerry Olson and Jacob Jacoby, "A Construct Validation Study of Brand Loyalty," in *Proceedings, 79th Annual Convention of the American Psychological Association*, Vol. 6 (1971), pp. 657–58.

[37]Kevin J. Clancy and David M Kweskin, "T.V. Commercial Recall Correlates," *Journal of Advertising Research*, Vol. 11 (April 1971), pp. 18–20; Shirley Young, "Copy Testing Without Magic Numbers," *Journal of Advertising Research*, Vol. 12 (February 1972), pp. 3–12.

[38]Young, ibid., p. 7.

[39]Gardner, same as reference 7 above, pp. 43–44.

[40]Joel Cohen, Presidential Address, untitled, *Association for Consumer Research Newsletter*, Vol. 3 (January 1973), pp. 3,5.

[41]Edward W. Hart, Jr., "Consumer Risk-Taking for Self and for Spouse," unpublished Ph.D. dissertation (Purdue University, 1974); Karl Weigl, "Perceived Risk and Information Search in a Gift Buying Situation," unpublished MS thesis (Purdue University, 1975).

[42]Jacob Jacoby, Carol K. Berning, and Thomas Dietvorst, "What About Disposition?" *Journal of Marketing*, Vol. 41 (April 1977), pp. 22–28.

[43]Eugene J. Webb, Donald T. Campbell, Richard D. Schwartz, and Lee Sechrest, *Unobtrusive Measures: Non-reactive Research in the Social Sciences* (Chicago: Rand-McNally, 1966).

DISCUSSION QUESTIONS

1. Randomly select a current issue of the *Journal of Consumer Research* and evaluate the articles based on Jacoby's crtiicisms. Compare the recent issue to an earlier issue of the *Journal of Consumer Research*.

2. What are the major deficiencies of the articles you have examined? Explain. What changes seem to have occurred from the older articles to the newer articles?

3. What are the major strengths of the articles you have examined? Explain. What changes seem to have occurred from the older articles to the newer articles.

FOUR

CHALLENGES TO MARKETING THEORY

Many of the essays contained in this volume offer appropriate challenges for the marketing discipline. Traditional assumptions of theory development and testing, research methods and theory's relationship to research have been reexamined, and new and creative approaches to marketing thought development have been introduced. Nevertheless, most of the preceding essays do not have challenges as their primary intent. This is not the case with the two closing papers; both were written primarily to provoke and stimulate thinking and changes in the marketing discipline.

Peter's clever and interesting appear is an original piece for this volume. The paper's tracing of a hypothetical professor's career and his relationship to his mentor provide numerous explicit and implicit challenges to the reader. The Zaltman and Bonoma paper provides an excellent capstone to this book by suggesting some potentially heretical but heuristic deviations from current academic marketing practices. Although some of the ideas are purposely overstated, the authors' ''heresy'' provokes thought and discussion regarding nontraditional and novel considerations pertinent to the marketing discipline.

28

ON IGNORING A RESEARCH EDUCATION*

J. PAUL PETER

Professor Bimbo, an excellent consumer researcher, was held in high esteem by his colleagues. He was a careful researcher who tested provocative hypotheses and usually found strong relationships and striking effects. However, in his latest series of studies, the results had been lackluster. Although he worked hard in designing these studies, there just wasn't much to write about.

Bimbo was worried that his brilliant career might falter, so, he contacted a good friend and colleague, Professor Hardbottom. Hardbottom was one of the grand old men in the field who lately spent most of his time reading about Eastern religions. Yet, in his day, he had been quite a researcher, and if he'd continued working hard, probably could have got a research chair at a major school. Bimbo was convinced that Hardbottom spent too much time reading metaphysical junk. However, he respected Hardbottom's knowledge of research methodology.

Bimbo brought his work to Hardbottom's office. Surprisingly, Hardbottom did not want to know much about the theory under investigation other than what direction the measures should correlate. He told Bimbo to leave the questionnaire, coding instructions, and data and to come back tomorrow.

When Bimbo returned the next day, Hardbottom explained: "It's quite clear what the problem is. Your questions are too difficult and you don't have enough items per scale. Simplify the questions a bit and double the number of items on each scale and I'm sure you'll find the relationships you're looking for."

Bimbo went back to his office and did as he was told. He then collected some more data and sure enough he got an R^2 of .79, quite good for the theory and quite high for studies in the field. Bimbo published the study in a prestigious journal, received a number of kudos, and even some feelers for research chairs at minor universities.

Bimbo was starting to feel better about his career

and resumed his work with renewed vigor. This time he designed a balanced replication of a previous study he had published on persuasion tactics. After collecting the data, though, the exact replication part of the study did not come out as expected. Because he had planned to use the study when being interviewed for better positions, he was panic-stricken with the results. He quickly called for a conference with Hardbottom.

After Bimbo explained the failure to achieve an exact replication and how important it was for the rest of the study, Hardbottom asked about what the manipulation was supposed to achieve. He then suggested that the main reason for the failure to replicate was the difference in sex of the interviewers. He explained that to get the positive result achieved in the earlier study, Bimbo should be sure the interviewers were the opposite sex of the interviewees. Also, he should be sure that the interviewers were the most attractive people in the class and that they smiled, said "thank you," and squeezed the subject's arm when the subject complied with their first request.

Bimbo protested that previous studies never reported anything like this and that the theory said nothing about it either. Although a bit irritated, Hardbottom smiled and said, "Don't get upset. All I'm saying is that you need a stronger manipulation to get the effect you want."

Bimbo went back to his office and thought a bit. He remembered a number of unpublished experiments he had read in various areas that did not achieve a positive result. Often these studies blamed the failure on a manipulation that was too weak. So, he thought, what's wrong with using a stronger manipulation to increase the probability of achieving the effect needed in the research?

He quickly set up the study and analyzed the data because his first new-job interview was but two weeks away. Sure enough, the exact replication worked out beautifully and with a few other tips from Hardbottom, the balanced replication extended previous research in the field. Bimbo presented the study at several universities and as the word traveled through the grapevine, even some

---

*Editors' Note: This article is being presented without a preface because it has never been published before and because a preface might weaken the message.

major universities started to call about the possibility of a chaired professorship.

Bimbo was really excited now and started turning the crank. Some of his studies were coming out great, but occasionally he would need to see Hardbottom for some advice. His resume and research reputation were growing by leaps and bounds.

Bimbo finally was offered and accepted a prestigious chair at a major university. Because the new university was some distance away, the occasional conversations with Hardbottom were now only by telephone. This seemed to bother Hardbottom not at all, and he could usually resolve the problem with a single simple sentence, such as "Design your measures more carefully," "Increase your sample size," "Use a more homogeneous sample," "Experimentally control this variable," "Statistically control that variable," "Move the setting to the laboratory," "Try a Bayesian rather than a classical approach," "Use a within-subjects design," "Use this other statistic." It seemed that Hardbottom had almost an endless list of methodological recommendations and could apply them easily to each new situation. By and large, they almost always worked!

Bimbo was now delirious with his success. His research budget was astronomical, and grant funding was little more than a phone call away. There were even rumors that he would receive an international research award.

The following year, Bimbo did receive a prestigious award for major contributions to knowledge. By this time, he no longer needed to call Hardbottom for advice as he never had any problems in conducting his research and obtaining impressive results.

A few weeks later, he was thinking about his success and decided to use some of his large travel budget to visit old Hardbottom. He was sure Hardbottom would be glad to see him and revel in his success. He even considered offering his old friend a job as a research associate. After all, "Bimbo and Hardbottom" would look great in print, and it would be a nice gesture for his earlier help.

Hardbottom *was* glad to see him, and they spent the afternoon drinking beer in a local pub. Most of the talk was about Bimbo's accomplishments and success. Finally, being a bit embarrassed, Bimbo decided to give his old friend a chance to brag a bit about himself. He reminded Hardbottom of all of the previous advice and help he had given. He also reminded him of how little information was needed before Hardbottom could determine a solution. In fact, other than the direction of the relationship between measures or the type of effect that a manipulation was supposed to achieve, little else was needed. "How do you do it, old friend?" asked Bimbo.

Surprisingly, and perhaps because of a few beers too many, Hardbottom became angry with the question and shouted, "Haven't you learned by now that it is the method that controls the results?"

Bimbo was a bit shaken and irritated with such a ridiculous challenge. "What about hypothesis testing, old man?" he said in a superior tone.

"What about it, sonny? Is hypothesis testing any more than a glorified method?" snapped Hardbottom.

"What about theory, you old bastard?" blasted Bimbo.

"The issue is not theory construction, you incompetent serf! The issue is obtaining desired empirical results! Given sufficient knowledge of a variety of methods, clever researchers should be able to orchestrate designs to support their predilections!" clarified Hardbottom loudly.

Trying to gather his composure and put the argument in perspective, Bimbo reasoned, "You're saying that the method controls the results and the researcher controls the method, is that your position?"

"Now you're *finally* getting a research education!" said Hardbottom triumphantly.

With that, Bimbo left the bar and decided not to offer the senile old fool a job. After all, everyone knows that theories are universal and data speak for themselves.

DISCUSSION QUESTIONS

1. Professor Hardbottom made a number of recommendations in this story that by and large almost always worked. Below is a list of those recommendations. On the scales to the right, please check what the effect of each of these recommendations has on obtaining statistically significant correlations and treatment effects to support a theory.

	Increases the Probability of Obtaining Supportive Results	Decreases the Probability of Obtaining Supportive Results
a. Increasing the reliability of measures by simplifying and adding items. (Also consider the effects of deleting items that decrease the reliability coefficient.)	_____	_____
b. Using stronger manipulations.	_____	_____
c. Increasing sample size.	_____	_____
d. Using more homogeneous samples.	_____	_____
e. Experimentally or statistically controlling other variables.	_____	_____
f. Using a laboratory setting when a different setting fails.	_____	_____
g. Using different statistics when the originally chosen statistic fails.	_____	_____
h. Redesigning the study after an initial failure to achieve supportive results.	_____	_____
i. Pretesting the method.	_____	_____

2. In light of your answers to question 1 and considering the biases journals seem to exhibit toward publishing only so-called positive results, are researchers more likely to be confirmationists or falsificationists? Do researchers' predilections concerning the veracity of the theory affect the role they play in conducting and reporting research?

3. Basic research reports can be divided into six parts: theory, hypotheses, measurement, sampling and data collection, data analysis, and results and interpretation. For each of these stages, a number of things can affect the outcomes of the research project. In the following table, there is a list of questions for each of the six stages and two categories for responses: the researcher and the nature of the phenomenon. Divide 100 points for each question between the researcher and the nature of the phenomenon in terms of the amount of *influence* they have on the research outcome. Be prepared to defend your choices.

	The Researcher Decides This	The Nature of the Phenomenon Decides This
Theory		
a. Which theory will be investigated in the research?	_____	_____
Hypotheses/Research Questions		
a. What specific hypotheses will be tested?	_____	_____
b. How many hypotheses will be tested?	_____	_____
c. What parts of the theory will not be tested?	_____	_____
d. How the constructs are defined?	_____	_____
Measurement		
a. How will the constructs be measured, i.e., what procedures will be used?	_____	_____
b. How much effort will be expended on developing and validating the measures?	_____	_____
c. How high will the reliability values have to be before the		

measure is considered appropriate for use in the substantive theory test?
d. What manipulations will be used?

Sampling and Data Collection
a. How is the sampling plan determined?
b. How large a final sample is acceptable?
c. How homogeneous or heterogeneous is the final sample?
d. How will the data be collected?

Data Analysis
a. What types of data analysis will be used?
b. What computer program(s) will be used?
c. What statistics will be used?

Results and Interpretation
a. What criteria will be used to determine whether the hypotheses are supported or not?
b. How the data are interpreted?
c. What determines the implications of the study?
d. What determines whether the results are generalizable?

4. Overall, how important are subjective researcher decisions and inferences in the research process?
5. Are theories universal and do data speak for themselves?
6. Which of these researchers was more successful?
7. Which of these researchers ignored a research education?

PREFACE TO

"The Lack of Heresy in Marketing"

We cannot offer the reader any profound or moving account of the origin of our ideas or even of the intent in writing this paper. The ideas surfaced first while we were sitting by a winter's fire imbiding in traditional holiday cheer. That relaxed setting somehow prompted a motivation to be mischievous with respect to the contents of an already overdue paper. The ideas and the impulse to be mischievous simply seemed like fun, although we seriously endorse the recommendations in this paper.

29

THE LACK OF HERESY IN MARKETING

GERALD ZALTMAN
THOMAS V. BONOMA

INTRODUCTION

Heresy, according to one source, is a set of ideas, opinions, or practices which deviate from the accepted body of beliefs, customs, and practices in an organized endeavor. Though the term is usually only applied in matters of faith and morals, such as religion, it is appropriate wherever training, custom, or ''right practice'' dictates the reactions of a majority or all of the practitioners in an area, such as in science. Clearly, to talk about heresy requires two logical components: an accepted body of customs, beliefs and practices endorsed by the majority of practitioners in a field, and a number of deviates proposing nontraditional or unaccepted ideas and practices.

It is our contention that marketing thought, theory, and research seem to have an overwhelming abundance of the first logical condition, and a dearth of the second. That is, the theme of our paper is that there is an insufficient volume of heresy in marketing thought, an insufficient number of deviant practices, thoughts, and beliefs. Our purpose here is to suggest some potentially heretical and at the same time heuristic deviations from current academic marketing practice as we understand it. In pursuing this theme we shall state certain ideas in their extreme form, primarily to provoke discussion and thought. Though we do not necessarily feel these ideas are valid in their extreme form, we do feel very strongly about the validity of the basic thrust and direction of the ideas. Additionally, we wish to point out at the outset that we do not except ourselves and our own work from many of the criticisms we make below; indeed, it has been observing our own behavior that has been a primary cause of many of the thoughts.

In order to provide at least a skeleton of organi-

zation to some of the ideas we shall propose, we will overlay a systems orientation on academic marketing. Like all systems, marketing has input, throughput, and output functions. We consider each in turn, moving through problem focus and theory construction issues (input) to variable selection, methodology and analytic modes (throughput), toward the output of our discipline, publications and conferences.

INPUT VARIABLES

Theory Construction

Theory building in marketing, when it is compared against the same endeavor in other social sciences, seems neither to be as frequently engaged nor as fruitfully directed as many of its sister disciplines. It is easy to say, as we have in other publications, that marketing is a young discipline, and therefore should not be expected to show much sophistication in theory development. Indeed, our ''borrowed'' psychological, sociological, and other theoretical notions seem to serve us rather well; again perhaps a sign of youth, or else an indicator of the close relationship of marketing to its admittedly behavioral foundations. Or, one can address the convenient truisms that marketing is only an ''applied'' science, and therefore is secondary in such ''basic'' science concerns as theory building, or that marketing after all is only art, and we need not be concerned with theoretical abstractions but only with empirical covariations. But, perhaps it is worthwhile to direct some attention to the traditional and customary theory-building practices in use in the marketing discipline to see if perhaps some of the reasons for our failure to develop integrated conceptual views of marketing phenomena may lie in the way we have chosen to approach this task.

Basically, we would argue that much more of an anthropological approach to marketing theory should be taken. If we really want to understand

Source: Revised for this volume from *Conceptual and Theoretical Developments in Marketing,* O. C. Ferrell, Stephen W. Brown, and Charles W. Lamb eds., Chicago, Ill.: American Marketing Association, 1979, 474–484.

329

what theory is, particularly which theories make sense or work, we should not always follow the deductive mode of thinking generally espoused in traditional science. We would argue first of all that there is *not* a difference between theory and practice. In fact, we feel that it is extremely unfortunate that such a dichotomy exists in the minds of practitioners and in the minds of academics. Thus, our most heretical thought is that we should abandon terms that imply false dichotomies, such as theory and practice. Specifically, we would argue for building marketing theory by following a theory-in-use approach.[1] That is, marketers can identify theory by observing very closely what it is that very effective managers do. We would then state those practices in the form of general rules of thumb. Following the derivation of several of these rules of thumb obtained by very close empirical observation, we could derive some propositions which these managers seem to hold or from which these rules of thumb seem to be derived. Having identified a set of propositions, we could start linking different components of these propositions in such a form as to develop a theory of interrelated concepts. In essence, we advocate moving "backward" from successful practice to sound theory. The logical path here, of course, is inductive, not deductive.

We must digress here. It is our contention that marketing managers who are very effective in the practice of their profession maintain in their minds a large inventory of ideas or concepts. Moreover, these ideas are interrelated. We would call such interrelationships, in the minimal form of two ideas, propositions. To the extent that there are several ideas linked, we would have a theory. In this case we are defining or treating a theory simply as a relationship among three or more concepts or ideas.

We suspect we would find, following this anthropological approach, that managers have a very good sense of the various conditions under which differing combinations of ideas are most important; that is, a sense for what types of situational factors would cause greater reliance on certain concepts or ideas, and less reliance on other concepts or ideas. Of course, if we told our manager that what has been described is a very rich or sophisticated theory, we would probably find ourselves facing a very offended person. That is, to say that effective managerial action results from theory is to suggest first that the concepts driving action are very abstract,

and managers will hasten to tell you that the way they think is not abstract. Secondly, since the term theory often implies something irrelevant, managers might be further offended by the implication that their thinking is irrelevant, and it is highly unlikely that they would be where they are if that were the case. But what *is* likely to be abstract and irrelevant is a theory arrived at in a more deductive mode in a more traditional fashion where the goal of the theory is to predict management behavior. Similar logic can be applied to developing theories of consumer behavior.

A few more words need to be said about a theory-in-use approach. What it requires is going out and being with people who are closest to the phenomena that we study. If we are concerned with theories about marketing management, it implies that we go out and work along with, or at least be participant observers with, marketing managers in the contexts of concern. If we want to understand consumers, it means in effect that we should live with our consumers. We should observe them very closely in a more anthropological and participative way. We should choose different kinds of laboratory settings in which to study consumers. This may mean much greater reliance on noninteractive unobtrusive measures than we customarily use.

The normal path of science suggests that we start out with a grand phenomenon that we would like to explain, like "marketing," and attempt to build our theories by deductively arguing specific consequences from the general framework while at the same time maintaining a customary and acceptable scientific detachment from the phenomena we observe. We challenge both of those notions, and argue that the best path toward theory building and marketing may well be an inductive one, working up from successful managerial practice or "expert" consumer behavior while at the same time maintaining an involved, participative interaction with the objects of our observation.

Writing Versus Thinking

Now there is a second problem. It will not behoove us to go out and spend a lot of time with managers, with consumers, and with the people who are closest to the phenomena with which we are concerned unless we simply have a richer set of ideas to bring to bear, a richer framework with which to filter the ideas our subjects or respondents bring to us. Toward that end we would like to make some radical suggestions. The most radical suggestion is that the marketing profession, at least the academics and others who are active authors, take a year's sabbatical from writing and that the time be spent simply in thinking—not in doing research, not in collecting data—but simply in reconceptualizing and construing the phenomena we are concerned with, perhaps through the anthropological approach that we are suggesting. What would be the cost or loss of a year's absence from writing by the marketing professor? We will return to that issue in the "Output" section. For those who are not sure what to think about, we suggest working with a marketing manager for half the year.

Of course, no amount of additional thinking will do any good if we are thinking about the wrong things, or thinking about them in the wrong way. The anthropological approach would do much toward insuring against that contingency. But, a third problem which characterizes not only marketing but many of the other social sciences is what we like to call "low variance" problem focus. Consider the notion of statistical variance or dispersion. It basically is intended to summarize the range of possible outcomes in a given distribution of events or measures. It is our contention that the social sciences in general, and marketing in particular, operate to work on problems where the variance of possible outcomes, and hence the contribution of theory or research to their explanation, is low. That is, we like to insure ourselves against surprises, against developing theories which fail because the world surprises us, against doing surveys or experiments which show nothing. That means, when we select a research problem or enter a subarea in marketing, we ordinarily like to restrict our attention so narrowly that we have a good chance of success with our efforts. That, of course, makes for a lot of hypothesis confirmation and tight-looking theory. It also makes for cliche-like theories and studies for "low-risk" science which grinds out minor contributions around minor themes, and for a rather self-serving approach which is more attuned to satisfying the political and career realities of those undertaking it than it is the needs of knowledge.

Instead of trying to develop a theory of marketing, for example, we continue partitioning the area until we feel more comfortable with its size. We then have industrial, consumer and not-for-profit marketing, and of course, with those three labels must come three distinct sets of theories, propositions, and empirical forays. We do not content ourselves with worrying about the product in the marketing mix, but persist in attempting to differentiate services and products in what sometimes seems an almost hair-splitting fashion so that we can reduce the variance and hence increase the predictability of our endeavors. When carried to its logical extreme, of course, this fractionization of discipline (social psychology is an excellent example) leads ultimately to theories and models so specific that they are nongeneralizable across cases, empirical endeavors which become minor variations on a theme, and generally a science which is so atomized as to be useless. We would like to encourage higher risk, unifying, even if you like "grand theoretical" attempts in marketing. Perhaps that means that heretically we would recommend that we all be more tolerant of failure, and even of negative results in dissertations. The one thing that is clear is that neither an individual nor a science over exceeds its aspirations; if those are of the conservative, low-risk variety, the output will often match. As one manager of our acquaintance puts it, "Don't chin yourself on a curb."

THROUGHPUT

Variables Selection and Use

Most of the little we have to say about variable selection is directly due to the state of affairs in theory development we talked about above. Our variables seem to come from two sources: the ones we "borrow" from other disciplines, and thin air. There is certainly nothing wrong with the first, as long as the researcher is willing to borrow not only the variables of interest but also the theoretical rationale underlying their original selection. But, as many of us seem to do, to just select a grab bag of unrelated psychological or economic or decision theory concepts, stick them together in one or another fashion, and run another survey or lab experiment is not an optimal approach for achieving increases in knowledge.

As many others have pointed out better than we can here, the investigatory method of choice in marketing is almost always the survey or a variant of it. Clearly, reliance on self-report measures is a chancy business at best, and a simple expedient decision when other methods are not used to "triangulate" these largely inconsistently related reports of behavior with actual behavior. Contrary to others, we do not feel that marketing's "salvation" lies solely in the experiment. We feel, rather, that it lies in a multimethod approach, one which employs the case study, the anthropological naturalistic observation we talked about above, tests and measurements, and experiments with the more self-report investigatory approaches in order to get a handle on behavior. To rely solely on what others say they will do, or have done, or feel or think is to put ease and expediency on altars where they do not belong.

Analytic Modes and Replications

Where our methods are often based on dubious indicators of behavior, our analytic modes are often based on the equally dubious measure of association instead of causality. Covariation is always an interesting and noteworthy event in the world, and there is certainly nothing wrong with pointing it out in marketing. But to rely solely or even largely on the statistics of covariation instead of those of causality is to put oneself in the position of having to say that because there is a .98 correlation between the softness of asphalt and the incidence of polio that the former causes the latter.

But, the reader should not get the impression that we are advocating the use only of sophisticated variance partitioning statistics. Indeed, we would like to put forth the notion that while much more sophisticated quantitative analysis of marketing problems is necessary for further understanding of those problems, that the application of those techniques will provide very little additional insight unless a substantial amount of qualitative sophistication has preceded that statistical sophistication. Unfortunately, we see a gross misuse, or rather overuse of statistical techniques *relative* to the qualitative dimensions of the work or data that those techniques are applied to. We strongly suggest much more thinking before doing, unless the more quantitative in our midst are content with their role of obfuscating the obvious via numbers.

Finally, on throughput, it has been and probably will always remain a heretical thought in the social sciences that an investigator is responsible for replicating his or her findings before disseminating them. For reasons that are well known to all of us,

this will never become common practice or indeed even a desirable rarity. But, we do feel compelled to nod in the direction of all those central points the *Journal of Consumer Research* puts in its guidelines under the title of "Would You Like to Be Rejected by JCR?"

OUTPUT

We suggested above that it might behoove all of us to take a year's sabbatical from writing, and to devote that time to thinking. At this point, it might be appropriate to ponder the potential costs or loss of a year's presence from writing by the total marketing community in the following fashion. Suppose all publication activity ceased in marketing. Operationally, let's say that the American Marketing Association would cease publication of its journals, proceedings, special workshops, and other publications for one calendar year. Would there be a great loss, apart perhaps from promotions not taking place? We think not. Let's assume that starting five years ago and going back for a period of, let's say, another five or ten years, that we were to randomly select and expunge from memory one volume of journals and that same year's conference proceedings and other published documents. We think that that one year's worth of publications selected at random would not be missed. That is, the number of seminal ideas appearing in that one year would be extremely few, if any. Most of the publications, we would find, would not even be missed in subsequent publications in terms of citations. It is not that these articles would not have been cited, but rather that there would be other writings that would serve the purposes these citations would have served. The increment in knowledge provided by that one year's volume as evidenced by what we would "not know" through its absence would be very minimal.

Our purpose here is not to suggest that none of us does good or important work, but only that the criteria for published work are perhaps less than optimal for many marketing academics, much less for the practitioners who are often so negatively vocal about our publications. Most of us marvel at the avidity with which our doctoral students consume the *Journal of Marketing Research*, when we try to struggle through at least the abstracts before the next issue comes out. Similar feelings are often generated by the conference proceedings, which we feel we cannot do without until we have bought them and carted them about for three or four days only to let them languish on a shelf back home (after we have looked up our own article, of course) until next year's volume disturbs the dust. Perhaps we could rethink some of our orientations toward output, and suggest some unusual criteria short of a full sabbatical (thought we still think that is the most valuable alternative) for the discipline.

One suggestion that might, if implemented, reduce the quantity of output while maintaining quality would be to apply the same standards to conference proceedings as we would apply, and do apply, to the *Journal of Marketing,* the *Journal of Marketing Research,* and the *Journal of Consumer Research.* We would very quickly find that most of the conference submissions would not be accepted. Moreover, there would probably be such an inadequate number of papers accepted to warrant not holding a conference at all. One could speculate on the value or merit of the conference papers by asking what attendance might be at AMA if the recruiting activities were not so prominent or did not take place at all at the Fall meetings. We suggest that attendance would at least be halved at those meetings, which might be an unobtrusive measure of the intellectual value of the gathering.

Of course, it might be argued that the types of papers and the purposes of conferences in general are to present more speculative, tentative thoughts that are not well documented but are meant to be provocative. In fact, that can be a very important function of a conference. An interesting test of that notion applied to AMA conferences would be to find out how many of the proceedings papers indeed stimulated additional research or further thought and made their way into major or even minor research efforts. We suspect that very little of what's presented at those conferences bears that fruit.

Another suggestion we have is that the journals, for example, be required to establish a higher threshold of contribution to knowledge than might currently be used. That is, we characterize the great majority of research or thinking in marketing as being rather minor extensions of existing thought. It is somewhat analogous to simply fine-tuning a rather large machine. (In many cases the machine isn't so large either.) We would find it difficult to establish a way of measuring what a significant contribution is. One operational measure, however,

might be the response to the following question: How much present thinking on the part of how many people would be changed if an idea or research finding were, in fact, correct? The greater the amount of thinking that a person has to change or discard as a result of a particular finding or conclusion, the greater the contribution of that research to that person. The more such people there are who have to discard or change their thinking, the greater the contribution of the research to the profession at large. We would therefore want to require all authors to respond to that question (perhaps empirically) in the context or body of their articles. They should indicate what practices by how many people would be changed as a result of their findings. This gets into the problem of research utilization. That is, conceivably a finding could have great impact in these terms, but not in fact be translated into action. We do not suggest authors/researchers be held accountable in that way, but only in the sense that their ideas have potential for utilization. We would build the same concerns into the referees' evaluations.

Finally, we find the notion that marketing holds two conferences, one for managers and another for educators, both dysfunctional and absurd. If academic marketing is as divorced from marketing practice as our professional association seems to feel and as many marketing managers would insist, then it is probably time to close down shop and find another endeavor. Our prime constituency, the marketing practitioner, is insulated from academics in a manner that can only contribute to further fractionization of our discipline, more irrelevance in academic activities, and retarded progress for the discipline as a whole.

SOME MORE HERESY

On the Importance of Illness, Showers, Driving Home, and Feeding the Dog

Where do ideas come from to do provocative, interesting research? We have asked a wide number of colleagues where they get their ideas and when they get their ideas. It is very interesting that seldom do they respond by saying in effect, "I was sitting at my desk thinking hard about this particular issue, or about what to do with my time, or which of several topics to allocate my resources and time to.'' Most responded by saying they get their most intriguing ideas that have led to their major research contributions when they are lying ill with a fever in bed, when they are taking a shower, while they are driving home, or, as in the case of one colleague, often when feeding or walking the dog. The significance of these comments is not that one ought to acquire a dog or become ill on some routine basis. Rather, they suggest that there are issues, ideas, and problems of concern to people which they never quite disengage from. That is, even when undertaking other activities—driving home, showering— there is something working in the unconscious which occasionally interrupts into the conscious mind in the form of a very significant or important idea. These people are not quite able to ever disengage from their activities as researchers and scholars. Indeed, it may be important to program such idle activities as walking the dog or driving home so that one is free from the normal course of pressures and distractions that might prevent the unconscious from projecting important ideas or perspectives into the conscious mind.

It is because we feel that so many ideas to develop in this fashion, that is, without a great deal of logical explicit thinking, that people have a hard time describing how or where they got ideas, the physical setting was mentioned almost consistently. People remembered where they got the idea and could respond most effectively in those terms, but not how the idea came to mind. Now certainly many ideas come directly to us from colleagues in conversation or in the reading of their work. Someone might make a suggestion that we ought to look at an issue this way or that way. Or someone may make a claim that there is an idea (however they arrived at it) that one ought to pursue, and indeed people may accept ideas generated by others and pursue them. That is all well and proper. But we think that most original research and thinking will come in the very uncontrolled and erratic way of unconscious thought processes projecting themselves forward. The important consideration is to allow this to happen.

Prostitution and Promiscuity

One often hears the term prostitution applied to contract and grant research, especially by academic institutions. This reference refers to the occurrence of organizations and individuals or teams of individuals responding to funding opportunities for research primarily on the basis of the need to bring in external funds to the research agency for various administration purposes, such as continuing one's job, contributing overhead to the institution, and supporting backup personnel. The explicit implication is that the funds are obtained and solicited or accepted for those reasons primarily. The other motivations for doing research—it's fun, it's challenging to oneself, to others, and so forth—apply only in a very secondary fashion. Prostitution is not at all uncommon. There are strong pressures to solicit funds. Confusion develops, however, in the following way. Many projects which may be of concern to many people have very significant consequences in terms of the number of people whose thinking would be changed, which require assumption challenging and so forth, do require substantial amounts of money. This is especially true for research which has policy implications as well as traditional theoretical implications. Pressure develops within the researcher to find funds adequate to his or her research objectives. Such funds are not always clearly available.

We feel that the term promiscuity applies when researchers have a special kind of interest, a special theme, or a special concern and are able to in effect seduce funding agencies into supporting those research concerns and those research interests. Indeed, it can be fun to show a federal official or a private foundation official how their concerns and needs are coincident with your skills, interests and research commitments. This can often be a very creative act whereby you make a connection between a particular body of research and a particular problem of concern to these officials. Typically, this will be a connection they had not previously perceived; in effect, they are seduced. Clearly, the seducer in this instance is the researcher and not the funding source. If the researcher obtains substantial benefit (as well as the funding source) in terms of not simply financial contributions to the research enterprise, but the ability to conduct and pursue their [sic] interests more effectively and vigorously, then they [sic] are indeed having lots of fun. We can only speak knowledgeably about promiscuity. We will have to leave it up to others to speak about prostitution. However, the crucial difference is that in the instance of promiscuity, researchers are having fun. They are doing the seducing which can be fun in and of itself; after all, whoever claimed courtship to be unpleasant? More importantly, as a result of the seduction researchers obtain resources which enable them to pursue their interests and their concerns. It just so happens that the pursuit of these concerns is of benefit to the sponsor of the research.

Prostitution (it seems to us) is an instance where the researcher does not have fun. The researcher is primarily a tool for the implementation of funding agency objectives only. We would urge young researchers to be very careful and very wary of the kinds of institutional pressures that cause one to be seduced as opposed to being the seducer. Promiscuity, we feel, will lead to much greater development of theory because it leads to potentially greater levels of a research activity, and the direction of research is much more at the control and discretion of the researcher. Prostitution, on the other hand, is more likely to lead to funding of policy-related research which may have significant theoretical development, but it is a theoretical development which is constrained by the direction the policy research is to take.

CONCLUSION

Our basic concern in this paper is with resolving a paradox. This paradox might be described in the following way. Our profession contains among its practitioners and academic scholars a substantial number of very bright, technically highly capable and energetic individuals who are very serious about their work. The contradiction that concerns us is that the summary results of these individuals is not what one would expect given such attributes. Clearly there are individual exceptions to this. However, in aggregate the boundaries of marketing knowledge are not being violated and then extended with the frequency our potential permits. There is a lack of daring to be different. We are more than a little reluctant to propose and pursue nontraditional or unaccepted ideas. Our field is well endowed with bright and earnest practitioners and scholars. Thus the most essential ingredient for having more heresy is present. The challenge is how to encourage, facilitate, and even protect those who dare to be different and provocative. What types of social innovations in our profession would encourage more theory construction, more creative thinking and more promiscuity? To encourage the reader to wrestle with this question we shall pose a few . . . discussion questions.

NOTES

[1]Gerald Zaltman, Karen LeMasters, and Michael P. Heffring, *Theory Construction in Marketing: Some Thoughts on Thinking,* N.Y.: John Wiley & Sons, 1982, Chapter 6.

DISCUSSION QUESTIONS

1. What are the distinguishing characteristics of an idea, research finding, or theory that is provocative? Are they typically well validated or fully developed? What are their sources? What might cause a potentially provocative idea to be rejected as either obvious or absurd?

2. How many heretical ideas have you encountered during the past year in the marketing literature? If one or more, what proportion do they represent of all ideas you have encountered during this same period? Do you think there may be an upper limit to the amount of tradition breaking a given field can tolerate within a given period of time? Just how many significant innovative ideas could be accepted in marketing over a period of say three or four years? Do you feel we are operating at that limit?

3. What are the conditions under which most of your interesting ideas first appear? Have you ever not put forth an idea about which you felt strongly because of a concern over ridicule or an inability to offer evidence others might demand? How many such ideas do you think stay hidden because they are not shared, are difficult to research, difficult to explain fully or because they are inconsistent with basic (but not necessarily correct) assumptions in the field? To what extent do you think that such hidden ideas represent the source of most ideas that lead a field? What might be done by any individual, group (such as AMA), or institution (such as a school) to uncover more hidden ideas more quickly? What are the sources of pressure for keeping heretical ideas hidden?

FIVE

TAXONOMICAL BIBLIOGRAPHY OF MARKETING THEORY

COMPILED BY STEPHEN J. GROVE AND RAYMOND P. FISK

Creating this taxonomical bibliography of marketing theory proved to be a rewarding but prodigious task. It was pursued in two parts: (1) creation of the taxonomy based on an analysis of prior classifications of theoretical phenomena in marketing and (2) categorization of articles, books, and manuscripts within the taxonomy.

A few caveats are necessary at the outset. First, with the exception of a relatively small collection of classic sources, the bibliography contains materials published during and after 1976. The year 1976 was chosen as a cut-off point because the last known marketing theory bibliography was published in 1976 by Thompson and Faricy. Second, space constraints prevented us from cross-referencing these sources. Hence, each source was listed in only one category. Third, every effort was made to include all marketing theory sources (including many from a variety of conferences). However, we have probably, and inadvertently, neglected some sources. Fourth, a rule for inclusion or exclusion is always necessary in classificatory tasks. To be included in this bibliography, a source must have concerned a theoretical/conceptual issue. We tried to err on the side of inclusion. Articles that contained both theoretical/conceptual material and empirical content were also included. However, for papers such as these, we chose to err on the side of exclusion.

The taxonomy for this bibliography was created after evaluating the subject classifications in prior marketing theory readers by Fisk (1971); Cox, Alderson, and Shapiro (1964); and Kernan and Sommers (1968). In addition, the subject headings from the three American Marketing Association theory conferences were examined. The Thompson and Faricy (1976) bibliography was also inspected.

The resultant taxonomy is as follows:

1. Marketing Theory: Its Nature and Content
2. The History of Marketing Thought and Theory
3. Research Contributions to Marketing Theory
4. Theory and Consumer Behavior
5. Theory and Strategic Marketing
6. Marketing Mix
   a. Product Theory
   b. Price Theory
   c. Promotion Theory
   d. Distribution Theory
7. Macromarketing Theory
8. Broadening Marketing

In the second stage of the bibliography, we sought to find and classify all relevant articles based on our criteria. The easy starting point was the AMA theory conferences. All papers from the three conferences were categorized into one of the headings. Next, the journals: *Journal of Marketing, Journal of Marketing Research, Journal of Consumer Research, Journal of the Academy of Marketing Science, Journal of Retailing,* and *Journal of Macromarketing* were examined. In addition, the conference proceedings for the American Marketing Association, the Association for Consumer Research, and the Southern Marketing Association were inspected. Also, the AMA marketing services conference, and the consumer satisfaction/dissatisfaction conferences were reviewed. We also examined all papers in the *Journal of Marketing*'s "Marketing Abstracts" section listed under the heading of marketing theory. Most of those listings were categorized in the bibliography.

Please note we have coded many of the entries in this bibliography to save space. For example the American Marketing Association Theory Conference Proceedings are each coded to avoid repeating the same bibliographic data 50 or 60 times. A complete list of all coded bibliographic data follows.

BIBLIOGRAPHIC CODING

ACR–77 = *Advances in Consumer Research*, 1977, William D. Perreault, Jr., Editor, Atlanta, Ga., Association for Consumer Research.

ACR–78 = *Advances in Consumer Research*, 1978, H. Keith Hunt, Editor, Ann Arbor, Mich., Association for Consumer Research.

ACR–79 = *Advances in Consumer Research*, 1979, William L. Wilkie, Editor, Ann Arbor, Mich., Association for Consumer Research.

ACR–80 = *Advances in Consumer Research*, 1980, Jerry C. Olson, Editor, Ann Arbor, Mich., Association for Consumer Research.

ACR–81 = *Advances in Consumer Research*, 1981, Kent B. Monroe, Editor, Ann Arbor, Mich., Association for Consumer Research.

ACR–82 = *Advances in Consumer Research*, 1982, Andrew A. Mitchell, Editor, Ann Arbor, Mich., Association for Consumer Research.

ACR–83 = *Advances in Consumer Research*, 1983, Richard P. Bagozzi, Alice M. Tybout, Editors, Ann Arbor, Mich., Association for Consumer Research.

AMA–76 = *Marketing: 1776–1976 and Beyond*, 1976, Kenneth L. Bernhardt, Chicago, American Marketing Association.

AMA–77 = *Contemporary Marketing Thought*, 1977, Barnett A. Greenberg, Danny N. Bellenger, Chicago, American Marketing Association.

AMA–78 = *Research Frontiers in Marketing: Dialogues and Directions*, 1978, Subhash C. Jain, Chicago, American Marketing Association.

AMA–79 = *1979 Educators' Conference Proceedings*, 1979, Neil Beckwith, Michael Houston, Robert Mittelstaedt, Kent B. Monroe, Scott Ward, Editors, Chicago, American Marketing Association.

AMA–80 = *Marketing in the 80's: Changes & Challenges*, 1980, Richard P. Bagozzi, Kenneth L. Bernhardt, Paul S. Busch, David W. Cravens, Joseph F. Hair, Jr., and Carol A. Scott, Editors, Chicago, American Marketing Association.

AMA–81 = *The Changing Marketing Environment: New Theories and Applications*, 1981, Kenneth L. Bernhardt, Ira Dolich, Michael Etzel, William Kehoe, Thomas Kinnear, William D. Perreault, Jr., and Kenneth Roering, Editors, Chicago, American Marketing Association.

AMA–82 = *An Assessment of Marketing Thought & Practice*, 1982, William O. Bearden, William R. Darden, Patrick E. Murphy, John R. Nevin, Jerry C. Olson, Bruce J. Walker, and Barton A. Weitz, Editors, Chicago, American Marketing Association.

AMA–83 = *1983 AMA Educators' Proceedings*, 1983, Patrick E. Murphy, Gene R. Laczniak, Paul F. Anderson, Russell W. Belk, O. C. Ferrell, Robert F. Lusch, Terence A. Shimp, and Charles B. Weinberg, Editors, Chicago, American Marketing Association.

CS/D–1 = *Conceptualization and Measurement of Consumer Satisfaction and Dissatisfaction*, 1977, H. Keith Hunt, Editor, Cambridge, Mass., Marketing Science Institute.

CS/D–2 = *Consumer Satisfaction, Dissatisfaction and Complaining Behavior*, 1977, Ralph L. Day, Editor, Bloomington, Indiana University.

CS/D–3 = *New Dimensions of Consumer Satisfaction and Complaining Behavior*, 1979, Ralph L. Day and H. Keith Hunt, Editors, Bloomington, Indiana University.

CS/D–4 = *Refining Concepts and Measures of Consumer Satisfaction and Complaining Behavior*, 1980, H. Keith Hunt and Ralph L. Day, Editors, Bloomington, Indiana University.

CS/D–5 = *New Findings on Consumer Satisfaction and Complaining*, 1982, Ralph L. Day and H. Keith Hunt, Editors, Bloomington, Indiana University.

CS/D–6 = *Conceptual and Empirical Contributions to Consumer Satisfaction and Complaining Behavior*, 1982, H. Keith Hunt and Ralph L. Day, Editors, Bloomington, Indiana University.

JM = *Journal of Marketing*.

JMR = *Journal of Marketing Research*.

SC–81 = *Marketing of Services*, 1981, James H. Donnelly and William R. George, Editors, Chicago, American Marketing Association.

SMA–76 = *Proceedings: Southern Marketing Association*, 1976, Henry W. Nash and Donald P. Robin, Editors, Mississippi State University, Southern Marketing Association.

SMA–77 = *Proceedings: Southern Marketing Association*, 1977, Donad P. Robin, Editors, Mississippi State University, Southern Marketing Association.

SMA–78 = *Proceedings: Southern Marketing Association*, 1978, Robert S. Franz, Robert M. Hopkins, and A. G. Toma, Editors, University of Southwestern Louisiana, Southern Marketing Association.

SMA–79 = *Proceedings: Southern Marketing Association*, 1979, Robert S. Franz, Robert M. Hopkins, and Alfred G. Toma, Editors, University of Southwestern Louisiana, Southern Marketing Association.

SMA–80 = *Evolving Marketing Thought for 1980,* 1980, John H. Summey and Ronald D. Taylor, Editors, Carbondale, Southern Marketing Association.

SMA–81 = *Progress in Marketing Theory and Practice,* 1981, Blaise J. Bergiel, Ronald D. Taylor, and John H. Summey, Editors, Carbondale, Southern, Marketing Association.

SMA–82 = *A Spectrum of Contemporary Marketing Ideas,* 1982, Carol H. Anderson, Blaise J. Bergiel, and John H. Summey, Editors, Carbondale, Southern, Marketing Association.

TC–79 = *Conceptual and Theoretical Developments in Marketing,* 1979, O. C. Ferrell, Stephen W. Brown, and Charles W. Lamb, Jr., Editors, Chicago, American Marketing Association.

TC–80 = *Theoretical Developments in Marketing,* 1980, Charles W. Lamb, Jr., and Patrick M. Dunne, Editors, Chicago, American Marketing Association.

TC–82 = *Marketing Theory: Philosophy of Science Perspectives,* 1982, Ronald F. Bush and Shelby D. Hunt, Editors, Chicago, American Marketing Association.

TAXONOMICAL BIBLIOGRAPHY OF MARKETING THEORY

1. Marketing Theory: Its Nature and Content

Alderson, Wroe, and Reavis Cox, 1948, "Towards a Theory of Marketing," *JM,* 13, October, pp. 137–152.

Alderson, Wroe, 1952, *Psychology for Marketing and Economics,"* *JM,* 17, October, pp. 119–135.

Alderson, Wroe, 1957, *Marketing Behavior and Executive Action,* Homewood, Ill.: Richard D. Irwin.

*Alderson, Wroe, 1958, "The Analytical Framework for Marketing," in *Proceedings: Conference of Marketing Teachers from Far Western States,* Delbert J. Duncan, ed., Berkeley: School of Business Administration, University of California.

Alderson, Wroe, 1965, *Dynamic Marketing Behavior: A Functionalist Theory of Marketing,* Homewood, Ill.: Richard D. Irwin.

*Anderson, Paul F., 1983, "Marketing, Scientific Progress, and Scientific Method," *JM,* 47, Fall, pp. 18–31.

Arndt, Johan, 1979, "The Market Is Dying: Long Live Marketing, *MSU Business Topics,* Vol. 27, No. 1, Winter, pp. 5–14.

Arndt, Johan, 1980, "Perspectives for a Theory of Marketing," *Journal of Business Research,* 8, September, pp. 389–402.

---

*Reading is reprinted in this collection.

Arndt, Johan, 1981, "The Conceptual Domain of Marketing: An Evaluation of Shelby Hunt's Three Dichotomies Model," *European Journal of Marketing,* 16, Fall, pp. 27–35.

Atwater, Thomas V., 1979, " 'Lost' or Neglected Components of a General Equilibrium Theory of Marketing," TC–79, pp. 184–186.

Bagozzi, Richard P., 1974, "Marketing as an Organized Behavioral System of Exchange," *JM,* 38, October, pp. 77–81.

*Bagozzi, Richard P., 1975, "Marketing as Exchange," *JM,* 39, October, pp. 32–39.

Bagozzi, Richard P., 1976, "Science, Politics, and the Social Construction of Marketing," AMA–76, pp. 586–592.

Bagozzi, Richard P., 1978, "Marketing as Exchange: A Theory of Transactions in the Marketplace," *American Behavioral Scientist,* 21, March–April, pp. 535–556.

*Bagozzi, Richard P., 1979, "Toward a Formal Theory of Marketing Exchanges," TC–79, pp. 431–447.

Bartels, Robert, 1944, "Marketing Principles," *JM,* 9, October, p. 151.

Bartels, Robert, 1951, "Can Marketing Be a Science?" *JM,* 15, January, pp. 319–328.

Bartels, Robert, 1968, "The General Theory of Marketing," *JM,* 32, January, pp. 29–33.

Bartels, Robert, 1970, *Marketing Theory and Metatheory,* Homewood, Ill.: Richard D. Irwin.

Bartels, Robert, 1974, "The Identity Crisis in Marketing," *JM,* 38, October, pp. 73–76.

Bartels, Robert, 1977, "General Theory of Marketing," AMA–77, pp. 549–550.

*Baumol, W. J., 1957, "On the Role of Marketing Theory," *JM,* 21, April, pp. 413–418.

Bell, Martin L., 1976, "The Foundering Marketing Concept," SMA–76, pp. 264–266.

*Brodbeck, May, 1982, "Recent Developments in the Philosophy of Science," TC–82, pp. 1–6.

Brown, Stephen W., and Raymond P. Fisk, eds., 1984, *Marketing Theory: Distinguished Contributions.* New York: Wiley.

Bush, Alan J., William C. Moncrief, and Clifford D. Scott, 1982, "On the Interpretation of Nomic Necessity: A Requirement for a Science of Marketing," TC–82, pp. 30–33.

Bush, Ronald F., and Shelby D. Hunt, eds., 1982, *Marketing Theory: Philosophy of Science Perspectives,* Chicago: American Marketing Association.

*Buzzell, Robert D., 1963, "Is Marketing a Science?" *Harvard Business Review,* 41, January–February, pp. 32–40, 166–170.

Caballero, Marjorie J., 1980, "Marketing: Science and Art," SMA–80, pp. 338–341.

Caballero, Marjorie J., and Tom L. Ingram, 1982, "The Marketing Profession: Analytic, Synthetic and Practical," TC–82, pp. 39–42.

Capella, Louis M., and Thomas J. Maronick, 1979, "Marketing Theory Courses: A New Direction?" SMA–79, pp. 12–15.

Carman, James M., 1973, "On the Universality of Marketing," *Journal of Contemporary Business,* 2, Autumn, pp. 1–16.

Carman, James M., 1980, "Paradigms for Marketing Theory," in Jagdish N. Sheth, ed., *Research in Marketing,* Vol. 3, Greenwich, Conn.: JAI Press.

Chonko, Lawrence B., and Patrick M. Dunne, 1982, "Marketing Theory: A Status Report," TC–82, pp. 43–46.

Cox, Reavis, Wroe Alderson, and Stanley J. Shapiro, 1964, *Theory in Marketing,* Homewood, Ill.: Richard D. Irwin.

Dawson, Leslie, 1971, "Marketing Science in the Age of Aquarius," *JM,* 35, July, pp. 66–72.

Dawson, Leslie, 1979, "Resolving the Crisis in Marketing Thought," *Management International Review,* 19, No. 3, pp. 77–84.

Demirdjian, Zohrab S., 1976, "Marketing as a Pluralistic Discipline: The Forestalling of an Identity Crisis," *Journal of the Academy of Marketing Science,* Vol. 4, No. 2, Fall, pp. 672–681.

El-Ansary, Adel I., 1979, "The General Theory of Marketing: Revisited," TC–79, pp. 399–407.

Ellis, Dean S., and Laurence W. Jacobs, 1977, "Marketing Utilities: A New Look," *Journal of the Academy of Marketing Science,* Vol. 5, Nos. 1 & 2, Winter, pp. 21–26.

Enis, Ben M., Robert Bartels, Richard J. Lutz, Richard P. Bagozzi, Shelby D. Hunt, and H. Robert Dodge, 1979, "Have We Reached Agreement on What the Marketing Discipline Should Be? A Panel Discussion," TC–79, pp. 1–14.

Enis, Ben M., 1982, "Toward a Taxonomy of Marketing Terms," TC–82, pp. 26–29.

Etgar, Michael, 1977, "Comment on the Nature and Scope of Marketing," *JM,* 31, October, pp. 15–16, 146.

Ferrell, O. C., Stephen W. Brown, and Charles W. Lamb, Jr., eds., 1979, *Conceptual and Theoretical Developments in Marketing,* Chicago: American Marketing Association.

Ferrell, O. C. and J. R. Perrachione, 1980, "An Inquiry into Bagozzi's Formal Theory of Marketing Exchanges," TC–80, pp. 158–161.

Fisk, George, 1971, *New Essays in Marketing Theory,* Boston: Allyn & Bacon.

Fulmer, Robert M., 1976, "The New Marketing and The New Realities," AMA–76, pp. 360–361.

Grether, E. T., 1949, "A Theoretical Approach to the Analysis of Marketing," in *Theory in Marketing,* Reavis Cox and Wroe Alderson, eds., Chicago: Richard D. Irwin.

Gumucio, F. R., 1977, "Comment on the Nature and Scope of Marketing," *JM,* 41, January, p. 8.

Halbert, M., 1965, *The Meaning and Sources of Marketing Theory,* New York: McGraw-Hill.

Howard, John A., 1965, *Marketing Theory,* Boston: Allyn & Bacon.

Hunerberg, Reinhard, 1978, "Marketing Discipline Program of Science," *Zeitschrift fur Betriebswirtschaft Forschung* (West-deutscher Verlag, Ophovenerster, 1–3, 567 Opladen, West Germany), 48, June, pp. 468–483.

Hunt, Shelby D., 1971, "The Morphology of Theory and the General Theory of Marketing," *JM,* 35, April, pp. 65–68.

Hunt, Shelby D., 1973, "Lawlike Generalizations and Marketing Theory," *JM,* 37, July, pp. 69–70.

Hunt, Shelby D., 1976, *Marketing Theory: Conceptual Foundations of Research in Marketing,* Columbus, Ohio: Grid.

*Hunt, Shelby D., 1976, "The Nature and Scope of Marketing," *JM,* 40, July, pp. 17–28.

Hunt, Shelby D., 1976, "The Three Dichotomies Model of Marketing: An Elaboration of Issues," in *Proceedings of Macro-Marketing Conference,* Charles C. Slater, ed., Boulder: University of Colorado.

Hunt, Shelby, D., 1977, "The Nature and Scope of Marketing Revisited: The Three Dichotomies Model," AMA–77, p. 547.

Hunt, Shelby D., 1978, "A General Paradigm of Marketing: In Support of the Three Dichotomies Model," *JM,* 42, April, pp. 107–110.

Hunt, Shelby D., 1979, "Positive vs. Normative Theory in Marketing: The Three Dichotomies Model as a General Paradigm for Marketing," TC–79, pp. 567–576.

Hunt, Shelby D., James A. Muncy, and Nina M. Ray, 1981, "Alderson's General Theory of Marketing: A Formalization," in *Review of Marketing, 1981,* Ben M. Enis and Kenneth J. Roering, eds., Chicago: American Marketing Association.

Hunt, Shelby D., and John J. Burnett, 1982, "The Macromarketing/Micromarketing Dichotomy: A Taxonomical Model," *JM,* 46, Summer, pp. 11–26.

*Hunt, Shelby D., 1983a, "General Theories and the Fundamental Explananda of Marketing," *JM,* 47, Fall, pp. 9–17.

Hunt, Shelby D., 1983b, *Marketing Theory: The Philosophy of Marketing Science,* Homewood, Ill.: Richard D. Irwin.

Hutchinson, Kenneth D., 1952, "Marketing as a Science: An Appraisal," *JM,* 16, January, pp. 286–293.

Kernan, Jerome B., and Montrose S. Sommers, eds., 1968, *Perspectives in Marketing Theory,* New York: Appleton-Century-Crofts.

*Kotler, Philip, 1972, "A Generic Concept of Marketing," *JM,* 36, April, pp. 46–54.

Kotler, Philip, 1979, "A Critical Assessment of Marketing Theory and Practice," in *Diffusing Marketing Theory and Research,* Alan R. Andreasen and David M. Gardner, eds., Chicago: American Marketing Association.

Krulis-Randa, Jan S., 1977, "Marketing—Theory and Practice," *Die Unternehmung,* Vol. 1, pp. 59–74.

Lamb, Charles W., Jr., and Patrick M. Dunne, eds., 1980, *Theoretical Developments in Marketing,* Chicago: American Marketing Association.

*Leone, Robert P., and Randall L. Schultz, 1980, "A Study of Marketing Generalizations," *JM,* 44, Winter, pp. 10–18.

Levitt, Theodore, 1960, "Marketing Myopia," *Harvard Business Review,* 38, July–August, pp. 45–56.

Lockley, Lawrence C., 1964, "An Approach to Marketing Theory," in *Theory in Marketing,* Reavis Cox, Wroe Alderson, and Stanley Shapiro, Homewood, Ill.: Richard D. Irwin.

Marketing Staff of The Ohio State University, 1965, "Statement of Marketing Philosophy," *JM,* 29, January, pp. 43–44.

*Mokwa, Michael P., and Kenneth R. Evans, 1982, "In Pursuit of Marketing Knowledge: An Exploration into Philosophies of Inquiry," TC–82, pp. 34–38. (Reading 16: "Knowledge and Marketing: Exploring the Foundations of Inquiry.")

Monroe, Kent B., Shelby D. Hunt, Gerald Zaltman, William L. Wilkie, and Thomas Tucker, 1979, "Graduate Marketing Theory Course: A Panel Discussion," TC–79, pp. 665–678.

Mount, Peter R., 1969, "Exploring the Commodity Approach in Developing Marketing Theory," *JM,* 33, April, pp. 62–64.

*Mowen, John C., 1979, "Retroduction and the Research Process in Consumer Behavior," TC–79, pp. 590–604. (Reading 19: "Retroduction and the Process of Discovery in Consumer Behavior.")

Nakamoto, Kent, and Shelby D. Hunt, 1980, "Deterministic Theory and Marketing," TC–80, pp. 244–247.

Nickels, William G., and Dennis Pitta, 1977, "Foundations for an Exchange Theory of Marketing," SMA–77, pp. 293–295.

O'Shaughnessy, John, and Michael J. Ryan, 1979, "Marketing, Science, and Technology," TC–79, pp. 577–89.

*Peter, J. Paul, Paul F. Anderson, May Brodbeck, Shelby D. Hunt, Richard Lutz, Jerry C. Olson, Michael J. Ryan, and Gerald Zaltman, 1982, "Current Issues in the Philosophy of Science: Implications for Marketing Theory—A Panel Discussion," TC–82, pp. 11–16.

Peters, William H., J. Howard Westing, George Schwartz, Jeffrey M. Maiken, John G. Myers, and William H. Peters, 1979, "What Is the Appropriate Orientation for the Marketing Academician? A Panel Discussion," TC–79, pp. 49–75.

Pinson, Christian R. A., Reinhard Angelmar, and Eduardo L. Roberto, 1972, "An Evaluation of the General Theory of Marketing," *JM,* 36, July, pp. 66–69.

Rethans, Arno J., 1979, "The Aldersonian Paradigm: A Perspective for Theory Development and Synthesis," TC–79, 197–209.

Robin, Donald P., 1970, "The Ethics of Science in Marketing," *JM,* 34, October, pp. 73–76.

Robin, Donald P., 1977, "The Boundaries of Marketing," AMA–77, p. 548.

Robin, Donald P., 1977, "Comment on the Nature and Scope of Marketing," *JM,* 41, January, pp. 136, 138.

Robin, Donald P., 1978, "Comment on the Nature and Scope of Marketing," *JM,* 42, July, pp. 6, 42.

Robin, Donald P., 1978, "A Useful Scope for Marketing," *Journal of the Academy of Marketing Science,* Vol. 6, No. 3, Summer, pp. 228–238.

Rockwood, Persis Emmett, 1980, "An Informal Integration of Marketing Theories and Concepts," TC–80, pp. 262–264.

Ross, Will H., 1977, "Comment on the Nature and Scope of Marketing," *JM,* 41, April, pp. 10, 146.

Ryan, Michael J., and John O'Shaughnessy, 1982, "Scientific Explanation and Technological Prediction," TC–82, pp. 22–25.

Sauer, William J., Nancy Nighswonger, and Gerald Zaltman, 1982, "Current Issues in Philosophy of Science: Implication for the Study of Marketing," TC–82, pp. 17–21.

Schwartz, George, 1965, "Nature and Goals of Marketing Science," in *Science in Marketing,* George Schwartz, ed., New York: Wiley.

Schwartz, George, ed., 1965, *Science in Marketing,* New York: Wiley.

Shaw, Eric H., and Donald F. Dixon, 1980, "Exchange: A Conceptualization," TC–80, pp. 150–153.

Smith, Wendell R., 1979, "The Interdependence of Theories, Strategies and Models," TC–79, pp. 639–640.

Solomon, Paul J., 1979, "Marketing Theory and Metatheory," TC–79, pp. 374–382.

Spratlen, Thaddeus, 1979, "Evolutionary Approaches to Marketing Science: A Reply and a Plea," *Management International Review,* (Gabler, K. G., Taunusstr. 54, Postfach 1546, 6200 Wiesbaden 1, W. Ger. BRD), 19, No. 3, pp. 85–87.

Stidsen, Bent, 1979, "Directions in the Study of Marketing," TC–79, pp. 383–398.

Taylor, Weldon J., 1965, "Is Marketing a Science? Revisited," *JM,* 29, July, pp. 49–53.

Tucker, W. T., 1974, "Future Directions in Marketing Theory," *JM,* 38, April, pp. 30–35.

Vaile, Roland S., 1949, "Towards a Theory of Marketing—Comment," *JM,* 13, April, pp. 520–522.

Vidali, Joseph J., 1977, "A Suggested Taxonomy for Marketing Thought: The Case of Lacking Applied Development and Research in Marketing," *Journal of the Academy of Marketing Science,* Vol. 5, No. 1, Winter, pp. 147–153.

Wales, Hugh G., and Lyndon E. Dawson, Jr., 1979, "The Anomalous Qualities Between Present-Day Conferences and Alderson's Marketing Theory Seminars," TC–79, pp. 222–227.

Weinberger, Marc G., 1977, "Positivism and Normativism: A Crossroad of Values in Marketing Education," AMA–77, pp. 50–54.

Wijnholds, Heiko de B., 1979, "Towards the Fundamentals of the Marketing Concept," TC–79, pp. 540 553.

Wynn, George W., 1980, "The Container of Marketing," SMA–80, pp. 329–331.

*Zaltman, Gerald, and Thomas Bonoma, 1979, "The Lack of Heresy in Marketing," TC–79, pp. 474 484.

Zaltman, Gerald, and Karen Lawther, 1979, "Let's at Least Be Interesting: The Art of Challenging Assumptions," TC–79, pp. 501–516.

Zaltman, Gerald, Karen LeMasters, and Michael P. Heffring, 1982, *Theory Construction in Marketing: Some Thoughts on Thinking,* New York: Wiley.

2. The History of Marketing Thought and Theory

Alderson, Wroe, and Miles W. Martin, 1965, "Toward a Formal Theory of Transactions and Transvections," *JM,* 2, May, pp. 117–127.

Barksdale, Hiram C., William J. Kelly, and Ian Macfarlane, 1978, "The Marketing Concept in the U.S. and the USSR: An Historical Analysis," *Journal of the Academy of Marketing Science,* Vol. 6, No. 4, Fall, pp. 258–277.

*Barksdale, Hiram C., 1980, "Wroe Alderson's Contributions to Marketing Theory," TC–80, pp. 1–3.

Bartels, Robert, 1962, *The Development of Marketing Thought,* Homewood, Ill.: Richard D. Irwin.

Bartels, Robert, 1976, *The History of Marketing Thought,* 2nd ed., Columbus, Ohio: Grid.

Berry, Leonard L., 1977, "Social and Economic Discontinuity and Marketing," AMA–77, p. 543.

Converse, Paul D., 1945, "The Development of a Science of Marketing," *JM,* 10, July, pp. 14–23.

Fox, Karen F. A. and Philip Kotler, 1980, "The Marketing of Social Causes: The First Ten Years," *JM,* 44, Fall, pp. 24–33.

Green, Paul, and Donald Tull, 1970, *Research for Marketing Decisions,* 2nd ed., Englewood Cliffs, N.J.: Prentice-Hall.

Hollander, Stanley C., 1978, "Can We Go Back?—The Case of Farmers' Stall Markets," AMA–78, pp. 301–303.

Hollander, Stanley C., 1980, "Some Notes on the Difficulty of Identifying the Marketing Thought Contributions of the 'Early Institutionalists'," TC–80, pp. 45–46.

Jackson, Donald W., Jr., 1979, "The Development of a Marketing Thought Course: An Approach," TC–79, 408–419.

Keith, Robert J., 1960, "The Marketing Revolution," *JM,* 24, January, pp. 35–38.

Kirkpatrick, Jerry, 1982, "Theory and History in Marketing," TC–82, pp. 47–51.

Lazer, William, 1979, "Some Observations on the Development of Marketing Thought," TC–79, pp. 652–664.

Lipson, Harry A., 1979, "Progress in the Development of Marketing Theory: A Retrospective View," TC–79, pp. 420–425.

Lusch, Robert F., 1980, "Alderson, Sessions, and the 1950s Manager," TC–80, pp. 4–6.

Meyer, Paul W., 1978, "Milestone of Marketing Development?" *Absatzwirtschaft,* (Sonderheft 10/1978), pp. 21–24.

Mitchell, Ted, 1980, "A General Law of Trade Relationships," TC–80, pp. 154–157.

Monieson, David D., and Stanley J. Shapiro, 1980, "Biological and Evolutionary Dimensions of Aldersonian Thought: What He Borrowed Then and What He Might Have Borrowed Now," TC–80, pp. 7–12.

Patti, Charles H., and Raymond P. Fisk, 1982, "National Advertising, Brands, and Channel Control: An Historical Perspective with Contemporary Options," *Journal of the Academy of Marketing Science,* Vol. 10, No. 1, p. 90.

Pollay, Richard W., 1979, "Lydiametrics: Applications of Econometrics to the History of Advertising," *Journal of Advertising History,* January, pp. 3–18.

Savitt, Ronald, 1980, "Historical Research in Marketing," *JM,* 44, Fall, pp. 52–58.

Schwartz, George, 1963, *Development of Marketing Theory,* Cincinnati, Ohio: South-Western Publishing.

*Sheth, Jagdish N., and David M. Gardner, 1982, "History of Marketing Thought: An Update," TC–82, pp. 52–58.

Thompson, Ralph B., and John H. Faricy, 1976, *A Selected and Annotated Bibliography of Marketing Theory,* 2nd ed., Austin: Bureau of Business Research, University of Texas.

Walters, C. Glenn, 1979, "Consumer Behavior: An Appraisal," *Journal of the Academy of Marketing Science,* Vol. 7, No. 4, Fall, pp. 273–284.

Wright, John S., and Parks B. Dimsdale, Jr., eds., 1974, *Pioneers in Marketing,* Atlanta: Georgia State University.

Wright, John S., 1979, "Variations on a Theme: The Marketing Thought Course," TC–79, pp. 426–430.

Wright, John S., 1980, "The Biographical Approach to the Study of Marketing Thought," TC–80, pp. 43–44.

3. Research Contributions to Marketing Theory

Allen, Chris T., 1982, "Perspectives of Mail Survey Response Rates: The Self-Perception Paradigm and Beyond," TC–82, pp. 307–310.

Anderton, E. J., R. Tudor, and K. Gorton, 1976, "Sequential Analysis: A Reappraisal for Market Research," *Journal of the Market Research Society,* 18, October, pp. 166–79.

Armstrong, J. Scott, and Alan C. Shapiro, 1974, "Analyzing Quantitative Models," *JM,* 38, April, pp. 61–66.

Arndt, Johan, 1977, "Comments on the Sociology of Marketing Research," AMA–77, pp. 185–190.

Bagozzi, Richard P., 1979, "The Role of Measurement in Theory Construction and Hypothesis Testing: Toward a Holistic Model," TC–79, pp. 15–33.

Bagozzi, Richard P., 1980, *Causal Models in Marketing,* New York: Wiley.

Bagozzi, Richard P., 1981, "Causal Modeling: A General Method for Developing and Testing Theories in Consumer Research," ACR–81, pp. 195–202.

Brown, Stephen W., and Kenneth C. Coney, 1976, "Building a Replication Tradition in Marketing," AMA–76, pp. 622–625.

*Brown, Stephen W., and Corbett F. Gaulden, 1980, "Replication and Theory Development," TC–80, pp. 240–243.

Bultez, Alain V., and Philippe A. Naert, 1979, "Does Lag Structure Really Matter in Optimizing Advertising Expenditures?" *Management Science,* 25, May, pp. 454–465.

Burnett, John J., and Lawrence B. Chonko, 1980, "The Role of Causality in Marketing: A Cautionary Note," TC–80, pp. 51–54.

Calder, Bobby J., 1977, "Focus Groups and the Nature of Qualitative Marketing Research," *JMR,* 14, August, pp. 353–364.

Calder, Bobby J., Alice M. Tybout, and Lynn W. Phillips, 1980, "The Design, Conduct, and Application of Consumer Research: Theory vs. Effects Oriented Studies," AMA–80, pp. 307–311.

*Calder, Bobby J., Lynn W. Phillips, and Alice M. Tybout, 1981, "Designing Research for Application," *Journal of Consumer Research,* 8, September, 197–207.

Calder, Bobby J., Lynn W. Phillips, and Alice M. Tybout, 1982, "The Concept of External Validity," *Journal of Consumer Research,* 9, December, pp. 240–244.

Calder, Bobby J., Lynn W. Phillips, and Alice M. Tybout, 1983, "Beyond External Validity," *JCR,* 10, June, pp. 112–114.

Cervantes, Fernando J., 1982, "A Projective Technique to Avoid Social Desirability Responses in Health Surveys," TC–82, pp. 311–313.

Chakravarti, Dipankar, Andrew Mitchell, and Richard Staelin, 1977, "A Cognitive Approach to Model-Building and Evaluation," AMA–77, pp. 213–218.

Churchill, Gilbert A., Jr., 1979, "A Paradigm for Developing Better Measures of Marketing Constructs," *JMR,* 16, February, pp. 64–73.

Darden, William R., 1981, "Review of Behavioral Modeling in Marketing," in *Review of Marketing 1981,* Ben Enis and Kenneth Roering, eds., Chicago: American Marketing Association.

Deshpande, Rohit P., 1983, "Paradigms Lost: On Theory and Method in Research in Marketing," *JM,* 47, Fall.

Dholakia, Nikhilesh, and A. Fuat Firat, 1980, "A Critical View of the Research Enterprise in Marketing," AMA–80, pp. 316–319.

Dillon, William R., Matthew Goldstein, and Leon G. Schiffman, 1978, "Appropriateness of Linear Discriminant and Multinomial Classification Analysis in Marketing Research," *JMR,* 15, February, pp. 103–112.

Dillon, William R., Matthew Goldstein, and Lucy Lement, 1981, "Analyzing Qualitative Predictors with Too Few Data: An Alternative Approach to Handling Sparse-Cell Values," *JMR,* 18, February, pp. 51–62.

Etzel, Michael J., Terrell G. Williams, John C. Rogers, and Douglas J. Lincoln, 1982, "The Comparability of Three Stapel Scale Forms in a Marketing Setting," TC–82, pp. 303–306.

Fornell, Claes, and George M. Zinkhan, 1982, "Classification Schemes for a New Generation of Multivariate Analysis," TC–82, pp. 295–299.

Goldman, Arieh, 1979, "Publishing Activity in Marketing as an Indicator of Its Structure and Disciplinary Boundaries," *JMR,* 16, November, pp. 485–494.

Green, Paul, 1978, "An AID/Logit, Procedure for Analyzing Large Multiway Contingency Tables," *JMR,* 15, February, pp. 132–6.

Hart, Sandra Hile, 1982, "Toward a Philosophy of Qualitative Research: The Value of Hermeneutics in Marketing," SMA–82, pp. 249–252.

Houston, Michael J., J. Paul Peter, and Alan G. Sawyer, 1983, "The Role of Meta-Analysis in Consumer Research," ACR–83, pp. 497–502.

*Jacoby, Jacob, 1978, "Consumer Research: A State of the Art Review," *JM,* 42, April, pp. 87–96.

LaTour, Stephen A., and Paul W. Miniard, 1983, "The Misuse of Repeated Measures Analysis in Marketing Research," *JMR,* 20, February, pp. 45–57.

Lazer, William, 1962, "The Role of Models in Marketing," *JM,* 26, April, pp. 9–14.

Lynch, John G., Jr., 1983, "The Role of External Validity in Theoretical Research," *JCR*, 10, June, pp. 109–112.

Madden, Charles Stanley, Lori Sharp Franz, and Robert Mittelstaedt, 1979, "The Replicability of Research in Marketing: Reported Content and Author Cooperation," TC–79, pp. 76–85.

Madden, Thomas J., William R. Dillon, and Marc G. Weinberger, 1982, "Causal Modeling in Marketing: A Latent Structure Analysis Approach," TC–82, pp. 289–294.

McGrath, Joseph E., and David Brinberg, 1983, "External Validity and the Research Process: A Comment on the Calder/Lynch Dialogue," *JCR*, 10, June, pp. 115–124.

Monroe, Kent B., and R. Krishnan, 1983, "A Procedure for Integrating Outcomes Across Studies," ACR–83, pp. 503–506.

Monroe, Kent B., and Susan Petroshius, 1979, "Developing Causal Priorities in Marketing," TC–79, 0p. 114–130.

*Morgan, Gareth, and Linda Smircich, 1980, "The Case for Qualitative Research," *Academy of Management Review*, Vol. 5, No. 4, October, pp. 491–500.

*Myers, John G., Stephen A. Greyser, and William F. Massy, 1979, "The Effectiveness of Marketing's 'R & D' for Marketing Management: An Assessment," *JM*, 43, January, pp. 17–29.

Myers, John G., William F. Massy, and Stephen A. Greyser, 1980, *Marketing Research and Knowledge Development: An Assessment for Marketing Management*, Englewood Cliffs, N.J.: Prentice-Hall.

Nighswonger, Nancy J., and Claude R. Martin, Jr., 1981, "On Using Voice Analysis in Marketing Research," *JMR*, 28, August, pp. 350–355.

*Olson, Jerry, C., 1982, "Presidential Address: 1981, Toward a Science of Consumer Behavior," ACR–82, pp. v–x.

Parasuraman, A., 1982, "Is a 'Scientist' Versus 'Technologist' Research Orientation Conducive to Marketing Theory Development?" TC–82, pp. 78–79.

Peter, J. Paul, 1977, "Reliability, Generalizability and Consumer Behavior," ACR–77, pp. 394–400.

Peter, J. Paul, 1979, "An Investigation of Some Criteria of Quality Measurement," TC–79, pp. 102–113.

Peter, J. Paul, 1981, "Construct Validity: A Review of Basic Issues and Marketing Practices," *JMR*, 28, May, pp. 133–145.

*Peter, J. Paul, 1983, "On Ignoring a Research Education."

Peter, J. Paul, and Jerry Olson, 1983, "Is Science Marketing?", *JM*, 47, Fall.

Punj, Girish, and David W. Stewart, 1983, "Cluster Analysis in Marketing: Review and Suggestions for Application," *JMR*, 20, May, pp. 134–148.

Rados, Davis L., 1980, "Two-Way Analysis of Tables in Marketing Research," *Journal of the Marketing Research Society*, (15 Belgrave Sq., London SWIX 8PF, England), 22, October, pp. 248–262.

Ray, Michael L., 1979, "The Critical Need for a Marketing Measurement Tradition: A Proposal," TC–79, pp. 34–48.

Reilly, Michael D., and Jerry N. Conover, 1983, "Meta-Analysis: Integrating Results From Consumer Research Studies," ACR–83, pp. 509–513.

Ryan, Michael J., and John O'Shaughnessy, 1980, "Theory Development: The Need to Distinguish Levels of Abstraction," TC–80, pp. 47–50.

Ryan, Michael J., and Donald W. Barclay, 1983, "Integrating Results From Independent Studies," ACR–83, pp. 491–496.

Sawyer, Alan G., and J. Paul Peter, 1983, "The Significance of Statistical Significance Tests in Marketing Research," *JMR*, 20, May, pp. 122–133.

Segal, Madhav, N., 1982, "On the Data Collection and Related Measurement Issues in Decompositional Multiattribute Preference Models," TC–82, pp. 300–302.

Theil, Henry, 1979, "Can Economists Contribute to Marketing Research?" *Sloan Management Review*, 20, Summer, pp. 19–29.

Tybout, Alice M., Bobby J. Calder, and Brian Sternthal, 1981, "Using Information Processing Theory to Design Marketing Strategies," *JMR*, 18, pp. 63–72.

Venkatesan, M., 1967, "Laboratory Experiments in Marketing: The Experimenter Effect," *JMR*, 4, pp. 142–147.

Weston, H., 1976, "The Estimation of Marketing Efficiency," *European Journal of Marketing*, 10, pp. 218–239.

Wilson, R. Dale, 1979, "The Role of Model Testing in Theory Development: The Case of Mathematical Marketing Models," TC–79, pp. 86–101.

Wind, Yoram, and Susan Douglas, 1980, "Comparative Methodology and Marketing Theory," TC–80, pp. 30–33.

Wright, Peter, and Mary Ann Kriewall, 1980, "State-of-Mind Effects on the Accuracy with Which Utility Functions Predict Marketplace Choice," *JMR*, 19, August, pp. 227–293.

Zentes, Joachim, 1976, "Possibilities and Limitations of Spectral Analysis in Marketing," *Der Markt*, 59, March, pp. 72–81.

Zikmund, William G., 1982, "Metaphors as Methodology," TC–82, pp. 75–77.

4.   Theory and Consumer Behavior

Adler, Keith, 1982, "Potential 'Control Mechanisms' for Theories of Consumer Behavior," TC–82, pp. 181–184.

Adler, Roy D., and Larry M. Robinson, 1980, "A Consumer Satisfaction Model Based on Job Satisfaction Theory," CS/D–4, pp. 19–22.

Andreasen, Alan R., 1965, "Attitudes and Consumer Behavior: A Decision Model," in *New Research in Marketing*, L. Preston, ed., Berkeley: Institute of Business and Economic Research, University of California.

Andreasen, Alan R., 1977, "A Taxonomy of Consumer Satisfaction/Dissatisfaction Measures," *Journal of Consumer Affairs*, 12, Winter, pp. 11–24.

Andreasen, Alan R., 1982, "Consumer Satisfaction in Loose Monopolies: The Case of Medical Care," TC–82, pp. 215–219.

Barach, Jeffrey A., 1981, "Conflicting Theories Concerning Self-Confidence and Persuasibility in Buyer Behavior—A Resolution," SMA–81, pp. 122–125.

Bauer, Raymond, 1960, "Consumer Behavior as Risk Taking," *Proceedings: 43rd Conference of the American Marketing Association*, Chicago: American Marketing Association, pp. 389–398.

Bearden, William O., and Jesse E. Teel, 1980, "An Investigation of Personal Influences on Consumer Complaining," *Journal of Retailing*, 56, Fall, pp. 3–20.

Belk, Russell W., 1975, "Situational Variables and Consumer Behavior," *Journal of Consumer Research*, 2, December, pp. 157–164.

Belk, Russell, W. 1982, "Acquiring, Possessing, and Collecting: Fundamental Processes in Consumer Behavior," TC–82, pp. 185–190.

Belk, Russell W., 1983, "Worldly Possessions: Issues and Criticisms," ACR–83, pp. 514–519.

Bellenger, Danny N., and George P. Moschis, 1982, "A Socialization Model of Retail Patronage," ACR–82, pp. 373–378.

Bernardo, John J., and Lawrence X. Tarpey, 1980, "Brand Loyalty as a Theoretical Construct," TC–80, pp. 198–201.

Bettman, James R., 1979, *An Information Processing Theory of Consumer Choice*, Reading, Mass.: Addison-Wesley.

Bhagat, Rabi S., P. S. Raju, and Jagdish N. Sheth, 1979, "Attitudinal Theories of Consumer Choice Behavior: A Comparative Analysis," *European Research*, 7, March, pp. 51–62.

Bonoma, Thomas V., and Leonard C. Felder, 1977, "Nonverbal Communication in Marketing: Toward a Communicational Analysis," *JMR*, 14, May, pp. 169–180.

Bozinoff, Lorne, and M. S. Sommers, 1982, "An Information Processing Perspective on the Product-Market Boundary Definition Question," TC–82, pp. 233–236.

Brown, Wilson, 1979, "The Family and Consumer Decision Making," *Journal of the Academy of Marketing Science*, Vol. 7, No. 4, Fall, pp. 335–345.

Burke, Marian, W. David Conn, and Richard J. Lutz, 1978, "Using Psychographic Variables to Investigate Product Disposition Behaviors," AMA–78, pp. 321–326.

Burns, Alvin C., 1977, "Husband and Wife Decision Making Roles: Agreed, Presumed, Conceded and Disputed," ACR–77, pp. 50–55.

Carman, James M., 1978, "Values and Consumption Patterns: A Closed Loop," ACR–78, pp. 403–407.

Chakravarti, Dipankar, and John C. Lynch, Jr., 1983, "A Framework for Exploring Context Effects on Consumer Judgment and Choice," ACR–83, pp. 289–297.

Clee, Mona, and Robert Wicklund, 1980, "Consumer Behavior and Psychological Reactance," *Journal of Consumer Research*, 6, March, pp. 389–405.

Czepiel, John A., and Larry J. Rosenberg, 1976, "Consumer Satisfaction: Toward an Integrative Framework," SMA–76, pp. 169–171.

Czepiel, John A., and Larry J. Rosenberg, 1977, "Consumer Satisfaction: Concept and Measurement," *Journal of the Academy of Marketing Science*, Vol. 5, No. 4, Fall, pp. 403–411.

Czepiel, John A., and Larry J. Rosenberg, 1977, "The Study of Consumer Satisfaction: Addressing the 'So What' Question," CS/D–1, pp. 92–121.

Czepiel, John A., Larry J. Rosenberg, and Carol Surprenant, 1980, "The Development of Thought, Theory and Research in Consumer Satisfaction," TC–80, pp. 216–219.

Darden, William R., Donna K. Darden, Roy Howell, and Shirley J. Miller, 1981, "Consumer Socialization Factors in a Patronage Model of Consumer Behavior," ACR–81, pp. 655–661.

Dawson, Lyndon E., Jr., and Hugh G. Wales, 1979, "Consumer Motivation Theory in Historical Perspective: An Aldersonian View," TC–79, pp. 210–221.

Day, Ralph L., "Extending the Concept of Consumer Satisfaction," ACR–77, pp. 149–154.

Day, Ralph L., 1980, "Research Perspectives on Consumer Complaining Behavior," TC–80, pp. 211–215.

Della Bitta, Albert J., 1982, "Consumer Behavior: Some Thoughts on Sheth's Evaluation of the Discipline," *Journal of the Academy of Marketing Science*, Vol. 10, No. 1, pp. 1–9.

Della Bitta, Albert J., 1982, "Rejoinder to 'Consumer Behavior: Some Thoughts on Sheth's Evaluation of the Discipline'," *Journal of the Academy of Marketing Science*, Vol. 10, No. 1, pp. 16–19.

DeLozier, M. Wayne, and Denis F. Healy, 1976, "A Theoretical Framework Relating the Concepts of Need, Want, Drive and Motivation," SMA–76, pp. 118–120.

Deshpande, Rohit, Wayne D. Hoyer, and Scott Jeffries, 1982,

"Low Involvement Decision Processes: The Importance of Choice Tactics," TC–82, pp. 155–158.

Dholakia, Nikhilesh, 1982, "Some Underpinnings for a Radical Theory of Consumption," ACR–82, pp. 296–301.

Dickinson, Roger, 1982, "Consumer Behavior: A Consumer Perspective," TC–82, pp. 202–205.

Dickson, Peter R., 1982, "Person-Situation: Segmentation's Missing Link," *JM*, 46, Fall, pp. 56–64.

Durand, Richard M., and Carl E. Ferguson, Jr., 1982, "The Environmentally Concerned Citizen: Demographic, Social-Psychological, and Energy Related Correlates," TC–82, pp. 211–214.

Feldman, Laurence P., and Jacob Hornik, 1981, "The Use of Time: An Integrated Conceptual Model," *Journal of Consumer Research*, 7, April, pp. 407–419.

Ferber, Robert, 1977, "Can Consumer Research be Interdisciplinary?" *Journal of Consumer Research*, 4, December, pp. 189–192.

Festervand, T. A., and W. J. Lundstrom, 1982, "Industrial Buyer Behavior: A Hobbesian Explanation," TC–82, pp. 195–197.

Fischer-Winkelmann, Wolf, 1976, "A New Theory of Buying Decisions: An Outline of the Problems," *Management International Review*, Vol. 16, No. 4, pp. 79–94.

Fisk, Raymond P., 1981, "Toward a Consumption/Evaluation Process Model for Services," SC–81, pp. 191–195.

Fisk, Raymond P., and Kenneth A. Coney, 1982, "Postchoice Evaluation: An Equity Theory Analysis of Consumer Satisfaction/Dissatisfaction with Service Choices," CS/D–6, pp. 9–16.

Foxall, Gorden R., 1980, "Marketing Models of Buyer Behavior," *European Research*, (European Society for Opinion—Market Research, 27 Lexington St., London W1R 3HQ, England), 8, September, pp. 195–206.

Gilly, Mary C., 1980, "Complaining Consumers and the Concept of Expectations," CS/D–4, pp. 44–49.

Gioia, Dennis A., and James M. Stearns, 1980, "A Unified Expectancy Approach to Consumer Satisfaction/ Dissatisfaction," CS/D–4, pp. 13–18.

Glassman, Myron, and Theodore Smith, 1980, "On the Process of Consumer Satisfaction, Dissatisfaction and Complaining Behavior," CS/D–4, pp. 62–66.

Graham, Robert J., 1981, "The Role of Perception of Time in Consumer Research," *Journal of Consumer Research*, 7, April, pp. 335–342.

Granzin, Kent, and John Painter, 1980, "An Investigation of Satisfaction as a Central Construct in the Buyer Decision Process," SMA–80, pp. 179–182.

Grønhaug, Kjell, 1977, "Exploring Consumer Complaining Behavior: A Model and Some Empirical Results," ACR–77, pp. 159–165.

Guseman, Dennis S., 1981, "Risk Perception and Risk Reduction in Consumer Services," SC–81, pp. 200–204.

Hagerty, Michael R., 1980, "A Deterministic-type Model of Consumer Choice," ACR–80, p. 129–133.

Hansen, Flemming, 1972, *Consumer Choice Behavior: A Cognitive Theory*, New York: Free Press.

Hansen, Flemming, 1981, "Hemispheral Lateralization: Implications for Understanding Consumer Behavior," *Journal of Consumer Research*, 8, June, pp. 23–36.

Harris, Brian F., and Michael K. Mills, 1982, "Towards a General Model of Distributive Buying," TC–82, pp. 191–194.

Hauser, John R., 1978, "Consumer Preference Axioms: Behavioral Postulates for Describing and Predicting Stochastic Choice," *Management Science*, 24, September, pp. 1331–1340.

Hawes, Douglass K., 1979, "Leisure and Consumer Behavior," *Journal of the Academy of Marketing Science*, Vol. 7, No. 4, Fall, pp. 391–403.

Hawes, Douglass K., 1979, "Time and Behavior," TC–79, pp. 281–295.

Hawes, Douglass K., 1980, "The Time Variable in Models of Consumer Behavior," ACR–80, pp. 442–447.

Hawkins, Del I., and Kenneth A. Coney, 1976, "Advertising and Differentiated Sex Roles in Contemporary American Society," *Journal of the Academy of Marketing Science*, Vol. 4, No. 1, Winter, pp. 418–428.

Hawkins, Del I., Don Roupe, and Kenneth A. Coney, 1981, "The Influence of Geographic Subcultures in the United States," ACR–81, pp. 713–717.

Hempel, Donald J., 1977, "Family Decision Making: Emerging Issues and Future Opportunities," AMA–77, pp. 428–431.

Hirschman, Elizabeth C., 1979, "Individual Creativity and Creativogenic Society," TC–79, pp. 264–280.

Hirschman, Elizabeth C., 1979, "Intratype Competition Among Department Stores," *Journal of Retailing*, 55, Winter, pp. 20–34.

Hirschman, Elizabeth C., 1980, "Consumer Creativity: Nature, Measurement and Application," TC–80, pp. 162–165.

Hirschman, Elizabeth C., 1980, "Potential Sources for a General Theory of Consumer Payment Systems," TC–80, pp. 202–205.

Hirschman, Elizabeth C., 1981, "American Jewish Ethnicity: Its Relationship to Some Selected Aspects," *JM*, 45, Summer, pp. 102–110.

Hirschman, Elizabeth C., 1981, "The Roles of Perception and

Preference in Consumer Decision Making,'' AMA–81, pp. 185–188.

Hirschman, Elizabeth C., and Morris B. Holbrook, 1982, ''Hedonic Consumption: Emerging Concepts, Methods and Propositions,'' *JM,* 46, Summer, pp. 92–101.

Holman, Rebecca H., 1981, ''The Imagination of the Future: A Hidden Concept in the Study of Consumer Decision Making,'' ACR–81, p. 187.

Houston, Michael J., and Michael L. Rothschild, 1978, ''Conceptual and Methodological Perspectives on Involvement,'' AMA–78, pp. 184–187.

Howard, John A., and Jagdish N. Sheth, 1967, ''A Theory of Buyer Behavior,'' in Reed Moyer, ed., *Changing Marketing Systems,* Chicago: American Marketing Association.

Howard, John A., and Jagdish N. Sheth, 1969, *The Theory of Buyer Behavior,* New York: Wiley.

Hoyer, Wayne D., and Mark I. Alpert, 1983, ''Additional Theory and Data Contrasting Measures of Attribute Importance,'' AMA–83, pp. 78–84.

Humphreys, Marie Adele, and James M. Kenderdine, 1979, ''Perceived Risk and Consumer Decision Making: An Alternative View of Uncertainty,'' AMA–79, pp. 283–285.

Humphreys, Marie Adele, and Charles A. Ingene, 1980, ''Perceptions of Risk: A Theory of Consumer and Producer Behavior,'' TC–80, pp. 194–197.

Hunt, James M., 1980, ''Consumer Responses to Inequitable Economic Exchanges: An Attribution Theoretical Analysis,'' CS/D–4, pp. 23–28.

Huppertz, John W., Sidney J. Arenson, and Richard H. Evans, 1978, ''An Application of Equity Theory to Buyer-Seller Exchange Situations,'' *JMR,* 15, May, pp. 250–260.

Ivy, Thomas T., and Louis E. Boone, 1976, ''A Behavioral Science Approach to Effective Sales Presentations,'' *Journal of the Academy of Marketing Science,* Vol. 4, No. 2, Spring, pp. 456–466.

Jacoby, Jacob, Carol K. Berning, and Thomas Dietvorst, 1977, ''What About Disposition?'' *JM,* 41, April, pp. 22–28.

Jones, J. Morgan, and Fred S. Zufryden, 1980, ''Adding Explanatory Variables to a Consumer Purchase Behavior Model: An Exploring Study,'' *JMR,* 17, August, pp. 323–334.

Jones, J. Morgan, and Fred S. Zufryden, 1982, ''An Approach for Assessing Demographic and Price Influences,'' *JM,* 46, Winter, pp. 36–46.

Kamen, Joseph M., 1979, ''How to Get Higher Ratings and Sell Less,'' *JMR,* 19, April, pp. 59–60.

Kassarjian, H. H., 1971, ''Personality and Consumer Behavior: A Review,'' *JMR,* 8, November, pp. 409–419.

Kassarjian, Harold, 1982, ''The Development of Consumer Behavior Theory,'' ACR–82, pp. 20–22.

Kelly, J. Patrick, and Scott M. Smith, 1983, ''Determinants of Retail Patronage: An Examination of Alternative Models,'' ACR–83, pp. 345–350.

Kotler, Philip, 1965, ''Behavioral Models for Analyzing Buyers,'' *JM,* 29, October, pp. 37–45.

Krapfel, Robert, 1982, ''Power in Organizational Buyer-Seller Relations: Synthesis and Extensions,'' TC–82, pp. 198–201.

Laczniak, Gene R., and Patrick E. Murphy, 1980, ''Fine Tuning Organizational Buying Models,'' TC–80, pp. 77–80.

LaForge, Raymond W., 1979, ''A New (?) Conceptualization of Consumer Satisfaction/Dissatisfaction,'' SMA–79, pp. 460–463.

Landon, E. Laird, 1977, ''A Model of Consumer Complaint Behavior,'' CS/D–2, pp. 31–35.

LaTour, Stephen A., and Nancy C. Peat, 1979, ''Conceptual and Methodological Issues in Consumer Satisfaction Research,'' ACR–79, pp. 431–437.

Lawther, Karen, S. Krishnan, and Valerie A. Valle, 1979, ''The Consumer Complaint Process: Directions for Theoretical Development,'' CS/D–3, pp. 10–14.

Leavitt, Clark, 1977, ''Consumer Satisfaction and Dissatisfaction: Bipolar or Independent,'' CS/D–1, pp. 132–152.

Leigh, James H., and Claude R. Martin, Jr., 1982, ''Collective Behavior in Consumer Behavior,'' TC–82, pp. 228–232.

LeLievre, K., 1980, ''A Dyadic Model for Negotiation of Consumer Complaint Settlements,'' CS/D–4, pp. 57–61.

Levy, Sidney J., 1963, ''Symbolism and Life Style,'' in S. A. Greyser, ed., *Toward Scientific Marketing,* Chicago: American Marketing Association.

Levy, Sidney J., 1966, ''Social Class and Consumer Behavior,'' in *On Knowing the Consumer,* Joseph W. Newman, ed., New York: Wiley.

Levy, Sidney J., 1981, ''Interpreting Consumer Mythology: A Structural Approach to Consumer Behavior,'' *JM,* 45, Summer, pp. 49–61.

Loken, Barbara, 1983, ''The Theory of Reasoned Action: Examination of the Sufficiency Assumption For A Television Viewing Behavior,'' ACR–83, pp. 100–105.

Louviere, Jordan L., 1983, ''Integrating Conjoint and Functional Measurement with Discrete Theory: An Experimental Design Approach,'' ACR–83, pp. 151–156.

Lynch, John G., Jr., 1982, ''On the External Validity of Experiments in Consumer Research,'' *Journal of Consumer Research,* 9, December, pp. 225–239.

McAlister, Leigh, 1982, *Consumer Choice Theory Models,* Greenwich, Conn.: JAI Press.

McAlister, Leigh, and Edgar Pessemier, 1982, ''Variety Seeking Behavior: An Interdisciplinary Review,'' *Journal of Consumer Research,* 9, December, pp. 311–322.

Miller, John A., 1977, "Studying Satisfaction, Modifying Models, Eliciting Expectations, Posing Problems, and Making Meaningful Measurements," CS/D–1, pp. 72–91.

Mills, Michael K., and Thomas V. Bonoma, 1979, "Deviant Consumer Behavior: A Different View," ACR 79, pp. 347–352.

Mills, Michael K., and Thomas V. Bonoma, 1979, "Deviant Consumer Behavior: New Challenge for Marketing Research," AMA–79, pp. 445–449.

Mills, Michael K., 1982, "Individuation-Deindividuation Theory: Applications/Propositions for Marketing Science," TC–82, pp. 220–223.

Mitchell, Andrew A., 1978, "An Information Processing View of Consumer Behavior," AMA–78, pp. 188–197.

Mitchell, Ted, 1982, "To Choose Y When X is Preferred to Y," TC–82, pp. 206–210.

Mittelstaedt, Robert A., 1971, "Criteria for a Theory of Consumer Behavior," in Robert L. Holloway, Robert A. Mittelstaedt, M. Venkatesan, eds., *Consumer Behavior: Contemporary Research in Action*, Boston: Houghton Mifflin, pp. 8–13.

Mizerski, Richard W., Linda L. Golden, and Jerome B. Kernan, 1979, "The Attribution Process in Consumer Decision Making," *Journal of Consumer Research*, 6, September, pp. 123–140.

Moschis, George P., 1976, "Shopping Orientations and Consumer Uses of Information," *Journal of Retailing*, 52, Summer, pp. 61–70.

Moschis, George P., and Gilbert A. Churchill, Jr., 1978, "Consumer Socialization: A Theoretical and Empirical Analysis," *JMR*, 15, November, pp. 599–609.

Motes, William H., 1982, "A Learned Helplessness Model of Consumer Behavior," TC–82, pp. 151–154.

Mowen, John C., 1982, "Reinforcement Timing Theory: On the Relation Between Time, Approach-Avoidance Conflict and Decision Making," TC–82, pp. 166–169.

Munch, James M., and John L. Swasy, 1983, A Conceptual View of Questions and Questioning in Marketing Communications," ACR–83, 209–214.

Munsinger, Gary M., and Gerald Albaum, 1976, "Manifest and Latent Functions in Marketing," *Marquette Business Review*, Vol. 20, No. 1, Spring, pp. 24–31.

Murphy, Patrick E., and William A. Staples, 1979, "A Modernized Family Life Cycle," *Journal of Consumer Research*, 6, June, pp. 12–22.

Nicosia, Francesco M., 1966, *Consumer Decision Processes: Marketing and Advertising Implications*, Englewood Cliffs, N.J.: Prentice-Hall.

Nicosia, Francesco M., and Robert N. Mayer, 1976, "Toward a Sociology of Consumption," *Journal of Consumer Research*, 3, September, pp. 65–75.

Nord, Walter R., and J. Paul Peter, 1980, "A Behavior Modification Perspective on Marketing," *JM*, 44, Spring, pp. 36–47.

O'Brien, Terrence, 1971, "Stages of Consumer Decision Making," *JMR*, 8, August, pp. 238–289.

Oliva, Terence A., and Alvin C. Burns, 1978, "Catastrophe Theory as a Model for Describing Consumer Behavior," ACR–78, pp. 273–276.

Oliver, Richard L., 1980, "Conceptualizing and Measurement of Disconfirmation Perceptions in the Prediction of Consumer Satisfaction," CS/D–4, pp. 2–6.

Oliver, Richard L., 1980, "Theoretical Bases of Consumer Satisfaction Research: Review, Critique, and Future Direction," TC–80, pp. 206–210.

Oliver, Richard L., and William O. Bearden, 1983, "The Role of Involvement in Satisfaction processes," ACR–83, pp. 250–255.

Olshavsky, Richard W., and Donald H. Granbois, 1979, "Consumer Decision Making—Fact or Fiction?" *Journal of Consumer Research*, 6, September, pp. 93–100.

Ortinau, David J., 1979, "A Conceptual Model of Consumers' Post Purchase Satisfaction/Dissatisfaction Decision Process," CS/D–3, pp. 35–40.

Oshikawa, S., 1969, "Can Cognitive Dissonance Theory Explain Consumer Behavior?" *JM*, 33, October, pp. 44–49.

Peter, J. Paul, and Walter R. Nord, 1982, "A Clarification and Extension of Operant Conditioning Principles in Marketing," *JM*, 46, Summer, pp. 102–107.

Peterson, Robin T., and Charles Gross, 1979, "Changing Attitudes Through Balance Theory," *Business*, 29, September–October, pp. 15–19.

Pfaff, Martin, 1977, "The Index of Consumer Satisfaction: Measurement Problems and Opportunities," CS/D–1, pp. 36–71.

Punj, Girish N., and Richard Staelin, 1978, "The Choice Process for Graduate Business Schools," *JMR*, 15, November, pp. 588–599.

Punj, Girish N., 1983, "A Model of Consumer Information Search Behavior for New Automobiles," *JCR*, 9, March, pp. 366–380.

Rau, Pradeep, and Saeed Samiee, 1981, "Models of Consumer Behavior: The State of the Art," *Journal of the Academy of Marketing Science*, Vol. 9, No. 3, Summer, pp. 300–316.

Reingen, Peter H., 1978, "On the Social Psychology of Giving: Door-in-the-Face and When Even a Penny Helps," ACR–78, pp. 1–4.

Richins, Marsha L., 1979, "Consumer Complaining Processes: A Comprehensive Model," CS/D–3, pp. 30–34.

Roberts, C. Richard, and James W. Cagley, 1982, "Behavioral Correlates of the Inflation Problem: An Investigation of the Consumer's Assessment Process," TC–82, pp. 224–227.

Robertson, T. S., and S. Ward, 1973, "Consumer Behavior Research: Promise and Prospects," in S. Ward and T. S. Robertson, eds., *Consumer Behavior: Theoretical Sources,* Englewood Cliffs, N.J.: Prentice-Hall.

Robertson, Thomas S., and Joan Zielinski, 1982, "Consumer Behavior Theory: Excesses and Limitations," ACR–82, pp. 8–12.

Roeder, Deborah L., Nicholas M. Didow, and Bobby J. Calder, 1978, "A Review of Formal Theories of Consumer Socialization," ACR–78, pp. 528–534.

Sarel, Dan, 1981, "Advances in Environmental Psychology—A New Perspective on Consumer Behavior," AMA–81, pp. 134–138.

Sarel, Dan, 1982, "Models of Behavioral Choice Under Risk—A Review," SMA–82, pp. 123–126.

Schweiger, G., J. Mazanec, and O. Weigele, 1976, "The Model of 'Perceived Risk,' Structure and Concepts of Operationalization," *Der Markt,* 59, April, pp. 93–102.

Scott, Carol A., 1978, "Attribution Theory in Consumer Research: Scope, Issues and Contribution," AMA–78, pp. 169–173.

Scott, Carol A., and Alice M. Tybout, 1981, "Theoretical Perspectives on the Impact of Negative Information: Does Valence Matter?" ACR–81, pp. 408–409.

Seagert, Joel, and Robert J. Hoover, 1976, "Learning Theory and Marketing: An Update," AMA–76, pp. 512–514.

Sethna, Beheruz N., 1980, "Some Important Determinants of Consumer Satisfaction/Dissatisfaction," CS/D–4, pp. 29–33.

Sheth, Jagdish N., 1973, "A Model of Industrial Buyer Behavior," *JM,* 37, October, pp. 50–56.

Sheth, Jagdish N., 1974, "A Theory of Family Buying Decisions," in J. N. Sheth, ed., *Models of Buyer Behavior,* New York: Harper & Row.

Sheth, Jagdish N., 1977, "Recent Developments in Organizational Buyer Behavior," in Arch G. Woodside, Jagdish N. Sheth, and Peter D. Bennett, eds., *Consumer and Industrial Buying Behavior,* New York: Elsevier North-Holland, 17–34.

Sheth, Jagdish N., 1979, "How Consumers Use Information," *European Research,* 7, July, 167–173.

Sheth, Jagdish N., 1979, "The Surpluses and Shortages in Consumer Behavior Theory and Research," *Journal of the Academy of Marketing Science,* Vol. 7, No. 4, Fall, pp. 414–427.

Sheth, Jagdish, 1982, "Consumer Behavior: Surpluses and Shortages," ACR–82, pp. 13–16.

Sheth, Jagdish N., 1982, "Reply to 'Consumer Behavior: Some Thoughts on Sheth's Evaluation of the Discipline'," *Journal of the Academy of Marketing Science,* Vol. 10, No. 1, Winter, pp. 10–15.

Shocker, Allen D., and Gerald Zaltman, 1977, "Validity Importance in Consumer Research: Some Pragmatic Issues," ACR–77, pp. 405–408.

Shugan, Steven M., 1980, "The Cost of Thinking," *Journal of Consumer Research,* Vol. 7, No. 2, December, pp. 99–111.

Sirgy, M. Joseph, 1982, "Self-Concept in Consumer Behavior: A Critical Review," *Journal of Consumer Research,* Vol. 9, No. 3, December, pp. 287–300.

Sirgy, M. Joseph, 1982, "Towards a Psychological Model of Consumer Satisfaction/Dissatisfaction," CS/D–5, pp. 40–47.

Sproles, George B., 1980, "New Theoretical and Empirical Perspectives of Consumer Efficiency," ACR–80, pp. 178–179.

Stone, Robert N., 1981, "A Reconceptualization of Risk," SMA–81, pp. 350–353.

Suprenant, Carol, 1977, "Consumer Attributions of the Cause of Their Product Satisfaction and Dissatisfaction," CS/D–2, pp. 36–37.

Swan, John E., and I. Fredrick Trawick, 1980, "Satisfaction Related to Predictive *vs* Desired Expectations," CS/D–4, pp. 7–12.

Swan, John E., and Alice Atkins Mercer, 1982, "Consumer Satisfaction as a Function of Equity and Disconfirmation," CS/D–6, pp. 2–8.

Swan, John E., and I. Fredrick Trawick, 1982, "Satisfaction, Disconfirmation, and Comparison of Alternatives," CS/D–6, pp. 17–24.

Swartz, Teresa A., 1982, "Development and Application of a Model of Social Influence Theory to the Study of the Effects of Source Credibility and Attractiveness," TC–82, pp. 163–166.

Syzbillo, George J., and Arlene Sosanie, 1977, "Family Decision Making: Husband, Wife, and Children," ACR–77, pp. 46–49.

Thaler, Richard, 1983, "Transaction Utility Theory," ACR–83, 229–232.

Thomas, Robert J., 1982, "A Conceptual Model of Interpersonal Purchase Influence in Organizations," AMA–82, pp. 7–11.

Thorelli, Hans B., 1977, "Philosophies of Consumer Information Programs," ACR–77, pp. 282–287.

Tucker, W. T., 1964, "The Development of Brand Loyalty," *JMR,* 1, August, pp. 32–35.

Tucker, W. T., 1967, *Foundations for a Theory of Consumer Behavior,* New York: Holt, Rinehart & Winston.

Tyebjee, Tyzoon T., 1978, "Cognitive Response and the Reception Environment of Advertising," AMA–78, pp. 174–177.

Uusitalo, Liisa, and Jyrki Uusitalo, 1981, "Scientific Progress and Research Traditions in Consumer Research," ACR–81, pp. 559–563.

van Raaij, W. Fred, and Kassaye Wandwossen, 1978, "Motivation-Need Theories and Consumer Behavior," ACR–78, pp. 590–595.

Venkatesh, Alladi, and Philip C. Burger, 1982, "Towards a Theory of Consumer Responses to Regulation," TC–82, pp. 159–162.

Vinson, Donald E., and Roger A. Strang, 1978, "Policy Implications of a Values Approach to Consumer Dissatisfaction," SMA–78, pp. 302–306.

Voss, Justin, and Roger D. Blackwell, 1979, "The Role of Time Resources in Consumer Behavior," TC–79, pp. 296–311.

Ward, Scott, and Thomas S. Robertson, eds., 1973, *Consumer Behavior: Theoretical Sources*, Englewood Cliffs, N.J.: Prentice-Hall.

Watkins, Thayer, 1978, "A Property of Optimal Consumption Policies for Decision-Making Under Uncertainty," *Southern Economic Journal*, 44, April, pp. 752–761.

White, Phillip D., 1978, "Situational Influences on Industrial Buying Behavior: Perspectives and Prospects," SMA–78, pp. 127–130.

Wiley, James B., and Gordon G. Bechtel, 1983, "Theory Based Monitoring of Social Constructs," ACR–83, pp. 157–162.

Wilson, R. Dale, and Rebecca H. Holman, 1980, "Economic Theories of Time in Consumer Behavior: A Philosophy of Science Perspective on Their Evolution," TC–80, pp. 265–268.

Wind, Yoram, 1977, "Reflections on Creativity and Relevance of Consumer Research," AMA–77, pp. 55–58.

Wind, Yoram, and Robert J. Thomas, 1980, "Conceptual and Methodological Issues in Organizational Buying Behavior," *European Journal of Marketing*, Vol. 14, No. 4, pp. 239–263.

Winter, Mary, and Earl W. Morris, 1979, "Satisfaction as an Intervening Variable," CS/D–3, pp. 15–25.

Withey, Stephen B., 1977, "Integrating Some Models About Consumer Satisfaction," CS/D–1, pp. 120–131.

Woodruff, Robert B., Ernest R. Cadotte, and Roger L. Jenkins, 1983, "Modeling Consumer Satisfaction Processes Using Experience-Based Norms," *JMR*, 20, August, pp. 206–304.

Wortzel, Lawrence H., 1982, "Consumer Decisions for High Involvement Products: An Extension and Elaboration of the Ray Three Orders Model and a Linkage to Information Processing Models," TC–82, pp. 167–170.

Zaltman, Gerald, Christian R. A. Pinson, and Reinhard Angelmar, 1973, *Metatheory and Consumer Research*, New York: Holt, Rinehart & Winston.

Zaltman, Gerald, and Melanie Wallendorf, 1977, "Sociology: The Missing Chunk or How We've Missed the Boat," AMA–77, pp. 235–238.

Zeithaml, Valarie A., 1981, "How Consumer Evaluation Processes Differ Between Goods and Services," SC–81, pp. 186–190.

Zeithaml, Valarie A., 1982, "The Acquisition, Meaning and Use of Price Information by Consumers of Professional Services," TC–82, pp. 237–241.

Zikmund, William G., 1977, "A Taxonomy of Black Shopping Behavior," *Journal of Retailing*, 53, Spring, pp. 61–72.

5. Theory and Strategic Marketing

Abell, Derek F., 1978, "Metamorphosis in Market Planning," AMA–78, pp. 257–259.

*Anderson, Paul F., 1982, "Marketing Strategic Planning, and the Theory of the Firm," *JM*, 46, Spring, pp. 15–26.

Arndt, Johan, and Thorolf Helgesen, 1981, "Marketing and Productivity: Conceptual and Measurement Issues," AMA–81, pp. 81–84.

Ayal, Igal, and Jehiel Zif, 1978, "Competitive Market Choice Strategies in Multinational Marketing," *Columbia Journal of World Business*, 13, Fall, pp. 72–81.

Bell, Martin L., 1981, "Tactical Service Marketing and the Process of Remixing," SC–81, pp. 163–167.

Biggadike, E. Ralph, 1981, "The Contributions of Marketing to Strategic Management," *Academy of Management Review*, Vol. 6, No. 4, October, pp. 621–632.

Borden, Neil H., 1964, "The Concept of the Marketing Mix," *Journal of Advertising Research*, 4, June, pp. 2–7.

Buss, W. C., 1982, "The Competitive-Exclusion Principle," TC–82, pp. 89–92.

Buzzell, Robert D., 1981, "Are There 'Natural' Market Structures," *JM*, 45, Winter, pp. 42–51.

Cardozo, Richard N., and David K. Smith, Jr., 1983, "Applying Financial Portfolio Theory to Product Portfolio Decisions: An Empirical Study," *JM*, 47, Spring, pp. 110–119.

Cook, Victor J., Jr., 1983, "Marketing Strategy and Differential Advantage," *JM*, 47, Spring, pp. 68–76.

Cooke, Ernest F., 1982, "The Fundamental Theorem of Market Share Determination," TC–82, pp. 84–88.

Cravens, David W., 1982, *Strategic Marketing*, Homewood, Ill.: Richard D. Irwin.

Day, George S., 1977, "Diagnosing the Product Portfolio," *JM*, 41, April, pp. 29–38.

Day, George S., and Robin Wensley, 1983, "Marketing Theory With A Strategic Orientation," *JM*, 47, Fall.

Demirdjian, Zohrab S., 1978, "Marketing Strategy: A Contingency and Systems Approach," SMA–78, pp. 403–406.

Enis, Ben M., and Michael P. Mokwa, 1979, "The Marketing Management Matrix—A Taxonomy for Strategy Comprehension," TC–79, pp. 485–500.

Enrick, Norbert L., and James H. Macomber, 1977, "The Matrix Approach to Market Analysis," *Journal of the Academy of Marketing Science*, Vol. 5, Nos. 1 & 2, Winter, pp. 94–105.

Fennell, Geraldine, 1982, "Terms v. Concepts: Market Segmentation, Brand Positioning and Other Aspects of the Academic-Practitioner Gap," TC–82, pp. 97–102.

Fraser, Cynthia, and John W. Bradford, 1983, "Competitive Market Structure Analysis: Principal Partitioning of Revealed Substitutabilities," *JCR*, 10, June, pp. 15–30.

Gobelli, David H., 1983, "Recasting the Marketing Concept," AMA–83, pp. 320–323.

Guseman, Dennis, and Peter L. Gillett, 1982, "Services Marketing: The Challenge of Stagflation," SC–81, pp. 182–185.

Hempel, Donald J., and Michael V. Laric, 1979, "Marketing Productivity Analysis, Strategic Implications for Consumer Services," TC–79, pp. 554–566.

Henderson, Bruce D., 1983, "The Anatomy of Competition," *JM*, 47, Spring, pp. 12–25.

Howard, John A., 1981, "The Empirical Theory of Managing the Market," in *Review of Marketing 1981*, Ben Enis and Kenneth Roering, eds., Chicago: American Marketing Association.

Howard, John A., 1983, "Normative Theory of the Firm," *JM*, 47, Fall.

Jain, Subhash C., 1981, *Marketing Planning and Strategy*, Cincinnati, Ohio: South-Western Publishing.

Johnson, Richard M., 1971, "Market Segmentation: A Strategic Marketing Tool," *JMR*, 8, February, pp. 13–18.

Keegan, Warren J., 1969, "Multinational Product Planning: Strategic Alternatives," *JM*, January, pp. 58–62.

Kotler, Philip, and Ravi Singh, 1981, "Marketing Warfare in the 1980's," *Journal of Business Strategy*, Winter, pp. 30–41.

Kotler, Philip, and Liam Fahe, 1982, "The World's Champion Marketers: The Japanese," *Journal of Business Strategy*, Summer, pp. 3–13.

Larreche, Jean-Claude, and Reza Moinpour, 1983, "Managerial Judgment in Marketing: The Concept of Expertise," *JMR*, 20, May, pp. 110–121.

Lovelock, Christopher H., Eric Langeard, John E. G. Bateson, and Pierre Eiglier, 1981, "Some Organizational Problems Facing Marketing in the Service Sector," SC–81, pp. 168–171.

Lovelock, Christopher, 1981, "Why Marketing Management Needs to Be Different for Services," SC–81, pp. 5–9.

Lusch, Robert F., 1979, "The Marketing-Accounting Interface," AMA–79, pp. 320–324.

Maile, Carlton A., and A. H. Kizilbash, 1978, "Improving Marketing Strategy with the Sleeper Effect," *Akron Business and Economic Review*, 9, Fall, pp. 32–36.

Massey, William, and Barton Weitz, 1977, "A Normative Theory of Market Segmentation," in *Behavioral Models for Marketing Action*, Francesco M. Nicosia and Yoram Wind, eds., Hinsdale, Ill.: Dryden Press.

McCullough, Charles D., and Larry T. Patterson, 1978, "Demographic Versus Psychographic Variables in Segmenting Markets," SMA–78, pp. 97–100.

Mentzer, John T., and Robert L. Cook, 1979, "The Consideration of Time Perception in Marketing Planning," AMA–79, pp. 435–439.

Meyer, Paul W., and Anton Meyer, 1981, "Brand Management Modelwise," *Absatzwirtschaft*, (Postfach 9225, D-4000 Dusseldorf, Germany), No. 4, pp. 122–129.

Miracle, Gordon, 1968, "Product Characteristics and Marketing Strategy," in *Perspectives in Marketing Theory*, Jerome B. Kennan and Montnose S. Sommers, eds., New York: Appleton-Century-Crofts.

Nevin, John R., 1978, "Using Experimental Data to Suggest and Evaluate Alternative Marketing Strategies," AMA–78, pp. 207–211.

Resnik, Alan J., Peter B. B. Turney, and J. Barry Mason, 1979, "Reconciling Marketing and Production Factors: A Neglected Area of Segmentation Theory," TC–79, pp. 346–362.

Rink, David, and H. Robert Dodge, 1978, "The Role of PLC Theory in Formulating and Implementing Effective Sales Strategies and Tactics," SMA–78, pp. 192–194.

Ryans, Adrian B., and Dick R. Wittink, 1977, "The Marketing of Services: A Categorization with Implications for Strategy," AMA–77, pp. 312–314.

Sandeman, Graham, 1981, "Implications of the Molecular Marketing Model in the Design of Retail Concepts," SC–81, pp. 230–235.

Sands, Saul, and Kenneth M. Warwick, 1976, "Pooled Marketing: The Challenge and the Opportunity," *Journal of the Academy of Marketing Science*, Vol. 4, No. 2, Spring, pp. 527–538.

Schiff, J. S., Jose Fernandez, and Leon Winer, 1977, "Segmentation as an Industrial Marketing Strategy," AMA–77, pp. 486–491.

Shapiro, Benson P., 1977, "Can Marketing and Manufacturing

Coexist?'' *Harvard Business Review,* 55, September–October, pp. 104–114.

Sheth, Jagdish N., and Gary L. Frazier, 1983, ''A Margin-Return Model for Strategic Market Planning,'' *JM,* 47, Spring, pp. 100–109.

Smith, Wendell R., 1956, ''Product Differentiation and Market Segmentation as Alternative Marketing Strategies,'' *JM,* 21, July, pp. 3–8.

Soldner, Helmut, 1976, ''Conceptual Models for Retail Strategy Formulation,'' *Journal of Retailing,* 52, Fall, pp. 47–56.

Spekman, Robert E., and Kjell Gronhaug, 1983, ''Insights on Implementation: A Conceptual Framework for Better Understanding the Strategic Marketing Planning Process,'' AMA–83, pp. 311–315.

Takeuchi, Hirotaka, 1982, ''Productivity as a Marketing Management Problem,'' TC–82, pp. 265–268.

Taylor, Ronald, Sion Raveed, John Summy, and Robert Butler, 1979, ''Demarketing Strategy—A Tool for the Future,'' SMA–79, pp. 60–63.

Tietz, Bruno, 1977, ''A Theory of Sequential Marketing,'' *Zeitschrift fur betriebswirtschaftliche Forschung*, 29, pp. 312–332.

Walters, C. Glenn, and Ronald D. Taylor, 1979, ''Contingency Marketing and Contemporary Marketing Management: A Comparison,'' TC–79, pp. 517–531.

Wensley, Robin, 1981, ''Strategic Marketing: Betas, Boxes, or Basics,'' *JM,* 45, Summer, pp. 173–182.

Williams, Robert J., and Colin F. Neuhaus, 1977, ''A Model for a Strategic Marketing Plan,'' AMA–77, p. 523.

Wilson, David T., and Morry Ghingold, 1980, ''Building Theory from Practice: A Theory-in-Use Approach,'' TC–80, pp. 236–239.

Wilson, Terry C., ''An Opportunity Screening Model,'' AMA–83, pp. 324–326.

Wind, Yoram, Vijay Mahajan, and Donald J. Swire, 1983, ''An Empirical Comparison of Standardized Portfolio Models,'' *JM,* 47, Spring, pp. 89–99.

Wind, Yoram, and Thomas S. Robertson, 1983, ''Marketing Strategy: New Directions for Theory and Research,'' *JM,* 47, Spring, pp. 12–25.

Zoltners, Andris A., and Joe A. Dodson, 1983, ''A Market Selection Model for Multiple End-Use Products,'' *JM,* 47, Spring, pp. 76–88.

6. Marketing Mix

a. Product Theory

Aspinwall, Leo V., 1962, ''The Characteristics of Goods Theory,'' in *Managerial Marketing; Perspectives and Viewpoints—a Source Book,* William Lazer and Eugene J. Kelley, eds., Homewood, Ill.: Richard D. Irwin, pp. 633–643.

Bass, Frank N., 1974, ''The Theory of Stochastic Brand Preference and Brand Switching,'' *JMR,* 11, February, pp. 1–20.

Bateson, John E. G., 1979, ''Why We Need Service Marketing,'' TC–79, pp. 131–146.

Bell, Martin L., 1981, ''A Matrix Approach to the Classification of Marketing Goods and Services,'' SC–81, pp. 208–212.

Bloch, Peter H., and Marsha L. Richins, 1980, ''What Is Product Importance? A Theoretical Analysis and Synthesis,'' TC–80, pp. 190–193.

Bloch, Peter H., and Marsha L. Richins, 1983, ''A Theoretical Model for the Study of Product Importance Perceptions,'' *JM,* 47, Summer, pp. 69–81.

Blute, Marion, 1982, ''Evolutionary and Ecological Processes in Marketing: The Product Life Cycle,'' TC–82, pp. 71–74.

Brown, Herbert E., and J. Taylor Sims, 1976, ''Market Segmentation, Product Differentiation, and Market Positioning as Alternative Marketing Strategies,'' AMA–76, pp. 483–487.

Brown, James R., and Edward F. Fern, 1981, ''Goods vs. Services Marketing: A Divergent Perspective,'' SC–81, pp. 205–207.

Bruner, Gordon C., II, and Tom L. Ingram, 1981, ''From Theory to Tactics: Adapting Risk Theory for an Unconventional Product Application,'' SMA–81, pp. 358–361.

Bucklin, Louis P., 1963, ''Retail Strategy and the Classification of Goods,'' *JM,* 27, January, pp. 50–55.

Burger, Philip C., 1980, ''How the Public Sector Hinders New Products,'' TC–80, pp. 233–235.

Calantone, Roger J., and Robert G. Cooper, 1977, ''A Typology of Industrial New Product Failure,'' AMA–77, pp. 492–497.

Cannon, Thomas, and Ronald W. Hasty, 1976, ''Managing for New Products—The Additional Dimension of Human Factors Research,'' AMA 76, pp. 488 492.

Chaterji, C. S., Ronald T. Lonsdale, and Stanley F. Stasch, 1981, ''New-Product Development: Theory and Practice,'' in *Review of Marketing 1981,* Ben M. Enis and Kenneth J. Roering, eds., Chicago: American Marketing Association.

Dholakia, Nikhilesh, 1980, ''Product Portfolio Optimality in Dynamic Market Situations,'' TC–80, pp. 108–111.

Dholakia, Nikhilesh, and David Dilts, 1981, ''Implications of Human Capital Theory for the Marketing of Services,'' SC–81, pp. 213–216.

Enis, Ben M., and Kenneth J. Roering, 1980, ''Product Classification Taxonomies: Synthesis and Consumer Implications,'' TC–80, pp. 186–189.

Enis, Ben M., and Kenneth J. Roering, 1981, "Services Marketing: Different Products, Similar Strategy," SC–81, pp. 1–4.

Giddy, Ian, 1978, "The Demise of the Product-Cycle Model in International Business Theory," *Columbia Journal of World Business*, 13, Spring, pp. 90–97.

Grinnell, D. Jacque, 1976, "Product Mix Decisions: Direct Costing vs. Absorption Costing," *Management Accounting*, 54, July/August, pp. 36–42.

Gummesson, Evert, 1981, "The Marketing of Professional Services—25 Propositions," SC–81, pp. 108–112.

Hughes, Joseph P., 1978, "Factor Demand in the Multi-Product Firm," *Southern Economic Journal*, 44, October, pp. 494–501.

Lovelock, Christopher H., 1979, "Theoretical Contributions from Services and Nonbusiness Marketing," TC–79, pp. 147–165.

Lovelock, Christopher H., 1980, "Towards a Classification of Services," TC–80, pp. 72–76.

Lovelock, Christopher H., 1983, "Classifying Services to Gain Strategic Marketing Insights," *JM*, 47, Summer, pp. 9–20.

Marcus, Burton H., 1980, "Product Development: The Need for Micro and Macro Concept Applications," TC–80, pp. 120–124.

Marton, Katherin, and Karen A. Berkman, 1976, "A Systems Approach for the Generation of New Product Ideas," *Journal of the Academy of Marketing Science*, 4, Spring, pp. 520–526.

Mason, Joseph Barry, Alan J. Resnik, and Peter B. Turney, 1979, "New Product Development and Strategic Planning for the 1980's," AMA–79, pp. 348–351.

Mason, William R., 1958, "A Theory of Packaging in the Marketing Mix," *Business Horizons*, 1, Summer, pp. 91–95.

May, Frederick E., Richard E. Homans, and R. Neil Maddox, 1980, "Regulating Demand in Innovative Maturity," TC–80, pp. 182–185.

Midgley, David F., 1981, "Toward a Theory of the Product Life Cycle: Explaining Diversity," *JM*, 45, Fall, pp. 109–115.

Murphy, Patrick E., and Richard K. Robinson, 1981, "Concept Testing for Services," SC–81, pp. 217–220.

Narasimhan, Chakravarthi, and Subrata K. Sen, 1983, "New Product Models for Test Market Data," *JM*, 47, Winter, pp. 11–25.

Rink, David R., and John E. Swan, 1979, "Product Life Cycle Theory: A Past, Present and Future Analysis," TC–79, pp. 312–327.

Rink, David R., and Peter F. Kaminski, 1981, "Product Life Cycle Theory: A Framework for Fashioning Transportation Strategies and Tactics," AMA–81, pp. 97–100.

Rothberg, Robert R., 1980, "Strategic Considerations in the Design and Use of New Product Screening Models," TC–80, pp. 81–84.

Sarel, Dan, 1980, "Product Positioning—A Reassessment," TC–80, pp. 116–119.

Shary, Philip B., and Boris W. Becker, 1976, "Product Availability and the Management of Demand," *European Journal of Marketing*, Vol. 10, No. 3, pp. 127–135.

*Shostack, Lynn G., 1977, "Breaking Free from Product Marketing," *JM*, April, pp. 73–80. (Reading 22: "A Framework for Service Marketing.")

Shostack, G. Lynn, 1981, "How to Design a Service," SC–81, pp. 221–229.

Tellis, Gerard J., and C. Merle Crawford, 1981, "An Evolutionary Approach to Product Growth Theory," *JM*, 45, Fall, pp. 125–132.

Weinberger, Marc, and Stephen W. Brown, 1977, "A Difference in Informational Influences: Services vs. Goods," *Journal of the Academy of Marketing Science*, Vol. 5. No, 1, Winter, pp. 389–407.

Wind, Yoram, and Henry J. Claycamp, 1976, "Planning Product Line Strategy: A Matrix Approach," *JM*, 40, January, pp. 2–9.

Wind, Yoram, 1982, *Product Policy: Concepts, Methods and Strategy*, Reading, Mass.: Addison-Wesley.

b. Price Theory

Anderson, Paul F., 1980, "Theoretical and Implementational Problems of ROI Pricing," TC–80, pp. 178–181.

Barker, Raymond F., 1976, "The Effect of Changes in the Product Line on Price-Quality Relationships," AMA–76, pp. 192–196.

Green, Paul, 1963, "Bayesian Decision Theory in Pricing Strategy," *JM*, 27, January, pp. 5–14.

Hanna, Nessim, 1980, "A Closer Look at Pricing Today: The Increasing Challenges of Inflation," TC–80, pp. 174–176.

Hansz, James E., and Kenneth P. Sinclair, 1978, "Target Return Pricing: Panacea or Paradox?" SMA–78, pp. 441–444.

Hayakawa, Hiroaki, 1976, "Consumer Theory When Prices and Real Income Affect Preference," *Southern Economic Journal*, 43, July, pp. 840–845.

Hawkins, Edward R., 1968, "Price Policies and Theory," *Perspectives in Marketing Theory*, Jerome B. Kernan and Montrose S. Sommers, eds., New York: Appleton-Century-Crofts.

Ingene, Charles A., and Michael Levy, 1982, "Cash Discounts to Retail Customers: An Alternative to Credit Card Sales," *JM*, 46, Spring, pp. 92–103.

Kamen, Joseph M., and Robert J. Toman, 1970, "Psychophysics of Prices," *JMR*, 7, November, pp. 27–35.

Lambert, David R., 1979, "On Paying Homage to a False God: Comments on the Theory of the Firm's Role in Marketing," TC–79, pp. 363–373.

Monroe, Kent B., 1973, "Buyers' Subjective Perceptions of Price," *JMR*, 10, February, pp. 70–80.

Monroe, Kent B., and David M. Gardner, 1976, "An Experimental Inquiry into the Effect of Price on Brand Preference," AMA–76, pp. 552–556.

Monroe, Kent B., 1979, *Pricing: Making Profitable Decisions*, New York: McGraw-Hill.

Monroe, Kent B., and Susan M. Petroshius, 1980, "A Theoretical Approach for Determining Product Line Prices," TC–80, pp. 21–24.

Olson, Jerry C., 1980, "Implications of an Information Processing Approach to Pricing Research," TC–80, pp. 13–16.

Park, C. Whan, V. Parker Lessig, and James R. Merrill, 1982, "The Elusive Role of Price in Brand Choice Behavior," ACR–82, pp. 201–205.

Rexeisen, Richard J., 1982, "Is There a Valid Price Quality Relationship?" ACR–82, pp. 190–194.

Ricsz, Peter C., 1978, "Price Versus Quality in the Marketplace, 1961–1975," *Journal of Retailing*, 54, Winter, pp. 15–28.

Rink, David R., 1980, "A Prescriptive Model for New Product Pricing," TC–80, pp. 170–173.

Shapiro, Benson P., 1973, "Price Reliance: Existence and Sources," *JMR*, 10, August, pp. 286–293.

Sherman, Roger, 1981, "Pricing Inefficiency Under Profit Regulation," *Southern Economic Journal*, 48, October, pp. 475–489.

Sproles, George B., 1977, "New Evidence on Price and Product Quality," *Journal of Consumer Affairs*, 11, Summer, pp. 63–77.

Weston, J. Fred, 1979, "Pricing Policy and the Meaning of Target Return Pricing," AMA–79, pp. 312–319.

Widrick, Stanley M., 1980, "Towards the Development of a Theory of Retail Price Image," TC–80, pp. 17–20.

c. Promotion Theory

Adams, W. J., and J. L. Yellen, 1977, "What Makes Advertising Profitable?" *Economic Journal*, 87, September, pp. 421–49.

Arndt, Johan, 1976, "Research into Advertising," *European Journal of Marketing*, Vol. 10, No. 4, pp. 178–197. (Monograph)

Arndt, Johan, 1982, "The Economies of Scale in Advertising: The Myth, the Concept, the Facts," AMA–82, pp. 341–345.

Arterburn, Alfred, and John Woodbury, 1981, "Advertising,

Price Competition and Market Structure," *Southern Economic Journal*, 47, January, pp. 763–775.

Asch, Peter, 1979, "The Role of Advertising in Changing Concentration, 1963–1972," *Southern Economic Journal*, 47, July, pp. 288–297.

Belch, Michael A., and Robert W. Haas, 1979, "Using the Buyer's Needs to Improve Industrial Sales," *Business*, 29, September–October, pp. 8–14.

Bloom, Paul N., 1977, "Advertising in the Professions: The Critical Issues," *JM*, 41, July, pp. 103–110.

Booms, Bernard H., and Jody L. Nyquist, 1981, "Analyzing the Customer/Firm Communication Component of the Services Marketing Mix," SC–81, pp. 172–177.

Bushman, F. Anthony, 1977, "A New Product Model for Direct Mail Promotion," SMA–77, pp. 261–264.

Chonko, Lawrence B., 1982, "On the Measurement of Sales Performance," TC–82, pp. 107–111.

Churchill, Gilbert A., Jr., Neil M. Ford, and Orville C. Walker, 1976, "Organizational Climate and Job Satisfaction in the Salesforce," *JMR*, 13, November, pp. 323–332.

Clabaugh, Maurice G., Jr., John M. Hawes, and Joanna Wallace, 1982, "Cass: Contingency Approach to Selling as a System," TC–82, pp. 103–106.

Darmon, Rene Y., 1980, "Economic Theory and Sales Force Compensation," TC–80, pp. 85–90.

Dubinsky, Alan J., and Thomas N. Ingram, 1981–1982, "A Classification of Industrial Buyers: Implications for Sales Training," *Journal of Personal Selling & Sales Management*, 2, Fall/Winter, pp. 46–51.

Duncan, Calvin P., 1979, "Humor in Advertising: A Behavioral Perspective," *Journal of the Academy of Marketing Science*, Vol. 7, No. 4, Fall, pp. 285–306.

Etgar, Michael, and Stephen A. Goodwin, 1978, "Comparative Advertising: Issues and Problems," ACR–78, pp. 63–71.

Frampton, G. Creighton, 1977, "Subliminally Induced Fear: An Extension of a Conceptual Fear Model," SMA–77, pp. 311–314.

Grønhaug, Kjell, and Thomas V. Bonoma, 1980, "Industrial-Organizational Buying: A Derived Demand Perspective," TC–80, pp. 224–228.

Hargrove, Earnestine C., and Kathleen A. Krentler, 1980, "Evaluating Sales Promotion: A Paradigm," SMA–80, pp. 93–96.

Homer, Pamela, 1981, "Towards a Theory of Media Selection," SMA–81, pp. 362–365.

Kelly, J. Steven, and Barbara M. Kessler, 1978, "Subliminal Seduction: Fact or Fantasy?" SMA–78, pp. 112–114.

La Barbera, Priscilla A., 1980, "Toward the Theoretical Development of Advertising Self-Regulation," TC–80, pp. 129–132.

LaForge, Raymond W., 1980, "Salesforce Decision Models: Trends in the 1970's, Directions for the 1980's," SMA–80, pp. 41–45.

LaForge, Raymond W., and David W. Cravens, 1981–1982, "A Marketing Response Model for Sales Management Decision Making," *Journal of Personal Selling & Sales Management,* 2, Fall/Winter, pp. 10–16.

LaForge, Raymond W., and David W. Cravens, 1982, "An Approach for Implementing Salesforce Decision Models," AMA–82, pp. 252–255.

LaForge, Raymond W., and Davis W. Cravens, 1982, "Steps in Selling Effort Deployment," *Industrial Marketing Management,* Vol. 11, July, pp. 183–194.

LaForge, Raymond W., Stephen J. Grove, and Gregory M. Pickett, 1983, "Sales Management Research: A Call for Integration," AMA–83, pp. 212–216.

Leigh, Thomas W., 1982, "Company Reputation as a Determinant of Sales Call Effectiveness: A Cognitive Social Learning Perspective," TC–82, pp. 171–176.

Leone, Robert P., 1983, "Modeling Sales-Advertising Relationships: An Integrated Time Series-Econometric Approach," *JMR,* 20, August, pp. 291–295.

Maile, C. A., and A. H. Kizilbash, 1977, "A Communications Model for Marketing Decisions," *Journal of the Academy of Marketing Science,* Vol. 5, Nos. 1 & 2, Winter, pp. 48–56.

McDonald, Colin, 1979, "Implications of a Person-Centered View of Advertising," *Admap* (10 Langston St., London SW100JH, England), 15, June, pp. 252–260.

McGarry, Edmund D., 1936, "The Importance of Scientific Method in Advertising," *JM,* 1, October, pp. 82–86.

McIntyre, Shelby H., and Albert V. Bruno, 1976, "Testimonials in Advertising: A Conceptual Perspective," AMA–76, pp. 63–66.

Meisel, John B., 1979, "Demand and Supply Determinants of Advertising Intensity Among Convenience Goods," *Southern Economic Journal,* 46, July, pp. 233–243.

Mowen, John C., Stephen W. Brown, and Meg Schulman, 1979, "Theoretical and Empirical Extentions of Endorser Effectiveness," AMA–79, pp. 258–262.

Mowen, John C., and Scott Painton, 1980, "An Outline of a General Theory of Consumer Mass Communications," TC–80, pp. 166–169.

Pagoulatos, Emilio, and Robert Sorensen, 1981, "A Simultaneous Equation Analysis of Advertising Concentration and Profitability," *Southern Economic Journal,* 47, January, pp. 728–741.

Patti, Charles H., 1977, "Evaluating the Role of Advertising," *Journal of Advertising,* Vol. 7, No. 4, Fall, pp. 30–35.

Phillips, Nick, 1979, "Measuring Attitudes and Behavior—Practical Implications for Advertising," *Admap,* 15, March, pp. 119–124.

Rothschild, Michael L., and William C. Gaidis, 1981, "Behavioral Learning Theory: Its Relevance to Marketing and Promotions," *JM,* 45, Spring, pp. 70–78.

Scammon, Debra L., Dennis L. McNeill, and Ivan L. Preston, 1980, "The FTC's Emerging Theory of Consumer Protection via Increased Information," TC–80, pp. 133–137.

Schramm, Wilbur, 1968, "How Communication Works," in *Perspectives in Marketing Theory,* Jerome B. Kennan and Montrose B. Sommers, eds., New York: Appleton-Century-Crofts.

Shimp, Terence A., 1982, "A Classification Schematum of Advertising Content: Toward General Advertising Theory," TC–82, pp. 80–83.

Simon, Julian L., and Johan Arndt, 1980, "The Shape of the Advertising Response Function," *Journal of Advertising Research,* 20, August, pp. 11–28.

Sissors, Jack Z., 1978, "Another Look at the Question: Does Advertising Affect Values?" *Journal of Advertising,* Vol. 7, No. 3, Summer, pp. 26–30.

Smith, D. Stanton, Gregory W. Danford, and Bryan E. Stanhouse, 1978, "The Advertising-Concentration Controversy: Comment," *Southern Economic Journal,* 44, January, pp. 653–660.

Smith, Robert E., and Shelby D. Hunt, 1978, "The Effectiveness of Personal Selling over Advertising: An Attributional Analysis," AMA–78, pp. 158–163.

Spiro, Rosanne L., and Kent D. VanLiere, 1982, "Salesperson Performance: A Conceptual Framework," SMA–82, pp. 36–41.

Taylor, Ronald D., and John H. Summey, 1980, The Promotional Mix and the Product Life Cycle: A Review of Their Interaction," TC–80, pp. 125–128.

Tyagi, Pradeep K., 1982, "Organizational Climate in Sales Force Organizations: A Critical Review and Future Directions," TC–82, pp. 112–115.

Weitz, Barton A., 1981, "Effectiveness in Sales Interactions: A Contingency Framework," *JM,* 45, Winter, pp. 85–103.

White, Irving S., 1959, "The Functions of Advertising in Our Culture," *JM,* 24, July, pp. 8–14.

Wilson, David T., and Lorne Bozinoff, 1980, "Role Theory and Buying-Selling Negotiations: A Critical Overview," AMA–80, pp. 118–121.

Wilson, R. Dale, and Noreen K. Moore, 1979, "The Role of Sexually-Oriented Stimuli in Advertising: Theory and Literature Review," ACR–79, pp. 55–61.

Winer, Russell S., 1980, "Analysis of Advertising Experiments," *Journal of Advertising Research,* 20, June, pp. 25–31.

Wiswede, Gunter, 1979, "Reactance—As to the Application of a Social Science Theory to Problems of Advertising and

Selling," *Jahrbuch der Absatz- und Verbrauchsforschung* Vol. 25, No. 2, pp. 81–110.

Young, Robert F., 1981, "The Advertising of Consumer Services and the Hierarchy of Effects," SC–81, pp. 196–199.

d. Distribution Theory

Achrol, Ravi Singh, Torger Reve, and Louis W. Stern, 1983, "The Environment of Marketing Channel Diads: A Framework for Comparative Analysis," *JM,* 47, Fall.

Allmon, Dean E., and Michael T. Troncalli, 1978, "Concepts of a Channel of Distribution for Services," SMA–78, pp. 209–210.

Bennion, Mark L., 1980, "A Discussion of the Role of the Product Line in the Calculation of a Manufacturer's Power in the Distribution Channel," TC–80, pp. 108–111.

Berens, John S., 1980, "Capital Requirements and Retail Institutional Innovation—Theoretical Observations," TC–80, pp. 248–250.

Berens, John S., and Larue W. Berens, 1980, "Cycle Theory in Distribution—Modification and Extension," SMA–80, pp. 304–307.

Berkowitz, Eric N., Terry Deutscher, and Robert A. Hansen, 1978, "Retail Image Research: A Case of Significant Unrealized Potential," AMA–78, pp. 62–66.

Berkowitz, Eric N., John R. Walton, and Orville C. Walker, Jr., 1979, "In-Home Shoppers: The Market for Innovative Distribution Systems," *Journal of Retailing,* 55, Summer, pp. 15–33.

Bloom, Gordon F., 1978, "The Future of the Retail Food Industry: Another View," *Journal of Retailing,* 54, Winter, pp. 3–14.

Brown, James R., 1980, "More on the Channel Conflict-Performance Relationship," TC–80, pp. 104–107.

Bucklin, Louis P., 1963, "Retail Strategy and the Classification of Consumer Goods," *JM,* 27, January, pp. 50–55.

Bucklin, Louis P., 1966, *A Theory of Distribution Channel Structure,* Berkeley: Institute of Business and Economic Research, University of California.

Bucklin, Louis P., 1973, "A Theory of Channel Control," *JM,* 37, January, pp. 39–47.

Childers, Terry L., and Robert W. Ruekert, 1982, "The Meaning and Determinants of Cooperation Within an Interorganizational Marketing Network," TC–82, pp. 116–119.

Chirouze, Yves, 1980, "Short-Circuit Distribution by Selling Direct" [Court-circuitez la distribution grâce à la vente directe"], *Harvard-L'Expansion,* (La Revue des Responsables, 67, Avenue Wagram 75017 Paris, France), Fall, pp. 103–113.

Clabaugh, Maurice G., Jr., 1977, "Image: A Key to Cognitive Behavioralism and Retail Spatial Movement," SMA–77, pp. 138–141.

Comer, James M., Alok K. Chakrabarti, and Robert L. Franczvai, 1976, "Channel Theory Revisited: The Industrial Service Exception," AMA–76, pp. 245–247.

Converse, Paul D., 1949, "New Laws of Retail Gravitation," *JM,* 14, October, 379–384.

Crask, Melvin R., and Fred D. Reynolds, 1978, "An Indepth Profile of the Department Store Shopper," *Journal of Retailing,* 54, Summer, pp. 23–32.

Dickson, Peter R., 1983, "Distributor Portfolio Analysis and the Channel Dependence Matrix: New Techniques for Understanding and Managing the Channel," *JM,* 47, Summer, pp. 35–44.

Dovel, Thomas D., and Denis F. Healy, 1977, "The Garage Sale—A New Retailing Phenomenon," SMA–77, pp. 164–167.

Dwyer, F. Robert, and Orville C. Walker, Jr., 1981, "Bargaining in an Asymmetrical Power Structure," *JM,* 45, Winter, pp. 104–115.

El-Ansary, Adel L., and Robert A. Robicheaux, 1974, "A Theory of Channel Control: Revisited," *JM,* 38, January, pp. 2–7.

Etgar, Michael, 1979, "Sources and Types of Intrachannel Conflict," *Journal of Retailing,* 55, Spring, pp. 61–78.

Etgar, Michael, and Dov Izraeli, 1982, "Behavioral and Economic Approaches to Channel Coordination," TC–82, pp. 128–131.

Frazier, Gary L., 1983, "Interorganizational Exchange Behavior in Marketing Channels: A Broadened Perspective," *JM,* 47, Fall.

Gautschi, David A., 1981, "Specification of Patronage Models for Retail Center Choice," *JMR,* 18, May, pp. 162–174.

George, William R., 1977, "The Retailing of Services—A Challenging Future," *Journal of Retailing,* 53, Fall, pp. 85–98.

Ginter, Peter M., and Jack M. Starling, 1978, "Reverse Distribution Channels: Concept and Structure," SMA–78, pp. 206–208.

Giraldi, Bernard, 1979, "The Future of the Mail-Order Business" [L'avenir de la vente par correspondence"], *Revue française du marketing,* 78, July/August/September, pp. 31–52.

Grimm, Jim L., and James B. Spalding, 1980, "Is Channel(s) Theory Lagging?" TC–80, pp. 255–258.

Hansen, Robert A., Terry Duetscher, and Eric N. Berkowitz, 1977, "Institutional Positioning: A Dynamic Concept for Retailing Strategy," *Journal of the Academy of Marketing Science,* Vol. 5, No. 3, Summer, pp. 185–194.

Harvey, Michael G., and John A. Stieber, 1982, "Franchise Agreements: The Initial Source of Conflict in Franchise Systems," TC–82, pp. 147–150.

Highland Arthur V., and Anthony F. McGann, 1977, "Physical Distribution, Ultimate Consumers, and Weber's Law," ACR–77, pp. 133–137.

Hirschman, Elizabeth C., 1978, "A Descriptive Theory of Retail Market Structure," *Journal of Retailing,* 54, Winter, pp. 29–48.

Hirschman, Elizabeth C., 1980, "Roles of Retailing in the Diffusion of Popular Culture: Microperspectives," *Journal of Retailing,* 56, Spring, pp. 16–36.

Hirschman, Elizabeth C., 1981, "Retail Research and Theory," in *Review of Marketing 1981,* Ben M. Enis and Kenneth J. Roering, eds., Chicago: American Marketing Association. pp. 120–133.

Hollander, Stanley C., 1960, "The Wheel of Retailing," *JM,* 25, July, pp. 37–42.

Hollander, Stanley C., 1979, "Retail Research Needs and Problems," AMA–79, pp. 406–407.

Hollander, Stanley C., 1981, "Retailing Theory: Some Criticism and Some Admiration," in *Theory in Retailing: Traditional and Nontraditional Sources,* Ronald W. Stampl and Elizabeth C. Hirschman, eds., Chicago: American Marketing Association.

Holton, Richard H., and Louis P. Bucklin, 1982, "Managing Distribution Systems in a Decentralized Communist Economy," TC–82, pp. 124–127.

Hunt, Kenneth A., and John T. Mentzer, 1982, "Distribution of Power as a Determinate in Predicting Coalition Formations Within Channels of Distribution," TC–82, pp. 120–123.

Ingene, Charles A., 1980, "Decision Making in an Uncertain Environment: The Case of Retail Display Space," TC–80, pp. 220–223.

Jackson, Donald M., and Michael F. d'Amico, 1979, "Channel Length and Channel Values," *Akron Business and Economic Review,* 10, Spring, pp. 19–23.

Jackson, Donald W., and Bruce J. Walker, 1980, "The Channel Manager: Marketing's Newest Aide?" *California Management Review,* Vol. 23, No. 2, Winter, pp. 52–58.

Kaminski, Peter F., and David R. Rink, 1982, "The Impact of Product Life Cycle Theory upon Physical Distribution Management: A Prescriptive Model," SMA–82, pp. 114–117.

Lambert, Douglas M., and James R. Stock, 1978, "Physical Distribution and Consumer Demands," *MSU Business Topics,* Vol. 26, No. 2, Spring, pp. 49–56.

Langeard, Eric, 1982, "Distribution Channels in Service Industries," TC–82 , pp. 132–137.

Lesser, Jack A., and James M. Stearns, 1982, "The Develop-

ment of Retailing Information Systems Based on Shopping Behavior Theory," TC–82., pp. 138–142.

Lusch, Robert F., 1980, "Estimation of a Production Function for Food Wholesalers," TC–80, pp. 37–39.

Lynagh, Peter M., and Richard F. Poist, 1977, "Physical Distribution and the Product Life Cycle: An Examination of Theoretical Relationships," SMA–77, pp, 95–98.

Mallen, Bruce, 1964, "Conflict and Cooperation in Marketing Channels," in L. George Smith ed., *Progress in Marketing,* Chicago: American Marketing Association.

Markin, Rom J., and Calvin P. Duncan, 1981, "The Transformation of Retailing Institutions: Beyond the Wheel of Retailing and Life Cycle Theories," *Journal of Macromarketing,* 1, Spring, pp. 58–66.

Mentzer, John T., A. Coskun Samli, and Mary Ann Lederhaus, 1980, "Stability and Efficiency in Marketing Channels: The Theory of Double Exchange," TC–80, pp. 251–254.

Robicheaux, Robert, and Adel El-Ansary, 1975, "A General Model for Understanding Channel Member Behavior," *Journal of Retailing,* 52, Winter, pp. 13–30, 90–94.

Rosenbloom, Bert, and Leon G. Schiffman, 1981, "Retailing Theory: Perspectives and Approaches," in *Theory in Retailing: Traditional and Nontraditional Sources,* Ronald W. Stampl and Elizabeth C. Hirschman, eds., Chicago: American Marketing Association.

Rosson, Philip, and Robert Sweitzer, 1979, "The Pluralistic Politics of Channel Decision-Making," TC–79, pp. 328–345.

Shooshtari, Nader, and Bruce Walker, 1980, "In Search of a Theory of Channel Behavior," TC–80, pp. 100–103.

Smith, Michael F., 1982, "Person Perception in the Manufacturer-Distributor Interaction Sequence," TC–82, pp. 143–146.

Wagenheim, George D., 1980, "Physical Distribution Functional Transfer: A Source of Competitive Advantage," TC–80, pp. 40–42.

Wilkinson, Ian F., 1979, "Power and Satisfaction in Channels of Distribution," *Journal of Retailing,* 55, Summer, pp. 79–94.

7.   Macromarketing Theory

Andreasen, Alan R., 1982, "Judging Marketing in the 1980's," *Journal of Macromarketing,* 2, Spring, pp. 7–13.

Arndt, Johan, 1978, "Marketing in the Age of Market Domestication: Macro-Marketing Reflections with Micro Implications," AMA–78, pp. 204–307.

Arndt, Johan, 1981, "The Political Economy of Marketing Systems: Reviving the Institutional Approach," *Journal of Macromarketing,* 1, Fall, pp. 36–47.

Arndt, Johan, 1983, "The Political Economy Paradigm," *JM*, 47, Fall.

Barnes, James H., Jr., 1982, "Recycling: A Problem in Reverse Logistics," *Journal of Macromarketing*, 2, Fall, pp. 31–37.

Bartels, Robert, and Roger L. Jenkins, 1977, "Macromarketing," *JM*, 41, October, pp. 17–20.

Bartels, Robert, 1983, "Is Marketing Defaulting Its Responsibilities?", *JM*, 47, Fall.

Bates, Albert D., 1978, "Macromarketing and the Isolation Syndrome," AMA–78, pp. 348–349.

Bruce, Grady D., 1978, "Information About Social and Cultural Change: An Analytical Framework for Managerial Use," SMA–78, pp. 298–301.

Bruce, Grady D., 1979, "A Tripartite Theory on the Effects of Inflation," TC–79, pp. 228–236.

Carman, James M., 1982, "Private Property and the Regulation of Vertical Channel Systems," *Journal of Macromarketing*, 2, Spring, pp. 20–26.

Chaganti, Rajeswararao, 1978, "Macro-marketing and Quality of Life: Some Issues and Opportunities for Research," *Proceedings of the Third Macro-Marketing Seminar*, August, p. 117.

Chaganti, Rajeswararao, 1981, "Macromarketing: Elements of a Framework for Normative Evaluation," *Journal of Macromarketing*, 1, Fall, pp. 56–59.

Cundiff, Edward W., 1982, "A Macromarketing Approach to Economic Development," *Journal of Macromarketing*, 2, Spring, pp. 14–19.

Dawson, Leslie M., 1980, "Marketing for Human Needs in a Humane Future," *Business Horizons*, 23, June, pp. 72–82.

Day, George S., and David Aaker, 1970, "A Guide to Consumerism," *JM*, 34, July, pp. 12–19.

Dholakia, Nikhilesh, A. Fuat Firat, and Richard P. Bagozzi, 1980, "The De-Americanization of Marketing Thought: In Search of a Universal Basis," TC–80, pp. 25–29.

Dholakia, Nikhilesh A., and Ruby Roy Dholakia, 1982, "Marketing in the Emerging World Order," *Journal of Macromarketing*, 2, Spring, pp. 47–56.

Dixon, Donald F., 1978, "The Origins of Macro-marketing Thought," *Proceedings of the Third Macro-Marketing Seminar*, August, pp. 9–28.

Dixon, Donald F., 1979, "The Economic Performance of Marketing," SMA–79, pp. 56–59.

Dixon, Donald F., 1981, "Whither Macromarketing: Some Further Considerations," SMA–81, pp. 223–226.

Dixon, Donald F., 1982, "The Ethical Component of Marketing: An Eighteenth Century View," *Journal of Macromarketing*, 2, Spring, pp. 38–46.

English, Wilke D., and Marye Tharp Hilger, 1978, "Consumer Alienation in the Marketplace," SMA–78, pp. 307–310.

Etgar, Michael, 1976, "Three Models of Distributive Change," in C. C. Slater, ed. *Macromarketing: Distributive Processes from a Societal Perspective*, Boulder: Business Research Division, Graduate School of Business, University of Colorado.

Evans, Joel R., and Kevin F. McCrohan, 1977, "A Model of Buyer Power: Understanding Monopsony and Oligopsony," SMA–77, pp. 17–20.

Falkenberg, Andreas W., and John R. Wish, 1980, "Efficiency, Equity and Freedom of Choice as Evaluative Criteria for Normative Marketing Management," TC–80, pp. 138–141.

Farley, John U., and Harold J. Leavitt, 1971, "Marketing and Population Problems," *JM*, 35, July, pp. 28–33.

Ferrell, O. C., and Dean M. Krugman, 1978, "The Role of Consumers in the Public Policy Process," *Journal of the Academy of Marketing Science*, Vol. 6, No. 3, Summer, pp. 167–175.

Firat, A. Fuat, and Nikhilesh Dholakia, 1982, "Consumption Choices at the Macro Level," *Journal of Macromarketing*, 2, Fall, pp. 6–15.

Fisk, George, 1967, *Marketing Systems: An Introductory Analysis*, New York: Harper & Row.

Fisk, George, 1974, *Marketing and the Ecological Crisis*, New York: Harper & Row.

Fisk, George, and R. W. Nason, eds., 1979, *Macromarketing: New Steps on the Learning Curve*, Boulder: Business Research Division, Graduate School of Business, University of Colorado.

Fisk, George, R. W. Nason, and P. D. White, eds., 1980, *Macromarketing: Evolution of Thought*, Boulder: Business Research Division, Graduate School of Business, University of Colorado.

Fisk, George, 1980, "Taxonomic Classification of Macromarketing Theory," TC–80, pp. 146–149.

Fisk, George, 1982, "Editor's Working Definition of Macromarketing," *Journal of Macromarketing*, 2, Spring, pp. 3–4.

*Fisk, George, and Patricia Meyers, 1982, "Macromarketers' Guide to Paradigm Development," TC–82, pp. 281–285.

Fisk, Raymond P., 1982, "Toward a Theoretical Framework for Marketing Ethics," TC–82, pp. 255–259.

Granzin, Kent L., 1982, "A Conceptual Systems Framework for Marketing," TC–82, pp. 246–249.

Grether, E. T., 1983, "Regional-Spatial Analysis in Marketing," *JM*, 47, Fall.

Groeneveld, Leonard, 1976, "Revamping the Meaning of Systems in Marketing," SMA–76, pp. 267–269.

Gunn, Bruce, 1976, ''The Macromarketing System—An Analog Model,'' *Marquette Business Review,* 20, Spring, pp. 1–11.

Gunn, Bruce, 1980, ''Competruism,'' *Journal of the Academy of Marketing Science,* Vol. 8, No. 3, Summer, pp. 243–254.

Heed, Søren, 1981, ''Marx and Marketing: A Radical Analysis of the Macro Effects of Marketing,'' AMA–81, pp. 431–433.

Heed, Søren, 1981, ''From Micromarketing to Macromarketing: Radical Social System Paradigms,'' *Journal of Macromarketing,* 1, Fall, p. 60–61.

Hibbert, E. P., 1979, ''The Cultural Dimension of Marketing and the Impact of Industrialization,'' *European Research,* January, pp. 41–47.

Hilger, Marye Tharp, 1978, ''The Role of Marketing Institutions in Consumer Alienation: A Neglected Social Externality,'' *Proceedings of the Third Macro-Marketing Seminar,* August, pp. 89–104.

Hirschman, Elizabeth C., and Michael R. Solomon, 1982, ''Competition and Cooperation Among Culture Production Systems,'' TC–82, pp. 269–272.

Hirschman, Elizabeth C., 1983, ''Aesthetics, Ideologies and the Limits of the Marketing Concept,'' *JM,* 47, Summer, pp. 45–55.

Holloway, Robert J., and Robert S. Hancock, 1973, *Marketing in a Changing Environment,* 2nd ed., New York: Wiley.

Horan, Patrick M., E. M. Beck, and Charles M. Tolbert, II, 1980, ''The Market Homogeneity Assumption: On the Theoretical Foundations of Empirical Knowledge,'' *Social Science Quarterly,* 61, September, pp. 279–291.

Hunt, Shelby D., 1981, ''Macromarketing as a Multidimensional Concept,'' *Journal of Macromarketing,* 1, Spring, p. 7.

Ingene, Charles A., 1982, ''Analyzing Productivity in Marketing: A Model and Some Hypotheses,'' TC–82, pp. 277–280.

Jacobson, Robert, and Franco M. Nicosia, 1981, ''Advertising and Public Policy: The Macroeconomic Effects of Advertising,'' *Journal of Marketing Research,* 18, February, pp. 29–38.

Kangun, Norman, 1972, *Society and Marketing,* New York: Harper & Row.

Keane, John G., 1976, ''Marketing Self-Renewal,'' SMA–76, pp. 63–67.

Kohlhagen, Steve W., 1977, ''Income Distribution and 'Representative Demand' in International Trade Flows—An Empirical Test of Linder's Hypothesis,'' *Southern Economic Journal,* 44, July, pp. 167–72.

Kotler, Philip, and Sidney J. Levy, 1971, ''Demarketing, Yes, Demarketing,'' *Harvard Business Review,* Vol. 49, November–December, pp. 71–80.

Kotler, Philip, and Gerald Zaltman, 1971, ''Social Marketing: An Approach to Planned Social Change,'' *JM,* 35, July, pp. 3–12.

Krapfel, Robert E., Jr., 1982, ''Marketing by Mandate,'' *JM,* 46, Summer, pp. 79–85.

Lambert, Zarrel V., 1980, ''Consumer Alienation, General Dissatisfaction, and Consumerism Issues: Conceptual and Managerial Perspectives,'' *Journal of Retailing,* 56, Summer, pp. 3–24.

Layton, Roger A., 1981, ''Trade Flows in Macromarketing Systems: Part I, A Macromodel of Trade Flows,'' *Journal of Macromarketing,* 1, Spring, pp. 35–48.

Lazer, William, 1969, ''Marketing's Changing Social Relationships,'' *JM,* 33, January, pp. 3–9.

Lazer, William, and Eugene J. Kelley, eds., 1973, *Social Marketing: Perspectives and Viewpoints,* Homewood, Ill.: Richard D. Irwin.

Lazer, William, 1977, ''The 1980's and Beyond: A Perspective,'' *MSU Business Topics,* Vol. 25, No. 2, Spring, pp. 21–35.

Lusch, Robert F., and Ray R. Serpkenci, 1982, ''Correlates of Working Capital Productivity in Marketing Channels: A Macromarketing Perspective,'' TC–82, pp. 273–276.

Matsusaki, Hiro, 1979, ''Marketing, Culture and Social Framework: The Need for Theory Development at the Macro Marketing Level,'' TC–79, pp. 679–693.

Miller, James Grier, 1981, A Commentary on ''General Living Systems Theory and Marketing: A Framework for Analysis,'' *JM,* Vol. 45, No. 4, Fall, p. 38.

Miller, Joseph C., and Michael D. Hutt, 1983, ''Assessing Societal Effects of Product Regulations: Toward an Analytic Framework,'' AMA–83, pp. 364–368.

Molitor, Graham T. T., 1981, ''Consumer Policy Issues: Global Trends for the 1980's,'' ACR–81, pp. 458–466.

Moyer, Reed, 1972, *Macromarketing,* New York: John Wiley & Sons.

Moyer, Reed, and Michael D. Hutt, 1978, *Macromarketing,* 2nd ed., Santa Barbara, Calif.: Wiley.

Nakanishi, Masao, 1981, ''Marketing Developments in Japan,'' *JM,* 45, Summer, pp. 106–108.

Norton, George, 1976, ''Consumer Markets in a Columbian Town,'' *Journal of Consumer Affairs,* Summer, pp. 48–61,

Palda, Kristian S., 1980, ''The Public Sector and Marketing: Should the Twain Meet?'' TC–80, pp. 229–232.

Peppas, Spero C., 1982, ''An Application of Marketing Theory to the Attraction of Foreign Investment,'' SMA–82, pp. 204–208.

Reidenbach, R. Eric, and Terence A. Oliva, 1982, ''An Extension of General Living Systems Theory as a Paradigm for Analyzing Marketing Behavior,'' TC–82, pp. 59–62.

Reidenbach, R., Eric, and Terence A. Oliva, 1982, "A Pre-analytic Approach to Modeling Macromarketing Behavior," TC–82, pp. 242–245.

Rethans, Arno J., and Jack L. Taylor, Jr., 1982, "Generic Problems Confronting Macromarketing Decisionmakers," TC–82, pp. 286–288.

Robin, Donald P., 1980, "Value Issues in Marketing," TC–80, pp. 142–145.

Rosenbloom, Bert, 1979, "A Theory of the Role of Marketing in Society as Derived from Marketing Thought of the First Quarter of the Twentieth Century," TC–79, pp. 641–651.

Samli, A. Coskun, and M. Joseph Sirgy, 1982, "Social Responsibility in Marketing: An Analysis and Synthesis," TC–82, pp. 250–254.

Shawver, Donald L., and William G. Nickels, 1981, "A Rationalization for Macromarketing Concepts and Definitions," *Journal of Macromarketing*, 1, Spring, p. 8.

Slater, Charles C., 1968, "Marketing Processes in Developing Latin American Societies," *JM*, 32, July, pp. 50–55.

Slater, Charles C., 1978, "Macromarketing: Some Speculation on Directions and Opportunities," AMA–78, pp. 346–347.

Slater, Charles C., and Dorothy Jenkins, 1978, "Systems Approach to Comparative Macro-Marketing," *Proceedings of the Third Macro-Marketing Seminar*, August, pp. 371–380.

Smith, Phyllis Stoll, and Leonard J. Konopa, 1980, "Macromarketing: Whence and Whither," SMA–80, pp. 332–337.

Srivastava, Rejendra K., and Rohit Deshpande, 1977, "The Management of Marketing-Conflict: Implications for Public Policy," AMA–77, p. 542.

Steiner, Robert L., 1976, "The Prejudice Against Marketing," *JM*, 40, July, pp. 2–9.

Stiff, Ronald, and Patrick E. Murphy, 1981, "Federal Trade Commission Activities in the Service Sector: Recent Experience and Potential Future Directions," SC–81, pp. 179–181.

Tinsley, Dillard, 1979, "Canadian and European Perspectives on Foundation Concepts of Marketing Theory," TC–79, pp. 694–707.

Turner, Ronald E., and Stephen J. Arnold, 1982, "Planned Social Change: Some Implications of Marketing," TC–82, pp. 260–264.

van Bulok, Hendrikus, and Richard R. Still, 1979, "Developing a Multifactor Theory of Global Orientation in International Marketing: A Re-examination of Current Decision Models," SMA–79, pp. 387–389.

Webster, Frederick E., Jr., 1974, *Social Aspects of Marketing*, Englewood Cliffs, N.J.: Prentice-Hall, 1974.

Weisenberger, T. M., and D. Keith Humphries, 1976, "Marketing's Role in Economic Development," SMA–76, pp. 17–19.

White, Phillip D., and C. C. Slater, eds., 1978, *Macromarketing: Distributive Processes from a Societal Perspective: An Elaboration of Issues*, Boulder: Business Research Division, Graduate School of Business, University of Colorado.

White, Phillip D., 1979, "Macromarketing Versus Micromarketing: Level of Aggregation as a Sufficient Definitional Criterion," AMA–79, pp. 619–623.

White, Phillip D., 1981, "The Systems Dimensions in the Definition of Macromarketing," *Journal of Macromarketing*, 1, Spring, pp. 11–13.

8. Broadening Marketing

Arndt, Johan, 1978, "How Broad Should the Marketing Concept Be?" *JM*, 42, January, pp. 101–103.

Arndt, Johan, 1980, "On the Political Economy of Marketing Systems: Untapped Potentials of an Institutional Approach to Marketing," TC–80, pp. 96–99.

Bagozzi, Richard P., 1975, "Social Exchange in Marketing," *Journal of the Academy of Marketing Science*, Vol. 3, No. 4, Fall, pp. 314–327.

Bagozzi, Richard P., 1977, "Is All Social Exchange Marketing? A Reply," *Journal of the Academy of Marketing Science*, Vol. 5, No. 4, Fall, pp. 315–326.

Barksdale, Hiram C., Jr., 1979, "The Broadening Controversy in Marketing," SMA–79, pp. 456–459.

Barksdale, Hiram C., Jr., and Jay E. Klompmaker, 1979, "Marketing Implications of the Split-Brain Phenomenon," SMA–79, pp. 284–287.

Bliss, Perry, 1980, "Marketing, the Generic Concept and Political Science," TC–80, pp. 34–36.

Brown, Stephen W., Zohrab S. Demirdjian, and Sandra E. McKay, 1977, "The Consumer in an Era of Shortages," *MSU Business Topics*, Vol. 25, No. 2, Spring, pp. 49–53.

Brown, Stephen W., and Robert W. Obenberger, 1977, "The Ownership Preoccupation of Marketing Thought: A Case for Consumer Leasing and Renting," SMA–77, pp. 296–298.

Dodge, H. Robert, and Dub Ashton, 1979, "A Decision Framework for Marketing," TC–79, pp. 624–638.

Enis, Ben, 1973, "Deepening the Concept of Marketing," *JM*, 37, October, pp. 57–62.

Ferrell, O. C., and Mary Zey-Ferrell, 1977, "Is All Social Exchange Marketing," *Journal of the Academy of Marketing Science*, Vol. 5, No. 4, Fall, pp. 307–314.

Fisk, Raymond P., and Stephen W. Brown, 1979, "Equity Theory: A Complement to the Understanding of Marketing Exchanges," SMA–79, pp. 53–55.

*Fisk, Raymond P., and Kirk D. Walden, 1979, "Naive Marketing: Further Extension of the Concept of Marketing," TC–79, pp. 459–473. (Reading 14: "Naive Marketing: A Neglected Dimension of Human Behavior.")

Granzin, Kent L., 1982, "A Proposed Path Toward Marketing Theory: An Illustration of Multidisciplinary Synthesis by Means of the Value Relation," TC–82, pp. 63–66.

Grönroos, Christian, 1981, "Internal Marketing—An Integral Part of Marketing Theory," SC–81, pp. 236–238.

Hampton, Gerald M., and C. Patrick Fleenor, 1979, "The Need for Value Based Marketing," TC–79, pp. 237–245.

Hills, Gerald E., 1976, "Social Marketing: A Definition Treatise," AMA–76, pp. 582–585.

Hirschman, Elizabeth C., 1979, "Communal and Associational Social Structure: Their Underlying Behavioral Components and Implications for Marketing," *Journal of the Academy of Marketing Science,* Vol. 7, No. 3, Summer, pp. 192–213.

Hollander, Stanley C., 1980, "Let Us Contemplate Our Navels: The Need for a Sociology of Marketers and Marketologists," TC–80, pp. 55–58.

Hugstad, Paul, and James W. Taylor, 1979, "Risk Theory and the Science of Marketing," TC–79, pp. 448–458.

Klein, Thomas A., 1979, "Contemporary Problems, Marketing Theory, and Futures Research," TC–79, pp. 258–263.

Kotler, Philip, and Sidney J. Levy, 1969, "Broadening the Concept of Marketing," JM, 33, January, pp. 10–15.

Kotler, Philip, and Sidney J. Levy, 1969, "A New Form of Marketing Myopia: Rejoinder to Professor Luck," JM, 33, July, pp. 55–57

Kotler, Philip, 1972, "Defining the Limits of Marketing," in *Marketing Education and the Real World, 1972 Fall Conference Proceedings,* Boris W. Becker and Helmut Becker, eds., Chicago: American Marketing Association.

Laczniak, Gene R., Robert F. Lusch, and Jon G. Udell, 1977, "Marketing in 1985: A View from the Ivory Tower," JM, 41, October, pp. 47–56.

Laczniak, Gene R., and Donald A. Michie, 1979, "Broadening Marketing and Social Order: A Reply," *Journal of the Academy of Marketing Science,* Vol. 7, No. 3, Summer, pp. 239–241.

Laczniak, Gene R., and Donald A. Michie, 1979, "The Social Disorder of the Broadened Concept of Marketing," *Journal of the Academy of Marketing Science,* Vol. 7, No. 3, Summer, pp. 214–232.

*Levy, Sidney J., 1976, "Macrology 101 or the Domain of Marketing," AMA–76, pp. 577–581.

Levy, Sidney J. and Philip Kotler, 1979, "Toward a Broader Concept of Marketing's Role in Social Order," *Journal of the Academy of Marketing Science,* Vol. 7, No. 3, Summer, pp. 233–238.

Luck, David J., 1969, "Broadening the Concept of Marketing—Too Far," JM, 33, July, pp. 53–54.

Luck, David J., 1974, "Social Marketing: Confusion Compounded," JM, 38, October, pp. 70–72.

Lusch, Robert F., and Gene R. Laczniak, 1979, "Does Futures Research Have a Role in Marketing Theory?" TC–79, pp. 246–257.

Lusch, Robert F., 1981, "Integration of Economic Geography and Social Psychological Models of Patronage Behavior," ACR–81, pp. 644–647.

Martinelli, Patrick A., 1969, "Can Marketing Theory Be Developed Through the Study of Social Institutions," JM, 33, April, pp. 60–62.

Mayer, Robert Nathan, and Francesco M. Nicosia, 1977, "New Contributions of Sociology to Consumer Research," AMA–77, pp. 239–242.

Murphy, Patrick E., 1980, "Marketing Nonprofit Organizations: Problems and Prospects for the 1980's," AMA–80, pp. 278–281.

Nickels, William G., and Earnestine Hargrove, 1977, "A New Societal Marketing Concept," AMA–77, p. 541.

Nickels, William G., 1979, "Theory Development and the Broadened Concept of Marketing," TC–79, pp. 614–623.

Obenberger, Robert W., and Stephen W. Brown, 1976, "A Marketing Alternative: Consumer Leasing and Renting," *Business Horizons,* 19, October, pp. 82–86.

O'Leary, Ray, and Ian Iredale, 1976, "The Marketing Concept: Quo Vadis?" *European Journal of Marketing,* 10, pp. 146–157.

Reidenbach, Eric R., and Terence A. Oliva, 1981, "General Living Systems Theory and Marketing: A Framework for Analysis," JM, 45, Fall, pp. 30–39.

Robin, Donald P., 1979, "Useful Boundaries for Marketing," TC–79, pp. 605–613.

Shama, Avraham, 1976, "The Marketing of Political Candidates," *Journal of the Academy of Marketing Science,* Vol. 4, No. 2, Fall, pp. 764–777.

Spratlen, Thaddeus H., 1979, "A Conceptual Analysis and Framework for Social Marketing Theory and Research," TC–79, pp. 166–183.

Tinney, Cathie H., 1982, "The Application of Exchange Theory to Marketing: A Recommended Perspective," SMA–82, pp. 245–248.

Zey-Ferrell, Mary, and O. C. Ferrell, 1980, "A Rejoinder: Is All Social Exchange Marketing? A Reply," *Journal of the Academy of the Marketing Science,* Vol. 8, No. 3, Summer, pp. 182–195.

Author Index

Subject Index

367